Islam at the Crossroads

Islam at the Crossroads

Lameh Fananapazir

OXFORD
GEORGE RONALD

George Ronald, Publisher
Oxford
www.grbooks.com

©Lameh Fananapazir 2015
All Rights Reserved
Reprinted 2016

A catalogue record for this book
is available from the British Library

ISBN 978-0-85398-598-3

Cover design: Steiner Graphics

CONTENTS

Preface, *by Glenford Mitchell* — ix
Foreword, *by Douglas Martin* — xix
Introduction — 1

PART I THE SUMMONS

1 The Summons of the Báb and Bahá'u'lláh and the '*Ajal*' of the '*Ummah*' of Islam — 13

2 Islam: The Promise of the Bible — 30

3 Islam: A Testimony of Direct Divine Intervention in Human Affairs — 48

PART II ISSUES FACING ISLAM

4 The Challenge and Failure of Islamic Fundamentalism and the Impotence of Liberal Secular Islam — 63

5 Religious Fanaticism and Intolerance — 73

6 Sectarian Hostility and Violence — 90

7 Excessive Reliance on Religious Leaders for Guidance — 110

8 Frustration of the Sacred Duty of Believers to Investigate the Truth and to Recognize their Lord — 138

9	Misinterpretation of the Divine Word	163
10	Corruption of the Divine Message (*tahrif*)	183
11	Christian-Islamic Doctrinal Conflicts	199
12	The 'Seal of the Prophets' (*khátam al-nabiyyín*), and the Finality of Islam	248

PART III SALVATION OF ISLAM

13	Promotion of True Religious Enquiry and Adherence to Valid Criteria for Ascertaining Truth	269
14	Responding to the Call the Summoner, Bahá'u'lláh	294
15	Embracing the 'Great Announcement' of the Qur'án and the 'Good News' of the Bible	325
16	Recognition of the Promised 'Day' and 'Hour'	356
17	Reaffirmation of the Unifying Principle of 'One Common Faith'	384
18	Abrogation of the Dispensation of Muhammad, and the Suspension and Modification of its Social Laws by Bahá'u'lláh	409
19	Participating in the Resurrection and Rebirth of the Faith of Islam	452

Bibliography — 487

Notes and References — 493

About the Author — 659

ACKNOWLEDGEMENTS

This book is dedicated to all those who have spent their lives reconciling faith and reason, fostering inter-religious understanding, and promoting the realization of the commonality of Faith. I am particularly indebted to Khazeh Fananapazir for his many generous contributions and insights. I would like to express my heartfelt gratitude to my wife Karen, without whose support, encouragement and many valuable suggestions this manuscript would not have been completed. Finally, I am profoundly grateful to May Hofman for her vast knowledge, depth of experience, and remarkable editorial skills.

PREFACE

The vitality of men's belief in God is dying out in every land; nothing short of His wholesome medicine can ever restore it. The corrosion of ungodliness is eating into the vitals of human society; what else but the Elixir of His potent Revelation can cleanse and revive it? . . . The world is in travail, and its agitation waxeth day by day. Its face is turned towards waywardness and unbelief. Such shall be its plight that to disclose it now would not be meet and seemly . . .

Bahá'u'lláh[1]

For more than a century and a half the world has been swirling in manifold turmoil. It increases, diversifies, intensifies, never stopping. The consequence has been an unexampled rush of change, at once bewildering and marvellous, whose effects are reflected in simultaneous occurrences of rise and fall, order and chaos, integration and disintegration. But in the heat of this turbulence can be discerned the shaping of some form of social cohesion of a totally new scope and force. The use of the term 'globalization' in the realm of politics is perhaps an attempt to identify what is not yet clearly definable but is, nonetheless, assuming greater importance in the interactions among peoples and nations.

See, for example, how, in a relatively brief period, dynasties fell, economies fluctuated, two world wars wreaked havoc, and a majority of the world's people resisted colonial domination, arranged themselves into independent nations, and are represented in a world organization known as the United Nations. Consider, too, that in the twentieth century unprecedented thrusts of scientific discovery vastly increased the breadth of knowledge, and that corollary rapid advances in technology shrank planet Earth into a mere neighbourhood. Similarly exceptional, the field of the arts greatly expanded by multifarious bursts of creative energy. The seeming suddenness and far-reaching impact of such breathtaking and apparently inexplicable change raise questions that demand answers, if the current disequilibrium affecting all human affairs is to be reckoned with.

Humanity has entered a new age. Convulsions on the monumental scale being experienced make that obvious. But how are the concurrent workings of these disruptive and productive phenomena to be understood and dealt with? By what light is clarity to be achieved and conviction assured?

Bahá'u'lláh is the Source of that light, many people in many countries believe. Increasing millions recognize Him as the Manifestation of God for our age, the latest prophetic Voice, Who appeared in Iran more than 150 years ago. His Message is primarily concerned with the issues of our time, offering guidance for a new world order towards which nations are gradually moving. 'The Day of the Promise is come,' Bahá'u'lláh proclaims, declaring that 'Every Prophet hath announced the coming of this Day, and every Messenger hath groaned in His yearning for this Revelation.'[2]

Bahá'u'lláh, alluding to the transformative impact of His Revelation, asserts:

> Through the movement of Our Pen of Glory, We have, at the bidding of the omnipotent Ordainer, breathed a new life into every human frame, and instilled into every word a fresh potency. All created things proclaim the evidences of this worldwide regeneration.[3]

Humanity is thus prompted to new forms of endeavour in every department of life, demonstrating the truth of Bahá'u'lláh's further assertion that 'every creature hath been endowed with all the potentialities it can carry'.[4]

The oneness of mankind is the central theme of the Revelation. It signalizes the 'coming of age of the entire human race'. Bahá'u'lláh's call for unity is compelling in what it proposes as solutions for the afflictions of human society and as features of the glorious future that it envisages. 'It beseemeth all men, in this Day . . .', He urges, 'to establish the unity of all mankind'.[5]

In setting forth requisites for meeting the spiritual and social challenges of the modern age, the Revelation of Bahá'u'lláh elucidates the mysteries that have for so many ages remained impenetrable in the prophecies and symbolic language of Holy Books of the past.

The Revelation of Bahá'u'lláh offers illuminating answers to critical questions. It affirms the advent of the Most Great Peace in fulfilment of the ancient promise recorded in all the sacred scriptures. It specifies the spiritual and practical measures for attaining the unity of humankind, the prerequisite of that peace. It identifies the Source of the power actuating the forces at work throughout the planet.

The call of Bahá'u'lláh for the unity of the human race emphasizes a significant verity: the evolution of human development has reached its stage of maturity. And so His principle of the oneness of mankind is meant to signify the consummation of human evolution – 'an evolution that has had its beginnings in the birth of family life, its subsequent development in the achievement of tribal solidarity, leading in turn to the constitution of the city-state, and expanding later into the institution of independent and sovereign nations'.[6]

'Abdu'l-Baha, the eldest Son of Bahá'u'lláh appointed by His Father to interpret the Bahá'í teachings, offers this elucidation:

> All created things have their degree, or stage, of maturity. The period of maturity in the life of a tree is the time of its fruit-bearing . . . The animal attains a stage of full growth and completeness, and in the human kingdom man reaches his maturity when the light of his intelligence attains its greatest power and development . . .
>
> Similarly, there are periods and stages in the aggregate world of humanity, which one time was passing through its degree of childhood, at another its time of youth but now has entered its long presaged perod of maturity, the evidences of which are everywhere visible and apparent . . . That which was applicable to human needs during the early history of the race could neither meet nor satisfy the demands of this day and period of newness and consummation. Humanity has emerged from its former degrees of limitation and preliminary training. Man must now become imbued with new virtues and powers, new moralities, new capacities. New bounties, bestowals and perfections are awaiting and already descending upon him. The gifts and graces of the period of youth, although timely and sufficient during the adolescence of the world of mankind, are now incapable of meeting the requirements of its maturity.[7]

At so advanced a stage a new statement of spiritual and social principles becomes necessary. These Bahá'u'lláh has provided, as was done at earlier stages of human development when Prophets of God arose to offer guidance required by the conditions of the times. In this sense, Bahá'u'lláh affirms that all the Prophets proclaim the same truth, thus His teaching that all the divine religions are one and their purpose similar. The following statement by 'Abdu'l-Bahá reaffirms this truth:

> The divine religions were founded for the purpose of unifying humanity and establishing universal peace. Any movement which brings about peace and agreement in human society is truly a divine movement; any reform which causes people to come together under the shelter of the same tabernacle is surely animated by heavenly motives. At all times and in all ages of the world, religion has been a factor in cementing together the hearts of men and in uniting various and divergent creeds. It is the peace element in religion that blends mankind and makes for unity . . .
>
> The cause of this fellowship and unity lies in the fact that the divine law has two distinct aspects or functions: one the essential or fundamental, the other the material or accidental. The first aspect of the revealed religion of God is that which concerns the ethical development and spiritual progress of mankind . . . These ordinances are changeless, essential, eternal. The second function of the divine religion deals with material conditions, the laws of human intercourse and social regulation. These are subject to change and transformation in accordance with the time, place and conditions. The essential ordinances of religion were the same during the time of Abraham, the day of Moses and the cycle of Jesus, but the accidental or material laws were abrogated and superseded according to the exigency and requirement of each succeeding age.[8]

By holding fast, without question, to traditional forms of belief and worship passed down from one generation to another, the followers of different Prophets have maintained false separations between religions – separations that have caused disunion and discord leading often to warfare. In exhorting individuals to investigate truth independently, Bahá'u'lláh lays down a principle that is essential to the establishment of unity. So firmly is this principle applied in the Bahá'í community, that when the children of Bahá'ís become adults, they are not automatically registered as believers, but must on their own apply for such registration on the basis of conviction independently derived from their investigation and study.

The disequilibrium of society caused by the visitation of a Manifestation of God at this time is the result of a 'transitory dislocation' in human affairs – this is an inescapable necessity as the inadequate and often corrupt institutions and practices of the old order slowly yield to the principles of a new world order which will reflect the maturity of the human race. Concerning this great prospect, Bahá'u'lláh's words are unequivocal: 'Soon,' He writes, 'will the present-day order be rolled up, and a new one spread out in its stead. Verily, thy Lord speaketh the truth, and is the Knower of things unseen.'[9] The sooner the states and nations adjust to the spiritual requisites of this new age, the sooner will they experience the stupendous reality of a united world in which the 'infinite diversity of its federated units' will acquire the splendour of a garden of multi-various flowers.

It is in the light of this great expectation, and with particular relevance to the issues of Islam, that this book is presented.

The recurrence of momentous happenings in the Middle East is an especially critical aspect of the world-transforming turmoil enveloping all of humanity. The situation which has arisen there since the collapse of the Ottoman Empire can be said to have had its beginning in Iran in 1844 when Mírzá Muḥammad-'Alí, the Báb, announced His mission, claiming to be the Qá'im long expected by Muslims. He revealed copious commentaries that elucidate verses of the Qur'án, which for the most part, as He explained, were allusions to the Promised Day of God and to the Promised One, of Whom the Báb was the Forerunner. Writing in His Persian Bayán, the Mother-Book of His Revelation, the Báb declares: 'The Bayán and whosoever is therein revolve round the saying of "Him Whom God shall make manifest", even as the Alif (the Gospel) and whosoever was therein revolved round the saying of Muḥammad, the Apostle of God.'[10] He further writes, 'Today the Bayán is in the stage of seed; at the beginning of the manifestation of "Him Whom God shall make manifest" its ultimate perfection will become apparent.'[11]

The rapid conversion of multitudes in Iran to the Bábí Faith alarmed a sceptical Muslim clergy whose violent rejection of the Báb's message forced His imprisonment and ultimate execution in dramatic circumstances when in July 1850 His body was riddled by the bullets aimed at him by a regiment of 750 soldiers.[12] A massive slaughter of His followers ensued. Mírzá Ḥusayn 'Alí, scion of a noble family, emerged as the most outstanding and respected supporter of the Bábí Faith and a fearless defender of the Bábís, whose spirits He endeavoured to uplift after the horrific demise of their leader. In 1853 He was thrown into a dungeon in Tehran, the notorious 'black pit', where He was forced to suffer for several months on false charges. In this dismal place, weighed down by the huge chain clasped to His neck, He received the first intimation of His prophetic mission.[13] He subsequently adopted the name Bahá'u'lláh (Glory of God) by which the Báb addressed Him, and He was eventually recognized by the great majority of the Bábís as the future One to Whom the Báb had repeatedly referred as 'Him Whom God shall make manifest'.

Even though Bahá'u'lláh was proven innocent, the clergy remained fearful of His influence. Consequently, He was exiled from His homeland to Baghdad in neighbouring Iraq, thence to Constantinople, to Adrianople, and finally to Akka in the Holy Land, where He was placed in prison for more than two years and thereafter kept under detention until His passing in 1892. Undeterred, Bahá'u'lláh proclaimed His message of peace and justice in missives addressed jointly, and in some instances individually, to the rulers and religious leaders of the day. The Writings of Bahá'u'lláh, comprising some 100 volumes, cover a vast array of subjects elucidating issues of the modern age and setting forth the principles for establishing a new world order.

The appearance of a Manifestation of God – a Moses, a Christ, or a Muhammad – is a spiritual and historic phenomenon of earth-shaking significance; this is documented in the annals of civilization. Thus it is against the background of Bábí–Bahá'í events in our time that the situation in the Middle East, no less than in all other parts of the world, must necessarily be viewed. The coming of twin Manifestations in that region exerted an immediate transformative influence on a considerable number of the Iranian people, among whom some of the most heroic episodes of faith and sacrifice took place and, to this day, continue with the unrelenting persecution of the Bahá'ís in Iran.

The primacy of the Middle East in the beginnings of the history of civilization has always been the object of the curiosity of people throughout the world. As the birthplace of so many religions, it evokes a special significance in the hearts and minds of countless souls. Stirrings in that region during the twentieth century aroused keen attention far and wide. That attention is now even more greatly heightened. As is commonly known, early in the twenty-first century the shock wave produced by attacks on Western interests in Africa, Asia and Europe, and particularly by 9/11 – the exceptional fiery attack on the twin towers in New York City – abruptly extended such stirrings to the Western hemisphere, with awesome impact. In its wake, Westerners have felt themselves caught in an enigmatic and perilous phenomenon that now, through the rise of the so-called 'Islamic State' or ISIS, threatens to engulf the entire world. More often than not, extremist elements who commit these horrors both at home and abroad adduce justification from what are purported to be their religious beliefs. This in itself is a telling example of the dangerous lengths to which misinterpretation of scripture can extend.

Despite the voluminous social and political commentaries of scholars and pundits attempting to offer explanations, people remain mystified as to the true meaning of these happenings. In Islamic nations, the citizens themselves seem woefully unaware of the reality underlying their predicament. And despite the early hopes inspired by what seemed in 2011 as the beginning of an 'Arab Spring', no clear and credible Muslim voice has articulated a generally acceptable rationale or offered a luminous direction as to the way forward.

Turning to the lessons of history, sociology and political science can, of course, be of inestimable value to those who search for a solution to the predicament overshadowing Islamic society. But beyond this effort an underlying reality must be recognized and comprehensively and profoundly dealt with: Religion lies at the heart of the troubles in the Islamic world; and, paradoxical as it may seem, the resolution of these troubles lies in religion.

Finding that solution requires an honest search that must begin at the centre of Islam, which for Muslims is the revealed Word – the text of the Holy Qur'án – and must involve authentic interpretations from authorized sources. It is the absence of authenticity in the plethora of free-floating interpretations by unauthorized and uninformed actors that is the main issue. Over the centuries, these illegitimate interpreters have ignored the clear distinction the Holy Qur'án makes between 'perspicuous' and 'figurative' expressions in the verses the Book contains.

The 'perspicuous' contents of the Qur'án are readily understood, needing no particular interpretation, as they clearly provide the laws and ordinances regarding such matters as prayer, fasting, marriage, divorce, inheritance – the distinctive marks of an independent community. To their eternal credit, Muslims have generally abided by these laws and ordinances. Unfortunately, by presuming to read the mind of God, their leaders have not heeded the directive of the Prophet concerning the 'figurative' contents of His Book. The deplorable outcome is the conspicuous display of confusion bedevilling the Islamic world and frustrating its inhabitants' aspirations for spiritual and social advancement. It makes for an overwhelming crisis in Islam.

The 'figurative' matter, the Book warns, should await future elucidation by 'those endued with knowledge'. But it also anticipates the grievous actions of those 'whose hearts are given to err', as clearly indicated in the Qur'án:

> He it is who hath sent down to thee 'the Book'. Some of its signs are of themselves perspicuous; – these are the basis of the Book – and others are figurative. But they whose hearts are given to err, follow its figures, craving discord, craving an interpretation; yet none knoweth its interpretation but God. And the stable in knowledge say 'we believe in it; all is from our Lord'. But none will bear this in mind, save men endued with understanding.[14]

Proper interpretation, the Writings of Bahá'u'lláh explain, needed to await His own Revelation and that of His Forerunner, the Báb. He elaborates on this matter in His *Kitáb-i-Íqán* (Book of Certitude). The following statement of Bahá'u'lláh is relevant:

> Consider that which hath been sent down unto Muḥammad, the Apostle of God. The measure of the Revelation of which He was the bearer had been clearly foreordained by Him Who is the Almighty, the All-Powerful. They that heard Him, however, could apprehend His purpose only to the extent of their station and spiritual capacity. He, in like manner, uncovered the Face of Wisdom in proportion to their ability to sustain the burden of His Message. No sooner had mankind attained the stage of maturity, than the Word revealed to

men's eyes the latent energies with which it had been endowed – energies which manifested themselves in the plenitude of their glory when the Ancient Beauty appeared, in the year sixty, in the person of 'Alí-Muḥammad, the Báb.[15]

The crisis is made worse by the rejection of the latest Manifestation of God, as well as by wilful disregard of the Source of authentic interpretations which He represents. This negative attitude woefully frustrates the will of Muslims to resolve their concerns.

Here, then, is an earnest attempt to aid any serious-minded search for solutions. The contents of this book are basically a compilation of extracts drawn primarily from Bahá'u'lláh's own words and the texts of the Qur'án and the Bible to explain the interrelationship between Islam and its sister Abrahamic religions, Judaism and Christianity, and His own Revelation. This is so since the Bahá'í belief system is grounded in scripture, and considers the divine Word as immune from unauthorized human interpretation. Furthermore, the Qur'án refers to the Jews and Christians as *Ahl al-Kitáb*, or 'the people of the Book' (scripture), and presents the Torah and the Gospels as the most reliable evidences of divine intervention. This presentation therefore frequently makes parallel comparisons of the Bible, the Qur'án, and the Writings of Bahá'u'lláh. It is hoped that reliance on the scriptures will enable the individual to 'see with his own eyes, hear with his own ears' and investigate the truth independently, so that he or she may 'follow the truth instead of indulging in blind acquiescence and imitation of ancestral beliefs'.[16]

The book examines the criteria offered by the teachings of Bahá'u'lláh for examining the validity of the Mission of the Prophet Muhammad, and some of the reasons why Islam and its fortunes are directly dependent on submission to God's Will and following His Straight Path in this day and age.

The intention is that the format of scriptural presentation will illustrate the progressive pattern and integral coherence of the divine Revelations as constituents of one common faith, and, furthermore, demonstrate the principle that 'God, Who at sundry times and in divers manners spake in time past unto the fathers by the prophets, hath in these last days spoken unto us,'[17] and, specifically, to followers of Islam, through Bahá'u'lláh.

Even though the book principally addresses immediate concerns of the people of Islam, it should hold an equal interest for people of the West who are in a quandary about events in the Middle East, which directly affect them too. A distinctive message is being communicated from the recurrent commotion throughout the Middle East, and this in perhaps the only effective way possible in a turbulent world. Western society, no less than every other portion of mankind, must sooner or later recognize what is most significant about the Middle East, whose contribution to a rising world civilization and culture is a critical though largely unappreciated fact. So pre-eminent a truth must, in time, be widely and gratefully acknowledged as the tumult of present-day conditions recedes in favour of a spiritually transformed and peaceful planet. After all, it is in the east that the sun rises, both physically and spiritually.

Glenford Mitchell

FOREWORD

It is difficult to remember that as recently as the beginning of this century the subject of Islam occupied a place on the periphery, if that, of the consciousness of most people in the West. The startling series of events that had accompanied the 1979 Islamic Revolution in Iran, while capturing international media attention, appeared to be a phenomenon limited to that country and largely understandable in familiar political and socio-economic terms. Much the same view was taken of the religiously inspired terrorism that sought to change the character of the Palestinian *intifadá*.

The horrific assaults carried out against the United States in September 2001 by squads of suicide bombers – together with the worldwide terrorist outrages that followed – ended abruptly Western confidence in its understanding of the culture of the one-and-a-quarter billion Muslims who share the planet with the rest of humankind. Less dramatic, but probably equally significant in the long term, has been the awakening of European populations to the implications of the presence in their midst of a vast number of Muslim immigrants – some now into the third generation – who, unlike new arrivals from other lands, appear essentially irreconcilable with certain foundational norms of Western culture. Perhaps not surprisingly, the shock and alarm has inspired widespread desire to understand the religious roots of such phenomena, awakening an interest in Islamic belief and practice unprecedented since the 16th century.

For followers of the Faith of Bahá'u'lláh, this unexpected turn of events comes as a sharp reminder of the emphasis Shoghi Effendi[1] very early placed on the importance of Western Bahá'ís undertaking a serious study of Islam. During the 1930s he began calling on believers to 'strive to obtain . . . a sound knowledge of the history and tenets of Islám', using for the purpose 'sources that are authoritative and unbiased'.[2] Without detracting from equal respect for the truths of all the great religions, the Guardian urged Bahá'ís to reflect on the fact that the Qur'án, apart from the scriptures of the Bahá'í Faith itself, 'constitutes the only Book which can be regarded as an absolutely authenticated Repository of the Word of God'.[3] A letter written on his behalf to an individual who proposed to prepare a course on the Islamic Faith for a Bahá'í summer school sets the subject in historical perspective:

> There is so much misunderstanding about Islám in the West in general that you have to dispel. Your task is rather difficult and requires a good deal of erudition. Your chief task is to acquaint the friends with the pure teaching of the Prophet as recorded in the Qur'án, and then to point out how these teachings have, throughout succeeding ages, influenced nay guided the course of human development . . .
>
> You should also cautiously emphasize the truth that due to the historical order of its appearance, and also because of the obviously more advanced character of its teachings, Islám constitutes a fuller revelation of God's purpose for mankind. The so-called Christian civilization of which the Renaissance is one of the most striking manifestations is essentially Muslim in its origins and foundations. When medieval Europe was plunged in darkest barbarism, the Arabs regenerated and transformed by the spirit released by the religion of Muhammad were busily engaged in establishing a civilization the kind of which their contemporary Christians in Europe had never witnessed before. It was eventually through Arabs that civilization was introduced to the West . . .
>
> From the standpoint of institutionalism Islám far surpasses true Christianity as we know it in the Gospels. There are infinitely more laws and institutions in the Qur'án than in the Gospel. While the latter's emphasis is mainly, not to say wholly, on individual and personal conduct, the Qur'án stresses the importance of society. This social emphasis acquires added importance and significance in the Revelation of Bahá'u'lláh.[4]

Whether because of the multitude of other tasks facing a body of people as relatively small and limited in resources as the Bahá'í community, or because historical circumstances did not yet seem to add their urgency to guidance of the kind cited, Bahá'í interest in the subject tended to lag. Courses were intermittently given at summer schools, Bahá'í writers such as Hasan Balyuzi[5] and Stanwood Cobb[6] attempted to fill the gap in Bahá'í literature and efforts were made at the local level to attract the participation of Muslim speakers in such events as World Religion Day. For most Bahá'ís, however, the issue remained peripheral until recent world events brought into focus the prescience of Shoghi Effendi's appeals.

The fact that impresses itself immediately on the observer is that Islam is in a condition of deep crisis. Political upheavals that dominate popular discussion of the subject are clearly no more than surface expressions of a problem of historic dimension: the inability of Islamic scholars and institutions to reconcile the teachings and perspectives of their Faith with the realities of modernity. Democratic and constitutional government, pluralistic societies, the authority of the sciences, such principles as gender equality and religious freedom, a rapidly integrating world – all these familiar features of contemporary civilization pose insurmountable challenges to anyone who attempts to accommodate them to religious guidance laid down fourteen centuries ago for an earlier, much simpler stage in humanity's social evolution. One sees in contemporary Islam a society desperately searching for, and failing always to find, a formula that will make it possible somehow to retain traditional Muslim faith in God while embracing the inescapable requirements of a world beyond the imagination of ages past.

The crisis is largely self-inflicted. The Qur'án succeeded in imprinting on religious consciousness an understanding of and respect for the successive stages in the revelation of a single Divine Will for humanity. In consequence, Islamic society demonstrated for several centuries a level of religious toleration unknown to Christian Europe and antithetical to established Christian theology. Had the full possibilities of this central truth been embraced by the Qur'án's immediate beneficiaries, there is every reason to assume that the majority of the peoples of Europe would in time have accepted the new Faith, as the majority of their co-religionists in Byzantine lands had done.

The unprecedented advances in intellectual, aesthetic, economic and technological life that followed on the spiritual awakening would have made this outcome all the more likely. In a remarkably short period, considered in terms of historical time, a vast multicultural Islamic community emerged, rivalling in scope the former Roman Empire although far more integrated in its submission to a universal moral code and its use of a single common language of immense power. Taught to prize knowledge 'wherever it may be found', Muslim scholars drew freely on the heritage of Greek learning and on the achievements of the cultures they encountered in Persia, China and India.

The results were dazzling. For five centuries, an apparently inexhaustible series of advances in mathematics, chemistry, physics, medicine, geography, philosophy, history, optics and engineering made 'Islam' synonymous with civilization itself – in present-day terms, with 'modernity'. To the scientific features of the progress were added brilliant accomplishments in the arts, in architecture, literature, music, graphic design, cuisine, horticulture and landscaping. Enormous libraries were founded, universities established, hospitals, public baths, lighted streets and vast irrigation systems created. Such practical pursuits as textiles, ceramics, jewellery, paper-making, water purification, agronomy and international banking ensured that the Muslim world would become – and for several centuries remain – the focal centre of economic power in the Mediterranean basin and throughout the Middle East.

The response of the medieval Church was to denounce Muhammad as a 'false prophet' and Islam as 'the handiwork of Satan'. The attempt of present-day commentators to explain so sudden and enormous an explosion of cultural energy with whatever lies at hand in the toolbox of Western historicism has not been a great deal more helpful. Nowhere in the long annals of humanity's social evolution is there a comparable example of a great and enduring civilization brought into existence in so brief a space of time through the efforts of a handful of primitive tribes. It is – or ought to be – at least sobering to remind oneself that the grandfathers of the scholars, poets, scientists, builders and administrators who were suddenly everywhere pushing back the frontiers of human achievement had themselves been brutal, illiterate herdsmen, as had been their forefathers through unnumbered generations. To modern Muslims, only perversity can fail to acknowledge the obvious connection between cause and effect. The Qur'án promises in the most emphatic language that 'And those who strive in Our (Cause), – We will certainly guide them to Our Paths',[7] and the divine promise was unarguably fulfilled time and again in every field of Muslim endeavour. Throughout the centuries, this unresolved issue has remained the unbridgeable gap separating Western and Islamic consciousness.

FOREWORD

Belated sympathy in our own day with the plight of Muslim societies, whatever the underlying motivations, cannot wish away the challenge.

As Islamic civilization leapt the Mediterranean to penetrate Spain and Sicily, it began to exert an irresistible attraction on the peoples living in northern lands. The material benefits that would follow during the later period of the Crusades have tended to dominate whatever attention has been given to the encounter by Western writers. Infinitely more important in the long run was the revolutionary impact of Islamic science, scholarship and spirit of inquiry on the minds of Europeans who studied at universities in Umayyad Spain, read the commentaries by Arab translators of Greek texts and debated with their Muslim and Jewish counterparts at the court of Frederic II in Palermo. Primitive universities sprang up, first in Italy, and subsequently in Paris, Oxford and elsewhere, setting in motion the aggressive challenge to church orthodoxy that would, in time, dissolve Europe's received certainties about reality. The closest approximation in recent history to the intellectual dominance attained in the early European renaissance by such Islamic scholars as Ibn Rushd (Averroes) and Ibn Sina (Avicenna) lies in the intellectual influence exercised by nineteenth-century Western thinkers like Darwin and Marx.

Ideally, the principle implicit in the process of divine revelation could have laid the foundation of Muslim understanding of the evolutionary nature of reality. Instead, in both Sunni and Shí'ih societies, authority for the interpretation of Quranic truths was increasingly surrendered into the hands of professional clergies. The political and other reasons for this intellectual and spiritual retreat are as controversial as they are complex, and lie far beyond the scope of this brief survey, but the consequence was to leave this most advanced segment of humankind tragically handicapped in addressing the ongoing challenges of historical change. The spirit of confident inquiry that had once animated scientific and cultural breakthroughs gradually atrophied, to be replaced by submission to theological dogma and by an obsessive preoccupation with the minutiae of ritual behaviour.

With rejection of the missions, first of the Báb and subsequently of Bahá'u'lláh, this dry timber burst into an all-consuming conflagration. A century and a half later, the Muslim world lies prostrate and impotent as the rest of humankind presses on into an apparently limitless achievement. Whatever response the generality of believing Muslims might have made to the fulfilment of the Qur'án's apocalyptic promises had been aborted by violent opposition on the part of the same clerical leadership who had gradually suffocated progressive thought of every kind. 'The foolish divines', Bahá'u'lláh comments,

> have laid aside the Book of God, and are occupied with that which they themselves have fashioned. The Ocean of Knowledge is revealed, and the shrill of the Pen of the Most High is raised, and yet they, even as earthworms, are afflicted with the clay of their fancies and imaginings. They are exalted by reason of their relationship to the one true God, and yet they have turned aside from Him! Because of Him have they become famous, and yet they are shut off as by a veil from Him![8]

The resolution of Islam's spiritual and historical dilemma is one of the central themes of Bahá'u'lláh's mission, dealt with at length in the *Kitáb-i-Íqán*. Bahá'u'lláh reminds His listeners that 'Islam' (surrender to the will of God) is the religion taught by all the Manifestations and prophets of the Divine throughout history, 'the changeless faith of God, eternal in the past, eternal in the future'.[9] Verses in the Qur'án itself leave no room for reasonable doubt on the point, emphasizing as they do that Abraham, Moses and all of the Hebrew prophets were Muslims.

> And strive in His cause as ye ought to strive, (with sincerity and under discipline). He has chosen you, and has imposed no difficulties on you in religion; it is the cult (faith) of your father Abraham. It is He Who has named you Muslims, both before and in this (Revelation) . . .[10]

To attempt to limit the religion of God to any one of its prophetic Dispensations, even to the concluding one inaugurated by Muhammad – as all traditional Muslim theology does – is to pervert one of the central teachings of the Qur'án.

The error was early compounded by the theological precept that the Qur'án represents God's final intervention in history. Again, the Qur'án itself exposes the fallacy: 'The Jews say: "God's hand is tied up." Be their hands tied up and be they accursed for the (blasphemy) they utter. Nay, both His hands are widely outstretched: He giveth and spendeth (of His bounty) as He pleaseth.'[11] Bahá'u'lláh remarks that 'For over a thousand years they [i.e. the Islamic clergy] have been reciting this verse, and unwittingly pronouncing their censure against the Jews, utterly unaware that they themselves, openly and in private, are voicing the sentiments and belief of the Jewish people!'[12]

In practical terms, the effect of misconceptions so fundamental has been to block unfettered study of the evolutionary nature of truth, a theme that, ironically, had begun tentatively to suggest itself in the writings of some of the great minds of early periods of Islamic civilization.

'Globalization' and 'modernity', far from being alien to the Faith taught in the Qur'án (or to any of the earlier stages in the unfolding of the Divine Will), are rather a fulfilment of the process, both spiritually and practically. Clearly, Muslims have as much right to this common heritage of humankind as do the people of any other religious background. Indeed, viewed objectively, the urgent and repeated summons of the Qur'án to prepare for the staggering changes to be expected in the Promised Day should have empowered its followers, to a far greater extent than any other religious community, to recognize and welcome the process of transformation in which the entire world is today caught up.

At the root of these failures of understanding was a betrayal of trust. The text of the Qur'án makes it clear that the power to interpret its figurative and prophetic verses rests solely in the hands of God and His Appointees. Believers are counselled to recite the holy Text and to observe its laws, while awaiting with patience and trust the Day when its full meaning will be made clear by the same Voice that revealed it: 'Move not thy tongue concerning (the Qur'án) to make haste therewith. Surely on Us (devolves) the collecting of it and the reciting of it. Therefore when We have recited it, follow its recitation. Again on Us (devolves) the explaining of it.'[13] The community of the faithful is warned in the strongest terms against succumbing again to the ancient temptation – exemplified by the Meccan idolaters – of 'joining partners with God'. The significance of the warning became clear when *ulamá* presumed on their misappropriated authority to defy God's Manifestation of Himself in the missions of the Báb and Bahá'u'lláh.

For the faithful Muslim, therefore, the words of the Qur'án represent the ultimate spiritual test. Far from endorsing the prejudices, dogmas and fanaticism that have gradually overlaid Islamic belief down through the centuries, the Text itself contains all that is required to dissolve these encrustations. The transformative influence exerted by Bahá'u'lláh on some of the most spiritually advanced minds of His age arose precisely from their recognition of Him as the authoritative Interpreter of the Book's words. Today, millions of Muslims view with feelings of outrage and helplessness the caricature of the Faith they love that an aggressive fundamentalism is determined to impose upon it. Equally painful to them is the precipitous decline that has paralysed Islamic societies everywhere – economically, politically, culturally and socially.

When Muhammad died in the year 632 AD, the devastated body of His followers were aroused from their grief by words that have rung down the centuries, uttered by Abu Bakr, who had undertaken to serve as Caliph ('commander') of the community: 'Whosoever worshipped Muhammad, know that Muhammad is dead. Whosoever worshipped God, know that God is alive and will never die!'

The same searching test today faces the entire Muslim world. The prophetic Dispensation inaugurated by the Prophet, with its attendant laws and institutions, has come to its predestined end, as did all those that preceded it. The universal faith of Islam, for which that Dispensation served as the vehicle, is eternal and immutable. No one who approaches the Cause of Bahá'u'lláh in a spirit of detachment will fail to discover in it the fulfilment and flowering of the enduring truths brought by the Qur'án: the inseparability of mind and heart, the rejection of distinctions based on race, the social role of religion, tolerance for differences of belief and, above all else, the soul's intended intimacy with the one God who is 'nearer than one's life vein'.[14]

The challenge faced by Bahá'ís is to assist Muslim enquirers – and indeed those of Christian and Jewish backgrounds – to approach a study of the Qur'án and its civilizing power in a spirit of the *Kitáb-i-Íqán*.

> O my brother, when a true seeker determineth to take the step of search in the path leading to the knowledge of the Ancient of Days, he must, before all else, cleanse and purify his heart, which is the seat of the revelation of the inner mysteries of God, from the obscuring dust of all acquired knowledge, and the allusions of the embodiments of satanic fancy.[15]

The present compilation is offered as a contribution to this effort.

Douglas Martin

INTRODUCTION

> Father, glorify[1] thy name. Then came there a voice from heaven, saying, I have both glorified it, and will glorify it again.
> *John 12:28*

Faith, according to the Baháʼí Writings,[2] is critical to our spiritual well-being and social advancement:

> Religion is the greatest of all means for the establishment of order in the world and for the peaceful contentment of all that dwell therein. The weakening of the pillars of religion hath strengthened the hands of the ignorant and made them bold and arrogant. Verily I say, whatsoever hath lowered the lofty station of religion hath increased the waywardness of the wicked, and the result cannot be but anarchy . . . Religion is a radiant light and an impregnable stronghold for the protection and welfare of the peoples of the world, for the fear of God impelleth man to hold fast to that which is good, and shun all evil. Should the lamp of religion be obscured, chaos and confusion will ensue, and the lights of fairness, of justice, of tranquillity and peace cease to shine.[3]

True religion, however, far from being harmful to humanity, must be demonstrably beneficial – it must yield goodly spiritual and social 'fruits'.[4]

> Religion should unite all hearts and cause wars and disputes to vanish from the face of the earth, give birth to spirituality, and bring life and light to each heart. If religion becomes a cause of dislike, hatred, and division, it were better to be without it, and to withdraw from such a religion would be a truly religious act. For it is clear

that the purpose of a remedy is to cure; but if the remedy should only aggravate the complaint it had better be left alone. Any religion which is not a cause of love and unity is no religion . . . thus any remedy that causes disease does not come from the great and supreme Physician.[5]

Bahá'u'lláh declares that all divine creeds are part of one common faith and emphasizes the urgent and desperate need for reconciliation of the religions of mankind.

> We desire but the good of the world and happiness of the nations . . . That all nations should become one in faith and all men as brothers; that the bonds of affection and unity between the sons of men should be strengthened; that diversity of religion should cease. . .[6]

> These principles and laws, these firmly-established and mighty systems, have proceeded from one Source, and are rays of one Light. That they differ one from another is to be attributed to the varying requirements of the ages in which they were promulgated.[7]

It has never been part of God's purpose to establish systems that increase hostility, death and destruction; it is rather to advance civilization and to strengthen bonds of affection and understanding. The Bahá'í Faith deplores the fragmentation of human society by religion. Therefore, its primary role is not to create a new religion but, more importantly, to renew belief, rekindle hope and resuscitate faith.

> Far from wishing to add to the number of religious systems, whose conflicting loyalties have for so many generations disturbed the peace of mankind, this Faith [of Bahá'u'lláh] is instilling into each of its adherents a new love for, and a genuine appreciation of, the unity underlying the various religions represented within its pale.[8]

> O ye that dwell on earth! The distinguishing feature that marketh the preeminent character of this Supreme Revelation consisteth in that We have, on the one hand, blotted out from the pages of God's holy Book whatsoever hath been the cause of strife, of malice and mischief amongst the children of men, and have, on the other, laid

down the essential prerequisites of concord, of understanding, of complete and enduring unity.⁹

Sadly, 'the decline of religion as a social force, of which the deterioration of religious institutions is but an external phenomenon, is chiefly responsible for so grave, so conspicuous an evil'¹⁰ as is currently prevalent.

And in this context, Islam, together with Judaism and Christianity, undeniably faces an increasing array of severe challenges today. The world is witnessing an alarming resurgence of religious fundamentalism, and an increasingly invasive, assertive, and militant Islam. Simultaneously, on multiple fronts, Sunni and Shí'ih Muslims exchange hostilities, and are in conflict with Jews, Christians, and members of other religions.

Twenty-six centuries ago, during a period of immense political instability, the Prophet Jeremiah advised the Jews who were experiencing a similar multitude of tests to pause and examine their options, remind themselves of earlier experiences that had led to their salvation, and look at the road ahead before continuing on the path to destruction:

> This is what the Lord says: 'Stand at the crossroads and look; ask for the ancient paths, ask where the good way is, and walk in it, and you will find rest for your souls. But you said, "We will not walk in it."'¹¹

This decision to travel the right road, Christ warned, is far from easy, and hence requires determination:

> Enter ye in at the strait gate: for wide is the gate, and broad is the way, that leadeth to destruction, and many there be which go in thereat: Because strait is the gate, and narrow is the way, which leadeth unto life, and few there be that find it.¹²

Muslims are today also at an important crossroads, and, together with Christians and Jews, have an appointment with destiny. They have a divinely-ordained choice, and a way is open to them to heed with due humility the invitation and the Call of the Summoner promised in the Qur'án:

On that day they follow the Summoner who deceiveth not, and voices are hushed for the Beneficent, and thou hearest but a faint murmur.

On that day no intercession availeth save him unto whom the Beneficent hath given leave and whose word He accepteth.

He knoweth (all) that is before them and (all) that is behind them, while they cannot compass it in knowledge.

And faces humble themselves before the Living, the Eternal...'[13]

This book has several aims.

First, relying predominantly on the Bible, the Qur'án and the Bahá'í Writings, it aims to explain the scriptural relationships of Judaism, Christianity, Islam and the Bahá'í Faith, their common aims and anticipations. Additionally, using mostly Bahá'u'lláh's own Words, it describes the divine prescription for mankind today. In this process, one comes to readily note the numerous indications of a fundamental principle proclaimed by Bahá'u'lláh, namely, that the interdependence of the religions is because they derive their inspiration from the same Source and vitally share a common faith that in its essentials is 'changeless . . . eternal in the past, eternal in the future'.[14] The emphasis on Judaism, Christianity and Islam in this presentation reflects simply the close relationship of the three Abrahamic religions, and by no means indicates that other divine religions are less valid or that the rest of humanity has been deprived of its share of divine grace.

Second, it aims to demonstrate that the Revelation of Muhammad was anticipated in the Bible, and that given the salutary influences of Islam, at least in its early history, that the Revelation of Muhammad constitutes a great proof of the very existence of God, *An-Náfi*, the Source of (all) good[15] and of divine direction in the unfolding spiritual destiny of mankind.

Third, it argues that for Islam to extricate itself from its current sorry state requires Muslims to rely less on their religious leaders for their daily guidance. They must instead trust that God will guide them if they make a sincere effort to investigate His Truth and to recognize their Lord. Only then will they escape radical and extreme ideologies, interfaith hostility and sectarian violence. Only then will they witness a spiritual rebirth of Islam at peace and in conformity with modernity.

Fourth, it aims to show that the Bible and the Qur'án itself indicate that every spiritual cycle or religious Dispensation, such as Judaism,

Christianity and Islam, have a beginning and, according to their own scriptures, a preordained end which is expected to be followed by a glorious Day, for these religions 'are doomed not to die, but to be reborn ... "Does not the child succumb in the youth and the youth in the man; yet neither child nor youth perishes?"'[16]

Judaism has now anticipated its Redeemer for several thousand years, and continues to eagerly await the coming of the Messiah. In the Tanakh, the Prophet Malachi promised the return of Elijah[17] and described that period as 'the great and dreadful day of the Lord' when 'the Sun of Righteousness' will 'arise, with healing in His wings'. Isaiah alluded to the coming of the 'Glory of the Lord',[18] the 'Wonderful, Counsellor, the mighty God, the everlasting Father, the Prince of Peace',[19] the 'Rod come forth out of the stem of Jesse' and the 'Branch grown out of its roots',[20] one who 'shall be established upon the throne of David',[21] who 'will come with strong hand',[22] who 'shall judge among the nations',[23] who 'shall smite the earth with the rod of His mouth, and with the breath of His lips shall he slay the wicked',[24] and who 'shall assemble the outcasts of Israel, and gather together the dispersed of Judah from the four corners of the earth'.[25] Of Him David had sung in his Psalms, acclaiming Him as the 'Lord of Hosts' and the 'King of Glory'.[26] To Him Haggai had referred as the 'Desire of all nations',[27] and Zachariah as the 'Branch' Who 'shall grow up out of His place',[28] and 'shall build the Temple of the Lord'.[29] Ezekiel and Joel had announced that His Day, 'the Day of the Lord', was 'near' and 'at hand'[30, 31]

In turn, Christ towards the end of His ministry reassured His disciples with the good news (gospel) of a future Revelation linked to His own:

> I have yet many things to say unto you, but ye cannot bear them now.
>
> Howbeit when he, the Spirit of truth, is come, he will guide you into all truth: for he shall not speak of himself; but whatsoever he shall hear, that shall he speak: and he will shew you things to come.
>
> He shall glorify me: for he shall receive of mine, and shall shew it unto you.[32]

The New Testament further teaches that God has spoken in the past through the Prophets 'at sundry times and in diverse manners'.[33]

Christians of numerous denominations have now prayed each Sunday for the past two thousand years for their 'daily bread' and for the coming of the Kingdom of God, when God's will shall 'be done on earth, as it is in heaven'.[34]

Yet Christian attitudes towards this 'good news' have today become ambivalent, according to one Bible scholar:

> we must think of the Christian teaching concerning the Second Coming of our Lord, and we will see that in modern times it has undergone a curious experience. For some people it is a belief which has simply vanished from the forefront of their minds, taking its place on the circumference, and even among the eccentricities of Christian doctrine. They seldom preach on it, and simply lay it aside. For other people it is the very centre of Christian belief. It dominates their whole thought and their whole thinking, and it is not far from the culmination of every sermon which they preach . . .[35]

The Qur'án expresses belief in the Psalms (*Zabur*), Torah (*Tawrát*) of Moses (*Musá*) and the Gospel (*Injíl*) of Jesus (*Ísá*), and mentions a long line of Prophets that have guided humanity, including the Old Testament Prophets Noah, Abraham, Jonah, Joseph, David, Moses and Aaron. It asserts that God has revealed His purpose to every section of humanity – 'to every people (*Ummah*) have we appointed rites and ceremonies which they must follow . . .'[36] And it emphasizes that God has sent more Prophets than the limited number mentioned in the Qur'án.[37]

The Qur'án, however, states unconditionally that an '*Ummah*', or people or nation, has a finite duration. It further indicates that religions decline when they age beyond their allotted time.[38] It is at these times that God renews His Covenant, elaborates on the spiritual and ethical principles that must govern the behaviour of individuals and society, and the laws that must be enacted to protect and advance civilization. Continued adherence to social teachings prescribed for an earlier Dispensation beyond their divinely-ordained expiration date causes harm. To allay undue concern the Qur'án moreover states:

> None of Our revelations do We abrogate or cause to be forgotten, but We substitute something better or similar: Knowest thou not that God Hath power over all things?

INTRODUCTION

> Knowest thou not that to God belongeth the dominion of the heavens and the earth? And besides Him ye have neither patron nor helper.[39]

Therefore, in anticipation of the end of the Dispensation of Islam and its rebirth, the Qur'án prepares Muslims for the awesome advent of Bahá'u'lláh's Revelation by describing the event in many ways:

> To Him Muḥammad, the Apostle of God, had alluded in His Book as the 'Great Announcement,' and declared His Day to be the Day whereon 'God' will 'come down' 'overshadowed with clouds,' the Day whereon 'thy Lord shall come and the angels rank on rank,' and 'The Spirit shall arise and the angels shall be ranged in order.' His advent He, in that Book, in a súrih said to have been termed by Him 'the heart of the Qur'án,' had foreshadowed as that of the 'third' Messenger, sent down to 'strengthen' the two who preceded Him. To His Day He, in the pages of that same Book, had paid a glowing tribute, glorifying it as the 'Great Day,' the 'Last Day,' the 'Day of God,' the 'Day of Judgment,' the 'Day of Reckoning,' the 'Day of Mutual Deceit,' the 'Day of Severing,' the 'Day of Sighing,' the 'Day of Meeting,' the Day 'when the Decree shall be accomplished,' the Day whereon the second 'Trumpet blast' will be sounded, the 'Day when mankind shall stand before the Lord of the world,' and 'all shall come to Him in humble guise,' the Day when 'thou shalt see the mountains, which thou thinkest so firm, pass away with the passing of a cloud,' the Day 'wherein account shall be taken,' 'the approaching Day, when men's hearts shall rise up, choking them, into their throats,' the Day when 'all that are in the heavens and all that are on the earth shall be terror-stricken, save him whom God pleaseth to deliver,' . . . the Day 'when the earth shall shine with the light of her Lord, and the Book shall be set, and the Prophets shall be brought up, and the witnesses; and judgment shall be given between them with equity; and none shall be wronged.'[40]

Muslims have moreover daily, and for many centuries, supplicated the Lord of the Day of Judgement to guide them to the 'Straight Path'. The Qur'án requires them to respond positively to the Call of their *Rabb* or

Lord,[41] and the Qur'án blesses those who 'desire to seek for the Countenance of their Lord Most High'.[42]

Fifth, this book suggests that Muslims 'consider the past'[43] and in so doing study the spiritual message of the Qur'án for themselves, diligently and without prejudice. They will then readily recognize that several of the social laws of the Qur'án are no longer applicable today, and importantly, that the difficulties that prevented individuals from recognizing Muhammad are identical to those that they may experience when presented with the Faith of Bahá'u'lláh.

> O my friend, were the bird of thy mind to explore the heavens of the Revelation of the Qur'án, were it to contemplate the realm of divine knowledge unfolded therein, thou wouldst assuredly find unnumbered doors of knowledge set open before thee. Thou wouldst certainly recognize that all these things which have in this day hindered this people from attaining the shores of the ocean of eternal grace, the same things in the Muḥammadan Dispensation prevented the people of that age from recognizing that divine Luminary, and from testifying to His truth.[44]

It is a tragedy that Muslims have now ignored the 'Call' of their 'Summoner', the only salvation for Islam, for more than one hundred and sixty years. Consequently, Islam faces many difficult issues today, several of which are outlined in this book.

Many political and military solutions have been proposed in response to this state of affairs, this threat to world peace. A great deal of effort has also been spent in improving inter-religious dialogue and understanding, and in appreciating each other's cultures. While these well-intentioned efforts are laudable, they have proven largely ineffective in creating an organic change in the attitudes of Muslims towards each other and towards Jews, Christians, and followers of other religions. Even if these efforts were to be successful in creating a lasting peace between the divergent interests, humanity would still need the redeeming principles of Bahá'u'lláh's Revelation to replace the current inadequate systems with a truly spiritual world civilization.

Today, the Bahá'í Faith invites Jews, Christians and Muslims, as well as members of other religions, to divest themselves of hollow and outworn institutions, obsolescent doctrines and beliefs, effete and discredited traditions, clerical control and manipulation, and instead to be true to their scriptures and to embrace the divine call that fulfils their highest aspirations and which represents the most recent stage in the evolution of the one common faith. Were Islam to awaken and heed the Message of Bahá'u'lláh, it would find itself freed from the burden of exclusivity, fanaticism, social devastation and economic upheaval, outdated social principles, internecine conflicts – at peace with itself and the rest of mankind, and in conformity with the purpose of God for humanity.

> Those who care for the future of the human race may well ponder this advice. 'If long-cherished ideals and time-honoured institutions, if certain social assumptions and religious formulae have ceased to promote the welfare of the generality of mankind, if they no longer minister to the needs of a continually evolving humanity, let them be swept away and relegated to the limbo of obsolescent and forgotten doctrines. Why should these, in a world subject to the immutable law of change and decay, be exempt from the deterioration that must needs overtake every human institution? For legal standards, political and economic theories are solely designed to safeguard the interests of humanity as a whole, and not humanity to be crucified for the preservation of the integrity of any particular law or doctrine.'[45]

The ultimate challenge therefore, and one articulated by Bahá'u'lláh, is whether Muslims, Christians and the followers of Moses are sufficiently in tune with the realities of their own faiths to be able to discard their shackles and to recognize His most glorious Cause. It is hoped that this presentation will stimulate further study and assist in this process.

> Say: If ye deny this Revelation, by what proof have ye believed in God? Produce it then. Thus hath the summons of God been sent down by the Pen of the Most High at the bidding of your Lord, the Most Glorious . . .[46]

PART I

THE SUMMONS

I

THE SUMMONS OF THE BÁB AND BAHÁ'U'LLÁH AND THE '*AJAL*' OF THE '*UMMAH*' OF ISLAM

> Therefore, (O Prophet) turn away from them. The day that the Caller (*Al-Dda̱ai*) will call (them) to a terrible affair,
>
> They will come forth – their eyes humbled – from their graves, (torpid) like locusts scattered abroad,
>
> Hastening, with eyes transfixed, towards the Caller! 'Hard is this Day!' the Unbelievers will say.
>
> Qamar, the Moon, 54:6–8[1]

Islam at its inception indubitably made major contributions to civilization. It created unity and harmony and promoted peace amongst diverse antagonistic populations, fusing them across a major part of the then known world into a 'Nation of Islam'. One may then question why Islam has fallen today into such disrepair and become prey to the many issues discussed in the following chapters. A possible explanation, and one considered here, is that this 'Nation of Islam' was never intended to last forever, but instead was meant to evolve into a new and more inclusive religious experience, adapted to the needs of mankind today. The thesis of this presentation, in part, is that the Faith of Bahá'u'lláh fulfils that need and expectation.

The need for a fresh revelation

> Who, contemplating the helplessness, the fears and miseries of humanity in this day, can any longer question the necessity for a fresh revelation of the quickening power of God's redemptive love and guidance? Who, witnessing on one hand the stupendous advance

achieved in the realm of human knowledge, of power, of skill and inventiveness, and viewing on the other the unprecedented character of the sufferings that afflict, and the dangers that beset, present-day society, can be so blind as to doubt that the hour has at last struck for the advent of a new Revelation, for a re-statement of the Divine Purpose, and for the consequent revival of those spiritual forces that have, at fixed intervals, rehabilitated the fortunes of human society?[2]

The Qur'án refers to Islam as an '*Ummah*', a nation, people, or a divinely-ordained religious system or Dispensation.

> Thus have We made of you an *Ummah* justly balanced, that ye might be witnesses over the nations, and the Messenger a witness over yourselves.[3]

It warns, however, that every '*Ummah*' has a preordained '*ajal*', 'term', a predestined end or demise. It announces that God will in due time send Messengers who will reveal His verses (*A'ráf*, the Heights, 7:35). It warns Muslims to 'listen for the Day when the Caller will call out from a place quite near' (*Qáf*, 50:41),[4] and invite them and the rest of humanity to 'a terrible affair'[5] – a Day that will be hard indeed for those who disbelieve (*Qamar*, the Moon, 54:6).

> To every people is a term appointed: when their term is reached, not an hour can they cause delay, nor (an hour) can they advance it.
> O ye Children of Adam! Whenever there come to you Apostles from amongst you, rehearsing My Signs unto you, those who are righteous and mend (their lives), – on them shall be no fear nor shall they grieve.[6]

> For those whose hopes are in the meeting with God; for the Term (appointed) by God is surely coming: and He hears and knows (all things).[7]

> Do they not reflect in their own minds? Not but for just ends and for a term appointed, did God create the heavens and the earth, and all between them: yet are there truly many among men who deny the meeting with their Lord![8]

The following pages will demonstrate as conclusively as possible that the twin Dispensations of the Báb and Bahá'u'lláh represent the promised Summons of 'the Lord of the Hosts' or *Rabb al Junood* (*Muddaththir*, One Wrapped up, 74:31; Isa. 2:12 and 28:5), and are a further 'Revelation from the Lord of the Worlds' or *Rabb alAAalameen* (*Wáqi'a*, the Inevitable Event, 56:80) – 'the twin trumpet blasts' (*Zumar*, the Crowds, 39:68) destined to call both the living and spiritually dead.

> Ah woe, that Day, to the rejectors of Truth!
> Have we not made the earth (as a place) to draw together –
> The living and the dead.[9]

> Who will give an account to him that is ready to judge the living and the dead.[10]

Bahá'u'lláh testifies:

> This is the Day whereon every man will fly from himself, how much more from his kindred, could ye but perceive it. Say: By God! The blast hath been blown on the trumpet, and lo, mankind hath swooned away before us! The Herald [the Báb] hath cried out, and the Summoner [Bahá'u'lláh] raised His voice saying: 'The Kingdom is God's, the Most Powerful, the Help in Peril, the Self-Subsisting.'[11]

Dawn of a new Revelation signalling the rebirth and resurrection of earlier Dispensations

Seventeen decades ago (1260 AH, 1844 AD), addressing the people of both the East and West, a twenty-five-year-old youth, the Báb (the Gate), announced that the period of prophecy and expectation, the last of which had been associated with the Prophet Muhammad, the 'Seal of the Prophets', had come to a close, and that His Revelation signalled the dawn of a new era.[12] The 'Summoner' promised in the Qur'án and anticipated in the Gospels when 'the Son of man shall come in the glory of his Father with his angels; and then he shall reward every man according to his works' (Matt. 16:27), and the 'Lord of Hosts' and the 'King of Glory' awaited in the Torah had finally issued His 'Call'.

For to us a child is born, to us a son is given; and the government will be upon his shoulder, and his name will be called 'Wonderful Counselor, Mighty God, Everlasting Father, Prince of Peace'.

Of the increase of his government and of peace there will be no end, upon the throne of David, and over his kingdom, to establish it, and to uphold it with justice and with righteousness from this time forth and for evermore. The zeal of the Lord of hosts will do this.[13]

Lift up your heads, O ye gates; and be ye lift up, ye everlasting doors; and the King of glory shall come in.

Who is the King of glory?

The Lord strong and mighty, the Lord mighty in battle.

Lift up your heads, O ye gates; even lift them up, ye everlasting doors; and the King of glory shall come in.

Who is this King of glory: The Lord of hosts, he is the King of glory.[14]

His Revelation was the 'Great Announcement' (*Nabaa*, the (Great) News, 78:1-2) promised in the Qur'án and the 'City of God' promised in the Bible.

And I saw a new heaven and a new earth: for the first heaven and the first earth were passed away; and there was no more sea.

And I John saw the holy city, new Jerusalem, coming down from God out of heaven, prepared as a bride adorned for her husband.

And I heard a great voice out of heaven saying, Behold, the tabernacle of God is with men, and he will dwell with them, and they shall be his people, and God himself shall be with them, and be their God.

And God shall wipe away all tears from their eyes; and there shall be no more death, neither sorrow, nor crying, neither shall there be any more pain: for the former things are passed away.

And he that sat upon the throne said, Behold, I make all things new. And he said unto me, Write: for these words are true and faithful.

And he said unto me, It is done. I am Alpha and Omega, the beginning and the end. I will give unto him that is athirst of the fountain of the water of life freely.

He that overcometh shall inherit all things; and I will be his God, and he shall be my son.[15]

His Faith was destined to guide mankind to the 'straight' and 'right Path' (*Fátiḥa*, the Opening Chapter, 1:5), and to establish the Kingdom of God on earth, as in the prayer of Jesus, 'Thy kingdom come' (Matt. 6:10).

The Báb addressed the Islamic world thus:

O people of the Qur'án! Ye are as nothing unless ye submit unto the Remembrance of God (the Báb) and unto this Book. If ye follow the Cause of God, We will forgive you your sins, and if ye turn aside from Our command, We will, in truth, condemn your souls in Our Book . . .[16]

In the manifestation of the Apostle of God (Muhammad) all were eagerly awaiting Him, yet thou hast heard how He was treated at the time of His appearance, in spite of the fact that if ever they beheld Him in their dreams they would take pride in them.

Likewise in the manifestation of the Point of the Bayán (the Báb), the people stood up at the mention of His Name and fervently implored His advent night and day, and if they dreamt of Him they gloried in their dreams; yet now that He hath revealed Himself, invested with the mightiest testimony, whereby their own religion is vindicated, and despite the incalculable number of people who yearningly anticipate His coming, they are resting comfortably in their homes, after having hearkened to His verses; while He at this moment is confined in the mountain of Mákú, lonely and forsaken.[17]

His Announcement ushered in the 'Day of Judgement', the 'Day of Resurrection', and the 'heaven on earth' promised in the Bible and in the Qur'án. Their common faith had been revived and the eternal divine purpose for humanity had been restated. Consequently, all earlier Dispensations, including that of Islam, were abrogated and their social laws that did not serve the interests of the new age and humanity were suspended. Their followers were challenged to liberate themselves from clerical tyranny, to investigate the truth unfettered by tradition, superstition and dogma, and to ascertain the divine purpose by valid criteria.

In His prolific Writings, the Báb in turn anticipated the imminent Revelation of '*Man-yazhur'u'lláh*' or 'Him whom God will manifest' (Bahá'u'lláh), and addressed Him with great love and humility:

> This is an epistle from this lowly servant to the All-Glorious Lord – He Who hath been aforetime and will be hereafter manifest, Verily He is the Most Manifest, the Almighty.
>
> In the name of the Sovereign Lord, the Lord of Power.
>
> Glorified is He before Whom all the dwellers of earth and heaven bow down in adoration and unto Whom all men turn in supplication . . . He is the One Who revealeth whatsoever He willeth and by His injunction 'Be Thou' all things have come into being.
>
> This is an epistle . . . unto Him Who will be made manifest through the power of Truth – He Who is the All-Glorious, the Best Beloved – to affirm that all created things as well as myself bear witness for all time that there is none other God but Thee . . . and that all men shall be raised to life through Thee.[18]

He warned His followers not to fail to recognize the future Revelation:

> Take good heed of yourselves, O people of the Bayán, lest ye perform such deeds as to weep sore for His sake night and day, to stand up at the mention of His Name, yet on this Day of fruition – a Day whereon ye should not only arise at His Name, but seek a path unto Him Who personifies that Name – ye shut yourselves out from Him as by as veil.[19]

The Báb's audacious Message spread like wildfire, and within six years had swept throughout Persia and neighbouring countries. People from all walks of life, including prominent Muslim theologians and clerics, rallied to His Cause. The phenomenal success of the Báb's Message greatly alarmed the Islamic ecclesiastical and civil authorities, resulting in an unimaginable persecution, unprecedented in religious history for its ferocity and cruelty. After two years the Báb was imprisoned and held a captive until His martyrdom in 1850 AD. His followers were decimated. Tragically and ironically, the primary perpetrator was the

Shí'ih Islamic clerical order that still today yearningly prays that God will hasten the appearance of the Promised One, '*Al-Qá'im*', or 'He Who shall arise'. Bahá'u'lláh laments this recurrent tragedy:

> How often have they expected His coming, how frequently have they prayed that the breeze of divine mercy might blow, and the promised Beauty step forth from behind the veil of concealment, and be made manifest to all the world. And whensoever the portals of grace did open, and the clouds of divine bounty did rain upon mankind, and the light of the Unseen did shine above the horizon of celestial might, they all denied Him, and turned away from His face – the face of God Himself. Refer ye, to verify this truth, to that which hath been recorded in every sacred Book.[20]

Twenty years after the declaration of His Forerunner, Bahá'u'lláh announced in 1863 that He was the One the Báb had referred to in His Book, the Bayán, and claimed that His Revelation fulfilled the expectations of all earlier religions, including Judaism, Christianity and Islam.

> The summons and the message which We gave were never intended to reach or to benefit one land or one people only. Mankind in its entirety must firmly adhere to whatsoever hath been revealed and vouchsafed unto it. Then and only then will it attain unto true liberty. The whole earth is illuminated with the resplendent glory of God's Revelation. In the year sixty He Who heralded the light of Divine Guidance – may all creation be a sacrifice unto Him – arose to announce a fresh revelation of the Divine Spirit, and was followed, twenty years later, by Him through Whose coming the world was made the recipient of this promised glory, this wondrous favour. Behold how the generality of mankind hath been endued with the capacity to hearken unto God's most exalted Word – the Word upon which must depend the gathering together and spiritual resurrection of all men . . .[21]

In innumerable revealed Writings, but primarily in the *Kitáb-i-Íqán*, Bahá'u'lláh declared that God, the Source of all Revelations, is One. To know the essentially unknowable God, the purpose of man's creation,[22] was to acknowledge His Divine Messengers, Who incarnated the Divine

Will and Purpose. Faith was still faith, no matter by which religion it had been revealed. Moreover, God's Faith was eternal and changeless in its foundational verities or essentials. Bahá'u'lláh thus explained that the various spiritual cycles or Dispensations differed only 'in the intensity of their revelation, and the comparative potency of their light'[23] due primarily to the different requirements and capacities of the people to whom the Message was revealed at any one time. The various religions were therefore distinguishable only by non-essentials – social laws that were relevant for only a finite period of time and which were destined to be abrogated or modified at a later date. Thus, the Divine Message had each time been revealed commensurate with the capacity and special needs of a particular people and age. Therefore, the Faith of Bahá'u'lláh considers itself not so much an additional religion but more accurately as the renewal of Faith. In the words of Shoghi Effendi:

> Far from wishing to add to the number of the religious systems, whose conflicting loyalties have for so many generations disturbed the peace of mankind, this Faith is instilling into each of its adherents a new love for, and a genuine appreciation of the unity underlying, the various religions represented within its pale.[24]

The Faith standing identified with the name of Bahá'u'lláh disclaims any intention to belittle any of the Prophets gone before Him, to whittle down any of their teachings, to obscure, however slightly, the radiance of their Revelations, to oust them from the hearts of their followers, to abrogate the fundamentals of their doctrines, to discard any of their revealed Books, or to suppress the legitimate aspirations of their adherents. Repudiating the claim of any religion to be the final revelation of God to man, disclaiming finality for His own Revelation, Bahá'u'lláh inculcates the basic principle of the relativity of religious truth, the continuity of Divine Revelation, the progressiveness of religious experience. His aim is to widen the basis of all revealed religions and to unravel the mysteries of their scriptures. He insists on the unqualified recognition of the unity of their purpose, restates the eternal verities they enshrine, coordinates their functions, distinguishes the essential and the authentic from the nonessential and spurious in their teachings, separates the God-given truths from the priest-prompted superstitions, and on this as a basis proclaims the possibility, and even prophecies the inevitability, of their unification, the consummation of their highest hopes.[25]

As with His Predecessors, Bahá'u'lláh taught that it is everyone's duty to arise, and undaunted by any hindrances with which friend or foe might unwittingly or deliberately obstruct his path, investigate the truth of the Divine Revelation – one's faith is simply too important to be left to chance alone and dictated solely by an accident of birth. Rather, an individual's beliefs should be the product of earnest study. He reminded the Muslims that the Qur'án had promised that such a sincere effort ('*jihád*', or spiritual struggle or endeavour) will be divinely assisted and recompensed (*Ibráhím*, Abraham, 14:24). True seekers will be rewarded with the ability to see with their own eyes and to hear the divine melody with their own ears. They will readily discern that the Tree of Bahá'u'lláh's Revelation is 'good' as demonstrated by its 'good fruits' (*Ibráhím*, Abraham, 14:24-7; Matt. 7:18-19) – evident in the genuine and organic unity of Bahá'í communities throughout the world, and in the shunning of all religious discord and animosity, the harmonization of science and faith, the promotion of the rights of women, and the establishment of justice. Shoghi Effendi writes:

> The Faith of Bahá'u'lláh has assimilated, by virtue of its creative, its regulative and ennobling energies, the varied races, nationalities, creeds and classes that have sought its shadow, and have pledged unswerving fealty to its cause. It has changed the hearts of its adherents, burned away their prejudices, stilled their passions, exalted their conceptions, ennobled their motives, coordinated their efforts, and transformed their outlook. While preserving their patriotism and safeguarding their lesser loyalties, it has made them lovers of mankind, and the determined upholders of its best and truest interests. While maintaining intact their belief in the Divine origin of their respective religions, it has enabled them to visualize the underlying purpose of these religions, to discover their merits, to recognize their sequence, their interdependence, their wholeness and unity, and to acknowledge the bond that vitally links them to itself. This universal, this transcending love which the followers of the Bahá'í Faith feel for their fellow-men, of whatever race, creed, class or nation, is neither mysterious nor can it be said to have been

artificially stimulated. It is both spontaneous and genuine. They whose hearts are warmed by the energizing influence of God's creative love cherish His creatures for His sake, and recognize in every human face a sign of His reflected glory.[26]

The followers of Bahá'u'lláh are instructed 'to think of all humankind as their friends; regarding the alien as an intimate, the stranger as a companion . . .'[27]

As a direct consequence of the assertion that the Dispensation of Islam was ended and that God had revealed once again His Purpose to humanity, Bahá'u'lláh and His followers were in turn persecuted savagely, as attested by Him:

> The people of the Qur'án have arisen against Us, and tormented Us with such a torment that the Holy Spirit lamented, and the thunder roared out, and the clouds wept over us . . .[28]

The hostility to the Revelation of Bahá'u'lláh continues unabated to this day, both in the land of its birth and in almost every Muslim domain. For forty years Bahá'u'lláh suffered imprisonment and torture. His last banishment was to Palestine, where he died – a prisoner of the Ottoman Empire.

> . . . Is it ever so, that, when there cometh unto you a messenger with that which ye yourselves desire not, ye grow arrogant, and some ye disbelieve and some ye slay?[29]

In Islamic lands the Faith of Bahá'u'lláh continues to be much maligned by a biased and misguided clergy that claims to represent the true interests of Islam. It has been maliciously misrepresented as being Zionist[30] and inspired and aided by foreign powers. Bahá'ís have been castigated as belonging to a misguided and detestable cult or sect, '*firqeh zállé*',[31] infidels, apostates (*murtadd*), causing 'corruption and mischief (*fasád*) on earth',[32] and 'those who wage war against God'[33] – inflammatory accusations that have been used to justify the extermination of individuals and communities under religious or Sharia law. Their basic freedoms have been curtailed, their properties confiscated, looted or burned, their right to education denied, their marriages annulled, and men, women, and children have been subjected to harsh imprisonment, torture and death.[34]

Despite all the adversities, the Faith of Bahá'u'lláh has triumphed and is now spread over the entire planet and recognized as one of the fastest growing religions.[35]

> Their intention is to extinguish God's Light (by blowing) with their mouths: but God will complete (the revelation of) His Light, even though the unbelievers detest it.[36]

> Those who reject God, hinder (men) from the Path of God, and resist the Messenger, after Guidance has been clearly shown to them, will not injure God in the least, but He will make their deeds of no effect.[37]

> Say: 'That is a Message Supreme (above all) –
> From which ye do turn away!'[38]

> But verily, this is a Message for the God-fearing.
> And We certainly know that there are amongst you those that reject (it).
> But truly (Revelation) is a cause of sorrow for the unbelievers.
> But, verily, it is Truth of assured certainty.
> So glorify the name of thy Lord Most High.[39]

A popular but unjust charge is that this innocent Faith is anti-Islamic. This could not be further from the truth; Bahá'ís revere Muhammad and believe in the Qur'án. The accusation is particularly malicious, as Bahá'ís have not allowed their mistreatment to deter them from acknowledging the validity of Islam and expressing their love for its Prophet. They naturally champion the cause of Islam to its detractors, as evident from 'Abdu'l-Bahá's addresses in synagogues and churches in the West.[40] Irrespective of their religious background, the followers of Bahá'u'lláh are taught, as an essential element of their Faith, to regard Islam as one link in the chain of continually progressive Revelations. They are well aware that their scriptures glorify Muhammad and refer to Him as 'the Apostle of God',[41] 'the Prophet of God',[42] 'the Messenger of God',[43] 'the Seal of the Prophets',[44] 'the Seal of the Prophets and Messengers',[45] 'the Most distinguished of God's chosen ones',[46] 'the Center of creation and Sun of prophethood',[47] 'the Messenger of reality',[48] 'that immortal Beauty' and 'that Divine Beauty',[49] 'the Beloved of God',[50] 'the Dayspring of Divine wisdom, the Dawning-Point of Revelation',[51] 'the King of Glory',[52] 'the Lord of Mankind',[53] 'the Lord of existing things',[54] 'the Source of Divine wisdom . . . that Manifestation of Universal prophethood',[55] 'the Day-star of Truth . . . that Flame of supreme Prophethood',[56] 'the King of the elect and the Sun of Truth',[57] 'the Ark of Salvation, the Luminous Countenance and Lord of Men',[58] 'the sovereign Lord of all',[59] 'the Dawning-Point of revelation, the Focus of the endless splendours of grace . . . that Wellspring of universal wisdom, that Mine of Divine knowledge',[60] and 'that Blessed Tree Whose light was "neither of the East nor of the West" and Who cast over all the peoples of the earth the sheltering shade of a measureless grace, [and] showed forth infinite kindness and forbearance in His dealings with every one'.[61]

The following tributes in the Bahá'í Writings bear testimony to this:

> And I praise and glorify the first sea which has branched from the ocean of the Divine Essence, and the first morn which hath glowed from the horizon of Oneness, and the first sun which hath risen in the Heaven of Eternity, and the first fire which was lit from the Lamp pf Preexistence in the lantern of singleness: He who was Aḥmad in the kingdom of the exalted ones, and Muhammad amongst the concourse of the near ones, and Maḥmúd in the realm of the sincere ones. '. . . by whichsoever (name) ye will, invoke Him: He Hath most excellent names' in the hearts of those who know. And upon His household and companions be abundant and abiding and eternal peace![62]

> Blessing and peace be upon Him through Whose advent Baṭḥá (Mecca) is wreathed in smiles, and the sweet savours of Whose raiment have shed fragrance upon all mankind – He Who came to protect men from that which would harm them in the world below. Exalted, immensely exalted is His station above the glorification of all beings and sanctified from the praise of the entire creation. Through His advent the tabernacle of stability and order was raised throughout the world and the ensign of knowledge hoisted among

the nations. May blessings rest also upon His kindred and His companions through whom the standard of the unity of God and of His singleness was uplifted and the banners of celestial triumph were unfurled. Through them the religion of God was firmly established among His creatures and His Name magnified amidst His servants. I entreat Him – exalted is He – to shield His Faith from the mischief of His enemies who tore away the veils, rent them asunder and finally caused the banner of Islám to be reversed amongst all peoples.[63]

O my friend, were the bird of thy mind to explore the heavens of the Revelation of the Qur'án, were it to contemplate the realm of divine knowledge unfolded therein, thou wouldst assuredly find unnumbered doors of knowledge set open before thee.[64]

As to Muhammad, the Apostle of God, let none . . . think for a moment that either Islám, or its Prophet, or His Book, or His appointed Successors, or any of His authentic teachings, have been, or are to be in any way, or to however slight a degree, disparaged. The lineage of the Báb, the descendant of the Imám Husayn; the divers and striking evidences, in Nabíl's Narrative, of the attitude of the Herald of our Faith towards the Founder, the Imáms, and the Book of Islám; the glowing tributes paid by Bahá'u'lláh in the Kitáb-i-Íqán to Muhammad and His lawful Successors, and particularly to the 'peerless and incomparable' Imám Husayn; the arguments adduced, forcibly, fearlessly, and publicly by 'Abdu'l-Bahá, in churches and synagogues, to demonstrate the validity of the Message of the Arabian Prophet . . . all proclaim, in no uncertain terms, the true attitude of the Bahá'í Faith . . .[65]

Bahá'ís realize that the subject of Islam is dealt with in a cursory fashion and unfairly in the West. They are prompted to study the Qur'án and the history of Islam:

They must strive to obtain, from sources that are authoritative and unbiased, a sound knowledge of the history and tenets of Islám – the source and background of their Faith – and approach reverently and with a mind purged from preconceived ideas the study of the Qur'án which, apart from the sacred scriptures of the Bábí and Bahá'í Revelations, constitutes the only Book which can be regarded as an absolutely authenticated Repository of the Word of God.[66]

> ... the Guardian would certainly advise, and even urge the friends to make a thorough study of the Qur'án, as the knowledge of this sacred Scripture is absolutely indispensable for every believer who wishes to adequately understand and intelligently read, the writings of Bahá'u'lláh.[67]

Apart from Muslims, many individuals who have to date espoused the Faith of Bahá'u'lláh were formerly Jews, Christians, Buddhists, Hindus, or did not subscribe to any religion. As Bahá'ís they have come to accept Islam, and to recognize it as an irrefutable evidence of divine intervention in human affairs, that, at least in its early period, was responsible for magnificent and amazing social and spiritual advances.

A notable illustration of this reverential attitude towards Islam is 'the written testimonial of the Queen of Rumania, who, born in the Anglican faith and notwithstanding the close alliance of her government with the Greek Orthodox Church, the state religion of her adopted country, had . . . been prompted to proclaim her recognition of the prophetic function of Muhammad . . .'[68] She wrote:

> God is All, everything. He is the power behind all beginnings . . . His is the Voice within us that shows us good and evil. But mostly we ignore or misunderstand this voice. Therefore, did He choose His Elect to come down amongst us upon earth to make clear His Word, His real meaning. Therefore, the Prophets; therefore, Christ, Muhammad, Bahá'u'lláh, for man needs from time to time a voice upon earth to bring God to him, to sharpen the realization of the existence of the true God. Those voices sent to us had to become flesh, so that with our earthly ears we should be able to hear and understand.[69]

Shoghi Effendi comments on her testimony:

> What greater proof, it may be pertinently asked, can the divine . . . require wherewith to demonstrate the recognition by the followers of

Bahá'u'lláh of the exalted position occupied by the Prophet Muhammad among the entire company of the Messengers of God? What greater service do these divines expect us to render the Cause of Islám? What greater evidence of our competence can they demand than that we should kindle, in quarters so far beyond their reach, the spark of an ardent and sincere conversion to the truth voiced by the Apostle of God, and obtain from the pen of royalty this public, and indeed historic, confession of His God-given Mission?[70]

Thus, to the many Muslims who have embraced His Faith, Bahá'u'lláh is the promise of the Qur'án, and they consider heeding His Call tantamount to being faithful to the Message of the Prophet of Islam – just as the Jews who accepted Jesus were considered to have truly known Moses and understood His Revelation (John 5:25), and the Jews and Christians who accepted Islam were considered as having been obedient to the teachings of Moses and Christ. Shoghi Effendi writes that:

the Bahá'í Revelation, claiming as it does to be the culmination of a prophetic cycle and the fulfilment of the promise of all ages, [does not] attempt, under any circumstances, to invalidate those first and everlasting principles that animate and underlie the religions that have preceded it. The God-given authority, vested in each one of them, it admits and establishes as its firmest and ultimate basis. It regards them in no other light except as different stages in the eternal history and constant evolution of one religion, Divine and indivisible, of which it itself forms but an integral part. It neither seeks to obscure their Divine origin, nor to dwarf the admitted magnitude of their colossal achievements. It can countenance no attempt that seeks to distort their features or to stultify the truths which they instil. Its teachings do not deviate a hairbreadth from the verities they enshrine, nor does the weight of its message detract one jot or one tittle from the influence they exert or the loyalty they inspire. Far from aiming at the overthrow of the spiritual foundation of the world's religious systems, its avowed, its unalterable purpose is to widen their basis, to restate their fundamentals, to reconcile their aims, to reinvigorate their life, to demonstrate their oneness, to restore the pristine purity of their teachings, to coordinate their functions and to assist in the realization of their highest aspirations.

These divinely-revealed religions, as a close observer has graphically expressed it, 'are doomed not to die, but to be reborn . . . "Does not the child succumb in the youth and the youth in the man; yet neither child nor youth perishes?"'[71]

It is the thesis of this presentation that it is largely due to the denial of Bahá'u'lláh's Message that Islam today faces many perplexing issues, and is in dire need of the 'resurrection' and regeneration that is such an integral and persistent message of the Qur'án. The current parlous state of Islam is directly due to resisting 'the straight Path'[72] that they have prayed for five times every day and which is delineated for them by Bahá'u'lláh. Hopefully, they will still heed His Call and save themselves from the severe consequences of disbelief recorded in their Holy Book.

The declaration by Bahá'u'lláh of His Divine Mission has therefore had far-reaching implications for the current version and state of Islam, a reality that is not lost on both the Sunni and Shí'ih institutions of Islam which have tried and failed to extirpate His nascent Faith.

> Islám, at once the progenitor and persecutor of the Faith of Bahá'u'lláh, is, if we read aright the signs of the times, only beginning to sustain the impact of this invincible and triumphant Faith.[73]

The twin processes of integration and disintegration are readily apparent today – on the one hand, a rapidly expanding and remarkably varied and united Bahá'í world community is working diligently to promote social and religious unity; and on the other hand, religious fanaticism and sectarian violence is daily causing havoc in the name of Allah. Religious terrorism has not spared any corner of the earth, and it is clear that politicians and statesmen are impotent to deal with its root causes – all that they can hope for is to limit and mitigate its consequences. This increasingly unmanageable crisis is by now of immediate and vital concern to every citizen of planet Earth.

Bahá'u'lláh invites the peoples of the world to examine His Revelation, 'a Faith which is at once the essence, the promise, the reconciler, and the unifier' of earlier Dispensations.[74] Muslims, as with followers of other religions, must, despite the pressures inherent in time-honoured tradition and obstacles inculcated and imposed by a dominant and powerful clergy that controls every aspect of their lives, belief and worship, face up to the clear choice before them, and fulfil their spiritual destiny. The stark alternatives are to either leave Islam, or to support, passively or actively, the increasingly destructive tendencies that in the eyes of many have unfairly tainted the noble name of Islam and made it synonymous with terrorism and with animosity and aggression towards all that is reasonable and modern.

In recognition of the difficulties that the heralded Revelation will face and in order to facilitate the response of Muslims, the Holy Qur'án thus prompts the seeker:

> O ye who believe! if a wicked person comes to you with any news, ascertain the truth, lest ye harm people unwittingly, and afterwards become full of repentance for what ye have done.[75]

The sincere seeker is further fortified in his or her spiritual effort, often fraught with difficulties and stumbling-blocks, by the promise of aid from the Almighty:

> And those who strive in Our (Cause), We will certainly guide them to Our Paths: for verily God is with those who do right.[76]

> But to those who receive guidance, He increases the (light of) Guidance . . .[77]

Faced with claims of the superiority and permanence of the Islamic Dispensation that preempt and thwart investigation of new teachings, the seeker is also reassured by this blessed Quranic verse that applies to all Dispensations:

> None of Our revelations do We abrogate or cause to be forgotten, but We substitute something better or similar; knowest thou not that God hath power over all things?[78]

2

ISLAM: THE PROMISE OF THE BIBLE

> . . . consider the people unto whom the Gospel was given. Having no access to the apostles of Jesus, they sought the pleasure of the Lord in their churches, hoping to learn that which would be acceptable unto God, but they found therein no path unto Him. Then when God manifested Muḥammad as His Messenger and as the Repository of His good-pleasure, they neglected to quicken their souls from the Fountain of living waters which streamed forth from the presence of their Lord and continued to rove distraught upon the earth seeking a mere droplet of water and believing that they were doing righteous deeds. They behaved as the people unto whom the Qur'án was given are now behaving.
>
> The Báb[1]

By the time the Qur'án was revealed, Christian Europe faced many challenges. The Christian 'house'[2] had become divided, with the Orthodox Eastern Church irreconcilably alienated from the Western Roman Catholic Church over dogma. In part, Christian belief had become indistinguishable from pagan superstition, and fatalism prevailed. The rich and powerful ruled, and the poor and powerless could hope only to survive. And, as yet, Christian Europe had to deal with the repercussions of the Reformation and the consequences of protracted wars between Protestants and Catholics.

Bahá'u'lláh declares that the Christians would have fared better if they had, through personal endeavour, recognized Muhammad as a Divine Messenger and had been transformed by His Message:

> Had these souls but clung steadfastly to the Handle of God manifested in the Person of Muḥammad, had they turned wholly unto God and cast aside all that they had learned from their divines, He

would assuredly have guided them through His grace and acquainted them with the sacred truths that are enshrined within His imperishable utterances. For far be it from His greatness and His glory that He should turn away a seeker at His door, cast aside from His Threshold one who hath set his hopes on Him, reject one who hath sought the shelter of His shade, deprive one who hath held fast to the hem of His mercy, or condemn to remoteness the poor one who hath found the river of His riches. But as these people failed to turn wholly unto God, and to hold fast to the hem of His all-pervading mercy at the appearance of the Daystar of Truth, they passed out from under the shadow of guidance and entered the city of error...[3]

Bahá'u'lláh blames this failure on their misapprehension of their scriptures and reliance on a literal interpretation of the Divine Word:

Inasmuch as the Christian divines have failed to apprehend the meaning of [the Words of Jesus concerning the Manifestation to come after Him] and did not recognize their object and purpose, and have clung to the literal interpretation of the words of Jesus, they therefore became deprived of the streaming grace of the Muhammadan Revelation and its showering bounties. The ignorant among the Christian community, following the example of the leaders of their faith, were likewise prevented from beholding the beauty of the King of glory, inasmuch as those signs which were to accompany the dawn of the sun of the Muhammadan Dispensation did not actually come to pass. Thus, ages have passed and centuries rolled away, and that most pure Spirit hath repaired unto the retreats of its ancient sovereignty. Once more hath the eternal Spirit breathed into the mystic trumpet, and caused the dead to speed out of their sepulchres of heedlessness and error unto the realm of guidance and grace. And yet, that expectant community still crieth out: When shall these things be? When shall the promised One, the object of our expectation, be made manifest . . .?[4]

Prerequisites for understanding Biblical references to Islam

According to the Bible itself, only the Prophets of God may interpret prophecy:

> We have also a more sure word of prophecy; whereunto ye do well that ye take heed, as unto a light that shineth in a dark place, until the day dawn, and the day star arise in your hearts:
>
> Knowing this first, that no prophecy of the scripture is of any private interpretation.
>
> For the prophecy came not in old time by the will of man: but holy men of God spake as they were moved by the Holy Ghost.[5]
>
> Ye shall not add unto the word which I command you, neither shall ye diminish aught from it, that ye may keep the commandments of the Lord your God which I command you.[6]
>
> What thing soever I command you, observe to do it: thou shalt not add thereto, nor diminish from it.[7]

Just as Christ had opened the eyes of the Jews who recognized Him to mysteries of the Tanakh, the Hebrew Bible, concerning His Revelation, today the authority to explain the scriptures resides with Bahá'u'lláh.[8] However, faith, spiritual receptivity and 'a hearing ear and a seeing eye' are essential requirements to appreciate the explanations of the Divine Word.

> And he [Jesus] turned him unto his disciples, and said privately, Blessed are the eyes which see the things that ye see:
>
> For I tell you, that many prophets and kings have desired to see those things which ye see, and have not seen them; and to hear those things which ye hear, and have not heard them.[9]

The Christian appreciates that it is sadly often the case that although the Word of God enlightens some, it has the potential to blind others:

> And Jesus said, For judgment I am come into this world, that they which see not might see; and that they which see might be made blind.[10]

> And in them is fulfilled the prophecy of Esaias, which saith, By hearing ye shall hear, and shall not understand; and seeing ye shall see, and shall not perceive:
>
> For this people's heart is waxed gross, and their ears are dull of

hearing, and their eyes they have closed; lest at any time they should see with their eyes and hear with their ears, and should understand with their heart, and should be converted, and I should heal them.

But blessed are your eyes, for they see: and your ears, for they hear.[11]

When studying Biblical references to Muhammad and to Islam, Christians do well to consider that every Bible text quoted in the New Testament as referring to Jesus is vehemently disputed by Jewish scholars, whose unanimous opinion is that the scripture is quoted out of context. The following are examples of their objections:[12]

1. Matt. 1:22–3

Now all this was done, that it might be fulfilled which was spoken of the Lord by the prophet, saying,

Behold, a virgin shall be with child, and shall bring forth a son, and they shall call his name Emmanuel, which being interpreted is, God with us.

This refers to Isa. 7:14–16:

Therefore the Lord himself shall give you a sign; Behold, a virgin shall conceive, and bear a son, and shall call his name Immanuel.

Butter and honey shall he eat, that he may know to refuse the evil, and choose the good.

For before the child shall know to refuse the evil, and choose the good, the land that thou abhorrest shall be forsaken of both her kings.

Objections

Matthew clearly regards the prophecy as referring to the virgin birth of Christ. Commentators however have pointed out that (a) the Prophet Isaiah wanted to restore faith in King Ahaz (732 BC) and to prevent him from making alliances with Assyria during a critical period, by offering him a sign from God; (b) there is no indication that the child would be the Messiah; (c) most Jewish sources translate '. . . the young woman is with child' – the timing of the pregnancy being in the past, present or imminent future; and (d) the reference is to a young woman (*almah*) and not to a virgin (*betulah*). Jewish tradition states that the young woman was indeed Isaiah's own wife. The Isaiah statement is also incompatible with the dietary practices of Jesus and the Church's teachings on immaculate (sinless) conception.

2. Matt. 2:14-15

> When he arose, he took the young child and his mother by night, and departed into Egypt:
> And was there until the death of Herod: that it might be fulfilled which was spoken of the Lord by the prophet, saying, Out of Egypt have I called my son.

This refers to Hos. 11:1:

> When Israel was a child, then I loved him, and called my son out of Egypt.

Objection

Hosea refers to the historical event of the Jews, God's son (Exod. 4:22), coming out of Egypt – not a Messianic expectation.

3. Matt. 2:17-18

> Then was fulfilled that which was spoken by Jeremy the prophet, saying,
> In Rama was there a voice heard, lamentation, and weeping, and great mourning, Rachel weeping for her children, and would not be comforted, because they are not.

This refers to Jer. 31:15-16:

> Thus saith the Lord; A voice was heard in Ramah, lamentation, and bitter weeping; Rahel weeping for her children refused to be comforted for her children, because they were not.

Objection

This is not a Messianic prophecy predicting the killing of 'innocents' by Herod (died 4 BC) but refers to the captivity of Rachel's children in Assyria. The subsequent verses describe their return to Israel.

4. Matt. 2:23

> And he came and dwelt in a city called Nazareth: that it might be fulfilled which was spoken by the prophets, He shall be called a Nazarene.

Objections

This does not appear to be a reference to any passage in the Tanakh, as the words 'Nazareth' and 'Nazarene' do not appear in that scripture. Also, there has never been a requirement for the Messiah to come from Nazareth.

5. Matt. 4:12–16

> Now when Jesus had heard that John was cast into prison, he departed into Galilee;
> And leaving Nazareth, he came and dwelt in Capernaum, which is upon the sea coast, in the borders of Zabulon and Nephthalim:
> That it might be fulfilled which was spoken by Esaias the prophet, saying,
> The land of Zabulon, and the land of Nephthalim, by the way of the sea, beyond Jordan, Galilee of the Gentiles;
> The people which sat in darkness saw great light; and to them which sat in the region and shadow of death light is sprung up.

This refers to Isa. 8:22 and 9:12:

> And they shall look unto the earth; and behold trouble and darkness, dimness of anguish; and they shall be driven to darkness.
> Nevertheless the dimness shall not be such as was in her vexation, when at the first he lightly afflicted the land of Zebulun and

the land of Naphtali, and afterward did more grievously afflict her by the way of the sea, beyond Jordan, in Galilee of the nations.

The people that walked in darkness have seen a great light: they that dwell in the land of the shadow of death, upon them hath the light shined.

Objection

Isaiah provides an historical account of the king of Assyria's assault on the Northern Kingdom of Israel, inflicting heavy losses and afflicting Zebulon, Naphtali and Galilee, as opposed to Matthew's claim that this is a Messianic prophecy, fulfilled by Jesus. Matthew's account twice eliminates wording about how the subject 'afflicted' these areas.

6. Matt. 12:15-18

But when Jesus knew it, he withdrew himself from thence: and great multitudes followed him, and he healed them all;

And charged them that they should not make him known:

That it might be fulfilled which was spoken by Esaias the prophet, saying,

Behold my servant, whom I have chosen; my beloved, in whom my soul is well pleased: I will put my spirit upon him, and he shall shew judgment to the Gentiles.

This refers to Isa. 42:1-4:

Behold my servant, whom I uphold; mine elect, in whom my soul delighteth; I have put my spirit upon him: he shall bring forth judgment to the Gentiles.

He shall not cry, nor lift up, nor cause his voice to be heard in the street.

A bruised reed shall he not break, and the smoking flax shall he not quench: he shall bring forth judgment unto truth.

He shall not fail nor be discouraged, till he have set judgment in the earth: and the isles shall wait for his law.

Objection

Christ's statement that He had only come for the lost sheep of Israel (Matt. 15:24) and His instructions to His twelve disciples, 'Go not into the way of the Gentiles, and into any city of the Samaritans enter ye not: But go rather to the lost sheep of the house of Israel' (Matt. 10:5–6).

7. Matt. 13:34–5

> All these things spake Jesus unto the multitude in parables; and without a parable spake he not unto them:
> That it might be fulfilled which was spoken by the prophet, saying, I will open my mouth in parables; I will utter things which have been kept secret from the foundation of the world.

This refers to Ps. 78:1–3:

> Give ear, O my people, to my law: incline your ears to the words of my mouth.
> I will open my mouth in a parable: I will utter dark sayings of old:
> Which we have heard and known, and our fathers have told us.

Objection

This is an inaccurate translation according to the Hebrew Tanakh, in which there is no mention of 'things which have been kept secret from the foundation of the world'.

8. Matt. 21:4–7

> All this was done, that it might be fulfilled which was spoken by the prophet, saying,
> Tell ye the daughter of Sion, Behold, thy King cometh unto thee, meek, and sitting upon an ass, and a colt the foal of an ass.
> And the disciples went, and did as Jesus commanded them,
> And brought the ass, and the colt, and put on them their clothes, and they set him thereon.

This refers to Zech. 9:9:

> Rejoice greatly, O daughter of Zion; shout, O daughter of Jerusalem: behold, thy King cometh unto thee: he is just, and having salvation; lowly, and riding upon an ass, and upon a colt the foal of an ass.

Objection

Both ass and colt are lowly animals compared to a horse and were used for double emphasis that the Messiah would be humble – Matthew has Jesus riding two animals! It is also not much of a prophecy if there was a deliberate attempt to purchase the animals so as to fulfil the prediction.

9. John 1:45

> Philip findeth Nathaniel, and saith unto him, We have found him, of whom Moses in the law, and the prophets, did write, Yeshua of Nazareth, the son of Joseph.

Objection

None of the Old Testament prophets including Moses wrote about Yeshua.

A prophecy may apply to one or all subsequent Prophets

That an allusion to one of them may apply generally to all of them may be concluded from Jesus's explanation that had the Jews known the reality of Moses and been in tune with the Divine Message they would also have recognized Him;[13] from Muhammad's teaching that no distinction should be made between any of the religions;[14] and from Bahá'u'lláh's assertion that the Prophets of God proclaim the same Divine Purpose.[15]

Moreover, the Prophets of God do not depend on the expectations of an earlier Dispensation for the validation of their Revelations. Christ's authority was not based on prophecies of the Tanakh, particularly as explained by the Jewish rabbis, nor did the legitimacy of Muhammad's mission derive solely from New Testament prophecies as interpreted by

Christian clergy. Their authority was from above, and the truth of their Cause was established and made evident by the fruits of their Revelations and the transforming power of their Faiths. Prophecies and their elucidation by the Author of a subsequent Dispensation are therefore more a means of demonstrating the continuity of Revelation and the essential unity of divinely-revealed religions. Had the Prophets of God conformed to the expectations of their time none of them would have been rejected and persecuted.

Muhammad and Islam, the promise of the Torah[16]

The Bahá'í Faith teaches that there is an indissoluble link between the various Dispensations. In this context Shoghi Effendi explains that the mission of the Prophet Muhammad was indeed part of the promise and 'good news' of the Bible.

> The Bahá'í view . . . is that the Dispensation of Muhammad, like all other Divine Dispensations, has been foreordained, and that as such it forms an integral part of the Divine plan for the spiritual, moral and social development of mankind. It is not an isolated phenomenon, but is closely and historically related to the Dispensation of Christ, and those of the Báb and Bahá'u'lláh. It was intended by God to succeed Christianity, and it was therefore the duty of the Christians to accept it as firmly as they had adhered to the religion of Christ.[17]

Deuteronomy announces that God will summon a Prophet from amongst the Arabs, Who will be of the stature of Moses, and similar to Moses will speak only as directed by the Almighty.

> The Lord [Hebrew *Yahweh*, thy God] thy God [Hebrew *ĕ-lō-he-kā*] will raise up unto thee a Prophet [Hebrew *nā-bî*][18] from the midst of thee, of thy brethren,[19] like unto me [Hebrew *kā-mō-nî*]; unto him ye shall hearken.[20]

And again,

> I . . . will raise them up a Prophet [Hebrew *nā-bî*] from among their brethren [Hebrew *'ă-ḥê-hem*], like unto thee,[21] and will put my

words in his mouth; and he shall speak unto them all that I shall command him.[22]

When John the Baptist preached many centuries later to 'prepare the way' for Christ, it is clear from the questions the Jewish leaders asked him that apart from the Messiah and the return of Elias or Elijah, they continued to expect the Prophet promised in Deuteronomy:

> And this is the record of John, when the Jews sent priests and Levites from Jerusalem to ask him, Who art thou?
> And he confessed, and denied not; but confessed, I am not the Christ.
> And they asked him, What then? Art thou Elias? And he saith, I am not. Art thou that prophet? And he answered, No.
> Then said they unto him, Who art thou? that we may give an answer to them that sent us . . .[23]

The Tanakh also bears witness to the coming of the 'Holy One' and 'Lord' from Mount Parán (a mountain range in Arabia), and the appearance of twelve princes who are offspring of Ishmael – a reference to the twelve successors or Imáms of Muhammad.

> God came from Temán,[24] and the Holy One [*u-qdush*] from mount Parán. Selah. His glory covered the heavens, and the earth was full of his praise.[25]

> And as for Ishmael . . . Behold, I have blessed him, and will make him fruitful, and will multiply him exceedingly; twelve princes shall he beget, and I will make him a great nation.[26]
> And this is the blessing, wherewith Moses the man of God blessed the children of Israel before his death.
> And he said, The Lord came from Sinai, and rose from Seir unto them; he shined forth from mount Parán and he came with ten thousand Saints from his right hand went a fiery law for them.[27]

The 95th Súrah of the Qur'án echoes the strong link between the three Abrahamic religions:

> By the fig!
> And by the olive!
> And by Mount Sinai!
> And by this safe land![28]

And Bahá'u'lláh, addressing 'Alí Páshá, the powerful Ottoman prime minister, uses identical references, reminding us of the oneness of faith and the unity of the religions:

> O Chief! We revealed Ourself unto thee at one time upon Mount Tina, and at another time upon Mount Zayta,[29] and yet again in this hallowed Spot. Following, however, thy corrupt inclinations, thou didst fail to respond and wert accounted with the heedless.[30]

The famous prophecy of Isaiah on the gathering and peace amongst wild 'animals' is an apt description of the savage tribes of Arabia that became civilized under the influence of Islam; it has also been understood as referring to the future unity and harmony of the peoples of the world 'in the knowledge of the Lord'.

> The wolf also shall dwell with the lamb, and the leopard shall lie down with the kid; and the calf and the young lion and the fatling together; and a little child shall lead them.
> And the cow and the bear shall feed; their young ones shall lie down together: and the lion shall eat straw like the ox.
> And the suckling child shall play on the hole of the asp, and the weaned child shall put his hand on the cockatrice' den.
> They shall not hurt nor destroy in all my holy mountain: for the earth shall be full of the knowledge of the Lord, as the waters cover the sea.[31]

The Bahá'í Faith, the reconciler of religions and peoples, sees itself as the fulfilment of the Isaiah prophecy and of a similar Quranic expectation: 'they (all animals) shall be gathered to their Lord in the end'.[32] However, it additionally maintains that the prophecy was also fulfilled by the Dispensation of Muhammad:

> This is what Muhammad taught His people concerning Jesus and

Moses, and He reproached them for their lack of faith in these great Teachers, and taught them the lessons of truth and tolerance. Muhammad was sent from God to work among a people as savage and uncivilized as the wild beasts. They were quite devoid of understanding, nor had they any feelings of love, sympathy and pity. Women were so degraded and despised that a man could bury his daughter alive, and he had as many wives to be his slaves as he chose.

Among these half animal people Muhammad was sent with His divine Message. He taught the people that idol worship was wrong, but that they should reverence Christ, Moses and the Prophets. Under His influence they became a more enlightened and civilized people and arose from the degraded state in which He found them. Was not this a good work, and worthy of all praise, respect and love?[33]

New Testament prophecies concerning Muhammad and Islam and fulfilment in the Dispensations of the Báb and Bahá'u'lláh

The Gospel of St John remarks that it is in the interest of His followers that Jesus 'goes away', as only then would Christians receive the 'Paraclete' or Comforter (also translates as the Counsellor, Helper, Encourager, and Advocate). The Bahá'í Faith accepts that one explanation is that the expected 'Paraclete' refers to the succeeding Dispensation of Muhammad.[34]

> And I will pray the Father, and he shall give you another Comforter, that he may abide with you for ever;
> Even the Spirit of truth; whom the world cannot receive, because it seeth him not, neither knoweth him: but ye know him; for he dwelleth with you, and shall be in you.[35]

> Nevertheless I tell you the truth; It is expedient for you that I go away: for if I go not away, the Comforter will not come unto you; but if I depart, I will send him unto you.
> And when he is come, he will reprove the world of sin, and of righteousness, and of judgment . . .
> I have yet many things to say unto you, but ye cannot bear them now.
> Howbeit when he, the Spirit of truth, is come, he will guide you

into all truth: for he shall not speak of himself; but whatsoever he shall hear, that shall he speak: and he will shew you things to come.

He shall glorify me: for he shall receive of mine, and shall shew it unto you.

All things that the Father hath are mine: therefore said I, that he shall take of mine, and shall shew it unto you.[36]

These things have I spoken unto you, being yet present with you.

But the Comforter, which is the Holy Ghost, whom the Father will send in my name, he shall teach you all things, and bring all things to your remembrance, whatsoever I have said unto you.[37]

But when the Comforter is come, whom I will send unto you from the Father, even the Spirit of truth, which proceedeth from the Father, he shall testify of me.[38]

The Book of Revelation (the Revelation of St John the Divine) contains many references that have puzzled Christians over the centuries and have led to many interpretations. Its importance has always been recognized in light of St John's admonition at the beginning of his book: 'Blessed is he that readeth, and they that hear the words of this prophecy . . . for the time is at hand' (Rev. 1:3).

Two chapters of the Book of Revelation are explained by 'Abdu'l-Bahá in detail as referring to Islam. His explanations are given in the notes and references for this chapter.

The birth of a 'child' (Dispensation of Islam) in the desert [39]

And there appeared a great wonder in heaven; a woman[40] clothed with the sun, and the moon under her feet,[41] and upon her head a crown of twelve stars:[42]

And she being with child cried, travailing in birth, and pained to be delivered.

And there appeared another wonder in heaven; and behold a great red dragon, having seven heads and ten horns, and seven crowns upon his heads.[43]

And his tail drew the third part of the stars of heaven, and did cast them to the earth: and the dragon stood before the woman which was ready to be delivered, for to devour her child as soon as it was born.⁴⁴

And she brought forth a man child, who was to rule all nations with a rod of iron: and her child was caught up unto God, and to his throne.⁴⁵

And the woman fled into the wilderness, where she hath a place prepared of God,⁴⁶ that they should feed her there a thousand two hundred and threescore days.⁴⁷

'Two witnesses', 'two olive trees', and 'two candle sticks' (Muhammad and His Successor, 'Alī)⁴⁸

And there was given me a reed like unto a rod:⁴⁹ and the angel stood, saying, Rise, and measure the temple of God, and the altar, and them that worship therein.⁵⁰

But the court which is without the temple leave out, and measure it not; for it is given unto the Gentiles:⁵¹ and the holy city shall they tread under foot forty and two months.⁵²

And I will give power unto my two witnesses, and they shall prophesy a thousand two hundred and threescore days, clothed in sackcloth.

These are the two olive trees, and the two candlesticks standing before the God of the earth.⁵³

And if any man will hurt them, fire proceedeth out of their mouth, and devoureth their enemies: and if any man will hurt them, he must in this manner be killed.

These have power to shut heaven, that it rain not in the days of their prophecy: and have power over waters to turn them to blood, and to smite the earth with all plagues, as often as they will.

And when they shall have finished their testimony, the beast that ascendeth out of the bottomless pit shall make war against them, and shall overcome them, and kill them.⁵⁴

And their dead bodies shall lie in the street of the great city, which spiritually is called Sodom and Egypt, where also our Lord was crucified.⁵⁵

And they of the people and kindreds and tongues and nations shall see their dead bodies three days and an half, and shall not suffer their dead bodies to be put in graves.⁵⁶

> And they that dwell upon the earth shall rejoice over them, and make merry, and shall send gifts one to another; because these two prophets tormented them that dwelt on the earth.
>
> And after three days and an half[57] the Spirit of life from God entered into them, and they stood upon their feet; and great fear fell upon them which saw them.
>
> And they heard a great voice from heaven saying unto them, Come up hither. And they ascended up to heaven in a cloud; and their enemies beheld them.[58]

'Abdu'l-Bahá further explains that the verses of the Revelation of St John 'have another explanation and a symbolic sense':

> the Law of God is divided into two parts. One is the fundamental basis which comprises all spiritual things – that is to say, it refers to the spiritual virtues and divine qualities; this does not change or alter: it is the Holy of Holies, which is the essence of the Law of Adam, Noah, Abraham, Moses, Christ, Muhammad, the Báb and Bahá'u'lláh, and which lasts and is established in all the prophetic cycles. It will never be abrogated . . .'[59]

These foundations of the Religion of God are renewed with each subsequent Dispensation. The other part of the Law of God comprises the social teachings that do change with every new Dispensation (the Holy City). Thus at the end of the Mosaic Dispensation,

> the Law of God disappeared, only a form without spirit remaining. The Holy of Holies departed from among them, but the outer court of Jerusalem – which is the expression used for the form of the religion – fell into the hands of the Gentiles. In the same way, the fundamental principles of the religion of Christ, which are the greatest virtues of humanity, have disappeared; and its form has remained in the hands of the clergy and the priests. Likewise, the foundation of the religion of Muhammad has disappeared, but its form remains in the hands of the official 'ulamá.[60]

The Praised One

The Bible teaches that the Jews should give thanks to God's Holy Name (*ḥamd*, see I Chron. 16:35); 'praise the Lord for His mercy endureth for ever' (II Chron. 20:21), and praise His glorious name (I Chron. 29:13). The Christians are instructed to 'shew forth the praises of him who hath called you out of darkness into his marvellous light' (I Pet. 2:9).

Bahá'u'lláh explains that the reality of the Prophets of God is one and the same. Therefore, the 'praise' referred to in the Bible applies not only abstractly to God but specifically to Moses and Christ, the Revealers of His Purpose and the Manifestations of His Names and Attributes. Indeed, the title 'the Praised One' applies to all of the Divine Messengers, including Muhammad, whose very name derives from the verb 'to praise' or 'to exalt'. Bahá'u'lláh confirms this title, referring to other forms of this name 'the Praised One':

> He who was Aḥmad in the kingdom of the exalted ones, and Muhammad amongst the concourse of the near ones, and Maḥmúd in the realm of the sincere ones. '. . . by whichsoever (name) ye will, invoke Him: He hath the most excellent names' in the hearts of those who know.[61]

The Bible also foretells that with the coming of the Lord who will explain the divine mysteries, all humanity will 'have praise of God':

> Therefore judge nothing before the time, until the Lord come, who both will bring to light the hidden things of darkness, and will make manifest the counsels of the hearts: and then shall every man have praise of God.[62]

> And in that day shall ye say, Praise the Lord, call upon his name, declare his doings among the people, make mention that his name is exalted.[63]

It is noteworthy that the Jews at the time of Muhammad cherished Messianic hopes, and their invitation for Him to join them in Medina was partly a reflection of their excitement that the call of monotheism had been raised from amongst the Arabs.[64] Yet despite all the glad-tidings in the Bible, the Jews and Christians failed to recognize the station of Muhammad. The Qur'án affirms that Jesus gave the good news of Muhammad (Ahmad, 'the Praised One'):

> And remember, Jesus, the son of Mary, said: 'O Children of Israel! I am the messenger of God (sent) to you, confirming the Law (which came) before me, and giving glad Tidings of a Messenger to come after me, whose name shall be Ahmad.' But when he came to them with Clear Signs, they said, 'This is evident sorcery!'[65]

In turn, the Muslims did not heed the very same prophecies which predicted the misfortunes that would befall Islam. In this context the Báb, the forerunner of Bahá'u'lláh, drew parallels between the failure of the Christian kings to acknowledge Muhammad as the One promised in the Bible, and the inability of the Muslim rulers of His own time to recognize Him as the One promised in the Qur'án:

> Gracious God! Within the domains of Islám there are at present seven powerful sovereigns ruling the world. None of them hath been informed of His [the Báb's] Manifestation, and if informed, none hath believed in Him. Who knoweth, they may leave this world below full of desire, and without having realized that the thing for which they were waiting had come to pass. This is what happened to the monarchs that held fast unto the Gospel. They awaited the coming of the Prophet of God [Muhammad], and when He did appear, they failed to recognize Him. Behold how great are the sums which these sovereigns expend without even the slightest thought of appointing an official charged with the task of acquainting them in their own realms with the Manifestation of God! They would thereby have fulfilled the purpose for which they have been created. All their desires have been and are still fixed upon leaving behind them traces of their names.[66]

3

ISLAM: A TESTIMONY OF DIRECT DIVINE INTERVENTION IN HUMAN AFFAIRS

From His retreat of glory His voice is ever proclaiming: 'Verily, I am God; there is none other God besides Me, the All-Knowing, the All-Wise. I have manifested Myself unto men, and have sent down Him Who is the Day Spring of the signs of My Revelation. Through Him I have caused all creation to testify that there is none other God except Him, the Incomparable, the All-Informed, the All-Wise.' He Who is everlastingly hidden from the eyes of men can never be known except through His Manifestation, and His Manifestation can adduce no greater proof of the truth of His Mission than the proof of His own Person.

Bahá'u'lláh[1]

... those Whom He [God] hath raised up in truth and sent forth with His guidance are the Manifestations of His most excellent names, the Revealers of His most exalted attributes, and the Repositories of His Revelation in the kingdom of creation; that through them the Proof of God hath been perfected unto all else but Him, the standard of Divine Unity hath been raised, and the sign of sanctity hath been made manifest; and that through them every soul hath found a path unto the Lord of the Throne on high.

Bahá'u'lláh[2]

The Qur'án manifests the creative power of the Word of God

The Judaic, Christian and Islamic Revelations deserve our close attention not only because of their profound consequences for mankind, but also because they constitute the greatest proof of God's very existence and involvement in human affairs. However, as Islam is historically closer to our time it provides more verifiable and ample material for analysis. Bahá'ís consider the study of Islam and of the Revelation of Muhammad to be essential and vitally important, affording us an even greater opportunity to examine the impact of this divine intervention in human affairs. Bahá'u'lláh declares: 'the unfailing testimony of God to both the East and the West is none other than the Qur'án'.[3]

As attested by Himself, Muhammad could not read or write. The Qur'án itself refers to Him as the illiterate Prophet (*alnnabiyya al-ommiyya*). Yet He provided the Arabs with their first Book, which despite severe persecution transformed them and later generations and wider sections of human society – a phenomenon that any unbiased student of history would attribute to the creative power of the Divine Word.

> Those who follow the Apostle, the unlettered Prophet, whom they find mentioned in their own (Scriptures); in the law (Torah) and the Gospel; for he commands them what is just and forbids them what is evil: he allows them as lawful what is good (and pure) and prohibits them from what is bad (and impure); He releases them from their heavy burdens and from the yokes that are upon them. So it is those who believe in him, honour him, help him, and follow the light which is sent down with him, it is they who will prosper.
>
> Say: 'O men! I am sent unto you all, as the Apostle of God, to Whom belongeth the dominion of the heavens and the earth: there is no god but He: it is He that giveth both life and death. So believe in God and His Apostle, the unlettered Prophet, who believed in God and His words: follow him that (so) ye may be guided.'[4]

Spiritual 'fruits' are evidence that the 'tree' is divine

Christ stated that 'every tree is known by his own fruit' and 'a good tree bringeth not forth evil fruit, neither can a corrupt tree bring forth good fruit'. He warned that 'every tree that brings not forth good fruit is hewn down, and cast into the fire' and instructed His followers, 'therefore by their fruits you shall know them' (Matt. 7:16-19).

What Judaism, Christianity and Islam have notably shared in common is their demonstrated ability to transmute individuals through the power of the Divine Word, and call into being a new race of men. This spiritual transformation is considered in Bahá'í Writings as a supreme function of God's Revelations. Bahá'u'lláh is emphatic in affirming their essential role in this regard:

> Is not the object of every Revelation to effect a transformation in the whole character of mankind, a transformation that shall manifest itself, both outwardly and inwardly, that shall affect both its inner life and external conditions? For if the character of mankind be not changed, the futility of God's universal Manifestations would be apparent.[5]

Indeed, it is Bahá'í belief that God reveals His Faith in the most difficult circumstances to illustrate this very fact, demonstrating His creative Power.

> How often have the Prophets of God, not excepting Bahá'u'lláh Himself, chosen to appear, and deliver their Message in countries and amidst peoples and races, at a time when they were either fast declining, or had already touched the lowest depths of moral and spiritual degradation. The appalling misery and wretchedness to which the Israelites had sunk, under the debasing and tyrannical rule of the Pharaohs, in the days preceding their exodus from Egypt under the leadership of Moses; the decline that had set in in the religious, the spiritual, the cultural, and the moral life of the Jewish people, at the time of the appearance of Jesus Christ; the barbarous cruelty, the gross idolatry and immorality, which had for so long been the most distressing features of the tribes of Arabia and brought such shame upon them when Muhammad arose to proclaim His Message in their midst; the indescribable state of decadence, with its attendant corruption, confusion, intolerance, and oppression, in both the civil and religious life of Persia, so graphically portrayed by the pen of a considerable number of scholars, diplomats, and travellers, at the hour of the Revelation of Bahá'u'lláh – all demonstrate this basic and inescapable fact . . . For it is precisely under such circumstances, and by such means that the Prophets have, from time immemorial, chosen and were able to demonstrate their redemptive power to raise from the depths of abasement and of misery, the

people of their own race and nation, empowering them to transmit in turn to other races and nations the saving grace and the energizing influence of their Revelation.[6]

Truthfulness, love, compassion and hospitality replace dishonesty, hatred, estrangement and rudeness; unity and peace triumph over conflict and contention; and enlightened behaviour is substituted for ignorance. In turn, this transformation promotes justice, education, and the sciences and the arts; the alteration in individual outlooks and collective strivings advance the evolution of human society.

Examples of the workings of this spiritual phenomenon, as history records, are noted in the saintly and heroic actions of the early Christians at Rome, and in the reformed behaviour of savage tribes of Arabia after the appearance of Muhammad. And those so affected attributed their new pattern of life to the influences of a higher authority. The depths of their conviction and consequent conversion, as well as their ability to bear with fortitude the horrors of the oppression they encountered, can be ascribed, as Bahá'u'lláh thus explains, solely to the Divine Word:

> Is it within human power . . . to effect in the constituent elements of any of the minute and indivisible particles of matter so complete a transformation as to transmute it into purest gold? Perplexing and difficult as this may appear, the still greater task of converting satanic strength into heavenly power is one that We have been empowered to accomplish. The Force capable of such a transformation transcendeth the potency of the Elixir itself. The Word of God, alone, can claim the distinction of being endowed with the capacity required for so great and far-reaching a change.[7]

Transformation of world society by Islam

The spiritual and cultural evolution of Arabia and Europe resulting from the Message of the Prophet Muhammad is frequently referred to in the Bahá'í teachings, as for example in a far-reaching and profound address by 'Abdu'l-Bahá to the Jewish community of San Francisco in 1912:

Consider that His Holiness Muhammad was born among the savage and barbarous tribes of Arabia, lived among them and was outwardly illiterate and uninformed of the Holy Books of God. The Arabian people were in the utmost ignorance and barbarism. They buried their infant daughters alive, considering this to be an evidence of a valorous and lofty nature. They lived in bondage and serfdom under the Iranian and Roman governments and were scattered throughout the desert engaged in continual strife and bloodshed. When the Light of Muhammad dawned, the darkness of ignorance was dispelled from the deserts of Arabia. In a short period of time those barbarous peoples attained a superlative degree of civilization which with Baghdad as its center extended far westward as Spain and afterward influenced the greater part of Europe. What proof of Prophethood could be greater than this, unless we close our eyes to justice and remain obstinately opposed to reason?[8]

Elsewhere 'Abdu'l-Bahá told a Christian audience: 'Muhammad was sent from God to work among a people as savage and uncivilized as the wild beasts.'[9] The social and spiritual edification and unification of the fiercely savage tribes of the Arabian Peninsula under the banner of a monotheistic Faith may be regarded as fulfilment of the following Biblical prophecy – incidentally, a unity amongst wild beasts that according to the Qur'án will require be repeated in the future (*Takwír*, Folding Up, 81:5).

> The wolf also shall dwell with the lamb, and the leopard shall lie down with the kid; and the calf and the young lion and the fatling together; and a little child shall lead them.
> And the cow and the bear shall feed; their young ones shall lie down together: and the lion shall eat straw like the ox.
> And the suckling child shall play on the hole of the asp, and the weaned child shall put his hand on the cockatrice den.
> They shall not hurt nor destroy in all my holy mountain.[10]

The following is a remarkable tribute from the Bahá'í Writings to the transforming power and influence of Islam:

> The noted historians of Europe, in describing the conditions,

A TESTIMONY OF DIVINE INTERVENTION IN HUMAN AFFAIRS

manners, politics, learning and culture, in all their aspects, of early, medieval and modern times, unanimously record that during the ten centuries constituting the Middle Ages, from the beginning of the sixth century of the Christian era till the close of the fifteenth, Europe was in every respect and to an extreme degree, barbaric and dark. The principal cause of this was that the monks, referred to by European peoples as spiritual and religious leaders, had given up the abiding glory that comes from obedience to the sacred commandments and heavenly teachings of the Gospel, and had joined forces with the presumptuous and tyrannical rulers of the temporal governments of those times. They had turned their eyes away from everlasting glory, and were devoting all their efforts to the furtherance of their mutual worldly interests and passing and perishable advantages. Ultimately things reached a point where the masses were hopeless prisoners in the hands of these two groups, and all this brought down in ruins the whole structure of the religion, culture, welfare and civilization of the peoples of Europe.

When the unworthy acts and thoughts and the discreditable purposes of the leaders had stilled the sweet savors of the Spirit of God (Jesus) and they ceased to stream across the world, and the darkness of ignorance and bigotry and of actions that were displeasing to God, encompassed the earth, then the dawn of hope shone out and the Divine spring drew on; a cloud of mercy overspread the world, and out of the regions of grace the fecund winds began to blow. In the sign of Muḥammad, the Sun of Truth rose over Yathrib (Medina) and the Ḥijáz and cast across the universe the lights of eternal glory. Then the earth of human potentialities was transformed, and the words 'The earth shall shine with the light of her Lord,' were fulfilled. The old world turned new again, and its dead body rose into abundant life. Then tyranny and ignorance were overthrown, and towering palaces of knowledge and justice were reared in their place. A sea of enlightenment thundered, and science cast down its rays. The savage peoples of the Ḥijáz, before that Flame of supreme Prophethood was lit in the lamp of Mecca, were the most brutish and benighted of all the peoples of the earth. In all the histories, their depraved and vicious practices, their ferocity and their constant feuds, are a matter of record. In those days the civilized peoples of the world did not even consider the Arab tribes of Mecca and Medina as human beings. And yet, after the Light of the World rose over them, they were – because of the education bestowed on them by that Mine of perfections, that Focal Center of Revelation, and the blessings vouchsafed by the Divine Law – within a brief interval gathered into the shelter of the principle of Divine oneness. This brutish people then attained such a high degree of human perfection and civilization that all their contemporaries marveled at them. Those very peoples who had always mocked the Arabs and held them up to ridicule as a breed devoid of judgment, now eagerly sought them out, visiting their countries to acquire enlightenment and culture, technical skills, statecraft, arts and sciences.

Observe the influence on material situations of that training which is inculcated by the true Educator. Here were tribes so benighted and untamed that during the period of the Jáhilíyyih they would bury their seven-year-old daughters alive – an act which even an animal, let alone a human being, would hate and shrink from but which they in their extreme degradation considered the ultimate expression of honor and devotion to principle – and this darkened people, thanks to the manifest teachings of that great Personage, advanced to such a degree that after they conquered Egypt, Syria and its capital Damascus, Chaldea, Mesopotamia and Iran, they came to administer single-handedly whatever matters were of major importance in four main regions of the globe.

The Arabs then excelled all the peoples of the world in science and the arts, in industry and invention, in philosophy, government and moral character. And truly, the rise of this brutish and despicable element, in such a short interval, to the supreme heights of human perfection, is the greatest demonstration of the rightfulness of the Lord Muḥammad's Prophethood.

In the early ages of Islám the peoples of Europe acquired the sciences and arts of civilization from Islám as practiced by the inhabitants of Andalusia. A careful and thorough investigation of the historical record will establish the fact that the major part of the civilization of Europe is derived from Islám; for all the writings of Muslim scholars and divines and philosophers were gradually collected in Europe and were with the most painstaking care weighed and debated at academic gatherings and in the centers of learning, after which their valued contents would be put to use. Today, numerous copies of the works of Muslim scholars which are not to be found in Islámic countries, are available in the libraries of Europe. Furthermore, the laws and principles current in all European countries are derived to a considerable degree and indeed virtually in their entirety from the works on jurisprudence and the legal decision of Muslim theologians.[11]

Bahá'í belief on the subject of the influence of Islam on European civilization is illustrated further by the following statement:

> ... due to the historical order of its appearance, and also because of the obviously more advanced character of its teachings, Islám constitutes a fuller revelation of God's purpose for mankind. The so-called Christian civilization of which the Renaissance is one of the most striking manifestations is essentially Muslim in its origins and foundations. When medieval Europe was plunged in darkest barbarism, the Arabs regenerated and transformed by the spirit released by the religion of Muhammad were busily engaged in establishing a civilization the like of which their contemporary Christians in Europe had never witnessed before. It was eventually through Arabs that civilization was introduced to the West. It was through them that the philosophy, science and culture which the old Greeks had developed found their way to Europe. The Arabs were the ablest translators, and linguists of their age, and it is thanks to them that the writings of such well-known thinkers as Socrates, Plato and Aristotle were made available to the Westerners. It is wholly unfair to attribute the efflorescence of European culture during the Renaissance period to the influence of Christianity. It was mainly the product of the forces released by the Muhammadan Dispensation.[12]

Introduction of nationhood: Al-Ummat-ul Islámiyyah, *the nation of Islam*

At a time when Europe was plagued by conflicts and in dire spiritual darkness, Islam introduced the concept of '*Ummah*', 'nation' or 'community'. It created a vast social and spiritual community that transcended earlier national boundaries. In this extended community Muslims of vastly different ethnic backgrounds were considered equal and were united in faith and vision, and entrusted with the duty of protecting the rights of minorities. This is fully acknowledged in the Bahá'í Writings:

> The Faith of Islám, the succeeding link in the chain of Divine Revelation, introduced . . . the conception of the nation as a unit and a vital stage in the organization of human society, and embodied it in its teaching. This indeed is what is meant by this brief yet highly significant and illumination pronouncement of Bahá'u'lláh: 'Of old [Islamic Dispensation] it hath been revealed: "Love of one's country is an element of the Faith of God."' This principle was established and stressed by the Apostle of God, inasmuch as the evolution of human society required it at that time. Nor could any stage above and beyond it have been envisioned, as world conditions preliminary to the establishment of a superior form of organization were as yet unobtainable. The conception of nationality, the attainment to the state of nationhood, may, therefore, be said to be the distinguishing characteristics of the Muhammadan Dispensation, in the course of which the nations and races of the world, and particularly in Europe and America, were unified and achieved political independence.[13]

Through the power released by the Divine Revelation of which it was the channel, Islam succeeded for an extended period in counteracting the doubts, misconceptions, prejudices, suspicions and narrow self-interest that affected diverse peoples in their relations one to another. The success of Islam was in part due to its tolerance of religious minorities, including Jews and Christians, allowing them to express their full potential. Within the first hundred and thirty years (622-750 AD) many nations and ethnic groups were united under the banner of Islam – a vast territory that extended from China to Spain.[14] It was to be only centuries later that these communities would be treated more harshly in countries under Islamic rule.

Advances in the status of women

At a time when Christian Europe debated whether women had souls (Council of Macon, 585 AD) and prominent Christians were apt to make disparaging statements about the so-called frailties of women, and when the custom of Arabs in the period of ignorance (*jáhiliyyah*) had been to bury their female infants alive, the Qur'án gave women many rights including their ability to defend themselves in a court of law, to inherit (*Nisaa*, the Women, 4:7), to refuse a marriage proposal, and to earn a lawful living. They were entitled to protection from tyranny and to be fed, clothed and sheltered. Compassion was to be shown to orphans and their rights were also to be protected. Female infanticide was strictly forbidden (*Takwír*, the Folding Up, 81:8).

Advances in sciences and arts

It was directly as a result of the liberating spirit of the Revelation of the Prophet Muhammad that the Islamic world became renowned for five hundred years (750–1257 AD) as the global centre for translating, correlating and corroborating scientific data. During this golden age of Islam, philosophers, scientists and engineers contributed to scientific knowledge, advances in civilization and cultural arts. Indeed, many inventions formerly attributed to Westerners are now recognized to have had their origins in Muslim endeavours, while the influence of Islamic art and architecture dating from that time can still be seen today in southern Europe and north Africa, perhaps most notably in the magnificent buildings in Spain – the palaces, gardens, and mosques in Cordova, Seville and Granada.

Muslim scholars have recorded the following among the numerous intellectual and scientific achievements stemming from the influence of Islam: the establishment of the world's first university –Al-Azhar in Egypt in 969 AD; the invention, construction, and testing of a flying object; glass mirrors; mechanical clocks; documentation of the oscillatory motion of the pendulum and its value for use in clocks; scientific advances in optics including refraction of light; the invention of glass lenses for improving vision; advances in algebra including definitions of *sine*, *cosine* and *tangent*, the adoption of zero (*sifr*) and its use in decimal fractions; the solution of complex equations, including quadratic and cubic equations; the use of symbols to develop and perfect the binomial theorem solving difficult cubic equations (x^3); logarithms and logarithmic tables; the discovery that algebra could be used to solve geometrical problems; the production of many highly accurate astronomical tables and star charts; the production of untold volumes of books on the geography of Africa, Asia, India, China and the Indies; scientific experiments and advances in chemistry and geology and the observation that fossils found on mountains indicated a watery origin of sections of dry land on earth; the first mention of the geological formation of valleys; advances in medicine, pathology, and surgery; the correct description of the nature of pleurisy, tuberculosis and pericarditis; the pathology of hydrocephalus and other congenital diseases; descriptions of the diseases of circulation and certain malignancies, including cancer of the stomach, bowel and esophagus; the development of pharmacotherapies for combatting microbes, such as the application of sulphur topically specifically to kill the scabies mite, or the use of mercurial compounds as topical antiseptics and the production of high grade alcohol through distillation as a solvent and antiseptic; the performance of surgery under inhalation anesthesia with the use of narcotic-soaked sponges which were placed over the face; the recognition of opium derivatives as anaesthetic agents; medical and surgical texts on preventive medicine, nutrition, cosmetics, drug therapy, surgical technique, anaesthesia, pre- and post-operative care; the writing of the first 'modern' pharmacopeia; the use of drugs for specific symptoms and illnesses, based on practical observation rather than accounts of the ancients; the description of cardiovascular circulation and the function of veins and their valves; the introduction of the practice of bedside teaching, and the practice and maintenance of special wards for the insane. With regard to the latter, they were treated kindly – it was presumed their illness was real, at a time when in other parts of the world the mentally ill or insane were outcast or treated brutally. In contrast, the mentally ill in the Islamic world were treated with supportive care, drugs and psychotherapy.[15]

These scientific and technological advances were instrumental in creating a surge in the social evolution of the then known world.

Furthermore, the Bahá'í Writings point out that at a time when most scholars in the Christian world were of the opinion that the sun moved around the earth, the Qur'án advanced the notion that the reverse was true:

> . . . during the first centuries and down to the fifteenth century of the Christian era – all the mathematicians of the world agreed that the earth was the center of the universe, and that the sun moved.

The famous astronomer [Copernicus] who was the protagonist of the new theory discovered the movement of the earth and the immobility of the sun. Until his time all the astronomers and philosophers of the world followed the Ptolemaic system, and whoever said anything against it was considered ignorant. Though Pythagoras, and Plato during the latter part of his life, adopted the theory that the annual movement of the sun around the zodiac does not proceed from the sun, but rather from the movement of the earth around the sun, this theory had been entirely forgotten, and the Ptolemaic system was accepted by all mathematicians. But there are some verses revealed in the Qur'án contrary to the theory of the Ptolemaic system. One of them is 'The sun moves in a fixed place' (*Yá-Sín*, 36:38), which shows the fixity of the sun, and its movement around an axis. Again, in another verse, 'And each star moves in its own heaven' (*Yá-Sín*, 36:40). Thus is explained the movement of the sun, of the moon, of the earth, and of other bodies. When the Qur'án appeared, all the mathematicians ridiculed these statements and attributed the theory to ignorance. Even the doctors of Islám, when they saw that these verses were contrary to the accepted Ptolemaic system, were obliged to explain them away.

It was not until after the fifteenth century of the Christian era, nearly nine hundred years after Muḥammad, that a famous astronomer [Galileo] made new observations and important discoveries by the aid of the telescope, which he had invented. The rotation of the earth, the fixity of the sun, and also its movement around an axis, were discovered. It became evident that the verses of the Qur'án agreed with existing facts, and that the Ptolemaic system was imaginary.

In short, many Oriental peoples have been reared for thirteen centuries under the shadow of the religion of Muḥammad. During the Middle Ages, while Europe was in the lowest depths of barbarism, the Arab peoples were superior to the other nations of the earth in learning, in the arts, mathematics, civilization, government and other sciences. The Enlightener and Educator of these Arab tribes, and the Founder of the civilization and perfections of humanity among these different races, was an illiterate Man, Muḥammad. Was this illustrious Man a thorough Educator or not? A just judgment is necessary.[16]

PART II

ISSUES FACING ISLAM

4

THE CHALLENGE AND FAILURE OF ISLAMIC FUNDAMENTALISM AND THE IMPOTENCE OF LIBERAL SECULAR ISLAM

> Gird up the loins of your endeavor, O people of Bahá, that haply the tumult of religious dissension and strife that agitateth the peoples of the earth may be stilled, that every trace of it may be completely obliterated. For the love of God, and them that serve Him, arise to aid this sublime and momentous Revelation. Religious fanaticism and hatred are a world-devouring fire, whose violence none can quench. The Hand of Divine power can, alone, deliver mankind from this desolating affliction.
>
> *Bahá'u'lláh*[1]

> We desire but the good of the world and happiness of the nations . . . That all nations should become one in faith and all men as brothers; that the bonds of affection and unity between the sons of men should be strengthened; that diversity of religion should cease . . .
>
> *Bahá'u'lláh*[2]

Despite its glorious past, Islam today is regrettably in a parlous state and faces seemingly insurmountable obstacles. The pristine purity of its spiritual teachings – unity, mercy, compassion, justice, fairness and truthfulness – requires resurrection and restoration. However, its fractionalism and hence competing interests must lead an unbiased observer to readily conclude that Islam is patently incapable of saving itself.

Just as the phenomenal rise of Islam and its transforming influence attested to the spiritual efficacy of Muhammad's Revelation, so the current spectacle testifies that divine inspiration has ceased to flow through the institutions that claim to represent the Faith, and now surges through new channels.

Fundamentalism in Judaism, Christianity and Islam

All three Abrahamic religions have their fundamentalists, conservatives and liberals. The fundamentalists, whether Jewish, Christian or Muslim, are remarkably similar in their beliefs and outlook, and share the same intolerance of the external world. They tend to interpret their respective scriptures – the Torah, the Gospels and the Qur'án – literally, and maintain dogmatically that their religion is the final, complete and immutable Word of God.

They know that their scriptures affirm that God has spoken to their ancestors through earlier Prophets and promises that He will speak again in the future. Yet with a defiant attitude they condemn anyone who may advocate the necessity for additional spiritual teachings and explanations. They consider it unforgivable, intolerable, even blasphemous, that anyone should dare to suggest that certain scriptural social laws no longer serve the needs of humanity today. They are so adamant in their convictions that they are often ready to shed innocent blood to vindicate their beliefs.

Fundamentalist outlook versus liberal expression of Islam

The world has in the past few decades witnessed a resurgence of Islamic fundamentalism. *Salafi*,[3] or fundamentalist Islam, is touted as the pure form of the religion and dictates the content of the Sharia[4] law or Islamic jurisprudence that invasively governs the lives of its adherents. Whether Sunni or Shí'ih, fundamentalist Muslims[5] reject and resent the success and dominant presence and influence of Western Judeo-Christian civilizations and democracies, and watch with consternation liberal and moderate Muslims' apparent tolerance of immodesty, lack of parental control, use of alcohol and drugs, and mundane indulgences and pursuits. They view with disdain and unconcealed hostility the many compromises of moderate Muslims with 'un-Islamic' societies that they consider to be a violation of the spiritual and social teachings of Islam, and which threaten hallowed traditions. It is clear to them that the liberal or moderate Muslims have strayed far from the righteous path, betrayed their *Ummah* and religion, disavowed their spiritual birthright, and adulterated the true Faith with alien ideologies and illegitimate secular practices. They castigate liberal Muslims for having bartered divine law for the crass materialism and immoral values of the Western societies where they have made their homes. Non-fundamentalists are seen as Muslim in name only, ill-informed of the teachings of the Qur'án and the true tenets of Islam.

Islamic fundamentalists consider themselves as promoting '*dár al-Islám*' or 'abode of Islam or peace', in conflict with the '*káfirs*' or unbelievers who preside in '*dár al-harb*' or 'abode of war'. This inevitably places them, with certain scriptural justifications, on a war footing with the West as well as with moderate Muslims residing in the East or the West They perceive it to be mandated by the Qur'án that holy war (*jihád*) be waged against enemy or infidel territories (*dár-al-harb*), the ultimate goal being to unfurl the banner of Islam in the very heart of Western capitals.

This distressing inability of fundamentalists to cope with modernity, and their uneasy relationship with the rest of the world, is characterized by recurrent and escalating crises. Islam, a religion that proclaims peace, is hence plagued by continued sectarianism and is at war with itself and its sister religions. Revealed by a 'Most Compassionate and the Most Merciful' God, it has tragically become increasingly associated with terrorism. The world witnesses the perversion of the Divine Word and acts of incomprehensible barbarity carried out in God's name.

Ominously, fundamentalist Muslims are convinced that the West has revived the medieval Crusades and is waging a war against Islam, and that it is their responsibility to protect God's religion; moderate Muslims, they feel, are simply oblivious of the danger that the West poses to Islam. They view the establishment of a Jewish homeland – although promised in the Qur'án – in Islamic lands with the support of the West as further proof of a Judeo-Christian collaboration against the interests of Islam. They regard the presence of Westerners in the holy lands associated with the birth of their religion as sacrilegious, and deeply resent the increased and aggressive proselytizing and evangelical activities of the Christian churches amongst them. In their opinion, conversion from Islam to any other religion deserves the death penalty. They contend that the salvation of Islam and total victory over the unbelievers or 'infidels' is possible only through a return to the pure teachings of the Qur'án and following closely the actions and sayings of Muhammad (*Sunnah*), as the teacher of Sharia and its best exemplar, and through strict imposition of Sharia laws. Western and Judeo-Christian influences in their countries are to be forcefully resisted and rooted out.

The alternative to fundamentalist Islam, namely, secular, moderate or liberal Islam, acknowledges that the social laws of Islam are demonstrably impracticable today, unacceptable to their host societies, and at odds with modernity – they are unlikely to promote unity and to advance the cause of oneness of humanity or to uphold human rights, and specifically the rights of women.

Moderate or liberal Muslims argue that whenever and wherever Islamic fundamentalism has come to power it has done little to promote the welfare of their societies, which instead have become less free. Many injustices have been visited on them in the name of Islam, and religious and other minorities have been persecuted – their societies have become more backward, economically more destitute and more morally bankrupt, and education, particularly of girls, has suffered greatly. Many liberals do try to conscientiously attend the local mosque, and to listen dutifully to the sermons of the local imam or spiritual leader and teacher, to pray five times a day, to fast during the holy month of Ramadan, and to participate in the festivals, and they may even undertake the prescribed pilgrimage to Mecca and Medina (*Al-Ḥajj*). At the same time they are offended by reports of maltreatment of women by the fundamentalists, and the inordinate emphasis on martyrdom and holy war. Some of them express dismay at the readiness of extremists to destroy innocent lives, including those of their fellow Muslims, and at their keenness to brand all non-fundamentalists as infidels worthy of death, imprisonment, annihilation and torture. Many liberal Muslims in the West are unhappy that extremists and violent elements have hijacked their religion. Understandably, they resent having to endure the unwelcome attention, suspicion and occasional violence that follow repeated acts of 'Islamic' extremism.

However, the liberal reinvention of Islam also ultimately fails because it lacks scriptural justification. Its readiness to make concessions and to find a middle ground is often at odds with the teachings of the Qur'án and its central belief that Islam owes its very existence to divine intervention and is therefore immune from human invention. Hence, while the practitioners of secular Islam may have achieved a degree of acceptability in the West, their practices lack legitimacy in the eyes of their fellow believers. They are perceived as having betrayed the Cause and substituted, for a vibrant Faith, a mundane and invented entity that involves a spiritually unsatisfying series of social activities.

Rising Western apprehension

At the same time, Western democracies are wary of the rise of radical (fundamentalist or *jihadist*) Islam in previously friendly countries and also amongst their own populations, and are fearful of the intentions of Islamic extremists. Recurring acts of terrorism have forced the Western democracies to be constantly vigilant against internal and external terrorism and to sacrifice their blood and wealth in defence.

Western countries are understandably proud of their ancient traditions and protective of their hard-won freedoms, particularly from the shackles of religious orthodoxy. They point out that it is those very same freedoms that permit the followers of so many imported religions, including Islam, to live and worship unhindered and protected amongst them. There is therefore a deepening anxiety about the phenomenal increase of Muslim populations amongst them that threatens to change the fundamental nature of their communities. This is coupled with an increasing frustration at the inability of Muslims to become integrated into their societies. There is therefore a genuine fear that the present trends will eventually force the collapse of Western cultures, only to be replaced by undemocratic, repressive and alien Islamic majorities. Prominent European leaders now openly concede that multiculturalism has failed, and express the need to adopt new policies to protect their national identities. They point out that rather than integration, the rapid growth of Islam and its influence in Western countries have led to a greater desire and confidence on the part of Muslim migrants to emphasize their own culture. Europeans have been challenged by practices such as Islamic mortgage lending, halal meat, and probably most controversial, the wearing of the veil.[6] The media, too, are quick to capitalize on widespread anxiety about the perceived threat of Islam to European identity.[7]

Lack of familiarity of Jews, Christians and Muslims with each others' religions

It is unfortunate that many Muslims in both the East and in the West are entirely unfamiliar with the teachings of the Torah and the Gospels, and the beliefs of the Jews and Christians among whom they live, even though the Jews and Christians are depicted as 'the people of the Book' in the Qur'án, and that much of its teaching is devoted to this very subject. It is equally true that most Westerners are also largely unfamiliar with the teachings and tenets of Islam. It is also probably the case that most Jews, Christians and Muslims are unaware of the contents of their own scriptures and unable to distinguish between the Divine Word and the superstition and misinformation originating from their spiritual rulers in the past. Many followers of these religions find it more convenient and acceptable to follow blindly rather than discover the truth personally.

Scepticism that Islam is 'a religion of peace', discomfort with expressed Islamic ideals, and uncertainty concerning what constitutes a 'good Muslim'

There are many aspects of Judaism, Christianity and Islam that would justify labelling them as 'religions of peace', despite obvious indications that all three religions when interpreted and influenced by extremists and fundamentalists have demonstrated a deplorable readiness to use religion to justify violence and barbarity. However, in recent years the many violent attacks perpetrated in the name of Islam have raised doubts in the minds of many Westerners that Islam is a religion of peace. The situation is not helped by unwise and aggressive statements by Muslim fundamentalists that are readily reported in the Western press.[8]

It is too easily forgotten that many millions of Christians have died in Europe at the hands of their fellow Christians in the course of numerous political, nationalistic or religious wars:

> History provides ample evidence of Christianity's harsh treatment of 'heretics', and its violence toward all other religions (for example, during the Crusades). By accusing Jews of the crime of deicide,

Christianity also laid the foundations for the world's oldest hatred, anti-Semitism. However, in the 21st century, the dominant interpretations and objectives of both mainstream Judaism and Christianity are unquestionably peaceful. Most Christians genuinely seek accommodation with other religions, and attempt to make amends for the anti-Semitism of their forbears.[9]

Not so with Islam today. The widespread persecution of non-Muslim religions and the frequent extreme violence waged against their followers under Islamic jurisdiction – death threats, judicial murder and mutilation for apostasy and blasphemy – are deeply offensive to many in the West who are frustrated by the silence of the 'moderates', reportedly constituting the majority of Muslims, in the face of the many examples of blatant human rights violations and religious intolerance by extremists.[10] Their inaction is attributed to their increasing marginalization and intimidation by more radical elements, or worse, tacit approval of the excesses. It has become popular among even moderate Muslims to brand any criticism as 'Islamophobia' and 'racism' that must be vigorously resisted.

It is perhaps valuable to remind ourselves that most of the Qur'án was revealed when Islam was fighting for its very survival against fierce tribes that lived ruthlessly by pillage and plunder, and were bent on destroying an infant Faith that they saw as a direct challenge to their time-honoured traditions and which they viewed as an existential challenge because of the threat it posed to their commerce. The Jewish and Christian communities in the Arabian Peninsula were also mostly hostile and tended to break their truces. Some of the language of the Qur'án, as well as the harsh treatment of infidels and mistrust of Jews and Christians, reflects this initial adverse experience. But the fortunes of Islam changed radically over a relatively short period of time and there is evidence that the stringent laws would have been mitigated by 'Alí Ibn Abí Tálib had He been allowed to succeed Muhammad earlier. When Muslims did eventually turn to Him for direction Islam had already taken many wrong turns and its armies continued to seek fresh conquests. He and all his successors were killed at the hands of fellow Muslims.

While the fundamentalists believe that the strict Islamic practices should continue to be observed, the moderates draw on verses of the

Qur'án that instead emphasize tolerance, mercy and justice. It is therefore expedient for the West to consider moderate Muslims as the 'true Muslims'. However, in so doing the West has no argument to counteract the many teachings in the Qur'án that are used by fundamentalists to radicalize Muslims. In other words, what the West terms a 'good Muslim' is considered an infidel by fundamentalist Muslims, and what the West terms a 'radical' Muslim may be hailed as a true follower of the teachings of the Qur'án and a holy warrior.

Sharia law

A further area of deep concern in the West concerns Sharia law. This system of Islamic jurisprudence is gaining popularity in Muslim countries, but is also increasingly adopted in the West, existing side by side with the older law of the land. Both are designed, at least in theory, to safeguard the freedoms of the individual. However, there is a wide gulf between Western and Muslim concepts of freedom. In Western democracies freedom of expression and association, and the right of individuals to control their own lives, are highly valued. In fundamentalist Muslim societies, as expressed by the Sufi master Ibn Arabi (d. 1240) perfect freedom or *hurriyya* is 'perfect slavery'. This calls for total obedience to Allah the 'master' on the part of his human 'slaves'. Belief that Sharia law embodies the Divine Will gives legitimacy to the subjugation of all Muslims to its totalitarian dictates and justifies at times severe limitations on personal freedoms. A Muslim is expected to consider subordination of his own freedom to the beliefs, morality and customs of the group as the only proper course of behaviour. An individual's ability to make choices is severely curtailed, and there is no escape from the Sharia law once he or she is determined to be within the jurisdiction of any court established to enforce it.

The replacement of autocratic regimes by Islamic regimes that espouse the Sharia system is frequently greeted initially with great enthusiasm by the masses. Once voted in by popular support, it is there to stay; the system does not brook any opposition since any resistance is itself considered against the Divine Purpose. It is feared that once the full implications are realized it will be too late to reverse the trend. Nor are the lives of non-Muslims and liberal Muslims untouched by the provisions of Sharia law that may directly and intimately affect their lives. For example, the Sharia does not recognize or tolerate marriage between a non-Muslim man and a Muslim woman, unless he converts to Islam.

Another curious development is the unfortunate tendency on the part of some Muslim liberal intellectuals to maintain against all the available evidence that certain of the harsher social laws of the Dispensation of Muhammad, elaborated in the Sharia law, practised widely by Muslim States and codified in their constitutions, are simply not part of the Quranic text.[11] They therefore directly or indirectly perpetuate the un-Quranic belief that the social laws of Islam are eternal and do not require to be abrogated. This powerful self-deception can only be understood by a strong desire to have one's cake and eat it – a misguided belief that Islam can be reformed from within and made to conform to modernity and still be compatible with all of the provisions of the Qur'án.

The effect of this unfortunate reluctance or inability to admit the end (*ajal*) of the Islamic *Ummah* is to further deprive the Islamic world of the saving grace of the grand design of the Summoner of Islam. Ultimately, it helps to frustrate the very goals and highest aspirations of the Muslim social reformers, such as the emancipation of Muslim women from Islamic orthodoxy.

The Faith of Bahá'u'lláh as the sole and ultimate salvation of Islam

It should be clear from the above discourse that none of the three religions currently at odds with each other can be reformed from within in any meaningful way that will ensure the tranquillity of humankind. Their rescue, and international peace, can only be assured by their allegiance to a new Divine Revelation. The Qur'án warns that Islam will undergo a spiritual death reminiscent of the condition of the Arabian tribes before their spiritual revival by Muhammad. God would then have to re-resurrect them.

> How can ye reject the faith in God? Seeing that ye were without life, and He gave you life; then will He cause you to die, and will again bring you to life; and again to Him will ye return.[12]

The Faith of Bahá'u'lláh affords Islam respite from the crises it faces today, and in so doing it also provides relief from the excesses of extremists. It inculcates reverence for the Qur'án and Muhammad, promotes the eternal values of Islam and embodies its essence and highest aspirations. It has the proven ability to reconcile Islam with modernity, and to unify it with other religions. Critically, the Faith of Bahá'u'lláh has the power and legitimacy to abrogate the harsher social laws of the Qur'án, which form the basis of Sharia law, to fundamentally alter the social agenda of Islam, and to free Muslims from the domination of its clerics and scholars.

5

RELIGIOUS FANATICISM AND INTOLERANCE

Religion should unite all hearts and cause wars and disputes to vanish from the face of the earth, give birth to spirituality, and bring life and light to each heart. If religion becomes a cause of dislike, hatred and division, it were better to be without it, and to withdraw from such a religion would be a truly religious act. For it is clear that the purpose of a remedy is to cure; but if the remedy should only aggravate the complaint it had better be left alone. Any religion which is not a cause of love and unity is no religion . . . any remedy that causes disease does not come from the great and supreme Physician.

'Abdu'l-Bahá[1]

. . . they whose hearts are warmed by the energizing influence of God's creative love cherish His creatures for His sake, and recognize in every human face a sign of His reflected glory.

Shoghi Effendi[2]

The rise of religious intolerance and hostility reminiscent of the pre-Islamic period of ignorance (*jáhiliyyah*)

How tragic that at a time when it has been demonstrated conclusively that we are genetically one we find that humanity is divided and mankind is repeatedly challenged by so many prejudices. We are prey to ethnic and colour prejudice for which there is no scientific justification, and are beset by tribal, national and political divisions. The many religions today, with their attendant bewildering array of subdivisions, contribute significantly to this alienation in the human family. Religion is currently responsible for fuelling numerous wasteful bloody conflicts worldwide, and is a notable impediment to universal peace and the achievement of the organic unity of mankind.

There is no need to dwell at length on the well-known and tragic details of the hostility and animosity that has for so many centuries characterized the adversarial relationships of three Abrahamic religions – Judaism, Christianity and Islam, and for that matter, between resurgent Islam and fundamentalist Hinduism and also Buddhism. Sadly, daily outrages supply news headlines.

> From the beginning of human history down to this time the world of humanity has not enjoyed a day of absolute rest and relaxation from conflict and strife. Most of the wars have been caused by religious prejudice, fanaticism and sectarian hatred. Religionists have anathematized religionists, each considering the other as deprived of the mercy of God, abiding in gross darkness and the children of Satan. For example, the Christians and Muslims considered the Jews satanic and the enemies of God. Therefore, they cursed and persecuted them. Great numbers of Jews were killed, their houses burned and pillaged, their children carried into captivity. The Jews in turn regarded the Christians as infidels and the Muslims as enemies and destroyers of the Law of Moses. Therefore, they call down vengeance upon them and curse them even to this day.[3]

This religious animosity is a sign of serious spiritual malaise and has encouraged scepticism about the value of faith, leading many to seek alternative pursuits:

> The resurgence of fanatical religious fervour occurring in many lands cannot be regarded as more than a dying convulsion. The very nature of the violent and disruptive phenomena associated with it testifies to the spiritual bankruptcy it represents. Indeed, one of the strangest and saddest features of the current outbreak of religious fanaticism is the extent to which, in each case, it is undermining not only the spiritual values which are conducive to the unity of mankind but also those unique moral victories won by the particular religion it purports to serve.
>
> However vital a force religion has been in the history of mankind, and however dramatic the current resurgence of militant religious

fanaticism, religion and religious institutions have, for many decades, been viewed by increasing numbers of people as irrelevant to the major concerns of the modern world. In its place they have turned either to the hedonistic pursuit of material satisfactions or to the following of man-made ideologies designed to rescue society from the evident evils under which it groans. All too many of these ideologies, alas, instead of embracing the concept of the oneness of mankind and promoting the increase of concord among different peoples, have tended to deify the state, to subordinate the rest of mankind to one nation, race or class, to attempt to suppress all discussion and interchange of ideas, or to callously abandon starving millions to the operations of a market system that all too clearly is aggravating the plight of the majority of mankind, while enabling small sections to live in a condition of affluence scarcely dreamed of by our forebears.[4]

'Abdu'l-Bahá tells us that Bahá'u'lláh 'exhorted the people to do away with strife and discord' and describes 'the principal reason of the unrest among nations':

> The chief cause is the misrepresentation of religion by the religious leaders and teachers. They teach their followers to believe that their own form of religion is the only one pleasing to God, and that followers of all other persuasions are condemned by the All-Loving Father and deprived of His Mercy and Grace. Hence arise among the peoples, disapproval, contempt, disputes and hatred. If these religious prejudices could be swept away, the nations would soon enjoy peace and concord.[5]

Islam, a religion of peace and compassion

The word 'Islam' is derived from '*salema*' or peace, purity, submission, and obedience to the divine Command (*amr*). In contrast to what is frequently and regrettably perpetrated in the name of that great religion, the Qur'án explains that Islam seeks to promote peace and religious tolerance. Indeed, the Qur'án opens with the clarion call that God is Most Compassionate and Most Merciful,[6] a prescriptive statement that adorns the beginning of most of the 114 chapters of the Book.

Other 'Beautiful Names' of God, or 'Al-Asmá al-Husná', mentioned in the Qur'án include *As-Salam* or the Source of Peace; *Al-Karim* or the Generous; *Al-Wadud* or the Loving One; *Al-Barr*, the Doer of Good, *Ar-Ra'uf* or the Clement, and *As-Sabur* or the Patient One.

The Qur'án discourages conceit and arrogance, religious or otherwise:

Nor walk on the earth with insolence . . .[7]

O my son! . . . enjoin what is just, and forbid what is wrong: and bear with patient constancy whatever betide thee; for this is firmness (of purpose) in (the conduct of) affairs.
And swell not thy cheek (for pride) at men, nor walk in insolence through the earth; for God loveth not any arrogant boaster.
And be moderate in thy pace, and lower thy voice...[8]

The Bible also emphatically recommends peace as a divine virtue and synonymous with righteousness:

[It is] an honour for a man to cease from strife . . .[9]

Thou shalt not avenge, nor bear any grudge against the children of thy people, but thou shalt love thy neighbour as thyself: I [am] the Lord.[10]

Blessed [are] the peacemakers: for they shall be called the children of God.[11]

Let him eschew evil, and do good; let him seek peace, and ensue it.[12]

If it be possible, as much as lieth in you, live peaceably with all men.[13]

Follow peace with all [men], and holiness, without which no man shall see the Lord.[14]

But the fruit of the Spirit is love, joy, peace, longsuffering, gentleness, goodness, faith.[15]

And the fruit of righteousness is sown in peace of them that make peace.[16]

> Recompense to no man evil for evil. Provide things honest in the sight of all men.[17]
>
> Let us therefore follow after the things which make for peace, and things wherewith one may edify another.[18]
>
> Glory to God in the highest, and on earth peace, good will toward men.[19]
>
> Now the God of peace [be] with you all. Amen.[20]
>
> See that none render evil for evil unto any [man]; but ever follow that which is good, both among yourselves, and to all [men].[21]
>
> Not rendering evil for evil, or railing for railing: but contrariwise blessing; knowing that ye are thereunto called, that ye should inherit a blessing.[22]

The Bible also promises the cessation of conflicts and the establishment of universal peace:

> The glory of this latter house shall be greater than of the former, saith the Lord of hosts: and in this place will I give peace, saith the Lord of hosts.[23]
>
> And he shall judge among the nations, and shall rebuke many people: and they shall beat their swords into plowshares, and their spears into pruninghooks: nation shall not lift up sword against nation, neither shall they learn war any more.[24]

Islam teaches that 'God is never unjust'

That today this mercy and compassion (*rahm*) mentioned so frequently in the Qur'án is not always evident in the actions of certain Muslims does not in any way indicate a deficiency of the pristine Faith of Muhammad – the emphasis of the revealed Word is on truth and on a Supreme Being Who is just and fair, and whose Bounty encompasses all. He rewards the righteous.

> God is never unjust in the least degree: if there is any good (done), He doubleth it, and giveth from His own presence a great reward.[25]
>
> God commands justice, the doing of good, and liberality to kith and kin, and He forbids all shameful deeds, and injustice and rebellion: He instructs you, that ye may receive admonition.[26]
>
> The Word of thy Lord doth find its fulfilment in truth and in justice: none can change His Words: for He is the one who heareth and knoweth all.[27]
>
> Whoever works righteousness benefits his own soul; whoever works evil, it is against his own soul: nor is thy Lord ever unjust (in the least) to His servants.[28]

Muslims are expected to likewise act justly and with truth. A true Muslim must not to allow any lingering hatred or prejudice to persuade him to act unjustly and unkindly.

> O ye who believe! stand out firmly for God, as witnesses to fair dealing, and let not the hatred of others to you make you swerve to wrong and depart from justice. Be just: that is next to piety: and fear God. For God is well-acquainted with all that ye do.[29]

As God is the one common source of guidance for all His children, there cannot be any justification for religious strife and persecution.

The Qur'án declares that the God that spoke through Abraham, Moses and the Prophets of the Torah, and through Jesus in the Gospels (*injil*) is identical to the God that has revealed the Qur'án – 'Allah' is merely the translation in Arabic of the word God, and is the term used in Arabic Bibles. Many early Aramaic references to God are derivatives of the word Allah such as Eloi, Eli, Elohim, etc. He is the source of spiritual guidance of all revealed faiths and aught beside His Command is darkness; the divine truth and the light do not belong to the 'East' or to the 'West'.

> And your God is One God: there is no god but He, Most Gracious, Most Merciful.[30]

God is the Light of the heavens and the earth. The parable of His Light is as if there were a Niche and within it a Lamp: the Lamp enclosed in Glass: the glass as it were a brilliant star: lit from a blessed Tree, an Olive, neither of the East nor of the West, whose oil is well-nigh luminous, though fire scarce touched it: Light upon Light! God doth guide whom He will to His Light: God doth set forth Parables for men: and God doth know all things.[31]

God is the Protector of those who have faith: from the depths of darkness He will lead them forth into light. Of those who reject faith the patrons are the Evil Ones: from light they will lead them forth into the depths of darkness. They will be Companions of the Fire, to dwell therein (for ever).[32]

The Torah and the Gospels also teach that God is the identical source of light and guidance at every stage in humanity's spiritual development

And God said, Let there be light: and there was light.[33]

This then is the message which we have heard of him, and declare unto you, that God is light, and in him is no darkness at all.[34]

Hear, O Israel: The Lord our God is one Lord:
   And thou shalt love the Lord thy God with all thine heart, and with all thy soul, and with all thy might.[35]

For there is one God . . .[36]

The oneness of the Prophets and the faith proclaimed by them is a fundamental article of the Faith of Bahá'u'lláh, which aims to unify mankind:

. . . all the Prophets are the Temples of the Cause of God, Who have appeared clothed in divers attire. If thou wilt observe with discriminating eyes, thou wilt behold them all abiding in the same tabernacle, soaring in the same heaven, seated upon the same throne, uttering the same speech, and proclaiming the same Faith. Such is the unity of those Essences of being, those Luminaries of infinite and immeasurable splendour.[37]

That the Jews, Christians and Muslims have come to consider themselves as belonging to different and seemingly irreconcilable religions is regrettable, for according to the Qur'án they are inspired by one heavenly Book, are part of one Faith or '*Din*', and follow one 'straight Path' or 'Way'.

> The Jews say: 'The Christians have naught (to stand) upon;' and the Christians say: 'The Jews have naught (to stand) upon.' Yet they (profess to) study the (same) Book. Like unto their word is what those say who know not, but God will judge between them in their quarrel on the Day of Judgment.[38]

Today, the synagogue, the church and the mosque promote religious exclusivity and emphasize doctrinal differences. But the Qur'án regards the divine teachings of the Prophets as integral parts of a common 'Religion of God':

> Do they seek for other than the Religion of God? – while all creatures in the heavens and on earth have, willing or unwilling, bowed to His Will (accepted Islam), and to Him shall they all be brought back.
>   Say: 'We believe in God, and in what has been revealed to us and what was revealed to Abraham, Ishmael, Isaac, Jacob, and the Tribes, and in (the Books) given to Moses, Jesus, and the Prophets, from their Lord; we make no distinction between one and another among them, and to God do we bow our will (in Islam).'[39]

Notably, Jesus thus defined a Christian:

> By this shall all men know that ye are my disciples, if ye have love one to another.[40]

In the Qur'án the appellation 'Muslim' is applied generically to all who have surrendered their will to the Will of God and who have been obedient to His Command as revealed by any of His chosen Prophets.

> Those to whom We sent the Book before this – they do believe in this (Revelation):

> And when it is recited to them, they say: 'We believe therein, for it is the Truth from our Lord: Indeed we have been Muslims (bowing to God's Will) from before this.'[41]

Thus we find that several individuals are described as having been Muslims when they had clearly lived long before the advent of Islam. For example, Noah revealed that He had been commanded by God to be a Muslim:

> Relate to them the story of Noah. Behold, he said to his people: 'O my people, if it be hard on your (mind) that I should stay (with you) and commemorate the Signs of God – yet I put my trust in God. Get ye then an agreement about your plan and among your partners, so your plan be not to you dark and dubious. Then pass your sentence on me, and give me no respite.
>
> 'But if ye turn back, (consider): no reward have I asked of you: my reward is only due from God, and I have been commanded to be of those who submit to God's Will (in Islam).'[42]

Abraham is declared to have been a Muslim:

> Abraham was not a Jew nor yet a Christian; but he was true in Faith, and bowed his will to God's (which is Islam), and he joined not gods with God.[43]

Moses exhorted the Jews to be Muslims:

> Moses said: 'O my People! if ye do (really) believe in God, then in Him put your trust if ye submit (your will to His).'[44]

Joseph is recounted as having confessed to being a Muslim:

> O my Lord! Thou hast indeed bestowed on me (Joseph) some power, and taught me something of the interpretation of dreams and events – O Thou Creator of the heavens and the earth! Thou art my Protector in this world and in the Hereafter. Take thou my soul (at death) as one submitting to Thy Will (as a Muslim), and unite me with the righteous.[45]

The Queen of Shebá (*Bilqis*) confessed to also being a Muslim:

> She said: 'O my Lord! I have indeed wronged my soul: I do (now) submit (in Islam), with Solomon, to the Lord of the Worlds.'[46]

Pharaoh's magicians declared themselves to be Muslims by confessing their belief in the God of Moses and Aaron:

> But the sorcerers fell down prostrate in adoration.
> Saying: 'We believe in the Lord of the worlds,
> 'The Lord of Moses and Aaron.'
> Said Pharaoh: 'Believe ye in him before I give you permission? Surely this is a trick which ye have planned in the City to drive out its people: but soon shall ye know (the consequences).
> 'Be sure I will cut off your hands and your feet on opposite sides, and I will cause you all to die on the cross.'
> They said: 'For us, we are but sent back unto our Lord:
> 'But thou dost wreak thy vengeance on us simply because we believed in the Signs of our Lord when they reached us! Our Lord! Pour out on us patience and constancy, and take our souls unto thee as Muslims (who bow to Thy will)!'[47]

The Disciples of Christ also reportedly claimed to be Muslims because they believed in Jesus and promoted the Christian Faith:
When Jesus found unbelief on their part he said: 'Who will be my helpers to (the work of) God?' Said the Disciples: 'We are God's helpers, we believe in God, and do thou bear witness that we are Muslims.'[48]

> And behold! I inspired the Disciples to have faith in Me and My Messenger (Jesus): they said, 'We have faith, and do thou bear witness that we bow to God as Muslims.'[49]

In the light of the above statements it is not surprising that the Qur'án considers it intolerable that anyone is denied worship of God in any place dedicated to that purpose by any religious community.

> And who is more unjust than he who forbids that in places for the worship of God, God's name should be celebrated? – whose zeal is

RELIGIOUS FANATICISM AND INTOLERANCE

(in fact) to ruin them? It was not fitting that such should themselves enter them except in fear. For them there is nothing but disgrace in this world, and in the world to come, an exceeding torment.[50]

The Qur'án also does not condone any coercion in religion:

> Let there be no compulsion in religion: Truth stands out clear from error; whoever rejects evil and believes in God hath grasped the most trustworthy hand-hold, that never breaks. And God heareth and knoweth all things.[51]

The Qur'án hence instructs Muslims to demonstrate dignity and a spirit of forgiveness, humility and tolerance towards individuals whose conduct does not meet with their approval.

> And the servants of (God) Most Gracious are those who walk on the earth in humility, and when the ignorant address them, they say: 'Peace!'[52]

> . . . And, if they pass by futility [hollow words or unseemly behaviour], they pass by it with honourable (avoidance) [with dignity].[53]

> And when they hear vain talk, they turn away therefrom and say: 'To us our deeds, and to you yours.'[54]

> Say: 'O People of the Book! Come to common terms as between us and you: that we worship none but God; that we associate no partners with Him; that we erect not, from among ourselves, lords and patrons other than God.'[55]

Tolerance is to be extended to unbelievers and to 'pagans' who appear to pray to an unfamiliar divine entity.

> Revile not ye those whom they call upon besides God, lest they out of spite revile God in their ignorance. Thus have We made alluring to each people its own doings. In the end will they return to their Lord, and We shall then tell them the truth of all that they did.[56]

But if any reject Faith, let not his rejection grieve thee: to Us is their return, and We shall tell them the truth of their deeds: for God knows well all that is in (men's) hearts.⁵⁷

Tell those who believe, to forgive those who do not look forward to the Days of God: it is for Him to recompense (for good or ill) each people according to what they have earned.⁵⁸

When God sent Moses and Aaron to a man who claimed to possess divinity, as the Pharaoh had done, He commanded them to be tolerant of his adversarial and arrogant attitudes and to speak softly to him.

> Go, both of you, to Pharaoh, for he has indeed transgressed all bounds;
> But speak to him mildly; perchance he may take warning or fear (God).⁵⁹

The letter written by 'Ali, son of Abú Tálib ('Alí Ibn Abí Tálib), an individual revered by both Sunni and Shí'ih, is an illustration of this. In it he instructs a local governor to behave tolerantly towards other religions. It describes how believers in a minority religion (Majus, or Zoroastrians) were to be treated and what those who held a different creed should expect of a Muslim ruler.

> ... be it known to you that villagers and farmers of the provinces under you complain of your harshness, arrogance and cruelty. They complain that you consider them mean, humble and insignificant and treat them scornfully. I deliberated over their complaint and found that if, on account of their paganism they do not deserve any favourable treatment of extra privileges, they do not deserve to be treated cruelly and harshly either. They are governed by us, they have made certain agreements with us and we are obliged to respect and honour the terms of those agreements.
>
> Therefore, be kind to them in future, tolerate them and give them due respect, but at the same time keep your prestige and guard well the position and honour of the authority which you hold. Always govern with a soft but strong hand. Treat them as they individually deserve, kindly or harshly and with respect or with contempt.⁶⁰

Christ also taught religious tolerance. He reminded His followers that the Father 'maketh his sun to rise on the evil and on the good, and sendeth rain on the just and on the unjust'.[61] They were instructed to pray to the Heavenly Father of all mankind to 'forgive their sins' and not to lead them 'into temptation'.[62]

The Gospels further describe an event that clearly illustrates that true faith transcends religious labels. On one occasion Jesus declared that he had not found belief as great as that of a Roman centurion in the whole of Israel. With this single pronouncement He opened the eyes of His followers to the possibility that a seemingly polytheistic Roman soldier, part of the occupying force that was trampling underfoot the Holy Land, could have faith that was greater than that of any of the devout followers of Moses who professed belief in the Lord of Hosts and assiduously adhered to the minutest aspects of the Law.

> And when Jesus was entered into Capernaum, there came unto him a centurion, beseeching him,
>
> And saying, Lord, my servant lieth at home sick of the palsy, grievously tormented.
>
> And Jesus saith unto him, I will come and heal him.
>
> The centurion answered and said, Lord, I am not worthy that thou shouldest come under my roof: but speak the word only, and my servant shall be healed.
>
> For I am a man under authority, having soldiers under me: and I say to this man, Go, and he goeth; and to another, Come, and he cometh; and to my servant, Do this, and he doeth it.
>
> When Jesus heard it, he marvelled, and said to them that followed, Verily I say unto you, I have not found so great faith, no, not in Israel.
>
> And I say unto you, That many shall come from the east and west, and shall sit down with Abraham, and Isaac, and Jacob, in the kingdom of heaven.
>
> But the children of the kingdom shall be cast out into outer darkness: there shall be weeping and gnashing of teeth.
>
> And Jesus said unto the centurion, Go thy way; and as thou hast believed, so be it done unto thee. And his servant was healed in the selfsame hour.[63]

The statement of Jesus recorded in the Gospel of Matthew is rendered more palatable by the author of the Gospel of St Luke (7:2–5) by the preliminary explanation that it was the Jewish elders who had pleaded the cause of the centurion. These leaders, who had earlier opposed the actions of Jesus, now desired that Christ perform a miracle and heal the centurion's servant because the centurion was 'worthy', as he loved Israel and had built a synagogue.

> And a certain centurion's servant, who was dear unto him, was sick, and ready to die.
> And when he heard of Jesus, he sent unto him the elders of the Jews, beseeching him that he would come and heal his servant.
> And when they came to Jesus, they besought him instantly, saying, That he was worthy for whom he should do this:
> For he loveth our nation, and he hath built us a synagogue.[64]

Nevertheless, the spiritual transformation resulting from this remarkable insight later led to Christians from Jewish, Roman, and Greek backgrounds to consider themselves as one, and to sacrifice their lives for each other in the murderous Roman arenas.

In a further example, Jesus ordered His disciple not to interfere with the teaching activities of a person who was not directly one of His followers:

> And John answered and said, Master, we saw one casting out devils in thy name; and we forbad him, because he followeth not with us.
> And Jesus said unto him, Forbid him not: for he that is not against us is for us.[65]

Sharing one's beliefs

The position of the Bahá'í Faith is that all faiths are valid expressions of the divine purpose; an appreciation of the spiritual purpose of one religion aids the understanding of all of them. Our concern must focus on promoting spiritual understanding – opening the eyes and ears, and bettering the spiritual and social conditions of humanity. There is therefore no place for undue apprehension and alarm when an individual changes his or her allegiance from one religion to another.

It may be objected that, if all the great religions are to be recognized as equally Divine in origin, the effect will be to encourage, or at least to facilitate, the conversion of numbers of people from one religion to another. Whether or not this is true, it is surely of peripheral importance when set against the opportunity that history has at last opened to those who are conscious of a world that transcends this terrestrial one – and against the responsibility that this awareness imposes. Each of the great faiths can adduce impressive and credible testimony to its efficacy in nurturing moral character. Similarly, no one could convincingly argue that doctrines attached to one particular belief system have been either more or less prolific in generating bigotry and superstition than those attached to any other. In an integrating world, it is natural that patterns of response and association will undergo a continuous process of shifting, and the role of institutions, of whatever kind, is surely to consider how these developments can be managed in a way that promotes unity. The guarantee that the outcome will ultimately be sound – spiritually, morally and socially – lies in the abiding faith of the unconsulted masses of the earth's inhabitants that the universe is ruled not by human caprice, but by a loving and unfailing Providence.[66]

Proclaiming one's faith should therefore be a sharing of the gift of Revelation and not of undue concern about religious affiliation.

> The responsibility of the Bahá'ís to teach the Faith is very great. The contraction of the world and the onward rush of events require us to seize every chance open to us to touch the hearts and minds of our fellowmen. The Message of Bahá'u'lláh is God's guidance for mankind to overcome the difficulties of this age of transition and move forward into the next stage of its evolution, and human beings have the right to hear it. Those who accept it incur the duty of passing it on to their fellowman. The slowness of the response of the world has caused and is causing great suffering; hence the historical pressure upon Bahá'ís to exert every effort to teach the Faith for the sake of their fellowmen. They should teach with enthusiasm, conviction, wisdom and courtesy, but without pressing their hearer, bearing in mind the words of Bahá'u'lláh: 'Beware lest ye contend with any one, nay, strive to make him aware of the truth with kindly

manner and most convincing exhortation. If your hearer respond, he will have responded to his own behoof, and if not, turn ye away from him, and set your faces towards God›s sacred Court, the seat of resplendent holiness.'[67]

Faith devoid of proselytizing, priestcraft and paid clergy

The Faith of Bahá'u'lláh does not rely on priesthood to defend its cause or to propagate its Message. Bahá'ís do not seek rank or privilege; it is the duty of each to present the verities of his or her Faith to the best of his or her abilities without proselytizing – the enticement or coercion of an individual to change his or her religion which is a major source of contention between Judaism, Christianity and Islam. Truth is in no need of such proselytizing, for the purpose of the divine Word is to open the eyes and ears, rather than to change religious labels or to win souls for God at any cost.

> It is true that Bahá'u'lláh lays on every Bahá'í the duty to teach His Faith. At the same time, however, we are forbidden to proselytize, so it is important for all believers to understand the difference between teaching and proselytizing. It is a significant difference and, in some countries where teaching a religion is permitted, but proselytizing is forbidden, the distinction is made in the law of the land. Proselytizing implies bringing undue pressure to bear upon someone to change his Faith. It is also usually understood to imply the making of threats or the offering of material benefits as an inducement to conversion. In some countries mission schools or hospitals, for all the good they do, are regarded with suspicion and even aversion by the local authorities because they are considered to be material inducements to conversion and hence instruments of proselytization.
>
> Bahá'u'lláh, in *The Hidden Words*, says, 'O Son of Dust! The wise are they that speak not unless they obtain a hearing, even as the cup-bearer, who proffereth not his cup till he findeth a seeker, and the lover who crieth not out from the depths of his heart until he gazeth upon the beauty of his beloved . . .', and [in] *The Advent of Divine Justice*, a letter which is primarily directed towards exhorting the friends to fulfil their responsibilities in teaching the Faith, Shoghi Effendi writes: 'Care, however, should, at all times, be exercised,

lest in their eagerness to further the international interests of the Faith they frustrate their purpose, and turn away, through any act that might be misconstrued as an attempt to proselytize and bring undue pressure upon them, those whom they wish to win over to their Cause.'[68]

6

SECTARIAN HOSTILITY AND VIOLENCE

> O ye children of men! The fundamental purpose animating the Faith of God and His Religion is to safeguard the interests and promote the unity of the human race, and to foster the spirit of love and fellowship amongst men. Suffer it not to become a source of dissension and discord, of hate and enmity. This is the straight Path, the fixed and immovable foundation. Whatsoever is raised on this foundation, the changes and chances of the world can never impair its strength, nor will the revolution of countless centuries undermine its structure ...
>
> *Bahá'u'lláh*[1]

Almost from its inception Islam, a religion that prides itself on standing for peace and order, has become plagued with sectarian violence, caused largely by disagreements as to who should lead the community following the passing of Muhammad (632 AD). The absence of a universally-accepted and reliable infallible interpreter of the Divine Word and an unchallengeable source of continued clear divine guidance added to the spiritual void, and Islam became divided into two factions, Sunni and Shí'ih. The majority Sunni sect[2] relies mainly on the Qur'án and the guidance of tradition. Historically, Sunnis have followed appointed leaders (Caliphs), the first four of whom, Abu Bekr, Omar, Othman and 'Alí Ibn Abi Tálib, are called *Al-Khulafah ar-Rashidun* or Rightly-Guided Caliphs. Those of the Shí'ih faction[3] believe that Imam 'Alí Ibn Abi Tálib[4] should have been recognized as the rightful successor of Muhammad. There are several divisions of Shí'ih, the largest, Twelver Shí'ih Islam (*Ithná'ashariyyah* or *Imámiyyah*) owe their allegiance to Ali and eleven subsequent divinely-ordained *Imams*. All but the last Imam were assassinated, but the twelfth, Imam Mahdi, is believed to be still alive. He is alleged to have disappeared after performing last rites for his father's death, and that He is still under *ghaybat* or 'occultation' but will eventually reappear on the face of the earth to establish truth and bring an end to tyranny and oppression. Both Sunni and Shí'ih sects have in turn multiple subdivisions. Hence, the animosities and internecine feuds between the rival sects date to Muhammad's passing and the inception of Islam. The violence has not abated and has only intensified in recent years, spasmodically affecting different regions of the world and disturbing the peace of mankind.

These divisions in Islam have occurred despite many admonitions in the Qur'án itself that God's Faith must not under any circumstances be splintered into sects. The Qur'án declares that God abhors divisions, and instructs Muslims to shun entirely those who split God's religion. It specifically warns against causing mischief in the guise of promoting peace.

> As for those who divide (create divisions within) their religion and break up into sects, thou hast no part in them in the least: their affair is with God: He will in the end tell them the truth of all that they did.[5]

> When it is said to them: 'Make not mischief on the earth,' they say: 'Why, we only want to make peace!'[6]

To emphasize the importance of unity, the Qur'án warns against the type of sectarianism that had infected Judaism and Christianity.

> And, verily, this Brotherhood ['*Ummah*', people or 'nation' of Islam] of yours is a single Brotherhood, and I am your Lord and Cherisher: therefore fear Me (and no other).
>   But people have cut off their affair (of unity), between them, into sects – each party rejoices in that which is with itself.
>   But leave them in their confused ignorance for a time.[7]

Specifically, Muslims were taught to avoid the disharmony that has its roots in interpretations of scripture and man-made dogma.

> But the sects [a reference to Christian denominations that differed in their teachings concerning the station of Jesus and the nature of

His 'sonship'] differ among themselves: and woe to the unbelievers because of the (coming) Judgment of a Momentous Day![8]

The Qur'án warns Muslims that every religious sect claims to have a monopoly on truth, and to be the sole source of salvation for its followers:

> Those who split up their religion, and become (mere) sects, each party rejoicing in that which is with itself![9]

The Qur'án points out that divisions occurred only after clear divine guidance was provided but was ignored, and consequently truth was discarded.

> Nor did the People of the Book make schisms, until after there came to them Clear Evidence.[10]

> Be not like those who are divided amongst themselves and fall into disputations after receiving clear Signs: for them is a dreadful penalty.[11]

> And they became divided only after knowledge reached them – through selfish envy as between themselves. Had it not been for a Word that went forth before from thy Lord, (tending) to a term appointed, the matter would have been settled between them: but truly those who have inherited the Book after them are in suspicious (disquieting) doubt concerning it.[12]

> And We granted them clear Signs in affairs: it was only after knowledge had been granted to them that they fell into schisms, through insolent envy among themselves. Verily thy Lord will judge between them on the Day of Judgment as to those matters in which they set up differences.[13]

Muslims are commanded not to follow those who stir up trouble, and are advised even to avoid building mosques that are sectarian in nature and promote disunity and disharmony.

> . . . do right, and follow not the way of those who do mischief.[14]

> And there are those who put up a mosque by way of mischief and infidelity – to disunite the Believers and in preparation for one who warred against God and His Apostle aforetime. They will indeed swear that their intention is nothing but good; But God doth declare that they are certainly liars.[15]

Sadly, these clear warnings were not heeded, thus ensuring the disintegration of Islam – a process analogous to physical death when the various bodily components lose their cohesion and become dispersed. Hence, the Qur'án predicts that the *insán*, or spiritual man that was 'created' through the Revelation of the Qur'án will suffer a reversal and will be abased.

> (God) Most Gracious!
> It is He Who has taught the Qur'án.
> He has created man [*insán*].[16]
>
> We have indeed created man [*insán*] in the best of moulds,
> Then ['*thumma*', implying a passage of time] do We abase him (to be) the lowest of the low – [17]

Man's salvation, spiritual rebirth, resurrection, reanimation will require divine intervention.

> How can ye reject the faith in God? – seeing that ye were without life, and He gave you life; then will He cause you to die, and will again bring you to life; and again to Him will ye return.[18]

'Alí Ibn Abí Tálib bemoaned the spiritual decline that had already overtaken Muslims within the short span of time following the death of Muhammad.

> I see you just bodies without spirits and spirits without bodies, devotees without good, traders without profits, wakeful but sleeping, present but unseen, seeing but blind, hearing but deaf and speaking but dumb.
> I notice that misguidance has stood on its centre and spread (all round) through its off-shoots. It weighs you with its weights and

confuses you with its measures. Its leader is an out-cast from the community. He persists on misguidance. So on that day none from among you would remain except as the sediment in a cooking pot or the dust left after dusting a bundle. It would scrape you as leather is scraped, and trample you as harvest is trampled, and pick out the believer as a bird picks out a big grain from the thin grain.

Where are these ways taking you, gloom misleading you, and falsehoods deceiving you? Whence are you brought and where are you driven? For every period there is a written document and everyone who is absent has to return. So listen to your godly leader and keep your hearts present. If he speaks to you be wakeful. The forerunner must speak truth to his people, should keep his wits together and maintain presence of mind. He has clarified to you the matter as the stitch-hole is cleared, and scraped it as the gum is scraped (from the twigs).

Nevertheless, now the wrong has set itself on its places and ignorance has ridden on its riding beasts. Unruliness has increased while the call for virtue is suppressed. Time has pounced upon like a devouring carnivore, and wrong is shouting like a camel after remaining silent. People have become brothers over ill-doings, have forsaken religion, are united in speaking lie but bear mutual hatred in the matter of truth.

When such is the case, the son would be a source of anger (instead of coolness of the eye to parents) and rain the cause of heat, the wicked would abound and the virtuous would diminish. The people of this time would be wolves, its rulers beasts, the middle class men gluttons and the poor (almost) dead. Truth would go down, falsehood would overflow, affection would be claimed with tongues but people would be quarrelsome at heart. Adultery would be the key to lineage while chastity would be rare and Islam would be worn overturned like the skin.[19]

Imám 'Alí also predicted a dire fate for Islam.

Amir al-mu'minin, peace be upon him said: A time will come when nothing will remain of the Qur'án except its writing, and nothing of Islám except its name. The mosques in those days will be busy with regards to construction but desolate with regard to guidance.

Those staying in them and those visiting them will be the worst of all on earth. From them mischief will spring up and towards them all wrong will turn. If anyone isolates himself from it (mischief) they will fling him back to it. And if any one steps back from it they will push him towards it.[20]

Again,

Certainly, a time will come upon you after me when nothing will be more concealed than rightfulness, nothing more apparent than wrongfulness – and nothing more current than untruth against Alláh and His prophet. For the people of this period nothing is more valueless than the Qur'án being recited as it ought to be recited, nor anything more valuable than the Qur'án being misplaced from its position. And in the towns nothing will be more hated than virtue, nor anything more acceptable than vice.

The holders of the book will throw it away and its memorizers would forget it. In these days the Qur'án and its people will be exiles and expelled. They will be companions keeping together on one path, but none will offer them asylum. Consequently at this time the Qur'án and its people will be among the people but not among them, will be with them but not with them, because misguidance cannot accord with guidance even though they may be together. The people will be united on division and will therefore cut away from the community, as though they were the leaders of the Qur'án and not the Qur'án their leader. Nothing of it will be left except its name, and they will know nothing save its writing and its words. Before that, they will inflict hardship on the virtuous, naming the latter's truthful views about Alláh false allegations, and enforcing for virtues the punishment of the vice.[21]

He foretells that the tragedy to be visited on Islam will be evident to all humanity:

O people! a time will come to you when Islám would be capsized as a pot is capsized with all its contents. O people, Alláh has protected you from that He might be hard on you but He has not spared from being put on trial.[22]

The *Bihár al-Anwár*, a voluminous compilation of traditions (*hadith*) considered authentic by Shi'ihs, predicts the same dreadful fate at 'the end of time' with the reappearance of Jesus, the Qá'im (He Who Shall Arise), and the Imám Zamán (the Lord or Leader of the Age). It describes the appalling tragedy in stark terms:

> The Prophet of God, upon Him and His Family be salutations, hath said/ sayeth:
>
> A time shall come when people shall have the faces of the Children of Adam but the hearts of devils.
>
> They shall be like ravenous beasts and shedders of blood. There is no wickedness that they will not perpetrate. Wert thou to follow them, they would cast thee into doubt and perplexity and wert thou to relate the *hadith* to them, they would gainsay it. And when thou art no longer amongst them, they would speak evil against thee and bite upon thy back. True prophetic practice and the sunna would, in their view, be called innovation, but their innovations they would claim as the true sunna. The forbearing amongst them will be cheated and the cheaters called kind. The true believers in that land will be brought low while the impious and the wicked will be honoured. Their young will be irreverent, their women impudent, and the mature amongst them shall neither command righteousness nor forbid evil.
>
> To seek succour from them would heap degradation on the seeker and to wish for glory from them would be humiliation itself. To desire what they desire would be the essence of poverty. In those days God will withhold His mercy in its rightful season and shall make it rain down in unseasonable times. The immoral amongst them will have ascendancy and these evil doers will 'set you hard tasks and punishments, slaughter your sons, and let your womenfolk live' [*Ibráhím*, Abraham, 14:6].
>
> They will invoke their invocations but these shall not be heard.
>
> The Prophet of God upon Him and His Family be salutations hath said:
>
> A time shall come upon my people when their appetites will be their gods, their women their points of adoration, their money their religion,[23] their honour a mere bargain. Naught shall remain of belief but its name, naught shall remain of Islam but its form.

Nothing will remain of the Qur'án but its external teachings. The mosques of that day will be well constructed but the hearts within them will be decadent and bereft of any guidance. The learned divines [*ulemá*] of that day will be the worst of God's creation on this earth. On that very day God will test them in these four ways:

The oppression of authority, all-embracing famine, cruelty of officials, the tyranny of rulers.

The companions of the Prophet were surprised and asked:

'O Messenger of God: will they truly worship idols again?'

The Prophet replied:

'Yes, their every dirham will be an idol for them.'

The Prophet of God, upon Him and His Family be salutations, hath said:

On the latter days, a group of my people will attend mosques. They will sit in rings in those mosques. Their remembrance will be this world. Their love will be the world and its vanities. Associate not with them for God has no need of them.

The Prophet of God, upon Him and His Family be salutations, said:

A Day will attend my people whereupon people will flee their divines as the sheep flee from the ravenous wolf. Three calamities will befall them. *Baraka* (blessings) will be uplifted away from their possessions. An oppressive ruler will oppress them and thirdly they will leave this world with no faith.

Anas narrated from the Prophet:

A time will transpire and come about when the one patiently holding on to faith is like the one holding in his hand red-hot coal.

The Prophet of God, upon Him and His Family be salutations, said:

A day will come upon my people (*ummah*) when their rulers will rule with injustice, their divines will be motivated by greed, the generality will be actuated by hypocrisy, their traders will trade only with usury, their women's main concern will be this life's luxuries, and their youth's only preoccupation to seek wedlock.

On that day the pointlessness of my people will be as the emptiness of the market where there is no true and genuine commodity to obtain.

The dead will recline in their graves because they have not

wrought any good. No righteous soul will live amongst them . . .

Then fleeing from them is preferable than staying amongst them.

The Prophet, upon Him and His Family be salutations, said:

A time is coming upon my people when its learned ones will be recognized only by their elegant clothes and the Qur'án will be known only by its fine voice of recitation, and God will not be worshipped except in the month of Ramadan, and when that day comes God will impose on them a ruler who shall have no knowledge, no forbearance nor any mercy.[24]

The *Bihár al-Anwár* further warns of deteriorating morals and diminishing faith prior to the advent of the promised Qá'im:

> What will be your condition when your women will be corrupted and your youth will be transgressors; and when you will neither encourage good nor forbid evil? . . . What will be your condition when you will order evil and forbid good? . . . What will be your condition when you will consider good as evil and evil as good?[25]

> . . . you will kill each other and all of this will occur among Muslims only.[26]

> A time will come when my *Ummah* will become impure from inside and attractive from outside in order to acquire wealth. They will do showoff (boastful actions) instead of gaining divine rewards. They will not fear Alláh. Alláh will punish all of them. At that time, people will supplicate like a drowning man, but their supplications will not be accepted.[27]

> A time will come on my *Ummah* when only the name of the Holy Qur'án will remain. They will have only the title of Islám, while they will be far from it (spiritual message or content). Their mosques will be filled (with people) apparently, but will be completely deprived of guidance. Their jurists will be the worst under this sky and mischief will start from them and return to them.[28]

> I said: O son of Alláh's Messenger, when will your Qaim appear? He [Aba Ja'far Muhammad bin 'Alí Báqir] replied: When the men will

resemble women and women will resemble men . . . false testimony will be accepted and true testimony will be obstructed. Murder will be accepted as minor thing. Adultery and usury will be common. People will fear the talks of the evil . . .²⁹

The Imam (Amir al-mu'minin, a.s.) Know that those signs (of the advent of Qaim) are as follows: When people will forget prayers. Trusts will be betrayed. Lying would be considered lawful. Usury will be common. Bribes will be rampant. Tall buildings would be constructed. Religion will be sold in exchange of worldly gains. Fools will be in power . . . Relationships will be broken off. Carnal desires will be widely followed. Bloodshed will be considered a minor matter.

Forbearance will be looked upon as weakness and oppression will be considered a matter of pride. Kings and rulers will be sinners and transgressors. Ministers shall be liars. The general public shall be dishonest. The reciters of the Qur'án will be transgressors. False testimony will be acceptable. Sins would be committed openly. Laying false allegations will be a common thing. Sinfulness and rebellion will be rife. The Qur'án will be looked down upon. Mosques will be decorated. Minarets will be elevated. Evil people will be accorded honor . . .³⁰

Before the coming of Qaim there will be deceitful years, in which a truthful one will be considered a liar, a liar will be considered truthful and a cheater will be respected.³¹

. . . whenever you see truth is extinct . . . and injustice and oppression have surrounded from all sides and Qur'án has become old-fashioned . . . and you see Qur'án interpreted by selfish motives and see religion is inverted like a bowl. And you see people of falsehood dominating over people of truth and see mischief becoming common but no one restraining it. Rather the mischief-makers will be defended and you will see transgressions openly committed . . . You will see that the believer will assume silence as his advice will not be accepted. You will see the transgressor lying and also see that his lies are being accepted and no one is refuting or falsifying his words. You will see the young insulting the elders . . . You will see when people see a believer making an effort and searching, they would seek the refuge of Alláh that they may not become like him . . .

You will see the path of good is closed and the path of mischief is open and full of people who walk upon it . . . You will see each one advising others what he himself has not done.

You will see that one possessing wealth is respected more than a believer . . .

You will see the believer always in sorrow, degradation and humiliation . . . You will see people competing with each other in testifying falsely . You will see that the prohibited has become permissible, the permissible has become prohibited. You will see people justifying their religion on the basis of their personal views and the Book of God and its commands are rendered useless . . .

You will see that no one is committing sins in the darkness of the night. Rather you will see them committing sins in broad daylight. You will see the believer, except by his heart, cannot refute the evils. You will see unprecedented wealth being squandered on activities hated by God. You will see wealthier people more deserving of leadership of the people . . . You will see people killed merely on allegations and doubts . . .

You will see that rebellion and injustice has come out in the open. You will see backbiting a sort of good and jovial manner and people would give glad-tidings to each other through it. You will see destructions dominating their lives . . . You will see that human life is a saleable commodity. You will see that bloodshed would become an easy and very common matter . . .

You will see that the hearts of the people have become hard and their eyes have no shame and the remembrance of Alláh is hard on them . . . You will see that if a worshipper goes to the worship house, he will do so with the intention of showing off . . . If you see a jurisprudent is contemplating something other than religious aim, it is that he intends to obtain material gains and worldly power. You will see that the people are supporting only those who are powerful and those who are victorious without any thought of whether they have been on the right or wrong . . .

You will see a person issuing good exhortation, but someone would stand up and say that Alláh does not want him to say these things . . . You will see that the paths of good are deserted and no one walks upon them . . .

You will see that people and groups do not follow anyone except the rich . . . You will see that the heavenly signs shall become apparent, but none would be afraid of them . . .

You will see children making allegations about their parents and criticizing them . . . You will see that conditions reach to such a stage that if a day passes for a man without having committed any sin, short-selling, misappropriation, usurpation, and wine-drinking, he would think that a day of his life is wasted . . .

You will see the mosques full of people who do not fear God. They have gathered to backbite and consume the flesh of the people of truth . . . You will see judges issuing judgments against divine commands . . .

You will see people advising good from the pulpit, but themselves not acting upon it . . .

You will see the signs of religion have become outdated, antiquated and old. Then beware of such a day for the sake of Alláh and beseech the Almighty for salvation . Know that in such days people shall be deep in Divine chastisement. . .[32]

Neighbors will harass each other. Cruelty will be done to relatives. Elders will have no kindness. Youngsters will lack shame and modesty . . . Servants will be oppressed. False testimonies will be common. Judgments will be given on the basis of injustice. The son will abuse the father. The brother will be jealous of his brother. Partners will cheat each other . . . Arrogance will permeate the people . . . There will be increase in crime . . . (unmindful of) the hereafter people will be busy in the world. There will be decrease in piety. Greed will increase. The believer will be degraded and the hypocrite will be exalted. Azann (call to prayer) will echo in the masjids (Mosques) but the hearts of the people will be without faith. The Qur'án will be considered light and unimportant. The believer will be degraded in every way.

At that time you will see that human beings are there but their hearts will be satanic; their words will be sweeter than honey, but the hearts will be more bitter than poison ivy. They will be wolves in the dress of humans. Every day the Almighty Alláh will say: Are you deceiving Me or you have in fact become disrespectful to me.[33]

> A time will come on the people when the sinners will gain respect, the shame will be loved and the equitable will be considered weak ... when worship will be considered useless ...³⁴

> When knowledge would be taken away from the world, when ignorance would be common. When there would be many reciters of the Qur'án and practical deeds would increase, when killings would increase; sincere jurisprudence would decrease and dishonest scholars would increase ...
> All this would happen when your Ummah will construct Masjids over graves and copies of the Qur'án will be embellished, masjids would be richly decorated. Oppressions would increase and sins would be committed openly and your Ummah would be ordered to commit sin and evil and they would be restrained from deeds of virtue ... Rulers would be infidels, their associates would be sinners, their helpers would be oppressors and their advisors would be transgressors ...
> Your society will pass through a period when cunning and crafty intriguers will be favored by status, when profligates will be considered as well-bred, and well-behaved and elegant elites of society, when just and honest persons will be considered weaklings ... when prayer and worship to Alláh will be taken up for the sake of show off to gain popularity and higher status at such times ...³⁵

> It is mentioned in a correct tradition of the Messenger of Alláh (s.a.w.s.) that he said: Very soon, all that has passed in Bani-Israel will come to pass in my Ummah also. That is, if someone entered a porpoise hole in Banu Israel, you would also enter it. (i.e. whatever bad happened to or was done by the Children of Israel will be occur to or will be committed by Muslims.)³⁶

The New Testament also preaches against division and sectarianism.

> And Jesus knew their thoughts, and said unto them, Every kingdom divided against itself is brought to desolation; and every city or house divided against itself shall not stand.³⁷

> That they all may be one; as thou, Father, art in me, and I in thee,

that they also may be one in us: that the world may believe that thou hast sent me.[38]

Finally, be ye all of one mind, having compassion one of another, love as brethren, be pitiful, be courteous.[39]

That ye may with one mind and one mouth glorify God, even the Father of our Lord Jesus Christ.[40]

Now I beseech you, brethren, by the name of our Lord Jesus Christ, that ye all speak the same thing, and that there be no divisions among you; but that ye be perfectly joined together in the same mind and in the same judgment.[41]

By this shall all men know that ye are my disciples, if ye have love one to another.[42]

Ye have heard that it hath been said, Thou shalt love thy neighbour, and hate thine enemy.
    But I say unto you, Love your enemies, bless them that curse you, do good to them that hate you, and pray for them which despitefully use you, and persecute you;
    That ye may be the children of your Father which is in heaven: for he maketh his sun to rise on the evil and on the good, and sendeth rain on the just and on the unjust.[43]

These admonitions were also sadly ignored, and Christianity has shared a fate similar to Islam.[44] Unfortunately, the love that Christ stated as defining His true followers was replaced relatively early on by intolerance, factional hatred and bloodshed.

> Religious wars have been many. Nine hundred thousand martyrs to the Protestant cause was the record of conflict and difference between that sect of Christians and the Catholics. Consult history and confirm this.[45] How many languished in prisons! How merciless the treatment of captives! All in the name of religion! Consider and estimate the outcome of other wars between the people and sects of religious belief.[46]

Interdenominational violence and animosity has stained the annals of the Christian church for centuries. The Thirty Years' War (1618–48) fought between Catholics and Protestants over control of Germany was one of the longest and most destructive conflicts in European history, resulting in the death of about 7.5 million followers of Christ at the hand of their co-religionists. The current lack of Christian love and unity is attested to by many scholars, such as in this statement by Reverend Barclay:

> It is the tragedy of the Church that it has been marked by division and disunity rather than by the supreme unity which ought to be the closest of all unities. We should surely regard it as an astonishing and shocking thing to go on repeating a creed which in action we deny, and to go on affirming a belief which our practice bluntly and flatly contradicts . . .[47]

The question that Christians need to ask themselves is whether they should have blindly followed self-proclaimed spiritual leaders and man-made institutions for so many centuries when the 'fruits' of that tree has been so evil. Inevitably, the Bible predicts that a time will come when Christ will not recognize His followers. Rather, He will condemn their supplications and solicitations in His Name and will regard their seemingly 'wonderful works' as evil and unjust.

> Not every one that saith unto me, Lord, Lord, shall enter into the kingdom of heaven; but he that doeth the will of my Father which is in heaven.
> Many will say to me in that day, Lord, Lord, have we not prophesied in thy name? and in thy name have cast out devils? and in thy name done many wonderful works?
> And then will I profess unto them, I never knew you: depart from me, ye that work iniquity.[48]

> And I say unto you, That many shall come from the east and west, and shall sit down with Abraham, and Isaac, and Jacob, in the kingdom of heaven.
> But the children of the kingdom shall be cast out into outer darkness: there shall be weeping and gnashing of teeth.[49]

Christians are reminded that the second coming of Christ will occur during a spiritual nighttime. They therefore need to be prepared by remaining awake and sober:

> But of the times and the seasons, brethren, ye have no need that I write unto you.
>
> For yourselves know perfectly that the day of the Lord so cometh as a thief in the night . . .
>
> But ye, brethren, are not in darkness, that that day should overtake you as a thief.
>
> Ye are all the children of light, and the children of the day: we are not of the night, nor of darkness.
>
> Therefore let us not sleep, as do others; but let us watch and be sober.
>
> For they that sleep sleep in the night; and they that be drunken are drunken in the night.
>
> But let us, who are of the day, be sober, putting on the breastplate of faith and love; and for an helmet, the hope of salvation.[50]

In common with Christianity and Islam, the Bible also foresees a time when Judaism will also slide or 'slip' into darkness.

> Wherefore their way shall be unto them as slippery ways in the darkness: they shall be driven on, and fall therein: for I will bring evil upon them, even the year of their visitation, saith the Lord.[51]

> And it shall come to pass in that day, that the Lord shall punish the host of the high ones that are on high, and the kings of the earth upon the earth.
>
> And they shall be gathered together, as prisoners are gathered in the pit . . .[52]

> And the songs of the temple shall be howlings[53] in that day, saith the Lord God: there shall be many dead bodies in every place; they shall cast them forth with silence.[54]

Unity is the hallmark of Bahá'u'lláh's Revelation.

> O contending peoples and kindreds of the earth! Set your faces towards unity, and let the radiance of its light shine upon you. Gather ye together, and for the sake of God resolve to root out whatever is the source of contention amongst you. Then will the effulgence of the world's great Luminary envelop the whole earth, and its inhabitants become the citizens of one city, and the occupants of one and the same throne. This wronged One hath, ever since the early days of His life, cherished none other desire but this, and will continue to entertain no wish except this wish.[55]

As its mandate and primary purpose is to create oneness of Faith and to promote harmony, the Divine Will has ensured that the Faith of Bahá'u'lláh be 'undenominational, non-sectarian, and wholly divorced from every ecclesiastical system, whatever its form, origin, or activities'.[56]

> Religion should unite all hearts and cause wars and disputes to vanish from the face of the earth, give birth to spirituality, and bring life and light to each heart. If religion becomes a cause of dislike, hatred and division, it were better to be without it, and to withdraw from such a religion would be a truly religious act. For it is clear that the purpose of a remedy is to cure; but if the remedy should only aggravate the complaint it had better be left alone. Any religion which is not a cause of love and unity is no religion. All the holy prophets were as doctors to the soul; they gave prescriptions for the healing of mankind; thus any remedy that causes disease does not come from the great and supreme Physician.[57]

Despite challenges, the hand of Providence has protected His Faith from sectarianism and division by ensuring a clear line of succession and interpreters ('Abdu'l-Bahá and Shoghi Effendi) and ensuring that, following them, ultimate authority resides with the Supreme Body, the Universal House of Justice, which adjudicates on matters not specifically dealt with by Bahá'u'lláh. 'Abdu'l-Bahá commented:

> The wisdom of this is that the times never remain the same, for change is a necessary quality and an essential attribute of this world, and of time and place. Therefore the House of Justice will take action accordingly . . .

> Briefly, this is the wisdom of referring the laws of society to the (Universal) House of Justice. In the religion of Islám . . . not every ordinance was explicitly revealed; nay not a tenth part of a tenth part was included in the Text; although all matters of major importance were specifically referred to, there were undoubtedly thousands of laws which were unspecified. These were devised by the divines of a later age according to the laws of Islamic jurisprudence, and individual divines made conflicting deductions from the original revealed ordinances. All these were enforced. Today this process of deduction is the right of the body of the House of Justice, and the deductions and conclusions of individual learned men have no authority, unless they are endorsed by the House of Justice. The difference is precisely this, that from the conclusions and endorsements of the body of the House of Justice whose members are elected by and known to the worldwide Bahá'í community, no differences will arise; whereas the conclusions of individual divines and scholars would definitely lead to differences, and result in schism, division, and dispersion. The oneness of the Word would be destroyed, the unity of the Faith would disappear, and the edifice of the Faith of God would be shaken.[58]

Disunity and sectarianism leads to darkness and signifies spiritual death. Hence, the rebirth of God's Faith is in conformity with the Quranic prophecy of a Day when the earth will shine with the light of its Lord (*Zumar*, the Crowds, 39:69), and the Biblical promise of a Day that shall not be followed by night, a Day of everlasting splendour, a Day when the Glory of God will provide the spiritual light of the City of God:

> Thy sun shall no more go down; neither shall thy moon withdraw itself: for the Lord shall be thine everlasting light, and the days of thy mourning shall be ended.[59]
> And they shall see his face; and his name shall be in their foreheads.
> And there shall be no night there; and they need no candle, neither light of the sun; for the Lord God giveth them light: and they shall reign for ever and ever.[60]

And the city had no need of the sun, neither of the moon, to shine in it: for the glory of God did lighten it, and the Lamb is the light thereof.

And the nations of them which are saved shall walk in the light of it: and the kings of the earth do bring their glory and honour into it.

And the gates of it shall not be shut at all by day: for there shall be no night there.

And they shall bring the glory and honour of the nations into it.

And there shall in no wise enter into it any thing that defileth, neither whatsoever worketh abomination, or maketh a lie . . .[61]

Bahá'u'lláh confirms that this scriptural promise has been fulfilled in this Day.

This is but an evidence of the bounty which God hath vouchsafed unto Thee, a bounty which shall last until the Day that hath no end in this contingent world. It shall endure so long as God, the Supreme King, the Help in Peril, the Mighty, the Wise, shall endure. For the Day of God is none other but His own Self, Who hath appeared with the power of truth. This is the Day that shall not be followed by night, nor shall it be bounded by any praise, would that ye might understand![62]

The followers of Bahá'u'lláh pray for unity and that all human beings may be illumined by the eternal divine light and partake of the heavenly bounty:

O Thou kind Lord! O Thou Who art generous and merciful! We are the servants of Thy threshold and are gathered beneath the sheltering shadow of Thy divine unity. The sun of Thy mercy is shining upon all, and the clouds of Thy bounty shower upon all. Thy gifts encompass all, Thy loving providence sustains all, Thy protection overshadows all, and the glances of Thy favor are cast upon all. O Lord! Grant Thine infinite bestowals, and let the light of Thy guidance shine. Illumine the eyes, gladden the hearts with abiding joy. Confer a new spirit upon all people and bestow upon them eternal life. Unlock the gates of true understanding and let the light of faith shine resplendent. Gather all people beneath the shadow of Thy bounty and cause them to unite in harmony, so that they may become as the rays of one sun, as the waves of one ocean, and as the fruit of one tree. May they drink from the same fountain. May they be refreshed by the same breeze. May they receive illumination from the same source of light. Thou art the Giver, the Merciful, the Omnipotent.[63]

7

EXCESSIVE RELIANCE ON RELIGIOUS LEADERS FOR GUIDANCE

> Tear asunder, in My Name, the veils that have grievously blinded your vision, and, through the power born of your belief in the unity of God, scatter the idols of vain imitation . . . Sanctify your souls from whatsoever is not of God, and taste ye the sweetness of rest within the pale of His vast and mighty Revelation, and beneath the shadow of His supreme and infallible authority. Suffer not yourselves to be wrapt in the dense veils of your selfish desires, inasmuch as I have perfected in every one of you My creation, so that the excellence of My handiwork may be fully revealed unto men. It follows, therefore, that every man hath been, and will continue to be, able of himself to appreciate the Beauty of God, the Glorified. Had he not been endowed with such a capacity, how could he be called to account for his failure? . . . For the faith of no man can be conditioned by any one except himself.
> *Bahá'u'lláh*[1]

The Qur'án proclaims that God is the only Truth or Reality (*Al-Haqq*):

> That is because God is the (only) Reality, and because whatever else they invoke besides Him is falsehood; and because God, – He is the Most High, Most Great.[2]

> Such is God, your real Cherisher and Sustainer: Apart from Truth, what (remains) but error? How then are ye turned away?
> . . . Say: 'It is God Who gives guidance towards Truth. Is then He Who gives guidance to Truth more worthy to be followed, or he who finds not guidance (himself) unless he is guided?'[3]

God is the 'Guide' (*Al-Hádí*) Who through His Revelation (the Book) steers human beings out of spiritual darkness, and redirects their steps to the Straight and Right Path(s).

> God guideth all who seek His good pleasure to ways [*sobul*] of peace and safety, and leadeth them out of darkness, by His Will, unto the light, – guideth them to a Path [*sirát*] that is Straight.[4]

> That which We have revealed to thee of the Book is the Truth, – confirming what was (revealed) before it.[5]

It is again God alone Who will clarify the Truth and decide on matters in the Day when His Revelation will unify mankind.

> Say: 'Our Lord will gather us together and will in the end decide the matter between us (and you) in truth and justice: and He is the One to decide, the One Who knows all.'[6]

Humanity must therefore turn to God only, as the 'Fountain of All Truth' in 'that Day', a Day that has now been ushered in by Bahá'u'lláh:

> On that Day God will pay them back (all) their just dues, and they will realize that God is the (very) Truth, that makes all things manifest.[7]

Before His crucifixion Christ reassured His disciples by announcing to them the coming of the Spirit of Truth, Who would reveal 'all truth' and further revelations of the Divine Purpose:

> I have yet many things to say unto you, but ye cannot bear them now.
> Howbeit when he, the Spirit of truth,[8] is come, he will guide you into all truth: for he shall not speak of himself; but whatsoever he shall hear, that shall he speak: and he will show you things to come.
> He shall glorify me: for he shall receive of mine, and shall show it unto you.[9]

The Qur'án warns, however, that humanity will be 'veiled' from the truth and the illumination of God's promised Revelation:

> Verily, from (the Light of) their Lord, that Day, will they be veiled.[10]

An essential element of God's Purpose is to remove the veils and sources of spiritual blindness:

> (It will be said:) 'Thou wast heedless of this; now have We removed thy veil, and sharp is thy sight this Day!'[11]

The veils that commonly prevent humanity from seeing the truth are usually idols of imagination and individuals who have assumed spiritual authority over their flock and have come to 'partner God':

> And they set up (idols) as equal to God, to mislead (men) from the Path! Say: 'Enjoy your brief power)! But verily ye are making straightway for hell!'[12]

The Qur'án warns against indulging in '*shirk*' (assigning 'partners to God')[13] and teaches that individuals should use their reason and not rebel against the truth; hasty and uninformed judgements are forbidden.

> Say: The things that my Lord hath indeed forbidden are: shameful deeds, whether open or secret; sins and trespasses against truth or reason;[14] assigning of partners to God, for which He hath given no authority; and saying things about God of which ye have no knowledge.[15]

The Bible, too, warns that human beings will be judged by their response to the truth that God will reveal in due course; they must therefore refrain from indulging in idle disputation.

> For he cometh, for he cometh to judge the earth: he shall judge the world with righteousness, and the people with his truth.[16]

> A good man out of the good treasure of the heart bringeth forth good things: and an evil man out of the evil treasure bringeth forth evil things.
> But I say unto you, That every idle word that men shall speak, they shall give account thereof in the day of judgment.

For by thy words thou shalt be justified, and by thy words thou shalt be condemned.[17]

The Báb and Bahá'u'lláh remind us of this truth:

> Say, verily, the criterion by which truth is distinguished from error shall not appear until the Day of Resurrection . . .
>
> How vast the number of people who will, on the Day of Resurrection, regard themselves to be in the right, while they shall be accounted as false through the dispensation of Providence, inasmuch as they will shut themselves out as by a veil from Him Whom God shall make manifest and refuse to bow down in adoration before Him Who, as divinely ordained in the Book, is the Object of their creation.[18]

> Verily this is that Most Great Beauty, foretold in the Books of the Messengers, through Whom truth shall be distinguished from error and the wisdom of every command shall be be tested. Verily He is the Tree of Life that bringeth forth the fruits of God, the Exalted, the Powerful, the Great . . .[19]

> When the Word of God is revealed unto all created things whoso then giveth ear and heedeth the Call is, indeed, reckoned among the most distinguished souls . . . And he who turneth away is accounted as the lowliest of His servants, though he be a ruler amongst men and the possessor of all the books that are in the heavens and on earth.[20]

Bahá'u'lláh reminds the Muslim clergy of the Quranic assertions that it is God and His Prophets Who define 'Truth' in every age.

> O Shaykh! Every time God the True One – exalted be his glory – revealed Himself in the person of His Manifestation, He came unto men with the standard of 'He doeth what He willeth, and ordaineth what he pleaseth.' None hath the right to ask why or wherefore, and he that doth so, hath indeed turned aside from God, the Lord of Lords.[21]

Moreover, acceptance of the new Revelation is independent of their scholarship:

> The understanding of His words and the comprehension of the utterances of the Birds of Heaven are in no wise dependent upon human learning. They depend solely upon purity of heart, chastity of soul, and freedom of spirit.[22]

He further reminds them that ultimately the legitimacy of their beliefs, acquired learning and judgements are evaluated by the standards of the new Revelation – they should not instead attempt to test the validity of the unfamiliar divine teachings by their understanding of an earlier Dispensation.

> O leaders of religion! Weigh not the Book of God with such standards and sciences as are current amongst you, for the Book itself is the unerring Balance established amongst men. In this most perfect Balance whatsoever the peoples and kindreds of the earth possess must be weighed, while the measure of its weight should be tested according to its own standard . . .[23]

> O ye leaders of religion! Who is the man amongst you that can rival Me in vision or insight? Where is he to be found that dareth to claim to be My equal in utterance or wisdom? No, by My Lord, the All-Merciful! All on the earth shall pass away; and this is the face of your Lord, the Almighty, the Well-Beloved . . . Say: This, verily, is the heaven in which the Mother Book is treasured, could ye but comprehend it. He it is Who hath caused the Rock to shout, and the Burning Bush to lift up its voice, upon the Mount rising above the Holy Land, and proclaim: 'The Kingdom is God's, the sovereign Lord of all, the All-Powerful, the Loving!' We have not entered any school, nor read any of your dissertations. Incline your ears to the words of this unlettered One, wherewith He summoneth you unto God, the Ever-Abiding. Better is this for you than all the treasures of the earth, could ye but comprehend it.[24]

Bahá'u'lláh informs the religious leaders that all their accomplishments, impressive titles and lofty positions will ill serve them if they oppose God's Revelation; their ultimate hope and salvation, and that of their followers, is to accept His Revelation.

O concourse of divines! This is the day whereon nothing amongst all things, nor any name amongst all names, can profit you save through this Name which God hath made the Manifestation of His Cause and the Dayspring of His Most Excellent Titles unto all who are in the kingdom of creation. Blessed is that man that hath recognized the fragrance of the All-Merciful and been numbered with the steadfast. Your sciences shall not profit you in this day, nor your arts, nor your treasures, nor your glory. Cast them all behind your backs, and set your faces towards the Most Sublime Word . . . Cast away, O concourse of divines, the things ye have composed with the pens of your idle fancies and vain imaginings.[25]

Every individual is responsible for his or her own faith

According to the sacred texts of Judaism, Christianity and Islam, people are accountable for their own spiritual welfare. However, they often abdicate this vital obligation, instead excessively revering their leaders and relying on their dictates for almost every matter of daily life, faith and even for matters of science. The Qur'án explains that it is often prominent individuals who deny the new Messenger because of their excessive attachment to power and to their ancestral religion. They thus play a major part in misleading their followers.

> Nay! They say: 'We found our fathers following a certain religion, and we do guide ourselves by their footsteps.'
>
> Just in the same way, whenever We sent a Warner before thee to any people, the wealthy ones[26] among them said: 'We found our fathers following a certain religion, and we will certainly follow in their footsteps.'
>
> He said: 'What! Even if I brought you better guidance than that which ye found your fathers following?' They said: 'For us, we deny that ye (prophets) are sent (on a mission at all).'
>
> So We exacted retribution from them: now see what was the end of those who rejected (Truth)!'[27]

The New Testament encourages investigation: 'Prove all things; hold fast that which is good,'[28] but predicts a time when individuals will not be inclined to listen to 'sound doctrine': instead, they will follow their own desires and surround themselves with teachers who tell them what they want to hear.

> For the time will come when they will not endure sound doctrine; but after their own lusts shall they heap to themselves teachers, having itching ears;
> And they shall turn away their ears from the truth, and shall be turned unto fables.[29]

> How can ye believe, which receive honour one of another, and seek not the honour that cometh from God only?[30]

Christians have therefore been given the following clear instruction:

> And be not conformed to this world: but be ye transformed by the renewing of your mind, that ye may prove what is that good, and acceptable, and perfect, will of God.[31]

Criteria of being learned

Quoting a tradition ascribed to the eleventh Imám, Abú Muḥammad al-Ḥasan al-'Askarí, Bahá'u'lláh writes:

> Concerning the prerequisites of the learned, He saith: 'Whoso among the learned guardeth his self, defendeth his faith, opposeth his desires, and obeyeth his Lord's command, it is incumbent upon the generality of the people to pattern themselves after him . . .'[32]

'Abdu'l-Bahá comments on this same tradition:

> An authoritative Tradition states: 'As for him who is one of the learned: he must guard himself, defend his faith, oppose his passions and obey the commandments of his Lord. It is then the duty of the people to pattern themselves after him.' Since these illustrious and holy words embody all the conditions of learning, a brief commentary on their meaning is appropriate. Whoever is lacking in these divine qualifications and does not demonstrate these inescapable requirements in his own life, should not be referred to as

learned and is not worthy to serve as a model for the believers.[33]

However, Bahá'u'lláh continues, this high standard is rarely met, and the requisite spiritual qualities are unfortunately rare:

> those who have been adorned with the attributes enumerated in this holy Tradition are scarcer than the philosopher's stone; wherefore not every man that layeth claim to knowledge deserveth to be believed.[34]

The 'people of the Book' (*'Ahli alkitáb*)

The Qur'án castigates those who, in possession of holy scripture, misinterpret the Divine Word, oppose God's Revelation, and thereby prevent the enlightenment of their followers. It was primarily the recipients of the 'Book', namely the clergy, who rejected Muhammad.

> Even if thou wert to bring to the people of the Book all the Signs (together), they would not follow thy Qibla; nor art thou going to follow their Qibla; nor indeed will they follow each other's Qibla. If thou after the knowledge hath reached thee, wert to follow their (vain) desires, – then wert thou indeed (clearly) in the wrong.
> The people of the Book know this as they know their own sons; but some of them conceal the truth which they themselves know.
> The Truth is from thy Lord; so be not at all in doubt.[35]

> Ye People of the Book! Why reject ye the Signs of God, of which ye are (yourselves) witnesses?
> Ye People of the Book! Why do ye clothe truth with falsehood, and conceal the Truth, while ye have knowledge?[36]

> Say: 'O People of the Book! why reject ye the signs of God, when God is Himself witness to all ye do?'
> Say: 'O ye People of the Book! why obstruct ye those who believe, from the path of God, seeking to make it crooked, while ye were yourselves witnesses (to God's Covenant)? But God is not unmindful of all that ye do.'[37]

> O ye who believe! There are indeed many among the priests and

anchorites, who in falsehood devour the substance of men and hinder (them) from the Way of God. And there are those who bury gold and silver and spend it not in the Way of God: announce unto them a most grievous penalty – [38]

Bahá'u'lláh explains that 'people of the Book', refers specifically to the Jewish, Christian and Muslim religious leaders, for it was they who possessed and interpreted the scriptures and who held the spiritual destiny of their followers in their grasp.

> It is evident that by the 'people of the Book', who have repelled their fellow-men from the straight path of God, is meant none other than the divines of that age . . . were you to observe with the eye of God . . .
> . . . The denials and protestations of these leaders of religion have, in the main, been due to their lack of knowledge and understanding . . . And yet, they have sought the interpretation of the Book from those that are wrapt in veils, and have refused to seek enlightenment from the fountainhead of knowledge.[39]

The Qur'án warns Muslims to heed the fate of Christians who failed to recognize the Divine Message and the Prophet Muhammad because they relied too heavily for guidance on their religious leaders whom they treated as 'lords' in preference to God.

> They take their priests and their anchorites to be their lords in derogation of God, and (they take as their Lord) Christ the son of Mary; Yet they were commanded to worship but One God: there is no god but He. Praise and glory to Him: (far is He) from having the partners they associate (with Him).[40]

The Qur'án decries wilful rejection of guidance. There is none more wicked than individuals who refuse to accept a Divine Revelation and who mislead others.

> And who doth more wrong than one who is reminded of the Signs of his Lord, but turns away from them, forgetting the (deeds) which his hands have sent forth? Verily We have set veils over their hearts

EXCESSIVE RELIANCE ON RELIGIOUS LEADERS FOR GUIDANCE

lest they should understand this, and over their ears, deafness. If thou callest them to guidance, even then will they never accept guidance.⁴¹

Canst thou then make the deaf to hear, or give direction to the blind or to such as (wander) in manifest error?⁴²

Those who, when they are admonished with the Signs of their Lord, droop not down at them as if they were deaf or blind.⁴³

The blind and the seeing are not alike;
Nor are the depths of Darkness and the Light;
Nor are the (chilly) shade and the (genial) heat of the sun:
Nor are alike those that are living and those that are dead. God can make any that He wills to hear; but thou canst not make those to hear who are (buried) in graves.⁴⁴

Or lest ye should say: 'If the Book had only been sent down to us, we should have followed its guidance better than they.' Now then hath come unto you a Clear (Sign) from your Lord, – and a guide and a mercy: then who could do more wrong than one who rejecteth God's Signs, and turneth away therefrom? In good time shall We requite those who turn away from Our Signs, with a dreadful penalty, for their turning away.⁴⁵

The Qur'án repeatedly reminds us that in every age it has been the spiritual and social leaders that have misled the believers, with the latter's acquiescence.

When it is said to them: 'Follow what God hath revealed:' They say: 'Nay! we shall follow the ways of our fathers.' What! even though their fathers were void of wisdom and guidance?⁴⁶

When they are told to follow the (Revelation) that God has sent down, they say: 'Nay, we shall follow the ways that we found our fathers (following).' What! even if it is Satan beckoning them to the Penalty of the (Blazing) Fire?⁴⁷

The Qur'án refers to the mutual culpability of the spiritual leaders and their flock: the former will be blamed by their followers for having woefully misled them. The latter, the 'arrogant ones', 'chiefs', great ones', 'wealthy ones', or 'protectors other than God', will in turn accuse their supporters for not having paid more attention to the truth – for they should have known that every 'Warner' is rejected by prominent people.

> The Day that their faces will be turned upside down in the Fire, they will say: 'Woe to us! Would that we had obeyed God and obeyed the Apostle!
>
> And they would say: 'Our Lord! We obeyed our chiefs and our great ones, and they misled us as to the (right) Path.
>
> 'Our Lord! Give them double penalty and curse them with a very great curse!'[48]

> They say: 'When will this promise (come to pass) if ye are telling the truth?'
>
> Say: 'The appointment to you is for a day, which ye cannot put back for an hour nor put forward.'
>
> The unbelievers say: 'We shall neither believe in this scripture nor in (any) that (came) before it.' Couldst thou but see when the wrongdoers will be made to stand before their Lord, throwing back the word (of blame) on one another! Those who had been despised will say to the arrogant ones: 'Had it not been for you, we should certainly have been believers!'
>
> The arrogant ones will say to those who had been despised: 'Was it we who kept you back from Guidance after it reached you? Nay, rather, it was ye who transgressed.'
>
> Those who had been despised will say to the arrogant ones: 'Nay! it was a plot (of yours) by day and by night. Behold! ye (constantly) ordered us to be ungrateful to God and to attribute equals to Him!' They will declare (their) repentance when they see the Penalty: We shall put yokes on the necks of the unbelievers: it would only be a requital for their (ill) deeds.
>
> Never did We send a Warner to a population, but the wealthy ones among them said: 'We believe not in the (Message) with which ye have been sent.'[49]

God will Himself demand an answer from those who are worshipped besides God, as to their role in misguiding their followers.

> The Day He will gather them together as well as those whom they worship besides God, He will ask; 'Was it ye who led these My servants astray, or did they stray from the Path themselves?'
>
> They will say: 'Glory to Thee! Not meet was it for us that we should take for protectors others besides Thee: but Thou didst bestow, on them and their fathers, good things (in life), until they forgot the Message: for they were a people (worthless and) lost.'
>
> (God will say): 'Now have they proved you liars in what ye say: so ye cannot avert (your penalty) nor (get) help.' And whoever among you does wrong, him shall We cause to taste of a grievous Penalty.[50]

'Ali Ibn Abi Tálib also spoke disparagingly about theological pronouncements and differences of opinion among spiritual leaders:

> When a problem is put before anyone of them he passes judgment on it from his imagination. When exactly the same problem is placed before another of them he passes an opposite verdict. Then these judges go to the chief who had appointed them and he confirms all the verdicts, although their Alláh is one (and the same), their Book (the Qur'án) is one (and the same).
>
> Is it that Alláh ordered them to differ and they obeyed Him? Or He prohibited them from it but they disobeyed Him? Or (is it that) Alláh sent an incomplete Faith and sought their help to complete it? Or they are His partners in the affairs, so that it is their share of duty to pronounce and He has to agree? Or is it that Alláh the Glorified sent a perfect faith but the Prophet fell short of conveying it and handing it over (to the people)?
>
> The fact is that Alláh the Glorified says: 'We have not neglected anything in the Book' (*An'ám*, Cattle, 6:38), and says one part of the Qur'án verifies another part and that there is no divergence in it as He says: 'And if it had been from any other Alláh, they would surely have found in it much discrepancy.' (*Nisaa*, the Women, 4:82)
>
> They said: 'Comest thou to us, that we may worship God alone, and give up the religion of our fathers? Bring us what thou threatenest us with, if so be that thou tellest the truth!' (*A'ráf*, the Heights, 7:70)[51]

The Bible also uses its most vehement language to describe such leaders. For example, the Prophet Ezekiel warns of a time when those who should be concerned for the spiritual welfare of their flock will instead feed on the flock.

> Son of man, prophesy against the shepherds of Israel, prophesy, and say unto them, Thus saith the Lord God unto the shepherds; Woe be to the shepherds of Israel that do feed themselves! should not the shepherds feed the flocks? [52]

> Thus saith the Lord God; Behold, I am against the shepherds; and I will require my flock at their hand, and cause them to cease from feeding the flock; neither shall the shepherds feed themselves any more; for I will deliver my flock from their mouth, that they may not be meat for them. [53]

John the Baptist and Christ also harshly criticized the Jewish leaders for their hypocrisy.

> But when he [John the Baptist] saw many of the Pharisees and Sadducees come to his baptism, he said unto them, O generation of vipers, who hath warned you to flee from the wrath to come? [54]

> Let them alone: they be blind leaders of the blind. And if the blind lead the blind, both shall fall into the ditch. [55]

> Then spake Jesus to the multitude, and to his disciples,
> Saying, The scribes and the Pharisees sit in Moses' seat:
> All therefore whatsoever they bid you observe, that observe and do; but do not ye after their works: for they say, and do not.
> For they bind heavy burdens and grievous to be borne, and lay them on men's shoulders; but they themselves will not move them with one of their fingers.
> But all their works they do for to be seen of men: they make broad their phylacteries, and enlarge the borders of their garments,
> And love the uppermost rooms at feasts, and the chief seats in the synagogues,
> And greetings in the markets, and to be called of men, Rabbi,

EXCESSIVE RELIANCE ON RELIGIOUS LEADERS FOR GUIDANCE

Rabbi . . .

But woe unto you, scribes and Pharisees, hypocrites! for ye shut up the kingdom of heaven against men: for ye neither go in yourselves, neither suffer ye them that are entering to go in.

Woe unto you, scribes and Pharisees, hypocrites! for ye devour widows' houses, and for a pretence make long prayer: therefore ye shall receive the greater damnation.

Woe unto you, scribes and Pharisees, hypocrites! for ye compass sea and land to make one proselyte, and when he is made, ye make him twofold more the child of hell than yourselves.

Woe unto you, ye blind guides, which say, Whosoever shall swear by the temple, it is nothing; but whosoever shall swear by the gold of the temple, he is a debtor!

Ye fools and blind: for whether is greater, the gold, or the temple that sanctifieth the gold? . . .

Woe unto you, scribes and Pharisees, hypocrites! for ye pay tithe of mint and anise and cummin, and have omitted the weightier matters of the law, judgment, mercy, and faith: these ought ye to have done, and not to leave the other undone.

Ye blind guides, which strain at a gnat, and swallow a camel.

Woe unto you, scribes and Pharisees, hypocrites! for ye make clean the outside of the cup and of the platter, but within they are full of extortion and excess.

Thou blind Pharisee, cleanse first that which is within the cup and platter, that the outside of them may be clean also.

Woe unto you, scribes and Pharisees, hypocrites! for ye are like unto whited sepulchres, which indeed appear beautiful outward, but are within full of dead men's bones, and of all uncleanness.

Even so ye also outwardly appear righteous unto men, but within ye are full of hypocrisy and iniquity.

Woe unto you, scribes and Pharisees, hypocrites! because ye build the tombs of the prophets, and garnish the sepulchres of the righteous,

And say, If we had been in the days of our fathers, we would not have been partakers with them in the blood of the prophets.

Wherefore ye be witnesses unto yourselves, that ye are the children of them which killed the prophets.

Ye serpents, ye generation of vipers, how can ye escape the damnation of hell?

> Wherefore, behold, I send unto you prophets, and wise men, and scribes: and some of them ye shall kill and crucify; and some of them shall ye scourge in your synagogues, and persecute them from city to city.[56]

It was also primarily the Jewish religious leaders who rejected Jesus and persecuted His followers, judging them according to their understanding of the (Mosaic) law – remarkably similar to the prosecution of the followers of Bahá'u'lláh by religious courts according to Islamic tradition and the Sharia law.

> Ananias the high priest descended with the elders, and with a certain orator named Tertullus, who informed the governor against Paul . . .
> For we have found this man a pestilent fellow, and a mover of sedition among all the Jews throughout the world, and a ringleader of the sect of the Nazarenes:
> Who also hath gone about to profane the temple: whom we took, and would have judged according to our law.[57]

Christ was also concerned that His own Faith would fall victim to ecclesiastical control, misdirection and oppression. He therefore reminded the Christians that His 'Kingdom' was 'not of this world' (John 18:36) and urged His followers not to become spiritual leaders or 'fathers' – commandments that did not prevent the Church from creating an elaborate spiritual hierarchy on earth.

> But be not ye called Rabbi: for one is your Master, even Christ; and all ye are brethren.
> And call no man your father upon the earth: for one is your Father, which is in heaven.
> Neither be ye called masters: for one is your Master, even Christ.
> But he that is greatest among you shall be your servant.
> And whosoever shall exalt himself shall be abased; and he that shall humble himself shall be exalted.[58]

He also warned that false teachers would appear at the second coming amongst the Christian flock, who would teach in His Name, Jesus, but would deceive many Christians:

EXCESSIVE RELIANCE ON RELIGIOUS LEADERS FOR GUIDANCE

> For many shall come in my name, saying, I am Christ; and shall deceive many . . .[59]

> Beware of false prophets, which come to you in sheep's clothing, but inwardly they are ravening wolves.[60]

These 'holy' deceivers would be recognized by the 'fruits' of their actions:

> Ye shall know them by their fruits. Do men gather grapes of thorns, or figs of thistles?
> Even so every good tree bringeth forth good fruit; but a corrupt tree bringeth forth evil fruit.
> A good tree cannot bring forth evil fruit, neither can a corrupt tree bring forth good fruit.
> Every tree that bringeth not forth good fruit is hewn down, and cast into the fire.
> Wherefore by their fruits ye shall know them.[61]
> And blessed is he, whosoever shall not be offended in me.[62]

The Bahá'í Faith also acknowledges that the masses have been misled, rendering them less able to turn to their Creator and His Revelation for spiritual and social guidance. The consequent loss of humanity's faith in God Himself, it asserts, rests primarily on the shoulders of the world's religious leaders.

> Bahá'u'lláh's severest condemnation is reserved for those who, presuming to speak in God's name, have imposed on credulous masses a welter of dogmas and prejudices that have constituted the greatest single obstacle against which the advancement of civilization has been forced to struggle. While acknowledging the humanitarian services of countless individual clerics, He points out the consequences of the way in which self-appointed religious elites, throughout history, have interposed themselves between humanity and all voices of progress, not excluding the Messengers of God Themselves. 'What "oppression" is more grievous,' He asks, 'than that a soul seeking the truth, and wishing to attain unto the knowledge of God, should know not where to go for it . . .?'[63]

Bahá'u'lláh therefore censures those clerics who deprive individuals of their share of divine grace through the influence and power that they exert over them.

> Leaders of religion, in every age, have hindered their people from attaining the shores of eternal salvation, inasmuch as they held the reins of authority in their mighty grasp. Some for the lust of leadership, others through want of knowledge and understanding, have been the cause of the deprivation of the people. By their sanction and authority, every Prophet of God hath drunk from the chalice of sacrifice, and winged His flight unto the heights of glory. What unspeakable cruelties they that have occupied the seats of authority and learning have inflicted upon the true Monarchs of the world, those Gems of Divine virtue! Content with a transitory dominion, they have deprived themselves of an everlasting sovereignty.[64]

Notably, the Qur'án warns that those who find themselves following the (religious) majority at the time of a new Dispensation are very likely to have been misled.

> The Hour will certainly come: therein is no doubt: yet most men believe not.[65]

> Wert thou to follow the common run of those on earth, they will lead thee away from the Way of God. They follow nothing but conjecture: they do nothing but lie.[66]

> Say: 'Not equal are things that are bad and things that are good, even though the abundance of the bad may dazzle thee; so fear God, O ye that understand; that (so) ye may prosper.[67]

The Qur'án also reminds us that it was blind imitation of others and excessive reverence for tradition that prevented many followers of earlier Dispensations from recognizing Muhammad.

> Never will the Jews or the Christians be satisfied with thee unless thou follow their form of religion. Say: 'The guidance of God – that is the (only) guidance.' Wert thou to follow their desires after the

knowledge which hath reached thee, then wouldst thou find neither protector nor helper against God.[68]

The fools among the people will say: 'What hath turned them from the Qibla[69] to which they were used?' Say: to God belong both East and West; He guideth whom He will to a Way that is straight.[70]

But when Our Clear Signs are rehearsed unto them, those who rest not their hope on their meeting with Us, say: 'Bring us a Reading other than this, or change this.' Say: 'It is not for me, of my own accord, to change it: I follow naught but what is revealed unto me: if I were to disobey my Lord, I should myself fear the Penalty of a Great Day (to come).' [71]

'Veils of Glory' (*Sobaháté-jalál*)

Bahá'u'lláh uses the term 'veils of glory' to refer to the temporal power and the pomp and glory surrounding certain religious leaders – the glitter and tinsel associated with their rank and offices that causes spiritual blindness and incapacitates their followers from being able to investigate reality for themselves, and hence to be receptive to the Divine Message.[72]

> Among these 'veils of glory' are the divines and doctors living in the days of the Manifestation of God, who, because of their want of discernment and their love and eagerness for leadership, have failed to submit to the Cause of God, nay, have even refused to incline their ears unto the Divine Melody.'They have thrust their fingers into their ears.'[73] And the people also, utterly ignoring God and taking them for their masters, have placed themselves unreservedly under the authority of these pompous and hypocritical leaders, for they have no sight, no hearing, no heart,[74] of their own to distinguish truth from falsehood. Notwithstanding the divinely inspired admonition of all the Prophets, the Saints, and Chosen Ones of God, enjoining the people to see with their own eyes and hear with their own ears, they have disdainfully rejected their counsels and have blindly followed, and will continue to follow, the leaders of their Faith. Should a poor and obscure person, destitute of the attire of

the men of learning, address them saying: 'Follow ye, O people, the Messengers of God,' they would, greatly surprised at such a statement, reply: 'What! Meanest thou that all these divines, all these exponents of learning, with all their authority, their pomp, and pageantry, have erred, and failed to distinguish truth from falsehood? Dost thou, and people like thyself, pretend to have comprehended that which they have not understood?' If numbers and excellence of apparel be regarded as the criterions of learning and truth, the peoples of a bygone age, whom those of today have never surpassed in numbers, magnificence and power, should certainly be accounted a superior and worthier people.[75]

In recognition of the inordinate influence that they exert over the masses of their followers, Bahá'u'lláh's counsels and admonitions are often directed at the Muslim clergy.

> The eye of My loving-kindness weepeth sore over you, inasmuch as ye have failed to recognize the One upon Whom ye have been calling in the daytime and in the night season, at even and at morn.[76]

> O concourse of divines! Fling away idle fancies and imaginings, and turn, then, towards the Horizon of Certitude. I swear by God! All that ye possess will profit you not, neither all the treasures of the earth, nor the leadership ye have usurped. Fear God, and be not of the lost ones.[77]

> O concourse of divines! . . . Lay aside that which ye possess, and hold your peace, and give ear, then, unto that which the Tongue of Grandeur and Majesty speaketh. How many the veiled handmaidens who turned unto Me, and believed, and how numerous the wearers of the turban who were debarred from Me, and followed in the footsteps of bygone generations![78]

He points out that their opposition to God's Revelation, which they consider to be strengthening their religion, has actually weakened Islam:

> We have invited all men to turn towards God, and have acquainted them with the Straight Path. They [divines] rose up against Us with

such cruelty as hath sapped the strength of Islám, and yet most of the people are heedless![79]

> O ye the dawning-places of knowledge! Beware that ye suffer not yourselves to become changed, for as ye change, most men will, likewise, change. This, verily, is an injustice unto yourselves and unto others... Ye are even as a spring. If it be changed, so will the streams that branch out from it be changed. Fear God, and be numbered with the godly. In like manner, if the heart of man be corrupted, his limbs will also be corrupted. And similarly, if the root of a tree be corrupted, its branches, and its offshoots, and its leaves, and its fruits, will be corrupted.[80]

And in one of his major general Tablets He writes:

> Our hope is that the world's religious leaders and the rulers thereof will unitedly arise for the reformation of this age and the rehabilitation of its fortunes. Let them, after meditating on its needs, take counsel together and, through anxious and full deliberation, administer to a diseased and sorely-afflicted world the remedy it requireth ... It is incumbent upon them who are in authority to exercise moderation in all things. Whatsoever passeth beyond the limits of moderation will cease to exert a beneficial influence.[81]

This is reminiscent of the humility and moderation commended in the Qur'án:

> Call on your Lord with humility and in private: for God loveth not those who trespass beyond bounds.[82]

Bahá'u'lláh further writes:

> O concourse of divines! Be fair, I adjure you by God, and nullify not the Truth with the things ye possess. Peruse that which We have sent down with truth. It will, verily, aid you, and will draw you nigh unto God, the Mighty, the Great. Consider and call to mind how when Muḥammad, the Apostle of God, appeared, the people denied Him. They ascribed unto Him what caused the Spirit (Jesus) to lament in

His Most Sublime Station, and the Faithful Spirit to cry out. Consider, moreover, the things which befell the Apostles and Messengers of God before Him, by reason of what the hands of the unjust have wrought. We make mention of you for the sake of God, and remind you of His signs, and announce unto you the things ordained for such as are nigh unto Him in the most sublime Paradise and the all-highest Heaven, and I, verily, am the Announcer, the Omniscient. He hath come for your salvation, and hath borne tribulations that ye may ascend, by the ladder of utterance, unto the summit of understanding . . . Peruse, with fairness and justice, that which hath been sent down. It will, verily, exalt you through the truth, and will cause you to behold the things from which ye have been withheld, and will enable you to quaff His sparkling Wine.[83]

And yet again,

> Say, O concourse of divines! Be fair in your judgement, I adjure you by God. Produce then whatever proofs and testimonies ye possess, if ye are to be reckoned among the inmates of this glorious habitation. Set your hearts towards the Dayspring of divine Revelation that We may disclose before your eyes the equivalent of all such verses, proofs, testimonies, affirmations and evidences as ye and other kindreds of the earth possess. Fear ye God and be not of them that well deserve the chastisement of God, the Lord of creation.[84]

> Time and again have We, for the sake of God, admonished the distinguished divines, and summoned them unto the Most Sublime Horizon, that perchance they might, in the days of His Revelation, obtain their portion of the ocean of the utterance of Him Who is the Desire of the world, and remain not utterly deprived thereof.[85]

Primary source of opposition

Sadly, it has again been the spiritual guides, particularly in this day and age those of Islam and perhaps to a lesser extent those of Christianity, who have become the primary cause of hostility towards God's Revelation. Bahá'u'lláh writes:

> When We observed carefully We discovered that Our enemies are, for the most part, the divines... Among the people are those who said: 'He hath repudiated the divines.' Say: 'Yea, by My Lord! I, in very truth, was the One Who abolished the idols!'... We, verily, have sounded the Trumpet, which is Our Most Sublime Pen, and lo, the divines and the learned, and the doctors and the rulers, swooned away except such as God preserved, as a token of His grace, and He, verily, is the All-Bounteous, the Ancient of Days.[86]

Muslim spiritual leaders, demanding respect and submission from their flock, have played a preponderant role in opposing and attempting to extirpate the Divine Cause:

> The foolish divines have laid aside the Book of God, and are occupied with that which they themselves have fashioned. The Ocean of Knowledge is revealed, and the shrill of the Pen of the Most High is raised, and yet they, even as earthworms, are afflicted with the clay of their fancies and imaginings. They are exalted by reason of their relationship to the one true God, and yet they have turned aside from Him! Because of Him have they become famous, and yet they are shut off as by a veil from Him![87]

> The pagan priests, and the Jewish and Christian divines, have committed the very things which the divines of the age, in this Dispensation, have committed, and are still committing. Nay, these have displayed a more grievous cruelty and a fiercer malice.[88]

Bahá'u'lláh draws the comparison between those spiritual leaders who maliciously persecuted Muhammad and those of His own day, who were again resolved to destroy and persecute God's Faith in the new Dispensation:

> You are well aware of what befell His Faith in the early days of His dispensation. What woeful sufferings did the hand of the infidel and erring, the divines of that age and their associates, inflict upon that spiritual Essence, that most pure and holy Being! How abundant the thorns and briars which they have strewn over His path! It is evident that wretched generation, in their wicked and satanic fancy, regarded

every injury to that immortal Being as a means to the attainment of an abiding felicity; inasmuch as the recognized divines of that age, such as 'Abdu'lláh-i-Ubayy, Abú-'Amír, the hermit, Ka'b-Ibn-i-Ashraf, and Naḍr-Ibn-i-Ḥárith, all treated Him as an impostor, and pronounced Him a lunatic and a calumniator. Such sore accusations they brought against Him that in recounting them God forbiddeth the ink to flow, Our pen to move, or the page to bear them. These malicious imputations provoked the people to arise and torment Him. And how fierce that torment if the divines of the age be its chief instigators, if they denounce Him to their followers, cast Him out from their midst, and declare Him a miscreant! Hath not the same befallen this Servant (Báb and Bahá'u'lláh), and been witnessed by all?[89]

Addressing a preeminent monarch of His time, Nasir'i-Din Shah of Persia, He writes,

Remember the days in which the Sun of Baṭḥá shone forth above the horizon of the Will of thy Lord, the Exalted, the Most High, and recall how the divines of that age turned away from Him, and the learned contended with Him, that haply thou mayest apprehend that which, in this day, remaineth concealed behind the veils of glory. So grievous became His plight on every side that He instructed His companions to disperse.[90]

Conversely, it was individuals of humble and low standing – ordinary people – who had recognized the truth and espoused Islam.

In like manner, when Muḥammad, the Prophet of God – may all men be a sacrifice unto Him – appeared, the learned men of Mecca and Medina arose, in the early days of His Revelation, against Him and rejected His Message, while they who were destitute of all learning recognized and embraced His Faith. Ponder a while. Consider how Balál, the Ethiopian, unlettered though he was, ascended into the heaven of faith and certitude, whilst 'Abdu'lláh Ubayy, a leader among the learned, maliciously strove to oppose Him. Behold, how a mere shepherd was so carried away by the ecstasy of the words of God that he was able to gain admittance into the habitation of his Best-Beloved, and was united to Him Who is the Lord of Mankind,

EXCESSIVE RELIANCE ON RELIGIOUS LEADERS FOR GUIDANCE

whilst they who prided themselves on their knowledge and wisdom strayed far from His path and remained deprived of His grace. For this reason He hath written: 'He that is exalted among you shall be abased, and he that is abased shall be exalted.' References to this theme are to be found in most of the heavenly Books, as well as in the sayings of the Prophets and Messengers of God.[91]

In summarizing Bahá'u'lláh's views, Shoghi Effendi writes,

> To these leaders who 'esteem themselves the best of all creatures,'[92] and have been regarded as the vilest by Him Who is the Truth,' who 'occupy the seats of knowledge and learning, and who have named ignorance knowledge, and called oppression justice,' and who, 'worship no God but their own desire, who bear allegiance to naught but gold, who are wrapt in the densest veils of learning, and who, enmeshed by its obscurities, are lost in the wilds of error' – to these Bahá'u'lláh has chosen to address these words: 'O concourse of divines! Ye shall not henceforward behold yourselves possessed of any power, inasmuch as We have seized it from you, and destined it for such as have believed in God, the One, the All-Powerful, the Almighty, the Unconstrained.'[93]

And quoting from Bahá'u'lláh's admonitions,

> How long will ye, O concourse of divines, level the spears of hatred at the face of Bahá? Rein in your pens. Lo, the Most Sublime Pen speaketh betwixt earth and heaven. Fear God, and follow not your desires which have altered the face of creation. Purify your ears that they may hearken unto the Voice of God. By God! It is even as fire that consumeth the veils, and as water that washeth the souls of all who are in the universe.[94]

> Say: O concourse of divines! Can any one of you race with the Divine Youth in the arena of wisdom and utterance, or soar with Him into the heaven of inner meaning and explanation? Nay, by My Lord, the God of mercy! All have swooned away in this Day from the Word of thy Lord. They are even as dead and lifeless, except him whom thy Lord, the Almighty, the Unconstrained, hath willed to exempt.

Such a one is indeed of those endued with knowledge in the sight of Him Who is the All-Knowing. The inmates of Paradise, and the dwellers of the sacred Folds, bless him at eventide and at dawn. Can the one possessed of wooden legs resist him whose feet God hath made of steel? Nay, by Him Who illumineth the whole of creation![95]

Not one Prophet of God was made manifest Who did not fall a victim to the relentless hate, to the denunciation, denial and execration of the clerics of His day! Woe unto them for the iniquities their hands have formerly wrought! Woe unto them for that which they are now doing! What veils of glory more grievous than these embodiments of error! By the righteousness of God! To pierce such veils is the mightiest of all acts, and to rend them asunder the most meritorious of all deeds! . . . On their tongue . . . the mention of God hath become an empty name; in their midst His holy Word a dead letter. Such is the sway of their desires, that the lamp of conscience and reason hath been quenched in their hearts . . . No two are found to agree on one and the same law, for they seek no God but their own desire, and tread no path but the path of error. In leadership they have recognized the ultimate object of their endeavour, and account pride and haughtiness as the highest attainments of their hearts' desire. They have placed their sordid machinations above the Divine decree, have renounced resignation unto the will of God, busied themselves with selfish calculation, and walked in the way of the hypocrite. With all their power and strength they strive to secure themselves in their petty pursuits, fearful lest the least discredit undermine their authority or blemish the display of their magnificence.[96]

Again,

Wherefore, then, do not these grovelling, worm-like men pause to meditate upon these traditions [concerning the Promised One], all of which are manifest as the sun in its noon-tide glory? For what reason do they refuse to embrace the Truth, and allow certain traditions, the significance of which they have failed to grasp, to withhold them from the recognition of the Revelation of God and His Beauty, and to cause them to dwell in the infernal abyss? Such things are to be attributed to naught but the faithlessness of the

EXCESSIVE RELIANCE ON RELIGIOUS LEADERS FOR GUIDANCE

divines and doctors of the age. Of these, Ṣádiq,[97] son of Muḥammad, hath said: 'The religious doctors of that age shall be the most wicked of the divines beneath the shadow of heaven. Out of them hath mischief proceeded, and unto them it shall return.'[98]

And yet again,

> . . . as they failed to recognize the accents of God and the divine mysteries and holy allusions enshrined in that which flowed from the tongue of Muḥammad, and as they neglected to examine the matter in their own hearts, and followed instead those priests of error who have hindered the progress of the people in past dispensations . . . they were thus veiled from the divine purpose, failed to quaff from the celestial streams, and deprived themselves of the presence of God, the Manifestation of His Essence, and the Dayspring of His eternity. Thus did they wander in the paths of delusion and the ways of heedlessness, and return to their abode in that fire which feedeth on their own souls. These, verily, are numbered with the infidels whose names have been inscribed by the Pen of God in His holy Book. Nor have they ever found, or will ever find, a friend or helper.[99]

By virtue of their opposition to His Cause, Bahá'u'lláh equated the Shí'ih clergy with the 'thick clouds' referred to in the Qur'án[100] and in the Bible (Zeph.1:15 and Rev.1:7) that prevent the light of Revelation from reaching the masses and transforming them.

> These thick clouds are the exponents of idle fancies and vain imaginings, who are none other than the divines of Persia . . . By 'divines' . . . is meant those men who outwardly attire themselves with the raiment of knowledge, but who inwardly are deprived therefrom . . . 'O ye that are foolish, yet have a name to be wise! Wherefore do ye wear the guise of the shepherd, when inwardly ye have become wolves, intent upon My flock? Ye are even as the star, which riseth ere the dawn, and which, though it seem radiant and luminous, leadeth the wayfarers of My city astray into the paths of perdition.' . . . 'O ye seemingly fair yet inwardly foul! Ye are like clear but bitter water, which to outward seeming is but crystal pure but of which, when tested by the Divine Assayer, not a drop is accepted. Yea, the sunbeam falleth alike upon

the dust and the mirror, yet differ they in reflection even as doth the star from the earth: nay, immeasurable is the difference!'[101]

Commenting on the persecution of the followers of the Báb and Bahá'u'lláh at the hands of the 'divines of Persia', Shoghi Effendi points out the tragic consequences of their acts:

> Were not the divines of Persia the first who hoisted the standard of revolt, who inflamed the ignorant and subservient masses against it, and who instigated the civil authorities, through their outcry, their threats, their lies, their calumnies, and denunciations, to decree the banishments, to enact the laws, to launch the punitive campaigns, and to carry out the executions and massacres that fill the pages of its history? So abominable and savage was the butchery committed in a single day, instigated by these divines, and so typical of the 'callousness of the brute and the ingenuity of the fiend' that Renan,[102] in his 'Les Apôtres', characterized that day as 'perhaps unparalleled in the history of the world'.
>
> It was these divines, who, by these very acts, sowed the seeds of the disintegration of their own institutions, institutions that were so potent, so famous, and appeared so invulnerable when the Faith was born. It was they who, by assuming so lightly and foolishly, such awful responsibilities were primarily answerable for the release of those violent and disruptive influences that have unchained disasters as catastrophic as those which overwhelmed kings, dynasties, and empires, and which constitute the most noteworthy landmarks in the history of the first century of the Bahá'í era.[103]

Commenting on the words of Jesus, 'The sun shall be darkened, and the moon shall not give its light, and the stars shall fall from heaven',[104] Bahá'u'lláh explains that, as with their followers, the clergy determine their own spiritual destiny:

> by these terms is intended the divines of the former Dispensation, who live in the days of the subsequent Revelations, and who hold the reins of religion in their grasp. If these divines be illumined by the light of the latter Revelation they will be acceptable unto God, and will shine with a light everlasting. Otherwise, they will

EXCESSIVE RELIANCE ON RELIGIOUS LEADERS FOR GUIDANCE

be declared as darkened, even though to outward seeming they be leaders of men, inasmuch as belief and unbelief, guidance and error, felicity and misery, light and darkness, are all dependent upon the sanction of Him Who is the Day-star of Truth. Whosoever among the divines of every age receiveth, in the Day of Reckoning, the testimony of faith from the Source of true knowledge, he verily becometh the recipient of learning, of divine favour, and of the light of true understanding. Otherwise, he is branded as guilty of folly, denial, blasphemy, and oppression.[105]

Given the difficulties they admittedly face and their awesome responsibilities, Bahá'u'lláh encourages respect for those religious leaders who are truly learned, fair, and detached from mundane desires, and who guide their followers to the truth.[106]

Great is the blessedness of that divine that hath not allowed knowledge to become a veil between him and the One Who is the Object of all knowledge, and who, when the Self-Subsisting appeared, hath turned with a beaming face towards Him. He, in truth, is numbered with the learned. The inmates of Paradise seek the blessing of his breath, and his lamp sheddeth its radiance over all who are in heaven and on earth. He, verily, is numbered with the inheritors of the Prophets. He that beholdeth him hath, verily, beheld the True One, and he that turneth towards him hath, verily, turned towards God, the Almighty, the All-Wise.[107]

Those divines . . . who are truly adorned with the ornament of knowledge and of a goodly character are, verily, as a head to the body of the world, and as eyes to the nations. The guidance of men hath, at all times, been, and is, dependent upon such blessed souls.[108]

The divine whose conduct is upright, and the sage who is just, are as the spirit unto the body of the world. Well is it with that divine whose head is attired with the crown of justice, and whose temple is adorned with the ornament of equity.[109]

The divine who hath seized and quaffed the most holy Wine, in the name of the sovereign Ordainer, is as an eye unto the world. Well is it with them who obey him, and call him to remembrance.[110]

8

FRUSTRATION OF THE SACRED DUTY OF BELIEVERS TO INVESTIGATE THE TRUTH AND TO RECOGNIZE THEIR LORD

> Notwithstanding the divinely-inspired admonitions of all the Prophets, the Saints, and Chosen ones of God, enjoining the people to see with their own eyes and hear with their own ears, they have disdainfully rejected their counsels and have blindly followed, and will continue to follow, the leaders of their Faith.
>
> *Bahá'u'lláh*[1]

> The challenge facing the religious leaders of mankind is to contemplate, with hearts filled with the spirit of compassion and a desire for truth, the plight of humanity, and to ask themselves whether they cannot, in humility before their Almighty Creator, submerge their theological differences in a great spirit of mutual forbearance that will enable them to work together for the advancement of human understanding and peace.
>
> *The Universal House of Justice*[2]

> The primary task of the soul will always be to investigate reality, to live in accordance with the truths of which it becomes persuaded and to accord full respect to the efforts of others to do the same.
>
> *The Universal House of Justice*[3]

All too often individuals hesitate to undertake the necessary effort to investigate their religion and faith in general, and thereby discover the truth for themselves. Instead, they either recklessly reject faith and religion, or follow blindly their spiritual leaders and find satisfaction and security in the familiar rituals and trappings of their often discredited religious institutions. They thus either espouse materialistic philosophies, or tenaciously adhere to effete traditions, content to be fed largely a diet of obsolescent man-made doctrines and beliefs that for the most part bear little resemblance to the divinely-ordained Revelation that originally inspired their Faith. They are merely grateful that they have been fortunate to belong to the 'right' religion, by virtue of having been born into a family with the correct religious credentials, oblivious of the fact that by inheriting their religion they have neglected a fundamental and personal spiritual duty:

> The nations and religions are steeped in blind and bigoted imitations. A man is a Jew because his father was a Jew. The Muslim follows implicitly the footsteps of his ancestors in belief and observance . . . they profess religious belief blindly and without investigation, making unity and agreement impossible . . . this condition will not be remedied without a reformation in the world of religion . . . the fundamental reality of the divine religions must be renewed, reformed, revoiced to mankind.[4]

The reasons for this regrettable paralysis of will to investigate truth and faith, and the factors that perpetuate it, are complex. It is clear however that 'religious institutions have too often been the chief agents in discouraging exploration of reality and the exercise of those intellectual faculties that distinguish humankind' as the Universal House of Justice wrote in the first years of the 21st century.[5]

Bahá'u'lláh testifies that 'all men are endowed with the capacity to see and hear' and yet they are 'deprived of the privilege of using these faculties'.[6] The very attempt to investigate faith and to discard outworn shibboleths will ensure the social and spiritual well-being of humanity. Unity will be facilitated when the human spirit is freed from the dictates of hollow, archaic institutions which by virtue of their senility have lost their cohesive and transforming power. Referring to his own countrymen who typify this debilitating problem, He writes:

> The people of Persia have turned away from Him Who is the Protector and the Helper. They are clinging to and have enmeshed themselves in the vain imaginings of the foolish. So firmly do they

adhere to superstitions that naught can sever them therefrom save the potent arm of God – exalted is His glory. Beseech thou the Almighty that He may remove with the fingers of divine power the veils which have shut out the divers peoples and kindreds, that they may attain the things that are conducive to security, progress and advancement and may hasten forth towards the incomparable Friend.[7]

Historical and social reasons

Perhaps the most benign and obvious explanation for clerical and institutional control has been societal imperatives. Due to limited resources only a few persons with sufficient qualifications could be assigned to lead. The majority of the people could participate in supporting the institutions, in particular financially, but the doctrinal issues were to be left to more qualified, spiritual and wiser individuals.

> In former ages priesthoods were necessary, because people were illiterate and uneducated and were dependent on priests for their religious instruction, for the conduct of religious rites and ceremonies, for the administration of justice, etc. Now, however, times have changed. Education is fast becoming universal, and if the commands of Bahá'u'lláh are carried out, every boy and girl in the world will receive a sound education. Each individual will then be able to study the Scriptures for himself, to draw the Water of Life for himself, direct from the Fountainhead. Elaborate rites and ceremonies, requiring the services of a special profession or caste, have no place in the Bahá'í system; and the administration of justice is entrusted to the authorities instituted for that purpose.[8]

Coerced conversion

In many cases the motivation to curb individual freedom to examine facts stems from anxiety that it may lead to loss of membership, adversely affecting the organization's revenues and influence relative to other denominations. The forceful conversion and baptism of individuals to Christianity as an official policy of the Church, particularly of the Jews from the time of Emperor Constantine and covering a period of many centuries, is well recorded. Forceful conversion to Islam of members of religious minorities tragically continues to this day as part of official policy or terrorist activities.

To assist individuals in their search is commended in the Bahá'í Faith, but coercion is forbidden:

> It is better to guide one soul than to possess all that is on earth, for as long as that guided soul is under the shadow of the Tree of Divine Unity, he and the one who hath guided him will both be recipients of God's tender mercy, whereas possession of earthly things will cease at the time of death. The path to guidance is one of love and compassion, not of force and coercion. This hath been God's method in the past, and shall continue to be in the future! He causeth him whom He pleaseth to enter the shadow of His Mercy. Verily, He is the Supreme Protector, the All-Generous.
>
> There is no paradise more wondrous for any soul than to be exposed to God's Manifestation in His Day, to hear His verses and believe in them, to attain His presence, which is naught but the presence of God, to sail upon the sea of the heavenly kingdom of His good-pleasure, and to partake of the choice fruits of the paradise of His divine Oneness.[9]

Inordinate influence of religious institutions and clerics

In Islam only certain qualified individuals have the authority to provide scriptural explanations (*tafsir*) that comply strictly with the accepted understanding of the Qur'án and traditions. Muslim clerics often employ a variety of methods designed to intimidate the faithful and to discourage them from evaluating reality. These include branding all unorthodox beliefs as 'blasphemy' and their followers as apostates, belonging to a 'cult' or a heresy, their very existence constituting an existential threat to Islam. The activities of other Faiths are declared as 'war on the religion of Islam', requiring decisive action to preserve virtue and prevent vice – in many cases justifying and mandating judicial punishment. This invasive clerical and organized community action is believed to be authorized by Quranic verses that enjoin good (*amr bil ma'ruf*) and forbid evil (*nahy anil munkar*), an instruction considered one of the greatest obligations (*wájibs*) in Islam:

> Ye are the best of peoples, evolved for mankind, enjoining what is right, forbidding what is wrong, and believing in God . . .[10]

> They believe in God and the Last Day; they enjoin what is right, and forbid what is wrong; and they hasten (in emulation) in (all) good works: they are in the ranks of the righteous.[11]

Notably, the checking of conduct is interpreted as being the responsibility of experts, scholars, and those considered qualified to lead the community.

> Let there arise out of you a band of people inviting to all that is good, enjoining what is right, and forbidding what is wrong: they are the ones to attain felicity.[12]

These Quranic verses all too often become a pretext to interfere in the social and spiritual affairs of others with different belief systems. However, the following verse indicates that the determination of 'good' and 'bad' is the duty of all believers:

> The believers, men and women, are protectors, one of another: they enjoin what is just, and forbid what is evil: they observe regular prayers, practise regular charity, and obey God and His Apostle. On them will God pour His mercy: for God is Exalted in power, Wise.[13]

In addition, Muslims are warned against indulging in hypocrisy that could result instead in the promotion of evil and denial of that which is good:

> The hypocrites, men and women, (have an understanding) with each other: they enjoin evil, and forbid what is just, and are close with their hands. They have forgotten God; so He hath forgotten them. Verily the hypocrites are rebellious and perverse.[14]

They must not in their zeal attack the faith of others, and must refrain from even provoking unbelievers by reviling their 'idols':

> Revile not ye those whom they call upon besides God, lest they out

of spite revile God in their ignorance. Thus have We made alluring
to each people its own doings. In the end will they return to their
Lord, and We shall then tell them the truth of all that they did.[15]

Clerical licence to enforce one's brand of Islam under the pretext of
'enjoining good and forbidding evil' is also moderated by the following
verses which forbid oppression and from profiting from religion:

> O my servants, I have made oppression unlawful for Me and unlawful for you, so do not commit oppression against one another. O My servants, all of you are liable to err except for those whom I guide on the right path . . .[16]

> The Signs (verses) of God have they sold for a miserable price, and (many) have they hindered from His Way: evil indeed are the deeds they have done.[17]

The *Bihár al-Anwár* warns of a day when individuals will be forbidden to express their faith and values:

> You will see a person issuing good exhortation, but someone would stand up and say that Alláh does not want him to say these things . . .[18]

In Christianity, one finds that the New Testament mentions the terms 'bishop' or 'overseer' *(episkopos)*, 'elder' or 'presbyter' *(presbuteros)* and 'pastor' *(poimen)* interchangeably (Acts 20:17, 28; Titus 1:5,7; I Pet. 5:1-2). The role of the bishop, elder or pastor was to lead by example and not to act as worldly lords (I Pet. 5:1-5; cf. Matt. 20:25-8; Mark 10:42-5).

St Paul cautions the bishops that wolves were likely to appear in their midst – a reminder of Christ's warning concerning the false teachers who are inwardly 'ravenous wolves' 'in sheep's clothing' who will prey on His followers (Matt. 7:15):

> Take heed therefore unto yourselves, and to all the flock, over the which the Holy Ghost hath made you overseers, to feed the church of God . . .

For I know this, that after my departing shall grievous wolves enter in among you, not sparing the flock.[19]

We also note that the New Testament warns against the rise of authoritarian elders who would be more interested in financial reward than in being good shepherds dedicated to guide the flock by example. They are also reminded that they will be answerable to the 'Chief Shepherd', or Bahá'u'lláh, who will appear in due course:

> The elders which are among you I exhort . . .
> Feed the flock of God which is among you, taking the oversight thereof, not by constraint, but willingly; not for filthy lucre, but of a ready mind;
> Neither as being lords over God's heritage, but being examples to the flock.
> And when the chief Shepherd shall appear, ye shall receive a crown of glory that fadeth not away.[20]

According to the New Testament, all Christians were initially collectively regarded as the people of God. The term 'laity' is not used, nor are there distinctions between 'clergy' and 'laity' in early Christianity. Later, clear distinctions emerged between the clergy and the laity;[21] the primary function of the latter was the financial support of the church. For this reason women were not considered part of the laity, as a woman was dependent on her husband who was the head and financial manager of his household. By the second century the position of 'monarchial bishop' was advocated, notably by Ignatius of Antioch, and by the fourth century the position of the bishops was greatly consolidated:

> The bishop, he is the minister of the word, the keeper of knowledge, the mediator between God and you in the several parts of your divine worship. He is the teacher of piety; and, next after God, he is your father, who has begotten you again to the adoption of sons by water and the Spirit. He is your ruler and governor; he is your king and potentate; he is, next after God, your earthly god, who has a right to be honoured by you . . . let the bishop preside over you as one honoured with the authority of God, which he is to exercise over the clergy, and by which he is to govern all the people.[22]

Suppression of freedom to worship and discuss faith by religious institutions and the state

Censorship of minority opinion has become a distressing policy of some Islamic countries relatively recently. However, suppression of religious discussion and enquiry by church and state occurred remarkably early in Christianity. Within three and a half centuries after the crucifixion of Jesus, the Christian Emperor Theodosius formally outlawed all public religious discourse.

> There shall be no opportunity for any man to go out to the public and to argue about religion or to discuss it or to give any counsel. If any person hereafter with flagrant and damnable audacity, should suppose that he may contravene any law of this kind or if he should dare to persist in his action of ruinous obstinacy, he shall be restrained with a due penalty and proper punishment.[23]

Violation of this edict carried a prison term in some instances, and the death penalty in all others. This was followed by a further attempt by the state and the church to clamp down on religious enquiry when, following the General Council of Chalcedon in 451 AD, Emperor Marcian and his ally Pope Leo forbade any public discussions on the nature of Christ.

It was only in 1522 that Martin Luther made it possible for the Bible to be studied by lay persons by completing a translation into German of the New Testament from the Greek. This was swiftly followed by William Tyndale's English translation in 1525, which the church authorities in England tried their best to confiscate and burn. After issuing a revised edition in 1535, Tyndale was arrested and imprisoned, and was then strangled and burned at the stake near Brussels a year later. Pope Pius IV forbade Christians from possessing and studying a list of books compiled and prohibited in the Index of Trent (*Index Librorum Prohibitorum*) of 1559.[24] Of the many more recent official decrees by the Catholic Church dissuading the flock from independently investigating scripture, the denouncement of Bible Societies by Pope Pius IX is of particular interest because firstly the Bible had announced that the 'gospel of the kingdom shall be preached in all the world for a witness unto all nations; and then shall the end come',[25] and secondly, he was the pontiff that Bahá'u'lláh would later address from prison proclaiming, 'O Pope! Rend the veils asunder. He Who is the Lord of Lords is come overshadowed with clouds . . .'[26] In 1846 the Pope wrote:

> You already know well, venerable brothers, the other portentous errors and deceits by which the sons of this world try most bitterly to attack the Catholic religion and the divine authority of the Church and its laws. They would even trample underfoot the rights both of the sacred and of the civil power. For this is the goal of the lawless activities against this Roman See in which Christ placed the impregnable foundation of His Church. This is the goal of those secret sects who have come forth from the darkness to destroy and desolate both the sacred and the civil commonwealth. These have been condemned with repeated anathema in the Apostolic letters of the Roman Pontiffs who preceded Us. We now confirm these with the fullness of Our Apostolic power and command that they be most carefully observed.
>
> This is the goal too of the crafty Bible Societies which renew the old skill of the heretics and ceaselessly force on people of all kinds, even the uneducated, gifts of the Bible. They issue these in large numbers and at great cost, in vernacular translations, which infringe the holy rules of the Church. The commentaries which are included often contain perverse explanations; so, having rejected divine tradition, the doctrine of the Fathers and the authority of the Catholic Church, they all interpret the words of the Lord by their own private judgment, thereby perverting their meaning. As a result, they fall into the greatest errors.[27]

Nor are the Protestant churches blameless in this regard. Martin Luther, the father of the Protestant Reformation and Lutheranism, one of the largest denominations of Christianity, vented his anger and frustration at recalcitrant Jews who had failed embrace his faith, by recommending strict restrictions on the study and worship of Judaism and on the livelihoods of its adherents. In his zeal to promote his brand of Christianity, he failed to entertain the possibility that the Jews were not persuaded by his arguments which were mostly products of reaction to church doctrine and alien to the teachings of the Prophets of the Tanakh.

FRUSTRATION OF THE SACRED DUTY OF BELIEVERS

What shall we Christians do with this rejected and condemned people, the Jews? Since they live among us, we dare not tolerate their conduct, now that we are aware of their lying and reviling and blaspheming. If we do, we become sharers in their lies, cursing and blasphemy. Thus we cannot extinguish the unquenchable fire of divine wrath, of which the prophets speak, nor can we convert the Jews . . . I shall give you my sincere advice:

First, to set fire to their synagogues or schools, and to bury and cover with dirt whatever will not burn, so that no man will ever again see a stone or cinder of them. This is to be done in honor of our Lord and of Christiandom, so that God may see that we are Christians . . .

Second, I advise that their houses also be razed and destroyed. For they pursue in them the same aims as in their synagogues . . .

Third, I advise that all their prayer books and Talmudic writings . . . be taken from them.

Fourth, I advise that their rabbis be forbidden to teach henceforth on pain of loss of life and limb . . .

Fifth, I advise that safe-conduct on the highways be abolished completely for the Jews. For they have no business in the countryside . . . Let them stay at home . . .

Sixth, I advise that usury be prohibited to them, and that all cash and the treasures of silver and gold be taken from them . . .

Seventh, I recommend putting a flail, an ax, a hoe, a spade, a distaff into the hands of the young, strong Jews and Jewesses and letting them earn their bread in the sweat of their brow (forced labour) . . .

And you, my dear gentlemen and friends who are pastors and preachers, I wish to remind very faithfully of your official duty, so that you too may warn your parishioners concerning their eternal harm . . . that they may be on their guard against the Jews and avoid them so far as is possible . . .[28]

Again,

all their books, their prayer books, their Talmudic writings, also the entire Bible, be taken from them, not leaving them one leaf . . . For they use all of these books to blaspheme the Son of God . . . they be forbidden on pain of death to praise God, to give thanks, to pray, and to teach publicly among us and in our country . . .[29]

In this manner Luther completely ignored the reassurances and admonitions of his Lord, Christ:

> Think not that I am come to destroy the law, or the prophets: I am not come to destroy, but to fulfil.
> For verily I say unto you, Till heaven and earth pass, one jot or one tittle shall in no wise pass from the law, till all be fulfilled.
> Whosoever therefore shall break one of these least commandments, and shall teach men so, he shall be called the least in the kingdom of heaven: but whosoever shall do and teach them, the same shall be called great in the kingdom of heaven.
> For I say unto you, That except your righteousness shall exceed the righteousness of the scribes and Pharisees, ye shall in no case enter into the kingdom of heaven.[30]

Deliberate distortion of facts to 'protect' the faith

Presenting scripture and doctrine selectively, and revising history, are sometimes considered as legitimate or simply good strategy in a perceived 'turf war' with other individuals and organizations. Thus, in a pious but misguided attempt to protect the flock from uncomfortable facts, the interpretation of the established church is often the only one tolerated and allowed to be received. Such deliberate obfuscation has included suppression of scriptural elements that encourage independent investigation and inform the individual of his and her divine right and responsibility to evaluate spiritual truth. Sadly, not a few religious leaders and institutions have felt that the average person, devoid of the right qualifications, training and rank, cannot be trusted to understand fully the content and context of the scriptures. They therefore routinely and intentionally select for general consumption only those portions of the scripture that they believe promote faith.

Ignoring specific scriptural teachings that are difficult to follow in this day and age, but at the same time adhering to traditions and the name of the religion

Religious institutions either resist long-overdue changes to their religious practices, or fail to admit to their adherents that the changes they have adopted, which are diametrically opposed to their scriptural teachings, are a clear indication that the time has arrived for their followers to accept God's latest Revelation. For example, Christ forbade divorce ('whosoever shall put away his wife, saving for the cause of fornication, causeth her to commit adultery: and whosoever shall marry her that is divorced committeth adultery', Matt. 5:32), but all Christian countries and most Christian churches now condone the practice. Christ forbade retaliation ('resist not evil: but whosoever shall smite thee on thy right cheek, turn to him the other also', Matt. 5:39; and 'I say unto you, Love your enemies, bless them that curse you, do good to them that hate you, and pray for them which despitefully use you, and persecute you', Matt. 5:44) but Christian states practise it, particularly when confronted with terrorism. Christ's teaching, 'Give to him that asketh thee, and from him that would borrow of thee turn not thou away' (Matt. 5:42), is incompatible with the commercial practices, banking systems, and stock markets of Christian nations. His teaching 'Swear not at all', and 'if any man will sue thee at the law, and take away thy coat, let him have thy cloak also' (Matt. 5:34, 40) are irreconcilable with Western legal systems. This is an example of how Christ's injunctions to individuals cannot be literally translated into social justice systems. Another such example is Christ's injunction, 'whosoever shall compel thee to go a mile, go with him twain' (Matt. 5:41), which may be followed by a Christian individual but is not the method by which Christian states can deal with, for example, hijacking.

Fear of change, and reluctance to abandon one's comfort zone

There is a natural tendency to follow unquestioningly the religion of one's parents, to imitate the practices of fellow believers, and follow ancestral traditions.

Be not then in doubt as to what these men worship. They worship nothing but what their fathers worshipped before (them): but verily we shall pay them back (in full) their portion without (the least) abatement.[31]

The individual's innate inertia is intensified by pressures from friends and foe intended to ensure that he or she does not meander too far away from the fold.[32] The fear of being shunned is illustrated by the following Gospel narrative of the reluctance of the parents of a man whose sight had been restored by Jesus to acknowledge Christ because of their apprehension that this could lead to being excluded from the synagogue.

> But the Jews did not believe concerning him, that he had been blind, and received his sight, until they called the parents of him that had received his sight.
>
> And they asked them, saying, Is this your son, who ye say was born blind? How then doth he now see?
>
> His parents answered them and said, We know that this is our son, and that he was born blind:
>
> But by what means he now seeth, we know not; or who has opened his eyes, we know not: he is of age; ask him: he shall speak for himself.
>
> These words spake his parent, because they feared the Jews: for the Jews had agreed already, that if any man did confess that he was Christ, he should be put out of the synagogue.[33]

This trepidation is further heightened by dire warnings from spiritual leaders that the aim of the new Revelation is to destroy their religion, when its real purpose is to enlighten and empower the individual spiritually and to confirm earlier expressions of God's indivisible Faith. This apprehension is exemplified by the account of the reaction to Noah's Revelation as described in the Qur'án:

> We sent Noah to his people: He said, 'O my people! Worship God! Ye have no other god but Him. Will ye not fear (Him)?'
>
> The chiefs of the unbelievers among his people said: 'He is no more than a man like yourselves: his wish is to assert his superiority over you: if God had wished (to send messengers), He could have

sent down angels: never did we hear such a thing (as he says), among our ancestors of old.'[34]

Pharaoh voiced identical misgivings about Moses, that he planned to create mischief or '*fasád*':

> Said Pharaoh: 'Leave me to slay Moses; and let him call on his Lord! What I fear is lest He should change your religion, or lest he should cause mischief to appear in the land!'[35]

The people of Thamud had similar concerns about their Prophet Sálih:

> They said: 'O Sálih! Thou hast been of us! – a centre of our hopes hitherto! Dost thou (now) forbid us the worship of what our fathers worshipped? But we are really in suspicious (disquieting) doubt as to that to which Thou invitest us.[36]

Bahá'u'lláh's prescription

To remedy such a deplorable state of affairs, and to free mankind from these impediments to progress, as in earlier Dispensations, Bahá'u'lláh has prescribed that unfettered search for truth be regarded a defining and guiding principle of His Faith. This emancipation is envisioned as a step towards securing the unity of mankind.

> The first teaching of Bahá'u'lláh is the investigation of reality. Man must seek the reality himself, forsaking imitations and adherence to mere hereditary forms. As the nations of the world are following imitations in lieu of truth and as imitations are many and various, differences of belief have been productive of strife and warfare. So long as these imitations remain, the oneness of the world of humanity is impossible. Therefore, we must investigate reality in order that by its light the clouds and darkness may be dispelled. Reality is one reality; it does not admit multiplicity or division. If the nations of the world investigate reality, they will agree and become united.[37]

> God has given man the eye of investigation by which he may see and recognize truth. He has endowed man with ears that he may hear

the message of reality and conferred upon him the gift of reason by which he may discover things for himself. This is his endowment and equipment for the investigation of reality. Man is not intended to see through the eyes of another, hear through another's ears nor comprehend with another's brain. Each human creature has individual endowment, power and responsibility in the creative plan of God. Therefore depend upon your own reason and judgement and adhere to the outcome of your own investigations; otherwise you will be utterly submerged in the sea of ignorance and deprived of all the bounties of God. Turn to God, supplicate humbly at His threshold, seeking assistance and confirmation, that God may rend asunder the veils that obscure your vision. Then will your eyes be filled with illumination, face to face you will behold the reality of God and your heart become completely purified from the dross of ignorance, reflecting the glories and bounties of the Kingdom.[38]

The Bahá'í Faith . . . enjoins upon its followers the primary duty of an unfettered search after truth, condemns all manner of prejudice and superstition, declares the purpose of religion to be the promotion of amity and concord, proclaims its essential harmony with science, and recognizes it as the foremost agency for the pacification and the orderly progress of human society . . .[39]

The Bahá'í discipline is that religious convictions must be validated by earnest search, free from preconceived notions. One's religious 'label' ought not to be attributable to the mere accident of birth and place. How else, it may be legitimately enquired, can individuals escape their past and the enslavement of outworn shibboleths of earlier Dispensations, and instead, accept the Revelation of Bahá'u'lláh in this new era – an essential and life-altering event promised so constantly, urgently and emphatically in the Torah, the Gospels, and the Qur'án?

Bahá'u'lláh thus exhorts individuals about their responsibility:

Tear asunder, in My Name, the veils that have grievously blinded your vision, and, through the power born of your belief in the unity of God, scatter the idols of vain imitation.[40]

It should therefore come as no surprise that to help their followers to recognize 'that Day', all three scriptures contain passages that stress this fundamental right and obligation of all individuals. Given the multiplicity of antagonistic religions and sects, the extent of religious bigotry, and the overpowering and suffocating clerical dominance that discourage any such independent enquiry, the investigation of truth freed from prejudice is of even greater importance today than when the Torah, Bible or the Qur'án were originally revealed.

What should an individual do?

The Qur'án commands that the individual ('I') seek the protection of the 'Lord of the Dawn' or 'Daybreak' (*Rabbi-alfalaq*) – the Lord of a new Day and the Author of a fresh Revelation, and implore Him to shelter him from the mischief-makers and from spiritual darkness.

> Say: I seek refuge with the Lord of the Dawn,
> From the mischief of created things;
> From the mischief of Darkness as it overspreads . . .[41]

All Muslims are required to implore God for guidance every day. This clearly would not be necessary if they have already been guided to the ultimate destination, the all truth, and do not need to make an effort or to take any individual action.

> Show us the straight way.[42]

In this context, the Qur'án assures us that God will guide individuals in His (multiple) Paths – but only those who fulfil their obligation to make a genuine effort to seek the truth.

> And those who strive in Our (Cause) – We will certainly guide them to Our Paths: for, verily, God is with those who do right.[43]

This conditional divine assistance is attested to by Bahá'u'lláh:

> When the detached wayfarer and sincere seeker hath fulfilled these essential conditions, then and only then can he be called a true seeker. Whensoever he hath fulfilled the conditions implied in the

verse: 'Whoso maketh efforts for Us,' he shall enjoy the blessing conferred by the words: 'In Our ways shall We assuredly guide him.'[44]

Bahá'u'lláh thus inspires us to undertake the first step (sincere and independent enquiry and desire for truth), confident that we will be rewarded by divine guidance toward our next step.

> O Son of Love! Thou art but one step away from the glorious heights above and from the celestial tree of love. Take thou one pace and with the next advance into the immortal realm and enter the pavilion of eternity. Give ear then to that which hath been revealed by the pen of glory.[45]

> O Son of Being. Love Me that I may love thee. If thou lovest Me not, My Love can in no wise reach thee. Know this, O servant.[46]

This reciprocity is also reflected in the following blessed Quranic verses:

> When My servants ask thee concerning Me, I am indeed close (to them); I listen to the prayer of every suppliant when he calleth on Me: let them also, with a will, listen to My call, and believe in Me: that they may walk in the right way.[47]

> Then do ye remember Me; I will remember you. Be grateful to Me, and reject not Faith.[48]

> And your Lord says: 'Call on Me; I will answer your (prayer): but those who are too arrogant to serve Me will surely find themselves in Hell in humiliation!'[49]

The Tanakh also requires the Jews to abandon the idols that they harbour in their hearts, to 'see' and to 'ask', i.e. investigate and examine 'the old paths' (earlier Dispensations), and in the process determine what Path and Way to follow:

> Son of man, these men have set up their idols in their heart, and put the stumblingblock of their iniquity before their face . . .[50]

> Thus saith the Lord, Stand ye in the ways, and see, and ask for the old paths, where is the good way, and walk therein, and ye shall find rest for your souls.⁵¹

Isaiah, one of the greatest Hebrew Prophets, taught the importance of calling upon (seeking) the Lord when He is near, remembering that God's way may not always accord with human wishes and desires.

> Seek ye the Lord while he may be found, call ye upon him while he is near:
> Let the wicked forsake his way, and the unrighteous man his thoughts: and let him return unto the Lord, and he will have mercy upon him; and to our God, for he will abundantly pardon.
> For my thoughts are not your thoughts, neither are your ways my ways, saith the Lord.
> For as the heavens are higher than the earth, so are my ways higher than your ways, and my thoughts than your thoughts.⁵²

The Psalms teach that spiritual life is gained only after seeking God's purpose:

> The humble shall see this, and be glad: and your heart shall live that seek God.⁵³

Jesus commanded His followers to cultivate a deep yearning for the truth and the Divine Will; only then would their supplications and spiritual enquires be answered.

> Blessed are they which do hunger and thirst after righteousness, for they shall be filled.⁵⁴

The quest is clearly for spiritual enlightenment and not for material gain, as indicated by the teaching of Christ, 'Take no thought for your life, what ye shall eat, or what ye shall drink' (Matt. 6:25).

> But blessed are your eyes, for they see: and your ears, for they hear.
> For verily I say unto you, That many prophets and righteous men have desired to see those things which ye see, and have not seen them;

and to hear those things which ye hear, and have not heard them.[55]

The Christian will be rewarded only after he or she makes the requisite effort:

> Ask and it shall be given you; seek, and ye shall find; knock, and it shall be opened unto you:
> For every one that asketh receiveth; and he that seeketh findeth; and to him that knocketh it shall be opened.
> Or what man is there of you, whom if his son ask bread, will he give him a stone?
> Or if he ask a fish, will he give him a serpent?
> If ye then, being evil, know how to give good gifts unto your children, how much more shall your Father which is in heaven give good things to them that ask him?[56]

This is echoed by the disciple Peter:

> As newborn babes, desire the sincere milk of the word, that ye may grow thereby.[57]

Encountering a new Revelation, Christians are expected to exhibit humility and not spiritual arrogance, as only when they sincerely admit that their cup is empty can it be filled – only then can they avoid rejecting the Divine kingdom.

> Blessed are the poor in spirit: for theirs is the kingdom of heaven.[58]

They must be prepared to examine God's Word, validate 'all things' independently and only then accept what is good and right.

> Pray without ceasing.
> In every thing give thanks . . .
> Quench not the Spirit.
> Despise not prophesyings.
> Prove all things; hold fast that which is good.[59]

> Proving what is acceptable unto the Lord.[60]

Otherwise they will fall into the same trap as the Jews, who failed to respond to Christ's Message and accused His Apostle Paul of being a heretic (a follower of a new detested cult, sect or heresy); 'for as concerning this sect, we know that everywhere it is spoken against' (Acts 28:22); and 'for we have found this man a pestilent fellow, and a mover of sedition among all the Jews throughout the world, and a ringleader of the sect of the Nazarenes' (Acts 24:5).

We may be surprised to discover that St Paul accepted the accusation of being a heretic. Furthermore, he claimed that this heresy was compatible with his continued belief in Moses and the Torah – 'But this I confess unto thee, that after the way which they call heresy, so worship I the God of my fathers, believing all things which are written in the law and in the prophets' (Acts 24:14).

This assertion is explained by the fact that the word 'heresy' comes from the Greek αἵρεσις, *hairesis* (from αιρεομαι, *haireomai*, to choose) and implies a *choice* of beliefs. As 'a Pharisee and the son of Pharisees' (Acts 23:6) St Paul was expected to act as an orthodox Jew (*ortho* = right + *doxa* or belief) or, as a Roman by birth (Acts 22:27) it would have been acceptable for him to worship the deities of the Roman Empire. What was entirely unacceptable to Jews and Romans alike was that instead he should exercise his choice to follow Jesus of Nazareth – consequently, he suffered imprisonment and was eventually beheaded by Nero in 67 AD.

The denunciation of the Bahá'í Faith as a heresy and a cult by some extreme Christian sources[61] and its condemnation as a detestable sect ('*firqeh zállé*') by some Muslim clergy (see Chapter 1) are reminiscent of similar condemnations of Christianity and Islam at their inception, and are simply futile attempts intended to discourage individuals from investigating truth for themselves.

As with the Apostle Paul, the followers of Bahá'u'lláh have reinvestigated the religion of their ancestors, evaluated the proclamation of Bahá'u'lláh and determined for themselves that the Bahá'í Faith is part of an eternal and continuous Divine Revelation with a life-giving and relevant message for this day and age. The accusation of '*firqeh*' or sect, related to the word '*fargh*' or difference, is particularly meaningless and undeserved, as the main themes of the Bahá'í Faith are unity and harmony, emphasizing the oneness of God, the oneness of religions and the oneness of mankind. Muslims who have accepted the Faith of

Bahá'u'lláh are familiar with the blessed Quranic verse, 'No difference (*lá nufarriqu*) do we make between any of them [Judaism, Christianity, and Islam]' (*Baqara*, the Heifer, 2:136). Each Dispensation accepts earlier Dispensations but has an issue with future Revelations.

Bahá'u'lláh declares that every human being is endowed with the capacity to recognize God's new Revelation, and to reflect His Glory:

> every man hath been, and will continue to be, able of himself to appreciate the Beauty of God, the Glorified. Had he not been endowed with such a capacity, how could he be called to account for his failure? If, in the Day when all the peoples of the earth will be gathered together, any man should, whilst standing in the presence of God, be asked: 'Wherefore hast thou disbelieved in My Beauty and turned away from My Self,' and if such a man should reply and say: 'Inasmuch as all men have erred, and none hath been found willing to turn his face to the Truth, I, too, following their example, have grievously failed to recognize the Beauty of the Eternal,' such a plea will, assuredly, be rejected. For the faith of no man can be conditioned by any one except himself.[62]

The Qur'án explains that Adam, the prototype human being, was endowed with the ability to hearken to the voice of God, and to discern truth, but humanity is ungrateful and neglectful of this bounty.

> But He (God) fashioned him (Adam) . . . and breathed into him something of His spirit. And He gave you (the faculties of) hearing and sight and feeling (and understanding): little thanks do ye give![63]

Scriptural warnings that the individual will experience trials

The Qur'án explains that the acquisition of true faith is fraught with difficulties, for God will test everyone who claims to believe.

> Do men think that they will be left alone on saying, 'We believe', and that they will not be tested?
> We did test those before them, and God will certainly know those who are true from those who are false.[64]

FRUSTRATION OF THE SACRED DUTY OF BELIEVERS

> Or do ye think that ye shall enter the Garden (of Bliss) without such (trials) as came to those who passed away before you? They encountered suffering and adversity, and were so shaken in spirit that even the Messenger and those of faith who were with him cried: 'When (will come) the help of God?' Ah! Verily, the help of God is (always) near![65]

Christians are also aware that many obstacles and 'stumbling blocks' are strewn in the path of a true seeker. They pray, therefore, that their feet do not slip in their earnest search.

> Enter ye in at the strait gate: for wide is the gate, and broad is the way, that leadeth to destruction, and many there be which go in thereat:
> Because strait is the gate, and narrow is the way, which leadeth unto life, and few there be that find it.[66]

> Hold up my goings in thy paths, that my footsteps slip not.[67]

The Qur'án moreover indicates that the faith of no one is conditioned by the faith of another: each individual is responsible for his or her own spiritual destiny:

> Namely, that no bearer of burdens can bear the burden of another;[68]

> On no soul doth God place a burden greater than it can bear. It gets every good that it earns, and it suffers every ill that it earns. (Pray) 'Our Lord! Condemn us not if we forget or fall into error; our Lord! Lay not on us a burden like that which Thou didst lay on those before us; our Lord! Lay not on us a burden greater than we have strength to bear. Blot out our sins, and grant us forgiveness. Have mercy on us. Thou art our Protector; help us against those who stand against Faith.'[69]

> Say: 'Shall I seek for Cherisher other than God, when He is the Cherisher of all things? Every soul draws the meed of its acts on none but itself: no bearer of burdens can bear the burden of another. Your goal in the end is towards God. He will tell you the truth of the things wherein ye disputed.'[70]

> Let them bear, on the Day of Judgement, their own burdens in full, and also of the burdens of those without knowledge, whom they misled. Alas, how grievous the burdens they will bear![71]
>
> Who receiveth guidance, receiveth it for his own benefit: who goeth astray doth so to his own loss: no bearer of burdens can bear the burden of another: nor would We visit with Our Wrath until We had sent a Messenger (to give warning).[72]
>
> Nor can a bearer of burdens bear another's burdens. If one heavily laden should call another to (bear) his load, not the least portion of it can be carried (by the other), even though he be nearly related... And whoever purifies himself does so for the benefit of his own soul; and the destination (of all) is to God.[73]
>
> If ye reject (God), truly God hath no need of you; but He liketh not ingratitude from His servants: if ye are grateful, He is pleased with you. No bearer of burdens can bear the burden of another. In the End, to your Lord is your Return, when He will tell you the truth of all that ye did (in this life). For He knoweth well all that is in (men's) hearts.[74]

Although all will be tested, none will be tested beyond his or her ability. Bahá'u'lláh therefore urges us to cleanse our sight so that we can make our own decisions concerning our spiritual destiny.

> Take heed lest ye allow yourselves to be shut out as by a veil from this Day Star that shineth above the dayspring of the Will of your Lord, the All-Merciful, and whose light hath encompassed both the small and the great. Purge your sight, that ye may perceive its glory with your own eyes, and depend not on the sight of any one except your self, for God hath never burdened any soul beyond its power. Thus hath it been sent down unto the Prophets and Messengers of old, and been recorded in all the Scriptures.[75]

Bahá'u'lláh further reminds us that the ultimate purpose of all learning is to recognize the day of humanity's 'meeting with its Lord', and not be veiled from that event.

Inasmuch as these undiscerning and wretched souls have failed to apprehend the true meaning of 'Resurrection' and of the 'attainment unto the divine Presence,' they therefore have remained utterly deprived of the grace thereof. Although the sole and fundamental purpose of all learning, and the toil and labour thereof, is attainment unto, and the recognition of, this station, yet they are all immersed in the pursuit of their material studies . . .

Consider, how can he that faileth in the day of God's Revelation to attain unto the grace of the 'Divine Presence' and to recognize His Manifestation, be justly called learned, though he may have spent aeons in the pursuit of knowledge, and acquired all the limited and material learning of men? It is surely evident that he can in no wise be regarded as possessed of true knowledge. Whereas, the most unlettered of all men, if he be honoured with this supreme distinction, he verily is accounted as one of those divinely-learned men whose knowledge is of God; for such a man hath attained the acme of knowledge, and hath reached the furthermost summit of learning.[76]

One phenomenon that may present a severe test is the fact that every Dispensation appears in a distinct new format. For instance, the *Bihár al-Anwár* prepares the Shi'íhs for the fact that the Promised One will alter their Faith:

He said: 'When he (the Qaim) rises, he will rule with a new method, new principles, new Sunnah and new judgments.'[77]

In Biblical language, the 'new Wine' will require a more appropriate and specific receptacle – a 'new goatskin'. The different presentation and structure, and the dissimilar social agenda should not however present a significant barrier to a true Christian, who will be well aware that the Gospels state that to succeed in our quest we must be prepared to discard dogma and to refute obsolete tradition.

. . . forgetting those things which are behind, and reaching forth unto those things which are before . . . Let us therefore, as many as be perfect, be thus minded . . .[78]

Your glorying is not good. Know ye not that a little leaven leaveneth the whole lump?

Purge out therefore the old leaven, that ye may be a new lump, as ye are unleavened. For even Christ our passover is sacrificed for us:

Therefore let us keep the feast, not with old leaven, neither with the leaven of malice and wickedness; but with the unleavened bread of sincerity and truth.[79]

And he spake also a parable unto them; No man putteth a piece of a new garment upon an old; if otherwise, then both the new maketh a rent, and the piece that was taken out of the new agreeth not with the old.

And no man putteth new wine into old bottles; else the new wine will burst the bottles, and be spilled, and the bottles shall perish.

But new wine must be put into new bottles; and both are preserved.[80]

The many followers of Bahá'u'lláh from Christian backgrounds are therefore ready, as in Gospel days, to embrace the divine testimony of the 'new testament' and not blindly follow the 'old'.

And such trust have we through Christ to God-ward:

Not that we are sufficient of ourselves to think any thing as of ourselves; but our sufficiency is of God;

Who also hath made us able ministers of the new testament . . .[81]

And he that sat upon the throne said, Behold, I make all things new. And he said unto me, Write: for these words are true and faithful.[82]

9

MISINTERPRETATION OF THE DIVINE WORD

> Thou dost witness how most of the commentaries and interpretations of the words of God, now current amongst men, are devoid of truth.
>
> *Bahá'u'lláh*[1]

Misrepresentation of reality due to inadequate understanding

The Bahá'í Writings observe that the 'different peoples of the world' are unaware that they are 'revolving around imaginations and are worshippers of the idols of thoughts and conjectures' devoid of any real substance[2] – a pattern of behaviour with inimical and debilitating spiritual consequences:

> Humanity has, alas, with increasing insistence, preferred, instead of acknowledging and adoring the Spirit of God as embodied in His religion in this day, to worship those false idols, untruths and half-truths, which are obscuring its religions, corrupting its spiritual life, convulsing its political institutions, corroding its social fabric, and shattering its economic structure.[3]

It is regrettable that despite a dearth of scriptural justification, the spiritual leaders of both Christianity and Islam have frequently pronounced, over many centuries, often in astonishing detail, and with the limited abilities of earthly minds, what transpires in the heavenly realm. They have not refrained from describing the nature of God's relationship to His Manifestations, or on pontificating on a wide variety of abstruse spiritual questions. Often, according to their imperfect understanding, there is only one correct interpretation for every subject in question, requiring that the doctrine be codified into their system of belief; any other explanation is considered as anathema. Yet Bahá'u'lláh explains:

> How great the multitude of truths which the garment of words can never contain! How vast the number of such verities as no expression can adequately describe, whose significance can never be unfolded, and to which not even the remotest allusions can be made! How manifold are the truths which must remain unuttered until the appointed time is come![4]

He further explains that divine insight, interpretation and authoritative explanations are provided by God alone:

> Know assuredly that just as thou firmly believest that the Word of God . . . endureth for ever, thou must, likewise, believe . . . that its meaning can never be exhausted. They who are its appointed interpreters, they whose hearts are the repositories of its secrets, are, however, the only ones who can comprehend its manifold wisdom. Whoso, while reading the Sacred Scriptures, is tempted to choose therefrom whatever may suit him with which to challenge the authority of the Representative of God among men, is, indeed, as one dead . . .[5]

> . . . they have sought the interpretation of the Book from those that are wrapt in veils, and have refused to seek enlightenment from the fountain-head of knowledge.[6]

The Bahá'í Writings therefore warn against enslavement to institutionalized explanations and interpretations of Divine Revelation:

> God has not intended man to imitate blindly his fathers and ancestors. He has endowed him with mind, or the faculty of reasoning, by the exercise of which he is to investigate and discover the truth, and that which he finds real and true he must accept . . . He must not rely implicitly upon the opinion of any man without investigation; nay, each soul must seek intelligently and independently, arriving at a real conclusion and bound only by that reality. The greatest cause of bereavement and disheartening in the world of humanity is

MISINTERPRETATION OF THE DIVINE WORD

> ignorance based upon blind imitation. It is due to this that wars and battles prevail; from this cause hatred and animosity arise continually among mankind.[7]

The misinterpretation of scriptural intent has contributed to religious strife and continues to impede the unity of mankind. The Revelations associated with Christ and Muhammad prescribed love, compassion, justice and unity. However, scriptural misinterpretation and misapprehension has been responsible for much of the hostility between these two great religions:

> Among the great religious systems of the world is Islám... For more than a thousand years there has been enmity and strife between Muslims and Christians owing to misunderstanding and spiritual blindness. If prejudices and imitations were abandoned there would be no enmity whatever between them...[8]

In the case of Christianity, attempts on the part of Christians to understand realities that were beyond their grasp divided the Christian Faith early on, such as the sectarian divisions caused by controversies over Church dogma, debates over original sin and whether Jesus was of 'similar' (*homoiousios*) substance to God or the exact same divine essence (*homoousios*). Some of these issues are discussed in Chapter 11.

Christ had warned that although His Revelation had the capacity to enlighten, it could also cause spiritual blindness, presumably through misapprehension of the divine intent.

> And Jesus said, For judgment I am come into this world, that they which see not might see; and that they which see might be made blind.
>
> And some of the Pharisees which were with him heard these words, and said unto him, are we blind also?
>
> Jesus said unto them, If ye were blind, ye should have no sin: but now ye say, We see; therefore your sin remaineth.[9]

The Qur'án explains that although the revealed Word has been sent down for guidance, it may mislead some, particularly if it involves explanation and interpretation of esoteric and figurative subjects.

... those who reject Faith say: 'What means God by this similitude?' By it He causes many to stray, and many He leads into the right path; but He causes not to stray, except those who forsake (the path).[10]

Similarity between adoration of physical idols and blind following of idols of conjecture

The Bible laments humanity's preoccupation with idols – whether objects that men fashion with their hands (Isa. 2:8) or products of imagination which they set up in their hearts, and which act as a 'stumblingblock' (Ezek. 14:3) to faith and the investigation of truth. God promises to 'sprinkle clean water' upon men and cleanse them from all of their idols (Exod. 36:25), obsessions which He pledges He will 'utterly abolish', for 'the Lord alone shall be exalted in that day' (Isa. 2:17-18). The Psalms thus describe physical idols:

> Their idols are silver and gold, the work of men's hands.
> They have mouths, but they speak not: eyes have they, but they see not:
> They have ears, but they hear not . . .[11]

but the Prophets of the Old Testament describe in a remarkable similar fashion those individuals who are devoid of spiritual insight and therefore at odds with the divine purpose:

> The word of the Lord also came unto me, saying,
>   Son of man, thou dwellest in the midst of a rebellious house, which have eyes to see, and see not; they have ears to hear, and hear not . . .[12]

> Seeing many things, but thou observest not; opening the ears, but he heareth not.[13]

> Hear now this, O foolish people, and without understanding; which have eyes, and see not; which have ears, and hear not.[14]

Christ also described spiritually unreceptive individuals in terms applied to inanimate idols – souls who because of their lack of response to the new Revelation did not deserve His Truth and explanations. His plea was: 'who hath ears to hear, let him hear', for as He had explained in the parable of the sower (Matt. 13:8–9) a receptive soul or fertile ground yielded an abundant harvest:

> And the disciples came, and said unto him, Why speakest thou unto them in parables?
>
> He answered and said unto them, Because it is given unto you to know the mysteries of the kingdom of heaven, but to them it is not given.
>
> For whosoever hath, to him shall be given, and he shall have more abundance: but whosoever hath not, from him shall be taken away even that he hath.
>
> Therefore speak I to them in parables: because they seeing see not; and hearing they hear not, neither do they understand.
>
> And in them is fulfilled the prophecy of Esaias, which saith, By hearing ye shall hear, and shall not understand; and seeing ye shall see, and shall not perceive:
>
> For this people's heart is waxed gross, and their ears are dull of hearing, and their eyes they have closed; lest at any time they should see with their eyes, and hear with their ears, and should understand with their heart, and should be converted, and I should heal them.
>
> But blessed are your eyes, for they see: and your ears, for they hear.[15]

Jesus then added that every new Dispensation provides new spiritual insights. Hence, the interpretations and understandings of an earlier Dispensation must not be allowed to hinder understanding and acceptance of the new:

> For verily I say unto you, That many prophets and righteous men have desired to see those things which ye see, and have not seen them; and to hear those things which ye hear, and have not heard them.[16]

This important point is reiterated by St Paul, who in turn quotes the Prophet Isaiah:

But as it is written [Isa. 64:4], Eye hath not seen, nor ear heard, neither have entered into the heart of man, the things which God hath prepared for them that love him.[17]

In turn, the Qur'án abhors the worship of idols and devotes a significant portion of its largest Súrah (*Baqara*, the Heifer) to the retelling of the event described in Exodus 32, when during the brief absence of Moses, the Israelites chose to worship a heifer or golden calf in place of the unseen God. Abraham had a similar issue with his father about worship of idols:

Behold, he said to his father: "O my father! Why worship that which heareth not and seeth not, and can profit thee nothing?"[18]

But as with the Bible, the Qur'án applies descriptions appropriate to 'idols' worshipped by pre-Islamic Arabs, to humans with similar deficiencies:

Deaf, dumb, and blind, they will not return (to the path).[19]

For the worst of beasts in the sight of God are the deaf and the dumb, – those who understand not.[20]

The Qur'án warns against '*shirk*' or assigning partners to God (*Ḥa-Mím*, or *Fuṣṣilat*, 41:6), and the inimical role of some clerics, particularly those motivated by power or profit. The term 'idols' includes individuals who have allowed themselves to become objects of worship to their followers, and it also refers to the unsound doctrines and effete traditions that they propagate. Bahá'u'lláh rebukes those spiritual leaders who have tacitly encouraged their followers to follow them blindly, without hesitation or reservation, and have thus played a critical role in deterring their followers from recognizing His Revelation.[21]

Through the actions of Muslim and Christian divines – 'idols,' whom Bahá'u'lláh has stigmatized as constituting the majority of His enemies – who failed, as commanded by Him, to lay aside their pens and fling away their fancies, and who, as He Himself testified, had they believed in Him would have brought about the conversion of the masses, Islám and Christianity have, it would be no exaggeration to say, entered the most critical phase of their history.[22]

> Had ye [spiritual leaders] believed in God, when He revealed Himself, the people would not have turned aside from Him, nor would the things ye witness today have befallen Us. Fear God, and be not of the heedless . . . This is the Cause that hath caused all your superstitions and idols to tremble . . . Blessed the man that observeth that whereunto he was bidden, and woe betide the negligent.[23]

> On their tongue the mention of God hath become an empty name; in their midst His holy Word a dead letter. Such is the sway of their desires, that the lamp of conscience and reason hath been quenched in their hearts . . . No two are found to agree on one and the same law, for they seek no God but their own desire, and tread no path but the path of error. In leadership they have recognized the ultimate object of their endeavour, and account pride and haughtiness as the highest attainments of their hearts' desire. They have placed their sordid machinations above the Divine decree, have renounced resignation unto the will of God, busied themselves with selfish calculation, and walked in the way of the hypocrite. With all their power and strength they strive to secure themselves in their petty pursuits, fearful lest the least discredit undermine their authority or blemish the display of their magnificence.[24]

> O concourse of divines! When My verses were sent down, and My clear tokens were revealed, We found you behind the veils. This, verily, is a strange thing . . . We have rent the veils asunder. Beware lest ye shut out the people by yet another veil. Pluck asunder the chains of vain imaginings, in the name of the Lord of all men, and be not of the deceitful.[25]

The Qur'án particularly condemns those who earn their livelihood by hiding the truth and misinterpreting the Divine Message.

> Then woe to those who write the Book with their own hands and then say: 'This is from God,' to traffic with it for a miserable price!

> Woe to them for what their hands do write, and for the gain they make thereby.[26]
>
> Those who conceal God's revelations in the Book, and purchase for them a miserable profit, they swallow into themselves naught but fire; God will not address them on the Day of Resurrection, nor purify them; grievous will be their penalty.[27]

The Bible also abhors the practice of profiting financially or otherwise from religion and in the process perverting divine justice, corrupting God's Word and violating the sanctity of His Faith.

> Thou shalt not wrest judgment; thou shalt not respect persons, neither take a gift: for a gift doth blind the eyes of the wise, and pervert the words of the righteous.[28]
>
> For we are not as many, which corrupt the word of God . . .[29]
>
> No man can serve two masters . . . Ye cannot serve God and mammon.[30]
>
> And Jesus said unto him, Foxes have holes, and the birds of the air have nests; but the Son of man hath not where to lay his head.[31]
>
> And he called unto him the twelve . . .
> And commanded them that they should take nothing for their journey, save a staff only; no scrip, no bread, no money in their purse:
> But be shod with sandals; and not put on two coats.[32]

Cautions against unwarranted interpretations of scripture

The Bible strictly forbids Jews and Christians from interpreting, deleting or adding to scripture (Deut. 4:1-2; Rev. 22:18-19), for only the One Who fulfils the prophecies and is God's Messenger can interpret the Divine Word:

> And they [Pharaoh's officers] said unto him [Joseph], We have dreamed a dream, and there is no interpreter of it. And Joseph said

MISINTERPRETATION OF THE DIVINE WORD

> unto them, Do not interpretations belong to God? tell me them, I pray you.[33]

> Knowing this first, that no prophecy of the scripture is of any private interpretation.
> For the prophecy came not in old time by the will of man: but holy men of God spake as they were moved by the Holy Ghost.[34]

> Therefore judge nothing before the time, until the Lord come, who both will bring to light the hidden things of darkness, and will make manifest the counsels of the hearts: and then shall every man have praise of God.[35]

These warnings were clearly not heeded, as is evident from the vast theological libraries and the numerous articles of faith on which the Jewish rabbis and Church elders have elaborated with little or no justification or divine authority.

The Bible also warns that uninformed and incompetent people will lead to perdition others who are similarly incapable of discerning the truth:

> Let them alone: they be blind leaders of the blind. And if the blind lead the blind, both shall fall into the ditch.[36]

> And he spake a parable unto them, Can the blind lead the blind? shall they not both fall into the ditch?[37]

With perhaps the intention of preventing scriptural controversies, the Qur'án explains that part of the Divine Revelation is clear but part of it is figurative. The ability to explain the abstruse scriptural passages ('*tavil*') belongs to God and 'those who are guided by God'. Therefore, not every pretender idolized by his followers possesses the authority to interpret the ambiguous (*mutishábihát*) verses of the Qur'án such as 'Seal of the Prophets', the 'Day of Judgement', 'the Resurrection', paradise and hell, 'the Balance', and so on:

> He it is Who has sent down to thee the Book: in it are verses basic or fundamental (of established meaning); they are the foundation

of the Book: others are allegorical. But those in whose hearts is perversity follow the part thereof that is allegorical, seeking discord, and searching for its hidden meanings, but no one knows its hidden meanings except God. And those who are firmly grounded in knowledge say: 'We believe in the Book; the whole of it is from our Lord'; and none will grasp the Message except men of understanding.[38, 39]

Additionally, the Qur'án cautions Muslims against making hasty interpretations of Quranic verses. Theeir duty is instead to recite the Qur'án, and to anticipate its full exposition or '*bayán*'[40] at a later date.

> Move not thy tongue concerning the (Qur'án) to make haste therewith.
> It is for Us to collect it and to promulgate it:
> But when We have promulgated it, follow thou its recital (as promulgated):
> Nay more, it is for Us to explain it (and make it clear – bring its *bayán*).[41]

Earlier Dispensations, the Qur'án explains, are provided with only a part of the 'Divine Book' but are promised a greater measure of Revelation which will help eliminate disagreements and restore unity.

> Hast thou not turned thy vision to those who have been given a portion of the Book? They are invited to the Book of God, to settle their dispute, but a party of them turn back and decline.[42]

The knowledge of the spiritual leaders of a former Dispensation is thus simply insufficient to comprehend the full meaning of the figurative verses. They do not possess the 'elucidation' ('*tavíl*').

> Nay, they charge with falsehood that whose knowledge they cannot compass, even before the elucidation thereof hath reached them: thus did those before them make charges of falsehood: but see what was the end of those who did wrong![43]

They therefore must also resist inventing fallible human explanations.

If any, after this, invent a lie and attribute it to God, they are indeed unjust wrongdoers.[44]

For We had certainly sent unto them a Book, based on knowledge, which We explained in detail,– a guide and a mercy to all who believe.

Do they just wait for the final fulfilment of the event? On the day the event is finally fulfilled, those who disregarded it before will say: 'The Prophets of our Lord did indeed bring true (tidings). Have we no intercessors now to intercede on our behalf? Or could we be sent back? Then should we behave differently from our behaviour in the past.' In fact they will have lost their souls, and the things they invented will leave them in the lurch.[45]

God promises to reveal in time the interpretation or '*taví*l' of the allegorical or figurative verses of the Qur'án, and today Bahá'u'lláh has explained many of its abstruse passages. He writes that while Revelation is susceptible to many spiritual explanations, only God's Prophets are the appointed interpreters of the Divine Word. He cautions people 'of insight' not to allow their interpretations of the Holy Scriptures to prevent them from recognizing the Manifestation of God, and proclaims that the knowledge or meaning of the figurative passages of the Qur'án has now been revealed, and all of the verses of God are 'perspicuous'.

> Know thou that the passages . . . called 'ambiguous' appear as such only in the eyes of them that have failed to soar above the horizon of guidance and to reach the heights of knowledge in the retreats of grace. For otherwise, unto them that have recognized the Repositories of divine Revelation and beheld through His inspiration the mysteries of divine authority, all the verses of God are perspicuous and all His allusions are clear. Such men discern the inner mysteries that have been clothed in the garment of words as clearly as ye perceive the heat of the sun or the wetness of water, nay even more distinctly.[46]

Indications in the Bible and the Qur'án that 'unsealing of the wine' of Revelation belongs to God and the Revealer of His Will

It is somewhat curious that despite the Prophet Daniel's admission that even he did not know the meaning of the prophecies revealed to him concerning the coming of the Messiah and the return of Christ, Christians continue to insist on their explanations of his dreams. It should be evident that only the Person who fulfils the prophecies is in a position to reveal their real meaning.

> But thou, O Daniel, shut up the words, and seal the book, even to the time of the end: many shall run to and fro, and knowledge shall be increased...
>
> And I heard, but I understood not: then said I, O my Lord, what shall be the end of these things?
>
> And he said, Go thy way, Daniel: for the words are closed up and sealed till the time of the end.
>
> Many shall be purified, and made white, and tried; but the wicked shall do wickedly; and none of the wicked shall understand; but the wise shall understand.[47]

Until the time arrives for clarifying the 'Words' and 'unsealing' the 'Book', the Gospels warn that no Christian is truly aware or 'knows . . . the hour' because its nature has been hidden from them, and hence, the Lord will appear unexpectedly to them. Christians must therefore remain vigilant.

> But of that day and that hour knoweth no man, no, not the angels which are in heaven, neither the Son, but the Father.[48]

> For yourselves know perfectly that the day of the Lord so cometh as a thief in the night.[49]

> Watch therefore, for ye know neither the day nor the hour wherein the Son of man cometh.[50]

It is an historical fact that many Christian groups, such as that led by William Miller, predicted from Biblical prophecies, mainly chapters 8 and 9 of Daniel, that Jesus would return in 1844 AD (the year that the

Báb declared His Mission). However, 100,000 Millerites were severely disappointed and grieved when Christ did not appear according to their expectations. They got the date right but still tragically missed the event![51]

The Qur'án also promises that at a future time the righteous will be given to drink of the 'choice sealed wine':

> Truly the Righteous will be in Bliss:
> On Thrones (of Dignity) will they command a sight (of all things):
> Thou wilt recognize in their Faces the beaming brightness of Bliss.
> Their thirst will be slaked with Pure Wine sealed:
> The seal thereof will be musk: and for this let those aspire, who have aspirations.[52]

In His Tablets, Bahá'u'lláh identifies the 'choice Wine' with His Revelation whose 'musk-laden fragrance' has been wafted 'upon all created things'. He states that He has 'unsealed' this 'Wine', thereby disclosing spiritual truths that were hitherto unknown and enabling those who quaff thereof to 'discern the splendours of the light of divine unity' and to 'grasp the essential purpose underlying the Scriptures of God'.[53]

He writes:

> The Best-Beloved is come. In His right hand is the sealed Wine of His name. Happy is the man that turneth unto Him, and drinketh his fill, and exclaimeth: 'Praise be to Thee, O Revealer of the signs of God!' By the righteousness of the Almighty! Every hidden thing hath been manifested through the power of truth. All the favours of God have been sent down, as a token of His grace. The waters of everlasting life have, in their fullness, been proffered unto men. Every single cup hath been borne round by the hand of the Well-Beloved. Draw near, and tarry not, though it be for one short moment.[54]

Again, based on Quranic verses and prophecies contained in the hadiths, certain Muslim sects such as the Shaykhis were able to deduce that the Promised One or Qá'im would appear in 1260 AH (corresponding to 1844 AD), but only some of them recognized the Báb as the object of their quest.

Literal interpretation of the scriptures

Amongst the idols at whose altar good sense is sacrificed is the insistence that only a literal explanation of the scriptures is valid. Many Christians have failed to heed the Bible's clear warning that literal interpretations destroy faith but spiritual explanations endow life:

> But the hour cometh,[55] and now is,[56] when the true worshippers shall worship the Father in spirit and in truth: for the Father seeketh such to worship him.
> God is a Spirit: and they that worship him must worship him in spirit and in truth.[57]

> It is the spirit that quickeneth; the flesh profiteth nothing: the words that I speak unto you, they are spirit, and they are life.[58]

> Which things also we speak, not in the words which man's wisdom teacheth, but which the Holy Ghost teacheth; comparing spiritual things with spiritual.
> But the natural man receiveth not the things of the Spirit of God: for they are foolishness unto him: neither can he know them, because they are spiritually discerned.[59]
> While we look not at the things which are seen, but at the things which are not seen: for the things which are seen are temporal; but the things which are not seen are eternal.[60]

> ... our sufficiency is of God.
> Who also hath made us able ministers of the new testament; not of the letter, but of the spirit: for the letter killeth, but the spirit giveth life.[61]

Some increasingly popular Christian denominations adhere tenaciously to a strictly literal interpretation of the scriptures, despite the numerous scriptural statements that can only be reasonably interpreted metaphorically, including the following.

Opening of eyes and ears

> . . . mine ears hast thou opened . . .
> Withhold not thou thy tender mercies from me, O Lord; let thy lovingkindness and thy truth continually preserve me.[62]

> Open thou mine eyes, that I may behold wondrous things out of thy law.[63]

> Hear, ye deaf; and look, ye blind, that ye may see.[64]

> And this is the will of him that sent me, that every one which seeth the Son, and believeth on him, may have everlasting life . . .[65]

Also, St Paul prays that through Jesus and the spirit of wisdom and revelation, 'the eyes of understanding' of the Christians may be 'enlightened'.[66]

Expectation that 'every eye' shall see Jesus at His second coming

> And all flesh shall see the salvation of God.[67]

> Behold, he cometh with clouds; and every eye shall see him . . .[68]

Divine Revelation described as 'bread' and 'water' to satisfy spiritual 'hunger' and 'thirst'

> And Jesus said unto them, I am the bread of life: he that cometh to me shall never hunger; and he that believeth on me shall never thirst.
> I am that bread of life.
> Your fathers did eat manna in the wilderness, and are dead.
> This is the bread which cometh down from heaven, that a man may eat thereof, and not die.
> I am the living bread which came down from heaven: if any man eat of this bread, he shall live for ever: and the bread that I will give is my flesh, which I will give for the life of the world.[69]

Perception of 'heaven' and 'descent from heaven'

Although born of Mary, Christ claimed to have come down from heaven, and whilst He was with His disciples on earth He claimed to be in heaven. This is a metaphor for the 'heaven of Divine Revelation' rather than an undefined region in the sky.

> And no man hath ascended up to heaven, but he that came down from heaven, even the Son of man which is in heaven.[70]

> For I came down from heaven, not to do mine own will, but the will of him that sent me.[71]

> The Jews then murmured at him, because he said, I am the bread which came down from heaven.
> And they said, Is not this Jesus, the son of Joseph, whose father and mother we know? how is it then that he saith, I came down from heaven?[72]

Spiritual life and death

In several Bible statements death appears to refer to mundane existence devoid of spiritual life.

> Verily, verily, I say unto you, If a man keep my saying, he shall never see death.
> Then said the Jews unto him, Now we know that thou hast a devil. Abraham is dead, and the prophets; and thou sayest, If a man keep my saying, he shall never taste of death.
> Art thou greater than our father Abraham, which is dead? and the prophets are dead: whom makest thou thyself?[73]

> We know that we have passed from death unto life, because we love the brethren. He that loveth not his brother abideth in death.[74]

> But she that liveth in pleasure is dead while she liveth.[75]

A certain disciple came to Christ and asked permission to go and bury his father. He answered, 'Let the dead bury their dead.'[76] Therefore, Christ designated as dead some who were still living. They were considered dead because they had not received the Holy Spirit and had not believed in Christ. Although physically alive, they were dead spiritually.

The Bahá'í Writings offer the following additional explanations:

> man, no matter how much he may advance in worldly affairs and make progress in material civilization, is imperfect unless he is quickened by the bounties of the Holy Spirit; for it is evident that until he receives that divine impetus he is ignorant and deprived. For this reason Jesus Christ said, 'Except a man be born of water and of the Spirit, he cannot enter into the kingdom of God.'[77] By this Christ meant that unless man is released from the material world, freed from the captivity of materialism and receiving a portion of the bounties of the spiritual world, he shall be deprived of the bestowals and favours of the Kingdom of God . . . In another place He said, 'That which is born of the flesh is flesh; and that which is born of the Spirit is spirit.'[78] The meaning of this is that if man is a captive of nature, he is like unto an animal because he is only a body physically born – that is, he belongs to the world of matter and remains subject to the law and control of nature. But if he is baptized with the Holy Spirit, if he is freed from the bondage of nature, released from animalistic tendencies and advanced in the human realm, he is fitted to enter into the divine Kingdom. The world of the Kingdom is the realm of divine bestowals and the bounties of God. It is attainment of the highest virtues of humanity; it is nearness to God; it is capacity to receive the bounties of the ancient Lord.[79]

Perception of time

> Your father Abraham rejoiced to see my day: and he saw it, and was glad.
>
> Then said the Jews unto him, Thou art not yet fifty years old, and hast thou seen Abraham?
>
> Jesus said unto them, Verily, verily, I say unto you, Before Abraham was, I am.
>
> Then took they up stones to cast at him.[80]

Portents of the 'first and second coming'

One example is St Peter's statement that they were witnessing the fulfilment of Biblical prophecies concerning the Messiah:

> But this is that which was spoken by the prophet Joel;
>   And I will shew wonders in heaven above, and signs in the earth beneath; blood, and fire, and vapour of smoke:
>   The sun shall be turned into darkness, and the moon into blood, before that great and notable day of the Lord come.[81]

Symbolic descriptions of life and death and divine intervention to resuscitate man are also evident from the following súrahs of the Qur'án:

> And if indeed thou ask them who it is that sends down rain from (Heaven) the sky, and gives life therewith to the earth after its death, they will certainly reply, 'God!' Say, 'Praise be to God!' But most of them understand not.[82]

> And among His Signs is this: thou seest the earth barren and desolate; But when We send down rain to it, it is stirred to life and yields increase. Truly, He Who gives life to the (dead) earth can surely give life to (men) who are dead. For He has power over all things.[83]

Many other passages in the Qur'án are also clearly metaphorical:

> Thou causest the Night to gain on the Day, and Thou causest the Day to gain on the Night; Thou bringest the Living out of the Dead, and Thou bringest the Dead out of the Living; and Thou givest sustenance to whom Thou pleasest, without measure.[84]

It was also the expectation of a literal fulfilment of the signs that were to accompany the coming of the Messiah that led the Jewish leaders, 'steeped in the literal interpretation and imitating the beliefs of fathers and ancestors,' to reject Christ.[85]

And yet, many fundamentalist Christians resolutely maintain the same stance today, despite the Gospel accounts of the difficulties that literal expectations of Messianic hopes posed for the Pharisees and

Sadducees at the First Coming, and which prevented the Jews from recognizing Jesus. Muslims should in turn consider that it was the literal interpretation of the Torah and of the Gospels that prevented the Jews and Christians from recognizing the Mission of Muhammad.

Bahá'u'lláh explains that had Christ's prophecies been fulfilled literally, it would have been impossible for anyone to doubt or deny the Mission of Muhammad. It would therefore be reasonable for Muslims to expect that their expectations would be fulfilled figuratively.

> They have even failed to perceive that were the signs of the Manifestation of God in every age to appear in the visible realm in accordance with the text of established traditions, none could possibly deny or turn away, nor would the blessed be distinguished from the miserable, and the transgressor from the God-fearing. Judge fairly: Were the prophecies recorded in the Gospel to be literally fulfilled; were Jesus, Son of Mary, accompanied by angels, to descend from the visible heaven upon the clouds; who would dare to disbelieve, who would dare to reject the truth, and wax disdainful? Nay, such consternation would immediately seize all the dwellers of the earth that no soul would feel able to utter a word, much less to reject or accept the truth. It was owing to their misunderstanding of these truths that many a Christian divine hath objected to Muhammad, and voiced his protest in such words: 'If Thou art in truth the promised Prophet, why then art Thou not accompanied by those angels our sacred Books foretold, and which must needs descend with the promised Beauty to assist Him in His Revelation and act as warners unto His people?' Even as the All-Glorious hath recorded their statement: 'Why hath not an angel been sent down to him, so that he should have been a warner with Him?'[86]

> Should they say: 'These words are indeed from God, and have no interpretation other than their outward meaning', then what objection can they raise against the unbelievers among the people of the Book? For when the latter saw the aforementioned passages in their Scriptures and heard the literal interpretations of their divines, they refused to recognize God in those who are the Manifestations of His unity, the Exponents of His singleness, and the Embodiments of His sanctity, and failed to believe in them and submit to their authority.

The reason was that they did not see the sun darken, or the stars of heaven fall to the ground, or the angels visibly descend upon the earth, and hence they contended with the Prophets and Messengers of God. Nay, inasmuch as they found them at variance with their own faith and creed, they hurled against them such accusations of imposture, folly, waywardness, and misbelief as I am ashamed to recount. Refer to the Qur'án, that thou mayest find mention of all this and be of them that understand its meaning. Even to this day do these people await the appearance of that which they have learned from their doctors and imbibed from their divines. Thus do they say: 'When shall these signs be made manifest, that we may believe?' But if this be the case, how could ye refute their arguments, invalidate their proofs, and challenge them concerning their faith and their understanding of their Books and the sayings of their leaders?[87]

In like manner, many Christians and Muslims insist on a literal interpretation of their expectations concerning Bahá'u'lláh. A sobering but inevitable conclusion is that ultimately all scriptural understanding that is not in tune with God's new Revelation and which hinders humanity from accepting the divine message is a misapprehension of the truth.

10

CORRUPTION OF THE DIVINE MESSAGE (*TAHRIF*)

That the divers communions of the earth, and the manifold systems of religious belief, should never be allowed to foster the feelings of animosity among men, is, in this Day, of the essence of the Faith of God and His Religion. These principles and laws, these firmly-established and mighty systems, have proceeded from one Source, and are rays of one Light.

Bahá'u'lláh[1]

The Quranic charge of Biblical *tahrif*

The Qur'án states that the scriptures of Jews and Christians have been subject to *tahrif* ('corruption', 'words changed from their original context', or 'displacement from its true meaning').

> Can ye entertain the hope that they will believe in you? – seeing that a party of them heard the word of God, and perverted it knowingly after they understood it.[2]

> O Messenger, let not those grieve thee, who race each other into unbelief: among those who say 'We believe' with their lips, but whose hearts have no faith; or it be among the Jews – men who will listen to any lie; will listen even to others who have never so much as come to thee. They change the words from their (right) times and places: For such, it is not God's will to purify their hearts. For them there is disgrace in this world, and in the Hereafter a heavy punishment.[3]

Muslims interpret this as referring to deliberate alteration of the text of the Holy Bible, and find proof of this in the absence of Muhammad's name in the Bible and the incompatibility of Christian creeds with the teachings of the Qur'án. Muslims have therefore concluded that the Qur'án is the only scripture that is reliable. Clearly, neither the assertion of *tahrif* nor the conclusion that the Bible is untrustworthy is acceptable to Jews and Christians,[4] further adding to the tensions and misunderstandings between the Judeo-Christian religions and Islam.

A primary concern of the Bahá'í Faith is to reveal the underlying unity amongst the religions. It upholds the authenticity and integrity of both the Bible and the Qur'án.

> ... (It) asserts the continuity of Divine Revelation; affirms the unity of the Prophets, the universality of their Message, the identity of their fundamental teachings, the sanctity of their scriptures ...[5]

And,

> preserves inviolate the sanctity of their authentic Scriptures ...[6]

The Bahá'í Faith provides a different perspective on *tahrif* which is consistent with known facts about the validity of the scriptures. Bahá'u'lláh explains that *tahrif* refers to false representations of the scriptures through unwarranted interpretations that add to or detract from the original divine message (see Chapter 9) – in other words, the theme of *tahrif* has itself been perverted.

> Verily by 'perverting' the text is not meant that which these foolish and abject souls have fancied, even as some maintain that Jewish and Christian divines have effaced from the Book such verses as extol and magnify the countenance of Muhammad, and instead thereof have inserted the contrary. How utterly vain and false are these words! Can a man who believeth in a book, and deemeth it to be inspired by God, mutilate it? Moreover, the Pentateuch had been spread over the surface of the earth, and was not confined to Mecca and Medina, so that they could privily corrupt and pervert its text.[7]

He further adds:

> And should they reply: 'The Books that are in the hands of this

people, which they call the Gospel and attribute to Jesus, the Son of Mary, have not been revealed by God and proceed not from the Manifestations of His Self,' then this would imply a cessation in the abounding grace of Him Who is the Source of all grace. If so, God's testimony to His servants would have remained incomplete and His favour proven imperfect. His mercy would not have shone resplendent, nor would His grace have overshadowed all. For if at the ascension of Jesus His Book had likewise ascended unto heaven, then how could God reprove and chastise the people on the Day of Resurrection, as hath been written by the Imams of the Faith and affirmed by its illustrious divines?[8]

Tahrif in Islam

Elaborating on this theme, Bahá'u'lláh warns that Muslims have been engaged in subjecting the precepts of the Qur'án to *tahrif*:

> by corruption of the text is meant that in which all Muslim divines are engaged today, that is the interpretation of God's holy Book in accordance with their idle imaginings and vain desires. And as the Jews, in the time of Muhammad, interpreted those verses of the Pentateuch, that referred to His Manifestation, after their own fancy, and refused to be satisfied with His holy utterance, the charge of 'perverting' the text was therefore pronounced against them. Likewise, it is clear, how in this day, the people of the Qur'án have perverted the text of God's holy Book, concerning the signs of the expected Manifestation, and interpreted it according to their inclination and desires.[9]

The Qur'án acknowledges that the Jews and Christians had received 'a portion of the Book', but notes that some of them had declined to accept God's latest Revelation. It attributes this rejection to an act of rebellion and not to falsification of the text of the scriptures.

> Hast thou not turned thy vision to those who have been given a portion of the Book? They are invited to the Book of God, to settle their dispute, but a party of them turn back and decline (the arbitration).[10]

The Qur'án also asserts that some Jews and Christians have been engaged in verbally misleading others through selective presentations of scripture, thus obscuring the truth and the divine purpose.

> There is among them a section who distort the Book with their tongues: (As they read) you would think it is a part of the Book, but it is no part of the Book; and they say, 'that is from God,' but it is not from God: It is they who tell a lie against God, and (well) they know it![11]

> ... they change the words from their (right) places and forget a good part of the Message that was sent them ...[12]

> Know they not that God knoweth what they conceal and what they reveal?
> And there are among them illiterates, who know not the Book but (see therein their own) desires, and they do nothing but conjecture.[13]

> Say: 'O People of the Book! exceed not in your religion the bounds (of what is proper), trespassing beyond the truth, nor follow the vain desires of people who went wrong in times gone by, who misled many, and strayed (themselves) from the even way.'[14]

Consistent with this view is the observation that only some of the *'ahli alkitáb'* or 'People of the Book' are condemned by the Qur'án: those who, due to their clerical position, have been in a position to interpret the *'Kitáb'* or Revelation, and have thus prevented others from believing. Sadly, this is common to all three religions: Judaism, Christianity, and Islam.[15]

> Of the Jews there are those who displace words from their (right) places ... God hath cursed them for their unbelief; and but few of them will believe.[16]

It is also evident that it would have been impossible to alter all the numerous and widespread copies of the Torah and the Gospels in such a way that no text would contain the original truth.

> Say: 'O ye People of the Book! why obstruct ye those who believe, from the path of God, seeking to make it crooked, while ye were yourselves witnesses (to God's Covenant)? But God is not unmindful of all that ye do.'
>
> O ye who believe! if ye listen to a faction among the People of the Book, they would (indeed) render you apostates after ye have believed![17]

Furthermore, there are references to 'those without faith' among the 'People of the Book', and with the skill and authority to hide the truth.[18]

> The People of the Book know this as they know their own sons; but some of them conceal the truth which they themselves know.[19]

> Quite a number of the People of the Book wish they could turn you (people) back to infidelity after ye have believed, from selfish envy, after the truth hath become manifest unto them; but forgive and overlook, till God accomplish His purpose; for God hath power over all things.[20]

> It is the wish of a section of the People of the Book to lead you astray. But they shall lead astray (not you), but themselves, And they do not perceive!
>
> Ye People of the Book! why reject ye the Signs of God, of which ye are (yourselves) witnesses?
>
> Ye People of the Book! why do ye clothe truth with falsehood, and conceal the truth, while ye have knowledge?
>
> A section of the People of the Book say: 'Believe in the morning what is revealed to the believers, but reject it at the end of the day; perchance they may (themselves) turn back.'[21]

The Qur'án also differentiates between those Jewish and Christian religious leaders who have true faith in the scriptures and those who do not.

> Those to whom We have sent the Book study it as it should be studied; they are the ones that believe therein; those who reject faith therein, the loss is their own.[22]

A distinction is also drawn between the 'learned' (religious leaders and scholars) and the 'unlearned' among the People of the Book.

> So if they dispute with thee, say: 'I have submitted my whole self to God and so have those who follow me.' And say to the People of the Book and to those who are unlearned: 'Do ye (also) submit yourselves?' If they do, they are in right guidance, but if they turn back, thy duty is to convey the Message; and in God's sight are (all) His servants.[23]

Importantly, the Qur'án confirms that the Torah and the Gospels are inerrant divine Revelations with spiritual guidance for mankind. Indeed, the Qur'án laments the fact that the Jews and Christians did not follow the divine Revelation recorded in their Holy Scriptures, for anyone who abides by the teachings of the Torah and the Gospels is blessed by God.

> If only the People of the Book (Jews and Christians) had believed and been righteous, We should indeed have blotted out their iniquities and admitted them to gardens of Bliss.
>
> If only they had stood fast by the Law, the Gospel, and all the revelation that was sent to them from their Lord, they would have enjoyed happiness from every side. There is from among them a party on the right course; but many of them follow a course that is evil.
>
> O Messenger! proclaim the (Message) which hath been sent to thee from thy Lord. If thou didst not, thou wouldst not have fulfilled and proclaimed His mission: and God will defend thee from men. For God guideth not those who reject Faith.
>
> Say: 'O People of the Book! ye have no ground to stand upon unless ye stand fast by the Law, the Gospel, and all the revelation that has come to you from your Lord.' It is the revelation that cometh to thee from thy Lord, that increaseth in most of them their obstinate rebellion and blasphemy. But sorrow thou not over (these) people without Faith.
>
> Those who believe, those who follow the Jewish (Scriptures), and the Sabians and the Christians, any who believe in God and the Last Day, and work righteousness, on them shall be no fear, nor shall they grieve.[24]

The Qur'án further affirms that the divine Word is eternal and unalterable:

> Rejected were the Messengers before thee: with patience and constancy they bore their rejection and their wrongs, until Our aid did reach them: there is none that can alter the Words of God. Already hast thou received some account of those Messengers.[25]

> The Word of thy Lord doth find its fulfilment in truth and in justice: none can change His Words: for He is the one who heareth and knoweth all.
> Wert thou to follow the common run of those on earth, they will lead thee away from the Way of God. They follow nothing but conjecture: they do nothing but lie.[26]

> For them are Glad Tidings, in the life of the Present and in the Hereafter: no change can there be in the Words of God. This is indeed the supreme Felicity.[27]

> He will say: 'Dispute not with each other in My Presence: I had already in advance sent you Warning.
> The word changes not before Me, and I do not the least injustice to My Servants.'[28]

Some examples of *tahrif* in Islam

Misinterpretation through mistranslation that ensures that the scripture conforms with preconceived notions of truth

The motivation for this type of *tahrif* in both Christianity and Islam is difficulty with texts that indicate that the Bible and the Qur'án are not the final Word of God and that there will be further outpourings of God's Revelation in due time through other Prophets, Apostles or Messengers. For example, the Qur'án announces that a Revelation that it refers to as 'that Book' (*dhálika alkitabu*) undoubtedly contains guidance 'to those who fear God' (*Baqara*, the Heifer, 2:2). Most translations interpret *dhálika* as 'this', a reference to the Qur'án, thus eliminating the blasphemous consideration of a future Revelation. However, we find that in other instances the Qur'án is referred to as *Kitábun*' (a Book)[29] and more specifically preceded by *háthá* (this) as in '*hátha Kitábun*' (this is a Book),[30] and '*Al-Kitáb*' (the Book).[31] Also, elsewhere in the Qur'án, *dhalika* is translated as 'that' and not as 'this'.[32]

A telling example is the mistranslation of '*immá ya-tiyyannakum rusulun*'. Contradicting the theory of finality of Revelation, the Qur'án explains that every '*ummah*', people or nation, including the Muslim community, has its '*ajal*' – a predestined end or predetermined demise. Therefore, as indicated by the verse that follows, God will in due course send additional Messengers who will explain His teachings or '*áyáts*'.

> Every nation (*umma*) hath its set time. And when their time is come, they shall not retard it an hour; and they shall not advance it.
>
> O children of Adam! there shall come to you Apostles (*immá ya-tiyyannakum rusulun*) from among yourselves, rehearsing my signs to you; and whoso shall fear God and do good works, no fear shall be upon them, neither shall they be put to grief.[33]

The starkly different translations of this verse demonstrate this bias and altered meaning or *tahrif*. Consistent with their belief in the finality of Islam and their understanding of the title of Muhammad as the 'Seal of the Prophets' (see *Ahzáb*, the Confederates, 33:40), most Muslim translators have interpreted *immá ya-tiyyannakum rusulun* as a conditional event.[34] This interpretation, however, merely gives the impression that the Qur'án is inconsistent, for why would it entertain even the possibility of future Messengers if this is entirely inconceivable?

According to the rules of grammar, when '*immá*' is combined with a future tense with an emphatic '*nun*' at the end of the future tense, it loses its conditionality and becomes emphatic.[35] The appropriate translation is probably provided by three of four non-Muslims who translate the phrase in the affirmative; as scholars in the Christian world they may have subscribed to the belief that the Gospels were the final Word of God, thus believing neither in Islam nor in Revelations that could come after Islam.[36] Only a minority of Muslim authors have faithfully translated the coming of *rusulun* or Messengers as a certainty.[37]

Notably, the identical clause containing *ya-tiyannakum* also appears in two other súrahs, where it is translated by several of the same translators in the affirmative and future emphatic and not in the conditional, perhaps presumably because there is no reference to future Messengers after Muhammad. Here, for instance, is Abdullah Yusuf Ali's translation:

> and if, as is sure (*fa-imma ya/tiyannakum*), there comes to you Guidance from Me, whosoever follows My guidance, on them shall be no fear, nor shall they grieve.[38]

> but if, as is sure, there comes to you (*fa-imma ya/tiyannakum*) Guidance from Me, whosoever follows My guidance, will not Lose his way, nor fall into misery.[39]

Vast collections of unverifiable hadith

Many of the *hadith* are admitted by Muslim scholars to be tenuous, partisan and contradictory, as well as impossible to substantiate. They are therefore suspected of having been fabricated (*mawdu*), because of their dubious content (*matn*) or defective chain of narration.

Some point out that although *hadith* may provide a degree of historical insight, according to the following Quranic verse they cannot be used to judge matters:

> Say: 'Shall I seek for judge [as a source of law] other than God? – When He it is Who hath sent unto you the Book, explained in detail.'[40]

There are even *hadith* that discourage the use of fabricated or questionable *hadith*:

> It was narrated that 'Amir bin Sa'd said: Husain bin Abi Waqqas said: I heard 'Uthman bin 'Affan say: What prevented me from narrating from the Messenger of Allah was not the fact that I was not the most knowledgeable of his companions about what he said, but I bear witness that I heard him say: 'Whoever says something about me that I did not say, let him take his place in Hell.'[41]

> It was narrated that 'Ali said: The Messenger of Allah said: 'Whoever tell a lie about me deliberately, let him take his place in Hell.'[42]

I heard 'Ali say: The Messenger of Allah said: 'Do not tell lies about me, for whoever tells lies about me will enter the Fire.'[43]

There are contradictory accounts of the same *hadith* being used to justify a Sunni or a Shí'ih position. For example, in a Sunni account of Muhammad's farewell speech (*khutbah*) on Mount Arafat He states:

> I leave behind me two things, the Qur'án and my example, the Sunnah and if you follow these you will never go astray.[44]

But a Shí'ih account conveys an entirely different understanding, supporting the succession of 'Alí and the eleven Imams that followed him:

> O People! Indeed, I am leaving among you that which if you hold on to, you shall never go astray: The Book of Allah (Qur'án), my kindred, my household (*Ahlul-Bait*).[45]

Rearrangement of verses to support sectarian viewpoints

The absence of punctuation in the Qur'án opens the way for rearrangement of the verses to support either Sunni or Shí'íh claims. For example, in the rendition of *Ál-i-'Imrán* (the Family of 'Imrán) 3:7 by Abdullah Yusuf Ali, the placement of a period before 'And' indicates that only God understands the abstruse verses:

> He it is Who has sent down to thee the Book: In it are verses Basic or fundamental (of established meaning); they are the foundation of the Book: others are allegorical. But those in whose hearts is perversity follow the part thereof that is allegorical, Seeking discord, and searching for its hidden meanings, but no one knows Its hidden meanings except God. And those who are firmly grounded in knowledge say: 'We believe in the Book; the whole of it is from our Lord:' and none Will grasp the Message except men of understanding.

In contradistinction, the absence of the period in the translation of Muhammad Ali allows 'those firmly grounded in understanding or knowledge' (e.g. the Imams) to also explain the abstruse verses.

And none knows its right interpretation except Allah and those who are firmly grounded in knowledge; they say, we believe in it; the whole is from our Lord – and none take heed except those gifted with understanding.

Introduction of personal interpretation

Some translations of the Qur'án include unwarranted editorial insertions in the text. The following two verses illustrate multiple interpolations (italicized) by the translator 'Al-Híllali:

> Answer the Call of your Lord (*i.e. accept the Islámic Monotheism, O mankind and jinn*) before there comes from Alláh a Day which cannot be averted (*i.e. the Day of Resurrection*). You will have no refuge on that Day nor will be for you any denying (*of your crimes as they are recorded in the Book of deeds*).⁴⁶

> Thus We have made you *[true Muslims – real believers of Islámic Monotheism, true followers of Prophet Muhammad and his Sunnah (legal ways)]*, a just *(and the best)* nation, that you may be witnesses over mankind and the Messenger (Muhammad) be a witness over you . . .⁴⁷

Suppression of the name Bahá or Glory, mentioned in the Dua-Sahar

This is an example of *tahrif* perpetrated in recent times. The *Dua-Sahar* or Dawn Prayer, also known as '*Dua Bahá*', is read during the fasting month of Ramadan. It was authored by Ja'far Ibn Muhammad Al-Sádiq (702–764 CE), the sixth Imam of the Shí'íhs, but is also revered by many Sunnis because of his piety and scholarly achievements. It is a beautiful prayer that invokes nineteen names of God (adopted by the Báb for the titles of the months of His calendar). The first invocation is Bahá or Glory:

> O God, I beseech Thee to bestow upon me Thy Glory (Bahá) that glorifies, and all Thy Glories are radiantly glorious; O God, I beseech Thee in the name of all Thy Glories.

*Allahuma ini asaluka min Bahá-ika bi-Abháu va kullun Bahá-ika
Bahi Allahuma ani as-aluka bi-Bahá-ika . . .*

The recent omission of the entire first paragraph by Islamic media and institutions is in reality an admission that the prayer contains a clear reference to Bahá and Bahá'u'lláh.[48]

Numerous unwarranted 'fatwás'

Fatwás are legally-binding often arrogant religious edicts by 'expert' clerics and jurists. They masquerade as representing the interests of Islam but are only tenuously related to the actual teachings of the Qur'án. They represent personal opinions and agendas. Not infrequently, *fatwás* are issued against the Bahá'í Faith with misleading assertions and unfounded accusations, proscribing association with Bahá'ís and justifying their persecution and elimination. A recent *fatwá* issued by the Supreme Leader of Iran, Ayatollah Ali Khameni, labels the Bahá'í Faith a 'deviant and misleading sect' and calls on Iranians to avoid Bahá'ís.[49] A further example is a *fatwá* by a prominent Egyptian Sunni cleric and theologian, Sheikh Yusuf Al-Qaradawi, President of the World Federation of Muslim Scholars, who issued a formal legal opinion that prohibits a Muslim man from marrying a Bahá'í woman.[50] There are also fabricated accusations against the Bahá'ís that misinterpret or distort historical facts. For instance, because the spiritual and administrative centre of the Bahá'í Faith is in Israel, its followers are sporadically accused of being agents and spies of Israel and Zionists, or colluding with foreign powers, charges that have been punishable, at least in Iran, by imprisonment and even execution.[51] These baseless allegations ignore entirely the point that Bahá'ís, as a matter of principle, scrupulously avoid partisan politics. Also, importantly, the fact that the Bahá'í Faith has its centre in what is Israel today was solely due to the successive banishments of Bahá'u'lláh by the Shí'ih Iranian government and the Sunni Ottoman Empire first to Iraq, then to Constantinople and Adrianople, and finally to the penal colony of Akka in Palestine almost a half century before the establishment of the State of Israel.

Tahrif in Christianity

In the Old Testament, we find Jeremiah lamenting the perversion of the 'Way' and loss of faith: 'for they have perverted their way, and they have forgotten the Lord their God',[52] while the New Testament exhorts the Christians to 'let no corrupt communication proceed out of your mouth, but that which is good to the use of edifying, that it may minister grace unto the hearers'.[53]

When the Pharisees and Sadducees desired that Jesus show them 'a sign from heaven', He rebuked them and called them 'a wicked and adulterous generation',[54] for by implication, they had added their human explanations to the Scriptures, similar to the adulteration of milk and wine with water – otherwise, they would have appreciated the validity of His Message and not instead demanded a physical miracle.[55]

Scripture altered to align it with doctrine

> God, who at sundry times and in divers manners spake in time past unto the fathers by the prophets,
>
> Hath in these last days spoken unto us by *his* Son, whom he hath appointed heir of all things, by whom also he made the worlds;
>
> Who being the brightness of his glory, and the express image of his person . . .[56]

At first glance St Paul appears here to be strongly endorsing the physical Sonship of Jesus, and hence the Trinity, until one notes that the italicized '*his*' ('υἱοῦ αὐτοῦ', 'the son of Him') is a substitution/interpretation in English of the original Greek 'a' son (υἱῷ). The original indefinite article is also more in keeping with the overall message of the passage, that Christ came as part of a sequence of Prophets who revealed God's Revelation during different Dispensations ('times') and in dissimilar ways. Also, that Christ was merely a reflection of God's Glory.

Interpretation of John 14:6

> Jesus saith unto him, I am the way, the truth, and the life: no man cometh unto the Father, but by me.[57]

This passage is usually interpreted as indicating that salvation is possible only through Christ. As observed earlier, God had spoken in the past (Heb. 1:1) and guided humanity through many Prophets before the appearance of Jesus. In the Dispensation of Moses God had led the way:

> Thus saith the Lord, thy Redeemer, the Holy One of Israel; I am the Lord thy God which teacheth thee to profit, which leadeth thee by the way that thou shouldest go.[58]

And in this context, it was the 'I AM' (God) that is always 'the way'.

> And God said unto Moses, I AM THAT I AM: and he said, Thus shalt thou say unto the children of Israel, I AM hath sent me to you.[59]

Again, John the Baptist had prepared the way and made it 'straight' for Christ.

> He said, I am the voice of one crying in the wilderness, Make straight the way of the Lord, as said the prophet E-sai'as.[60]

Furthermore, this mindset of exclusivity contradicts several of Christ's other statements, such as that there are other sheep (non-Christians) that belong to other flocks (religions or Dispensations).

> And other sheep I have, which are not of this fold: them also I must bring, and they shall hear my voice; and there shall be one fold, and one shepherd.[61]

Formulation of elaborate and irrational doctrines and edicts

Christians were instructed not to judge matters until the coming of the Lord:

> Therefore judge nothing before the time, until the Lord come, who both will bring to light the hidden things of darkness, and will make manifest the counsels of the hearts: and then shall every man have praise of God.[62]

CORRUPTION OF THE DIVINE MESSAGE

However, shortly after achieving temporal power, the Church set out to establish God's kingdom on earth although Jesus had warned that His kingdom was not of this world and that His disciples were assigned only the task of giving the 'good news' of its 'coming'.

> ... the fundamental reason why the unity of the Church of Christ was irretrievably shattered, and its influence was in the course of time undermined, was that the Edifice which the Fathers of the Church reared after the passing of His First Apostle was an Edifice that rested in nowise upon the explicit directions of Christ Himself. The authority and features of their administration were wholly inferred, and indirectly derived, with more or less justification, from certain vague and fragmentary references which they found scattered amongst His utterances as recorded in the Gospel. Not one of the sacraments of the Church; not one of the rites and ceremonies which the Christian Fathers have elaborately devised and ostentatiously observed; not one of the elements of the severe discipline they rigorously imposed upon the primitive Christians; none of these reposed on the direct authority of Christ, or emanated from His specific utterances. Not one of these did Christ conceive, none did He specifically invest with sufficient authority to either interpret His Word, or to add to what He had not specifically enjoined.
>
> For this reason, in later generations, voices were raised in protest against the self-appointed Authority which arrogated to itself privileges and powers which did not emanate from the clear text of the Gospel of Jesus Christ, and which constituted a grave departure from the spirit which that Gospel did inculcate. They argued with force and justification that the canons promulgated by the Councils of the Church were not divinely-appointed laws, but were merely human devices which did not even rest upon the actual utterances of Jesus ... Had it been possible for the Church Fathers, whose unwarranted authority was thus fiercely assailed from every side, to refute the denunciations heaped upon them by quoting specific utterances of Christ regarding the future administration of His Church, or the nature of the authority of His Successors, they would surely have been capable of quenching the flame of controversy, and preserving the unity of Christendom. The Gospel, however, the only repository of the utterances of Christ, afforded no such shelter to these

harassed leaders of the Church, who found themselves helpless in the face of the pitiless onslaught of their enemy, and who eventually had to submit to the forces of schism which invaded their ranks.[63]

The charge of deicide against the Jews

Whatever the origins of this ethno-religious slur,[64] it has sustained an anti-Semitic hatred that has fuelled many pogroms by the Church.[65] Recently, the Catholic Church has considered it necessary to repudiate this belief concerning the collective Jewish guilt for the crucifixion of Jesus.[66]

Instead of apportioning blame, the Bahá'í Faith focuses on the reasons why the people of faith reject a Revelation that they have long anticipated.

The 'times of refreshing' and 'restitution of all things'[67]

Bahá'u'lláh has purified Christianity and Islam of their *taḥríf*, and the Bahá'í Faith is itself immune from its nefarious effects, as the interpretation of the Holy Text is restricted to only two appointed successors.[68] In addition,

> those elements which in past Dispensations have, without the least authority from their Founders, been a source of corruption and of incalculable harm to the Faith of God, have been strictly excluded by the clear text of Bahá'u'lláh's writings. Those unwarranted practices, in connection with the sacrament of baptism, of communion, of confession of sins, of asceticism, of priestly domination, of elaborate ceremonials . . . have one and all been rigidly suppressed by the Pen of Bahá'u'lláh . . .[69]

11
CHRISTIAN–ISLAMIC DOCTRINAL CONFLICTS

> O concourse of divines! Fling away idle fancies and imaginings, and turn, then, towards the Horizon of Certitude . . . Say: O concourse of divines! Lay aside all your veils and coverings. Give ear unto that whereunto calleth you the Most Sublime Pen, in this wondrous Day . . . The world is laden with dust, by reason of your vain imaginings . . . Fear God, and be of them that judge equitably.
>
> *Bahá'u'lláh*[1]

Theological differences between Christians and Muslims render it difficult for them to regard each other's religion as integral components of one common faith. Muslims unfortunately consider the disparities as further evidence of the untrustworthiness of the Bible. For their part, Christian scholars point out that since the Bible originated earlier than the Qur'án, any discrepancy between the two scriptures is evidence that the Qur'án is fabricated, and hence Islam is a false religion. The position of the Bahá'í Faith is that the apparent inconsistencies are not scriptural but emanate from the literal interpretation of scriptural passages, excessive reliance on Church dogma and misapprehension of the spiritual message of the Qur'án.

Underlying reasons

Literal interpretation

It is worth remembering that it was adherence to the letter of the Mosaic Law that prevented the Jews from recognizing Jesus as their Messiah. The Gospels state that 'God is a Spirit: and they that worship him must worship him in spirit and in truth' (John 4:24). St Paul reiterates that a literal interpretation of the scriptures causes death but a spiritual interpretation confers life (II Cor. 3). He moreover states that the Word of God must be discerned spiritually (I Cor 2:14). The Qur'án explains that no one fully understands the allegorical parts of scripture, which require explanation by those empowered to do so (*Ál-i-'Imrán*, the Family of 'Imrán, 3:7). The Bahá'í Writings provide the spiritual understanding of the scriptures that is essential to reconciling apparent inconsistencies between the Bible and the Qur'án.

Church doctrine

The Church has in the course of the past two thousand years incrementally burdened itself with an elaborate doctrinal system that defines a 'Christian'. This composite, in its multitude forms, bears little resemblance to the pristine teachings of Jesus of Nazareth. Examples of accretional changes to Gospel ordinances include the prohibition of monastic marriage, the revering and bowing down before icons and statues of Jesus, Mary, the apostles and past Christian leaders, papal infallibility,[2] forgiveness of sins by priests, and various other practices and ceremonies. As observed by an astute Christian, 'there is religion enough, and Churchianity enough, but a great famine of real Christianity'.[3]

Largely due to their more advanced age, doctrinal adulteration of the Faith of Christ is most prominently a feature of the Catholic and Eastern Orthodox churches. The Reformation empowered the Protestant churches to shed many but not all of the human additions in an effort to return to the Gospel teachings. It is also worth noting that doctrine has perhaps a much greater place in Christianity than in Islam.

Influence of pagan religions in Christianity

Many of the most cherished Church doctrines and rituals have well-described correlations with Mithraism and other pagan and 'mystery' religions that were rivals to Christianity during the first four centuries of its existence. Mithraism predated Christianity and was very popular in the Roman Empire. The followers of Mithra dedicated the first day of the week to their Sun God, which they termed Sun-day. The Jewish thinker Philo of Alexandria had earlier identified the *Logos* with the Sun.

In time, Sunday became established as the Lord's Day for the Christians as well. From this observance of Sunday, the myth eventually evolved to connect the rising of Jesus with that day. The birthday of Mithra was 25 December and he was also described variously as 'the Way', 'the Truth', 'the Light', 'the Life', 'the Word', 'the Son of God', 'the Good Shepherd'.[4] The early Church Fathers, alarmed by the remarkable resemblances to Christian dogma, explained the similarities as the work of the devil, designed to sow seeds of doubt in the minds of the faithful. Whatever their interpretation, it is difficult to deny the influence of the cult of Mithra and additionally of the Alexandrian school of thought, the precepts of Zoroastrianism and of Greek philosophy on nascent Christianity.[5]

Detrimental consequences

Man-made doctrines and rituals, derived indirectly from fragmentary reports and not expressly condoned by the Gospels, have been the principal cause of the divisions and fragmentations of the Christian 'house'.[6] As explained here, it is largely Church dogma and explanations, and not the actual teachings of Christ, that are alien to the Torah and at odds with the Qur'án.

The apparently irreconcilable inconsistencies between Christian doctrine and Islamic belief have been a source of friction between the two religions over many centuries. While a detailed analysis of the subject is beyond the scope of this book, a brief examination of an early Church Creed serves to illustrate the main areas of contention.

The Apostles' Creed consists of twelve tenets[7] that summarize mainstream Christian belief for most, but not all, Christians. It is very commonly repeated by the congregation at church services and was developed between the second and ninth century as a baptismal rite for new Christian converts. The following provides a brief summary of various elements of the Creed, areas of accord and disagreement between Christianity and Islam, and attempts to reconcile the divergent viewpoints by the Bahá'í Faith:

1. I believe in God the Father Almighty, Maker of heaven and earth

This initial statement is consistent with the Torah:

> In the beginning God created the heaven and the earth.
> And the earth was without form, and void; and darkness was upon the face of the deep. And the Spirit of God moved upon the face of the waters.
> And God said, Let there be light: and there was light.[8]

The concept is amplified in the Qur'án with the mention of the creation of several heavens (raised through earlier Dispensations) to reveal the Divine Command (*Amr*), and to enlighten the earth of human understanding through divine knowledge and inspiration:

> God is He Who created seven Firmaments (Heavens) and of the earth a similar number. Through the midst of them (all) descends His Command: that ye may know that God has power over all things, and that God comprehends all things in (His) Knowledge.[9]

Bahá'u'lláh reminded Pope Pius IX that God is the Creator of heaven and earth:

> O Pope! Rend the veils asunder. He Who is the Lord of Lords is come overshadowed with clouds, and the decree hath been fulfilled by God, the Almighty, the Unrestrained . . . He, verily, hath again come down from Heaven even as He came down from it the first time. Beware that thou dispute not with Him even as the Pharisees disputed with Him [Jesus] without a clear token or proof . . . Beware lest any name debar thee from God, the Creator of earth and heaven. Leave thou the world behind thee, and turn towards thy Lord, through Whom the whole earth hath been illumined.[10]

However, the Bahá'í Faith regards the Biblical and Quranic references to creation, and the descriptions of heaven and hell, as symbolic, not intended to be interpreted literally. Heaven is considered as the state of perfection, the condition of spirituality and harmony with God's Will.

Hell is the state of imperfection, rebellion against the divine decree, alienation from God's purpose, and the condition of spiritual death. The delights of heaven are spiritual raptures and the tortures of hell are deprivation of the heavenly joys.

In the same vein, Jews and Christians are also reminded that a 'new heaven' of conformity with the divine Will, and a 'new earth' of understanding and social order, must replace the earlier heaven and earth and that the 'former things' will pass away and 'shall not be remembered, nor come into mind'.[11]

2. And in Jesus Christ His only Son our Lord

A literal understanding of the Sonship of Christ and the Trinity are at greatest variance with the teachings of the Qur'án. The doctrine of the Trinity is also inconsistent with the teachings of the Torah.

Sonship

The terms 'Son', 'Son of God' and 'begotten Son' that refer to Jesus are used in several ways in the New Testament, but not in any form that suggests a physical begetting by God. The New Testament uses the term 'son' to describe a spiritually transformed human being, as for example in the Gospel of St John, which labels any individual who was transformed by Christ's Revelation as the son of God, born of God and spiritually transformed by God, irrespective of his physical birth or parenthood.[12]

In accordance with St Paul's explanation that the things of God must be discerned spiritually (I Cor. 2:14), the appellation 'son of God' may apply to any individual who at the 'second coming' overcomes the anticipated spiritual hurdles and recognizes the truth:

> He that overcometh shall inherit all things; and I will be his God, and he shall be my son.[13]

Notably, St Paul called one of his converts, Timothy, his beloved (spiritual) son:

> For this cause have I sent unto you Timotheus, who is my beloved

son, and faithful in the Lord, who shall bring you into remembrance of my ways which be in Christ, as I teach every where in every church.[14]

The Trinity

The concept of the Trinity predates Christianity. It was adopted by the Church two to three hundred years after the inception of the Faith of Christ, an attempt doomed by the very nature of the quest: to define the unknowable nature of Christ and His relationship to the Holy Spirit and to God.

Espoused by the Church as the highest and most mysterious doctrine of the Christian Faith, the concept of the Trinity – Father, Son, and Holy Spirit – was derived largely from the pagan religions amongst which the Church grew and recruited its converts, especially those from Greek, Roman and Egyptian religions, who brought with them many of their ancient rites and terms into their newly adopted Faith. Its eventual formulation was closer to the beliefs of the mystery religions that prevailed in the Roman Empire than to its predecessor monotheistic Faith. Its adoption was far from universal, and it is probably true that this dogma, which plagued the infant Faith for centuries, was, more than any other, instrumental in the Church's early irretrievable and acrimonious schism.

With few exceptions, perhaps the best known of which is Unitarianism, Christian denominations maintain that the Trinity is one of the central doctrines of Christian faith. This belief is based on Jesus's frequent mention of God as the Heavenly Father and as His Own Father, His claim to be the Eternal Son of God, and His promise when His ministry was drawing to a close, that the Father would send another Divine Personage, the Holy Spirit, in His place. After His resurrection, He apparently revealed the doctrine in more explicit terms, bidding them 'go . . . and teach all nations, baptizing them in the name of the Father, and of the Son, and of the Holy Ghost'.[15] A divine trinity may also be inferred from the following New Testament statement:

> For there are three that bear record in heaven, the Father, the Word, and the Holy Ghost: and these three are one.[16]

CHRISTIAN–ISLAMIC DOCTRINAL CONFLICTS

As elaborated in the Nicene Creed (used in the Ordinary of the Catholic Mass) and the Athanasian Creed, the doctrine of the Trinity became even less susceptible to a spiritual rendition and more alien to both Biblical and Quranic assertions.[17] No number of creative theological arguments can entirely reconcile the Church's literal interpretation of a triune God with many of the Biblical statements concerning the supremacy and oneness of God:

> . . . and one of the scribes came, and having heard them reasoning together, and perceiving that he had answered them well, asked him, Which is the first commandment of all?
> And Jesus answered him, The first of all the commandments is, Hear, O Israel; The Lord God is one Lord:
> And thou shalt love the Lord thy God with all thy heart, and with all thy soul, and with all thy mind, and with all thy strength: this is the first commandment.[18]

> For one is your Father, the heavenly one . . .[19]

> For there is one God...[20]

> Now unto the King, eternal, immortal, invisible, the only wise God, be honour and glory for ever and ever. Amen.[21]

> That thou keep this commandment without spot, unrebukeable, until the appearing of our Lord Jesus Christ: Which in his times he shall shew, who is the blessed and only Potentate, the King of kings, and Lord of lords; Who only hath immortality, dwelling in the light which no man can approach unto; whom no man hath seen, nor can see: to whom be honour and power everlasting. Amen.[22]

> . . . we know that an idol is nothing in the world, and that there is none other God but one . . . But to us there is but one God, the Father, of whom are all things . . . and one Lord Jesus Christ, by Whom are all things . . .[23]

Jesus never claimed to be God or a god. He did not at any time during His three-year ministry desire His followers to worship Him, either as

God or as the Son of God, in the sense that the Church now preaches. He declared that the Father was greater than Himself:

> Ye have heard how I said unto you, I go away, and come again unto you. If ye loved me, ye would rejoice, because I said, I go unto the Father: for my Father is greater than I.[24]

Only the Father was to be worshipped:

> But the hour cometh, and now is, when the true worshippers shall worship the Father . . .[25]

His will was subordinate to the will of the Father:

> And he said, Abba, Father, all things are possible unto thee; take away this cup from me: nevertheless not what I will, but what thou wilt.[26]

> For I came down from heaven, not to do mine own will, but the will of him that sent me.[27]

He taught that supreme authority belongs to God only. In response to the request of the two brothers James and John that Jesus grant that one sit at the right hand, and the other at the left hand of Jesus in His glory, He replied:

> But to sit on my right hand and on my left hand is not mine to give; but it shall be given to them for whom it is prepared.[28]

Only the Father was All-Wise and knew the circumstances of the second coming:

> But of that day and that hour knoweth no man, no, not the angels which are in heaven, neither the Son, but the Father.[29]

The source of all Revelations is the Father alone:

> For I have not spoken of myself; but the Father which sent me, he

CHRISTIAN–ISLAMIC DOCTRINAL CONFLICTS

> gave me a commandment, what I should say, and what I should speak. And I know that his commandment is life everlasting: whatsoever I speak therefore, even as the Father said unto me, so I speak.[30]

> ... the word which ye hear is not mine, but the Father's which sent me.[31]

All glory belongs to God alone:

> And I seek not mine own glory: there is one that seeketh and judgeth.[32]

> Jesus answered, If I honour myself, my honour is nothing: it is my Father that honoureth me; of whom ye say, that he is your God.[33]

All good is to be attributed to God alone:

> And a certain ruler asked him, saying, Good Master, what shall I do to inherit eternal life?
> And Jesus said unto him, Why callest thou me good? none is good, save one, that is, God.[34]

> I can of mine own self do nothing: as I hear, I judge; ... because I seek not mine own will, but the will of the Father which hath sent me.[35]

> Verily, verily, I say unto you, The Son can do nothing of himself...[36]

> I do nothing of myself; but as my Father hath taught me, I speak these things.[37]

> If I bear witness of myself, my witness is not true.[38]

The ultimate source of all spiritual life is God only:

> ... God, who quickeneth all things ...[39]

The ability to recognize the truth comes solely from God:

And he said, Therefore said I unto you, that no man can come unto me, except it were given unto him of my Father.[40]

Christ was in the image of God, and declared the Father. What Jesus manifested was not God's Person but His divine attributes and His Glory:

> Jesus cried and said, He that believeth on me, believeth not on me, but on him that sent me.
> And he that seeth me seeth him that sent me.[41]

Jesus was but a reflection of God, the Author of all Revelations:

> [God] Hath in these last days spoken unto us by *his* [correct translation is 'a'] Son.
> Who being the brightness [reflection] of his glory, and the express image of his person.[42]

Jesus 'declared the Father'. His statements such as 'I and the Father are one' (John 10:30) were an indication of the oneness of His teachings with the divine purpose, rather than identity of His person with that of the Almighty. The Light that Jesus manifested was God's Light:

> No man hath seen God at any time, the only begotten Son, which is in the bosom of the Father, he hath declared him.[43]

Notably, Jesus predicted that this identity of divine purpose would be re-manifested and re-established at the 'second coming':

> At that day ye shall know that I am in my Father, and ye in me, and I in you.[44]

Jesus taught that blasphemy against the Son of Man can be forgiven but blasphemy against the Spirit of God is unforgivable:

> Wherefore I say unto you, All manner of sin and blasphemy shall be forgiven unto men: but the blasphemy against the Holy Ghost shall not be forgiven unto men.

> And whosoever speaketh a word against the Son of man, it shall be forgiven him: but whosoever speaketh against the Holy Ghost, it shall not be forgiven him, neither in this world, neither in the world to come.[45]

Belief in Christ was not a belief in Jesus but in the Revelation of the Father:

> Jesus cried and said, He that believeth on me, believeth not on me, but on him that sent me.[46]

It was preferable to accept the divine teachings than to believe in Jesus:

> If I do not the works of my Father, believe me not.
>
> But if I do, though you believe not me, believe the works . . .[47]

Jesus had other titles that again were unrelated to a belief in a triune God. In some instances He described Himself as a prophet, and was similarly referred to by others:

> And he (Jesus) said, Verily I say unto you, No prophet is accepted in his own country.[48]

> Many of the people therefore, when they heard this saying, said, Of a truth this is the Prophet.[49]

> Then those men, when they had seen the miracle that Jesus did, said, This is of a truth that prophet that should come into the world.[50]

He described Himself figuratively as 'bread' from God:

> I am that bread of life.[51]

> Your fathers did eat manna in the wilderness, and are dead.
> This is the bread which cometh down from heaven, that a man may eat thereof, and not die.

> I am the living bread which came down from heaven: if any man eat of this bread, he shall live for ever . . .⁵²

Other symbolic titles of Jesus include that of 'High Priest' and 'Apostle' (Hebr. 3:1). Considered together they do not provide a basis for asserting a physical identity with God, but suggest instead an identity of divine purpose. It was in this context that to know Christ was to know God:

> If ye had known me, ye should have known my Father also; and from henceforth ye know him, and have seen him.⁵³

> Philip saith unto him, Lord, shew us the Father, and it sufficeth us.
> Jesus saith unto him, Have I been so long time with you, and yet hast thou not known me, Philip? he that hath seen me hath seen the Father; and how sayest thou then, Shew us the Father?
> Believest thou not that I am in the Father, and the Father in me? the words that I speak unto you I speak not of myself: but the Father that dwelleth in me, he doeth the works.⁵⁴

It was not only some of the Churches that misinterpreted Jesus's teachings; the followers of Moses also misunderstood their spiritual significance and considered them blasphemous. Identical purpose was mistaken for equality of person.

> I [Jesus] and my Father are one.
> Then the Jews took up stones again to stone him.⁵⁵

Judaism, the parent religion of Christianity, uncompromisingly teaches monotheism and the Torah emphatically declares:

> Hear O Israel, the Lord our God, the Lord is one!⁵⁶

It would therefore have been entirely unthinkable to the early converts from the Jewish Faith to consider Jesus as God or a god:

> I am the Lord, and there is none else, there is no God beside me: I girded thee (satisfied your spiritual needs) though thou hast not

CHRISTIAN–ISLAMIC DOCTRINAL CONFLICTS

> known me: That they may know from the rising of the sun, and from the west, that there is none beside me. I am the Lord, and there is none else.[57]

> I am the first, and I am the last; and beside me, there is no God.[58]

In addition to these words, the Prophet Isaiah declares that God is unknowable:

> Hast thou not known? hast thou not heard, that the everlasting God, the Lord, the Creator of the ends of the earth, fainteth not, neither is weary? there is no searching of his understanding.[59]

> When, therefore, the Jews began to stone Jesus on hearing his words 'I and my Father are one', Jesus asked them why. They replied:
> . . . for blasphemy; and because that thou, being a man, makest thyself God.
> Jesus answered them, Is it not written in your law, I said, Ye are gods?
> If he called them gods, unto whom the word of God came, and the scripture cannot be broken;
> Say ye of him whom the Father hath sanctified, and sent into the world, Thou blasphemest; because I said, I am the Son of God?[60]

The description 'son' is often used in the Tanakh, but never in a literal sense as begetting by God. It is used to denote the Jewish nation:

> . . . where it was said unto them, Ye are not my people, there it shall be said unto them, Ye are the sons of the Living God.[61]

> When Israel was a child, then I loved him, and called my son out of Egypt.[62]

In other instances, the description 'son(s) of God' refers to humanity in general:

> And it came to pass, when men began to multiply on the face of the earth, and daughters were born unto them,

That the sons of God saw the daughters of men that they were fair; and they took them wives of all which they chose.[63]

Any person who recognized Jesus is described as having been born of God:

But as many as received him, to them gave he power to become the sons of God . . .
Which were born, not of blood, nor of the will of the flesh, nor of the will of man, but of God.[64]

Whosoever believeth that Jesus is the Christ is born of God.[65]

According to the Jewish scriptures, God had other 'begotten sons', one of whom was King David. Furthermore, he was begotten by God not at conception but when he was much older and, presumably, could reflect God's attributes:

. . . the Lord hath said unto me, Thou art my Son; this day have I begotten thee.[66]

Therefore, the phrase 'begotten son' is synonymous with 'derived from the Spirit of God', and does not imply a physical relationship with God. The word 'only' used in association with 'begotten son' (John 1:18) describes the special or specific relationship that the Manifestation of God has with God.

No man hath seen God at any time; the only begotten Son, which is in the bosom of the Father, he hath declared him.[67]

For example, God tells Abraham to sacrifice His 'only' son Isaac (Gen. 22:2) when clearly Abraham had another son called Ishmael who was fourteen years older (Gen. 28:9).

The view of the Qur'án

The Qur'án finds the notion of God physically procreating abhorrent and blasphemous, and emphatically condemns the belief in a triune

God. It declares that there are no gods beside God. It regards literal trinity as '*shirk*' – blatant polytheism and worshipping gods other than God. God is Single (*Al-Fard*) and God is One (*Al-Ahad*):

Say: He is God, the One and Only;
God, the Eternal, Absolute;
He begetteth not, Nor is He begotten;
And there is none like unto Him.[68]

There is no god but He, the Exalted in Might, the Wise.[69]

Not a messenger did We send before thee without this inspiration sent by Us to him: that there is no god but I; therefore, worship and serve Me.[70]

They say: 'God hath begotten a son': Glory be to Him – Nay, to Him belongs all that is in the heavens and on earth: everything renders worship to Him . . .[71]

They do blaspheme who say: 'God is Christ the son of Mary.' But said Christ: 'O Children of Israel! Worship God, my Lord and your Lord.' Whoever joins other gods with God – God will forbid him the Garden, and the Fire will be his abode. There will for the wrong-doers be no one to help.

They do blaspheme who say: God is one of three in a Trinity: for there is no god except One God. If they desist not from their word (of blasphemy), verily a grievous penalty will befall the blasphemers among them.

Why turn they not to God, and seek His forgiveness? For God is Oft-Forgiving, Most Merciful.[72]

Say: 'O People of the Book! Come to common terms as between us and you: that we worship none but God; that we associate no partners with Him; that we erect not, from among ourselves, lords and patrons other than God.' If then they turn back, say ye: 'Bear witness that we (at least) are Muslims (bowing to God's Will).'[73]

They take their priests and their anchorites to be their lords in derogation of God, and (they take as their Lord) Christ the son of Mary; yet they were commanded to worship but One God: There is no god but He. Praise and glory to Him (far is He) from having the partners they associate (with Him).[74]

The Qur'án also points out there is lack of unanimous belief concerning the Trinity, and indicates that the truth and a spiritual understanding will only be established in the Promised Day, namely with the coming of Bahá'u'lláh:

> But the sects differ among themselves: and woe to the unbelievers because of the (coming) Judgment of a momentous Day!
> How plainly will they see and hear, the Day that they will appear before Us! But the unjust today are in error manifest![75]

The Bahá'í perspective

The Bahá'í Writings refer to Christ as the 'Son' and to Bahá'u'lláh as 'the Establisher of the Kingdom of the Father foretold by the Son'.[76] The advent of Bahá'u'lláh is considered the coming of Jesus Christ again in the Glory of the Father:

> He Who is the Father is come, and the Son (Jesus Christ), in the holy vale, crieth out: 'Here am I, here am I, O Lord, my God!', whilst Sinai circleth round the House, and the Burning Bush calleth aloud: 'The All-Bounteous is come mounted upon the clouds! Blessed is he that draweth nigh unto Him, and woe betide them that are far away.'[77]

> The churches are waiting for the coming of Jesus Christ; we believe He has come again in the Glory of the Father.[78]

The Bahá'í Faith accepts the New Testament statements and explains the Sonship of Christ and the Trinity in spiritual terms. The designations of Christ in Bahá'í scriptures include those mentioned in the Bible: the Son of Man, the Son, Son of Mary, the Holy Spirit, the Spirit, and the Spirit of God.[79]

CHRISTIAN–ISLAMIC DOCTRINAL CONFLICTS

For the Faith of Bahá'u'lláh – if we would faithfully appraise it – can never, and in no aspect of its teachings, be at variance, much less conflict, with the purpose animating, or the authority invested in, the Faith of Jesus Christ.[80]

The Founder of the Christian Faith is designated by Bahá'u'lláh as the 'Spirit of God', is proclaimed as the One Who 'appeared out of the breath of the Holy Ghost', and is even extolled as the 'Essence of the Spirit'. His mother is described as 'that veiled and immortal, that most beauteous, countenance', and the station of her Son eulogized as a 'station which hath been exalted above the imaginings of all that dwell on earth' . . .[81]

The Bahá'í Faith explains that the Qur'án does not deny the title 'Son of God' but understands it spiritually:

In reality there is no contradiction at all; when the Qur'án denies Christ is the Son of God it is not refuting His words but the false interpretation of them by the Christians who read into them a relationship of an almost corporeal nature, whereas Almighty God has no parents or offspring. What is meant by Christ, is His Spirit's relation to the Infinite Spirit, and this the Qur'án does not deny. It is in a sense attributable – this kind of Sonship – to all the Prophets.[82]

These mirrors are the Messengers of God Who tell the story of Divinity, just as the material mirror reflects the light and disc of the outer sun in the skies. In this way the image and effulgence of the Sun of Reality appear in the mirrors of the Manifestations of God. This is what Jesus Christ meant when He declared, 'the father is in the son,' the purpose being that the reality of that eternal Sun had become reflected in its glory in Christ Himself. It does not signify that the Sun of Reality had descended from its place in heaven or that its essential being had effected an entrance into the mirror, for there is neither entrance nor exit for the reality of Divinity; there is no ingress or egress; it is sanctified above all things and ever occupies its own holy station. Changes and transformations are not applicable to that eternal reality. Transformation from condition to condition is the attribute of contingent realities.[83]

Bahá'u'lláh explains that Jesus Christ was the complete incarnation not of the essence of God but of His names and attributes:

> Know thou of a certainty that the Unseen can in no wise incarnate His Essence and reveal it to unto men. He is, and hath ever been, immensely exalted beyond all that can either be recounted or perceived. From His retreat of glory His voice is ever proclaiming: 'Verily, I am God; there is none other God besides Me, the All-Knowing, the All-Wise. I have manifested Myself unto men, and have sent down Him Who is the Day Spring of the signs of My Revelation.' . . . He Who is everlastingly hidden from the eyes of men can never be known except through His Manifestation, and His Manifestation can adduce no greater proof of the truth of His Mission than the proof of His own Person.[84]

> . . . all the Prophets of God, His well-favoured, His holy, and chosen Messengers, are, without exception, the bearers of His names, and the embodiments of His attributes.[85]

> These Tabernacles of Holiness, these primal Mirrors which reflect the light of unfading glory, are but expressions of Him Who is the Invisible of the Invisibles.[86]

And Shoghi Effendi, Guardian of the Bahá'í Faith, writes:

> The human temple that has been made the vehicle of so overpowering a Revelation must . . . ever remain entirely distinguished from that 'innermost Spirit of Spirits' and 'eternal Essence of Essences' – that invisible yet rational God Who, however much we extol the divinity of His Manifestation on earth, can in no wise incarnate His infinite, His unknowable, His incorruptible and all-embracing Reality in the concrete and limited frame of a mortal being. Indeed, the God Who could so incarnate His own reality would, in the light of the teachings of Bahá'u'lláh, cease immediately to be God. So crude and fantastic a theory of Divine incarnation is . . . incompatible with the essentials of Bahá'í belief . . .[87]

Hence, Bahá'u'lláh, Who in unnumbered passages claims His utterance to be the Voice of Divinity, the Call of God Himself, solemnly affirms:

> To every discerning and illumined heart it is evident that God, the unknowable Essence, the divine Being, is immensely exalted beyond every human attribute, such as corporeal existence, ascent and descent, egress and regress . . . He is and hath ever been veiled in the ancient eternity of His Essence, and will remain in His Reality everlastingly hidden from the sight of men . . . He standeth exalted beyond and above all separation and union, all proximity and remoteness . . . 'God was alone; there was none else beside Him' . . .[88]

> He is a true believer in Divine unity who . . . refuseth to allow any notion of multiplicity to becloud his conception of the singleness of God, who will regard the Divine Being as One Who, by His very nature, transcendeth the limitations of numbers.[89]

> Beware, beware, lest thou be led to join partners with the Lord, thy God. He is, and hath from everlasting been, one and alone, without peer or equal, eternal in the past, eternal in the future, detached from all things, ever-abiding, unchangeable, and self-subsisting. He hath assigned no associate unto Himself in His Kingdom, no counsellor to counsel Him, none to compare unto Him, none to rival His glory. To this every atom of the universe beareth witness, and beyond it the inmates of the realms on high, they that occupy the most exalted seats, and whose names are remembered before the Throne of Glory.
>
> Bear thou witness in thine inmost heart unto this testimony which God hath Himself and for Himself pronounced, that there is none other God but Him, that all else besides Him have been created by His behest, have been fashioned by His leave, are subject to His Law, are as a thing forgotten when compared to the glorious evidences of His oneness, and are as nothing when brought face to face with the mighty revelations of His unity.
>
> He, in truth, hath, throughout eternity, been one in His Essence, one in His attributes, one in His works. Any and every comparison is applicable only to His creatures, and all conceptions of association are conceptions that belong solely to those that serve Him. Immeasurably exalted is His Essence above the descriptions of His

creatures. He, alone, occupieth the Seat of transcendent majesty, of supreme and inaccessible glory. The birds of men's hearts, however high they soar, can never hope to attain the heights of His unknowable Essence . . .[90]

Thus, to His followers, Bahá'u'lláh, notwithstanding the overwhelming intensity of His revelation, is regarded as essentially one of these Manifestations of God, never to be identified with that invisible Reality, the Essence of Divinity itself.

From time immemorial . . . He, the Divine Being, hath been veiled in the ineffable sanctity of His exalted Self, and will everlastingly continue to be wrapt in the impenetrable mystery of His unknowable Essence. . .[91]

. . . whatever pertaineth to the former [Prophet, Divine Messenger], all His acts and doings, whatever He ordaineth or forbiddeth, should be considered, in all their aspects, and under all circumstances, and without any reservation, as identical with the Will of God Himself.[92]

'Abdu'l-Bahá gave the following explanation of the Trinity:

The Divine Reality, which is purified and sanctified from the understanding of human beings and which can never be imagined by the people of wisdom and of intelligence, is exempt from all conception. That Lordly Reality admits of no division; for division and multiplicity are properties of creatures which are contingent existences, and not accidents which happen to the self-existent.

The Divine Reality is sanctified from singleness, then how much more from plurality. The descent of that Lordly Reality into conditions and degrees would be equivalent to imperfection and contrary to perfection, and is, therefore, absolutely impossible. It perpetually has been, and is, in the exaltation of holiness and sanctity. All that is mentioned of the Manifestations and Dawning-places of God signifies the divine reflection, and not a descent into the conditions of existence.

God is pure perfection, and creatures are but imperfections.

For God to descend into the conditions of existence would be the greatest of imperfections; on the contrary, His manifestation, His appearance, His rising are like the reflection of the sun in a clear, pure, polished mirror. All the creatures are evident signs of God, like the earthly beings upon all of which the rays of the sun shine. But upon the plains, the mountains, the trees and fruits, only a portion of the light shines, through which they become visible, and are reared, and attain to the object of their existence, while the Perfect Man is in the condition of a clear mirror in which the Sun of Reality becomes visible and manifest with all its qualities and perfections. So the Reality of Christ was a clear and polished mirror of the greatest purity and fineness. The Sun of Reality, the Essence of Divinity, reflected itself in this mirror and manifested its light and heat in it; but from the exaltation of its holiness, and the heaven of its sanctity, the Sun did not descend to dwell and abide in the mirror. No, it continues to subsist in its exaltation and sublimity, while appearing and becoming manifest in the mirror in beauty and perfection.

Now if we say that we have seen the Sun in two mirrors – one the Christ and one the Holy Spirit – that is to say, that we have seen three Suns, one in the heaven and the two others on the earth, we speak truly. And if we say that there is one Sun, and it is pure singleness, and has no partner and equal, we again speak truly.

The epitome of the discourse is that the Reality of Christ was a clear mirror, and the Sun of Reality – that is to say, the Essence of Oneness, with its infinite perfections and attributes – became visible in the mirror. The meaning is not that the Sun, which is the Essence of the Divinity, became divided and multiplied – for the Sun is one – but it appeared in the mirror. This is why Christ said, 'The Father is in the Son,' meaning that the Sun is visible and manifest in this mirror.

The Holy Spirit is the Bounty of God which becomes visible and evident in the Reality of Christ. The Sonship station is the heart of Christ, and the Holy Spirit is the station of the spirit of Christ. Hence it has become certain and proved that the Essence of Divinity is absolutely unique and has no equal, no likeness, no equivalent.

This is the signification of the Three Persons of the Trinity. If it were otherwise, the foundations of the Religion of God would rest upon an illogical proposition which the mind could never conceive, and how can the mind be forced to believe a thing which it cannot conceive? A thing cannot be grasped by the intelligence except when it is clothed in an intelligible form; otherwise, it is but an effort of the imagination.

It has now become clear, from this explanation, what is the meaning of the Three Persons of the Trinity. The Oneness of God is also proved.[93]

3. Who was conceived by the Holy Ghost, born of the Virgin Mary

There is some ambiguity concerning the Gospel reports of the virgin birth, for they are at odds with two accounts of the genealogy of Jesus which trace His ancestry not through Mary but Joseph (Matt. 1:16 and Luke 3:23). It is also noteworthy that St Paul reminds the Jews that Jesus was not unique in not having a physical father for Melchisedech also did not have a father, neither, for that matter, a mother:

> For this Melchisedec, king of Salem, priest of the most high God . . .;
> To whom also Abraham gave a tenth part of all; first being by interpretation King of righteousness, and after that also King of Salem, which is, King of peace;
> Without father, without mother, without descent, having neither beginning of days, nor end of life; but made like unto the Son of God; abideth a priest continually.[94]

The Qur'án speaks of Jesus with reverence and describes Him as following a line of Messengers sent to preach the Gospel:

> We sent after them Jesus the son of Mary, and bestowed on him the Gospel; and We ordained in the hearts of those who followed him Compassion and Mercy . . .[95]

Islam has a high regard for Mary as a sublime model of both purity and piety, and dedicates the entire 19th Súrah of the Qur'án to *Maryam*, or Mary, praising her holiness, nobility of character and exemplary obedience to God. She is given prominent status as a supreme feminine model of sanctity and maternal virtue. The Qur'án also confirms the virgin birth of Christ but at the same time denies that God was the physical father.

> And (remember) her who guarded her chastity: We breathed into her of Our Spirit, and We made her and her son a sign for all peoples.[96]

It describes the announcement of the birth of the child to Mary and her surprise on hearing the news:

> Then We sent to her Our angel . . .
> He said: 'Nay, I am only a messenger from thy Lord, (to announce) to thee the gift of a holy son.'
> She said: 'How shall I have a son, seeing that no man has touched me, and I am not unchaste?'
> He said: 'So (it will be): thy Lord saith, "That is easy for Me: and (We Wish) to appoint him as a Sign unto men and a Mercy from Us": It is a matter (So) decreed.'
> So she conceived him, and she retired with him to a remote place.[97]

The Qur'án explains that Jesus's birth without the intervention of a father was brought about simply by the divine decree 'Be' (*kun*), 'and it is' (*fayakoonu*). When God ordains a matter, it is so, by the creative power of His command 'Be'.[98]

> Such (was) Jesus the son of Mary: (it is) a statement of truth, about which they (vainly) dispute.
> It is not befitting to (the majesty of) God that He should beget a son. Glory be to Him! When He determines a matter, He only says to it, 'Be', and it is.
> Verily God is my Lord and your Lord: Him therefore serve ye: this is a Way that is straight.[99]

This event, it asserts, was similar to the creation of Adam, the first human being who was born without a human mother or a human father.

> The similitude of Jesus before God is as that of Adam; He created him from dust,
> Then said to him, 'Be': And he was.[100]

The Bahá'í perspective

In the Bahá'í Writings, 'immaculate conception' concerns the virgin birth of Jesus, and it is in this context that 'immaculacy of Mary'[101] is referred to. In line with the Qur'án, it is accepted that Jesus came into this world through the direct intervention of the Holy Spirit, and consequently His birth was quite miraculous – the possibility of miracles by an omnipotent Creator is entertained but their importance as proof of faith is minimized. In contrast, the 'immaculacy of Mary' is understood particularly by the Catholic Church as the conception of the Virgin Mary in her mother's womb free from 'original sin'. Bahá'ís consider original sin to be a Church doctrine, but again, as they accept that Mary was sinless they have no issue with the the concept of the immaculacy of Mary:

> As to the position of Christianity, let it be stated without any hesitation or equivocation that its divine origin is unconditionally acknowledged, that the Sonship and Divinity of Jesus Christ are fearlessly asserted, that the divine inspiration of the Gospel is fully recognized, that the reality of the mystery of the Immaculacy of the Virgin Mary is confessed . . .[102]

> It would be a sacrilege for a Bahá'í to believe that the parents of Jesus were illegally married and that the latter was consequently of an illegal union. Such a possibility cannot be conceived by a believer who recognizes the high station of Mary . . . The only alternative therefore is to admit that the birth of Jesus has been miraculous. The operation of miracles is not necessarily irrational or illogical . . . The belief in the possibilities of miracles, on the contrary, implies that God's power is beyond any limitation whatsoever . . .[103]

4. He suffered under Pontius Pilate, was crucified, dead, and buried

The Qur'án asserts that Jesus was neither not killed nor crucified but was taken up by God.

> That they said (in boast), 'We killed Christ Jesus the son of Mary, the Apostle of God'; –

CHRISTIAN–ISLAMIC DOCTRINAL CONFLICTS

> But they killed him not, nor crucified him, but so it was made to appear to them, and those who differ therein are full of doubts, with no (certain) knowledge, but only conjecture to follow, for of a surety they killed him not: –
>
> Nay, God raised him up unto Himself; and God is Exalted in Power, Wise.[104]

> Behold! God said: 'O Jesus! I will take thee and raise thee to Myself and clear thee (of the falsehoods) of those who blaspheme; I will make those who follow thee superior to those who reject faith, to the Day of Resurrection: then shall ye all return unto me, and I will judge between you of the matters wherein ye dispute.'[105]

At first glance, this assertion appears entirely inconsistent with both the Jewish and Christian understanding that Jesus was crucified by Roman soldiers and died on the Cross.

A Bahá'í explanation

This centres on the intention of the Jews and their lack of success in achieving the desired result. Clearly, the Jews wished to eradicate the teachings of Jesus which were a threat to the established order. Their mistake was that they believed that by crucifying His body they would be able to frustrate the divine Will. The Quranic assertion that Jesus was not crucified and was not killed therefore refers to the failure to kill Christ, as the Word of God (*Kalimah*).

The Qur'án recounts the announcement to Zechariah of the birth of his son, John the Baptist (Yahyá), Who would bear witness to the truth of Christ, the Divine Word (*muṣaddiqan bikalimatin mina Alláhi*):

> There here did Zakaríya pray to his Lord, saying: 'O my Lord! Grant unto me from Thee a progeny that is pure: for Thou art He that heareth prayer!'
>
> While he was standing in prayer in the chamber, the angels called unto him: 'God doth give thee Glad tidings of Yahyá, Witnessing the truth of a Word from God, and (be besides) noble, chaste, and a Prophet, of the (goodly) company of the righteous.'[106]

Again, Christ is described as a 'Word' in the announcement of Jesus's birth to Mary:

> Behold! the angels said: 'O Mary! God giveth thee Glad tidings of a Word (*bikalimatin*) from Him: his name will be Christ Jesus, the son of Mary, held in honour in this world and the Hereafter and of (the company of) those nearest to God . . .'[107]

This is identical to the reference of Christ as 'the Word' in the Gospel of St. John:

> And the Word was made flesh, and dwelt among us, (and we beheld his glory, the glory as of the only begotten of the Father,) full of grace and truth.[108]

In addition, the Qur'án teaches that the Divine Word manifested in Christ had also been revealed in the past, thereby establishing God's Truth.

> Moses said: . . .'And God by His Words (*bikalimátihi*) doth prove and establish His Truth, however much the sinners may hate it!'[109]

> Already has Our Word (*kalimatuna*) been passed before (this) to Our Servants sent (by Us).[110]

In the same context Bahá'u'lláh warns that we should be on our guard in case the 'Book', the record of the revealed Word of earlier Revelations, hinder us from recognizing the 'Living Book', the Person of the Manifestation in this Day:

> Take heed lest ye be prevented by aught that hath been recorded in the Book from hearkening unto this, the Living Book.[111]

5. He descended into hell; the third day he rose again from the dead[112]

Some maintain that before His resurrection Jesus descended to hell or *sheol* (*Hades* in Greek), the 'place of the dead', and preached to the dead. This belief is not elaborated upon and is derived indirectly from the following New Testament statement:

> By which also he went and preached unto the spirits in prison;[113]

The Hebrew Bible mentions the ability of God to cause death and resurrection of individuals. However, this is usually understood figuratively and not as a literal expectation of a descent into hell followed by a raising up:

> the Lord deals death, and gives life,
> Casts down into Sheol and raises up.
> The lord makes poor and makes rich;
> He casts down, He also lifts high.
> He raises the poor from the dust . . .[114]

There are also references to a resurrection of Israel:

> Oh, let your dead revive!
> Let corpses arise!
> Awake and shout for joy,
> You who dwell in the dust! . . .[115]

> O dry bones, hear the word of the Lord!
> Thus said the Lord God to these bones: I will cause breath to enter you and you shall live again . . .[116]

According to these scriptures, the Prophet Elijah never died but was observed to ascend to heaven in a fiery chariot. Several individuals were also raised – presumably temporarily – from the dead (I Kings 17:23 and II Kings 4:36) back to life. Contact with the Prophet Elisha's bones was sufficient to raise a dead man (II Kings 13:21).

It would be more in keeping with the many other Biblucal statements that interpret life and death spiritually, to interpret the statement 'He descended into hell' as a reiteration that Christ preached also to the spiritually dead and freed their spirits from the chains of the mundane world, so that they too could ascend to heaven.

All four Gospels describe Jesus's crucifixion, death and subsequent burial in a tomb late on Friday. The tomb was later found to be empty (early on Sunday morning) and Jesus thereafter appeared to His followers. The Bible teaches that the accounts were handed down to us by those 'which from the beginning were eyewitnesses' (Luke 1:2).

There are several minor inconsistencies in the accounts: Christian scholars agree that the accounts of the Resurrection were actually written down several decades after the event and only by proselytizers. Inconsistencies include how many individuals visited Jesus's tomb; whether it was still dark outside; how many angels there were; whether they were inside the tomb or outside; whether Mary Magdalene told people about the tomb; whether she revisited the tomb; whether Jesus appeared to St Peter first; whether He appeared at all to Mary Magdalene; and whether he appeared to the twelve disciples or to several hundred.

However, these are insufficient to deny the whole event. Importantly, the historical authenticity of the crucifixion and death of Jesus is not denied by the Jews. Thus, both the Jews and Christians agree on the crucifixion and the death of Christ. It is therefore difficult to understand how the Qur'án can then deny this event. An example of the literal interpretation of the Quranic verse is to be found in the teachings of the Ahmadiyya sect, who believe that Jesus came down or was led down from the Cross and travelled to India to die in Kashmir at the age of one hundred and twenty years.[117]

Many of the pagan religions amongst whom Christians lived and preached the Gospel worshipped gods that had died and were resurrected. These included the Egyptian god Osiris, the Babylonian god Tammuz, and Mithra. The historian Edward Gibbon explains that one of the reasons for the rapid spread of Christianity in the Roman Empire was the alleged miraculous powers of the Church. As an illustration he records that the death and resurrection of ordinary Christians had become a not too unfamiliar occurrence:

> But the miraculous cure of disease of the most inveterate or even preternatural kind can no longer occasion any surprise, when we recollect that in the days of Irenaeus, about the end of the second century, the resurrection of the dead was very far from being esteemed an uncommon event; that the miracle was frequently performed on necessary occasions, by great fasting and the joint supplication of the church of the place, and that the persons thus

restored to their prayers had lived afterwards among them many years. At such a period, when faith could boast of so many wonderful victories over death, it seems difficult to account for the skepticism of those philosophers who still rejected and derided the doctrine of the resurrection. A noble Grecian had rested on this important ground the whole controversy, and promised Theophilus, bishop of Antioch, that, if he could be gratified with the sight of a single person who had been actually raised from the dead, he would immediately embrace the Christian religion. It is somewhat remarkable that the prelate of the first eastern church, however anxious for the conversion of his friend, thought proper to decline this fair and reasonable challenge.[118]

As mentioned previously, the Qur'án also maintains that Jesus went to heaven. Again, apart from the fact that there is no scientific basis for the assertion of a vertical ascent to heaven three days after the Crucifixion, the literal interpretation has scriptural objections, an important one being the following statement of Jesus to one of two individuals who were crucified with Him:

And Jesus said unto him, Verily I say unto thee, To day shalt thou be with me in paradise.[119]

Bahá'í explanations

The resurrections of the Divine Manifestations are not of the body. All Their states, Their conditions, Their acts, the things They have established, Their teachings, their expressions, Their parables and Their instructions have a spiritual and divine signification, and have no connection with material things . . .

Therefore, we say that the meaning of Christ's resurrection is as follows: the disciples were troubled and agitated after the martyrdom of Christ. The Reality of Christ, which signifies His teachings, His bounties, His perfections and His spiritual power, was hidden and concealed for two or three days after His martyrdom, and was not resplendent and manifest. No, rather it was lost, for the believers were few in number and were troubled and agitated. The Cause of Christ was like a lifeless body; and when after three days the disciples became assured and steadfast, and began to serve the Cause of Christ, and resolved to spread the divine teachings, putting His counsels into practice, and arising to serve Him, the Reality of Christ became resplendent and His bounty appeared; His religion found life; His teachings and His admonitions became evident and visible. In other words, the Cause of Christ was like a lifeless body until the life and the bounty of the Holy Spirit surrounded it.

Such is the meaning of the resurrection of Christ, and this was a true resurrection. But as the clergy have neither understood the meaning of the Gospels nor comprehended the symbols, therefore, it has been said that religion is in contradiction to science, and science in opposition to religion, as, for example, this subject of the ascension of Christ with an elemental body to the visible heaven is contrary to the science of mathematics. But when the truth of this subject becomes clear, and the symbol is explained, science in no way contradicts it; but, on the contrary, science and the intelligence affirm it.[120]

As to the resurrection of the body of Christ three days subsequent to His departure: This signifies the divine teachings and spiritual religion of His Holiness Christ, which constitute His spiritual body, which is living and perpetual forevermore.

By the 'three days' of His death is meant that after the great martyrdom, the penetration of the divine teachings and the spread of the spiritual law became relaxed on account of the crucifixion of Christ. For the disciples were somewhat troubled by the violence of divine tests. But when they became firm, that divine spirit resurrected and that body – which signifies the divine word – arose.

Likewise the address of the angels to the people of Galilee, 'That this Christ will return in the same way and that He will descend from heaven,' is a spiritual address. For when Christ appeared, He came from heaven, although He was outwardly born from the womb of Mary. For He said: 'No man hath ascended up to heaven, but he that came down from heaven.'

He said: 'I came down from heaven and likewise will go to heaven.' By 'heaven' is not meant this infinite phenomenal space, but 'heaven' signifies the world of the divine kingdom which is the supreme station and seat of the Sun of Truth.[121]

... concerning the meeting of His Highness Christ after the crucifixion and that some of the apostles perceived Him but did not recognize Him; but that they did recognize Him after the breaking of bread.

Know thou that the Messianic Spirit and the outpouring of the Holy Spirit is always manifest, but capacity and ability (to receive it) is more in some and less in others. After the crucifixion the apostles had not in the beginning the capacity and ability of witnessing the Messianic reality. For they were agitated. But when they found firmness and steadfastness their inner sight became opened, and they saw the reality of the Messiah as manifest. For the body of Christ was crucified and vanished, but the Spirit of Christ is always pouring upon the contingent world, and is manifest before the insight of the people of assurance.[122]

The Faith of Bahá'u'lláh emphasizes the spiritual significance of Christ's resurrection, and explains that the mistake of those who persecuted Christ was that they anticipated that by crucifying Him, they would extirpate the Word of God. The Word of God, the Logos, aided by the Holy Spirit, was clearly not destroyed but ultimately triumphed. Hence, although the Jews succeeded in destroying the physical body of Jesus, yet they were impotent to destroy the divine reality in Him.[123]

The Bahá'í Faith also clarifies that by the resurrection of the 'body' of Jesus is meant the resurrection of the 'body' of the Christian Faith and congregation, a concept that is consistent with New Testament statements.[124] Christ had also reassured His disciples that 'where two or three are gathered in my name, there am I in the midst of them' (Matt. 18:2). This presence is clearly not physical. Hence, the resurrection stories more aptly describe the profound spiritual transformation that the early Christian community underwent following the Crucifixion when they realized that the spirit of Christ and His teachings had conquered death, and was alive and was with them.

When Jesus Christ died upon the cross, the disciples who witnessed His crucifixion were disturbed and shaken. Even Peter, one of the greatest of His followers, denied Him thrice. Mary Magdalene brought them together and confirmed their faith, saying, 'Why are ye doubting? Why have ye feared? O thou Peter! Why didst thou deny Him? For Christ was not crucified. The reality of Christ is ever-living, everlasting, eternal. For that divine reality there is no beginning, no ending, and, therefore, there can be no death. At most, only the body of Jesus has suffered death.'[125]

This spiritual explanation of the events in no way diminishes the importance of the martyrdom of Christ. Indeed, Bahá'u'lláh, true to the promise of Christ that the Comforter would glorify Him, pays the following glowing tribute to the sacrifice of Christ and the spiritual power released by His crucifixion:

> Know thou that when the Son of Man (Jesus Christ) yielded up His breath to God, the whole creation wept with a great weeping. By sacrificing Himself, however, a fresh capacity was infused into all created things... The deepest wisdom which the sages have uttered, the profoundest learning which any mind hath unfolded, the arts which the ablest hands have produced, the influence exerted by the most potent of rulers, are but manifestations of the quickening power released by His transcendent, His all pervasive and resplendent Spirit.
>
> We testify that when He came into the world, He shed the splendour of His glory upon all created things. Through Him the leper recovered from the leprosy of perversity and ignorance. Through Him the unchaste and wayward were healed. Through His power born of Almighty God, the eyes of the blind were opened, and the soul of the sinner sanctified... He it is Who purified the world. Blessed is the man who, with a face beaming with light, hath turned towards Him.[126]

6. He ascended into heaven, and sitteth on the right hand of God the Father Almighty

There is no Gospel account to indicate that heaven is a physical place somewhere in the cosmos. Christ's ascension to heaven must be understood in the context of His other statements about 'heaven'. Although born of Mary in Bethlehem, Judea, Jesus maintained that He had come down from heaven:

> For I came down from heaven, not to do mine own will, but the will of him that sent me.[127]

On the same occasion at Capernaum, Jesus stated that He was 'the bread of life: he that cometh to me shall never hunger; and he that believeth on me shall never thirst'.[128] This claim clearly mystified His audience as, if taken literally, it could not be reconciled with the facts of Jesus's birth and upbringing amongst them:

> The Jews then murmured at him, because he said, I am the bread which came down from heaven.
> And they said, Is not this Jesus, the son of Joseph, whose father and mother we know? how is it then that he saith, I came down from heaven?[129]

In another instance, Jesus added to the confusion of Nicodemus, 'a ruler of the Jews', by declaring that whilst talking to him, He, 'the Son of man' was 'in heaven'. Moreover, He asserted that only a person who had come from heaven would go to heaven:

> And no man hath ascended up to heaven, but he that came down from heaven . . .[130]

The question to ponder, therefore, is what aspect of Jesus 'came down from heaven', 'was in heaven' and 'went to heaven'. It becomes evident that if we understand heaven as referring to God's presence and in conformity with His divine purpose, then Jesus was in heaven whilst on earth. Furthermore it was His teachings, the heavenly bread and water, that satisfied humanity's spiritual hunger and thirst that came down from the heaven of God's Will.

> . . . though, apparently, Christ was born from the womb of Mary, in reality He came from heaven, from the centre of the Sun of Reality, from the Divine World, and the Spiritual Kingdom. And as it has become evident that Christ came from the spiritual heaven of the Divine Kingdom, therefore, His disappearance under the earth for three days has an inner signification and is not an outward fact. In the same way, His resurrection from the interior of the earth is also symbolical; it is a spiritual and divine fact, and not material; and likewise His ascension to heaven is a spiritual and not material ascension.[131]

7. From whence he shall come to judge the quick and the dead

In view of the above considerations it is clear that the anticipated descent of Christ at a future date will be similar to the 'first coming'. Once again, God will reveal His purpose and by His teachings generate a new heaven and a new earth (Rev. 21:1). Through the power of His Word, both 'the quick' (or the spiritually aware) and 'the dead' (or the spiritually unresponsive) will be judged, for the kingdom of the Father Who is in heaven will come and His 'will be done in earth, as it is in heaven'.[132] Humanity will again receive the 'daily bread' (Matt. 6:9-11) and the spiritually dead Christians will be summoned to arise:

> For the Lord himself shall descend from heaven with a shout, with the voice of the archangel, and with the trump of God: and the dead in Christ shall rise first . . .[133]

> Marvel not at this: for the hour is coming, in the which all that are in the graves shall hear his voice . . .[134]

There are also verses in the Qur'án stating that God will re-resurrect and re-create man.

> From the (earth) did We Create you, and into it shall We return you, and from it shall We bring you out once again . . .[135]

Bahá'u'lláh quotes this passage in a letter to a minister of the Shah in Constantinople, 'to refute the argument of the Muslims who attach a purely literal interpretation to this verse of the Qur'án, and therefore consider it as implying bodily resurrection. To these Muslims, He says, that you who literally believe that the human body will return to dust and will be raised from it again, and therefore attach so much importance to this mortal world, how then can you wax so proud, and boast over things which are but perishable and consequently void of any true and lasting value.'[136] The passage reads:

> Rememberest thou not God's warning uttered in times past, that thou mayest be of them that heed His warning? He said, and He, verily, speaketh the truth: 'From it (earth) have We created you, and

unto it will We return you, and out of it will We bring you forth a second time.' This is what God ordained unto all them that dwell on earth, be they high or low. It behoveth not, therefore, him who was created from dust, who will return unto it, and will again be brought forth out of it, to swell with pride before God, and before His loved ones, to proudly scorn them, and be filled with disdainful arrogance. Nay, rather it behoveth thee and those like thee to submit yourselves to them Who are the Manifestations of the unity of God, and to defer humbly to the faithful, who have forsaken their all for the sake of God, and have detached themselves from the things which engross men's attention, and lead them astray from the path of God, the All-Glorious, the All-Praised. Thus do We send down upon you that which shall profit you and profit them that have placed their whole trust and confidence in their Lord.[137]

8. I believe in the Holy Spirit

The Holy Spirit may be likened to the rays that emanate from the sun and which are transmitted by individuals such as Christ Who convey the divine light to mankind. It is this Spirit of God that educates and spiritually transforms humanity:

> And He came to Nazareth where He had been brought up. And as His custom was, He went into the synagogue on the Sabbath day and stood up to read.
> And there was delivered unto Him the book of the prophet Isaiah. And when He had opened the book, He found the place where it was written:
> 'The Spirit of the Lord is upon Me, because He hath anointed Me to preach the Gospel to the poor. He hath sent Me to heal the brokenhearted, to preach deliverance to the captives, and recovering of sight to the blind, to set at liberty them that are bruised, to preach the acceptable year of the Lord . . .
> . . . 'This day is this Scripture fulfilled in your ears.'
> . . . And they said, 'Is not this Joseph's son?'[138]

The Holy Spirit is responsible for the transformation of the world and is the underlying inspiration of all earlier Dispensations:

In the beginning God created the heaven and the earth. And the earth was without form, and void; and darkness was upon the face of the deep. And the Spirit of God moved upon the face of the waters.[139]

For the prophecy came not in old time by the will of man: but holy men of God spake as they were moved by the Holy Ghost.[140]

Biblical statements such as 'For there are three that bear record in heaven, the Father, the Word, and the Holy Ghost: and these three are one'[141] are compatible with Bahá'í belief and teachings. The statements are understood in the context that Jesus did not speak or reveal anything of Himself but, as noted earlier, like a mirror only reflected and transmitted God's Light.

The Holy Spirit (*al-Rúh al-Quddus*), or simply the Spirit (*al-Ruh*), is mentioned several times in the Qur'án, and is generally interpreted as being the same as the Holy Spirit that is referred to in the Bible. Man – the spiritual man – was created through the breath of the Holy Spirit:

When I have fashioned him (in due proportion) and breathed into him of My Spirit, fall ye down in obeisance unto him.[142]

But He fashioned him in due proportion, and breathed into him something of His Spirit. And He gave you (the faculties of) hearing and sight and feeling (and understanding): little thanks do ye give![143]

The Qur'án describes the Holy Spirit as the source of inspiration of Islam, as well as of Jesus and all Dispensations:

Say, the Holy Spirit has brought the revelation from thy Lord in Truth, in order to strengthen those who believe, and as a Guide and Glad Tidings to Muslims.[144]

We gave Jesus the son of Mary Clear (Signs) and strengthened him With the holy spirit . . .[145]

(The Day) When will God say: O Jesus the son of Mary! Recount My favour to thee and to thy mother. Behold! I strengthened thee with the holy spirit, so that thou didst speak to the people in childhood and in maturity. Behold! I taught thee the Book and Wisdom ...[146]

Raised high above ranks (or degrees), (He is) the Lord of the Throne (of Authority): by His Command doth He send the Spirit (of inspiration) to any of His servants he pleases, that it may warn (men) of the Day of Mutual Meeting.[147]

The Holy Spirit sustains the faith of the individual believer:

Thou wilt not find any people who believe in God and the Last Day, loving those who resist God and His Apostle, even though they were their fathers or their sons, or their brothers, or their kindred. For such He has written Faith in their hearts, and strengthened them with a Spirit from Himself.[148]

The Bahá'í Faith teaches that the individual cannot ignore his or her spiritual nature; human beings are thus dependent on the Holy Spirit and divine assistance:

The world of humanity cannot advance through mere physical powers and intellectual attainments; nay, rather, the Holy Spirit is essential. The Divine Father must assist the human world to attain maturity. The body of man is in need of physical and mental energy, but his spirit requires the life and fortification of the Holy Spirit. Without its protection and quickening the human world would be extinguished. Jesus Christ declared, 'Let the dead bury their dead.' He also said, 'That which is born of the flesh is flesh; and that which is born of the Spirit is spirit.' It is evident, therefore, according to Christ that the human spirit which is not fortified by the presence of the Holy Spirit is dead and in need of resurrection by that divine power; otherwise, though materially advanced to high degrees, man cannot attain full and complete progress.[149]

Spiritual progress is through the breaths of the Holy Spirit and is the awakening of the conscious soul of man to perceive the reality of Divinity.[150]

The spirit of man is in need of the protection of the Holy Spirit. Just as he advances by progressive stages from the mere physical world of being into the intellectual realm, so must he develop upward in moral attributes and spiritual graces. In the process of this attainment he is ever in need of the bestowals of the Holy Spirit. Material development may be likened to the glass of a lamp whereas divine virtues and spiritual susceptibilities are the light within the glass. The lamp chimney is worthless without the light; likewise man in his material condition requires the radiance and vivification of the divine graces and merciful attributes. Without the presence of the Holy Spirit he is lifeless. Although physically and mentally alive he is spiritually dead. His Holiness Christ announced, 'That which is born of the flesh is flesh and that which is born of the Spirit is spirit,' meaning that man must be born again.[151]

9. The holy catholic Church, the communion of saints

The word 'catholic' means of interest to all, universal. As applied to the Roman Church in 1554 AD, it referred to a united Christian community that felt the presence of Christ amongst them. The following is a remarkably frank appraisal by Professor Reverend William Barclay[152] of the disunity that has infected the body of the Church:

> Those who have been, and who are still, responsible for the divisions within the Church and within individual congregations have much to answer for. The Church ought to be a united body, but the body which should be united is disintegrated into fragments. And since it is so, the weakness and the ineffectiveness of the Church are as inevitable as they are tragic . . .[153]

Explaining the 'communion of saints', he writes:

> The saints are not those who have the word 'Saint' prefixed to their names; they are not the famous examples of holiness and piety who have been canonized into saints . . . They are not so much the people who *are* different as they are people who with the help of Jesus Christ are *trying* to be different and to be Christ like . . . The phrase *the communion of saints* (is) a description of *the way in which Christian*

people in mutual care and love share everything with each other. This caring and sharing have always been the mark of the Church when it was truly Christian.

It was the mark of the life of the early Church. All those who believed had all things in common. There was not a needy person in the Christian fellowship . . . The Christians were like the members of a body. Each member had care for every other member. The need of one was the need of all and the suffering of one was the suffering of all (I Cor. 12:25-26) . . . There was in the Church a true sympathy in which each felt for and with all the others . . . A Church which has forgotten, not the obligation but the privilege of sharing, has lost the mark of a Christian Church . . .[154]

He adds:

It is the tragedy of the Church that it has been marked by division and disunity rather than by this supreme unity which ought to be the closest of all unities. We should surely regard it as an astonishing and a shocking thing to go on repeating a creed which in action we deny, and to go on affirming a belief which our practice bluntly and flatly contradicts. It is time that we remembered that the Communion Table or Altar, as the case may be, belongs to no branch of the Church, but to our Lord, and that any believer in him has the privilege of a share in holy things.[155]

Shoghi Effendi had earlier, during World War II, made a similar observation concerning this affliction of the Christian community:

What a sorry spectacle of impotence and disruption does this fratricidal war, which Christian nations are waging against Christian nations – Anglicans pitted against Lutherans, Catholics against Greek Orthodox, Catholics against Catholics, and Protestants against Protestants – in support of a so-called Christian civilization, offer to the eyes of those who are already perceiving the bankruptcy of the institutions that claim to speak in the name, and to be the custodians, of the Faith of Jesus Christ! The powerlessness and despair of the Holy See to halt this internecine strife, in which the children of the Prince of Peace – blessed and supported by the benedictions and harangues of the prelates of a hopelessly divided church – are engaged, proclaim the degree of subservience into which the once all-powerful institutions of the Christian Faith have sunk, and are a striking reminder of the parallel state of decadence into which the hierarchies of its sister religion have fallen.[156]

An inevitable analogy that may be drawn from Barclay's vivid description of the disintegration and fragmentation of the Christian community is the decomposition of a corpse. However, this Christian body is destined to be resurrected, not by its own efforts but through divine intervention.

The community of saints was reborn and magnified with the concept of *Ummah*, nation, introduced by the Qur'án, a community of believers with common beliefs, ethics, social agenda and participating in an identical divine plan of salvation. The united and sharing community derived its inspiration from the following Quranic verse:

> Verily, this Brotherhood of yours (your *Ummah*) is a single Brotherhood, and I am your Lord and Cherisher: therefore serve Me (and no other).[157]

Tragically, as described earlier, this Islamic community has suffered the same fate as the Christian community. Both are today resurrected in the community of Bahá'u'lláh:

> O army of God! Today, in this world, every people is wandering astray in its own desert, moving here and there according to the dictates of its fancies and whims, pursuing its own particular caprice. Amongst all the teeming masses of the earth, only this community of the Most Great Name is free and clear of human schemes and hath no selfish purpose to promote. Alone amongst them all, this people hath arisen with aims purified of self, following the Teachings of God, most eagerly toiling and striving toward a single goal: to turn this nether dust into high heaven, to make of this world a mirror for the Kingdom, to change this world into a different world, and cause all humankind to adopt the ways of righteousness and a new manner of life.
>
> O army of God! Through the protection and help vouchsafed by

the Blessed Beauty – may my life be a sacrifice to His loved ones – ye must conduct yourselves in such a manner that ye may stand out distinguished and brilliant as the sun among other souls. Should any one of you enter a city, he should become a centre of attraction by reason of his sincerity, his faithfulness and love, his honesty and fidelity, his truthfulness and loving-kindness towards all the peoples of the world, so that the people of that city may cry out and say: 'This man is unquestionably a Bahá'í, for his manners, his behaviour, his conduct, his morals, his nature and disposition reflect the attributes of the Bahá'ís.' Not until ye attain this station can ye be said to have been faithful to the Covenant and Testament of God. For he hath, through irrefutable Texts, entered into a binding Covenant with us all, requiring us to act in accordance with His sacred instructions and counsels.[158]

10. The forgiveness of sins

Praying directly to God for forgiveness of sins forms part of the worship of many faiths, including Judaism, as illustrated by the following prayer of King Solomon delivered before the elders of Israel.

> Then hear thou in heaven, and forgive the sin of thy servants . . .[159]

> Then hear thou from heaven thy dwelling place, and forgive, and render unto every man according unto all his ways, whose heart thou knowest; (for thou only knowest the hearts of the children of men) . . .[160]

The Psalms portray a sin-covering God Who responds to the petitions of His creation.

> Thou hast forgiven the iniquity of thy people, thou hast covered all their sin.[161]

> For thou, Lord, art good, and ready to forgive; and plenteous in mercy unto all them that call upon thee.[162]

All Christians are required to forgive each other's trespasses.

And forgive us our debts, as we forgive our debtors.[163]

But if ye forgive not men their trespasses, neither will your Father forgive your trespasses.[164]

Christian leaders who have been ordained have for centuries been given the sacramental duty of absolving others from their sins on behalf of God, notably through confession and repentance. This practice is based on Gospel statements that may also, however, be interpreted spiritually:

Whose soever sins ye remit, they are remitted unto them; and whose soever sins ye retain, they are retained.[165]

Confession of sins before a priest is also at variance with Christ's instructions that His followers should ask for forgiveness privately and directly from the Father:

But thou, when thou prayest, enter into thy closet, and when thou hast shut thy door, pray to thy Father . . .
 . . . when ye pray, use not vain repetitions, as the heathen do: for they think that they shall be heard for their much speaking.
 After this manner therefore pray ye: Our Father which art in heaven, Hallowed be thy name . . . forgive us our debts [sins], as we forgive our debtors.[166]

God is also described in the Qur'án as *Al-Afuw*,–'Eraser of sins' or 'Pardoner'; *Al-Ghaffár* (the title of the 40th Súrah) – 'the Forgiving'; and *Al-Ghaffur*, – 'the All-Forgiving' or 'the Oft-Forgiving'.[167]

The Bahá'í Faith prohibits confession to, and seeking absolution of one's sins from, a human being. Instead, one should beg forgiveness from God:

When the sinner findeth himself wholly detached and freed from all save God, he should beg forgiveness and pardon from Him. Confession of sins and transgressions before human beings is not permissible, as it hath never been nor will ever be conducive to divine forgiveness. Moreover such confession before people results in one's humiliation and abasement, and God – exalted be His glory – wisheth not the humiliation of His servants. Verily He is the Compassionate, the Merciful. The sinner should, between himself and God, implore mercy from the Ocean of mercy, beg forgiveness from the Heaven of generosity . . .[168]

To none is it permitted to seek absolution from another soul; let repentance be between yourselves and God. He, verily, is the Pardoner, the Bounteous, the Gracious, the One Who absolveth the repentant.[169]

[Bahá'ís] . . . are forbidden to confess to any person, as do the Catholics to their priests, our sins and shortcomings, or to do so in public, as some religious sects do. However, if we spontaneously desire to acknowledge we have been wrong in something, or that we have some fault of character, and ask another person's forgiveness or pardon, we are quite free to do so.[170]

Bahá'ís therefore implore the ever-forgiving God to pardon their sins and those of others:

Cast, then, upon me, O my God, the glances of Thy mercy, and forgive me my trespasses and the trespasses of them that are dear to Thee, and which come in between us and the revelation of Thy triumph and Thy grace. Cancel Thou, moreover, our sins which have shut off our faces from the splendours of the Day-Star of Thy favours. Powerful art Thou to do Thy pleasure.[171]

O God, my God! I have turned in repentance unto Thee, and verily Thou art the Pardoner, the Compassionate.
    O God, my God! I have returned to Thee, and verily Thou art the Ever-Forgiving, the Gracious.
    O God, my God! I have clung to the cord of Thy bounty, and with Thee is the storehouse of all that is in heaven and earth.
    O God, my God! I have hastened toward Thee, and verily Thou art the Forgiver, the Lord of grace abounding.
    O God, my God! I thirst for the celestial wine of Thy grace, and verily Thou art the Giver, the Bountiful, the Gracious, the Almighty.[172]

Original sin, and salvation through the blood of Christ

The Church canon of 'original sin' or 'ancestral sin' holds that the disobedience of Adam and Eve in the Garden of Eden corrupted human nature morally and ethically, the 'Fall' of mankind. Consequently, according to this doctrine, all individuals born into the world are tainted by the Fall and are ethically disabled and powerless to free themselves from this ancestral sin, unless they are rescued by the blood and sacrifice of Christ. The following Pauline statement is interpreted as justifying this belief:

> For as in Adam all die, even so in Christ shall all be made alive.[173]

Original sin was adopted as a Church doctrine largely through the arguments of St Augustine (354-430 AD). However, there are wide-ranging disagreements among Christian denominations as to the exact understanding of this doctrine, with some Christian groups rejecting it altogether.

Judaism, the Eastern Orthodox Church, and Islam acknowledge that the introduction of sin into the human race has had profound effects for mankind, but deny any inherited guilt or necessary corruption of man's nature.

The following Tanakh statement appears to justify that, through exercising his free will and obeying Divine statutes, man can overcome spiritual death, and attain spiritual life and salvation:

> When the son hath done that which is lawful and right, and hath kept all my statutes, and hath done them, he shall surely live.
>
> The soul that sinneth, it shall die. The son shall not bear the iniquity of the father, neither shall the father bear the iniquity of the son: the righteousness of the righteous shall be upon him, and the wickedness of the wicked shall be upon him.
>
> But if the wicked will turn from all his sins that he hath committed, and keep all my statutes, and do that which is lawful and right, he shall surely live, he shall not die.
>
> All his transgressions that he hath committed, they shall not be mentioned unto him: in his righteousness that he hath done he shall live.[174]

That man does not inherit sin and will be judged according to his own actions may also be concluded from by the following New Testament statements:

> ... revelation of the righteous judgment of God;
> Who will render to every man according to his deeds.[175]

> and they were judged every man according to their works.[176]

Although the Qur'án gives a similar account to the Bible of the insubordination of Adam and Eve, it also clearly states that no one receives divine punishment until sin is defined by the Author of an new Revelation, and no one bears the sins of others. It explains that 'thy Lord (is never) unjust (in the least) to His servants' (*Há-mím* or *Fuṣṣilat*, 41:46):

> Who receiveth guidance, receiveth it for his own benefit: who goeth astray doth so to his own loss: no bearer of burdens can bear the burden of another: nor would We visit with Our wrath until We had sent an apostle (to give warning).[177]

In the future Day of God every individual will also be accountable for his own deeds:

> One Day every soul will come up struggling for itself, and every soul will be recompensed (fully) for all its actions, and none will be unjustly dealt with.[178]

> O mankind! do your duty to your Lord, and fear (the coming of) a Day when no father can avail aught for his son, nor a son avail aught for his father. Verily, the promise of God is true: let not then this present life deceive you . . .[179]

The Bahá'í Writings explain that this passage alludes to the physical nature of man, inherited symbolically through Adam, and his spiritual nature, born from the bounty of the Holy Spirit:

> The Christ sacrificed Himself so that men might be freed from the

imperfections of the physical nature and might become possessed of the virtues of the spiritual nature. This spiritual nature, which came into existence through the bounty of the Divine Reality, is the union of all perfections and appears through the breath of the Holy Spirit. It is the divine perfections; it is light, spirituality, guidance, exaltation, high aspiration, justice, love, grace, kindness to all, philanthropy, the essence of life. It is the reflection of the splendor of the Sun of Reality . . . [Adam was] the cause of the physical life of mankind . . . but He is not the giver of spiritual life, whereas Christ is the cause of the spiritual life of man . . . Adam is a living soul; Christ is a quickening spirit . . .[180]

11. The resurrection of the body

There is a great emphasis here on the physical body (in the Greek, *anastasis sarkis*, and in the Latin, *resurrectio carnis*), indicating literally the resurrection of the flesh. This resurrection may also be considered to apply more aptly to the body of the community of believers – the Church and the *Ummah*. Otherwise, it is an absurd belief scientifically, and in conflict with the spiritual message of Christ in the Gospels:

> And fear not them which kill the body, but are not able to kill the soul: but rather fear him which is able to destroy both soul and body in hell.[181]

> It is the spirit that quickeneth; the flesh profiteth nothing: the words that I speak unto you, they are spirit, and they are life.[182]

It is clear from many of the statements of the disciples that they defined death and resurrection in spiritual terms:

> We know that we have passed from death unto life, because we love the brethren. He that loveth not his brother abideth in death.[183]

The Qur'án similarly is more concerned with spiritual rather than physical life and death. For example, as noted earlier it denies that Christ died, and it denounces the notion that the martyrs were dead:

> And say not of those who are slain in the way of God: 'They are dead.' Nay, they are living, though ye perceive (it) not.[184]

> Think not of those who are slain in God's way as dead. Nay, they live, finding their sustenance in the Presence of their Lord.[185]

The Qur'án also describes the Arabs as having been dead before the coming of Islam and the need for another spiritual resuscitation in the future:

> How can ye reject the faith in God? – Seeing that ye were without life, and He gave you life then will He cause you to die, and will again bring you to life; and again to Him will ye return.[186]

12. And the life everlasting

The Gospels define everlasting life as belief in 'one God' and the Author of His revelation:

> And this is life eternal, that they might know thee the only true God, and Jesus Christ, whom thou hast sent.[187]

> And this is the will of him that sent me, that every one which seeth the Son, and believeth on him, may have everlasting life: and I will raise him up at the last day.[188]

The Qur'án states that eternal paradise is the abode of the righteous:

> Say: Shall I give you glad tidings of things far better than those? For the righteous are Gardens in nearness to their Lord, with rivers flowing beneath; therein is their eternal home; with Companions pure (and holy); and the good pleasure of God. For in God's sight are (all) His servants . . .
>
> Those who show patience, firmness and self control; who are true (in word and deed); who worship devoutly; who spend (in the way of God); and who pray for forgiveness in the early hours of the morning.[189]

The Bahá'í Writings provide the following insights concerning the eternal life gained through faith:

> Whosoever acknowledged His truth and turned unto Him, his good works outweighed his misdeeds, and all his sins were remitted and forgiven... Thus God turneth iniquity into righteousness... In like manner, whosoever partook of the cup of love, obtained his portion of the ocean of eternal grace and of the showers of everlasting mercy, and entered into the life of faith – the heavenly and everlasting life. But he that turned away from that cup was condemned to eternal death. By the terms 'life' and 'death', spoken of in the scriptures, is intended the life of faith and the death of unbelief...[190]

> ... the spirit of Christ is a heavenly grace which descends from heaven; whosoever receives light from that spirit in abundance – that is to say, the heavenly teachings – finds everlasting life...[191]

The Divinity reveals His love and purpose for humanity in these words revealed by Bahá'u'lláh:

> O Son of Man! I loved thy creation, hence I created thee. Wherefore, do thou love Me, that I may name thy name and fill thy soul with the spirit of life.[192]

He thus counsels man not to barter away an eternal life because of transient aspirations:

> O My Servant! Abandon not for that which perisheth an everlasting dominion, and cast not away celestial sovereignty for a worldly desire. This is the river of everlasting life that hath flowed from the well-spring of the pen of the merciful; well is it with them that drink![193]

Christ also states that God sent Jesus because of his love for humanity 'that whosoever believeth in him should not perish, but have everlasting life' (John 3:6). The Gospels further define 'life eternal' as knowing 'thee the only true God, and Jesus Christ, whom thou hast sent' (John 17:3). In the sense that God can only be known through His Manifestations, eternal life is also theirs who acknowledge all those Revealers of the Truth. Admittedly, 'in them is life and the life is the life of men' (John 1:4), and they have all 'come that they (humanity) might have life, and that they might have it more abundantly' (John 10:10) – 'he that heareth' their 'word, and believeth on' the God that sent them, 'hath everlasting life, and shall not come into condemnation; but is passed from death unto life' (John 5:24). Similarly, the teachings of each of them 'is the bread which cometh down from heaven, that a man may eat thereof, and not die' (John 6:50). In the words of Bahá'u'lláh:

> . . . through the rise of these Luminaries of God the world is made new, the waters of everlasting life stream forth, the billows of loving-kindness surge, the clouds of grace are gathered, and the breeze of bounty bloweth upon all created things. It is the warmth that these Luminaries of God generate, and the undying fires they kindle, which cause the light of the love of God to burn fiercely in the heart of humanity. It is through the abundant grace of these Symbols of Detachment that the Spirit of life everlasting is breathed into the bodies of the dead.[194]

12

THE 'SEAL OF THE PROPHETS' (*KHÁTAM AL-NABIYYÍN*) AND THE FINALITY OF ISLAM

Consider the past. How many, both high and low, have, at all times, yearningly awaited the advent of the Manifestations of God in the sanctified persons of His chosen Ones. How often have they expected His coming, how frequently have they prayed that the breeze of divine mercy might blow, and the promised Beauty step forth from behind the veil of concealment, and be made manifest to all the world. And whensoever the portals of grace did open, and the clouds of divine bounty did rain upon mankind, and the light of the Unseen did shine above the horizon of celestial might, they all denied Him, and turned away from His face – the face of God Himself.

Bahá'u'lláh[1]

It is frequently asserted that a particular religion is superior to others. This arrogant assumption is based on misrepresentation of the divine intent and inconsistent with the total message of the scriptures. The contention is a potent source of religious intolerance, strife and discord, and often leads to denial of a promised Revelation.

They teach their followers to believe that their own form of religion is the only one pleasing to God, and that followers of any other persuasion are condemned by the All-Loving Father and deprived of His Mercy and Grace. Hence arise among the peoples, disapproval, contempt, disputes and hatred. If these religious prejudices could be swept away, the nations would soon enjoy peace and concord.[2]

Exclusivity in Islam

Muhammad – the 'Seal of the Prophets'

This title of Muhammad is considered by many Muslims to preclude the appearance of any future Prophet or Revelation.

> Muhammad is not the father of any of your men, but (he is) the Messenger of God (*rasúl-ulláh*), and the Seal of the Prophets (*khátam al-nabiyyín*) and God has full knowledge of all things.[3]

Islam: a 'complete' and 'perfected' religion

Hence, Islam does not require any addition or modification.

> The Religion before God is Islam . . .[4]

> This day have I perfected your religion for you, completed my favour upon you, and have chosen for you Islam as your religion.[5]

Islam: the only religion acceptable to God

> If anyone desires a religion other than Islam (submission to God), never will it be accepted of him; and in the Hereafter he will be in the ranks of those who have lost (all spiritual good).[6]

Islam: a religion of truth destined to triumph over other beliefs

> He it is who sent His Apostle with the Guidance and a religion of the truth, that He may make it victorious over every other religion.[7]

Exclusivity in Judaism and Christianity

Bahá'u'lláh exhorts Muslims to 'consider the past',[8] because as with many of the other issues facing Islam, the belief in the exclusivity of the Dispensation of Muhammad is best understood against the background of similar convictions held equally dogmatically by Jews and Christians. Confident in the finality and exclusivity of the Word of God vouchsafed to them, respectively, they too have not felt any need to abandon their hallowed traditions and embrace a subsequent Revelation. It was this opinion that persuaded the Jews to deny Jesus and, as attested by the Qur'án, for the Jews and Christians to reject Muhammad as an imposter.

The Jews believed that the Mosaic Law was divinely established, eternal and immutable.

And the Lord spake unto Moses, saying,

> Speak thou also unto the children of Israel, saying, Verily my sabbaths ye shall keep: for it is a sign between me and you throughout your generations; that ye may know that I am the Lord that doth sanctify you.
>
> Ye shall keep the sabbath therefore; for it is holy unto you: every one that defileth it shall surely be put to death: for whosoever doeth any work therein, that soul shall be cut off from among his people.
>
> Six days may work be done; but in the seventh is the sabbath of rest, holy to the Lord: whosoever doeth any work in the sabbath day, he shall surely be put to death.[9]

Nothing was to be added to or subtracted from the Torah:

> Now therefore hearken, O Israel, unto the statutes and unto the judgments, which I teach you, for to do them, that ye may live, and go in and possess the land which the Lord God of your fathers giveth you.
>
> Ye shall not add unto the word which I command you, neither shall ye diminish ought from it, that ye may keep the commandments of the Lord your God which I command you.[10]

What thing soever I command you, observe to do it: thou shalt not add thereto, nor diminish from it.

If there arise among you a prophet, or a dreamer of dreams, and giveth thee a sign or a wonder,

And the sign or the wonder come to pass, whereof he spake unto thee, saying, Let us go after other gods, which thou hast not known, and let us serve them;

Thou shalt not hearken unto the words of that prophet, or that dreamer of dreams . . .

Ye shall walk after the Lord your God, and fear him, and keep his commandments, and obey his voice, and ye shall serve him, and cleave unto him.[11]

After the death of Moses the servant of the Lord, it came to pass that the Lord spoke to Joshua . . . saying:

. . . be thou strong and very courageous, that thou mayest observe to do according to all the law which Moses My servant commanded thee; turn not from it to the right hand or to the left, that thou mayest prosper whithersoever thou goest.[12]

In the light of these firm injunctions of the Torah only a minority of the Jews were prepared to abandon their cherished traditions and social customs and embrace Christ as their Lord, Redeemer and Messiah,[13] or for that matter, the succeeding Dispensations of Muhammad and Bahá'u'lláh.

Initially, Jesus reassured the Jews that the laws of the Torah were eternal:

Think not that I am come to destroy the law, or the prophets: I am not come to destroy, but to fulfil.

For verily I say unto you, Till heaven and earth pass, one jot or one tittle shall in no wise pass from the law, till all be fulfilled.

Whosoever therefore shall break one of these least commandments, and shall teach men so, he shall be called the least in the kingdom of heaven: but whosoever shall do and teach them, the same shall be called great in the kingdom of heaven.

For I say unto you, That except your righteousness shall exceed the righteousness of the scribes and Pharisees, ye shall in no case enter into the kingdom of heaven.[14]

But shortly afterwards Christ abrogated and modified many of the most cherished and fundamental laws of the Torah. For example, He changed the laws concerning retaliation and divorce, and forbade oaths and passing judgement on anyone (Matt. 5:21; 5:31-5; 5:39-40); adversaries and evil were not to be resisted (Matt. 5:25; 5:38; 5:40). He re-defined adultery and mitigated the recommended punishment.

The Jewish spiritual leaders were particularly perturbed when Christ's disciples openly broke the Sabbath, one of the Ten Commandments, and in consequence they questioned His authority to preach and act as He did in open disregard of tradition and Holy Scripture. Christ's response to their objections was that as the Lord of a new Dispensation He had the necessary authority to change the social laws of the Mosaic Dispensation.

> ... the chief priests and the elders of the people came unto him as he was teaching, and said, By what authority doest thou these things? and who gave thee this authority?[15]

> And the Pharisees said unto him, Behold, why do they (disciples) on the sabbath day that which is not lawful?
> And he said unto them, The sabbath was made for man, and not man for the sabbath:
> Therefore the Son of man is Lord also of the sabbath.[16]

A new Dispensation requires a new format and a fresh set of social laws

> And Jesus said unto them ...
> No man putteth a piece of new cloth unto an old garment, for that which is put in to fill it up taketh from the garment, and the rent is made worse.
> Neither do men put new wine into old bottles: else the bottles break, and the wine runneth out, and the bottles perish: and they put new wine into new bottles, and both are preserved.[17]

The one God changes the social laws from one Dispensation to another

Jesus introduces several of the changes to the Laws of the Torah by stating 'Ye have heard that it was said of old ... but I say unto you ...' The original teachings had been given to the Jews a thousand years earlier by Moses, as He had been bidden by Jehovah. We can infer that the same God, now referred to as the Heavenly Father, intended the Jews to follow the new teachings brought by Jesus. The 'I' in Christ's statements refers to the Will of the Father:

> Verily, verily, I say unto you, the Son can do nothing of himself . . .[18]

> I can of mine own self do nothing . . .[19]

> For I came down from heaven, not to do mine own will, but the will of him that sent me.[20]

It is evident therefore that, although man cannot alter revelation during the period of a particular Dispensation, God is free to change His own teachings in future Dispensations.

Christianity in turn has been debilitated by its followers' belief that redemption is only possible through acceptance of Christ's Message. This belief led Christians to reject Islam. Today, it has cast the 'children of the kingdom' into 'outer darkness' (Matt. 8:12), and prevented them from embracing the Revelation of Bahá'u'lláh that they have prayed for every Sunday for the past two thousand years.

In their zeal to demonstrate that salvation is possible only through Jesus and none other, Christians frequently fail to comprehend the deeper meanings of 'I am', 'the way', 'the truth', 'the life', and coming 'unto the Father' (see Chapter 10):

> Jesus saith unto him, I am the way, the truth, and the life: no man cometh unto the Father, but by me.[21]

His Words are deemed to be eternal and sufficient for all time:

> Heaven and earth shall pass away: but my words shall not pass away.[22]

Nothing is to be added or subtracted from the Gospels:

> For I testify unto every man that heareth the words of the prophecy of this book, If any man shall add unto these things, God shall add unto him the plagues that are written in this book:

> And if any man shall take away from the words of the book of this prophecy, God shall take away his part out of the book of life, and out of the holy city, and from the things which are written in this book.[23]

Bahá'u'lláh reminds Muslims who believe in the exclusivity of Islam of the difficulties that a similar belief has posed for the followers of Jesus, preventing them from recognizing Muhammad:

> As is clear and evident . . . these words outwardly mean that the Books of the Gospel will remain in the hand of people till the end of the world, that their laws shall not be abrogated, that their testimony shall not be abolished, and that all that hath been enjoined, prescribed, or ordained shall endure forever.
>
> O My brother! Sanctify thy heart, illumine thy soul and sharpen thy sight, that thou mayest . . . apprehend the inner meaning of these utterances and their hidden mysteries. For otherwise, wert thou to interpret these words according to their outward meaning, thou couldst never prove the truth of the Cause of Him Who came after Jesus (Muḥammad), nor silence the opponents, nor prevail over the contending disbelievers. For the Christian divines use this verse to prove that the Gospel shall never be abrogated and that, even if all the signs recorded in their Books were fulfilled and the Promised One appeared, He would have no recourse but to rule according to the ordinances of the Gospel. They contend that if He were to manifest all the signs indicated in the Books, but decree aught besides that which Jesus had decreed, they would neither acknowledge nor follow Him, so clear and self-evident is this matter in their sight.
>
> Thou canst indeed hear the learned and the foolish amongst people voice the same objections in this day . . .[24]

Exclusivity and finality recognized as impediments

In response to Jewish and Christian objections, the Qur'án declares that salvation is achieved through deeds and is not by affiliation.

> And they say: 'None shall enter paradise unless he be a Jew or a Christian.' Those are their (vain) desires. Say: 'Produce your proof if ye are truthful.'

> Nay, whoever submits his whole self to God and is a doer of good, he will get his reward with his Lord; on such shall be no fear, nor shall they grieve.²⁵

Further to the New Testament proclamation that 'the Word of God is not bound' (II Tim. 2:9) the Qur'án brands as blasphemous notions of finality of the Torah that limit the ability of the Almighty to reveal new truths:

> The Jews say: 'God's hand is tied up (bound).' Be their hands tied up and be they accursed for the (blasphemy) they utter. Nay, both His hands are widely outstretched: He giveth and spendeth (of His bounty) as He pleaseth. But the revelation that cometh to thee from God increaseth in most of them their obstinate rebellion and blasphemy . . .²⁶

Tragically, Muslims today are committing the same 'blasphemy', allowing the term 'Seal of the Prophets' to deprive them of the divine bounty and grace.

> . . . how many are those who, through failure to understand its meaning, have allowed the term 'Seal of the Prophets' to obscure their understanding, and deprive them of the grace of all His manifold bounties!²⁷

> For, what blasphemy is greater than to turn unto the manifestations of Satan, to follow the doctors of oblivion and the people of rebellion? What impiety is more grievous than to deny the Lord on the day when faith itself is renewed and regenerated by God, the Almighty, the Beneficent?²⁸

An authoritative *hadith* predicts that Muslims would follow the erroneous ways of the Jews and Christians:

> The Prophet (Muhammad) said, 'You will follow the wrong ways, of your predecessors so completely and literally that if they should go into the hole of a mastigure (Egyptian sand-lizard), you too will go there.' We said 'O Allah's Apostle! Do you mean the Jews and the

Christians?' He replied, 'Whom else?' (Meaning, of course, the Jews and Christians).[29]

Explanations of 'Seal of the Prophets'

Khátam and Khátim

Some have argued that as the original text did not have modern diacritical marks, the title of Muhammad could easily have been either '*khátim al-nabiyyín*' (the closer or the terminator of the Prophets who preceded Him, namely, the preceding Dispensations), or '*khátam al-nabiyyín*' ('the Seal of the Prophets'), in the sense of 'the final or best of the Prophets' or 'the be-all or ultimate Prophet', similar to a seal authenticating a letter, and not a finality of any other future communications.

The theme of 'progressive revelation' is central to Bahá'í teachings.

> The fundamental principle enunciated by Bahá'u'lláh . . . is that religious truth is not absolute but relative, that Divine Revelation is a continuous and progressive process, that all the great religions of the world are divine in origin, that their basic principles are in complete harmony, that their aims and purposes are one and the same, that their teachings are but facets of one truth, that their functions are complementary, that they differ only in the non-essential aspects of their doctrines and that their missions represent successive stages in the spiritual evolution of human society.[30]

Bahá'u'lláh declares that the Manifestations of God are in essence and purpose one.

> These Countenances are the recipients of the Divine Command, and the day-springs of His Revelation. This Revelation is exalted above the veils of plurality and the exigencies of number.[31]

> 'All the Prophets of God,' asserts Bahá'u'lláh in the Kitáb-i-Íqán, 'abide in the same tabernacle, soar in the same heaven, are seated upon the same throne, utter the same speech, and proclaim the same Faith.' From the 'beginning that hath no beginning,' these Exponents of the Unity of God and Channels of His incessant

utterance have shed the light of the invisible Beauty upon mankind, and will continue, to the 'end that hath no end,' to vouchsafe fresh revelations of His might and additional experiences of His inconceivable glory. To contend that any particular religion is final, that 'all Revelation is ended, that the portals of Divine mercy are closed, that from the daysprings of eternal holiness no sun shall rise again, that the ocean of everlasting bounty is forever stilled, and that out of the Tabernacle of ancient glory the Messengers of God have ceased to be made manifest' would indeed be nothing less than sheer blasphemy.[32]

They only differ in the intensity of their revelation, and the comparative potency of their light . . . That a certain attribute of God hath not been outwardly manifested by these Essences of Detachment doth in no wise imply that they Who are the Daysprings of God's attributes and the Treasuries of His holy names did not actually possess it.[33]

Seeking the Countenance of God and the Seat of Truth

Seeking 'the Countenance of God' (*Rúm*, the Roman Empire, 30:38–9) and attaining 'the Seat of Truth' and 'the Presence of a Sovereign Omnipotent' (*Qamar*, the Moon, 54:55), lauded in the Qur'án, are interpreted in the Bahá'í Writings as attaining the presence of God's Manifestation for this age, Bahá'u'lláh.

According to the Qur'án, the 'eternal God' (*Aṣ-Ṣamad*) does not differentiate between any of the Prophets, regarding them as one (*Baqara*, the Heifer, 2:136) and establishing the same religion or *deen* (*Shúráa*, Consultation, 42:13). Bahá'u'lláh therefore does not interpret the 'Seal of the Prophets' as indicating that no further Messengers from God are possible, but rather, in the context of unity and oneness of the Prophets, the term 'Seal of the Prophets' does not apply to Muhammad only, but to each of the Prophets.

> . . . were they all to proclaim, 'I am the Seal of the Prophets,' they, verily, utter but the truth, beyond the faintest shadow of doubt. For they are all but one person, one soul, one spirit, one being, one revelation. They are all the manifestation of the 'Beginning' and the

'End,' the 'First' and the 'Last,' the 'Seen' and the 'Hidden' – all of which pertain to Him Who is the Innermost Spirit of Spirits and Eternal Essence of Essences.[34]

All the religions are hence seen as guiding humanity to the 'Right Path or Way', and no one achieves 'heaven' without their guidance. Each of the Prophets receives His decree from the same single God, Who according to the Bible is the 'Alpha and Omega' and 'the Beginning and the End' (Rev. 22:13), and Who is referred to in the Qur'án as 'the First' (*Al-Awwal*) and 'the Last' (*Al-Akhir*). Within the duration of His Dispensation the authority of a Prophet is therefore absolute and binding, and His Revelation is the ultimate expression of the Truth.

It is also in this context that certain seemingly exclusivist statements by Bahá'u'lláh are to be understood:

> The Book of God is wide open, and His Word is summoning mankind unto Him. No more than a mere handful, however, hath been found willing to cleave to His Cause, or to become the instruments for its promotion. These few have been endued with the Divine Elixir that can, alone, transmute into purest gold the dross of the world, and have been empowered to administer the infallible remedy for all the ills that afflict the children of men. No man can obtain everlasting life, unless he embraceth the truth of this inestimable, this wondrous, and sublime Revelation.[35]

'Seal of the Prophets' indicates the end of a cycle of prophecy and the beginning of a cycle of fulfilment

From time immemorial countless Prophets, including Muhammad, have announced the coming of the Báb and Bahá'u'lláh. Therefore, one sense in which the 'Seal of the Prophets' may be understood is that He was the final Prophet to predict this event. It is again in this context that Bahá'u'lláh gave the title 'King of the Messengers' (*sultán al-rusúl*) to the Báb, and the title 'Sender or Revealer of the Messengers' (*mursil al-rusúl*) to Himself.

'Seal of the Prophets' does not preclude the manifestation of Messengers

Notably, *Aḥzáb* (the Confederates), 33:40 appears to differentiate between Muhammad's two titles: Messenger of God (*rasul-u'lláh*), and Seal of the Prophets (*khátam al-nabiyyín*). Other verses also make a distinction between a Prophet (*nabi*) and a Messenger (*rasul*) e.g. *Ḥajj* (the Pilgrimage), 22:52. In general, a *rasúl*, such as Moses or Jesus, inaugurates a new Dispensation, but a *nabi*, such as the Prophets of the Old Testament, are 'warners' who remind people about ethical and spiritual values and guide individuals back to God's way, but do not abrogate previous laws or establish a new Dispensation. Some of the Prophets of the Bible expressly referred to in the Qur'án as *rasul* include Abraham (*A'ráf*, the Heights, 7:104), Noah (ibid. 7:61), Elijah (*Ṣáffát*, Those Ranged in Ranks, 37:123), and Jesus (*Ṣaff*, Battle Array, 61:6). Broadly, a *rasul* is also a *nabi* but not vice versa, as implied in the following verse:

> Those who follow the Apostle, the unlettered Prophet, Whom they find mentioned in their own (Scriptures), – In the Law and the Gospel; – For he commands them what is just and forbids them what is evil; he allows them as lawful what is good (and pure) and prohibits them from what is bad (and impure); He releases them from their heavy burdens and from the yokes that are upon them. So it is those who believe in him, honour him, help him, and follow the Light which is sent down with him, – It is they who will prosper.
>
> Say: 'O men! I am sent unto you all, as the Apostle of God, to Whom belongeth the dominion of the heavens and the earth: there is no god but He: it is He that giveth both life and death. So believe in God and His Apostle, the unlettered Prophet, who believeth in God and His Words: follow him that (so) ye may be guided.'[36]

Hence, the title of Muhammad as the 'Seal of the Prophets' negates neither a future Book (*Baqara*, the Heifer, 2:2), nor the specific promise contained in *A'ráf*, the Heights, 7:35 concerning the certain *coming* of Messengers (*rusulun*) who normally would inaugurate new Dispensations. Again, the emphatic promise that God will guide those who make an effort in His paths (*'Ankabút*, the Spider, 29:69), makes little sense if the last and best path had already been revealed and completed – the advice is more instructive if it refers also to future Revelations by a *rasul*. Bahá'u'lláh laments the fact that the clergy's reluctance to accept any new teachings has led Muslims to deny His Revelation despite the fulfilment of the many promises in the Qur'án.

> . . . their divines proclaim: 'Should all these signs come to pass and the long-awaited Qá'im[37] appear, and should He ordain, with respect to even our secondary laws, aught beyond that which hath been revealed in the Qur'án, we would assuredly charge Him with imposture, put Him to death, and refuse forever to acknowledge Him'. . . And all this, when the Day of Resurrection hath been ushered in, and the Trumpet hath been sounded, and all the denizens of earth and heaven have been gathered, and the Balance hath been appointed, and the Bridge hath been laid, and the Verses have been sent, and the Sun hath shone forth, and the stars have been blotted out, and the souls have been raised to life, and the breath of the Spirit hath blown, and the angels have been arrayed in ranks, and the Paradise hath been brought nigh, and Hell made to blaze! These things have all come to pass, and yet to this day not a single one of these people hath recognized them! They all lie as dead within their own shrouds, save those who have believed and repaired unto God, who rejoice in this day in His celestial paradise, and who tread the path of His good-pleasure.[38]

Bahá'u'lláh further explains:

> Even as He saith: 'Muhammad is not the father of any man among you, but He is the Messenger of God.'[39] Viewed in this light, they (prophets of God) are all but Messengers of that ideal King, that unchangeable Essence. And were they all to proclaim: 'I am the Seal of the Prophets' they verily utter but the truth, beyond the faintest shadow of doubt. For they are all but one person, one soul, one spirit, one being, one revelation. They are all the manifestation of the 'Beginning' and the 'End,' the 'First' and the 'Last,' the 'Seen' and 'Hidden' – all of which pertain to Him Who is the innermost Spirit of Spirits and eternal Essence of Essences.[40]

The progressive and evolutionary nature of revelation

Some indications of the progressive and evolutionary nature of revelation are also evident in the Qur'án (see Chapter 18). Certain Quranic laws were modified within the two decades of Muhammad's Ministry. For example, the Qur'án is initially neutral on the subject of wine:

> And of the fruits of the date-palm, and grapes, whence ye derive strong drink and (also) good nourishment. Lo! therein is indeed a portent for people who have sense.[41]

Later it discourages but does not forbid it:

> They ask thee concerning wine and gambling. Say: 'In them is great sin, and some profit, for men; but the sin is greater than the profit' . . .[42]

Certain restrictions were then placed on drinking:

> O ye who believe! approach not prayers with a mind befogged, until ye can understand all that ye say, nor in a state of ceremonial impurity (except when travelling on the road), until after washing your whole body if ye are ill, or on a journey, or one of you cometh from offices of nature, or ye have been in contact with women, and ye find no water, then take for yourselves clean sand or earth, and rub therewith your faces and hands. For God doth blot out sins and forgive again and again.[43]

Finally, drinking and gambling were entirely forbidden:

> O ye who believe! Intoxicants and gambling, (dedication of) stones, and (divination by) arrows, are an abomination,– of Satan's handwork: eschew such (abomination), that ye may prosper.
>
> Satan's plan is (but) to excite enmity and hatred between you, with intoxicants and gambling, and hinder you from the remembrance of God, and from prayer: will ye not then abstain?
>
> Obey God, and obey the Messenger, and beware (of evil): if ye do turn back, know ye that it is Our Messenger's duty to proclaim

(the Message) in the clearest manner.[44]

Again, the severe injunctions in the Qur'án to fight were later modified, and were further amended by 'Alí Ibn Abí Tálib (Imám 'Alí).

The Qur'án:

> O Prophet! Rouse the believers to the fight. If there are twenty amongst you, patient and persevering, they will vanquish two hundred: if a hundred, they will vanquish a thousand of the unbelievers: for these are a people without understanding.[45]

> Fight (kill) in the cause of God those who fight (kill) you, but do not transgress limits; For God loveth not transgressors.
> And slay them wherever ye catch them, and turn them out from where they have turned you out; for tumult and oppression are worse than slaughter; But fight them not at the Sacred Mosque, unless they (first) fight you there; But if they fight you, slay them. Such is the reward of those who suppress faith.[46]

'Alí Ibn Abí Tálib:

> Do not fight them unless they initiate the fighting, because, by the grace of Alláh, you are right and to leave them till they begin fighting will be another point from your side against them . . .[47]

The very harshness of many of the Qur'án's social laws is an indication that they will require to be abrogated at a future time (see Chapter 19).

The Qur'án reminds Muslims that God is omnipotent, and His Prophets and Messengers are therefore not to be questioned about their actions or the new teachings that they reveal.

> . . . for God doth command according to His will and plan.[48]

> He cannot be questioned for His acts, but they will be questioned (for theirs).[49]

> . . . for God carries out all that He wills.[50]

> Seest thou not that God merges Night into Day and he merges Day into Night; that He has subjected the sun, and the moon, each running its course for a term appointed . . .⁵¹

Bahá'u'lláh reminds the followers of religions of this essential truth:

> Blessed is the man that hath acknowledged his belief in God and in His signs, and recognized that 'He shall not be asked of His doings'. Such a recognition hath been made by God the ornament of every belief and its very foundation. Upon it must depend the acceptance of every goodly deed. Fasten your eyes upon it, that haply the whisperings of the rebellious may not cause you to slip.
>
> Were He to decree as lawful the thing which from time immemorial had been forbidden, and forbid that which had, at all times, been regarded as lawful, to none is given the right to question His authority.⁵²

God changes the Book from one Dispensation to another. The Qur'án therefore anticipates that certain of its own teachings will be cancelled and substituted for others:

> God doth blot out or confirm what He pleaseth: with Him is the Mother of the Book.⁵³

> When We substitute one revelation for another, – and God knows best what He reveals (in stages) – they say, 'Thou art but a forger': but most of them understand not.⁵⁴

Muhammad is the 'Seal' but also 'the Opener'. His Ministry ended the period of prophetic expectation and opened the period of fulfilment by announcing the coming of Bahá'u'lláh's Revelation, as also stated in the Visitation Address (*Ziyárát*) of Imam 'Alí:

> Peace be upon Thee, O Muhammad, the Seal (*khátam*) of the Prophets, the Lord of the Divine Envoys, the Trustee of God in mediating divine revelation, the One that closeth (*khátim*) that which preceded Him, the One Who openeth (*fátih*) that which will unfold in the future . . .⁵⁵

It is expected that the Promised Qá'im (He Who Shall Arise) will bring new teachings:

> How blessed is he, who lives until the appearance of the Qaim and becomes one of his assistants and woe unto whoever opposes him, objects to his orders and becomes one of his opponents.
>
> He said: 'When he (the Qaim) rises, he will rule with a new method, new principles, new Sunnah and new judgments . . . without caring for any blame, because he will act according to the will of Allah.'[56]

> Thus it is related in the 'Biháru'l-Anvár,' the ''Aválím,' and the 'Yanbú' of Ṣádiq, son of Muḥammad, that he spoke these words: 'Knowledge is twenty and seven letters. All that the Prophets have revealed are two letters thereof. No man thus far hath known more than these two letters. But when the Qá'im shall arise, He will cause the remaining twenty and five letters to be made manifest.' Consider; he hath declared Knowledge to consist of twenty and seven letters, and regarded all the Prophets, from Adam even unto the 'Seal,' as Expounders of only two letters thereof and as having been sent down with these two letters. He also saith that the Qá'im will reveal all the remaining twenty and five letters. Behold from this utterance how great and lofty is His station! His rank excelleth that of all the Prophets, and His Revelation transcendeth the comprehension and understanding of all their chosen ones.[57]

According to the Qur'án, the followers of every Dispensation or 'nation' will be judged by the contents, promises and injunctions of their own Book, and the extent to which they have been true to their specific divine revelation:

> And thou wilt see every sect bowing the knee: every sect will be called to its record: 'This Day shall ye be recompensed for all that ye did!'[58]

People are only held accountable after God has sent His Apostle and completed His testimony to them:

> Nor was thy Lord the one to destroy a population until He had sent to its Centre a messenger, rehearsing to them Our Signs; nor are We going to destroy a population except when its members practice iniquity.[59]

> Never did We destroy a population, but had its warners.[60]

Islam is considered in the Qur'án to be a 'middle' Dispensation, one interposed between earlier Dispensations and the anticipated Day of God:

> Thus We have appointed you a middle nation, that ye may be witnesses against mankind, and that the messenger may be a witness against you. And We appointed the qiblah which ye formerly observed only that We might know him who followeth the messenger, from him who turneth on his heels . . .[61]

The Revelation of the Qur'án led to the creation of (spiritual) man, but this would be followed by God teaching man the 'Bayán' – the 'Exposition' or 'Utterance':

> (God) Most Gracious!
> It is He Who has taught the Qur'án,
> He has created man:
> He has taught him (*Bayán*) speech (and intelligence).[62]

As explained by Bahá'u'lláh, the verses of God are thus revealed in direct proportion to the understanding of men:

> The measure of the Revelation of which He [Muhammad] was the bearer had been clearly foreordained by Him Who is the Almighty, the All-Powerful. They that heard Him, however, could apprehend His purpose only to the extent of their station and spiritual capacity. He, in like manner, uncovered the Face of Wisdom in proportion to their ability to sustain the burden of His Message. No sooner had mankind attained the stage of maturity, than the Word revealed to men's eyes the latent energies with which it had been endowed – energies which manifested themselves in the plenitude of their glory

when the Ancient Beauty appeared, in the year sixty, in the person of 'Alí-Muḥammad, the Báb.[63]

Hence, Bahá'u'lláh counsels Muslims:

> If ye have been careless of the Qur'án, the Bayán[64] cannot be regarded to be remote from you. Behold it open before your eyes. Read ye its verses, that perchance ye desist from committing that which will cause the Messengers of God to mourn and lament.[65]

Anticipation of a Day when the divine light of revelation will envelop the whole earth

> And the earth will shine with the glory (light) of its Lord: the record will be placed; the prophets and the witnesses will be brought forward; and a just decision pronounced between them; and they will not be wronged.[66]

PART III

SALVATION OF ISLAM

13

PROMOTION OF TRUE RELIGIOUS ENQUIRY AND ADHERENCE TO VALID CRITERIA FOR ASCERTAINING TRUTH

اِنَّ اَوَّلَ ما كتبَ اللهُ على العبادِ عرفانَ مشرقِ وحيهِ و مطلعِ امرهِ الَّذي كانَ مقامَ نفسهِ في عالَمِ الامرِ و الخلقِ مَن فازَ بهِ قد فازَ بكلِّ الخيرِ و الَّذي مُنعَ انَّهُ من اهلِ الضَّلالِ و لو أتى بكلِّ الاعمالِ

The first duty prescribed by God for His servants is the recognition of Him Who is the Dayspring of His Revelation and the Fountain of His laws, Who representeth the Godhead in both the Kingdom of His Cause and the world of creation. Whoso achieveth this duty hath attained unto all good; and whoso is deprived thereof, hath gone astray, though he be the author of every righteous deed.

Bahá'u'lláh[1]

The spiritual obligation of every Muslim to investigate the truth

Bahá'u'lláh has unequivocally declared that He is the *Nabaa Al-Azim*, the 'Great News' or the 'Great Announcement' promised in the Qur'án. It is therefore every Muslim's priority to investigate the divine Revelation destined for today. He must resist dismissing it out of hand, remembering that, without exception, all God's Prophets, including Muhammad, were branded as mischief-makers by the spiritual leaders of their time. Therefore, anticipating that Bahá'u'lláh's Message will also be misconstrued and rejected, the Qur'án warns that Muslims must evaluate any *nabaa* (message), even if its source has been labelled an evil-doer.

O ye who believe! If a wicked person comes to you with any news, ascertain the truth, lest ye harm people unwittingly, and afterwards become full of repentance for what ye have done.[2]

Prerequisites for success

Spiritual preparedness

Christ taught that only those endowed with spiritual receptivity deserved true understanding.

> Therefore speak I to them in parables: because they seeing see not; and hearing they hear not, neither do they understand.
> And in them is fulfilled the prophecy of Esaias [Isa. 6:10 and 44:18], which saith, By hearing ye shall hear, and shall not understand; and seeing ye shall see, and shall not perceive:
> For this people's heart is waxed gross, and their ears are dull of hearing, and their eyes they have closed; lest at any time they should see with their eyes and hear with their ears, and should understand with their heart, and should be converted, and I should heal them.[3]

The Qur'án also emphasizes that the expected Revelation will be recognized only by those possessed of faith and endued with righteousness.

> The day that certain of the Signs of thy Lord do come, no good will it do to a soul to believe in them then, if it believed not before nor earned righteousness through its Faith . . .[4]

It warns that those who are wilfully unjust and irrational will not discern the Light of the Promised Day.

> Nay, here are Signs self-evident in the hearts of those endowed with knowledge: And none but the unjust reject Our Signs.[5]

> . . . and God guideth not those who are perversely rebellious.[6]

> Verily, from (the Light of) their Lord, that Day, will they be veiled.[7]

Trust in God and freedom from prejudicial opinions of others

Christians are advised not to heed popular leaders who will preach what people like to hear, but to instead rigorously consider teachings that may be less familiar or palatable.

> For the time will come when they will not endure sound doctrine; but after their own lusts shall they draw to themselves teachers, having itching ears.[8]

Recognizing the difficulties faced by a seeker in this respect, Bahá'u'lláh writes:

> they that tread the path of faith, they that thirst for the wine of certitude, must cleanse themselves of all that is earthly – their ears from idle talk, their minds from vain imaginings, their hearts from worldly affections, their eyes from that which perisheth. They should put their trust in God, and, holding fast unto Him, follow in His way. Then will they be made worthy of the effulgent glories of the sun of divine knowledge and understanding, and become the recipients of a grace that is infinite and unseen, inasmuch as man can never hope to attain unto the knowledge of the All-Glorious, can never quaff from the stream of divine knowledge and wisdom, can never enter the abode of immortality, nor partake of the cup of divine nearness and favour, unless and until he ceases to regard the words and deeds of mortal men as a standard for the true understanding and recognition of God and His Prophets.[9]

He also advises against trusting the type of learning and theological wisdom that is inimical to recognizing the truth.

> O Son of Dust! Blind thine eyes, that thou mayest behold My beauty; stop thine ears, that thou mayest hearken unto the sweet melody of My voice; empty thyself of all learning, that thou mayest partake of My knowledge; and sanctify thyself from riches, that thou mayest obtain a lasting share from the ocean of My eternal wealth. Blind thine eyes, that is, to all save My beauty; stop thine ears to all save My word; empty thyself of all learning save the knowledge of

Me; that with a clear vision, a pure heart and an attentive ear thou mayest enter the court of My holiness.[10]

Realization that it is the Author of a new Dispensation Who is the standard of truth

In every new Dispensation, it is the Author of the new Revelation Who distinguishes truth from falsehood and light from darkness, and defines heaven and hell, life and death, salvation and falling from divine grace. His judgement is God's and His Revelation is neither subject to human analysis or criticism, nor is it conditioned and constrained by tradition or former teachings and understanding. The seeker must therefore readily acknowledge that God's Manifestation must not be asked of His doings, for 'He it is Who is the manifestation of "God doeth whatsoever He pleaseth", and abideth upon the throne of "He ordaineth whatsoever He chooseth" '.[11]

> Such a recognition hath been made by God the ornament of every belief and its very foundation. Upon it must depend the acceptance of every goodly deed. Fasten your eyes upon it, that haply the whisperings of the rebellious may not cause you to slip.[12]

The Pharisees and the Scribes were convinced that they were the repository of all truth and were acting in accordance with the divine will, but they were reminded that although they had the Law of Moses, they had to embrace the 'grace and truth' brought by Jesus (John 1:17) and accept Christ's teachings. They would then 'know the truth, and the truth shall make (them) free' from the shackles of misconceptions (John 8:32). Unfortunately, they were not ready to accept the truth in its latest format as attested by Jesus: 'And because I tell you the truth, ye believe me not' (John 8:45). Today, Bahá'u'lláh issues the same warning:

> O leaders of religion! Weigh not the Book of God with such standards and sciences as are current amongst you, for the Book itself is the unerring Balance established amongst men. In this most perfect Balance whatsoever the peoples and kindreds of the earth possess must be weighed, while the measure of its weight should be tested according to its own standard, did ye but know it.[13]

The seeker is empowered to discern the truth by his or her own efforts

> . . . Truth stands out clear from error; whoever rejects evil and believes in God hath grasped the most trustworthy hand-hold, that never breaks. And God heareth and knoweth all things.[14]

> God has given man the eye of investigation by which he may see and recognize truth. He has endowed man with ears that he may hear the message of reality and conferred upon him the gift of reason by which he may discover things for himself. This is his endowment and equipment for the investigation of reality. Man is not intended to see through the eyes of another, hear through another's ears nor comprehend with another's brain. Each human creature has individual endowment, power and responsibility in the creative plan of God. Therefore, depend upon your own reason and judgement and adhere to the outcome of your own investigation; otherwise you will be utterly submerged in the sea of ignorance and deprived of all the bounties of God. Turn to God, supplicate humbly at His threshold, seeking assistance and confirmation, that God may rend asunder the veils that obscure your vision. Then will your eyes be filled with illumination . . .[15]

> Rely upon God, thy God and the Lord of thy fathers. For the people are wandering in the paths of delusion, bereft of discernment to see God with their own eyes, or hear His Melody with their own ears. Thus have We found them, as thou also dost witness.[16]

He or she must rely on the assurance that God will assist those who undertake this spiritual endeavour (*jahd*) in any of His many Ways or Paths.

> And those who strive in Our (Cause) We will certainly guide them to Our Paths: for verily God is with those who do right.[17]

No one should be coerced to accept a faith, for God alone decides who will be guided

> Let there be no compulsion in religion . . .[18]

> For God leaves to stray whom He wills, and guides whom He wills. So let not thy soul go out in (vainly) sighing after them: for God knows well all that they do![19]

Valid criteria must be used to ascertain the truth

The Báb encourages Muslims to use the same proofs when evaluating truth today as they require of the Jews and Christians.

> If the followers of the Qur'án had applied to themselves proofs similar to those which they advance for the non-believers in Islám, not a single soul would have remained deprived of the Truth, and on the Day of Resurrection everyone would have attained salvation.[20]

In turn, in validating Islam and the Faith of Bahá'u'lláh, Christians must use the same criteria as they believe would convince the Jews of the truth of the Mission of Christ.

Scriptural criteria for recognizing the truth

Divine Revelations are not products of human learning

None of the Prophets had formal intellectual training. Moses had the additional impediment of stammering and His Message had to be relayed to the Israelites by Aaron.[21] Although Jesus was called 'teacher'[22] the available accounts of His childhood indicate that He did not have any rabbinical training. The Qur'án refers to Muhammad as the 'illiterate prophet'. Bahá'u'lláh also refers to the fact that He had no formal academic training or education:

> We have not entered any school, nor read any of your dissertations. Incline your ears to the words of this unlettered One, wherewith He summoneth you unto God, the Ever-Abiding. Better is this for

you than all the treasures of the earth, could ye but comprehend it.[23]

The Prophets deny ownership of their Message

The Prophets do not speak of their own volition. They deny ownership of the divine Message and instead attribute authorship to God alone; they simply abide by His will.

The Torah describes Moses, as well as a promised future Prophet, as speaking only as bidden by God.

> I [God] will raise them up a Prophet from among their brethren, like unto thee (Moses), and will put my words in his mouth; and he shall speak unto them all that I shall command him.
>
> And it shall come to pass, that whosoever will not hearken unto my words which he shall speak in my name, I will require it of him.[24]

Jesus ascribed the source of the 'Word' and His 'good works' to the Heavenly Father alone.

> I (Jesus) can of mine own self do nothing: as I hear, I judge: and my judgment is just; because I seek not mine own will, but the will of the Father which hath sent me.[25]

The Gospels add that the one who will inaugurate the 'second coming' will also not speak of Himself:

> when he, the Spirit of truth, is come, he will guide you into all truth: for he shall not speak of himself; but whatsoever he shall hear, that shall he speak . . . [26]

The Qur'án states that Muhammad revealed only what He had been taught to recite by God.

> Your Companion (Muhammad) is neither astray nor being misled,
> Nor does he say (aught) of (his own) Desire.
> It is no less than inspiration sent down to him:
> He was taught by one mighty in Power.[27]

As attested by Bahá'u'lláh in a Tablet addressing Nasiri'd-Din Shah, the monarch of Persia in whose 'black pit' dungeon (*síyáh-chál*) he had languished, He too was not the author of the Revelation vouchsafed to Him.

> By My life! Not of Mine own volition have I revealed Myself, but God, of His own choosing, hath manifested Me. In the Tablet, addressed to His Majesty the Sháh – may God, blessed and glorified be He, assist him – these words have streamed from the tongue of this Wronged One:
>
> O King! I was but a man like others, asleep upon My couch, when lo, the breezes of the All-Glorious were wafted over Me, and taught Me the knowledge of all that hath been. This thing is not from Me, but from One Who is Almighty and All-Knowing. And He bade Me lift up My voice between earth and heaven, and for this there befell Me what hath caused the tears of every man of understanding to flow. The learning current amongst men I studied not; their schools I entered not. Ask of the city wherein I dwelt, that thou mayest be well assured that I am not of them who speak falsely. This is but a leaf which the winds of the will of thy Lord, the Almighty, the All-Praised, have stirred. Can it be still when the tempestuous winds are blowing? Nay, by Him Who is the Lord of all Names and Attributes! They move it as they list.[28]

> By God! He, the Glory of God (Bahá), hath spoken not from mere impulse. He that hath given Him a voice is He that hath given a voice unto all things, that they may praise and glorify Him. There is none other God but Him, the One, the Incomparable, the Lord of strength, the Unconditioned.[29]

Power of the Word of God

The divine origin of a Revelation is established by goodly spiritual outcomes that are only possible through the creative power of the Word of God. The divine Word resurrects the spiritually dead, transforms humanity, provides a fresh impetus, and advances civilization.

The seeker can readily ascertain that the Revelations of Christ, Muhammad and Bahá'u'lláh were the cause of spiritual transformation in individuals and societies. The seeker can then attribute their teachings to God, for only the Divine, the Source of all good, can bring about such a profound change.

The Torah teaches that a Prophet must be recognized by the creative power of His Word:

> And if thou say in thine heart, How shall we know the word which the Lord hath not spoken?
> When a prophet speaketh in the name of the Lord, if the thing follow not, nor come to pass, that is the thing which the Lord hath not spoken, but the prophet hath spoken it presumptuously: thou shalt not be afraid of him.[30]

It is by this criterion that the Gospels expect Christ's teachings to be judged:

> He came unto his own, and his own received him not.
> But as many as received him, to them gave he power to become the sons of God, even to them that believe on his name:
> Which were born, not of blood, nor of the will of the flesh, nor of the will of man, but of God.[31]

> Either make the tree good, and his fruit good; or else make the tree corrupt, and his fruit corrupt: for the tree is known by his fruit.[32]

The Apostle Paul testified to this spiritual rebirth:

> Therefore if any man be in Christ, he is a new creature: old things are passed away; behold, all things are become new.[33]

Jesus also required that Christians judge future claims of prophethood by this same standard:

> Ye shall know them by their fruits. Do men gather grapes of thorns, or figs of thistles?
> Even so every good tree bringeth forth good fruit; but a corrupt tree bringeth forth evil fruit.
> A good tree cannot bring forth evil fruit, neither can a corrupt tree bring forth good fruit.

Every tree that bringeth not forth good fruit is hewn down, and cast into the fire.
Wherefore by their fruits ye shall know them.[34]

The Gospels regard Christ and the divine Word (*logos*), capable of new creation, as one and the same:

In the beginning was the Word, and the Word was with God, and the Word was God.
The same was in the beginning with God.
All things were made by him; and without him was not any thing made that was made.
In him was life; and the life was the light of men.[35]

And then shall they see the Son of man coming in the clouds with great power and glory.[36]

As stated in the Lord's Prayer, the kingdom is God's and Christ will return again with great 'power' and 'glory' (*Bahá*) for the refreshing and 'restitution of all things'(Acts 3:19, 21).

And lead us not into temptation, but deliver us from evil: For thine is the kingdom, and the power, and the glory, for ever. Amen.[37]

Using an identical parable to the one cited above (Matt. 7:16–20), the Qur'án indicates that God assists those who truly believe and will not guide those who do not do good:

. . . a goodly Word like a goodly tree, whose root is firmly fixed, and its branches (reach) to the heavens –
It brings forth its fruit at all times, by the leave of its Lord. So God sets forth parables for men, in order that they may receive admonition. . .
God will establish in strength those who believe, with the Word that stands firm, in this world and in the Hereafter; but God will leave, to stray, those who do wrong: God doeth what He willeth.[38]

Bahá'u'lláh also, in several of His Writings, reminds us that all

Revelations including His own must be judged by this standard:

> The Word of God may be likened unto a sapling, whose roots have been implanted in the hearts of men. It is incumbent upon you to foster its growth through the living waters of wisdom, of sanctified and holy words, so that its root may become firmly fixed and its branches may spread out as high as the heavens and beyond.[39]

> Verily this is that Most Great Beauty, foretold in the Books of the Messengers, through Whom truth shall be distinguished from error and the wisdom of every command shall be tested. Verily He is the Tree of Life that bringeth forth the fruits of God, the Exalted, the Powerful, the Great.[40]

> We ask for neither meed nor reward. 'We nourish your souls for the sake of God; we seek from you neither recompense nor thanks.' This is the food that conferreth everlasting life upon the pure in heart and the illumined in spirit. This is the bread of which it is said: 'Lord, send down upon us Thy bread from heaven.' This bread shall never be withheld from them that deserve it, nor can it ever be exhausted. It groweth everlastingly from the tree of grace; it descendeth at all seasons from the heavens of justice and mercy. Even as He saith: 'Seest thou not to what God likeneth a good word? To a good tree; its root firmly fixed, and its branches reaching unto heaven: yielding its fruit in all seasons.'[41]

Thus, initially a Muslim may begin his or her search by examining the fruits of the tree of the Bahá'u'lláh's Revelation. If the fruit is good, and if the new teachings advance the truest interests of Islam and advance the process of its regeneration and resurrection, then the seeker has to acknowledge the validity of its message.

Today the transforming power of the Faith of Bahá'u'lláh is evident to every unbiased observer:

> the primary reason why the Báb and Bahá'u'lláh chose to appear in Persia, and to make it the first repository of their Revelation, was because, of all the peoples and nations of the civilized world, that race and nation had . . . sunk to such ignominious depths, and

manifested so great a perversity, as to find no parallel among its contemporaries. For no more convincing proof could be adduced demonstrating the regenerating spirit animating the Revelations proclaimed by the Báb and Bahá'u'lláh than their power to transform what can be truly regarded as one of the most backward, the most cowardly, and perverse of peoples into a race of heroes, fit to effect in turn a similar revolution in the life of mankind. To have appeared among a race or nation which by its intrinsic worth and high attainments seemed to warrant the inestimable privilege of being made the receptacle of such a Revelation would in the eyes of an unbelieving world greatly reduce the efficacy of that Message, and detract from the self-sufficiency of its omnipotent power.[42]

The Prophet Daniel had alluded to truths that were as yet sealed,[43] and the Qur'án has promised the unsealing of pure or choice wine.[44] With reference to these pronouncements Bahá'u'lláh proclaims:

> Think not that We have revealed unto you a mere code of laws. Nay, rather, We have unsealed the choice Wine with the fingers of might and power.[45]

A new divine Revelation invariably attracts hostility from leaders of earlier Dispensations

The bright light of divine guidance often induces spiritual blindness. To this testifies the Tanakh:

> Declare this in the house of Jacob, and publish it in Judah, saying,
>   Hear now this, O foolish people, and without understanding; which have eyes, and see not; which have ears, and hear not.[46]

> And he said, Go, and tell this people, Hear ye indeed, but understand not; and see ye indeed, but perceive not.
>   Make the heart of this people fat, and make their ears heavy, and shut their eyes; lest they see with their eyes, and hear with their ears, and understand with their heart, and convert, and be healed.[47]

The Gospels also bear witness to the same misfortune:

But though he had done so many miracles before them, yet they believed not on him:

That the saying of Esaias the prophet might be fulfilled, which he spake, Lord, who hath believed our report? and to whom hath the arm of the Lord been revealed?

Therefore they could not believe, because that Esaias said again,

He hath blinded their eyes, and hardened their heart; that they should not see with their eyes, nor understand with their heart, and be converted, and I should heal them.[48]

The Qur'án too bewails this tragedy:

Among them are some who (pretend to) listen to thee: but canst thou make the deaf to hear – even though they are without understanding?

And among them are some who look at thee: but canst thou guide the blind – even though they will not see?[49]

Such are the men whom God has cursed for He has made them deaf and blinded their sight.[50]

Had We sent this as a Qur'án (in a language) other than Arabic, they would have said: 'Why are not its verses explained in detail? What! (a Book) not in Arabic and (a Messenger) an Arab?' Say: 'It is a guide and a healing to those who believe; and for those who believe not, there is a deafness in their ears, and it is blindness in their (eyes); they are (as it were) being called from a place far distant!'[51]

Deaf, dumb, and blind, they will not return (to the path).[52]

The divine Word survives and triumphs despite unrelenting opposition and fierce persecution

The light of the Gospels triumphed over darkness:

And the light shineth in darkness; and the darkness comprehended it not.[53]

The Qur'án declares that a corrupt tree does not survive – it has 'no staying power'[54] and is 'wholly unable to endure'[55]

> And the similitude of a bad saying is as a bad tree, uprooted from upon the earth, possessing no stability.[56]

> We will, without doubt, help Our apostles and those who believe, (both) in this world's life and on the Day when the Witnesses will stand forth.[57]

> God has decreed: 'It is I and My Messenger who must prevail': For God is One full of strength, able to enforce His Will.[58]

> And say: 'Truth has (now) arrived, and falsehood perished: for falsehood is (by its nature) bound to perish.'[59]

Constancy of the Prophet

Only through divine assurance and assistance can the Prophets of God even contemplate undertaking the arduous task ahead of them. For example, Nicodemus, a member of the Sanhedrin, admitted that Jesus had to have been assisted by God:

> The same came to Jesus by night and said to Him, 'Rabbi, we know that thou art a teacher come from God: for no man can do these miracles that thou doest, except God be with him.'[60]

The Qur'án advances 'constancy' of the Messengers as evidence of the divine origin of their Message:

> Rejected were the Apostles before thee: with patience and constancy they bore their rejection and their wrongs, until Our aid did reach them: there is none that can alter the Words (and Decrees) of God. Already hast thou received some account of those Apostles.[61]

Bahá'u'lláh explains that the 'constancy' of the Báb is a proof of His Mission:

Another proof and evidence of the truth of this Revelation, which amongst all other proofs shineth as the sun, is the constancy of the eternal Beauty in proclaiming the Faith of God. Though young and tender of age, and though the Cause He revealed was contrary to the desire of all the peoples of earth, both high and low, rich and poor, exalted and abased, king and subject, yet He arose and steadfastly proclaimed it. All have known and heard this. He was afraid of no one; He was regardless of consequences.[62]

He exclaims:

Could such a thing be made manifest except through the power of a Divine Revelation and the potency of God's invincible Will? By the righteousness of God! Were any one to entertain so great a Revelation in his heart the thought of such a declaration would alone confound him! Were the hearts of all men to be crowded into his heart, he would still hesitate to venture upon so awful an enterprise. He could achieve it only by the permission of God, only if the channel of his heart were to be linked with the Source of divine grace, and his soul be assured of the unfailing sustenance of the Almighty. To what, We wonder, do they ascribe so great a daring?[63]

Referring to His own Revelation Bahá'u'lláh writes:

Unveiled and unconcealed, this Wronged One hath, at all times, proclaimed before the face of all the peoples of the world that which will serve as the key for unlocking the doors of sciences, of arts, of knowledge, of well-being, of prosperity and wealth. Neither have the wrongs inflicted by the oppressors succeeded in silencing the shrill voice of the Most Exalted Pen, nor have the doubts of the perverse or of the seditious been able to hinder Him from revealing the Most Sublime Word.[64]

And again:

Can anyone speak forth of his own accord that for which all men, both high and low, will protest against him? Nay, by Him Who taught the Pen the eternal mysteries, save him whom the grace of the Almighty, the All-Powerful, hath strengthened.⁶⁵

'Desire for death'

The word 'martyr', which is Greek in origin, and its Arabic equivalent '*shahid*' translate as 'testimony' or 'witness'. Embracing sacrifice in God's Path differentiates people imbued with living faith from those for whom religion is defined by tradition and ceremonies and has simply become a convenience:

> Say: 'O ye that stand on Judaism! If ye think that ye are friends to God, to the exclusion of (other) men, then express your desire for death, if ye are truthful!'
> But never will they express their desire (for death), because of the (deeds) their hands have sent on before them! And God knows well those that do wrong!⁶⁶

In the Bible, the martyrdom of Stephen, the first Christian to give his life for Christ, dramatically illustrates this testimony of Faith.

> When they (members of the Jewish council) heard these things, they were cut to the heart, and they gnashed on him (Stephen) with their teeth.
> But he, being full of the Holy Ghost, looked up steadfastly into heaven, and saw the glory of God, and Jesus standing on the right hand of God,
> And said, Behold, I see the heavens opened, and the Son of man standing on the right hand of God.
> Then they cried out with a loud voice, and stopped their ears, and ran upon him with one accord,
> And cast him out of the city, and stoned him: and the witnesses laid down their clothes at a young man's feet, whose name was Saul.
> And they stoned Stephen, calling upon God, and saying, Lord Jesus, receive my spirit.
> And he kneeled down, and cried with a loud voice, Lord, lay not this sin to their charge. And when he had said this, he fell asleep.⁶⁷

The sufferings of Muhammad and Christ, and indeed of all the Prophets of God, are attested to by Bahá'u'lláh. Their sacrifice and fortitude, and that of their followers, should have been ample evidence of their sincerity and the truth of their Cause.

> Since the Seal of the Prophets (Muhammad) – may all else but Him be His sacrifice – and before Him the Spirit of God (Jesus), as far back as the First Manifestation, all have at the time of Their appearance suffered grievously. Some were held to be possessed, others were called impostors, and were treated in a manner that the pen is ashamed to describe. By God! There befell Them what hath made all created things to sigh, and yet the people are, for the most part, sunk in manifest ignorance! We pray God to assist them to return unto Him, and to repent before the door of His mercy. Potent is He over all things.[68]

The intense sufferings of the Báb and Bahá'u'lláh and of their followers are a dramatic ongoing example of this testimony. The following statements of Bahá'u'lláh concerning its importance of are self-explanatory:

> Glory to Thee, O my God! But for the tribulations which are sustained in Thy path, how could Thy true lovers be recognized; and were it not for the trials which are borne for love of Thee, how could the station of such as yearn for Thee be revealed? Thy might beareth me witness! The companions of all who adore Thee are the tears they shed, and the comforters of such as seek Thee are the groans they utter, and the food of them who haste to meet Thee is the fragments of their broken hearts.
>
> How sweet to my taste is the bitterness of death suffered in Thy path, and how precious in my estimation are the shafts of Thine enemies when encountered for the sake of the exaltation of Thy word! Let me quaff in Thy Cause, O my God, whatsoever Thou didst desire, and send down upon me in Thy love all Thou didst ordain. By Thy glory! I wish only what Thou wishest, and cherish what Thou cherishest. In Thee have I, at all times, placed my whole trust and confidence.[69]

Consider these martyrs of unquestionable sincerity, to whose truthfulness testifieth the explicit text of the Book, and all of whom, as thou hast witnessed, have sacrificed their life, their substance, their wives, their children, their all, and ascended unto the loftiest chambers of Paradise. Is it fair to reject the testimony of these detached and exalted beings to the truth of this pre-eminent and Glorious Revelation, and to regard as acceptable the denunciations which have been uttered against this resplendent Light by this faithless people, who for gold have forsaken their faith, and who for the sake of leadership have repudiated Him Who is the First Leader of all mankind? This, although their character is now revealed unto all people who have recognized them as those who will in no wise relinquish one jot or one tittle of their temporal authority for the sake of God's holy Faith, how much less their life, their substance, and the like.[70]

... they [followers of Bahá'u'lláh] have been tormented by day and by night with the fierceness of the Royal anger, and . . . they have been cast each one into a [different] land by the blasts of the tempests of the King's wrath. How many children have been left fatherless! How many fathers have become childless! How many mothers have not dared, through fear and dread, to mourn over their slaughtered children! Many [were] the servants [of God] who at eve were in the utmost wealth and opulence, and at dawn were beheld in the extreme of poverty and abasement! There is no land but hath been dyed with their blood and no air whereunto their groanings have not arisen. And during these few years the arrows of affliction have rained down without intermission from the clouds of fate. Yet, notwithstanding all these visitations and afflictions, the fire of divine love is in such fashion kindled in their hearts that, were they all to be hewn in pieces, they would not forswear the love of the Beloved of all the dwellers upon earth; nay rather with their whole souls do they yearn and hope for what may befall [them] in the way of God.

O King! . . . The Merciful Lord saith in the Furqán [the Qur'án], which is the enduring proof amidst the host of existences, 'Desire death, then, if ye be sincere.' He hath declared the desiring of death to be the proof of sincerity; and it will be apparent in the mirror of the [King's] luminous mind which party it is that hath this day foregone life in the way of Him [Who is] adored by the dwellers upon earth. Had the doctrinal books of this people, [composed] in proof of that wherein they are, been written with the blood which has been shed in His way (exalted is He), books innumerable would assuredly have been apparent and visible amongst mankind.

How, then, can one repudiate this people, whose words and deeds are consistent, and accept those persons who neither have foregone nor will forego one atom of the consideration [which they enjoy] in the way of [God] the Sovereign?[71]

One example recorded in Bahá'í historical documents will suffice here amongst the numerous accounts of martyrdom that testify of faith.

In Yazd, at the instigation of the mujtahid of that city, and by order of . . . the governor . . . seven were done to death in a single day in horrible circumstances. The first of these, a twenty-seven year old youth, 'Alí-Aṣghar, was strangled, his body delivered into the hands of some Jews who, forcing the dead man's six companions to come with them, dragged the corpse through the streets, surrounded by a mob of people and soldiers beating drums and blowing trumpets, after which, arriving near the Telegraph Office, they beheaded the eighty-five year old Mullá Mihdí and dragged him in the same manner to another quarter of the city, where, in view of a great throng of onlookers, frenzied by the throbbing strains of the music, they executed Áqá 'Alí in like manner. Proceeding thence to the house of the local mujtahid, and carrying with them the four remaining companions, they cut the throat of Mullá 'Alíy-i-Sabzivárí, who had been addressing the crowd and glorying in his imminent martyrdom, hacked his body to pieces with a spade, while he was still alive, and pounded his skull to a pulp with stones. In another quarter, near the Mihríz gate, they slew Muḥammad-Báqir, and afterwards, in the Maydán-i-Khán, as the music grew wilder and drowned the yells of the people, they beheaded the survivors who remained, two brothers in their early twenties, 'Alí-Aṣghar and Muḥammad-Ḥasan. The stomach of the latter was ripped open and his heart and liver plucked out, after which his head was impaled on a spear, carried aloft, to the accompaniment of music, through the streets of the city, and suspended on a mulberry tree, and stoned by a great concourse of people. His body was cast before the door of his mother's house, into which women deliberately entered to dance and make merry. Even pieces of their flesh were carried away to be used as a medicament. Finally, the head of Muḥammad-Ḥasan was attached to the lower part of his body and, together with those of the other martyrs, was borne to the outskirts of the city and so viciously pelted with stones that the skulls were broken, whereupon they compelled the Jews to carry the remains and throw them into a pit in the plain of Salsabíl. A holiday was declared by the governor for the people, all the shops were closed by his order, the city was illuminated at night, and festivities proclaimed the consummation of one of the most barbarous acts perpetrated in modern times.[72]

Bahá'u'lláh described the circumstances of the martyrdom of these seven in a Tablet addressed to *The Times* of London. Mullá 'Alíy-i-Sabzivárí, one of the seven, 'proclaimed the Cause of God at the very moment of martyrdom, and testified to its truth with his own life-blood. Just before he was beheaded, he cried aloud to the teeming multitudes who had assembled around him, these soul-stirring words: 'At the time of his martyrdom on the plane of Karbilá, Imám Ḥusayn, the Prince of Martyrs,[73] called out to those around him, "Is there any one capable of helping, to help me [*hal min násiren yansoroni*]." And I say to you: Is there any one capable of beholding, to behold me [*hal min náziren yanzoroni*]![74] – a reminder of Christ's frequent plea, 'He that hath eyes to see, let him see.'

The concept of martyrdom (*shahádat*) – death suffered as a consequence of compassionately, lovingly and peacefully testifying to one's faith – has today been debased. True martyrdom is suffering and death that is inflicted on a believer by tyrannical elements that attempt to extirpate the nascent Faith of God. This must be differentiated from the so-called 'martyrdom' of fanatics and radicals today, who die in the process of terrorizing and killing others by despicable and evil methods, and whose motivation is anticipated mundane rewards in the next world.

Consistency of the Divine Message

Defending the Qur'án, Muhammad stated that its Message had not wavered during the period of its revelation; if it had been the product of human endeavour it would be full of contradictions.

Do they not consider the Qur'án (with care)? Had it been from other than God, they would surely have found therein much discrepancy.[75]

It is noteworthy that the duration of Bahá'u'lláh's Ministry was almost twice as long as that of Muhammad. Hence, the consistency of His Message of love, amity and the oneness of God, oneness of faith, and oneness of humanity – despite forty years of exile and imprisonment – should according to this Súrah provide Muslims with a powerful proof of the validity of Bahá'u'lláh's Mission.

Physical miracles and literal fulfilment of prophecies are not valid criteria

Most religions attribute miracles to their Prophets. However, it is their followers who emphasize alleged miracles as evidence of the authenticity and superiority of their faiths – their Founders de-emphasize the relevance of miracles and resist calls to perform extraordinary deeds in support of their Missions.

The Gospels record Christ's refusal to perform any miracle in His lifetime:

> Then certain of the scribes and of the Pharisees answered, saying, Master we would see a sign from thee.
>
> But he answered and said unto them, An evil and adulterous generation seeketh a sign; and there shall no sign given to it, but the sign of the prophet Jonas;
>
> For as Jonas was three days and three nights in the whale's belly; so shall the Son of man be three days and three nights in the heart of the earth.[76]

Hence, although the Bible attributes many apparently physical miracles to Jesus, He vehemently declined to perform any miraculous deeds to induce acceptance of His Message. The only miracle the Jews were going to witness would be His death and resurrection, and even then no one witnessed an actual physical resurrection.

Furthermore, the miracles attributed to Jesus often did not convince even those who witnessed them.

> Then was brought unto him one possessed with a devil, blind, and dumb: and he healed him, insomuch that the blind and dumb both spake and saw.
>
> And all the people were amazed, and said, Is not this the son of David?
>
> But when the Pharisees heard it, they said, This fellow doth not cast out devils, but by Beelzebub the prince of the devils.[77]

The Qur'án also dismisses miracles:

> The unbelievers say: 'Why is not a sign sent down to him from his Lord?' Say: 'Truly God leaveth, to stray, whom He will; but He guideth to Himself those who turn to Him in penitence.'[78]

> Yet they say: 'Why are not Signs sent down to him from his Lord?' Say: 'the Signs are indeed with God: and I am indeed a clear Warner.'
>
> And is it not enough for them that We have sent down to thee the Book which is rehearsed to them? Verily, in it is mercy and a reminder to those who believe.[79]

The view expressed in Bahá'í scripture is that since the Prophets derive their power from God, they are certainly capable of performing physical miracles. However, the miracles attributed to them must not be used as proofs of the validity of their Message.

The Holy Manifestations are the sources of miracles and the originators of wonderful signs. For Them, any difficult and impracticable thing is possible and easy. For through a supernatural power wonders appear from Them; and by this power, which is beyond nature, They influence the world of nature. From all the Manifestations marvellous things have appeared.

> But in the Holy Books an especial terminology is employed, and for the Manifestations these miracles and wonderful signs have no importance. They do not even wish to mention them. For if we consider miracles a great proof, they are still only proofs and arguments for those who are present when they are performed, and not for those who are absent.[80]

. . . miracles are proofs for the eyewitness only, and even he may regard them not as a miracle but as an enchantment. Extraordinary feats have also been related of some conjurors.[81]

Many of the miracles, such as healing the blind and the deaf, or raising the dead, also have spiritual explanations that are more in keeping with a prophetic mission. Many of the Tanakh statements that refer to the 'deafness' and 'blindness' of the people, and their ability to see are clearly intended to be understood allegorically:

And the glory of the Lord shall be revealed, and all flesh shall see it together: for the mouth of the Lord hath spoken it.[82]

. . . so He will sprinkle many nations. Kings will shut their mouths because of Him, For they will see what had not been told them, and they will understand what they had not heard.[83]

The New Testament emphasizes spiritual explanations in preference to literal interpretations – an approach which the Gospels explain was valid both at the first and the second coming.

But the hour cometh, and now is, when the true worshippers shall worship the Father in spirit and in truth: for the Father seeketh such to worship him.
God is a Spirit: and they that worship him must worship him in spirit and in truth.[84]

Now we have received, not the spirit of the world, but the spirit which is of God; that we might know the things that are freely given to us of God.
Which things also we speak, not in the words which man's wisdom teacheth, but which the Holy Ghost teacheth; comparing spiritual things with spiritual.
But the natural man receiveth not the things of the Spirit of God: for they are foolishness unto him: neither can he know them, because they are spiritually discerned.[85]

And such trust have we through Christ to God-ward:

> Not that we are sufficient of ourselves to think any thing as of ourselves; but our sufficiency is of God;
> Who also hath made us able ministers of the new testament; not of the letter, but of the spirit: for the letter killeth, but the spirit giveth life.[86]
>
> While we look not at the things which are seen, but at the things which are not seen: for the things which are seen are temporal; but the things which are not seen are eternal.[87]

It is evident from the following Gospel account that Jesus was using the terms 'bread' and 'heaven' in a spiritual context:

> This is that bread which came down from heaven: not as your fathers did eat manna, and are dead: he that eateth of this bread shall live for ever . . .
> Many therefore of his disciples, when they had heard this, said, This is an hard saying; who can hear it?
> When Jesus knew in himself that his disciples murmured at it, he said unto them, Doth this offend you?
> What and if ye shall see the Son of man ascend up where he was before?
> It is the spirit that quickeneth; the flesh profiteth nothing: the words that I speak unto you, they are spirit, and they are life.[88]

It is also reasonable to assume from the following pronouncements of Christ that He intended the terms 'dead', 'light' and 'darkness', 'sight' and 'blindness' to be understood allegorically:

> Another of the disciples said to Him, 'Lord, permit me first to go and bury my father.'
> But Jesus said to him, 'Follow Me, and allow the dead to bury their own dead.'[89]

> For this people's heart is waxed gross, and their ears are dull of hearing, and their eyes they have closed; lest at any time they should see with their eyes, and hear with their ears, and should understand with their heart, and should be converted, and I should heal them.[90]

I am come a light into the world, that whosoever believeth on me should not abide in darkness.[91]

It is also clearly in the same context that He calls the Jewish religious leaders 'blind' (Matt. 23:26, 46).

The Qur'án differentiates between explicit or firm texts (*muhkam*) and allegorical (*mutáshabih*) statements (*Ál-i-'Imrán*, the Family of 'Imrán, 3:7). It often refers to its use of metaphors ('similitudes') to illustrate spiritual concepts.

> And such are the parables we set forth for mankind,
> But only those understand them who have Knowledge.[92]

Those gifted with hearing will believe. The spiritually dead will have to be resurrected by God:

> Those who listen (in truth), be sure, will accept: as to the dead, God will raise them up; then will they be turned unto Him.[93]

Finally, the Bahá'í writings offer the following criteria for accepting the Faith of Bahá'u'lláh:

> Not by the material resources which the members of this infant community can now summon to their aid; not by the numerical strength of its present-day supporters; nor by any direct tangible benefits its votaries can as yet confer upon the multitude of the needy and the disconsolate among their countrymen, should its potentialities be tested or its worth determined. Nowhere but in the purity of its precepts, the sublimity of its standards, the integrity of its laws, the reasonableness of its claims, the comprehensiveness of its scope, the universality of its programme, the flexibility of its institutions, the lives of its founders, the heroism of its martyrs, and the transforming power of its influence, should the unprejudiced observer seek to obtain the true criterion that can enable him to fathom its mysteries or to estimate its virtue.[94]

14

RESPONDING TO THE CALL OF THE SUMMONER, BAHÁ'U'LLÁH

> The Revelation which, from time immemorial, hath been acclaimed as the Purpose and Promise of all the Prophets of God, and the most cherished Desire of His Messengers, hath now, by virtue of the pervasive Will of the Almighty and at His irresistible bidding, been revealed unto men. The advent of such a Revelation hath been heralded in all the sacred Scriptures. *Bahá'u'lláh*[1]

The necessity for both spiritual and social renewal

It should be clear to any observer of current affairs that the Promised Day of change is long overdue.

In His time, Jesus explained that a new revelation, although an integral part of an eternal Faith of God, nevertheless requires a new outward form, not only to distinguish it from past Dispensations but also to act as an adequate and appropriate vehicle for the new.

> No man also seweth a piece of new cloth on an old garment: else the new piece that filled it up taketh away from the old, and the rent is made worse.
>
> And no man putteth new wine into old bottles: else the new wine doth burst the bottles, and the wine is spilled, and the bottles will be marred: but new wine must be put into new bottles.[2]

Today, there is even a greater and more urgent requirement for divine intervention:

> The vitality of men's belief in God is dying out in every land; nothing short of His wholesome medicine can ever restore it. The corrosion

of ungodliness is eating into the vitals of human society; what else but the Elixir of His potent Revelation can cleanse and revive it?[3]

And, once again, changes in the spiritual character of humanity must be coupled with necessary changes in the social order that embody the new divine principles.

> Does not the very operation of the world-unifying forces that are at work in this age necessitate that He Who is the Bearer of the Message of God in this day should not only reaffirm that self-same exalted standard of individual conduct inculcated by the Prophets gone before Him, but embody in His appeal, to all governments and peoples, the essentials of that social code, that Divine Economy, which must guide humanity's concerted efforts in establishing that all-embracing federation which is to signalize the advent of the Kingdom of God on this earth?[4]

Transformative power of the Word of God

In line with the teachings of the Gospel, the Qur'án associates the transforming power of Christ with the 'Word' (*Kalimah*):

> Behold! the angels said: 'O Mary! God giveth thee glad tidings of a Word from Him: his name will be Christ Jesus, the son of Mary, held in honour in this world and the hereafter and of (the company of) those nearest to God.'[5]

It is this divine Word that has the unique capacity to bring about a spiritual rebirth and social revival.

> In the beginning was the Word, and the Word was with God, and the Word was God.
> The same was in the beginning with God.
> All things were made by him; and without him was not any thing made that was made.
> In him was life; and the life was the light of men.
> And the light shineth in darkness; and the darkness comprehended it not.[6]

Bahá'u'lláh declares that this divine Word has once again been revealed, and that it 'alone, can claim the distinction of being endowed with the capacity required for so great and far-reaching a change'.[7]

> Hearken . . . to the voice of God, the Sovereign, the Help in Peril, the Self-Subsisting. He, verily, calleth aloud between heaven and earth, summoning all mankind unto the scene of transcendent glory. . . The whole world hath been set ablaze by the Word of thy Lord, the All-Glorious . . . It hath been manifested in the form of the human temple, and through it God hath quickened the souls of the sincere among His servants. In its inner essence, this Word is the living water by which God hath purified the hearts of such as have turned unto Him and forgotten every other mention, and through which He draweth them nigh unto the seat of His mighty Name. We have sprinkled it upon the people of the graves, and lo, they have risen up, with their gaze fixed upon the shining and resplendent Beauty of their Lord.[8]

The Word of God confers new life; it generates a new consciousness, transforms and regulates individual conduct, and fosters and advances human relationships.

> Every word that proceedeth out of the mouth of God is endowed with such potency as can instill new life into every human frame . . . All the wondrous works ye behold in this world have been manifested through the operation of His supreme and most exalted Will, His wondrous and inflexible Purpose . . . No sooner is this resplendent word uttered, than its animating energies, stirring with all created things, give birth to the means and instruments whereby such arts can be produced and perfected . . . In the days to come, ye will, verily, behold things of which ye have never heard before . . . Every single letter proceeding out of the mouth of God is indeed a mother letter, and every word uttered by Him Who is the Well Spring of Divine Revelation is a mother word . . .[9]

As in earlier Dispensations, the primary duty of the followers of Bahá'u'lláh in this day and age is therefore to transmit the Word and to centre their energies in the propagation of the Faith of God.

This is the day in which to speak. It is incumbent upon the people of Bahá to strive, with the utmost patience and forbearance, to guide the peoples of the world to the Most Great Horizon. Every body calleth aloud for a soul. Heavenly souls must needs quicken, with the breath of the Word of God, the dead bodies with a fresh spirit. Within every word a new spirit is hidden. Happy is the man that attaineth thereunto, and hath arisen to teach the Cause of Him Who is the King of Eternity . . . Say: O servants! The triumph of this Cause hath depended, and will continue to depend, upon the appearance of holy souls, upon the showing forth of goodly deeds, and the revelation of words of consummate wisdom.[10]

The invitation and the promise

All the divine Messengers have in the past bidden diverse sections of humanity to undergo this transformation and to return to the 'Straight Path' of Faith, its sole salvation and refuge (see Chapter 17). Bahá'u'lláh explains that God's Prophets 'one and all summon the people of the earth to acknowledge the Unity of God, and herald unto them the *Kawthar* [river of water of life in paradise] of an infinite grace and bounty. They are all invested with the robe of prophethood, and are honored with the mantle of glory'.[11] Today, Bahá'u'lláh invites all humanity to undergo the ordained changes necessary to create a new race of men and usher in a world spiritual civilization. The numerous references to this momentous event in the scriptures attest to its importance.

The designations 'Summoner', 'Crier' and 'Caller' are used in the Qur'án to describe the Promised One Who will announce the changes:

'The Summoner', 'the Caller' (*Almunádi*):
   And listen for the Day when the Caller will call out from a place quite near.[12]

'The Crier' (*mu-aththinun*):
   The companions of the garden (paradise) will call out to the companions of the fire: 'We have indeed found the promises of our Lord to us true: have you also found your Lord's promises true?' They shall say, 'Yes;' but a crier shall proclaim between them: 'The curse of God is on the wrongdoers.'[13]

'The One Who Invites', 'the Caller' (*al-Dda̲a̲i*):

> Therefore, (O Prophet,) turn away from them. The Day that the Caller will call (them) to a terrible affair.[14]

> It will be on a Day when He will call you, and ye will answer (His call) with (words of) His praise, and ye will think that ye tarried but a little while![15]

This 'Call' or 'Summons' of Bahá'u'lláh to renew God's eternal Faith had also earlier emanated from Muhammad, Who is similarly described in the Qur'án as a Warner, Caller, Summoner, and Inviter (to God's Faith), and One Calling to Faith, (*Munádi*).

> O our people, hearken to the one who invites (you) to God, and believe in him: He will forgive you your faults, and deliver you from a Penalty Grievous.[16]

> O Prophet! Truly We have sent thee as a Witness, a Bearer of Glad Tidings, and a Warner –
> And as one who invites to God's (Grace) by His leave, and as a Lamp spreading Light.
> Then give the glad tidings to the believers, that they shall have from God a very great Bounty.[17]

> Say thou: 'This is my way: I do invite unto God, on evidence clear as the seeing with one's eyes, – I and whoever follows me. Glory to God! and never will I join gods with God!'[18]

> Our Lord! we have heard the call of one calling (us) to Faith, 'Believe ye in the Lord,' and we have believed. Our Lord! Forgive us our sins, blot out from us our iniquities, and take to Thyself our souls in the company of the righteous.[19]

The Qur'án promises a renewal of creation and a transformation of heart and vision.

> The Day that We roll up the heavens like a scroll rolled up for books (completed) – even as We produced the first Creation, so shall We

produce a new one: a promise We have undertaken: truly shall We fulfil it.[20]

... men whom neither traffic nor merchandise can divert from the Remembrance of God, nor from regular Prayer, nor from the practice of regular Charity: their (only) fear is for the Day when hearts and eyes will be transformed (in a world wholly new).[21]

A new Book

God had sent down His verses and revealed the Qur'án, but He would reveal a new Book in the Day of Resurrection:

> ... on the Day of Resurrection, We shall bring out for him a Book which he will find wide open.[22]

Mankind will be judged by the standards and teachings of the new Revelation. It is expected that the radically different teachings will prove a severe test for some Muslims, as they proved a great difficulty and a test for the people in the time of Muhammad. The changes will be resisted, as they will not accord with the accepted traditions and explanations of the spiritual leaders.

> Thus have We sent down Clear Signs (the Qur'án); and verily, God doth guide whom He will![23]

> When We substitute one revelation for another, and God knows best what He reveals (in stages), they say, 'Thou art but a forger': but most of them understand not.[24]

The Jewish and Christian scriptures are also replete with God's promise to renew His Faith. The Tanakh declares that humanity will be baptized and purified.[25] God will 'create new heavens and a new earth: and the former shall not be remembered, nor come into mind'.[26] He will 'do a new thing', 'make a way in the wilderness, and rivers in the desert', [27] and endow mankind with 'a new wine', [28] 'a new name', [29] 'a new heart' and 'a new spirit'.[30]

The New Testament explains that with the coming of Christ 'old things' had 'passed away' and 'all things' had been made 'new',[31] but that at His second coming there will be 'a new heaven and a new earth' because the 'first (earlier) heaven and the earth were passed away' and perished and there will be 'no more sea'.[32] Humanity will witness a gloriously decked 'new Jerusalem' which will come 'down from God out of heaven prepared as a bride adorned for her husband'.[33] 'Another book' will be opened[34] and there will be 'a new song'.[35] There will be a need for 'refreshing and restitution of all things',[36] and for God to again 'renew all things'.[37] However, only those who are thirsty will drink from 'the fountain of the water of life freely'.[38]

In addition to the reference to 'another Book', the Bible emphasizes in so many ways that the divine visitation will bring a new Revelation and usher in a new Dispensation:

> we, according to His promise, look for new heavens and a new earth, wherein dwelleth righteousness.[39]

> To him that overcometh will I give to eat of the hidden man-na, and will give him a white stone, and in the stone a new name written, which no man knoweth, saving he that receiveth it.[40]

> Him that overcometh will I make a pillar in the temple of my God . . . I will write upon him the name of my God, which is new Jerusalem, which cometh down out of heaven from my God: and I will write upon him my new name.[41]

> And they sung as it were a new song before the throne. . .[42]

> And they sung a new song, saying, Thou art worthy to take the book, and to open the seals thereof.[43]

> Sing unto the Lord, a new song, and his praise from the end of the earth . . .[44]

Jesus evidently did not desire that even His own Person should become a distraction to hinder acceptance of the new revelation:

> Nevertheless I tell you the truth; It is expedient for you that I go

away: for if I go not away, the Comforter will not come unto you; but if I depart, I will send him unto you.[45]

Furthermore, the Bible emphasizes the importance of the spiritual and social laws that will be ordained compared to the diminished relevance of those of earlier Dispensations.

> And I will bring the blind by a way that they knew not; I will lead them in paths that they have not known: I will make darkness light before them, and crooked things straight. These things will I do unto them, and not forsake them.[46]

> For as the new heavens and the new earth, which I will make, shall remain before me, saith the Lord, so shall your seed and your name remain.[47]

> For, behold, I create new heavens and a new earth: and the former shall not be remembered, nor come into mind.[48]

The New Testament explains that all individuals, whatever their rank or privilege, will be presented with a new Book of spiritual life. Their own scriptures should guide them to the new Revelation, but only if they have remained faithful to the divine exhortations.

> And I saw the dead, small and great, stand before God; and the books were opened: and another book was opened, which is the book of life: and the dead were judged out of those things which were written in the books, according to their works.[49]

The promise of the coming of the Mahdi and the return of Jesus

In Shi'ih and Sunni eschatology, *al-Mahdi* ('the Guided One') will come before '*Yawm al-Qiyamah*', the Day of Judgement or 'the Day of Resurrection', and, alongside Jesus, will rid the world of wrongdoing, injustice and tyranny, and reform Islam. In Shi'ih Islam, belief in the *Mahdi*, the *Qá'im* or 'He Who Arises' or 'the Resurrector' is closely related to the appearance or return of Twelfth Imam, *Muhammad al-Mahdi,* and the reappearance of the martyred Imam Husayn.

The announcements by the Báb and Bahá'u'lláh

The Revelations of the Báb and Bahá'u'lláh are associated with the advents of *al-Mahdi* and the *Qá'im*. Expounding on this theme the Báb writes:

> Thou beholdest how vast is the number of people who go to Mecca each year on pilgrimage and engage in circumambulation, while He, through the potency of Whose Word the Ka'bah [the sanctuary in Mecca] hath become the object of adoration, is forsaken in this mountain. He is none other but the Apostle of God Himself, inasmuch as the Revelation of God may be likened to the sun. No matter how innumerable its risings, there is but one sun, and upon it depends the life of all things. It is clear and evident that the object of all preceding Dispensations hath been to pave the way for the advent of Muḥammad, the Apostle of God. These, including the Muḥammadan Dispensation, have had, in their turn, as their objective the Revelation proclaimed by the Qá'im. The purpose underlying this Revelation, as well as those that preceded it, has, in like manner, been to announce the advent of the Faith of Him Whom God will make manifest. And this Faith – the Faith of Him Whom God will make manifest – in its turn, together with all the Revelations gone before it, have as their object the Manifestation destined to succeed it. And the latter, no less than all the Revelations preceding it, prepare the way for the Revelation which is yet to follow. The process of the rise and setting of the Sun of Truth will thus indefinitely continue – a process that hath had no beginning and will have no end.[50]

> Since thou hast faithfully obeyed the true religion of God in the past, it behooveth thee to follow His true religion hereafter, inasmuch as every religion proceedeth from God, the Help in Peril, the Self-Subsisting.
>
> He Who hath revealed the Qur'án unto Muḥammad, the Apostle of God, ordaining in the Faith of Islám that which was pleasing unto Him, hath likewise revealed the Bayán, in the manner ye have been promised, unto Him Who is your Qá'im, your Guide, your Mihdí, your Lord, Him Whom ye acclaim as the manifestation of God's most excellent titles. Verily the equivalent of that

which God revealed unto Muḥammad during twenty-three years, hath been revealed unto Me within the space of two days and two nights. However, as ordained by God, no distinction is to be drawn between the two. He, in truth, hath power over all things.[51]

To His Shí'íh followers Bahá'u'lláh also represents the return of Imam Husayn:

> Consider the eagerness with which certain peoples and nations have anticipated the return of Imám-Ḥusayn, whose coming, after the appearance of the Qá'im, hath been prophesied, in days past, by the chosen ones of God, exalted be His glory. These holy ones have, moreover, announced that when He Who is the Day Spring of the manifold grace of God manifesteth Himself, all the Prophets and Messengers, including the Qá'im, will gather together beneath the shadow of the sacred Standard which the Promised One will raise. That hour is now come. The world is illumined with the effulgent glory of His countenance. And yet, behold how far its peoples have strayed from His path! None have believed in Him except them who, through the power of the Lord of Names, have shattered the idols of their vain imaginings and corrupt desires and entered the city of certitude. The seal of the choice Wine of His Revelation hath, in this Day and in His Name, the Self-Sufficing, been broken. Its grace is being poured out upon men. Fill thy cup, and drink in, in His Name, the Most Holy, the All-Praised.[52]

All humanity is summoned today

Whereas in past Dispensations only certain sections of mankind received the Divine Message, in this Day Bahá'u'lláh addresses His Call to all religions and peoples.

> From the horizon of His prison-city He summoneth mankind unto the Dayspring of God, the Exalted, the Great. Exultest thou over the treasures thou dost possess, knowing they shall perish?[53]

> This Wronged One hath, at all times, summoned the peoples of the world unto that which will exalt them, and draw them nigh unto

God. From the Most Sublime Horizon there hath shone forth that which leaveth no room unto any one for vacillation, repudiation or denial. The wayward, however, have failed to profit therefrom; nay, it shall only increase their loss.[54]

Great indeed is this Day! The allusions made to it in all the sacred Scriptures as the Day of God attest its greatness. The soul of every Prophet of God, of every Divine Messenger, hath thirsted for this wondrous Day. All the divers kindreds of the earth have, likewise, yearned to attain it. No sooner, however, had the Day Star of His Revelation manifested itself in the heaven of God's Will, than all, except those whom the Almighty was pleased to guide, were found dumbfounded and heedless.[55]

This is the King of Days, the Day that hath seen the coming of the Best-beloved, Him Who through all eternity hath been acclaimed the Desire of the World . . . The world of being shineth in this Day with the resplendency of this Divine Revelation. All created things extol its saving grace and sing its praises. The universe is wrapt in an ecstasy of joy and gladness. The Scriptures of past Dispensations celebrate the great jubilee that must needs greet this most great Day of God. Well is it with him that hath lived to see this Day and hath recognized its station.[56]

Bahá'u'lláh also specifically summoned and warned the most powerful Muslim and Christian monarchs and potentates of His time and addressed their subjects. Clearly, the destiny of Islam and, for that matter, the whole of humanity, is therefore dependent on its response to the call of the long-awaited Reformer and Saviour.

Verily I say, this is the Day in which mankind can behold the Face, and hear the Voice, of the Promised One. The Call of God hath been raised, and the light of His countenance hath been lifted up upon men. It behoveth every man to blot out the trace of every idle word from the tablet of his heart, and to gaze, with an open and unbiased mind, on the signs of His Revelation, the proofs of His Mission, and the tokens of His glory.[57]

Hearken, O King [Sulṭán 'Abdu'l-'Azíz], to the speech of Him that speaketh the truth, Him that doth not ask thee to recompense Him with the things God hath chosen to bestow upon thee, Him Who unerringly treadeth the straight Path. He it is Who summoneth thee unto God, thy Lord, Who showeth thee the right course, the way that leadeth to true felicity, that haply thou mayest be of them with whom it shall be well.[58]

Ye are but vassals, O kings of the earth! He Who is the King of Kings hath appeared, arrayed in His most wondrous glory, and is summoning you unto Himself, the Help in Peril, the Self-Subsisting. Take heed lest pride deter you from recognizing the Source of Revelation, lest the things of this world shut you out as by a veil from Him Who is the Creator of heaven. Arise, and serve Him Who is the Desire of all nations, Who hath created you through a word from Him, and ordained you to be, for all time, the emblems of His sovereignty.[59]

O Pope! [Pope Pius IX] Rend the veils asunder. He Who is the Lord of Lords is come overshadowed with clouds, and the decree hath been fulfilled by God, the Almighty, the Unrestrained... He, verily, hath again come down from Heaven even as He came down from it the first time. Beware that thou dispute not with Him even as the Pharisees disputed with Him [Jesus] without a clear token or proof. On His right hand flow the living waters of grace, and on His left the choice Wine of justice, whilst before Him march the angels of Paradise, bearing the banners of His signs. Beware lest any name debar thee from God, the Creator of earth and heaven. Leave thou the world behind thee, and turn towards thy Lord, through Whom the whole earth hath been illumined.
　... Dwellest thou in palaces whilst He Who is the King of Revelation liveth in the most desolate of abodes? Leave them unto such as desire them, and set thy face with joy and delight towards the Kingdom.[60]

Addressing the entire Christendom, Bahá'u'lláh reminds them of their earlier failure to recognize Muhammad. In this Day they are presented with yet another spiritual opportunity to acknowledge the fulfilment of the Lord's Prayer:

> Say: O concourse of Christians! We have, on a previous occasion, revealed Ourself unto you, and ye recognized Me not. This is yet another occasion vouchsafed unto you. This is the Day of God; turn ye unto Him . . . The Beloved One loveth not that ye be consumed with the fire of your desires. Were ye to be shut out as by a veil from Him, this would be for no other reason than your own waywardness and ignorance. Ye make mention of Me, and know Me not. Ye call upon Me, and are heedless of My Revelation . . . O people of the Gospel! They who were not in the Kingdom have now entered it, whilst We behold you, in this day, tarrying at the gate.[61]

He thus exhorts Christians to reflect on Christ's warnings concerning the spiritual darkness that will engulf the 'children of the kingdom', in contrast to the diverse people from non-Judeo-Christian backgrounds who will come to recognize God's Revelation and enter His heavenly kingdom.

> And I say unto you, That many shall come from the east and west, and shall sit down with Abraham, and Isaac, and Jacob, in the kingdom of heaven.
> But the children of the kingdom shall be cast out into outer darkness: there shall be weeping and gnashing of teeth.[62]

The Qur'án promises a future Day when unbelievers will be tested concerning their lack of positive response to the Message of the Summoner.[63]

> O our people, hearken to the one who invites (you) to God, and believe in him: He will forgive you your faults, and deliver you from a Penalty Grievous.
> If any does not hearken to the one who invites (us) to God, he cannot frustrate (God's Plan) on earth, and no protectors can he have besides God such men (wander) in manifest error.
> See they not that God, Who created the heavens and the earth, and never wearied with their creation, is able to give life to the dead? Yea, verily He has power over all things.
> And on the Day that the unbelievers will be placed before the Fire, (they will be asked,) 'Is this not the Truth?' They will say, 'Yea,

by our Lord!' (one will say:) 'Then taste ye the penalty, for that ye were wont to deny (truth)!'[64]

The Qur'án admits that the Call of the Summoner will indeed be a difficult experience for Muslims, and it will be particularly painful for those who lack faith.

> They will come forth, their eyes humbled – from (their) graves, (torpid) like locusts scattered abroad,
> Hastening, with eyes transfixed, towards the Caller! – 'Hard is this Day!', the unbelievers will say.[65]

Today, the followers of Islam have an appointment with destiny. They face the challenge of heeding and responding to the invitation and summons of the promised 'Caller', or continuing in their futile attempts to frustrate, suppress and eradicate the divine purpose. The Qur'án warns that, if Muslims neglect their spiritual obligations, God is capable of substituting them for another people:

> . . . If ye turn back (from the Path), He will substitute in your stead another people; then they would not be like you![66]

> Now I do Call to witness the Lord of all points in the East and the West that We can certainly –
> Substitute for them better (men) than they; and We are not to be defeated (in Our Plan).
> So leave them to plunge in vain talk and play about, until they encounter that Day of theirs which they have been promised! –
> The Day whereon they will issue from their sepulchers in sudden haste as if they were rushing to a goal-post (fixed for them), –
> Their eyes lowered in dejection, ignominy covering them (all over)! Such is the Day the which they are promised![67]

> As to these, they love the fleeting life, and put away behind them a Day (that will be) hard.
> It is We Who created them, and We have made their joints strong; but, when We will, We can substitute the like of them by a complete change.

> This is an admonition: whosoever will, let him take a (straight) Path to his Lord.[68]
>
> If He so pleased, He could blot you out and bring in a New Creation.[69]
>
> Thy Lord is Self-sufficient, Full of Mercy: if it were His Will, He could destroy you, and in your place appoint whom He will as your successors, even as He raised you up from the posterity of other people.
> All that hath been promised unto you will come to pass: Nor can ye frustrate it (in the least bit).[70]
>
> Seest thou not that God created the heavens and the earth in Truth? If He so will, He can remove you and put (in your place) a new Creation?
> Nor is that for God any great matter.[71]

Muslims are further counselled that the sole source of spiritual guidance will be the promised 'Summoner' and no one else. Hence, when He appears no one may speak on spiritual or temporal matters without His permission and blessing.

> On that day they follow the summoner who deceiveth not, and voices are hushed for the Beneficent, and thou hearest but a faint murmur.[72]
>
> The day it arrives, no soul shall speak except by His leave: of those (gathered) some will be wretched and some will be blessed.[73]

Bahá'u'lláh writes:

> In these days, praise be to God, the power of His Word hath obtained such ascendancy over men, that they dare breathe no word.[74]

It is therefore every Muslim's responsibility today to investigate the Message of Bahá'u'lláh, Who unequivocally and consistently has declared that He is the promised Summoner of Islam. 'The Crier hath cried out . . .'[75] and His Message could not be clearer:

The thing that must come hath come suddenly; behold how they flee from it! The inevitable hath come to pass; witness how they have cast it behind their backs! This is the Day whereon every man will fly from himself, how much more from his kindred, could ye but perceive it. Say: By God! The blast hath been blown on the trumpet, and lo, mankind hath swooned away before us! The Herald hath cried out, and the Summoner raised His voice saying: 'The Kingdom is God's, the Most Powerful, the Help in Peril, the Self-Subsisting.'[76]

The most grievous veil hath shut out the peoples of the earth from His glory, and hindered them from hearkening to His call. God grant that the light of unity may envelop the whole earth, and that the seal, 'the Kingdom is God's', may be stamped upon the brow of all its peoples.[77]

This is the day which God hath announced through the tongue of His Apostle. Reflect, that thou mayest apprehend what the All-Merciful hath sent down in the Qur'án and in this inscribed Tablet. This is the day whereon He Who is the Dayspring of Revelation hath come with clear tokens which none can number. This is the day whereon every man endued with perception hath discovered the fragrance of the breeze of the All-Merciful in the world of creation, and every man of insight hastened unto the living waters of the mercy of His Lord, the King of Kings.[78]

Every new revelation, without exception, has been initially rejected

As attested by Bahá'u'lláh, all the Prophets of God have appeared contrary to the desires of the people of their time:

Hath, from the foundation of the world until the present day, any Light or Revelation shone forth from the dayspring of the will of God which the kindreds of the earth have accepted, and Whose Cause they have acknowledged? Where is it to be found, and what is its name? Since the Seal of the Prophets (Muhammad) – may all else but Him be His sacrifice – and before Him the Spirit of God (Jesus), as far back as the First Manifestation, all have at the time of Their appearance suffered grievously. Some were held to be possessed, others were called impostors, and were treated in a manner that the pen is ashamed to describe. By God! There befell Them what hath made all created things to sigh, and yet the people are, for the most part, sunk in manifest ignorance! We pray God to assist them to return unto Him, and to repent before the door of His mercy. Potent is He over all things.[79]

All Messengers faced rejection and opposition, and have had to deal with enemies.

> The unbelievers say: 'We shall neither believe in this scripture nor in (any) that (came) before it . . .'[80]

> And when there comes to them a Book from God, confirming what is with them,– although from of old they had prayed for victory against those without Faith – when there comes to them that which they (should) have recognized, they refuse to believe in it; but the curse of God is on those without Faith.[81]

> Then sent We Our apostles in succession: every time there came to a people their apostle, they accused him of falsehood . . .[82]

> Ah! Alas for (My) Servants! There comes not a messenger to them but they mock him![83]

> But never did a single one of the Signs of their Lord reach them, but they turned away therefrom.[84]

> But (there were people) before them, who denied (the Signs) – the people of Noah, and the Confederates (of evil) after them; and every people plotted against their prophet, to seize him, and disputed by means of vanities, therewith to condemn the Truth; but it was I that seized them! and how (terrible) was My Requital![85]

> We did send Messengers before thee amongst the religious sects of old:
> But never came a Messenger to them but they mocked him.[86]

> And to you there came Joseph in times gone by, with clear Signs, but ye ceased not to doubt of the (mission) for which he had come: at length, when he died, ye said: 'No Messenger will God send after him.' Thus doth God leave to stray such as transgress and live in doubt.[87]
>
> Never comes (aught) to them of a renewed Message from their Lord, but they listen to it as in jest.[88]
>
> But there comes not to them a newly-revealed Message from (God) Most Gracious, but they turn away therefrom.[89]
>
> Likewise did We make for every Messenger an enemy, – evil ones among men and Jinns, inspiring each other with flowery discourses by way of deception. If thy Lord had so planned, they would not have done it: so leave them and their inventions alone.[90]
>
> Thus have We made for every prophet an enemy among the sinners: but enough is thy Lord to guide and to help.[91]
>
> ... Even thus, as they now speak, spake those (who were) before them. Their hearts are all alike. We have made clear the revelations for people who are sure.[92]

The Qur'án denounces the resources and money expended to oppose God's Faith, aware that 'If any does not hearken to the one who invites (us) to God, he cannot frustrate (God's Plan) on earth':[93]

> The unbelievers spend their wealth to hinder (men) from the path of God, and so will they continue to spend; but in the end they will have (only) regrets and sighs . . .[94]

Objections to Muhammad and His Revelation

The Qur'án instructively details the many objections that were levelled against Muhammad by those who were 'deaf, dumb and blind' and who consequently refused to 'return' to the straight Path (*Baqara*, the Heifer, 2:18).

Bahá'u'lláh explains that examination and study of these protestations strengthens one's faith and provides certitude:

> Should you acquaint yourself with the indignities heaped upon the Prophets of God, and apprehend the true causes of the objections voiced by their oppressors, you will surely appreciate the significance of their position. Moreover, the more closely you observe the denials of those who have opposed the Manifestations of the divine attributes, the firmer will be your faith in the Cause of God.[95]

A cavil was that the Revelation of Muhammad was fabricated:

> If they treat thy (mission) as false, so did the peoples before them (with their Prophets) – the People of Noah, and Ád and Thámud;
> Those of Abraham and Lut;
> And the companions of the Madyan people; and Moses was rejected (in the same way). But I granted respite to the unbelievers, and (only) after that did I punish them: but how (terrible) was my rejection (of them)![96]

> Nay, but there came to thee My Signs, and thou didst reject them: thou wast haughty, and became one of those who reject faith!'[97]

The Qur'án was considered the product of plagiarism and produced in collaboration with others.

> But the misbelievers say: 'Naught is this but a lie which he has forged, and others have helped him at it.' In truth it is they who have put forward an iniquity and a falsehood.[98]

> We know indeed that they say, 'It is a man that teaches him.' The tongue of him they wickedly point to is notably foreign, while this is Arabic, pure and clear.[99]

The Qur'án was further objected to because it was not revealed 'miraculously' and all at once, but in segments over a period of more than two decades.

> Those who reject Faith say: 'Why is not the Qur'án revealed to him all at once?' Thus (is it revealed), that We may strengthen thy heart thereby, and We have rehearsed it to thee in slow, well-arranged stages, gradually.[100]

Muhammad was charged with failing to bring anything that was new, and His Revelation was accused of being nothing but mere forgery.

> And when it is said unto them: What hath your Lord revealed? they say: (mere) fables of the men of old.[101]

> When Our Signs are rehearsed to them, they say: 'We have heard this (before): if we wished, we could say (words) like these: these are nothing but tales of the ancients.'[102]

> Then the Messenger will say: 'O my Lord! Truly my people took this Qur'án for just foolish nonsense.'[103]

> When Our clear Signs are rehearsed to them, they say, 'This is only a man who wishes to hinder you from the (worship) which your fathers practised.' And they say, 'This is only a falsehood invented!' and the Unbelievers say of the Truth when it comes to them, 'This is nothing but evident magic!'[104]

> And they say: 'Tales of the ancients, which he has written down, and they are dictated to him morning and afternoon.'[105]

As with other Messengers of God, Muhammad was labelled a liar.

> Certainly We made a covenant with the children of Israel and We sent to them apostles; whenever there came to them an apostle with what that their souls did not desire, some (of them) did they call liars and some they slew.[106]

> (The prophet) said: 'O my Lord! Help me: for that they accuse me of falsehood.'[107]

> And they wonder that a warner has come to them from among

themselves! And the disbelievers say: 'This (the Prophet Muhammad) is a sorcerer, a liar.'[108]

Because His Divine Message had not been received by the leaders of His time, it was not considered worthy of consideration:

> Also, they say: 'Why is not this Qur'án sent down to some leading man (chief) in either of the two cities?' (*Makkah* or Mecca, and *Tá'if*).[109]

Similarly, Christ's Word was deemed undeserving of serious attention because it had been accepted only by insignificant individuals who were poorly versed in the scriptures and unschooled in the Mosaic Law.

> Then answered them the Pharisees, Are ye also deceived?
> Have any of the rulers or of the Pharisees believed on him [Jesus]?
> But this people [Jesus' followers] who knoweth not the law are cursed.[110]

Because Muhammad's Message challenged hallowed tradition and threatened the civil and ecclesiastical order, He was accused of being mad, possessed; and the Qur'án was dismissed as nothing other than mere poetry.

> We know best why it is they listen, when they listen to thee; and when they meet in private conference, behold, the wicked say, 'Ye follow none other than a man bewitched!'[111]

> Or do they say, 'He is possessed'? Nay, he has brought them the Truth, but most of them hate the Truth.[112]

> And say: 'What! Shall we give up our gods for the sake of a Poet possessed?'[113]

> Say: 'I do admonish you on one point: that ye do stand up before God . . . and reflect (within yourselves): your Companion is not possessed: he is no less than a warner to you, in face of a terrible Penalty.'[114]

Jesus Christ and His forerunner, John the Baptist, were also accused of being possessed.

> For John came neither eating nor drinking, and they say, He hath a devil.[115]

> And the scribes which came down from Jerusalem said, He hath Beelzebub, and by the prince of the devils casteth he out devils.
> And he called them unto him, and said unto them in parables, How can Satan cast out Satan?
> And if a kingdom be divided against itself, that kingdom cannot stand.
> And if a house be divided against itself, that house cannot stand [the inference being that a religion that becomes divided into sects does not survive with an intact message].[116]

A further severe test for some individuals has been the fact that the Prophets of God appear as ordinary human beings and lead seemingly mundane lives.

> And the apostles whom We sent before thee were all (men) who ate food and walked through the streets: We have made some of you as a trial for others: will ye have patience? for God is One Who sees (all things).[117]

> And they say: 'What sort of a messenger is this, who eats food, and walks through the streets? Why has not an angel been sent down to him to give admonition with him?'[118]

> And the chiefs of his people, who disbelieved and denied the Meeting in the Hereafter, and to whom We had given the luxuries and comforts of this life, said: 'He is no more than a human being like you, he eats of that which you eat, and drinks of what you drink.'[119]

> What kept men back from belief when Guidance came to them, was nothing but this: they said, 'Has God sent a man (like us) to be (His) Apostle?'[120]

That was because there came to them messengers with Clear Signs, but they said: 'Shall (mere) human beings direct us?' So they rejected (the Message) and turned away. But God can do without (them): and God is free of all needs, worthy of all praise.[121]

As recorded by the Gospels, Jesus was likewise objected to because of His ordinariness, apparent lack of asceticism, and the undesirable company that He kept.

> The Son of man is come eating and drinking; and ye say, Behold a gluttonous man, and a winebibber, a friend of publicans and sinners![122]

> Then came to him (Jesus) the disciples of John, saying, why do we and the Pharisees fast oft, but thy disciples fast not?[123]

Bahá'u'lláh comments on this potent source of spiritual blindness:

> In another sense, [the clouds] mean the appearance of that immortal Beauty in the image of mortal man, with such human limitations as eating and drinking, poverty and riches, glory and abasement, sleeping and waking, and such other things as cast doubt in the minds of men, and cause them to turn away. All such veils are symbolically referred to as 'clouds'.
>
> These are the 'clouds' that cause the heavens of the knowledge and understanding of all that dwell on earth to be cloven asunder. Even as He hath revealed: 'On that day shall the heaven be cloven by the clouds.' Even as the clouds prevent the eyes of men from beholding the sun, so do these things hinder the souls of men from recognizing the light of the divine Luminary. To this beareth witness that which hath proceeded out of the mouth of the unbelievers as revealed in the sacred Book: 'And they have said: "What manner of apostle is this? He eateth food, and walketh the streets. Unless an angel be sent down and take part in His warnings, we will not believe."' Other Prophets, similarly, have been subject to poverty and afflictions, to hunger, and to the ills and chances of this world. As these holy Persons were subject to such needs and wants, the people were, consequently, lost in the wilds of misgivings and doubts, and were afflicted with bewilderment and perplexity. How,

they wondered, could such a person be sent down from God, assert His ascendancy over all the peoples and kindreds of the earth, and claim Himself to be the goal of all creation, – even as He hath said: 'But for Thee, I would not have created all that are in heaven and on earth,' – and yet be subject to such trivial things?'[124]

Community leaders demanded the miraculous as proof of the divine mission of Muhammad.

> And those who have no knowledge say: Why doth not God speak unto us, or some sign come unto us?[125]

> You are but a human being like us. Then bring us a sign if you are of the truthful.[126]

> Those who disbelieve say: If only a portent were sent down upon him from his Lord! Say: Lo! God sendeth whom He will astray, and guideth unto Himself all who turn (unto Him).[127]

> They who look not forward to meet Us say, 'If the angels be not sent down to us, or unless we behold our Lord . . .' Ah! they are proud of heart, and exceed with great excess![128]

> They say: 'We shall not believe in thee, until thou cause a spring to gush forth for us from the earth,
>   'Or (until) thou have a garden of date trees and vines, and cause rivers to gush forth in their midst, carrying abundant water;
>   'Or thou cause the sky to fall in pieces, as thou sayest (will happen), against us; Or thou bring God and the angels before (us) face to face;
>   'Or thou have a house adorned with gold, or thou mount a ladder right into the skies. No, we shall not even believe in thy mounting until thou send down to us a book That we could read.' Say: 'Glory to my Lord! Am I aught but a man, – an apostle?'[129]

As with earlier Prophets, Muhammad was challenged by disbelievers to bring the wrath of God if His mission was indeed divine:

> Remember how they said: 'O God! if this is indeed the Truth from

Thee, rain down on as a shower of stones from the sky, or send us a grievous penalty.'[130]

(The same are) those who say: Lo! God hath charged us that we believe not in any messenger until he brings us an offering which fire (from heaven) shall devour. Say (unto them, O Muhammad): Messengers came unto you before me with miracles, and with that (very miracle) which ye describe. Why then did ye slay them ? (Answer that) if ye are truthful! [131]

Jesus was also pressed to perform miracles to establish that He had indeed been sent by God – this despite His many 'wonders' recorded in the gospels.

And the Pharisees came forth, and began to question with him, seeking of him a sign from heaven, tempting him.
And he sighed deeply in his spirit, and saith, Why doth this generation seek after a sign? verily I say unto you, There shall no sign be given unto this generation.[132]

They said therefore unto him, What sign shewest thou then, that we may see, and believe thee? what dost thou work?
Our fathers did eat manna in the desert; as it is written, He gave them bread from heaven to eat.[133]

The rejection of the Bábi and Bahá'í Revelations

The Qur'án predicts that the followers of the next Revelation will also encounter similar objections, disbelief and opposition.

And when mankind are gathered (Day of Resurrection, Day of Judgment), they will become enemies for them and will deny their worshipping.[134]

Not unexpectedly, the Báb and Bahá'u'lláh were also reviled and subjected to relentless persecution, derision, and unfathomable suffering. Bahá'u'lláh remarks on the similarity between the opposition to His Revelation and to that of the Báb:

> What aileth this people that they speak of that which they understand not? They raise the same objections as did the followers of the Qur'án when their Lord came unto them with His Cause ... The very words and deeds of these men bear eloquent testimony to the truth of My words, if ye be of them that judge with fairness ... Those whom the Lord hath endued with knowledge shall find, in the very objections raised by the unbelievers, conclusive proofs to invalidate their claims and vindicate the truth of this manifest Light.[135]

Bahá'u'lláh warns Muslims that it is unreasonable and reckless to treat His mighty Revelation frivolously and to reject it out of hand.

> By the righteousness of God! Were any one to entertain so great a Revelation in his heart, the thought of such a declaration would alone confound him! Were the hearts of all men to be crowded into his heart, he would still hesitate to venture upon so awful an enterprise. He could achieve it only by the permission of God, only if the channel of his heart were to be linked with the Source of divine grace, and his soul be assured of the unfailing sustenance of the Almighty. To what, We wonder, do they ascribe so great a daring? Do they accuse Him of folly as they accused the Prophets of old? Or do they maintain that His motive was none other than leadership and the acquisition of earthly riches?[136]

> Consider these days in which He Who is the Ancient Beauty hath come in the Most Great Name, that He may quicken the world and unite its peoples. They, however, rose up against Him with sharpened swords, and committed that which caused the Faithful Spirit to lament, until in the end they imprisoned Him in the most desolate of cities ... Were anyone to tell them: 'The World Reformer is come,' they would answer and say: 'Indeed it is proven that He is a fomenter of discord!', and this notwithstanding that they have never associated with Him, and have perceived that He did not seek, for one moment, to protect Himself. At all times He was at the mercy of the wicked doers. At one time they cast Him into prison, at another they banished Him, and at yet another hurried Him from land to land. Thus have they pronounced judgment against Us, and God, truly, is aware of what I say.[137]

As observed earlier, Bahá'u'lláh blames directly and specifically the Muslim clerics for the failure of most of their followers to recognize His Revelation.

> The first to turn away from Us have been the world's spiritual leaders in this age – they that call upon Us in the daytime and in the night season and mention My Name while resting on their lofty thrones. However, when I revealed Myself unto men they rose against Me in such wise that even the stones groaned and lamented bitterly.[138]

They have misrepresented the promised and long-awaited 'Summoner' as the enemy of Islam rather than its sole salvation, and falsely accused His followers of 'waging war with God and His Messenger', allowing them licence to pass the sentence of death on His followers.

> The punishment of those who wage war against God and His Messenger (*allatheena yuháriboona Alláha warasoolahu*), and strive with might and main for mischief through the land is execution, or crucifixion, of the cutting off of hands and feet from opposite sides, or exile from the land: that is their disgrace in this world, and a heavy punishment is theirs in the Hereafter.[139]

They continue to do their utmost to frustrate the work of the promised Redeemer of Islam, and continue their futile attempts to extirpate His Faith. Bahá'u'lláh accuses specifically the Shí'ih clerics for the rejection and persecution of His Faith.

> The divines of Persia committed that which no people amongst the peoples of the world have committed.[140]

Bahá'u'lláh denounces this denial of His Revelation as blasphemy, and describes it as symptomatic of a profound spiritual malaise and spiritual death.

> O My brother! Forsake thine own desires, turn thy face unto thy lord, and walk not in the footsteps of those who have taken their corrupt inclinations for their god . . . For they who turn away from their Lord in this day are in truth accounted amongst the dead,

though to outward seeming they may walk upon the earth, among the deaf, though they may hear, and among the blind, though they may see....[141]

For, what blasphemy is greater than to turn unto manifestations of Satan, to follow the doctors of oblivion and the people of rebellion? What impiety is more grievous than to deny the Lord on the day when faith itself is renewed and regenerated by God, the Almighty, the Beneficent? What death is more wretched than to flee from the Source of everlasting life? What fire is fiercer on the Day of Reckoning than that of remoteness from the divine beauty and the celestial Glory?[142]

He further considers the rejection of His Divine Message as tantamount to a repudiation of all prior Revelations.

Be thou assured in thyself that verily, he who turns away from this Beauty hath also turned away from the Messengers of the past and showeth pride towards God from all eternity to all eternity.[143]

Bahá'u'lláh observes that while many Jews, generally reviled by Muslims and recipients of a more ancient Dispensation, had recognized His Revelation, Shí'ih Islam, the direct recipient of the Divine Revelation, tragically remained largely excluded and deprived of this redemption.

The children of Him Who is the Friend of God [Abraham] ... and heirs of the One Who discoursed with God [Moses], who were accounted the most abject of men, have split the veils asunder, and rent the coverings, and seized the Sealed Wine from the hands of the bounty of Him Who is the Self-Subsisting, and drunk their fill, whilst the detestable Shí'ih divines have remained, until the present time, hesitant and perverse.[144]

He reminded a particularly cruel Shí'ih cleric, Shaykh Muḥammad Taqíy-i-Najafí, that the Faith of God was destined to triumph.

How numerous the oppressors before thee, who have arisen to quench the light of God, and how many the impious who murdered and pillaged until the hearts and souls of men groaned by reason of their cruelty! The sun of justice hath been obscured, inasmuch as the embodiment of tyranny hath been stablished upon the throne of hatred, and yet the people understand not. O foolish one! Thou hast slain the children of the Apostle and pillaged their possessions. Say: Was it, in thine estimation, their possessions or themselves that denied God? Judge fairly, O ignorant one that hath been shut out as by a veil from God. Thou hast clung to tyranny, and cast away justice; whereupon all created things have lamented, and still thou art among the wayward. Thou hast put to death the aged, and plundered the young. Thinkest thou that thou wilt consume that which thine iniquity hath amassed? Nay, by Myself! Thus informeth thee He Who is cognizant of all. By God! The things thou possessest shall profit thee not, nor what thou hast laid up through thy cruelty. Unto this beareth witness thy Lord, the All-Knowing. Thou hast arisen to put out the light of this Cause; erelong will thine own fire be quenched, at His behest. He, verily, is the Lord of strength and of might. The changes and chances of the world, and the powers of the nations, cannot frustrate Him. He doeth what He pleaseth, and ordaineth what He willeth through the power of His sovereignty.[145]

Consequences for Islam

Had Islam heeded 'the Call' and the invitation of Bahá'u'lláh it would certainly not have found itself in its current dire condition, for it is quite clear to those who have witnessed the transforming power of the Message of Bahá'u'lláh that the repudiation of His Revelation has deprived Islam of its vitally needed spiritual reformation, its reanimation and revitalization, restatement of its original purpose, and rechannelling of its energies. Without the necessary divine guidance Islam has continued to remain fractured, unable to cope with modernity, and in dire conflict with itself and the rest of human race. Islam's redemption, on which in turn depends the peace of mankind, rests on whether it will yet respond at this late hour and accept Bahá'u'lláh's prescription.

> The All-Knowing Physician hath His finger on the pulse of mankind. He perceiveth the disease, and prescribeth, in His unerring wisdom, the remedy. Every age hath its own problem and every

soul its particular aspiration. The remedy the world needeth in its present-day afflictions can never be the same as that which a subsequent age may require. Be anxiously concerned with the needs of the age ye live in, and center your deliberations on its exigencies and requirements.

We can well perceive how the whole human race is encompassed with great, with incalculable afflictions. We see it languishing on its bed of sickness, sore-tried and disillusioned. They that are intoxicated by self-conceit have interposed themselves between it and the Divine and infallible Physician. Witness how they have entangled all men, themselves included, in the mesh of their devices. They can neither discover the cause of the disease, nor have they any knowledge of the remedy. They have conceived the straight to be crooked, and have imagined their friend an enemy.[146]

> Brimful and bitter indeed is the cup of humanity that has failed to respond to the summons of God as voiced by His Supreme Messenger, that has dimmed the lamp of its faith in its Creator, that has transferred, in so great a measure, the allegiance owed Him to the gods of its own invention, and polluted itself with the evils and vices which such a transference must necessarily engender.[147]

Bahá'u'lláh attributes the regrettable plight of Islam and its *Ummah* directly to the rejection of His Divine Message.

> We have invited all men to turn towards God, and have acquainted them with the Straight Path. They [divines] rose up against Us with such cruelty as hath sapped the strength of Islám, and yet most of the people are heedless![148]

> O concourse of Muslim Divines! Because of you the people were abased, and the banner of Islám was hauled down, and its mighty throne subverted.[149]

> O concourse of Muslim divines! By your deeds the exalted station of the nation hath been abased, the standard of Islám hath been reversed and its mighty throne hath fallen. Whenever the Divine Reformer has sought to ennoble the rank of the people, ye have

tumultuously risen against Him and prevented Him from executing His purpose, wherefore the realm hath remained in grievous loss.[150]

He warns of divine retribution that will afflict the cruel oppressors of God's Holy Faith.

> O people of the Qur'án! Verily the prophet of God, Muhammad, sheddeth tears at the sight of your cruelty. Ye have assuredly followed your evil and corrupt desires and turned away your face from the light of guidance. Erelong will ye witness the result of your deeds; for the Lord My God lieth in wait and is watchful of your behavior . . . Erelong He will raise in every city the standard of His sovereignty, and will wipe away the traces of them that have denied Him on the day of His return . . .[151]

He pleads with Muslims to open their eyes and recognize the Divine Revelation, for otherwise, they will be subjected to the dire predictions of the Qur'án.

> Behold how He hath come down from the heaven of His grace, girded with power and invested with sovereignty. Is there any doubt concerning His signs? Open ye your eyes, and consider His clear evidence. Paradise is on your right hand, and hath been brought nigh unto you, while Hell hath been made to blaze. Witness its devouring flame. Haste ye to enter into Paradise, as a token of Our mercy unto you, and drink ye from the hands of the All-Merciful the Wine that is life indeed.[152]

15

EMBRACING THE 'GREAT ANNOUNCEMENT' OF THE QUR'ÁN AND THE 'GOOD NEWS' OF THE BIBLE

> We have truly revealed the signs, demonstrated the irrefutable testimonies and have summoned all men unto the straight Path. Among the people there are those who have turned away and repudiated the truth, others have pronounced judgement against Us without any proof or evidence.
>
> *Bahá'u'lláh*[1]

'The Great News or Announcement' (*Nabaa Azim*), 'the Inevitable' or 'the Great Event' (*Al- Wáqi'a*), and 'the Great Catastrophe' (*alṭammatu alkubrá*)

A major and recurring theme of the Qur'án concerns a future spiritual experience which it depicts as a commotion, a truly momentous, awesome and dreadful occurrence the like of which humanity has never before witnessed. By implication, its very anticipation must regulate the conduct of all Muslims. The 78th Súrah of the Qur'án, *Nabaa*, the (Great) News, or the Announcement, is entirely devoted to this event.

> Of what do they ask one another?
> About the great event (great news, announcement).[2]
>
> When the Event Inevitable cometh to pass,
> Then will no (soul) entertain falsehood concerning its coming.[3]
>
> Then on that Day shall the (Great) Event befall.[4]

> Therefore, when there comes the great, overwhelming (Catastrophic Event)
> The Day when Man shall remember (all) that he strove for,
> And Hell-Fire shall be placed in full view for (all) to see,
> Then, for such as had transgressed all bounds,
> And had preferred the life of this world,
> The Abode will be Hell-Fire;
> And for such as had entertained the fear of standing before their Lord's (tribunal) and had restrained (their) soul from lower Desires,
> Their abode will be the Garden.[5]

Bahá'u'lláh declares unequivocally that His Revelation is the '*Nabaa Azim*' or the 'Great News or Announcement' that humanity and all religions, and particularly Islam, must heed.

> Say: I am come to you, O people, from the Throne of glory, and bear you an announcement from God, the Most Powerful, the Most Exalted, the Most Great.[6]

> This is the Announcement, the greatness of which hath been mentioned in most of the Books of old and of more recent times. This is the Announcement that hath caused the limbs of mankind to quake, except such as God, the Protector, the Helper, the Succorer, hath willed to exempt. Men have indeed with their own eyes witnessed how all men and all things have been thrown into confusion and been sore perplexed, save those whom God hath chosen to exempt.
> ... Great is the Cause, and great the Announcement! Patiently and calmly ponder thou upon the resplendent signs and the sublime words, and all that hath been revealed in these days, that haply thou mayest fathom the mysteries that are hid in the Books ...[7]

He moreover affirms that the 'Great Event' has come to pass:

> ... by Him Who is the Revealer of clear tokens! Verily, the Inevitable is come, and He, the True One, hath appeared with proof and testimony ...[8]

The Tanakh also announces the appearance of the 'good tidings' of the coming of the salvation of the Lord, which may be understood as a reference to the Revelations following the Mosaic Dispensation, including Christ and Bahá'u'lláh:

> . . . they that rule over them make them to howl, saith the Lord; and my name continually every day is blasphemed.
>
> Therefore my people shall know my name: therefore they shall know in that day that I am he that doth speak: behold, it is I.
>
> How beautiful upon the mountains are the feet of him that bringeth good tidings, that publisheth peace; that bringeth good tidings of good, that publisheth salvation; that saith unto Zion, Thy God reigneth!
>
> . . . The Lord hath made bare his holy arm in the eyes of all the nations; and all the ends of the earth shall see the salvation of our God.[9]

The Gospel of St Mark interprets the prophecies of Isaiah as referring to John the Baptist, who gave the gospel or 'good news' of the coming of Messiah or Christ.[10] Jesus, in His turn, gave the good news that God's Kingdom would come, and that God would establish it on earth (Matt. 6:9–10), explaining that His own Kingdom was not of this world (John 18:36):

> When ye pray, say, Our Father which art in heaven, Hallowed be thy name. Thy kingdom come. Thy will be done, as in heaven, so in earth.[11]

Therefore, the Gospel or 'good news' that the disciples were instructed to preach concerned, at least in part, Christ's return and the coming in the Glory of the Father (Matt. 16:27). St Paul was engaged in this proclamation and preaching of the Kingdom (Acts 20:25):

> And he said unto them, Go ye into all the world, and preach the gospel (good news) to every creature.[12]

Bahá'u'lláh announces the fulfilment of the Jewish and Christian expectations.

'Followers of the Gospel, behold the gates of heaven are flung open. He that had ascended unto it is now come. Give ear to His voice calling aloud over land and sea, announcing to all mankind the advent of this Revelation – a Revelation through the agency of which the Tongue of Grandeur is now proclaiming: "Lo, the sacred Pledge hath been fulfilled, for He, the Promised One, is come!"' 'The voice of the Son of Man is calling aloud from the sacred vale: "Here am I, here am I, O God my God!" . . . whilst from the Burning Bush breaketh forth the cry: "Lo, the Desire of the world is made manifest in His transcendent glory!" The Father hath come. That which ye were promised in the Kingdom of God is fulfilled. This is the Word which the Son veiled when He said to those around Him that at that time they could not bear it . . . Verily the Spirit of Truth is come to guide you unto all truth . . . He is the One Who glorified the Son and exalted His Cause . . .' 'The Comforter Whose advent all the scriptures have promised is now come that He may reveal unto you all knowledge and wisdom. Seek Him over the entire surface of the earth, haply ye may find Him.'[13]

The advent of 'the Lord' (*Rabb*) and 'the Lord of the Worlds' (*Rabb'u'Álamin*)

He will announce His Message to mankind:

> The day when (all) mankind stand before the Lord of the Worlds.[14]

Isaiah describes the coming of the Lord in dramatic terms:

> The wilderness and the solitary place shall be glad for them; and the desert shall rejoice, and blossom as the rose.
> It shall blossom abundantly, and rejoice even with joy and singing: the glory of Lebanon shall be given unto it, the excellency of Carmel and Sharon, they shall see the glory of the Lord, and the excellency of our God.[15]

> Enter into the rock, and hide thee in the dust, for fear of the Lord, and for the glory of his majesty.
> . . . and the Lord alone shall be exalted in that day.[16]

With reference to the latter announcement Bahá'u'lláh writes:

> No man that meditateth upon this verse can fail to recognize the greatness of this Cause, or doubt the exalted character of this Day – the Day of God Himself . . . This is the Day which the Pen of the Most High hath glorified in all the holy Scriptures.[17]

The Gospels express the desire that Christians will not fail to sincerely expect their Lord:

> Blessed [are] those servants, whom the lord when he cometh shall find watching.[18]

Similarly, the Qur'án expresses the hope that Muslims will not be disgraced in that Day:

> Our Lord! and grant us what Thou hast promised us by Thy apostles; and disgrace us not on the day of resurrection; surely Thou dost not fail to perform the promise.[19]

Muslims are hence required to pray that the *Rabb* will assist them to remain steadfast and not deviate from the truth.

> Our Lord! Let not our hearts deviate now after Thou hast guided us, but grant us mercy from Thine own Presence; for Thou art the Grantor of bounties without measure.[20]

They are instructed to single-mindedly seek only the Lord, the Most High Lord (*rabbihi al-aAAlá*)[21] and praise Him. Those seekers who are sincere will be rewarded:

> Those who spend their wealth for increase in self-purification,
> And have in their minds no favour from anyone for which a reward is expected in return,
> But only the desire to seek for the Countenance of their Lord Most High;
> And soon will they attain (complete) satisfaction.[22]

Glorify the name of thy Lord, Most High.[23]

Therefore be patient with constancy to the Command[24] of thy Lord, and hearken not to the sinner or the ingrate among them.
    And celebrate the name of thy Lord morning and evening
    And part of the night, prostrate thyself to Him; and glorify Him a long night through.[25]

Clearly, one explanation is that 'the Lord' refers to God, but according to Bahá'u'lláh, '*Rabb*' more specifically depicts the station of the Divine Messenger, Who is the '*Murabbí*' or educator and spiritual teacher of all mankind (*Nás*, Mankind, 114:1), and Who is sent by God to usher in His Day, as in 'the coming of the Father' and 'the Day of the Father' in the Bible. Hence, the term applies to both the Báb and Bahá'u'lláh.

The Qur'án explains that only those who are patient and humble and have faith may meet with their Lord.

Nay, seek (God's) help with patient perseverance and prayer: it is indeed hard, except to those who bring a lowly spirit.
    Who bear in mind the certainty that they are to meet their Lord, and that they are to return to Him.[26]

Only those individuals who are unaffected by worldly desires are predicted to recognize that Day and to receive its spiritual benefits.

The Companions of the Fire will call to the companions of the Garden: 'Pour down to us water or anything that God doth provide for your sustenance.' They will say: 'Both these things hath God forbidden to those who rejected Him.
    'Such as took their religion to be mere amusement and play, and were deceived by the life of the world.' That day shall We forget them as they forgot the meeting of this day of theirs, and as they were wont to reject Our Signs.[27]

The coming of the 'Balance' (*Mizán*)

In every succeeding Dispensation God redefines 'right' and 'wrong', discriminating between light and darkness, justice and injustice, and moderation and extremism or fanaticism. It is by means of this divine 'Balance' that all human conduct is judged and regulated.

According to the Qur'án, this 'Balance' was revealed in the Dispensation of Muḥammad but also by all the preceding divine Messengers:

> It is God Who has sent down the Book in truth, and the Balance.[28]

> And the Firmament has He raised high, and He has set up the Balance (of Justice)
> In order that ye may not transgress (due) balance.[29]

> We sent aforetime Our apostles with Clear Signs and sent down with them The Book and the Balance (of right and wrong), that men may stand forth in justice . . .[30]

The 'Balance' is to be re-revealed, and right again distinguished from error:

> The balance that Day will be true: those whose scale (of good) will be heavy, will prosper.[31]

> That Day, the dominion as of right and truth, shall be (wholly) for (God) Most Merciful: it will be a Day of dire difficulty for the Misbelievers.[32]

In the Bible, it was by means of this Balance that the Prophet Daniel found King Belshazzar to be spiritually deficient.

> Thou art weighed in the balances, and art found wanting.[33]

It is by means of this Balance that Christians are told that they can be free of sin 'and ye shall know the truth, and the truth shall make you free (from error) and sin'.[34]

And Bahá'u'lláh proclaims that in His Revelation the Balance has again 'been appointed':

The Balance hath been appointed, and all them that dwell on earth have been gathered together. The Trumpet hath been blown, and lo, all eyes have stared up with terror, and the hearts of all who are in the heavens and on the earth have trembled, except them whom the breath of the verses of God hath quickened, and who have detached themselves from all things.[35]

Signs accompanying the coming of the Lord of Hosts, the Kingdom of God, and the 'Great Event'

The Bible and the Qur'án are replete with signs that herald the Day of Bahá'u'lláh. Several of these seemingly physical portents have been understood to also apply to the Dispensations of Christ and Muhammad allegorically and have been explained in spiritual terms. Similarly, predictions concerning the divine visitation are accompanied by the warning that 'of that day and that hour knoweth no man, no, not the angels which are in heaven, neither the Son, but the Father'.[36] In the Qur'án the figurative statements may be considered as part of the *mushtabihat*, whose meanings are understood by those with firm faith who have been guided (*Ál-i-'Imrán*, the Family of 'Imrán, 3:7). Any investigation must therefore avoid folklore and theological speculation and rely solely on the Divine Word. Bahá'u'lláh exhorts the true seeker to cleanse and purify his heart 'from the obscuring dust of all acquired knowledge' and idle fancy, derived mostly from ephemeral and materialistic considerations.[37]

Descent in clouds

The divine visitation will come down in clouds, at which time all questions of faith are to be addressed to the Author of God's new Revelation:

> Will they wait until God comes to them in canopies of clouds, with angels (in His train) and the question is (thus) settled? But to God do all questions go back (for decision).[38]

The Tanakh also warns that it will be a day of darkness and clouds:

> A day of darkness and of gloominess, a day of clouds and of thick darkness, as the morning spread upon the mountains: a great people

and a strong; there hath not been ever the like, neither shall be any more after it, even to the years of many generations.[39]

That day is a day of wrath, a day of trouble and distress, a day of wasteness and desolation, a day of darkness and gloominess, a day of clouds and thick darkness.[40]

The Gospels similarly refer to a period of darkness and the shaking of the powers of heaven:

Immediately after the tribulation of those days shall the sun be darkened, and the moon shall not give her light, and the stars shall fall from heaven, and the powers of the heavens shall be shaken.[41]

Christ will return in 'clouds':

And then shall appear the sign of the Son of man in heaven: and then shall all the tribes of the earth mourn, and they shall see the Son of man coming in the clouds of heaven with power and great glory.[42]

Jesus saith unto him, Thou hast said: nevertheless I say unto you, Hereafter shall ye see the Son of man sitting on the right hand of power, and coming in the clouds of heaven.[43]

Behold, he cometh with clouds; and every eye shall see him . . .[44]

Darkening of the sun and moon

When the sun (with its spacious light) is folded up.[45]

The Hour has drawn near, and the moon has been cleft asunder.[46]

And the moon will be eclipsed,
And the sun and moon will be joined together.[47]

The Qur'án equates darkness with spiritual ignorance and abasement.

> A Book which We have revealed unto thee, in order that thou mightest lead mankind out of the depths of darkness into light – by the leave of their Lord – to the Way of (Him) the Exalted in power, worthy of all praise![48]

> From the depths of darkness He will lead them forth into light. Of those who reject faith the patrons (leaders) the evil ones: from light they will lead them (their followers) forth into the depths of darkness. They will be companions of the fire, to dwell therein (for ever).[49]

> We sent Moses with Our signs (and the command). 'Bring out thy people from the depths of darkness into light, and teach them to remember the Days of God.' Verily in this there are Signs for such as are firmly patient and constant, – grateful and appreciative.[50]

> He is the One Who sends to His Servant Manifest Signs, that He may lead you from the depths of Darkness into the Light and verily God is to you most kind and Merciful.[51]

> But those who have earned evil will have a reward of like evil: ignominy will cover their (faces): No defender will they have from (the wrath of) God: Their faces will be covered, as it were, with pieces from the depth of the darkness of night: they are companions of the Fire: they will abide therein (for aye)![52]

The Qur'án further describes a recurring spiritual cycle: brilliant Days of God alternating with dark nights of despair.

> He merges Night into Day, and He merges Day into Night; and He has full knowledge of the secrets of (all) hearts.[53]

The Tanakh also describes the 'darkening' of the sun, the moon and the stars, when the reign of the Lord of Hosts will be accompanied by spiritual darkness and violence.

> For the stars of heaven and the constellations thereof shall not give their light: the sun shall be darkened in his going forth, and the moon shall not cause her light to shine.[54]

> Then the moon shall be confounded, and the sun ashamed, when the Lord of hosts shall reign in mount Zion, and in Jerusalem, and before his ancients gloriously.[55]

> Arise, shine; for thy light is come, and the glory of the Lord is risen upon thee.
> For, behold, the darkness shall cover the earth, and gross darkness the people: but the Lord shall arise upon thee, and his glory shall be seen upon thee.[56]

> The sun shall be turned into darkness, and the moon into blood, before the great and the terrible day of the Lord come.[57]

Notably, the disciple Peter announced that all the signs predicted by the Prophet Joel, including the darkening of the sun and the turning of the moon into blood, had come to pass with the coming of Christ, indicating that the signs were understood figuratively.

> For these are not drunken, as ye suppose, seeing it is but the third hour of the day.
> But this is that which was spoken by the prophet Joel:
> And it shall come to pass in the last days, saith God, I will pour out of my Spirit upon all flesh: and your sons and your daughters shall prophesy, and your young men shall see visions, and your old men shall dream dreams:
> And on my servants and on my handmaidens I will pour out in those days of my Spirit; and they shall prophesy:
> And I will show wonders in heaven above, and signs in the earth beneath; blood, and fire, and vapour of smoke:
> The sun shall be turned into darkness, and the moon into blood, before that great and notable day of the Lord come.[58]

Christ predicted the darkening of the sun and the moon at His second coming, and equated, respectively, light and darkness with the presence and absence of spiritual guidance.

> But in those days, after that tribulation, the sun shall be darkened, and the moon shall not give her light.[59]

I am come a light into the world, that whosoever believeth on me should not abide in darkness.[60]

In him [Jesus] was life, and the life was the light of men.
 And the light shineth in darkness; and the darkness comprehended it not.[61]

In other words, Christ was the source of spiritual life versus spiritual death, and His spiritual teachings were a source of light intended to guide humanity out of its darkness. The people dwelling in the darkness were unreceptive to the divine Light, but despite their opposition they could not put it out.

For ye were sometimes darkness, but now are ye light in the Lord: walk as children of light: (For the fruit of the Spirit is in all goodness and righteousness and truth.)[62]

The New Testament predicts future loss of faith, false asceticism, and mass apostasy.

Now the Spirit speaketh expressly, that in the latter times some shall depart from the faith, giving heed to seducing spirits, and doctrines of devils;
 Speaking lies in hypocrisy; having their conscience seared with a hot iron.
 Forbidding to marry, and commanding to abstain from meats, which God hath created to be received with thanksgiving of them which believe and know the truth.[63]

It anticipates that man will once again be preoccupied with purely materialistic pursuits and be less concerned with spiritual growth and achievements.

And as it was in the days of Noah, so shall it be also in the days of the Son of man.
 They did eat, they drank, they married wives, they were given in marriage, until the day that Noah entered into the ark, and the flood came, and destroyed them all . . .

> Even thus shall it be in the day when the Son of man is revealed.[64]

> . . for that day shall not come, except there come a falling away first . . .[65]

The Tanakh also describes that the darkening of the horizons of religion will, as in the past, be associated with lack of spiritual receptivity.

> Seeing many things, but thou observest not; opening the ears, but he heareth not.[66]

> Son of man, thou dwellest in the midst of a rebellious house, which have eyes to see, and see not; they have ears to hear, and hear not: for they are a rebellious house.[67]

> Behold, the days come, saith the Lord God, that I will send a famine in the land, not a famine of bread, nor a thirst for water, but of hearing the words of the Lord:
> And they shall wander from sea to sea, and from the north even to the east, they shall run to and fro to seek the word of the Lord, and shall not find it.[68]

> I will make waste mountains and hills, and dry up all their herbs; and I will make the rivers islands, and I will dry up the pools.[69]

Bahá'u'lláh explains that terms such as 'sun', 'moon' and 'stars' as used in the Holy Books have manifold explanations:

> Thus, by the 'sun' in one sense is meant those Suns of Truth Who rise from the dayspring of ancient glory, and fill the world with a liberal effusion of grace from on high. These Suns of Truth are the universal Manifestations of God in the worlds of His attributes and names, even as the visible sun that assisteth, as decreed by God, the true One, the Adored, in the development of all earthly things, such as the trees, the fruits, and colours thereof, the minerals of the earth, and all that may be witnessed in the world of creation, so do the divine Luminaries, by their loving care and educative influence, cause the trees of divine unity, the fruits of His oneness, the

leaves of detachment, the blossoms of knowledge and certitude, and the myrtles of wisdom and utterance, to exist and be made manifest. Thus it is that through the rise of these Luminaries of God the world is made new, the waters of everlasting life stream forth, the billows of loving-kindness surge, the clouds of grace are gathered, and the breeze of bounty bloweth upon all created things. It is the warmth that these Luminaries of God generate, and the undying fires they kindle, which cause the light of the love of God to burn fiercely in the heart of humanity. It is through the abundant grace of these Symbols of Detachment that the Spirit of life everlasting is breathed into the bodies of the dead. Assuredly the visible sun is but a sign of the splendour of that Day-star of Truth, that Sun Which can never have a peer, a likeness, or rival. Through Him all things live, move, and have their being. Through His grace they are made manifest, and unto Him they all return. From Him all things have sprung, and unto the treasuries of His revelation they all have repaired. From Him all created things did proceed, and to the depositories of His law they did revert.[70]

The term 'suns' hath many a time been applied in the writings of the 'immaculate Souls' unto the Prophets of God, those luminous Emblems of Detachment. Among those writings are the following words recorded in the 'Prayer of Nudbih': 'Whither are gone the resplendent Suns? Whereunto have departed those shining Moons and sparkling Stars?' Thus, it hath become evident that the terms 'sun', 'moon', and 'stars' primarily signify the Prophets of God, the saints, and their companions, those Luminaries, the light of Whose knowledge hath shed illumination upon the worlds of the visible and the invisible.[71]

In another sense, by the terms 'sun', 'moon', and 'stars' are meant such laws and teachings as have been established and proclaimed in every Dispensation, such as the laws of prayer and fasting. These have, according to the law of the Qur'án, been regarded, when the beauty of the Prophet Muhammad had passed beyond the veil, as the most fundamental and binding laws of His dispensation.[72]

The 'fall', 'darkening' and 'dispersal' of the 'stars'

The New Testament predicts the fall of the stars.

> Immediately after the tribulation of those days shall the sun be darkened, and the moon shall not give her light, and the stars shall fall from heaven, and the powers of the heavens shall be shaken.[73]

> And the stars of heaven shall fall, and the powers that are in heaven shall be shaken.[74]

> And there shall be signs in the sun, and in the moon, and in the stars; and upon the earth distress of nations, with perplexity; the sea and the waves roaring.[75]

The Qur'án also predicts the fall and dispersion of stars.

> And when the stars shall disperse.[76]

> Verily that which ye are promised is imminent. When the stars, therefore, shall be blotted out . . .[77]

> When the stars fall, losing their lustre.[78]

> When the stars shall disperse . . .[79]

Bahá'u'lláh explains that the fall of stars also refers to the plight of religious leaders who, because of their denial of the following Revelation, have lost influence over their flock.

> In another sense, by these terms [sun, moon and stars] is intended the divines of the former Dispensation, who live in the days of the subsequent Revelations, and who hold the reins of religion in their grasp. If these divines be illumined by the light of the latter Revelation they will be acceptable unto God, and will shine with a light everlasting. Otherwise, they will be declared as darkened, even though to outward seeming they be leaders of men, inasmuch as belief and unbelief, guidance and error, felicity and misery, light

and darkness, are all dependent upon the sanction of Him Who is the Day-star of Truth. Whosoever among the divines of every age receiveth, in the Day of Reckoning, the testimony of faith from the Source of true knowledge, he verily becometh the recipient of learning, of divine favour, and of the light of true understanding. Otherwise, he is branded as guilty of folly, denial, blasphemy, and oppression.

It is evident and manifest unto every discerning observer that even as the light of the star fadeth before the effulgent splendour of the sun, so doth the luminary of earthly knowledge, of wisdom, and understanding vanish into nothingness when brought face to face with the resplendent glories of the Sun of Truth, the Day-star of divine enlightenment.[80]

... by the words 'the sun shall be darkened, and the moon shall not give her light, and the stars shall fall from heaven' is intended the waywardness of the divines, and the annulment of laws firmly established by divine Revelation, all of which, in symbolic language, have been foreshadowed by the Manifestation of God. None except the righteous shall partake of this cup, none but the godly can share therein. 'The righteous shall drink of a cup tempered at the camphor fountain' [*Insán*, Man, 76:5].[81]

O concourse of divines! This is the day whereon nothing amongst all things, nor any name amongst all names, can profit you save through this Name which God hath made the Manifestation of His Cause and the Dayspring of His Most Excellent Titles unto all who are in the kingdom of creation. Blessed is that man that hath recognized the fragrance of the All-Merciful and been numbered with the steadfast. Your sciences shall not profit you in this day, nor your arts, nor your treasures, nor your glory. Cast them all behind your backs, and set your faces towards the Most Sublime Word through which the Scriptures and the Books and this lucid Tablet have been distinctly set forth. Cast away, O concourse of divines, the things ye have composed with the pens of your idle fancies and vain imaginings. By God! The Day-Star of Knowledge hath shone forth above the horizon of certitude.[82]

The term 'stars' also includes Christian spiritual leaders:

> O concourse of bishops! Ye are the stars of the heaven of My knowledge. My mercy desireth not that ye should fall upon the earth. My justice, however, declareth: 'This is that which the Son hath decreed.' And whatsoever hath proceeded out of His blameless, His truth-speaking, trustworthy mouth, can never be altered. The bells, verily, peal out My Name, and lament over Me, but My spirit rejoiceth with evident gladness.[83]

> These 'fallen stars' of the firmament of Christendom, these 'thick clouds' that have obscured the radiance of the true Faith of God, these princes of the Church that have failed to acknowledge the sovereignty of the 'King of kings', these deluded ministers of the Son who have shunned and ignored the promised Kingdom which the 'Everlasting Father' has brought down from heaven, and is now establishing upon earth – these are experiencing, in this 'Day of Reckoning', a crisis, not indeed as critical as that which the Islamic sacerdotal order, the inveterate enemies of the Faith, has had to face, but one which is no less widespread and significant. 'Power hath been seized' indeed, and is being increasingly seized, from these ecclesiastics that speak in the name, and yet are so far away from the spirit, of the Faith they profess.[84]

Those leaders, however, that truly guide their followers must be respected:

> O people of God! Righteous men of learning who dedicate themselves to the guidance of others and are freed and well guarded from the promptings of a base and covetous nature are, in the sight of Him Who is the Desire of the world, stars of the heaven of true knowledge. It is essential to treat them with deference. They are indeed fountains of soft-flowing water, stars that shine resplendent, fruits of the blessed Tree, exponents of celestial power, and oceans of heavenly wisdom. Happy is he that followeth them. Verily such a soul is numbered in the Book of God, the Lord of the mighty Throne, among those with whom it shall be well.[85]

O friends! Be not careless of the virtues with which ye have been endowed, neither be neglectful of your high destiny. Suffer not your labours to be wasted through the vain imaginations which certain hearts have devised. Ye are the stars of the heaven of understanding, the breeze that stirred at the break of day, the soft-flowing waters upon which must depend the very life of all men, the letters inscribed upon His sacred scroll. With the utmost unity, and in a spirit of perfect fellowship, exert yourselves, that ye may be enabled to achieve that which beseemeth this Day of God. Verily I say, strife and dissension, and whatsoever the mind of man abhorreth are entirely unworthy of his station. Center your energies in the propagation of the Faith of God. Whoso is worthy of so high a calling, let him arise and promote it.[86]

'Stars' may also refer to the laws of a Revelation, as in the case of the *Kitáb-i-Aqdas*, the Most Holy Book of the Revelation of Bahá'u'lláh:

'This Book', He [Bahá'u'lláh] Himself testifies, 'is a heaven which We have adorned with the stars of Our commandments and prohibitions.' 'Blessed the man', He, moreover, has stated, 'who will read it, and ponder the verses sent down in it by God, the Lord of Power, the Almighty.'[87]

Stars are also equated with guidance and protection from evil, as in the Qur'án:

It is He Who maketh the stars (as beacons) for you, that ye may guide yourselves,
　　With their help, through the dark spaces of land and sea: We detail Our Signs for people who know.[88]

Verily, verily, your God is One! –
　　Lord of the heavens and of the earth, and all between them, and Lord of every point at the rising of the sun!
　　We have indeed decked the lower heaven with beauty (In) the stars,–
　　(For beauty) and for guard against all obstinate rebellious evil spirits.[89]

Also, the spectacular display of falling stars while Bahá'u'lláh was in Adrianople may be considered a literal fulfilment of the prophecies.

> In November 1866 when Bahá'u'lláh was residing in the house of Riḍá Big, a spectacular meteoric shower took place. Thousands of shooting-stars lit up the sky as they blazed their way through the atmosphere. This event, which has been called the 'star-fall' of 1866, was watched by millions in the East and West and for many the experience was terrifying.[90]

Those that guide people to righteousness are referred to as stars.

> And they that be wise shall shine as the brightness of the firmament; and they that turn many to righteousness as the stars for ever and ever.[91]

> . . . there shall come a Star out of Jacob, and a Sceptre shall rise out of Israel . . .[92]

The spiritual leaders of that day will no longer be able to enlighten their followers and will consequently fall from the lofty positions that they occupy.

> The earth shall quake . . . , the heavens shall tremble: the sun and the moon shall be dark, and the stars shall withdraw their shining: And the Lord shall utter his voice before his army . . .[93]

> The sun and the moon shall be darkened, and the stars shall withdraw their shining.[94]

> Behold, the day of the Lord cometh, cruel both in wrath and fierce anger, to lay the land desolate: and he shall destroy the sinners thereof out of it. For the stars of heaven and the constellations thereof shall not give their light: the sun shall be darkened in his going forth, and the moon shall not cause her light to shine.[95]

A Day that shall not be followed by night

Paradoxically, that 'Day' is expected to be eternally and brilliantly bright.

> No falsehood can approach it from before or behind it: It is sent down by One Full of Wisdom, Worthy of all Praise.[96]

> And when the chief Shepherd shall appear, ye shall receive a crown of glory that fadeth not away.[97]

> And the city [New Jerusalem] had no need of the sun, neither of the moon, to shine in it: for the glory of God [translated as 'Bahá'u'lláh' in certain early Arabic translations of the Bible until the late 19th century] did lighten it . . .[98]

> And the gates of it shall not be shut at all by day: for there shall be no night there.[99]

> And they shall see his face; and his [God's] name shall be in their foreheads.
> And there shall be no night there; and they need no candle, neither light of the sun; for the Lord God giveth them light: and they shall reign for ever and ever.[100]

> The sun shall be no more thy light by day; neither for brightness shall the moon give light unto thee; but the Lord shall be unto thee an everlasting light, and thy God thy glory.
> Thy sun shall no more go down; neither shall thy moon withdraw itself: for the Lord shall be thine everlasting light, and the days of thy mourning shall be ended.
> Thy people also shall be all righteous: they shall inherit the land for ever, the branch of my planting, the work of my hands, that I may be glorified.
> A little one shall become a thousand, and a small one a strong nation: I the Lord will hasten it in his time.[101]

> Moreover the light of the moon shall be as the light of the sun, and the light of the sun shall be sevenfold, as the light of seven days,

EMBRACING 'THE GREAT ANNOUNCEMENT' OF THE QUR'ÁN

> in the Day that the Lord bindeth up the breach of his people, and healeth the stroke of their wound.[102]

> But unto you that fear my name shall the Sun of righteousness arise with healing in his wings . . .[103]

In past Dispensations, the light of revelation has been darkened by sectarian violence and controversies over who was the legitimate successor of the Prophet, and further obscured by bitter arguments over dogma and tradition. It is therefore noteworthy in this context that the Author of the Bahá'í Revelation, Bahá'u'lláh, has invested the Universal House of Justice with absolute authority to adjudicate on matters not specifically dealt with in His Most Holy Book, the *Kitáb-i-Aqdas*. The unity of the Bahá'í Faith has also been ensured by clear statements concerning succession at each stage of its unfolding destiny.

The Day of Destruction and of the 'passing away of mountains'

The Qur'án frequently uses the imagery of mountains 'crumbling' or 'passing away':

> And you will see the mountains and think them solid, but they shall pass away as the passing away of the clouds. The Work of God, Who perfected all things, verily! He is well-acquainted with what you do.[104]

> And the mountains shall be like flocks of carded wool.[105]

> The day cometh when the earth and the mountains shall be shaken; and the mountains shall become a loose sand heap.[106]

> They will ask thee of the mountains (on that day). Say: My Lord will break them into scattered dust.[107]

> And the mountains shall be made to crumble with (an awful) crumbling.[108]

> And the earth is moved, and its mountains, and they are crushed to powder at one stroke.[109]

And the mountains will be like wool . . .[110]

When the mountains are scattered (to the winds) as dust . . .[111]

And the mountains shall vanish, as if they were a mirage.[112]

And when the mountains are made to pass away.[113]

One explanation of 'mountains' is that it refers to individuals such as the clergy who sustain the heaven of a religion. Bahá'u'lláh explains that the passing of the mountains refers to the plight of the clerical authorities who occupy high positions formerly viewed as unassailable:

> So blind hath become the human heart that neither the disruption of the city, nor the reduction of the mountain in dust, nor even the cleaving of the earth, can shake off its torpor. The allusions made in the Scriptures have been unfolded, and the signs recorded therein have been revealed, and the prophetic cry is continually being raised. And yet all, except such as God was pleased to guide, are bewildered in the drunkenness of their heedlessness![114]

> We beseech God to purge the hearts of certain divines from rancor and enmity, that they may look upon matters with an eye unbeclouded by contempt. May He raise them up unto so lofty a station that neither the attractions of the world, nor the allurements of authority, may deflect them from gazing upon the Supreme Horizon, and that neither worldly benefits nor carnal desires shall prevent them from attaining that Day whereon the mountains shall be reduced to dust. Though they now rejoice in the adversity that hath befallen Us, soon shall come a day whereon they shall lament and weep.[115]

Similar Biblical prophecies support this interpretation:

> Hear ye now what the Lord saith; Arise, contend thou before the mountains, and let the hills hear thy voice.
> Hear ye, O mountains, the Lord's controversy, and ye strong foundations of the earth: for the Lord hath a controversy with his people, and he will plead with Israel.[116]

> And the mountains shall be molten under him, and the valleys shall be cleft, as wax before the fire, and as the waters that are poured down a steep place.[117]

What is 'earthly' will be levelled or made plain: all will be made clear and there will be equalization of ranks and privileges through the promotion of new principles and social laws such as the oneness of humanity, and the equality of men and women.

> And (remember) the Day We shall cause the mountains to pass away (like clouds of dust), and you will see the earth as a leveled plain, and we shall gather them all together so as to leave not one of them behind.[118]

> They ask thee concerning the mountains: say, 'My Lord will uproot them and scatter them as dust;'
> 'He will leave them as plains smooth and level,
> Nothing crooked or curved wilt thou see in their place.'
> On that Day will they follow the Caller (straight): no crookedness (can they show) him: all sounds shall humble themselves in the presence of (God) Most Gracious: nothing shalt thou hear but the tramp of their feet (as they march).[119]

> On that day ye will be exposed; not a secret of you will be hidden.[120]

'The 'cleaving asunder'[121] 'rolling up' or 'folding' of the heavens

These momentous events are frequently referred to in the Qur'án:

> And when the heaven shall be cleft . . .[122]

> When the heaven shall have split asunder and duteously obeyed its Lord.[123]

> When the heaven is cleft asunder.[124]

> The very heaven being then rent asunder. His promise is to be fulfilled.[125]

> When the Heaven shall be cleft asunder, and become rose red, like stained leather.[126]

The Bible refers to the moon turning into blood, which is also coloured red, thereby predicting that the religion will become embroiled in bloodshed. Its social laws (its moon) will engender strife.

> And I will show wonders in heaven above, and signs in the earth beneath; blood, and fire, and vapour of smoke:
> The sun shall be turned into darkness, and the moon into blood, before that great and notable day of the Lord come.[127]

Emission of smoke from heaven enshrouding humanity

> Then watch thou for the Day that the sky will bring forth a kind of smoke (or mist) plainly visible,
> Enveloping the people: this will be a penalty grievous.
> (They will say:) 'Our Lord! Remove the penalty from us, for we do really believe!'
> How shall the Message be (effectual) for them, seeing that an Apostle explaining things clearly has (already) come to them, –
> Yet they turn away from him and say: 'tutored (by others), a man possessed!'[128]

The Torah declares that the Lord of Hosts is the Creator of heavens and earth, and describes the creation of new heavens and earth.

> O Lord of hosts, God of Israel, that dwellest between the cherubims, thou art the God, even thou alone, of all the kingdoms of the earth: thou hast made heaven and earth.[129]

> For as the new heavens and the new earth, which I will make, shall remain before me, saith the Lord, so shall your seed and your name remain.[130]

> For, behold, I create new heavens and a new earth: and the former shall not be remembered, nor come into mind.[131]

The New Testament also promises the dissipation of the old heavens and the birth of new heavens and a new earth.

> Nevertheless we, according to his promise, look for new heavens and a new earth, wherein dwelleth righteousness.[132]

> And I saw a new heaven and a new earth: for the first heaven and the first earth were passed away; and there was no more sea.[133]

The 'earth' will be subjected to 'earthquakes' (al-zilzál)

The Tanakh:

> Thou shalt be visited of the Lord of hosts with thunder, and with earthquake, and great noise, with storm and tempest, and the flame of devouring fire.[134]

The Gospels:

> For nation shall rise against nation, and kingdom against kingdom: and there shall be famines, and pestilences, and earthquakes, in divers places.[135]

The Qur'án:

> O mankind! Fear your Lord! For the convulsion of the Hour (of Judgment) will be a thing terrible![136]

The violent commotions experienced by the 'earth' will coincide with the Revelation or Inspiration that it will receive.

> When the earth is shaken to her (utmost) convulsion,
> And the earth throws up her burden,
> And man cries: 'What is the matter with her?'
> On that Day will she declare her tidings:
> For that thy Lord will have given her inspiration.[137]

The whole earth will be in God's hands

> No just estimate have they made of God, such as is due to Him: on the Day of Judgement the whole of the earth will be but His handful, and the heavens will be rolled up in His right hand: Glory to Him! High is He above the partners they attribute to Him![138]

Just as the 'heaven' of religion will be renewed, so will the 'earth' of human understanding be transformed; it will be revived and resurrected, as in the past.

> Have they not considered within themselves that God hath not created the Heavens and the Earth and all that is between them but for a serious end, and for a fixed term? But truly most men believe not that they shall meet their Lord.[139]

> On the day when the Earth shall be changed into another Earth, and the Heavens also, men shall come forth unto God, the Only, the Victorious.[140]

> It is He Who brings out the living from the dead, and brings out the dead from the living, and Who gives life to the earth after it is dead: and thus shall ye be brought out (from the dead).[141]

> A token unto them is the dead earth. We revive it, and We bring forth from it grain so that they eat thereof.[142]

The earth will shine with the light of its Lord

> And the earth will shine with the glory (light) of its Lord: the record will be placed; the prophets and the witnesses will be brought forward; and a just decision pronounced between them; and they will not be wronged.[143]

'The mystery of reversal' (sirr al-tankís)

With every new Dispensation, certain values that were previously considered sacrosanct are rejected, but other precepts flourish and are promoted.

Similarly, based largely on their reactions to the Divine Purpose, certain individuals of humble origin achieve exalted ranks while others who were previously in positions of authority are abased. This 'reversal' affecting hallowed principles and personalities is predicted in the Bible and the Qur'án to be a prominent feature of the Bahá'í Revelation.

> The lofty looks of man shall be humbled, and the haughtiness of men shall be bowed down . . .
> For the day of the Lord of hosts shall be upon every one that is proud and lofty, and upon every one that is lifted up; and he shall be brought low.[144]

The Prophet Isaiah predicts that while mountains (perhaps individuals with lofty titles) will be brought low, simultaneously valleys (lowly people who are not from a clerical background and who are not versed in theology) will be elevated in rank. The crooked paths (false ideas and clerical misinterpretations) will be corrected and rendered straight.

> Prepare ye the way of the Lord, make straight in the desert a highway for our God.
> Every valley shall be exalted, and every mountain and hill shall be made low: and the crooked shall be made straight, and the rough places plain.[145]

The Gospels promise that the abasement of the mountains and the exaltation of the valleys will be repeated with the second return of Elijah[146] when all humanity will witness divine intervention.

> As it is written in the book of the words of Esaias the prophet, saying, The voice of one crying in the wilderness, Prepare ye the way of the Lord, make his paths straight.
> Every valley shall be filled, and every mountain and hill shall be brought low; and the crooked shall be made straight, and the rough ways shall be made smooth;
> And all flesh shall see the salvation of God.[147]

Jesus also alludes to this reversal in the spiritual and social fortunes of individuals:

So the last shall be first, and the first last: for many be called, but few chosen.[148]

The Qur'án reminds us of this dire consequence of the anticipated Day:

> When the day that must come shall have come suddenly,
> None shall treat that sudden coming as a lie:
> Day that shall abase! Day that shall exalt!
> When the earth shall be shaken with a shock . . .[149]

Warning His own followers concerning the Revelation of Bahá'u'lláh, the Báb writes:

> O people of the Bayán! Be on your guard; for on the Day of Resurrection no one shall find a place to flee to. He will shine forth suddenly, and will pronounce judgement as He pleaseth. If it be His wish He will cause the abased to be exalted, and the exalted to be abased, even as He did in the Bayán, couldst thou but understand. And no one but Him is equal unto this. Whatever He ordaineth will be fulfilled, and nothing will remain unfulfilled.[150]

Bahá'u'lláh explains that this principle of reversal has been operative in earlier Dispensations:

> Consider the Dispensation of Jesus Christ. Behold, how all the learned men of that generation, though eagerly anticipating the coming of the Promised One, have nevertheless denied Him. Both Annas, the most learned among the divines of His day, and Caiaphas, the high priest, denounced Him and pronounced the sentence of His death.
> In like manner, when Muḥammad, the Prophet of God – may all men be a sacrifice unto Him – appeared, the learned men of Mecca and Medina arose, in the early days of His Revelation, against Him and rejected His Message, while they who were destitute of all learning recognized and embraced His Faith. Ponder a while. Consider how Balál, the Ethiopian, unlettered though he was, ascended into the heaven of faith and certitude, whilst 'Abdu'lláh Ubayy, a leader among the learned, maliciously strove to oppose Him . . . For this

reason He hath written: 'He that is exalted among you shall be abased, and he that is abased shall be exalted.' References to this theme are to be found in most of the heavenly Books, as well as in the sayings of the Prophets and Messengers of God.[151]

Bahá'u'lláh states further that this reversal of fortunes will be recognized also as a prominent feature of His Dispensation:

> . . . in one of His Tablets [He] refers to the 'symbol and allusion' of the 'mystery of the Great Reversal in the Sign of the Sovereign'. He states: 'Through this reversal He hath caused the exalted to be abased and the abased to be exalted,' and He recalls that 'in the days of Jesus, it was those who were distinguished for their learning, the men of letters and religion, who denied Him, whilst humble fishermen made haste to gain admittance into the Kingdom'.[152]

> Behold, the 'mystery of the Great Reversal in the Sign of the Sovereign' hath now been made manifest . . . How many the outwardly pious who have turned away, and how many the wayward who have drawn nigh, exclaiming: 'All praise be to Thee, O Thou the Desire of the worlds!'. . . How many an embodiment of heedlessness who came unto Us with purity of heart have We established upon the seat of Our acceptance; and how many an exponent of wisdom have We in all justice consigned to the fire. We are, in truth, the One to judge. He it is Who is the manifestation of 'God doeth whatsoever He pleaseth', and abideth upon the throne of 'He ordaineth whatsoever He chooseth'.[153]

Specifically:

> 'From two ranks amongst men,' is His terse and prophetic utterance, 'power hath been seized: kings and ecclesiastics.' 'If ye pay no heed,' He thus warned the kings of the earth, 'unto the counsels which . . . We have revealed in this Tablet, Divine chastisement will assail you from every direction . . . On that day ye shall . . . recognize your own impotence.[154]

The generality of mankind will be able to respond to His Call

He will be the Promised One of all revealed religions. 'Every eye', 'many nations', 'all nations', and 'many people' will behold that Day – that is, will be endowed with the spiritual capacity to discern and to recognize that Day, because not only has their particular religion alluded to the Event, but the Revelation of Bahá'u'lláh has also provided the spiritual insight and explanations of the scriptures.

> And the glory of the Lord [in Arabic, Bahá'u'lláh] shall be revealed, and all flesh shall see it together; for the mouth of the Lord hath spoken it.[155]

> And it shall come to pass in the last days, that the mountain of the Lord's house shall be established in the top of the mountains, and shall be exalted above the hills; and all nations shall flow unto it.
> And many nations shall go and say, Come ye, and let us go up to the mountain of the Lord, to the house of the God of Jacob; and he will teach us of his ways, and we will walk in his paths: for out of Zion shall go forth the Law, and the word of the Lord from Jerusalem.
> And he shall judge among many people, and rebuke strong nations afar off; and they beat their swords into pruning hooks: nation shall not lift up a sword against nation, neither shall they learn war any more.[156]

> So shall he sprinkle many nations . . .[157]

> And the Lord shall be king over all the earth: In that day shall there be one Lord and his name one.[158]

> Behold, he cometh with clouds; and every eye shall see him, and they also which pierced him: and all kindreds of the earth shall wail because of him. Even so, Amen.[159]

Hence, both the Jews and the gentiles shall see the light (Glory) of God:

> And the Gentiles shall come to thy light, and the kings to the brightness of thy rising.[160]

> And in that day there shall be a root of Jesse, which shall stand for an ensign of the people, to it shall the Gentiles seek: and his rest shall be glorious.[161]

> And it shall come to pass afterward, that I will pour out my spirit upon all flesh . . .[162]

The 'Desire of all nations' shall come:

> And I will shake all nations, and the desire of all nations shall come; I will fill this house with glory, saith the Lord of hosts.[163]

16

RECOGNITION OF THE PROMISED 'DAY' AND 'HOUR'

'This . . . is the king of days' [*Sultán-i-Ayám*], the 'Day of God Himself' [*Yawmu-lláh*], the 'Day which shall never be followed by night', the 'Springtime which autumn will never overtake', 'the eye to past ages and centuries', for which 'the soul of every Prophet of God, of every Divine Messenger, hath thirsted', for which 'all the divers kindreds of the earth have yearned'. . .   *Bahá'u'lláh*[1]

The Revelation of Bahá'u'lláh announces the beginning of the time promised in all the Holy Books as the 'Day of God', 'the Day that hath seen the coming of the Best-Beloved, Him Who, through all eternity, hath been acclaimed the Desire of the World'.[2] He further explains:

> The Scriptures of past Dispensations celebrate the great Jubilee that must needs greet this most great Day of God. Well is it with him that hath lived to see this Day and hath recognized its station.[3]

> It is evident that every age in which a Manifestation of God hath lived is divinely ordained, and may, in a sense, be characterized as God's appointed Day. This Day, however, is unique, and is to be distinguished from those that have preceded it. The designation 'Seal of the Prophets' fully revealeth its high station. The Prophetic Cycle hath, verily, ended. The Eternal Truth is now come. He hath lifted up the Ensign of Power, and is now shedding upon the world the unclouded splendour of His Revelation.[4]

> That which hath been made manifest in this preeminent, this most exalted Revelation, stands unparalleled in the annals of the past, nor will future ages witness its like.[5]

A unique Day

In the Qur'án the Day of God is designated in many different ways.

The promised Day (Al-Yawmi Al-Maw'údi)[6]

> The Great Terror will bring them no grief: but the angels will meet them (with mutual greetings): 'This is your Day, – (the Day) that ye were promised.'[7]

> Woe, then, to the unbelievers, on account of that Day of theirs which they have been promised![8]

> So leave them to plunge in vain talk and play about, until they encounter that Day of theirs which they have been promised![9]

A well-known Day (Yawmin Ma'lúmin)

> All will certainly be gathered together for the meeting appointed for a Day well-known.[10]

The Day of time appointed (Yawmi Al-Waqti Al-Ma'lúmi)

> (God) said: 'Respite is granted thee –
> 'Till the Day of the Time Appointed.'[11]

That Day (Dhálika Al-Yawmi, Yawma'idhin); the Day (Yawma)

> But God will deliver them from the evil of that Day, and will shed over them a Light of Beauty and a (blissful) Joy.[12]

> And man cries (distressed): 'What is the matter with her?' –
> On that Day will she (earth) declare her tidings.[13]

> That Day shall a man flee from his own brother.
> And from his mother, and his father.
> And from his wife and his children.[14]

Friends on that Day will be foes, one to another, except the righteous. My devotees! no fear shall be on you that Day, nor shall ye grieve.[15]

So on that Day no excuse of theirs will avail the transgressors, nor will they be invited (then) to seek grace (by repentance).[16]

... on that Day shall the believers rejoice ... [17]

On that Day those who reject Faith and disobey the Apostle will wish that the earth were made one with them: but never will they hide a single fact from God![18]

The Day it arrives, no soul shall speak except by His leave: of those (gathered) some will be wretched and some will be blessed.[19]

And a cup full (to the brim).
   No vanity shall they hear therein, nor untruth –
   Recompense from thy Lord, a gift, (amply) sufficient –
   (From) the Lord of the heavens and the earth, and all between – (God) Most Gracious: none shall have power to argue with Him.
   The Day that the Spirit and the angels will stand forth in ranks, none shall speak except any who is permitted by (God) Most Gracious, and he will say what is right.
   That Day will be the sure Reality: therefore, whoso will, let him take a (straight) return to his Lord![20]

A Glorious Day, a Mighty Day (Yawmin 'Ažímin); a Great Day (Yawmin Kabírin)

By the Day as it appears in glory.[21]

Do they not think that they will be called to account? –
On a Mighty Day.[22]

Say: 'I would, if I disobeyed my Lord, indeed have fear of the penalty of a Mighty Day.'[23]

'Seek ye the forgiveness of your Lord, and turn to Him in repentance; that He may grant you enjoyment, good (and true), for a term appointed, and bestow His abounding grace On all who abound in merit! But if ye turn away, then I fear for you the penalty of a Great Day.'[24]

The Last Day; the Final Day (Al-Yawma Al-'Ákhira)

The Qur'án reports that followers of several Messengers and Faiths expected the Last Day:

> There was indeed in them (Abraham and His followers) an excellent example for you to follow – for those whose hope is in God and in the Last Day. But if any turn away, truly God is free of all wants, worthy of all praise.[25]

> To the Madyan (people) (We sent) their brother Shu'aib. Then he said: 'O my people! serve God, and fear the Last Day: nor commit evil on the earth, with intent to do mischief.'[26]

> Of the people there are some who say: 'We believe in God and the Last Day,' but they do not (really) believe.
> Fain would they deceive God and those who believe, but they only deceive themselves and realize (it) not![27]

> They (people of the Book that stand for right) believe in God and the Last Day; they enjoin what is right, and forbid what is wrong; and they (hasten in emulation) in (all) good works; they are in the ranks of the righteous.[28]

> Ye have indeed in the Messenger of God a beautiful pattern of (conduct) for anyone whose hope is in God and the Final Day, and who engages much in the praise of God.[29]

The Day of Resurrection[30] (Yawmi Al-Qiyámati; Yawmu Al-Ba'thi); Day of Requital or Day of Judgment (Yawma Ad-Díni); The Day of Hell Fire

But those endued with knowledge and faith will say: 'Indeed ye did tarry, within God's Decree, to the Day of Resurrection, and this is the Day of Resurrection: but ye – ye were not aware!'[31]

But man wishes to do wrong (even) in the time in front of him.
He questions: 'when is the Day of Resurrection?'
At length, when the sight is dazed . . .[32]

No just estimate have they made of God, such as is due to Him: on the Day of Judgment the whole of the earth will be but His handful, and the heavens will be rolled up in His right hand: Glory to Him! High is He above the partners they attribute to Him![33]

Such will be their entertainment on the Day of Requital![34]

Master of the Day of Judgment.
Thee do we worship, and Thine aid we seek.
Show us the straight way.[35]

And (ask) of the sinners:
'What led you into hell-fire?'
They will say: 'We were not of those who prayed;
Nor were we of those who fed the indigent;
But we used to talk vanities with vain talkers
And we used to deny the Day of Judgment.
Until there came to us (the Hour) that is certain.'[36]

On the Day of Judgment wilt thou see those who told lies against God; – their faces will be turned black; is there not in hell an abode for the haughty?[37]

Those who (flounder) heedless in a flood of confusion:
They ask, 'When will be the Day of Judgment and justice?'
(It will be) a Day when they will be tried (and tested) over the Fire![38]

Some Christians and Muslims believe that the Day of Resurrection refers to a physical reanimation of the dead at an end of a time period. The following verse of the Qur'án indicates that at the dawn of a new Dispensation humanity is given spiritual life, but that spiritual death ensues before the advent of the next Dispensation:

> Say: 'It is God Who gives you life, then gives you death; then He will gather you together for the Day of Judgement about which there is no doubt': but most men do not understand.[39]

Hence, the anticipated Resurrection more aptly refers to a spiritual reawakening similar to that experienced by those spiritually dead people who were given life through the Revelation of Muhammad:

> How can ye reject the faith in God? – Seeing that ye were without life, and He gave you life then will He cause you to die, and will again bring you to life; and again to Him will ye return.[40]

> It is God Who begins (the process of) creation; then repeats it; then shall ye be brought back to Him.[41]

The Báb bemoans the fact that some have preferred to remain dead:

> As to those who have debarred themselves from the Revelation of God, they have indeed failed to understand the significance of a single letter of the Qur'án, nor have they obtained the slightest notion of the Faith of Islám, otherwise they would not have turned away from God, Who hath brought them into being, Who hath nurtured them, hath caused them to die and hath proffered life unto them, by clinging to parts of their religion, thinking that they are doing righteous work for the sake of God.[42]

The Day when the Holy Spirit and the angels will stand forth in ranks and everyone who wishes can take the straight path of return to his Lord

> The Day that the Spirit and the angels will stand forth in ranks, none shall speak except any who is permitted by (God) Most Gracious,

and he will say what is right.

That Day will be the sure Reality: therefore, whoso will, let him take a (straight) Return to his Lord!

Verily, We have warned you of a Penalty near – the Day when man will see (the deeds) which his hands have sent forth, and the unbeliever will say, 'Woe unto me! Would that I were (mere) dust!'[43]

And thy Lord shall come with angels, rank on rank.[44]

Bahá'u'lláh explains:

> By 'angels' is meant those who, reinforced by the power of the spirit, have consumed, with the fire of the love of God, all human traits and limitations, and have clothed themselves with the attributes of the most exalted Beings and of the Cherubim.[45]

The Day when God will judge schisms

We settled the Children of Israel in a beautiful dwelling-place, and provided for them sustenance of the best: it was after knowledge had been granted to them, that they fell into schisms. Verily God will judge between them as to the schisms amongst them, on the Day of Judgment.[46]

The Day of Account, the Day of Reckoning (Yawmi Al-Ḥisábi)

This is a Message (of admonition): and verily, for the righteous, is a beautiful place of (final) Return,–
   Gardens of eternity, whose doors will (ever) be open to them ...
   Such is the promise made to you for the Day of Account![47]

... for those who wander astray from the Path of God, is a penalty grievous, for that they forget the Day of Account.[48]

'O our Lord! Cover (us) with Thy forgiveness – me (Abraham), my parents, and (all) believers, on the Day that the Reckoning will be established!'[49]

The Day of Decision or 'Sorting Out' (Yawma Al-Faşli)

The 'Day of Judgement' will be a period of decision for Muslims, Jews and Christians – a Day when the believer will be judged as to his or her response to the Message.

> Verily the Day of Sorting Out is a thing appointed . . .[50]

> Verily the Day of Sorting Out is the time appointed for all of them . . .[51]

The Torah predicts that humanity will in that Day be besieged by many problems and perplexing issues. It will be a Day when the truth will not be clear to most people, but the wise will understand.

> Multitudes, multitudes in the valley of decision: for the day of the Lord is near in the valley of decision.[52]

> And it shall come to pass in that day, that the light shall not be clear, nor dark.[53]

The Qur'án indicates that the final resolution of perplexing issues should be left to God and will be determined in the Last Day:

> O ye who believe! Obey God, and obey the Messenger, and those charged with authority among you. If ye differ in anything among yourselves, refer it to God and His Messenger, if ye do believe in God and the Last Day: that is best, and most suitable for final determination.[54]

A Day of Testimony; a Day that shall be testified to or witnessed by all (Yawmun Mashhúdun)

> In that is a Sign for those who fear the penalty of the Hereafter: that is a Day for which mankind will be gathered together: that will be a Day of Testimony.
> Nor shall We delay it but for a term appointed.[55]

The Day of Victory *(Yawma Al-Fatĥi)*

Say (unto them): On the day of the victory the faith of those who disbelieve (and who then will believe) will not avail them, neither will they be reprieved.[56]

A stern, fateful, spiritually distressing, or wrathful Day *(Yawmáan 'Abúsáan Qamţaríráan); a Day of Distress (Yawmun 'Asírun); a Day of regret and remorse (Yawma Al-Ĥasrati); a Grievous Day, a Painful Day, a Woeful Day, or a Momentous Day (Yawmin 'Alímin)*

Hearts that Day will be in agitation.[57]

We only fear a Day of distressful wrath from the side of our Lord.[58]

That will be – that Day – a Day of Distress.[59]

But warn them of the Day of Distress, when the matter will be determined: for (behold,) they are negligent and they do not believe![60]

We sent Noah to his people (with a mission): 'I have come to you with a clear warning:
 That ye serve none but God: verily I do fear for you the penalty of a Grievous Day.'[61]

The Day when faces will be sad and eyes will gaze in horror; Day of violent commotion

And some faces, that Day, will be sad and dismal
 In the thought that some back-breaking calamity was about to be indicted on them.[62]

Think not that God doth not heed the deeds of those who do wrong. He but giveth them respite against a Day when the eyes will fixedly stare in horror.[63]

The Bible also describes the Day of the Lord as a day of wrath:

Enter into the rock, and hide thee in the dust, for fear of the Lord, and for the glory of his majesty.[64]

... the mighty man shall cry there bitterly.
That day is a day of wrath, a day of trouble and distress, a day of wasteness and desolation, a day of darkness and gloominess, a day of clouds and thick darkness,
A day of the trumpet and alarm against the fenced cities, and against the high towers.
And I will bring distress upon men, that they shall walk like blind men, because they have sinned against the Lord: and their blood shall be poured out as dust, and their flesh as the dung.[65]
Behold, I will send you Elijah the prophet before the coming of the great and dreadful day of the Lord.[66]

A Day of Deliverance when God will change distress into joy

But God will deliver them from the evil of that Day, and will shed over them a light of Beauty and a (blissful) Joy.[67]

The Day of the Trumpet

The advent of a Revelation is referred to as a trumpet blast that results in the spiritual resuscitation of humankind through the operation of the Holy Spirit (Greek *pneúma* or breath of God):

And the Trumpet shall be blown: that will be the Day whereof Warning (had been given).[68]

The trumpet shall be sounded, when behold, from the sepulchers (men) will rush forth to their Lord![69]

The Day that the Trumpet shall be sounded, and ye shall come forth in crowds . . .[70]

And the Day that the Trumpet will be sounded – then will be smitten with terror those who are in the heavens, and those who are on earth, except such as God will please (to exempt): and all shall come to His (Presence) as beings conscious of their lowliness.[71]

The Bible also refers to a special trumpet blast that will endow mankind with life:

> And it shall come to pass in that day, that the great trumpet shall be blown . . .[72]

> Blow ye the trumpet in Zion, and sound an alarm in my holy mountain: let all the inhabitants of the land tremble: for the day of the Lord cometh, for it is nigh at hand . . .[73]

> And he shall send his angels with a great sound of a trumpet, and they shall gather together his elect from the four winds, from one end of heaven to the other.[74]

> In a moment, in the twinkling of an eye, at the last trump: for the trumpet shall sound, and the dead shall be raised incorruptible, and we shall be changed.[75]

> For the Lord himself shall descend from heaven with a shout, with the voice of the archangel, and with the trump of God: and the dead in Christ shall rise first . . .[76]

The Day of earthquakes and violent commotions, when the earth and the heavens will be altered

> When the earth is shaken to her (utmost) convulsion,
> And the Earth throws up her burdens (from within) . . .[77]

> Nay! When the earth is pounded to powder . . .[78]

> One Day everything that can be in commotion will be in violent commotion,
>   Followed by oft-repeated (commotions) . . .
>   Cast down will be (their owners') eyes.[79]

> One day the earth will be changed to a different earth, and so will

be the heavens, and (men) will be marshaled forth, before God, the One, the Irresistible . . .⁸⁰

A Day of Assembly or Gathering (Yawmi Al-Jam'i); a Day of loss for some and gain for others (Yawmu At-Taghábuni)

God! There is no god but He: of a surety He will gather you together against the Day of Judgment, about which there is no doubt. And whose word can be truer than God's?⁸¹

The Day that He assembles you (all) for a Day of Assembly, – that will be a day of mutual loss and gain (among you). And those who believe In God and work righteousness, – He will remove from them their ills, and He will admit them to gardens beneath which rivers flow, to dwell therein for ever: that will be the supreme achievement.⁸²

. . . and warn (them) of the Day of Assembly, of which there is no doubt: (when) some will be in the Garden (paradise), and some in the Blazing Fire (hell).⁸³

One day We shall call together all human beings with their (respective) Imáms (spiritual leaders, scriptures): those who are given their record in their right hand will read it (with pleasure), and they will not be dealt with unjustly in the least.⁸⁴

It is he whom God guides, that is on true guidance; but he whom He leaves astray – for such wilt thou find no protector besides Him. On the Day of Judgment We shall gather them together, prone on their faces, blind, dumb, and deaf: their abode will be hell: every time it shows abatement, We shall increase for them the fierceness of the Fire.⁸⁵

One Day shall We gather them all together. Then shall We say to those who joined gods (with Us): 'To your place! ye and those ye joined as "partners".' We shall separate them, and their 'partners' shall say: It was not us that ye worshipped!⁸⁶

The Day when the Lord God will bring all humanity together

God is responsible for the spiritual education of all His creation, for according to the Qur'án He is the Lord of the Worlds (*Rabbi Al-'Álam'ina*), and the Lord of Mankind (*Rabbi An-Nási*), the King or Ruler of Humanity (*Máliki An-Nási*) and the God of all mankind (*'Iláhi An-Nási*).[87] Furthermore, the Qur'án promises that whereas in the past humanity has been separated by religious and geographic boundaries, all mankind will find themselves unified and sharing the same fate when they are all presented before God in that Day.

> 'Our Lord!' (they say), 'Let not our hearts deviate now after Thou hast guided us, but grant us mercy from Thine own Presence; for Thou art the Grantor of bounties without measure.
> Our Lord! Thou art He that will gather mankind together against a day about which there is no doubt: for God never fails in His promise.[88]

> Do they not think that they will be called to account? –
> On a Mighty Day,
> A Day when (all) mankind will stand before the Lord of the Worlds?[89]

> Assuredly it is thy Lord who will gather them together: for He is Perfect in Wisdom and Knowledge.[90]

> One day He will gather them together: (it will be) as if they had tarried but an hour of a day: they will recognise each other: assuredly those will be lost who denied the meeting with God and refused to receive true guidance.[91]

> Say: 'Our Lord will gather us together and will in the end decide the matter between us (and you) in truth and justice: and He is the One to decide, the One Who knows all.'[92]

> One Day He will gather them all together . . .[93]

> In that is a Sign for those who fear the penalty of the Hereafter: that is a Day for which mankind will be gathered together: that will be a

Day of Testimony.⁹⁴

On the day when the earth shall swiftly cleave asunder over the dead, will this gathering be easy to Us.⁹⁵

The Day when all Messengers will be gathered

This promise foreshadows the unification of religions and their followers:

One day will God gather the Messengers together, and ask: 'What was the response ye received (from men to your teaching)?'⁹⁶

The followers of every Dispensation will be gathered together

To each is a goal to which God turns him; then strive together (as in a race) towards all that is good. Wheresoever ye are, God will bring you together, for God hath power over all things.⁹⁷

The establishment of the oneness of humanity is also a promise of the Bible, fulfilled by Bahá'u'lláh, the 'Gatherer' of humanity:

And David my servant shall be king over them; and they all shall have one shepherd: they shall also walk in my judgments, and observe my statues, and do them.⁹⁸

And the nations of them which are saved shall walk in the light of it: and the kings of the earth do bring their glory and honour into it.⁹⁹

And before him shall be gathered all nations.¹⁰⁰

And other sheep I have, which are not of this fold: them also I must bring, and they shall hear my voice; and there shall be one fold, and one shepherd.¹⁰¹

The unification of humanity is also a prayer of the Báb:

Glorified art Thou, O Lord! Thou wilt surely gather mankind for the Day of whose coming there is no doubt – the Day whereon everyone shall appear before Thee and find life in Thee. This is the Day of the One true God – the Day Thou shalt bring about as Thou pleasest through the power of Thy behest.[102]

The Day of harmony and unity

The Qur'án refers to unbelievers as beasts (*Anfál*, the Spoils of War, 8:55), hence, an explanation is that adherents of other beliefs and warring and beast-like communities of mankind will be pacified, spiritualized, and unified.

And when the wild beasts are herded together. . .[103]

A similar expectation is recorded in the Bible:

The wolf also shall dwell with the lamb, and the leopard shall lie down with the kid; and the calf and the young lion and the fatling together; and a little child shall lead them.
And the cow and the bear shall feed; their young ones shall lie down together: and the lion shall eat straw like the ox.
And the suckling child shall play on the hole of the asp, and the weaned child shall put his hand on the cockatrice den.
They shall not hurt nor destroy in all my holy mountain.[104]

The Day when men shall be scattered; the Day of Noise and Clamour

The 'Day of Gathering' will paradoxically coincide with a Day of separation of men – separation of believers from unbelievers, and greater sectarianism and spiritual uncertainty:

On the Day that the Hour will he established, – That Day shall (all men) be sorted out (separated or scattered).[105]

The (Day) of Noise and Clamour:
What is the (Day) of Noise and Clamour?
And what will explain to thee what the (Day) of Noise and Clamour is?[106]

A Day of Visitation, of meeting with God

Clearly, 'meeting with God' cannot apply to the Godhead, the Omnipresent, the Infinite and the Unknowable Essence, but rather to the appointed Revealer of His Divine Purpose. Although statements concerning this event are traditionally taken to refer to life after physical death, they are also compatible with expectations of future divine visitation and meeting.

> He doth regulate all affairs, explaining the Signs in detail, that ye may believe with certainty in the meeting with your Lord.[107]

> Lost indeed are they who treat it as a falsehood that they must meet God, until on a sudden the hour is on them, and they say: 'Ah! Woe unto us that we took no thought of it'; for they bear their burdens on their backs, and evil indeed are the burdens that they bear?[108]

A new 'term' will commence, presumably following the end or '*ajal*' of earlier Dispensations:

> For those whose hopes are in the meeting with God; for the Term (appointed) by God is surely coming: and He hears and knows (all things).[109]

> ... they (unbelievers) deny the Meeting with their Lord![110]

> Those who reject the Signs of God and the Meeting, with Him (in the Hereafter) – it is they who shall despair of My Mercy: it is they who will (suffer) a most grievous Penalty.[111]

> They are those who deny the Signs of their Lord and the fact of their having to meet Him (in the Hereafter): vain will be their works, nor shall We, on the Day of Judgment, give them any weight.[112]

> If God were to hasten for men the ill (they have earned) as they would fain hasten on the good – then would their respite be settled at once. But We leave those who rest not their hope of their meeting with Us, in their trespasses, wandering in distraction to and fro.[113]

Those who rest not their hope on their meeting with Us, but are pleased and satisfied with the life of the present, and those who heed not Our Signs,

Their abode is the Fire, because of the (evil) they earned.[114]

In the Torah, the Prophets Isaiah and Micah also speak of 'the Day of Visitation':

And what will ye do in the day of visitation, and in the desolation which shall come from far? to whom will ye flee for help? and where will ye leave your glory?[115]

... the day of thy watchmen and thy visitation cometh ...[116]

The disciple Peter prepares the Jewish converts of this event:

Having your conversation honest among the Gentiles: that, whereas they speak against you as evildoers, they may by your good works, which they shall behold, glorify God in the day of visitation.[117]

The Torah also promises the advent of the 'day of the Lord', an inconceivably great and unprecedented Day.

Alas! for that day is great, so that none is like it ...[118]

The great day of the Lord is near, it is near, and hasteth greatly, even the voice of the day of the Lord ...[119]

Alas for the day! for the day of the Lord is at hand, and as a destruction from the Almighty shall it come.[120]

Behold, I will send my messenger, and he shall prepare the way before me: and the Lord, whom ye seek, shall suddenly come to his temple, even the messenger of the covenant, whom ye delight in: behold, he shall come, saith the Lord of hosts.

But who may abide the day of his coming? and who shall stand when he appeareth? for he is like a refiner's fire, and like fullers' soap.[121]

For unto us a child is born, unto us a son is given: and the government shall be upon his shoulder: and his name shall be called Wonderful, Counsellor, The mighty God, The everlasting Father, The Prince of Peace.

Of the increase of his government and peace there shall be no end, upon the throne of David, and upon his kingdom, to order it, and to establish it with judgment and with justice from henceforth-even forever. The zeal of the Lord of hosts will perform this.[122]

The Coming of the 'Lord' and the 'Day of God' is the 'good news' of the Gospels ('Gospel' or 'evangel': Arabic *injil*, which means good news).

Blessed are those servants, whom the lord when he cometh shall find watching.[123]

And I heard a great voice out of heaven saying, Behold, the tabernacle of God is with men, and he will dwell with them, and they shall be his people, and God himself shall be with them, and be their God.[124]

Advent and establishment of the 'Hour' (As-Sá'ah)

This is also referred to as 'the Final Hour', 'the Hour of Judgment', the terrible Hour of 'Convulsions', the 'Resurrection':

And the Hour is surely coming . . .[125]

The unbelievers say, 'Never to us will come the Hour': say, 'Nay! But most surely, by my Lord, it will come upon you' . . .[126]

And on the Day that the Hour will be established – that Day shall (all men) be sorted out.[127]

Verily the Hour is coming – My design is to keep it hidden – for every soul to receive its reward by the measure of its endeavour.[128]

They ask thee about the Hour – when will be its appointed time?

Say: 'The knowledge thereof is with my Lord (alone): none but He can reveal as to when it will occur. Heavy were its burden through the heavens and the earth. Only, all of a sudden will it come to you.' They ask thee as if thou wert eager in search thereof: say: 'The knowledge thereof is with God (alone), But most men know not.'[129]

... the promise of God is true, and that there can be no doubt about the Hour of Judgment ...[130]

To Him is referred the Knowledge of the Hour (of Judgment: He knows all) ...[131]

And blessed is He to Whom belongs the dominion of the heavens and the earth, and all between them: with Him is the knowledge of the Hour (of Judgment): And to Him shall ye be brought back.[132]

And what will make thee realize that perhaps the Hour is close at hand?
    Only those wish to hasten it who believe not in it: those who believe hold it in awe, and know that it is the Truth. Behold, verily those that dispute concerning the Hour are far astray.[133]

To God belongs the dominion of the heavens and the earth, and the Day that the Hour of Judgment is established – that Day will the dealers in falsehood perish![134]

O mankind! Fear your Lord! For the convulsion of the Hour will be a thing terrible![135]

And, verily, the Hour will come: there can be no doubt about it, or about (the fact) that God will raise up all who are in the graves.[136]

Those who reject Faith will not cease to be in doubt concerning (Revelation) until the Hour comes suddenly upon them, or there comes to them the penalty of a Day of Disaster.[137]

Nay, they deny the Hour: but We have prepared a Blazing Fire for such as deny the Hour ...[138]

> On the Day that the Hour will be established, the guilty will be struck dumb with despair.[139]

> Nay, the Hour is the time promised them: and that Hour will be most grievous and most bitter.[140]

The Gospels also anticipate an apocalyptic 'hour', an event that, similar to the first coming of Christ, will result in the resuscitation of the spiritually dead.

> Jesus saith unto her, Woman, believe me, the hour cometh, when ye shall neither in this mountain, nor yet at Jerusalem, worship the Father.[141]

> But the hour cometh, and now is, when the true worshippers shall worship the Father in spirit . . .[142]

> Verily, verily, I say unto you, the hour is coming, and now is, when the dead shall hear the voice of the Son of God: and they that hear shall live.[143]

> Marvel not at this: for the hour is coming, in the which all that are in the graves shall hear his voice . . .[144]

Anticipation of two Revelations in rapid succession

Two trumpet blasts

> The Trumpet will be sounded, when all that are in the heavens and on earth will swoon, except such as it will please God (to exempt). Then will a second one be sounded, when, behold, they will be standing and looking on![145]

According to Bahá'í scripture, these trumpet blasts refer to the twin Revelations of the Báb and Bahá'u'lláh. The Dispensation of the Báb preceded the Revelation of Bahá'u'lláh by only twenty years. It anticipated the advent of 'Him Whom God shall Manifest' but had its own independent scripture and laws.

I swear by the righteousness of God! The Blast hath been blown on the Trumpet of the Bayán as decreed by the Lord, the Merciful, and all that are in the heavens and on the earth have swooned away except such as have detached themselves from the world, cleaving fast unto the Cord of God, the Lord of mankind. This is the Day in which the earth shineth with the effulgent light of thy Lord, but the people are lost in error and have been shut out as by a veil. We desire to regenerate the world . . .[146]

Arise, and proclaim unto the entire creation the tidings that He Who is the All-Merciful hath directed His steps towards the Riḍván and entered it. Guide, then, the people unto the garden of delight which God hath made the Throne of His Paradise. We have chosen thee to be our most mighty Trumpet, whose blast is to signalize the resurrection of all mankind.[147]

Verily We have sounded the Trumpet which is none other than My Pen of Glory . . .[148]

Two Gardens

And those who are blessed shall be in the Garden (paradise): they will dwell therein for all the time that the heavens and the earth endure, except as thy Lord Willeth: a gift without break.[149]

But those who believe and work righteousness, and humble themselves before their Lord, – they will be companions of the Garden, to dwell therein (for ever)![150]

But for such as fear the time when they will stand before (the Judgment Seat Of) their Lord, there will be two Gardens (*jannatani*).[151]

Then which of the favors of your Lord will ye deny?
  They will recline on carpets, whose inner linings will be of rich brocade: the fruit of the Gardens (*aljannatayni*) will be near (and easy of reach).[152]

And besides these two, there are two other Gardens . . .[153]

The Báb defines the anticipated paradise thus:

> There is no paradise more wondrous for any soul than to be exposed to God's Manifestation in His Day, to hear His verses and believe in them, to attain His presence, which is naught but the presence of God, to sail upon the sea of the heavenly kingdom of His good-pleasure, and to partake of the choice fruits of the paradise of His divine Oneness.[154]

> Since that Day is a great Day it would be sorely trying for thee to identify thyself with the believers. For the believers of that Day are the inmates of Paradise, while the unbelievers are the inmates of the fire. And know thou of a certainty that by Paradise is meant recognition of and submission unto Him Whom God shall make manifest, and by the fire the company of such souls as would fail to submit unto Him or to be resigned to His good-pleasure. On that Day thou wouldst regard thyself as the inmate of Paradise and as a true believer in Him, whereas in reality thou wouldst suffer thyself to be wrapt in veils and thy habitation would be the nethermost fire, though thou thyself wouldst not be cognizant thereof.[155]

Humanity has therefore been offered two opportunities and summons to enter the paradise of the Divine Presence, as Bahá'u'lláh proclaims:

> Lo, the Nightingale of Paradise singeth upon the twigs of the Tree of Eternity, with holy and sweet melodies, proclaiming to the sincere ones the glad tidings of the nearness of God, calling the believers in the Divine Unity to the court of the Presence of the Generous One, informing the severed ones of the message which hath been revealed by God, the King, the Glorious, the Peerless, guiding the lovers to the seat of sanctity and to this resplendent Beauty.
>   Verily this is that Most Great Beauty, foretold in the Books of the Messengers, through Whom truth shall be distinguished from error and the wisdom of every command shall be tested. Verily He is the Tree of Life that bringeth forth the fruits of God, the Exalted, the Powerful, the Great.[156]

O Ye Dwellers in the Highest Paradise! Proclaim unto the children of assurance that within the realms of holiness, nigh unto the celestial paradise, a new garden hath appeared, round which circle the denizens of the realm on high and the immortal dwellers of the exalted paradise. Strive, then, that ye may attain that station, that ye may unravel the mysteries of love from its wind-flowers and learn the secret of divine and consummate wisdom from its eternal fruits. Solaced are the eyes of them that enter and abide therein![157]

Two Fountains or two Springs of the water of life in the Gardens of Paradise

In them (each) will be Two Springs flowing (free)...[158]

The merging of two Oceans or Seas

He has let free the two bodies of flowing water, meeting together ...[159]

Bahá'u'lláh has invited humanity to the Ocean of His Revelation:

... every drop of the waters of which crieth out, proclaiming unto all that are in heaven and on earth that He is, in truth, the Fountain of all life, and the Quickener of the entire creation, and the Object of the adoration of all worlds, and the Best-Beloved of every understanding heart, and the Desire of all them that are nigh unto Thee.[160]

He explains:

O My servants! My holy, My divinely ordained Revelation may be likened unto an ocean in whose depths are concealed innumerable pearls of great price, of surpassing luster. It is the duty of every seeker to bestir himself and strive to attain the shores of this ocean, so that he may, in proportion to the eagerness of his search and the efforts he hath exerted, partake of such benefits as have been pre-ordained in God's irrevocable and hidden Tablets. If no one be willing to direct his steps towards its shores, if every one should fail to arise and find Him, can such a failure be said to have robbed this ocean of its power or to have lessened, to any degree, its treasures? . . . O My servants! The one true God is My witness! This most great, this fathomless and surging Ocean is near, astonishingly near, unto you.[161]

He further writes:

Blessed is the man of insight who hath perceived, and the sore athirst who hath quaffed from this luminous Fountain. Blessed the man who acknowledgeth the truth, earnestly striving to serve the Cause of his Lord, the Powerful, the Almighty.[162]

His followers pray that they may be connected to the Ocean of His Bounty and Revelation:

Praise be to Thee, O Lord my God! I implore Thee, by Thy Name which none hath befittingly recognized, and whose import no soul hath fathomed; I beseech Thee, by Him Who is the Fountain-Head of Thy Revelation and the Day-Spring of Thy signs, to make my heart to be a receptacle of Thy love and of remembrance of Thee. Knit it, then, to Thy most great Ocean, that from it may flow out the living waters of Thy wisdom and the crystal streams of Thy glorification and praise.[163]

Two acknowledgments of the 'Great News' or 'Announcement'

Concerning what are they disputing?
Concerning the Great News,
About which they cannot agree.
Verily, they shall soon (Come to) know!
Verily, verily (*thumma*)[164] they shall soon (come to) know![165]

Two Easts and two Wests

The Qur'án further promises that there will be two Easts (dawning places of Revelation) and two Wests (final illumination), fulfilled by the twin Revelations of the Báb and Bahá'u'lláh:

Now I do call to witness the Lord of all points in the East and the West (*almasháriqi waalmagháribi*, the Lord of Easts and Wests) that we can certainly substitute for them better (men) than they . . .¹⁶⁶

(He is) Lord of the two Easts and Lord of the two Wests.¹⁶⁷

The Qur'án, moreover, indicates that the promised Faith will have a universal aim and appeal: 'a blessed Tree, an Olive, neither of the East nor of the West . . . light upon light! God doth guide whom He will to His Light'.¹⁶⁸

Bahá'u'lláh explains that the many dawning places and Revelations that are referred to describe different stages in the evolution of one common eternal Faith – different points in the orbit of the earth around the same sun:

> in every Dispensation the light of Divine Revelation hath been vouchsafed to men in direct proportion to their spiritual capacity. Consider the sun. How feeble its rays the moment it appeareth above the horizon. How gradually its warmth and potency increase as it approacheth its zenith, enabling meanwhile all created things to adapt themselves to the growing intensity of its light. How steadily it declineth until it reaches its setting point. Were it, all of a sudden, to manifest the energies latent within it, it would, no doubt, cause injury to all created things . . . In like manner, if the Sun of Truth were suddenly to reveal, at the earliest stages of its manifestation, the full measure of the potencies which the providence of the Almighty hath bestowed upon it, the earth of human understanding would waste away and be consumed; for men's hearts would neither sustain the intensity of its revelation, nor be able to mirror forth the radiance of its light.¹⁶⁹

The New Testament additionally speaks of 'two witnesses', 'two olive trees', and 'two candlesticks'.¹⁷⁰

Bahá'u'lláh attests that all the scriptural promises and predictions have been fulfilled by His Revelation.

> By Him Who is the Great Announcement! The All-Merciful is come invested with undoubted sovereignty. The Balance hath been

appointed, and all them that dwell on earth have been gathered together. The Trumpet hath been blown, and lo, all eyes have stared up with terror, and the hearts of all who are in the heavens and on the earth have trembled, except them whom the breath of the verses of God hath quickened, and who have detached themselves from all things.

This is the Day whereon the earth shall tell out her tidings. The workers of iniquity are her burdens, could ye but perceive it. The moon of idle fancy hath been cleft, and the heaven hath given out a palpable smoke. We see the people laid low, awed with the dread of thy Lord, the Almighty, the Most Powerful. The Crier hath cried out, and men have been torn away, so great hath been the fury of His wrath. The people of the left hand sigh and bemoan. The people of the right abide in noble habitations: they quaff the Wine that is life indeed, from the hands of the All-Merciful, and are, verily, the blissful.

The earth hath been shaken, and the mountains have passed away, and the angels have appeared, rank on rank, before Us. Most of the people are bewildered in their drunkenness and wear on their faces the evidences of anger. Thus have We gathered together the workers of iniquity. We see them rushing on towards their idol. Say: None shall be secure this Day from the decree of God. This indeed is a grievous Day. We point out to them those that led them astray. They see them, and yet recognize them not. Their eyes are drunken; they are indeed a blind people. Their proofs are the calumnies they uttered; condemned are their calumnies by God, the Help in Peril, the Self-Subsisting. The Evil One hath stirred up mischief in their hearts, and they are afflicted with a torment that none can avert. They hasten to the wicked, bearing the register of the workers of iniquity. Such are their doings.

Say: The heavens have been folded together, and the earth is held within His grasp, and the corrupt doers have been held by their forelock, and still they understand not. They drink of the tainted water, and know it not. Say: The shout hath been raised, and the people have come forth from their graves, and arising, are gazing around them. Some have made haste to attain the court of the God of Mercy, others have fallen down on their faces in the fire of Hell, while still others are lost in bewilderment. The verses of God have been revealed, and yet they have turned away from them. His proof hath been manifested, and yet they are unaware of it. And when they behold the face of the All-Merciful, their own faces are saddened, while they are disporting themselves. They hasten forward to Hell Fire, and mistake it for light. Far from God be what they fondly imagine! Say: Whether ye rejoice or whether ye burst for fury, the heavens are cleft asunder, and God hath come down, invested with radiant sovereignty. All created things are heard exclaiming: 'The Kingdom is God's, the Almighty, the All-Knowing, the All-Wise.'[171]

Vague fancies have encompassed the dwellers of the earth and debarred them from turning towards the Horizon of Certitude, and its brightness, and its manifestations and its lights. Vain imaginings have withheld them from Him Who is the Self-Subsisting. They speak as prompted by their own caprices, and understand not. Among them are those who have said: 'Have the verses been sent down?' Say: 'Yea, by Him Who is the Lord of the heavens!' 'Hath the Hour come?' 'Nay, more; it hath passed, by Him Who is the Revealer of clear tokens! Verily, the Inevitable is come, and He, the True One, hath appeared with proof and testimony. The Plain is disclosed, and mankind is sore vexed and fearful. Earthquakes have broken loose, and the tribes have lamented, for fear of God, the Lord of Strength, the All-Compelling.' Say: 'The stunning trumpet blast hath been loudly raised, and the Day is God's, the One, the Unconstrained.' 'Hath the Catastrophe come to pass?' Say: 'Yea, by the Lord of Lords!' 'Is the Resurrection come?' 'Nay, more; He Who is the Self-Subsisting hath appeared with the Kingdom of His signs.' 'Seest thou men laid low?' 'Yea, by my Lord, the Exalted, the Most High!' 'Have the tree-stumps been uprooted?' 'Yea, more; the mountains have been scattered in dust; by Him the Lord of attributes!' They say: 'Where is Paradise, and where is hell?' Say: 'The one is reunion with Me; the other thine own self, O thou who dost associate a partner with God and doubtest.' They say: 'We see not the Balance.' Say: 'Surely, by my Lord, the God of Mercy! None can see it except such as are endued with insight.' 'Have the stars fallen?' Say: 'Yea, when He Who is the Self-Subsisting dwelt in the Land of Mystery (Adrianople). Take heed, ye who are endued with discernment!' All the signs appeared when We drew forth the Hand of Power from the bosom of majesty and might. Verily, the Crier hath cried out, when the promised time came, and they that have recognized the splendours of Sinai have swooned away in the wilderness of hesitation, before the awful majesty of thy Lord, the Lord of creation. The trumpet asketh: 'Hath the Bugle been sounded?' Say: 'Yea, by the King of Revelation!, when He mounted the throne of His Name, the All-Merciful.' Darkness hath been chased away by the dawning-light of the mercy of thy Lord, the Source of all light. The breeze of the All-Merciful hath wafted, and the souls have been quickened in the tombs of their bodies. Thus hath the decree been fulfilled by God, the Mighty, the Beneficent. They that have gone astray have said: 'When were the heavens cleft asunder?' Say: 'While ye lay in the graves of waywardness and error.' Among the heedless is he who rubbeth his eyes, and looketh to the right and to the left. Say: 'Blinded art thou. No refuge hast thou to flee to.' And among them is he who saith: 'Have men been gathered together?' Say: 'Yea, by my Lord!, whilst thou didst lie in the cradle of idle fancies.' And among them is he who saith: 'Hath the Book been sent down through the power of the true Faith?' Say: 'The true Faith itself is astounded. Fear ye, O ye men of understanding heart!' And among them is he who saith: 'Have I been assembled with others, blind?' Say: 'Yea, by Him that rideth upon the clouds!' Paradise is decked with mystic roses, and hell hath been made to blaze with the fire of the impious. Say: 'The light hath shone forth from the horizon of Revelation, and the whole earth hath been illumined at the coming of Him Who is the Lord of the Day of the Covenant!' The doubters have perished, whilst he that turned, guided by the light of assurance, unto the Dayspring of Certitude hath prospered. Blessed art thou, who hast fixed thy gaze upon Me . . .'[172]

17

REAFFIRMATION OF THE UNIFYING PRINCIPLE OF 'ONE COMMON FAITH'

If thou be of the inmates of this city[1] . . . thou wilt view all the Prophets and Messengers of God as one soul and one body, as one light and one spirit, in such wise that the first among them would be last and the last would be first. For they have all arisen to proclaim His Cause and have established the laws of divine wisdom. They are, one and all, the Manifestations of His Self, the Repositories of His might, the Treasuries of His Revelation, the Dawning-Places of His splendor, and the Daysprings of His light. Through them are manifested the signs of sanctity in the realities of all things and the tokens of oneness in the essences of all beings . . . And since in their inmost Beings they are the same Luminaries and the self-same Mysteries, thou shouldst view their outward conditions in the same light, that thou mayest recognize them all as one Being, nay, find them united in their words, speech, and utterance.

Bahá'u'lláh[2]

The recognition of the oneness of faiths is dependent on the realization that the source of all revelations, God, is One (*Wahidun*), Indivisible and Single (*Fardun*), even though He is referred to by many names and titles.[3]

In the Bible God refers to Himself as 'I Am That I Am'[4] and is also known by several other Aramaic and Hebrew names: Jehovah (YWHW, Self-Existing One), Yahweh (JAH), El, Elohim, Elah, Eloah, Eli (my God), Eloi, El-Shadai (God Almighty, God All-Sufficient), Adonai (Lord), Melekh (the King), Emmanuel (God with us), Palet (Deliverer), Yeshua (Saviour), the Lord of Hosts, the Ancient of Days, the Word (Logos), the Heavenly Father, the Everlasting Father (Abbá), the 'First and the Last'.

Nevertheless, 'there is no searching of his understanding',[5] 'we know him not',[6] and He is 'unsearchable',[7] prompting Isaiah to state 'Verily thou art a God that hidest thyself, O God of Israel, the Saviour'[8] and to pose the following rhetorical question:

> To whom then will ye liken God? or what likeness will ye compare unto him?[9]

Apart from Alláh, the Qur'án describes God by ninety-nine 'Beautiful Names' (*Al-'Asma al-Husná*).[10] However, whether singly or collectively, none of the Names defines God's Unknowable Essence. They are all relative terms that apply more aptly to His Messenger, Who manifests the divine attributes.

The concept of progressive revelation in the Bible

An illustration from the Bible that truth is progressive and not absolute is provided by the fact that over time the character of God seems to undergo significant change. This can only be attributed, not to changes in the unknowable God, but to mankind's increased appreciation of His attributes. For example, the Jehovah of the Old Testament is a more feared God, Who is more apt to punish transgressions severely, but the Heavenly Father of the New Testament is more inclined to forgive, as brought by the teachings of Christ.

The Bible is also a narrative of a series of Prophets sent down by the one God to progressively reveal His Purpose to the children of Israel and the rest of humanity. The Tanakh promises that additional truths enshrined in a previously sealed Book will be revealed:

> But thou, O Daniel, shut up the words, and seal the book, even to the time of the end: many shall run to and fro, and knowledge shall be increased.[11]

> And I heard, but I understood not: then said I, O my Lord, what shall be the end of these things?
> And he said, Go thy way, Daniel: for the words are closed up and sealed till the time of the end.
> Many shall be purified, and made white, and tried; but the

wicked shall do wickedly: and none of the wicked shall understand; but the wise shall understand.[12]

Although the children of Israel had been endowed with spiritual life earlier, the Gospels report that Jesus's mission was to bestow the Jews and the rest of humanity with even greater spiritual life.

> I am come that they might have life, and that they might have it more abundantly.[13]

The New Testament predicts that at a future time earlier Revelations will be affirmed and their Books will be opened, and, importantly, another Book will be added to them:

> And I saw the dead, small and great, stand before God; and the books were opened: and another book was opened, which is the book of life: and the dead were judged out of those things which were written in the books, according to their works.[14]

An identical light of divine guidance

The Gospels affirm that the light that shone through Christ is the same source of inspiration that has enlightened every man:

> That was the true Light, which lighteth every man that cometh into the world.[15]

This concept is ratified and emphasized in the Bahá'í Writings:

> No one truth can contradict another truth. Light is good in whatsoever lamp it is burning! A rose is beautiful in whatsoever garden it may bloom! A star has the same radiance if it shines from the East or from the West! Be free from prejudice; so will you love the Sun of Truth from whatever point in the horizon it may arise. You will realize that if the Divine Light of Truth shone in Jesus Christ, it also shone in Moses and Buddha.[16]

In accordance with this understanding, Christ promoted tolerance of others who promote the same spiritual objectives under a different name, discouraging exclusivity and intolerance:

> In my Father's house are many mansions: if it were not so, I would have told you. I go to prepare a place for you.[17]

> And John answered him [Jesus], saying, Master, we saw one casting out devils in thy name, and he followed not us: and we forbad him, because he followed not us.
> But Jesus said, Forbid him not: for there is no man which shall do a miracle in my name, that can lightly speak evil of me.
> For he that is not against us is on our part.[18]

The New Testament reports God as having spoken many times and in many different ways. Clearly, God does not speak directly but addresses humanity through His various mouthpieces. The New Testament records many modifications of the social laws, but the spiritual message remains identical and is merely amplified. St Paul in his epistle to the Jews describes Jesus as the latest Prophet in a succession of Divine Messengers that had come to them, manifesting God's Glory.

> God, who at sundry times and in divers manners spake in time past unto the fathers by the prophets
> Hath in these last days spoken unto us by his Son, whom he hath appointed heir of all things, by whom also he made the worlds;
> Who being the brightness of his glory, and the express image of his person . . .[19]

Promise of future divine appearances and Revelations

The same Lord will manifest Himself in different places and under different circumstances:

> And he said, The Lord came from Sinai (Moses), and rose up from Seir (Jesus) unto them; he shined forth from mount Parán (Muhammad), and he came with ten thousands of saints (Bahá'u'lláh): from his right hand went a fiery law for them.[20]

Jesus also promised that a greater measure of truth would be revealed later. All truth would be revealed by the Spirit of Truth in the Day of the Father, Who is All-Knowing and All-Wise.

> I have yet many things to say unto you, but you cannot bear them now.
>
> Howbeit when he, the Spirit of truth, is come, he will guide you unto all truth; for he will not speak of himself but whatsoever he shall hear that shall he speak; and he will shew you things to come.
>
> He shall glorify me; for he shall receive of mine and shall shew it unto you.[21]

St Paul considered early Christians as mere infants who had been fed only with milk, more adapted to their as yet unevolved digestive systems but at the same time as nutritious as meat. They would have to wait for more solid and concentrated spiritual food as nourishment:

> ... a guide of the blind, a light of them which are in darkness,
> An instructor of the foolish, a teacher of babes ...[22]

> And I, brethren, could not speak unto you as unto spiritual, but as unto carnal, even as unto babes in Christ.
>
> I have fed you with milk, and not with meat: for hitherto ye were not able to bear it, neither yet now are ye able.
>
> For ye are yet carnal ...[23]

Timothy also preached that Christ would be manifested at several 'times' or Dispensations:

> I give thee charge in the sight of God ...
>
> That thou keep this commandment without spot, unrebukeable, until the appearing of our Lord Jesus Christ:
>
> Which in his times (God) shall shew, who is the blessed and only Potentate, the King of kings, and Lord of lords;
>
> Who only hath immortality, dwelling in the light which no man can approach unto; whom no man hath seen, nor can see: to whom be honour and power everlasting. Amen.[24]

The relatively increased spiritual potency and advancing civilization evident with succeeding Revelations is described in symbolic language by the Prophet Isaiah as improvements in physical domains:

> The bricks are fallen down, but we will build with hewn stones: the sycamores are cut down, but we will change them into cedars.[25]

The Gospels further explain that although born of Mary, Jesus was endowed with an eternal reality that transcended human limitations of time and place, and human comprehension:

> Your father Abraham rejoiced to see my day: and he saw it and was glad.
> Then said the Jews unto him, thou are not yet fifty years old, and hast thou seen Abraham?
> Jesus said unto them, Verily, verily, I say unto you, Before Abraham was, I am.
> Then took they up stones to cast at him: but Jesus hid himself.[26]

Being truly in tune with one Prophet and His scriptural teachings leads to belief in another – 'like recognizes like'.

> Do not think that I will accuse you to the Father: there is one that accuseth you, even Moses, in whom ye trust.
> For had ye believed Moses, ye would have believed me: for he wrote of me.
> But if ye believe not his writings, how shall ye believe my words?[27]

The concept of progressive revelation in the Qur'án

God's Revelation is inexhaustible:

> And if all the trees on earth were pens and the ocean (were ink), with seven oceans behind it to add to its (supply), yet would not the Words of God be exhausted (in the writing): for God is Exalted in Power, Full of Wisdom.[28]

> Say: 'If the ocean were ink (wherewith to write out) the words of my

Lord, sooner would the ocean be exhausted than would the words of my Lord, even if we added another ocean like it, for its aid.'[29]

The God that revealed the Qur'án is identical to the Lord God mentioned in the Bible.[30]

> Say: Will ye dispute with us about God, seeing that He is our Lord and your Lord; that we are responsible for our doings and ye for yours; and that we are sincere (in our faith) in Him?[31]

Muhammad's Revelation and inspiration is the same as that sent to the Prophets of the Bible. The Qur'án teaches that divine guidance (the Book) had also been 'sent down' to the Jews through Moses as 'the Law', and to the Christians through Jesus as 'the *Injeel* or *Injil*' ('Evangel', 'the Gospels', or the 'Good News').

> We sent Moses with Our signs (and the command). 'Bring out thy people from the depths of darkness into light, and teach them to remember the Days of God.' Verily, in this there are Signs for such as are firmly patient and constant – grateful and appreciative.[32]

> In the past We granted to Moses and Aaron the Criterion (for judgment), and a Light and a Message for those who would do right.[33]

> We gave Moses the Book and followed him up with a succession of Messengers; we gave Jesus the son of Mary clear (signs) and strengthened him with the Holy Spirit . . .[34]

> Moreover, We gave Moses the Book, completing (Our favor) to those who would do right, and explaining all things in detail, and a guide and a mercy, that they might believe in the meeting with their Lord.
> And this (Revelation of Muhammad) is a Book which We have revealed as a blessing: so follow it and be righteous, that ye may receive mercy.
> Lest ye should say: 'The Book was sent down to two peoples before us (i.e. the same Book to Jews and Christians), and for our part, we remained unacquainted with all that they learned by assiduous study.'[35]

REAFFIRMATION OF THE UNIFYING PRINCIPLE OF 'ONE COMMON FAITH'

> We have sent thee inspiration, as We sent it to Noah and the Messengers after him; We sent inspiration to Abraham, Ismail, Isaac, Jacob, and the Tribes, to Jesus, Job, Jonah, Aaron, and Solomon, and to David We gave the Psalms.
>
> Of some Messengers We have already told thee the story; of others We have not; and to Moses God spoke direct.
>
> Messengers who gave good news as well as warning, that mankind, after (the coming) of the Messengers, should have no plea against God: for God is Exalted in Power, Wise.[36]

> Can they be (like) those who accept a Clear (Sign) from their Lord, and whom a witness from Himself doth teach, as did the Book of Moses before it – a guide and a mercy? They believe therein . . .[37]

> And when there comes to them a Book from God, confirming what is with them, – although from of old they had prayed for victory against those without Faith, – when there comes to them that which they should) have recognized, they refuse to believe in it but the curse of God is on those without Faith.[38]

Divine guidance has come to humanity before Islam through a succession of Prophets (*Nabi*) and Messengers (*Rasul*). The Qur'án confirms earlier Revelations ('Days of God' or *'Ayyám-u-lláh*), and considers them as part of the same religion (*deen*) as Islam – each brings 'the Criterion' (*Furqán*) by which truth is distinguished from error.

> This Qur'án . . . is a confirmation of (revelations) that went before it and a fuller explanation of the Book . . .[39]

The Qur'án refers to the people of faith as the 'people of the Book'. The Prophets and Messengers bear 'good news', and are charged with distinguishing truth from error.

> Mankind was one single nation, and God sent Messengers with glad tidings and warnings; and with them He sent the Book in truth, to judge between people in matters wherein they differed; But the people of the Book, after the clear Signs Came to them, did not differ among themselves, except through selfish contumacy. God

by His Grace guided the believers To the Truth, concerning that wherein they differed. For God guides whom He will to a path that is straight.[40]

No distinction is to be made between any of the divine Messengers. A Muslim cannot entertain any distinction between Islam and earlier Revelations such Judaism and Christianity.

> Say ye: 'We believe in God, and that which hath been sent down to us, and that which hath been sent down to Abraham and Ismael and Isaac and Jacob and the tribes: and that which hath been given to Moses and to Jesus, and that which was given to the prophets from their Lord. No difference do we make between any of them: and to God are we resigned (Muslims).'[41]

> The Messenger believeth in what hath been revealed to him from his Lord, as do the men of faith. Each one (of them) believeth in God, His angels, His books, and His Messengers. 'We make no distinction (they say) between one and another of His Messengers.' And they say: 'We hear, and we obey: (we seek) Thy forgiveness, Our Lord, and to Thee is the end of all journeys.'[42]

The following has been attributed to Muhammad in the book *Sulaym ibn Qays*:

> I heard the Messenger of God, may God send His salutations upon Him and His Family, say: My *ummat* shall follow in the steps of the children of Israel, footstep by footstep, trace upon trace. Should the former enter a hole, the latter will enter it too.
> In truth the Torah and the Qur'án were written by the one and the same angel upon the one and the same scroll with the self-same Pen. And the similitudes and traditions are the same.[43]

Those who make distinctions between the various divine Messengers are charged with *shirk*, similar to multiplying the Godhead as in the literal interpretation of the Trinity.

> The same religion has He established for you as that which He

> enjoined on Noah – the which We have sent by inspiration to thee – and that which We enjoined on Abraham, Moses, and Jesus: Namely, that ye should remain steadfast in Religion, and make no divisions therein: to those who worship other things than God (*mushrikún*), hard is the (way) to which thou callest them. God chooses to Himself those whom He pleases, and guides to Himself those who turn (to Him).[44]

The particular brand of religion and its rituals are less important than belief in God, in His eternal Faith (Book), in His Prophets, and in anticipation of the Last Day, and leading a pious life.

> It is not righteousness that ye turn your faces toward East or West; but it is righteousness to believe in God and the Last Day, and the angels, and the Book, and the Messengers; to spend of your substance, out of love for Him, for your kin, for orphans, for the needy, for the wayfarer, for those who ask, and for the ransom of slaves; to be steadfast in prayer, and practice regular charity . . .[45]

Every nation has received spiritual and social teachings through a Prophet.

> To every people have We appointed rites and ceremonies which they must follow . . .[46]

> And the unbelievers say: 'Why is not a Sign sent down to him from his Lord?' But thou art truly a warner, and to every people a guide.[47]

> Verily We have sent thee in truth, as a bearer of Glad Tidings, and as a warner: and there never was a people, without a warner having lived among them (in the past).[48]

> For We assuredly sent amongst every people a Messenger, (with the Command), 'Serve God, and eschew evil': of the people were some whom God guided, and some on whom error became inevitably (established). So travel through the earth, and see what was the end of those who denied (the Truth).[49]

Indeed, there have been many Prophets other than those mentioned in the Qur'án:

> Of some Messengers We have already told thee the story; of others we have not . . .⁵⁰

> We did aforetime send messengers before thee: of them there are some whose story We have related to thee, and some whose story We have not related to thee. It was not (possible) for any messenger to bring a Sign except by the leave of God: but when the Command of God issued, the matter was decided in truth and justice, and there perished, there and then, those who stood on falsehoods.⁵¹

Humanity was resurrected by the Revelation of Muhammad, but will require to be resuscitated again at a future date.

> How can ye reject 'the faith in God?' – Seeing that ye were without life, and He gave you life then will He cause you to die, And will again bring you to life; and again to Him will ye return.⁵²

Every 'Day of God' or Dispensation has been inspired by a fresh Revelation or Book.

> We did send Messengers before thee and it was never the part of a Messenger to bring a Sign except as God permitted (or commanded). For each period is a Book (revealed).⁵³

God's Purpose is revealed progressively, and the common 'Book' of Revelation is revealed in sequential steps. The Qur'án describes a series of Prophets and Messengers sent by God to reveal His Will to humanity.

> Then sent We Our Messengers in succession of Messengers . . .⁵⁴

> It is He Who sent down to thee (step by step), in truth, the Book, confirming what went before it; and He sent down the Law (of Moses) and the Gospel (of Jesus) before this, as a guide to mankind, and He sent down the Criterion (of judgment between right and wrong) . . .⁵⁵

The 'Straight Path'

There have been multiple Paths, but at the same time there is one 'Straight Path'. The Qur'án teaches that there have been and will continue to be multiple ways of peace, and it is God who 'guides whom He will to a Path that is straight, upright, pure, unadulterated, and trustworthy'.

> Wherewith God guideth all who seek His good pleasure to ways of peace and safety, and leadeth them out of darkness, by His Will, unto the light, – guideth them to a Path that is Straight.[56]

> And those who strive In Our (Cause), – We will certainly guide them to Our Paths: For verily God is with those who do right.[57]

The Gospels explain that seeking the Path of God that 'leadeth unto [spiritual] life' is difficult and entails hardship and 'few there be that find it'.[58] Jesus's statement that He was the Way (John 14:6) can be reconciled with the numerous Gospel expectations of the 'Day of the Father' when God will 'make all things new' (Rev. 21:5) only if it is taken to indicate He was the specific guide to God's good pleasure in the Christian Dispensation. In turn, the Qur'án states that Muhammad and those who believed in Him were on the right Path (*Baqara*, the Heifer, 2:137). However, apparent exclusivist statements can only be reconciled with the coming of God's Day when 'the earth will shine with the Light of its Lord' (*Zumar*, the Crowds, 39:69) when it is taken to indicate that for the duration of Muhammad's Dispensation, Islam is the 'straight Way'.

> Verily this is My Way. Leading straight: follow it: follow not (other) paths: they will scatter you from (His) great Path.[59]

But so were all of the other Prophets of God. We learn for instance that Abraham invited His father to the Path of God and monotheism.

> Also mention in the book (the story of) Abraham: he was a man of Truth, a prophet.
> Behold, he said to his father: 'O my father! Why worship that which heareth not and seeth not, and can profit thee nothing?

> 'O my father! To me hath come knowledge which hath not reached thee: so follow me: I will guide thee to a Way that is even and straight.'[60]

The Qur'án further recounts the Prophet Húd stating that it was God, and by inference all His Divine Prophets, Who was on the straight Path.

> I put my trust in God, my Lord and your Lord! There is not a moving creature, but He hath grasp of its fore-lock. Verily, it is my Lord that is on a straight Path.[61]

Indeed, the straight Path of Muhammad was identical to that of Abraham:

> Say: 'Verily, my Lord hath guided me to a Way that is straight, – A religion of right, the Path (trod) by Abraham the true in faith, and he (certainly) joined not gods with God.'[62]

Again, the Qur'án reassures the children of Israel that if they followed their divine injunctions they would remain on the Path of rectitude.

> God did aforetime take a Covenant from the Children of Israel, and We appointed twelve Captains among them. And God said: 'I am with you: if ye (but) establish regular prayers, practice regular charity, believe in My apostles, honour and assist them, and loan to God a beautiful loan, verily I will wipe out from you your evils, and admit you to Gardens with rivers flowing beneath; But if any of you, after this, resisteth faith, he hath truly wandered from the path of rectitude.'[63]

Every Dispensation (religion), including Islam, has a finite duration:

> No people can hasten their term, nor can they delay (it).[64]

> To every people is a term appointed: when their term is reached, not an hour can they cause delay, or (an hour) can they advance (it in anticipation).[65]

Nor shall We delay it but for a term appointed.[66]

Neither can a people anticipate its term, nor delay it.[67]

Indeed, the Qur'án alludes to the fact that when a Dispensation ages, i.e. continues to dominate beyond its allotted time or its *ajal*, it shows signs of senescence.

If we grant long life to any, we cause him to be reversed in nature: will they not understand.[68]

The abrogation of a Dispensation is followed by a Revelation of better or similar 'verses':

None of Our revelations do We abrogate or cause to be forgotten, but We substitute something better or similar: Knowest thou not that God hath power over all things?[69]

The duty of the Prophets of God is only to deliver the Message and invite humanity to the Straight Path. God further informs Muhammad, and hence, Muslims, that 'it is not required of thee to set them on the right Path but (He) God sets on the right Path whom He pleaseth'.[70] The purpose of God's Messenger is only to invite all receptive souls to the Straight Path.

Verily this is an Admonition: therefore, whoso will, let him take a (straight) path to his Lord![71]

The Qur'án does not claim to be the sole source of truth, but at the time of the Prophet Muhammad it was the latest and a fuller expression of the Divine Will (the Book):

And we sent to you an apostle from among yourselves to rehearse our signs unto you, and to purify you, and to instruct you in 'the Book', and in the wisdom, and to teach you that which ye knew not.[72]

This Qur'án is not such as can be produced by other than God; on the contrary it is a confirmation of (revelations) that went before it, and a fuller explanation of the Book – wherein there is no doubt – from the Lord of the Worlds.[73]

The 'Mother Book' (*ommul Kitáb*) is with God, the Source of all Revelations. In the Qur'án the term is used to describe the Qur'án itself.

> That is the book! there is no doubt therein; a guide to the pious . . .[74]

> God doth blot out or confirm what He pleaseth: with Him is the Mother of the Book.[75]

As mentioned previously, Islam is depicted as a 'middle *Ummat*', which may be translated as one juxtaposed between earlier Dispensations and an anticipated Revelation:

> Thus have We made of you an Ummat justly balanced (*ommatan wasa<u>t</u>an*),[76] that ye might be witnesses over the nations.[77]

The acceptance of God's latest Revelation is simultaneously a declaration of belief in earlier revelations. And conversely, as attested by both the Báb and Bahá'u'lláh, rejection of His Revelation is a denial of God and His earlier Prophets and Messengers, including Moses, Christ and Muhammad:

> O people . . . Ye have disbelieved your Lord. If ye are truly faithful to Muhammad, the Apostle of God and the Seal of the Prophets, and if ye follow His Book, the Qur'án, which is free from error, then here is the like of it – this Book, which We have, in truth and by the leave of God, sent down unto Our Servant. If ye fail to believe in Him, then your faith in Muhammad and His Book which was revealed in the past will indeed be treated as false in the estimation of God. If ye deny Him, the fact of your having denied Muhammad and His Book will, in very truth and with absolute certainty, become evident unto yourselves.[78]

> They Who are the Luminaries of Truth and the Mirrors reflecting the light of Divine Unity, . . . in whatever age and cycle they are sent down from their invisible habitations of ancient glory unto this world

to educate the souls of men and endue with grace all created things, are invariably endowed with an all-compelling power and invested with invincible sovereignty . . . These sanctified Mirrors, these Day-Springs of ancient glory are one and all the exponents on earth of Him Who is the central Orb of the universe, its essence and ultimate purpose. From Him proceed their knowledge and power; from Him is derived their sovereignty. The beauty of their countenance is but a reflection of His image, and their revelation a sign of His deathless glory . . . Through them is transmitted a grace that is infinite, and by them is revealed the light that can never fade . . . Human tongue can never befittingly sing their praise, and human speech can never unfold their mystery . . . Inasmuch as these Birds of the celestial Throne . . . are all sent down from the heaven of the Will of God, and as they all arise to proclaim His irresistible Faith, they therefore are regarded as one soul and the same person. They all abide in the same tabernacle, soar in the same heaven, are seated upon the same throne, utter the same speech, and proclaim the same Faith . . .[79]

Be thou assured in thyself that verily, he who turns away from this Beauty hath also turned away from the Messengers of the past and showeth pride towards God from all eternity to all eternity.[80]

This belief is illustrated by the following testimony of the maternal uncle of the Báb, Ḥájí Mírzá Siyyid 'Alí, just before his martyrdom and after attempts to bribe and persuade him to recant his faith:

My repudiation of the truths enshrined in this Revelation would be tantamount to a rejection of all the Revelations that have preceded it. To refuse to acknowledge the Mission of the Siyyid-i-Báb would be to apostatise from the Faith of my forefathers and to deny the Divine character of the Message which Muhammad, Jesus, Moses, and all the Prophets of the past have revealed.[81]

To know God implies knowing His representative and mouthpiece

The Prophets of God express the divine purpose and manifest His attributes. Their station is immensely glorified above human understanding.

Any apparent difference in their stations is simply a reflection of the potency of the light that shines through their Revelations.

Recognition of the divine Messenger testifies to one's belief in God; allegiance to Him is allegiance to God and submission to Him demonstrates submission to the divine Will. It is in this context that the following statements of Bahá'u'lláh are understood.

> The praise which hath dawned from Thy most august Self, and the glory which hath shone forth from Thy most effulgent Beauty, rest upon Thee, O Thou Who art the Manifestation of Grandeur, and the King of Eternity, and the Lord of all who are in heaven and on earth! I testify that through Thee the sovereignty of God and His dominion, and the majesty of God and His grandeur, were revealed, and the Day-Stars of ancient splendor have shed their radiance in the heaven of Thine irrevocable decree, and the Beauty of the Unseen hath shone forth above the horizon of creation. I testify, moreover, that with but a movement of Thy Pen Thine injunction 'Be Thou' hath been enforced, and God's hidden Secret hath been divulged, and all created things have been called into being, and all the Revelations have been sent down.
>
> I bear witness, moreover, that through Thy beauty the beauty of the Adored One hath been unveiled, and through Thy face the face of the Desired One hath shone forth, and that through a word from Thee Thou hast decided between all created things, causing them who are devoted to Thee to ascend unto the summit of glory, and the infidels to fall into the lowest abyss.
>
> I bear witness that he who hath known Thee hath known God, and he who hath attained unto Thy presence hath attained unto the presence of God. Great, therefore, is the blessedness of him who hath believed in Thee, and in Thy signs, and hath humbled himself before Thy sovereignty, and hath been honored with meeting Thee, and hath attained the good pleasure of Thy will, and circled around Thee, and stood before Thy throne. Woe betide him that hath transgressed against Thee, and hath denied Thee, and repudiated Thy signs, and gainsaid Thy sovereignty, and risen up against Thee, and waxed proud before Thy face, and hath disputed Thy testimonies, and fled from Thy rule and Thy dominion, and been numbered with the infidels whose names have been inscribed by the fingers of

Thy behest upon Thy holy Tablets.[82]

> Were any of the all-embracing Manifestations of God to declare: 'I am God', He, verily, speaketh the truth, and no doubt attacheth thereto. For it hath been repeatedly demonstrated that through their Revelation, their attributes and names, the Revelation of God, His name and His attributes, are made manifest in the world.[83]

This identity of purpose is implicit in several Quranic statements. Allegiance to Muhammad signifies submission to the Divine Will:

> Verily, those who give Bai'á (pledge) to you (O Muhammad) they are giving Bai'á to God. The Hand of God is over their hands. Then whosoever breaks his pledge, breaks only to his own harm, and whosoever fulfills what he has covenanted with God, He will bestow on him a great reward.[84]

To love God implies to obey and follow His Prophet:

> Say: 'If you (really) love God then follow me, God will love you and forgive you of your sins. And God is Oft-Forgiving, Most Merciful.'[85]

Muhammad's actions were to be considered as the actions of God Himself:

> It is not ye who slew them; it was God: when thou threwest (a handful of dust), it was not thy act, but God's: in order that He might test the believers by a gracious trial from Himself: for God is He who heareth and knoweth (all things).[86]

In this context, the Gospels also claim that to know Jesus is to know God, and to recognize Christ is to 'see' God:

> Philip saith unto him, Lord, shew us the Father, and it sufficeth us.
>   Jesus saith unto him, Have I been so long time with you, and yet hast thou not known me, Philip? he that hath seen me hath seen the Father; and how sayest thou then, Shew us the Father?[87]

Then said they unto him, Where is thy Father? Jesus answered, Ye neither know me, nor my Father: if ye had known me, ye should have known my Father also.[88]

If ye had known me, ye should have known my Father also: and from henceforth ye know him, and have seen him.[89]

Blessed are the pure in heart: for they shall see God.[90]

The Torah also describes Moses as a special Prophet and as 'God':

> And thou (Moses) shalt speak unto him (Aaron), and put words in his mouth: and I (God) will be with thy mouth, and with his mouth, and will teach you what ye shall do.
> And he (Aaron) shall be thy spokesman unto the people: and he shall be, even he shall be to thee instead of a mouth, and thou (Moses) shalt be to him instead of God.[91]

> And he (the Lord) said, Hear now my words: If there be a prophet among you, I the Lord will make myself known unto him in a vision, and will speak unto him in a dream.
> My servant Moses is not so, who is faithful in all mine house.
> With him will I speak mouth to mouth, even apparently, and not in dark speeches; and the similitude of the Lord shall he behold: wherefore then were ye not afraid to speak against my servant Moses?[92]

> And the Lord said unto Moses, See, I have made thee a god to Pharaoh: and Aaron thy brother shall be thy prophet.[93]

Bahá'u'lláh explains that despite these considerations the divine Messengers and Prophets must in no wise to be confused with the Godhead:

> I am but a servant of God Who hath believed in Him and in His signs, and in His Prophets and in His angels. My tongue, and My heart, and My inner and My outer being testify that there is no God but Him, that all others have been created by His behest, and been fashioned through the operation of His Will. There is none other God but Him, the Creator, the Raiser from the dead, the

> Quickener, the Slayer. I am He that telleth abroad the favours with which God hath, through His bounty, favoured Me. If this be My transgression, then I am truly the first of the transgressors.[94]

God's chosen Messengers reveal His will and purpose to humanity. They do not incarnate the Godhead, but manifest the divine attributes. In this respect all the Prophets of God are considered as one, and the various religions they have inaugurated are regarded as part of an indivisible Faith of God.

> Exalted, immeasurably exalted art Thou above any attempt to measure the greatness of Thy Cause, above any comparison that one may seek to make, above the efforts of the human tongue to utter its import! From everlasting Thou hast existed, alone with no one else beside Thee, and wilt, to everlasting, continue to remain the same, in the sublimity of Thine essence and the inaccessible heights of Thy glory.
>
> And when Thou didst purpose to make Thyself known unto men, Thou didst successively reveal the Manifestations of Thy Cause, and ordained each to be a sign of Thy Revelation among Thy people, and the Day-Spring of Thine invisible Self amidst Thy creatures . . .[95]

> . . . there must needs be manifested a Being, an Essence Who shall act as a Manifestation and Vehicle for the transmission of the grace of the Divinity Itself, the Sovereign Lord of all. Through the Teachings of this Day Star of Truth every man will advance and develop until he attaineth the station at which he can manifest all the potential forces with which his inmost true self hath been endowed. It is for this very purpose that in every age and dispensation the Prophets of God and His chosen Ones have appeared amongst men, and have evinced such power as is born of God and such might as only the Eternal can reveal.[96]

Progressive revelation in the Bahá'í Faith

As attested by Bahá'u'lláh, each Dispensation has revealed a Path of God and represents the 'Straight Path':

The Prophets and Messengers of God have been sent down for the sole purpose of guiding mankind to the straight Path of Truth. The purpose underlying their revelation hath been to educate all men . . .[97]

. . . know thou that We bear witness unto that whereunto God hath Himself borne witness ere the creation of the heavens and of the earth, that there is none other God but Him, the Almighty, the All-Bounteous. We testify that He is One in His Essence, One in His attributes. He hath none to equal Him in the whole universe, nor any partner in all creation. He hath sent forth His Messengers, and sent down His Books, that they may announce unto His creatures the Straight Path.[98]

Bahá'u'lláh in turn declares that His Faith is the Straight Path re-revealed in this Day:

In this Day the Straight Path is made manifest, the Balance of divine justice is set and the light of the sun of His bounty is resplendent . . .[99]

Thus doth the Lord make plain the ways of truth and guidance, ways that lead to one way, which is this Straight Path. Render thanks unto God for this most gracious favour; offer praise unto Him for this bounty that hath encompassed the heavens and the earth; extol Him for this mercy that hath pervaded all creation.[100]

O ye children of men! The fundamental purpose animating the Faith of God and His Religion is to safeguard the interests and promote the unity of the human race, and to foster the spirit of love and fellowship amongst men. Suffer it not to become a source of dissension and discord, of hate and enmity. This is the straight Path, the fixed and immovable foundation. Whatsoever is raised on this foundation, the changes and chances of the world can never impair its strength, nor will the revolution of countless centuries undermine its structure.[101]

We have truly revealed the signs, demonstrated the irrefutable testimonies and have summoned all men unto the straight Path. Among the people there are those who have turned away and repudiated the truth, others have pronounced judgement against Us without any proof or evidence.[102]

And, once again, in this Day Bahá'u'lláh declares the oneness of God:

> Beware, beware, lest thou be led to join partners with the Lord, thy God. He is, and hath from everlasting been, one and alone, without peer or equal, eternal in the past, eternal in the future, detached from all things, ever-abiding, unchangeable, and self-subsisting. He hath assigned no associate unto Himself in His Kingdom, no counselor to counsel Him, none to compare unto Him, none to rival His glory . . .
> Bear thou witness in thine inmost heart unto this testimony which God hath Himself and for Himself pronounced, that there is none other God but Him, that all else besides Him have been created by His behest, have been fashioned by His leave, are subject to His law, are as a thing forgotten when compared to the glorious evidences of His oneness, and are as nothing when brought face to face with the mighty revelations of His unity.[103]

> [The Revelation of Bahá'u'lláh] unhesitatingly acknowledges itself to be but one link in the chain of continually progressive Revelations, supplements their teachings with such laws and ordinances as conform to the imperative needs, and are dictated by the growing receptivity, of a fast evolving and constantly changing society, and proclaims its readiness and ability to fuse and incorporate the contending sects and factions into which they have fallen into a universal Fellowship, functioning within the framework, and in accordance with the precepts, of a divinely conceived, a world-unifying, a world-redeeming Order.[104]

Bahá'u'lláh has come, as promised in the Torah, Gospels, and the Qur'án and in the scriptures of other divine religions,[105] to reveal the eternal faith of God. The following analogy exemplifies the Bahá'í attitude towards earlier Revelations:

> These divinely-revealed religions . . . 'are doomed not to die, but to be reborn . . . "Does not the child succumb in the youth and the youth in the man; yet neither child nor youth perishes?"'[106]

A primary purpose of the Bahá'í Faith is to enable Jews, Christians and Muslims to understand more fully the religion with which they stand identified; not to introduce another religion but rather to demonstrate the 'oneness' of faith. An important distinction is that although the Revelation of Bahá'u'lláh abrogates earlier Dispensations and some of their social laws, it does not abrogate their spiritual teachings or the religions themselves, as they form part of an indivisible eternal Faith.

> The Revelation, of which Bahá'u'lláh is the source and centre, abrogates none of the religions that have preceded it, nor does it attempt, in the slightest degree, to distort their features or to belittle their value. It disclaims any intention of dwarfing any of the Prophets of the past, or of whittling down the eternal verity of their teachings. It can, in no wise, conflict with the spirit that animates their claims, nor does it seek to undermine the basis of any man's allegiance to their cause. Its declared, its primary purpose is to enable every adherent of these Faiths to obtain a fuller understanding of the religion with which he stands identified, and to acquire a clearer apprehension of its purpose.[107]

The Bahá'í Faith therefore believes in Islam as an eternal Faith, reveres the Qur'án as the absolutely authentic Word of God, and testifies that Muhammad is the Apostle of God and the 'Seal of the Prophets'.

> For when God – blessed and exalted is He – sealed the station of prophethood in the person of Him Who was His Friend, His Chosen One, and His Treasure amongst His creatures, as hath been revealed from the Kingdom of glory: 'but He is the Apostle of God and the Seal of the Prophets', He promised all men that they shall attain unto His own presence in the Day of Resurrection. In this He meant to emphasize the greatness of the Revelation to come, as it hath indeed been manifested through the power of truth. And there is of a certainty no paradise greater than this, nor station higher, should ye reflect upon the verses of the Qur'án.[108]

The followers of Bahá'u'lláh are therefore encouraged to study the Qur'án and the history of Islam, as well as the Bible.

> Say: Perused ye not the Qur'án? Read it, that haply ye may find the Truth, for this Book is verily the Straight Path. This is the Way of God unto all who are in the heavens and all who are on the earth.[109]
>
> God sent His Prophets into the world to teach and enlighten man, to explain to him the mystery of the Power of the Holy Spirit, to enable him to reflect the light, and so in his turn, to be the source of guidance to others. The Heavenly Books, the Bible, the Qur'án, and the other Holy Writings have been given by God as guide into the paths of Divine virtue, love, justice and peace.
>
> Therefore I say unto you that ye should strive to follow the counsels of these Blessed Books, and so order your lives that ye may, following the examples set before you, become yourselves the saints of the Most High![110]

The Bahá'í Faith also believes in Moses, the Prophets recounted in the Tanakh and in Jesus, and teaches that the Bible contains the inspired Word of God:

> This book is the Holy Book of God, of celestial Inspiration. It is the Bible of Salvation, the Noble Gospel. It is the mystery of the Kingdom and its light. It is the Divine Bounty, the sign of the guidance of God.[111]

Bahá'ís do not engage in qualitative comparisons of the Prophets and their Dispensations. Bahá'u'lláh explains that any apparent superiority, such as that implied in the verse 'of those messengers, some of whom We have caused to excel others',[112] is to be attributed to differences in the intensity of the Revelations, and to the need to adapt the divine message to the requirements of each age: light is light and is nothing but light, and its source is the same identical Sun. The religions differ

> 'only in the intensity of their revelation and the comparative potency of their light'. And this, not by reason of any inherent incapacity of any one of them to reveal in a fuller measure the glory of the Message with which He has been entrusted, but rather because of the immaturity and unpreparedness of the age He lived in to apprehend and absorb the full potentialities latent in that Faith.[113]

It is for this reason that the Qur'án forbids idle disputations with the Jews and Christians and instead enjoins harmony:

> And dispute ye not with the People of the Book, except with means better (than mere disputation), unless it be with those of them who inflict wrong (and injury): But say, 'We believe in the Revelation which has come down to us and in that which came down to you; our God and your God is One; and it is to Him we bow (in Islam or obedience).'[114]

18

SUBMISSION TO THE DIVINE WILL: ABROGATION OF THE DISPENSATION OF MUHAMMAD, AND THE SUSPENSION AND MODIFICATION OF ITS SOCIAL LAWS BY BAHÁ'U'LLÁH

> ... the Revelation identified with Bahá'u'lláh abrogates unconditionally all the Dispensations gone before it, upholds uncompromisingly the eternal verities they enshrine, recognizes firmly and absolutely the Divine origin of their Authors, preserves inviolate the sanctity of their authentic Scriptures, disclaims any intention of lowering the status of their Founders or of abating the spiritual ideals they inculcate, clarifies and correlates their functions, reaffirms their common, their unchangeable and fundamental purpose, reconciles their seemingly divergent claims and doctrines, readily and gratefully recognizes their respective contributions to the gradual unfoldment of one Divine Revelation ...
>
> *Shoghi Effendi*[1]

'Essential' versus 'non-essential' aspects of religion

The Bahá'í Writings regard Judaism, Christianity and Islam as part of one common faith, and consider their spiritual, moral and ethical teachings to be timeless. 'They instil and awaken the knowledge and love of God, love for humanity, the virtues of the world of mankind, the attributes of the divine Kingdom, rebirth and resurrection from the kingdom of nature.'[2] This is considered the 'essential' aspect of these divinely-revealed religions, as the spiritual principles are everlasting.

They are not abrogated from one Dispensation to another but only reaffirmed:

> The Revelation, of which Bahá'u'lláh is the source and center, abrogates none of the religions that have preceded it, nor does it attempt, in the slightest degree, to distort their features or to belittle their value. It disclaims any intention of dwarfing any of the Prophets of the past, or of whittling down the eternal verity of their teachings. It can, in no wise, conflict with the spirit that animates their claims, nor does it seek to undermine the basis of any man's allegiance to their cause.[3]

The second feature of these religions comprises social laws that must be adhered to for the duration of a Dispensation, as they cater for critical human needs and conditions. These ordinances provide the Dispensations with their outward form and characteristics,[4] and are intended to bind their followers in a common practice of faith. This aspect of religion which deals with human transactions is considered 'non-essential', as the ordinances and institutions vary according to exigencies of time and place, and therefore are destined to change and evolve with a succeeding Revelation. Hence, it should never be made a cause or source of contention.

Eternal faith versus 'Dispensation' with a finite duration

The term 'Dispensation(s)' corresponds to 'hour', 'Day(s) of God or God', and 'term' or *ajal* in the Qur'án,[5] and 'season(s)', 'times', 'day(s)', 'hour' referred to in the Bible.[6] The Bahá'í Writings similarly distinguish between faith or religion and 'Dispensation'. Faith is renewed from time to time but is eternal. In contrast, 'Dispensation' is the defined period of time that extends from the proclamation of a Prophet of His Mission until the appearance of the next divine Messenger. It refers to the ordering or management of the affairs of a religion for a prescribed period. Dispensations provide the social laws that guide the many facets of the life of the individual and of the community, and their relationships with the outside world. These include laws that govern dietary habits, prescribe prayers and meditations for specific events, specify the method and period of fasting, dictate holy day observances, and define places of worship.

As described earlier, every religion confirms the validity and divine origin of preceding religions but abrogates their Dispensations and ushers in a Dispensation of its own. It is for this reason that although the Bahá'í Faith does not rescind the essentials of Judaism, Christianity and Islam, it does abrogate or modify their social principles, a divinely-ordained prescription acutely needed in this day and age.

> This Book [the Arabic Bayán] at once abrogated the laws and ceremonials enjoined by the Qur'án regarding prayer, fasting, marriage, divorce and inheritance, and upheld, in its integrity, the belief in the prophetic mission of Muhammad, even as the Prophet of Islám before Him had annulled the ordinances of the Gospel and yet recognized the Divine origin of the Faith of Jesus Christ.[7]

> The call of Bahá'u'lláh is primarily directed against all forms of provincialism, all insularities and prejudices. If long-cherished ideals and time-honored institutions, if certain social assumptions and religious formulae have ceased to promote the welfare of the generality of mankind, if they no longer minister to the needs of a continually evolving humanity, let them be swept away and relegated to the limbo of obsolescent and forgotten doctrines. Why should these, in a world subject to the immutable law of change and decay, be exempt from the deterioration that must needs overtake every human institution? For legal standards, political and economic theories are solely designed to safeguard the interests of humanity as a whole, and not humanity to be crucified for the preservation of the integrity of any particular law or doctrine.[8]

> We should also bear in mind that the distinguishing character of the Bahá'í Revelation does not solely consist in the completeness and unquestionable validity of the Dispensation which the teachings of Bahá'u'lláh . . . have established. Its excellence lies also in the fact that those elements which in past Dispensations have, without the least authority from their Founders, been a source of corruption and of incalculable harm to the Faith of God, have been strictly excluded

by the clear text of Bahá'u'lláh's writings. Those unwarranted practices, in connection with the sacrament of baptism, of communion, of confession of sins, of asceticism, of priestly domination, of elaborate ceremonials, of holy war and of polygamy, have one and all been rigidly suppressed by the Pen of Bahá'u'lláh; whilst the rigidity and rigor of certain observances, such as fasting, which are necessary to the devotional life of the individual, have been considerably abated.[9]

This break with tradition, signalling the dawn of a new age, is often a severe test for individuals who have come to regard the traditions and social teachings as core principles or 'pillars' of their Faith. They do well to remind themselves that acceptance of God's new design must be the hallmark of a true follower of Moses, Christ or Muhammad. Bahá'u'lláh declares that acceptance of all good is indeed dependent on acquiescence to the Divine Will:

> Blessed is the man that hath acknowledged his belief in God and in His signs, and recognized that 'He shall not be asked of His doings'. Such a recognition hath been made by God the ornament of every belief, and its very foundation. Upon it must depend the acceptance of every goodly deed. Fasten your eyes upon it, that haply the whisperings of the rebellious may not cause you to slip.
>
> Were He to decree as lawful the thing which from time immemorial had been forbidden, and forbid that which had, at all times, been regarded as lawful, to none is given the right to question His authority.[10]

The heightened perception of spiritual values and the requisite changes in the social laws correspond to the 'new heaven and a new earth' anticipated in the Bible. It is also of interest that in this context, Muḥammad ibn 'Alí al-Báqir, revered by Shí'ihs and highly respected by Sunnis for his knowledge and Islamic scholarship, stated 'when he (the Qá'im) rises, he will rule with a new method, new principles, new Sunnah and new judgments . . .'[11]

* * *

The following sections provide examples of new social laws in the Dispensation of Bahá'u'lláh and compare them to their predecessors in Judaism, Christianity and Islam.

Implications of Bahá'u'lláh's declaration of the oneness of mankind

Judaism, Christianity and Islam make clear demarcations between believers and 'outsiders', and even slavery was accepted and condoned by all three until quite recent times. Since Bahá'u'lláh unequivocally declares that humanity is one, His Faith does not recognize characterizations of the family of man that do not acknowledge this reality. Today the Faith of Bahá'u'lláh forbids distinctions between individuals that are inimical to the well-being of mankind, such as Jew versus gentile (*goim*), circumcised versus uncircumcised, pure (*táhir or pák*) versus unclean (*najis*), worthy of association versus untouchable, believer or '*mu'min*' versus an unbeliever, heathen or '*káfir*'. To Bahá'ís, what differentiates a believer and an unbeliever is simply that the former has attained to a measure of the Truth whilst the latter has yet to become spiritually aware of it.

The oneness of mankind is not a feature of the Dispensation of Moses, and in the Tanakh slavery is a fact of life. Moreover, the children of Israel are set apart from the uncircumcised gentiles, perhaps largely to protect the purity of the religion as the Jews moved through many lands and peoples and were likely to be influenced by the worship of diverse gods. The Bible is full of accounts of what was regarded justifiable homicide and destruction of the gentiles. The non-Jew is not to be trusted, and he is to be uncompromisingly excluded from the congregation. There was to be no compromise or attempt at integration or conversion:

> But if thou shalt . . . do all that I speak; then I will be an enemy unto thine enemies, and an adversary unto thine adversaries . . .
>
> Thou shalt not bow down to their gods, nor serve them, nor do after their works: but thou shalt utterly overthrow them, and quite break down their images.[12]

The New Testament introduces the concept that in the sight of God humanity is one:

> There is neither Jew nor Greek, there is neither bond nor free, there is neither male nor female: for ye are all one in Christ Jesus.[13]

However, equality of humanity is not a consistent Gospel teaching. Christ is described as a friend to publicans and sinners (Matt. 11:19) but He also taught that faith and hope were for the deserving:

> Give not that which is holy unto dogs, neither cast ye your pearls before swine . . .[14]

Christ explicitly commanded that His Message was primarily intended for the Jews. While He did respond compassionately to the pleadings of a non-Jew, He explained His reluctance to provide spiritual nourishment by indicating that He had been sent specifically to the house of Israel.

> These twelve Jesus sent forth and commanded them, saying, Go not into the way of the gentiles and into any city of the Samaritans enter ye not:
> But go rather to the lost sheep of the house of Israel.[15]

> And, behold, a woman of Canaan [described in Mark 7:26 as 'Greek, a Syrophenician by nation') came out of the same coasts, and cried unto him, saying,
> Have mercy on me, O lord, Thou Son of David; my daughter is grievously vexed with a devil.
> But he answered her not a word. And his disciples came and besought him, saying, Send her away; for she crieth after us.
> But he answered and said, I am not sent but unto the lost sheep of the house of Israel.
> Then came she and worshipped him, saying, Lord help me.
> But he answered and said, It is not meet to take the children's bread, and cast it to the dogs.
> And she said, Truth, Lord: yet the dogs eat of the crumbs which fall from their masters' table.
> Then Jesus answered and said unto her, O woman, great is thy faith: be it unto thee even as thou wilt.[16]

It was the Apostle Paul who undertook the evangelization of the gentiles in the face of opposition from the mother church in Jerusalem, which closely followed the traditional Jewish line. However, even he appears to admit that the Jews had a greater right to the new Revelation.

> For I am not ashamed of the gospel of Christ: for it is the power of God unto salvation to every one that believeth; to the Jew first, and also to the Greek.[17]

> Tribulation and anguish, upon every soul of man that doeth evil, of the Jew first, and also of the Gentile;
> But glory, honour, and peace, to every man that worketh good, to the Jew first, and also the gentile.
> For there is no respect of persons with God.[18]

The New Testament also appears less concerned with the rights and freedom of the slave as with the fact that the slave should be a good Christian and not engage in any action that would bring disrepute to the Faith.

> Slaves, be obedient to them that are your masters according to the flesh, with fear and trembling, in singleness of your heart, as unto Christ.[19]

> Bondservants (slaves), obey in all things your masters according to flesh; not with eyeservice, as menpleasers; but in singleness of heart, fearing God.[20]

> Let as many bondservants as are under the yoke count their own masters worthy of all honour, that the name of God and his doctrine be not blasphemed.
> And they that have believing masters, let them not despise them, because they are brethren; but rather do them service, because they are faithful and beloved, partakers of the benefit. These things teach and exhort.[21]

> Exhort bondservants to be obedient unto their own masters, and to please them well in all things; not answering again;

> Not purloining, but showing all good fidelity; that they may adorn the doctrine of God our Saviour in all things.[22]

> Servants (slaves), be subject to your masters with all fear; not only to the good and gentle, but also to the froward.[23]

A remarkable example of this is the spiritual transformation of the slave Oneismus who, after his conversion in prison, is sent back to his master by St Paul, bearing his Epistle to the Colossians (Philem. 1:8-12).

The oneness of mankind is not a primary concern of the Islamic Dispensation; although from early on Islam was adopted by individuals from many different backgrounds, there are significant differentiations. For example, the Qur'án discourages friendship with the Jews and Christians, at least with those who at an earlier time had continuously opposed Islam and plotted with its enemies.

> O ye who believe! Take not the Jews and the Christians for your friends and protectors: they are friends and protectors to each other. And he amongst you that turns to them (for friendship) is of them. Verily God guideth not a people unjust.[24]

> O believers! Take not for friends and protectors those who take your religion for a mockery or sport – whether among those who received the Scripture before you, or among those who reject Faith; but fear ye God, if ye have Faith (indeed).[25]

In contrast to the Jewish and Christian Dispensations, the Qur'án makes several provisions for the freeing of slaves. However, slavery is not forbidden but is generally accepted. Further, laws concerning justice do not apply equally to the free and the slave. For example, a free man cannot be killed for the death of a slave:

> O ye who believe, the law of equality is prescribed to you in cases of murder, the free for the free, the slave for the slave, the woman for the woman . . .[26]

The Qur'án states several times that had God willed it, He would have created 'a single people' earlier, the clear implication being that its time as a social principle had not yet come.

> To each among you have We prescribed a Law and an Open Way. If God had so willed, He would have made you a single people, but (His plan is) to test you in what He hath given you . . .[27]

> If thy Lord had so willed He could have made mankind one people: but they will not cease to dispute.[28]

> If God so willed, He could make you all one people: but He leaves straying whom He pleases, and He guides whom He pleases: but ye shall certainly be called to account for all your actions.[29]

> If God had so willed, He could have made them a single people; but He admits whom He will to His Mercy; and the wrongdoers will have no protector nor helper.[30]

Bahá'u'lláh has today condemned slavery:

> It is forbidden you to trade in slaves, be they men or women. It is not for him who is himself a servant to buy another of God's servants, and this hath been prohibited in His Holy Tablet. Thus, by His mercy, hath the commandment been recorded by the Pen of justice. Let no man exalt himself above another; all are but bondslaves before the Lord . . .[31]

That 'no-one should exalt himself over another' finds myriad expressions in the Writings of Bahá'u'lláh, centering around the fundamental Bahá'í principle of the oneness of mankind, a theme which is further discussed in Chapter 19.

Equality of women and men

For the first time in the history of religion, gender equality is made a specific and fundamental principle in the Revelation of Bahá'u'lláh (see Chapter 19). This has implications for new social laws such as those governing education, marriage, divorce, inheritance, and others.

The equality of women and men is not part of Bible teaching. The Tanakh allows men to own women, and monogamy is not enforced. However, fairness is advised.

> When thou goest forth to war against thine enemies, and the Lord thy God hath delivered them into thine hands, and thou hast taken them captive,
> And seest among the captives a beautiful woman, and hast a desire unto her, that thou wouldest have her to thy wife;
> Then thou shalt bring her home to thine house; and she shall shave her head, and pare her nails;
> And she shall put the raiment of her captivity from off her, and shall remain in thine house, and bewail her father and her mother a full month: and after that thou shalt go in unto her, and be her husband, and she shall be thy wife.
> And it shall be, if thou have no delight in her, then thou shalt let her go whither she will; but thou shalt not sell her at all for money, thou shalt not make merchandise of her, because thou hast humbled her.[32]

> If a man have two wives, one beloved, and another hated, and they have born him children, both the beloved and the hated; and if the firstborn son be hers that was hated:
> Then it shall be, when he maketh his sons to inherit that which he hath, that he may not make the son of the beloved firstborn before the son of the hated, which is indeed the firstborn:
> But he shall acknowledge the son of the hated for the firstborn, by giving him a double portion of all that he hath: for he is the beginning of his strength; the right of the firstborn is his.[33]

The New Testament teaches that bishops should limit themselves to one wife. It is unclear whether the same restriction applied to lay persons.

> A bishop then must be blameless, the husband of one wife, vigilant, sober, of good behaviour, given to hospitality, apt to teach.[34]

However, as advocated largely by St Paul, women are subject to the will of man, and there is a significant difference in the ranks of the two sexes.

> Wives, submit yourselves unto your own husbands, as unto the Lord.
> For the husband is the head of the wife, even as Christ is the head of the Church: and he is the Saviour of the body.
> Therefore as the church is subject unto Christ, so let the wives be to their husbands in every thing.
> Husbands, love your wives, even as Christ also loved the church, and gave himself for it.[35]

> Wives, submit yourselves unto your own husbands, as it is fit in the Lord.
> Husbands, love your wives, and be not bitter against them.[36]

Women are ordered not to preach and are commanded to observe silence in church. They are to rely on their husbands for information and knowledge.

> Let your women keep silence in the churches: for it is not permitted unto them to speak; but they are commanded to be under obedience, as also saith the law.
> And if they will learn anything, let them ask their husbands at home: for it is a shame for a woman to speak in the church.[37]

> But I suffer not a woman to teach, nor to usurp authority over the man, but to be in silence.
> For Adam was first formed, then Eve.
> And Adam was not deceived, but the woman being deceived was in the transgression.
> Notwithstanding she shall be saved in childbearing, if they continue in faith and charity and holiness with sobriety.[38]

The Christian churches continue to be divided on this issue, and there has been a divisive battle, such as that in the Anglican Church, about whether women should be ordained as bishops, resolved only in late 2014 through the decision to allow it. The arguments centred around whether to follow this scriptural guidance because the Bible is the Word of God, or to ignore it because this teaching is so patently at variance with modern times. The Church of England allowed the ordination of women as late as 1985. Mainstream Catholic and Orthodox churches do not as yet accept this practice.

Similarly, an epistle attributed to St Peter states that women must defer to their husbands, and encourages them to call their husbands 'lord', following the example of the wife of the patriarch Abraham.

> Likewise, ye wives, be in subjection to your husbands . . .
>
> While they behold your chaste conversations coupled with fear.
>
> Whose adorning let it not be that outward adorning of plaiting the hair, and of wearing of gold, or of putting on of apparel . . .
>
> For after this manner in the old time the holy women also, who trusted in God, adorned themselves, being in subjection unto their own husbands:
>
> Even as Sara obeyed Abraham, calling him Lord . . .[39]

The Qur'án demands respect for women:

> O mankind! Reverence your Guardian-Lord, Who created you from a single person, created, of like nature, his mate, and from them twain scattered countless men and women; reverence God through Whom ye demand your mutual (rights) and reverence the wombs (that bore you): for God watches over you.[40]

However, the Qur'án does not fully embrace the principle of equality of men and women. Infractions of the Quranic and Sharia laws have dire consequences for women in several Islamic countries – women found guilty risk lashing, imprisonment, and being stoned to death.

Irrespective of how affluent the wife may be, it is the duty of the husband to provide for her.

> Men are the protectors and maintainers of women, because God has given the one more (strength) than the other, and because they support them from their means . . .[41]

Females inherit half that of a male:

> The male having twice the share of the female . . .⁴²

This significant gender inequality is also evident in the Islamic marriage laws. Muslim men are advised to marry single women, including good handmaidens. They are encouraged to be faithful to their wives and not to take concubines.

> (Lawful unto you in marriage) are (not only) chaste women who are believers, but chaste women among the People of the Book (Jews and Christians), revealed before your time, when you give them due dowers, and desire chastity not lewdness, nor secret intrigues ...⁴³

> Marry those among you who are single, or the virtuous ones among your slaves, male or female: if they are in poverty, God will give them means out of His grace: for God encompasseth all, and knoweth all things.⁴⁴

Marriage between a Muslim and an unbeliever is strongly discouraged, a prohibition of marrying outside one's Faith similar to that in the Torah (Deut. 25:5).

> Do not marry unbelieving women (idolaters), until they believe; a slave woman who believes is better than an unbelieving woman, even though she allure you. Nor marry (your girls) to unbelievers until they believe: a man slave who believes is better than an unbeliever, even though he allure you. Unbelievers do (but) beckon you to the fire. But God beckons by His grace to the Garden (of Bliss) and forgiveness, and makes His Signs clear to mankind: that they may celebrate His praise.⁴⁵

A Muslim man may marry more than one wife, with a limit of four wives but on condition that he is able to deal justly between them – as it may be argued that that this impossible, the verse actually recommends monogamy.

If ye fear that ye shall not be able to deal justly with the orphans, marry women of your choice, two, or three, or four; but if ye fear that ye shall not be able to deal justly (with them) then one (only) or (the captives) that your right hands possess. Thus it is more likely that ye will not do injustice.[46]

Laws governing divorce

In the Torah divorce is permitted and is a relatively easy matter for men. However, women cannot divorce their husbands – a divorced woman, however, was free to marry another man (Deut. 24:2).

> When a man takes a wife and marries her, and it come to pass that she find no favour in his eyes, because he hath found some uncleanliness in her, then let him write her a bill of divorcement, and give it in her hand, and send her out of his house.[47]

Christ forbade divorce except for fornication, and equated marriage to a divorced woman with adultery.

> It has been said that, whosoever shall put away his wife, let him give her a writing of divorcement:
> But I say unto you, That whosoever shall put away his wife, saving for the cause of fornication, causeth her to commit adultery; and whosoever shall marry her that is divorced committeth adultery.[48]

The Catholic and Anglican Churches refuse to marry a divorced person, but Christians have largely abandoned this teaching. Before the passage of the 1857 Divorce and Matrimonial Causes Act in Britain divorces could only be granted by Parliament. This act created the Court for Divorce and Matrimonial Causes in London, which allowed men to divorce their wives for adultery and women for abuse or desertion. Despite opposition from the Catholic Church divorce became legal in Italy in 1974, in Spain in 1981, and in Ireland in 1997.

Gender parity is absent in Islam with regard to divorce. A man is allowed to divorce his wife. He may dismiss her but is required to provide for her. There are no provisions for a woman to divorce her husband.

> O ye who believe! when ye marry believing women, and then divorce them before ye have touched them, no period of *'iddat* (prescribed period of waiting) have ye to count in respect of them: so give them a present, and then set them free in a handsome manner.[49]

A Muslim must however be kind to his divorced wife. Repeated divorce of the same woman is discouraged.

> A divorce is only permissible twice: after that, the parties should either hold together on equitable terms or separate with kindness . . .
>
> So if a husband divorces his wife (irrevocably), he cannot, after that, re-marry her until after she has married another husband and he has divorced her. In that case there is no blame on either of them if they re-unite . . .[50]

To circumvent this restriction, some Muslims pay another man – the *muhallil*, or the 'one who makes it legal', to marry the ex-wife and then to divorce her for a brief period so that the original husband may marry her again. According to Muslim tradition[51] this cannot be a *pro forma* marriage (i.e. they cannot marry only to register the marriage), but the woman must engage in sexual intercourse with the man before she can return to her former husband. Others consider this '*taheel* marriage' as forbidden and invalid.

Another custom practised by certain members of the Shi'ih sect is that of '*sigeh*', or temporary marriage, whereby the man contracts with a woman or her guardian to marry her for a specified period of time only.

The divorced woman must be supported for a prescribed length of time ('*iddat*) to ensure that the relationship has not resulted in pregnancy:

> When ye divorce women, and they fulfil the term of their (*'iddat*), either take them back on equitable terms or set them free on equitable terms . . .
>
> When ye divorce women, and they fulfil the term of their (*'iddat*), do not prevent them from marrying their (former) husbands, if they mutually agree on equitable terms . . .[52]

> Divorced women shall wait concerning themselves for three monthly periods. Nor is it lawful for them to hide what God hath created in their wombs, if they have faith in God and the Last Day. And their husbands have the better right to take them back in that period, if they wish for reconciliation . . .[53]

Bahá'u'lláh abrogates all earlier laws that treated men preferentially and which led to the subjugation and mistreatment of women. With regard to marriage and divorce, Bahá'í law is governed by the principle of gender equality. (For a general discussion of gender equality in the Bahá'í Faith, see Chapter 19.) Marriage is the physical, intellectual, and spiritual union of two souls and the bringing up of children who will mention God. As for divorce, it is permissible but

> is strongly condemned in the Bahá'í Teachings. If, however, antipathy or resentment develop between the marriage partners, divorce is permissible after the lapse of one full year. During this year of patience, the husband is obliged to provide for the financial support of his wife and children, and the couple is urged to strive to reconcile their differences . . . both the husband and wife 'have equal right to ask for divorce' whenever either partner 'feels it absolutely essential to do so'.[54]

Abolition of monasticism and asceticism

Solitude and contemplation have been a pillar of many religious organizations, including in Christian society. However, the New Testament criticizes monastic and ascetic lifestyles and St Paul associates the practices with departure from faith 'in latter times'.

> Now the Spirit speaketh expressly, that in the latter times some shall depart from the faith, giving heed to seducing spirits, and doctrines of devils;
>
> Speaking lies in hypocrisy: having their conscience seared with a hot iron;
>
> Forbidding to marry, and commanding to abstain from meats, which God hath created to be received with thanksgiving of them which believe and know the truth.[55]

Certain New Testament statements attributed to Paul disapprove of marriage. But this was only because he considered it a distraction from God's urgent work at the time – nevertheless, he appreciated its necessity for the less fortunate.

> For I would that all men were even as I myself. But every man hath his proper gift of God, one after this manner, and another after that.
> Now concerning the things whereof ye wrote unto me: It is good for a man not to touch a woman.
> Nevertheless, to avoid fornication, let every man have his own wife, and let every woman have her own husband.[56]

> I say therefore to the unmarried and widows, It is good for them if they abide even as I.
> But if they cannot contain, let them marry, for it is better to marry than to burn.
> And unto the married I command, yet not I, but the Lord, Let not the wife depart from her husband:
> But and if she depart, let her remain unmarried, or be reconciled to her husband: and let not the husband put away his wife.[57]

> But I would have you without carefulness. He that is unmarried careth for the things that belong to the Lord, how he may please the Lord.
> But he that is married careth for the things that are of the world, how he may please his wife.
> There is difference also between a wife and a virgin. The unmarried woman careth for the things of the Lord, that she may be holy both in body and in spirit: but she that is married careth for the things of the world, how she may please her husband.[58]

The Qur'án considers monasticism a man-made invention and an addition.

> We sent after them Jesus the son of Mary, and bestowed on him the Gospel; and We ordained in the hearts of those who followed him compassion and mercy. But the monasticism which they invented for themselves, We did not prescribe for them . . .[59]

Although Bahá'u'lláh acknowledges the contribution made to Christian civilization by monks and nuns, he abrogates the laws of monasticism and asceticism:

> The pious deeds of the monks and priests among the followers of the Spirit . . . are remembered in His presence. In this Day, however, let them give up the life of seclusion and direct their steps towards the open world and busy themselves with that which will profit themselves and others. We have granted them leave to enter into wedlock that they may bring forth one who will make mention of God, the Lord of the seen and the unseen, the Lord of the Exalted Throne.[60]

> Say: O concourse of monks! Seclude not yourselves in your churches and cloisters. Come ye out of them by My leave, and busy, then, yourselves with what will profit you and others. Thus commandeth you He Who is the Lord of the Day of Reckoning. Seclude yourselves in the stronghold of My love. This, truly, is the seclusion that befitteth you, could ye but know it. He that secludeth himself in his house is indeed as one dead. It behoveth man to show forth that which will benefit mankind. He that bringeth forth no fruit is fit for the fire. Thus admonisheth you your Lord; He, verily, is the Mighty, the Bountiful. Enter ye into wedlock, that after you another may arise in your stead. We, verily, have forbidden you lechery, and not that which is conducive to fidelity. Have ye clung unto the promptings of your nature, and cast behind your backs the statutes of God? Fear ye God, and be not of the foolish. But for man, who, on My earth, would remember Me, and how could My attributes and My names be revealed? Reflect, and be not of them that have shut themselves out as by a veil from Him, and were of those that are fast asleep. He that married not [Jesus] could find no place wherein to abide, nor where to lay His head, by reason of what the hands of the treacherous had wrought. His holiness consisted not in the things ye have believed and imagined, but rather in the things which belong unto Us. Ask, that ye may be made aware of His station which hath been exalted above the vain imaginings of all the peoples of the earth. Blessed are they that understand.[61]

Sexual immorality and indecent behaviour

All divine religions prescribe fidelity and moral behaviour in sexual matters. However, whereas in Judaism, Christianity and Islam punishments are usually – although not entirely – specifically directed towards women, the Bahá'í Faith makes both men and women equally responsible.

According to the Tanakh, indecency committed by a virgin is punishable by death, but is limited to scourging in the case of a female slave.

> But if this thing be true, and the tokens of virginity be not found for the damsel . . .
> Then they shall bring out the damsel to the door of her father's house, and the men of her city shall stone her with stones that she die: because she hath wrought folly in Israel, to play the whore in her father's house: so shalt thou put evil away from among you.[62]

> And whosoever lieth carnally with a woman, that is a bondmaid, betrothed to an husband, and not at all redeemed, nor freedom given her; she shall be scourged; they shall not be put to death, because she was not free.[63]

Adultery is punishable by stoning of both the man and the woman.

> If a man be found lying with a woman married to an husband, then they shall both of them die, both the man that lay with the woman, and the woman: so shalt thou put away evil from Israel.
> If a damsel that is a virgin be betrothed unto an husband, and a man find her in the city, and lie with her;
> Then ye shall bring them both out unto the gate of that city, and ye shall stone them with stones that they die; the damsel, because she cried not, being in the city; and the man, because he hath humbled his neighbour's wife: so thou shalt put away evil from among you.[64]

As advocated by both St Paul and St Peter in the New Testament, women are instructed to abide by strict rules of conduct and modesty, so as to promote the Word of God – however, no punishment is prescribed for the guilty.

. . . women adorn themselves in modest apparel, with shamefacedness and sobriety; not with braided hair, or gold, or pearls, or costly array;

But (which becometh women professing godliness) with good works.

Let the woman learn in silence with all subjection.[65]

The aged women likewise, that they be in behaviour as becometh holiness, not false accusers, not given to much wine, teachers of good things;

That they may teach the young women to be sober, to love their husbands, to love their children,

To be discreet, chaste, keepers at home, good, obedient to their own husbands, that the word of God be not blasphemed.[66]

Likewise, ye wives, be in subjection to your own husbands; that, if any obey not the word, they also may without the word be won by the conversation of the wives;

While they behold your chaste conversation coupled with fear.

Whose adorning let it not be that outward adorning of plaiting the hair, and of wearing of gold, or of putting on of apparel;

But let it be the hidden man of the heart, in that which is not corruptible, even the ornament of a meek and quiet spirit, which is in the sight of God of great price.

For after this manner in the old time the holy women also, who trusted in God, adorned themselves, being in subjection unto their own husbands:

Even as Sara obeyed Abraham, calling him lord: whose daughters ye are, as long as ye do well, and are not afraid with any amazement.

Likewise, ye husbands, dwell with them according to knowledge, giving honour unto the wife, as unto the weaker vessel, and as being heirs together of the grace of life; that your prayers be not hindered.[67]

The Qur'án prescribes that women guard their modesty and not display their beauty.

And say to the believing women that they should lower their gaze and guard their modesty; that they should not display their beauty [*zínat* or beauty could be interpreted as natural beauty and/or external ornaments, hence, the grades of restrictions imposed on Muslim women by various religious authorities] and ornaments except what (must ordinarily) appear thereof; that they should draw their veils over their bosoms and not display their beauty except to their husbands, their fathers, their husband's fathers, their sons, their husbands' sons, their brothers or their brothers' sons, or their sisters' sons, or their women, or the slaves whom their right hands possess, or male servants free of physical needs, or small children who have no sense of the shame of sex; and that they should not strike their feet in order to draw attention to their hidden ornaments. And O ye Believers! turn ye all together towards God, that ye may attain Bliss.[68]

O Prophet! Tell thy wives and daughters, and the believing women, that they should cast their outer garments over their persons (when abroad): that is most convenient, that they should be known (as such) and not molested. And God is Oft-Forgiving, Most Merciful.[69]

Only women who cannot bear children are permitted not to wear an outer garment.

Such elderly women as are past the prospect of marriage – there is no blame on them if they lay aside their garments, provided they make not a wanton display of their beauty; but it is best for them to be modest: and God is One Who sees and knows all things.[70]

Individuals who falsely accuse a woman of indecent behaviour are cursed.

Those who slander chaste women, indiscreet but believing, are cursed in this life and in the Hereafter: for them is a grievous Penalty.[71]

And those who launch a charge against chaste women, and produce not four witnesses (to support their allegations) – flog them with eighty stripes: and reject their evidence ever after: for such men are wicked transgressors.[72]

In the case of an accusation of adultery that cannot be proven, the man and the woman may avoid punishment by swearing oaths that they are not guilty and in addition invoking the curse of God on their own selves if they are guilty. This is similar to the Torah (Num. 5:12–31).

> And for those who launch a charge against their spouses, and have (in support) no evidence but their own,– their solitary evidence (can be received) if they bear witness four times (with an oath) by God that they are solemnly telling the truth;
> And the fifth (oath) (should be) that they solemnly invoke the curse of God on themselves if they tell a lie.
> But it would avert the punishment from the wife, if she bears witness four times (with an oath) By God, that (her husband) is telling a lie;
> And the fifth (oath) should be that she solemnly invokes the wrath of God on herself if (her accuser) is telling the truth.[73]

However, proven indecent behaviour is severely punished.

> If any of your women are guilty of lewdness [*fāhishah*, any flagrant impropriety not necessarily amounting to fornication or adultery], take the evidence of four (reliable) witnesses from amongst you against them; and if they testify, confine them to houses until death do claim them, or God ordains for them some (other) way.
> If two men among you are guilty of lewdness, punish them both. If they repent and amend, Leave them alone; for God is Oft-returning, Most Merciful.[74]

Punishment for adultery (*zinā*) is equal flogging of both men and women.

> The woman and the man guilty of illegal sexual intercourse, flog each of them with a hundred stripes. Let not pity withhold you in their case, in a punishment prescribed by God, if you believe in

God and the Last Day. And let a party of the believers witness their punishment.[75]

Historically, Muslim women found guilty of adultery or fornication were punished by being literally immured. But this sentence was changed to 100 stripes and a year of banishment in the case of a maiden, and to death by stoning in the case of a married woman.[76] A male adulterer may only marry an adulteress or a polytheist (*mushrik*).

Let no man guilty of adultery or fornication marry any but a woman similarly guilty, or an unbeliever nor let any but such a man or an unbeliever marry such a woman: to the believers such a thing is forbidden.[77]

Women impure are for men impure, and men impure are for women impure; and women of purity are for men of purity, and men of purity are for women of purity: these are not affected by what men say: for them there is forgiveness, and a provision honorable.[78]

Severe but graded punishment is also prescribed for women suspected of misbehaviour or indecency.

Virtuous women are obedient, careful, during the husband's absence, because God hath of them been careful. But chide those for whose refractoriness ye have cause to fear; remove them into beds apart, and scourge them: but if they are obedient to you, then seek not occasion against them: verily, God is High, Great![79]

Some interpret the duration of abstention from conjugal relations as four months (*Baqara*, the Heifer, 2:227). 'If the husband deems the affair to be sufficiently grave, he will have to observe the conditions mentioned in *Nisā'*, the Women, 4:16.'[80] Others contend that the Quranic directive is less severe than it appears. They quote a *hadith* according to Thirmidhi and Muslim which reports that Muhammad had indicated that the beating should not leave marks on the wife.

As shown above, most warnings (and punishments) for immorality or indecency in the Abrahamic religions specifically concern women rather than men. In contrast, a chaste and moral life is prescribed in Bahá'í Writings for both men and women:

> Say: He is not to be numbered with the people of Bahá who followeth his mundane desires, or fixeth his heart on things of the earth. He is My true follower who, if he come to a valley of pure gold, will pass straight through it aloof as a cloud, and will neither turn back, nor pause. Such a man is, assuredly, of Me. From his garment the Concourse on high can inhale the fragrance of sanctity . . . And if he met the fairest and most comely of women, he would not feel his heart seduced by the least shadow of desire for her beauty. Such an one, indeed, is the creation of spotless chastity. Thus instructeth you the Pen of the Ancient of Days, as bidden by your Lord, the Almighty, the All-Bountiful.[81]

However, a dress code is not enforced, and asceticism is discouraged.

> . . . a chaste and holy life, with its implications of modesty, purity, temperance, decency, and clean-mindedness, involves no less than the exercise of moderation in all that pertains to dress, language, amusements, and all artistic and literary avocations. It demands daily vigilance in the control of one's carnal desires and corrupt inclinations. It calls for the abandonment of a frivolous conduct, with its excessive attachment to trivial and often misdirected pleasures. It requires total abstinence from all alcoholic drinks, from opium, and from similar habit-forming drugs. It condemns the prostitution of art and of literature, the practices of nudism and of companionate marriage, infidelity in marital relationships, and all manner of promiscuity, of easy familiarity, and of sexual vices. It can tolerate no compromise with the theories, the standards, the habits, and the excesses of a decadent age. Nay rather it seeks to demonstrate, through the dynamic force of its example, the pernicious character of such theories, the falsity of such standards, the hollowness of such claims, the perversity of such habits, and the sacrilegious character of such excesses.[82]

It must be remembered, however, that the maintenance of such a high standard of moral conduct is not to be associated or confused with any form of asceticism, or of excessive and bigoted puritanism. The standard inculcated by Bahá'u'lláh, seeks, under no circumstances, to deny anyone the legitimate right and privilege to derive the fullest advantage and benefit from the manifold joys, beauties, and pleasures with which the world has been so plentifully enriched by an All-Loving Creator. 'Should a man,' Bahá'u'lláh Himself reassures us, 'wish to adorn himself with the ornaments of the earth, to wear its apparels, or partake of the benefits it can bestow, no harm can befall him, if he alloweth nothing whatever to intervene between him and God, for God hath ordained every good thing, whether created in the heavens or in the earth, for such of His servants as truly believe in Him. Eat ye, O people, of the good things which God hath allowed you, and deprive not yourselves from His wondrous bounties. Render thanks and praise unto Him, and be of them that are truly thankful.'[83]

Alcohol and other recreational drugs

Strong drink is discouraged in the Tanakh. Certain priests, the mother of Samson, the Prophet Daniel, and John the Baptist avoided alcohol altogether.

> Do not drink wine nor strong drink, thou, nor thy sons with thee, when ye go into the tabernacle of the congregation, lest ye die: it shall be a statute for ever throughout your generations.[84]

> Wine is a mocker, strong drink is raging: and whosoever is deceived thereby is not wise.[85]

> Woe unto them that rise up early in the morning, that they may follow strong drink; that continue until night, till wine inflame them![86]

> Woe unto them that are mighty to drink wine, and men of strength to mingle strong drink.[87]

> For he [John the Baptist] shall be great in the sight of the Lord, and

shall drink neither wine nor strong drink; and he shall be filled with the Holy Ghost, even from his mother's womb.[88]

The New Testament includes drunkenness amongst other serious sins.

> But now I have written unto you not to keep company, if any man that is called a brother be a fornicator, or covetous, or an idolater, or a railer, or a drunkard, or an extortioner; with such an one no not to eat.[89]

> Know ye not that the unrighteous shall not inherit the kingdom of God? Be not deceived: neither fornicators, nor idolaters, nor adulterers, nor effeminate, nor abusers of themselves with mankind,
> Nor thieves, nor covetous, nor drunkards, nor revilers, nor extortioners, shall inherit the kingdom of God.[90]

> Envyings, murders, drunkenness, revellings, and such like: of the which I tell you before, as I have also told you in time past, that they which do such things shall not inherit the kingdom of God.[91]

> And be not drunk with wine, wherein is excess; but be filled with the Spirit.[92]

At the beginning of the Revelation the Qur'án appears to tolerate alcohol, but gradually and eventually forbids it. This is confirmed in the Dispensation of Bahá'u'lláh:

> It is inadmissible that man, who hath been endowed with reason, should consume that which stealeth it away.[93]

> Beware lest ye exchange the Wine of God for your own wine, for it will stupefy your minds, and turn your faces away from the Countenance of God, the All-Glorious, the Peerless, the Inaccessible. Approach it not, for it hath been forbidden unto you by the behest of God, the Exalted, the Almighty.[94]

The Bahá'í Faith also strictly forbids habit-forming drugs and drugs that interfere with one's reasoning unless they are used for medicinal purposes:

> this prohibition includes ... 'everything that deranges the mind' ... the use of alcohol is permitted only when it constitutes part of a medical treatment which is implemented 'under the advice of a competent and conscientious physician, who may have to prescribe it for the cure of some special ailment'.[95]

The law of retaliation

The code of Hammurabi, King of Babylon, 1792–1750 BC, allowed equal retaliation – an eye for an eye and a tooth for a tooth. This injunction is also part of the Law of Moses and applies to some extent even to animals:

> Burning for burning, wound for wound, stripe for stripe.
> And if a man smite the eye of his servant, or the eye of his maid, that it perish; he shall let him go free for his eye's sake.
> And if he smite out his manservant's tooth, or his maidservant's tooth; he shall let him go free for his tooth's sake.
> If an ox gore a man or a woman, that they die: then the ox shall be surely stoned, and his flesh shall not be eaten; but the owner of the ox shall be quit.
> But if the ox were wont to push with his horn in time past, and it hath been testified to his owner, and he hath not kept him in, but that he hath killed a man or a woman; the ox shall be stoned, and his owner also shall be put to death.
> If there be laid on him a sum of money, then he shall give for the ransom of his life whatsoever is laid upon him.
> Whether he have gored a son, or have gored a daughter, according to this judgment shall it be done unto him.
> If the ox shall push a manservant or a maidservant; he shall give unto their master thirty shekels of silver, and the ox shall be stoned.
> And if a man shall open a pit, or if a man shall dig a pit, and not cover it, and an ox or an ass fall therein;
> The owner of the pit shall make it good, and give money unto the owner of them; and the dead beast shall be his.

> And if one man's ox hurt another's, that he die; then they shall sell the live ox, and divide the money of it; and the dead ox also they shall divide.
>
> Or if it be known that the ox hath used to push in time past, and his owner hath not kept him in; he shall surely pay ox for ox; and the dead shall be his own. Eye for eye, tooth for tooth, hand for hand, foot for foot.[96]

And he that killeth any man shall surely be put to death.
> And he that killeth a beast shall make it good; beast for beast.
> And if a man cause a blemish in his neighbour; as he hath done, so shall it be done to him;
> Breach for breach, eye for eye, tooth for tooth: as he hath caused a blemish in a man, so shall it be done to him again.
> And he that killeth a beast, he shall restore it: and he that killeth a man, he shall be put to death.[97]

> And thine eye shall not pity; but life shall go for life, eye for eye, tooth for tooth, hand for hand, foot for foot.[98]

Both Moses and Jesus conveyed the decrees of the same God, Who presumably was not capricious. One can conclude, therefore, that the tougher social laws of the Torah addressed harsher realities of societal life.

The message of Christ concerned more the conduct of the individual and his spiritual outlook, and in this context Jesus prohibited personal retaliation entirely. Evil was not to be resisted but overcome with kindness. The Gospels however do not provide any guidance as to how society should deal with various grievances.

> Ye have heard that it had been said, An eye for an eye, and a tooth for a tooth: But I say unto you, That ye resist not evil; but whosoever shall smite thee on thy right cheek, turn to him the other also.
>
> And if any man shall sue thee at the law, and take away thy coat, let him have thy cloak also. And whosoever shall compel thee to go a mile, go with him twain.[99]

> But I say unto you, Love your enemies, bless them that curse you, do good to them that hate you, and pray for them which despitefully use you, and persecute you;
>
> That ye may be the children of your Father which is in heaven: for he maketh his sun to rise on the evil and on the good, and sendeth rain on the just and on the unjust.[100]

Justice would only be established at the 'second coming', when as promised in the Lord's Prayer, there shall be done 'on earth as it is in heaven'. Christians were, in the meantime, urged to obey their civil government.

> Ye have heard that it hath been said, An eye for an eye, and a tooth for a tooth:
>
> Tell us therefore, What thinkest thou? Is it lawful to give tribute unto Caesar, or not?
>
> But Jesus perceived their wickedness, and said, Why tempt ye me, ye hypocrites?
>
> Show me the tribute money. And they brought unto him a penny. And he saith unto them, Whose is this image and superscription?
>
> They say unto him, Caesar's. Then saith he unto them, Render therefore unto Caesar the things which are Caesar's; and unto God the things that are God's.[101]

The Bahá'í Writings elaborate on this theme:

> The Revelation associated with the Faith of Jesus Christ focused attention primarily on the redemption of the individual and the molding of his conduct, and stressed, as its central theme, the necessity of inculcating a high standard of morality and discipline into man, as the fundamental unit in human society. Nowhere in the Gospels do we find any reference to the unity of nations or the unification of mankind as a whole. When Jesus spoke to those around Him, He addressed them primarily as individuals rather than as component parts of one universal, indivisible entity. The whole surface of the earth was as yet unexplored, and the organization of all its peoples and nations as one unit could, consequently, not be envisaged, how much less proclaimed or established. What other

interpretation can be given to these words, addressed specifically by Bahá'u'lláh to the followers of the Gospel, in which the fundamental distinction between the Mission of Jesus Christ, concerning primarily the individual, and His own Message, directed more particularly to mankind as a whole, has been definitely established: 'Verily, He [Jesus] said: "Come ye after Me, and I will make you to become fishers of men." In this day, however, We say: "Come ye after Me, that We may make you to become the quickeners of mankind."'[102]

Al-Qiṣáṣ or 'the Law of equitable retaliation' is prescribed in the Qur'án – a law that it teaches confers spiritual benefits.

> And there is life for you in (the law of) retaliation, O men of understanding, that you may guard yourselves.[103]

> O you who believe! The law of equality is prescribed to you in cases of murder: the free for the free, the slave for the slave, and the woman for the woman. But if any remission is made by the brother of the slain, then grant a reasonable demand, and compensate him with handsome gratitude; this is a concession and a Mercy from your Lord. After this whoever exceeds the limits shall be in grave penalty.[104]

Public reprisal is also considered a spiritual duty of Muslims, and is allowed even during the sacred month.

> The prohibited month for the prohibited month, and so for all things prohibited, there is the law of equality. If then anyone transgresses the prohibition against you, transgress ye likewise against him. But fear God, and know that God is with those who restrain themselves.[105]

Later on there is less stress on retaliation and greater emphasis on forgiveness and patience in the face of aggression.

> And if ye do catch them out, catch them out no worse than they catch you out: but if ye show patience, that is indeed the best (counsel) for those who are patient.

> And do thou be patient, for thy patience is from God; nor grieve over them: and distress not thyself because of their plots.[106]

In the Dispensation of Bahá'u'lláh, personal retaliation is entirely abrogated:

> Know ye that to be killed in the path of His good pleasure is better for you that to kill. The beloved of the Lord must, in this day, behave in such wise amidst His servants that they may by their very deeds and actions guide all men unto the paradise of the All-Glorious.[107]

Bahá'ís are further admonished:

> O army of God! Beware lest ye harm any soul, or make any heart to sorrow; lest ye wound any man with your words, be he known to you or a stranger, be he friend or foe. Pray ye for all; ask ye that all be blessed, all be forgiven. Beware, beware, lest any of you seek vengeance, even against one who is thirsting for your blood. Beware, beware, lest ye offend the feelings of another, even though he be an evil-doer, and he wish you ill. Look ye not upon the creatures, turn ye to their Creator. See ye not the never-yielding people, see but the Lord of Hosts.[108]

Abrogation of the law of '*jihád*', holy war

Jews, Christians, and Muslims have a long history of waging 'holy wars' to promote or defend their religion. The Bible is replete with Jewish military exploits of the Children of Israel as they struggled to reach the Promised Land. While Jesus encouraged personal forgiveness and forbade retaliation and reprisal, He also anticipated the violence that His teachings would generate:

> Think not that I am come to send peace on earth: I came not to send peace, but a sword.
> For I am come to set a man at variance against his father, and the daughter against her mother, and the daughter in law against her mother in law.

And a man's foes shall be they of his own household.[109]

Extrapolating from the Bible passages, early Church fathers such as Augustine of Hippo and Thomas Aquinas, as well as most Christian Churches, have justified and promoted the concept of 'just wars'.

The word *jihád* appears 41 times in the Qur'án. It is an essential part of the spiritual duties of a Muslim. It is considered by some Sunnis as the sixth pillar of Faith and by some Shí'ihs as one of their foremost ten principles. In Islamic jurisprudence (the Sharia), developed in the first few centuries after the Prophet's death, *jihád* is the only form of warfare permissible under Islamic law, and may consist in wars against unbelievers, apostates, rebels, highway robbers, and dissenters renouncing the authority of Islam. The primary aim of *jihád* is not conversion of non-Muslims to Islam by force, but rather the expansion and defence of the Islamic State. In later centuries, especially following the colonization of large parts of the Muslim world, non-militant interpretation of *jihád* was emphasized. However, there is considerable debate today as to how *jihád* should be implemented. Based on a tradition (*hadith*), a distinction is made between *al-jihád al-akbar* (the greater *jihád*) – the struggle against one's self (*nafs*), a spiritual effort to lead a moral life as a good Muslim and to build a good Muslim society – and *al-jihád al-asghar* (the lesser *jihád*) – military expeditions undertaken to defend Islam. Most Muslims believe that the term refers predominantly to a military struggle. Today, Muslim authors recognize as legitimate only wars with the aim of territorial defence as well as the defence of religious freedom.

Origins of jihád

The Bahá'í Writings emphasize the non-offensive nature of the military actions of Islam during the lifetime of Muhammad:

> The military expeditions of Muhammad . . . were always defensive actions: a proof of this is that during thirteen years, in Mecca, He and His followers endured the most violent persecutions. At this period they were the target for the arrows of hatred: some of His companions were killed and their property confiscated; others fled to foreign lands. Muhammad Himself, after the most extreme persecutions by the Qurayshites, who finally resolved to kill Him, fled

to Medina in the middle of the night. Yet even then His enemies did not cease their persecutions, but pursued Him to Medina, and His disciples even to Abyssinia ...

It was under such circumstances that Muhammad was forced to take up arms ... to free these [tyrannical and barbarous] tribes from their bloodthirstiness was the greatest kindness, and to coerce and restrain them was a true mercy. They were like a man holding in his hand a cup of poison, which, when about to drink, a friend breaks and thus saves him. If Christ had been placed in similar circumstances, it is certain that with a conquering power He would have delivered the men, women and children from the claws of these bloodthirsty wolves.

Muhammad never fought against the Christians; on the contrary, He treated them kindly and gave them perfect freedom.[110]

Jihád was originally intended for the nearby neighbours of the Muslims, but as time passed and more enemies arose, the Quranic injunctions were updated for the new adversaries.

The injunction of jihád *is constrained by several important considerations*

Life is regarded as sacred (*Má'ida*, the Table Spread, 5:32) and homicide is strongly condemned. For example, infanticide was forbidden although it was a common and accepted practice in Arabia:

> kill not your children on a plea of want; – We provide sustenance for you and for them; ... take not life, which God hath made sacred, except by way of justice and law: thus doth He command you, that ye may learn wisdom.[111]

No one should be compelled to change his or her religion:

> Let there be no compulsion in religion. Truth stands out clear from error; whoever rejects evil and believes in God hath grasped the most trustworthy hand-hold, that never breaks. And God heareth and knoweth all things.[112]

A genuine offer of peace should be accepted:

> But if the enemy incline towards peace, do thou (also) incline towards peace, and trust in God: for He is the one that heareth and knoweth (all things).[113]

It is not God's wish to force individuals to believe, it is God Who bestows the gift of belief:

> If it had been the Lord's Will, they would all have believed – all who are on earth! Wilt thou then compel mankind, against their will, to believe!
> No soul can believe, except by the Will of God, and He will place doubt (or obscurity) on those who will not understand.[114]

A Muslim's duty is to invite humanity to heed divine guidance, but not to interfere with an individual's freedom of choice in action and in belief: it is not a Muslim's right to judge others for their 'unbelief' or to punish their apparent waywardness – reward and punishment are left to the Day of Judgement.

> To every people have we appointed rites and ceremonies which they must follow, let them not then dispute with thee on the matter, but do thou invite (them) to thy Lord: for thou art assuredly on the Right Way.
> If they do wrangle with thee, say, 'God knows best what it is ye are doing.'
> God will judge between you on the Day of Judgment concerning the matters in which ye differ.[115]

> O you who believe! When you go in the Cause of God, verify (the truth), and say not to anyone who greets you: 'You are not a believer'; seeking the perishable goods of the worldly life. There are much more profits and booties with God. Even as he is now, so were you yourselves before till God conferred on you His Favours, therefore, be cautious in discrimination. God is ever well-aware of what you do.[116]

The Qur'án prohibits the shedding of innocent blood and the committing of excesses. This allegedly is a teaching of the Torah, but also one that applies to Islam.

> On that account: We ordained for the Children of Israel that if anyone slew a person – unless it be for murder or for spreading mischief in the land – it would be as if he slew the whole people: and if anyone saved a life, it would be as if he saved the life of the whole people. Then although there came to them Our apostles with clear Signs, yet, even after that, many of them continued to commit excesses in the land.[117]

Some point out that the great *jihád* is the internal struggle to transform oneself. It is also instructive that *jihád* was, at least initially, defensive and part of the realities of life in a dangerous neighbourhood, but is tempered by the knowledge that Islam was inspired by a God Who is kind, merciful, compassionate, just, and concerned with the welfare of orphans. Nevertheless, admittedly, there are many injunctions in the Qur'án that recommend the waging of *jihád* against infidels and unbelievers, couched in a language that many today may find unacceptable.

> Then fight in the Cause of God, and know that God heareth and knoweth all things.[118]

> God hath granted a grade higher to those who strive and fight with their goods and persons than to those who sit (at home): unto all (in faith) hath God promised good: but those who strive and fight hath He distinguished above those who sit (at home) by a special reward.[119]

> O Prophet! Rouse the believers to the fight. If there are twenty amongst you, patient and persevering, they will vanquish two hundred: if a hundred, they will vanquish a thousand of the unbelievers: for these are a people without understanding.[120]

> And fight them on until there is no more tumult or oppression (disbelief), and there prevail justice and faith in God altogether and everywhere . . .[121]

> Fighting is prescribed for you, and ye dislike it. But it is possible

that ye dislike a thing which is good for you and that ye love a thing which is bad for you. But God knoweth, and ye know not.

. . . Tumult and oppression are worse than slaughter. Nor will they cease fighting you until they turn you back from your faith if they can. And if any of you turn back from their faith and die in unbelief, their works will bear no fruit in this life and in the Hereafter; they will be Companions of the Fire and will abide therein.[122]

. . . fight and slay the pagans wherever ye find them and seize them, beleaguer them and lie in wait for them in every stratagem (of war); but if they repent, and establish regular prayers and practise regular charity, then open the way for them: for God is Oft-Forgiving, Most Merciful.[123]

Therefore, when ye meet the unbelievers (in fight), smite at their necks; at length, when ye have thoroughly subdued them, bind a bond firmly (on them): thereafter (is the time for) either generosity or ransom . . .[124]

O Prophet! Strive hard against the unbelievers and the hypocrites, and be firm against them. Their abode is hell, an evil refuge indeed.[125]

If thou comest on them in the war, deal with them so as to strike fear in those who are behind them, that haply they may remember.
And if thou fearest treachery from any folk, then throw back to them (their treaty) fairly. Lo! God loveth not the treacherous.[126]

Fight those who believe not in God nor the Last Day, nor hold that forbidden which hath been forbidden by God and His Messenger, nor acknowledge the religion of truth, (even if they are) of the People of the Book, until they pay the *Jizyah*[127] with willing submission, and feel themselves subdued.[128]

. . . fight the pagans (*Mushrikún*) all together as they fight you all together. But know that God is with those who restrain themselves.[129]

Abolition of jihád *in the Bahá'í Faith*

Bahá'u'lláh has abolished 'holy wars' fought in the name of religion.

> The first Glad-Tidings which the Mother Book hath, in this Most Great Revelation, imparted unto all of the peoples of the world is that the law of holy war hath been blotted out from the Book. Glorified be the All-Merciful, the Lord of grace abounding . . .[130]

> Beware lest ye shed the blood of any one. Unsheathe the sword of your tongue from the scabbard of utterance, for therewith ye can conquer the citadels of men's hearts. We have abolished the law to wage holy war against each other.[131]

> Know thou that We have annulled the rule of the sword, as an aid to Our Cause, and substituted for it the power born of the utterance of men . . . Say: O people! Sow not the seeds of discord among men, and refrain from contending with your neighbor . . .[132]

Capital punishment

The death penalty, often carried out publicly, has been usual in most historical societies, including those associated with Judaism, Christianity and Islam. In the Qur'án it is reserved for two types of crime:

> *Wilful murder:* The victim's family is given a choice to either insist on the death penalty or to pardon the perpetrator and accept monetary compensation for their loss.

> *Spreading mischief in the land (fasád fil-ardh):* This crime has been open to a great deal of interpretation. It has been interpreted as applying to espousing different and unorthodox religious beliefs, blasphemy, apostasy, treason, terrorism, piracy, rape, adultery, drug trafficking, and homosexuality.

According to the Bahá'í Faith, religious belief and practice are part of human rights. Capital punishment for wilful murder is considered as one of those social laws that must vary with the exigencies of the time.

It is not entirely ruled out but an alternative of life imprisonment is also provided:

> while capital punishment is permitted, an alternative, 'life imprisonment', has been provided 'whereby the rigours of such a condemnation can be seriously mitigated' . . . 'Bahá'u'lláh has given us a choice and has, therefore, left us free to use our own discretion within certain limitations imposed by His law'. In the absence of specific guidance concerning the application of this aspect of Bahá'í law, it remains for the Universal House of Justice to legislate on the matter in the future.[133]

Apostasy

In Islam, *irtád*, *murtad* and '*ridda*', turning back or apostasy, are considered a profound insult to God and a failure of piety.[134] An individual born of Muslim parents who rejects Islam is called *murtad fitri* (natural apostate) (not based on the Qur'án), and a person who converted to Islam and later rejects the religion is called a *murtad milli* (apostate from the community).

> Those who turn back as apostates after Guidance was clearly shown to them, the Evil One has instigated them and buoyed them up with false hopes.[135]

Apostasy implies a turning back. For instance, an apostate from Islam who returns to his earlier religion denies the religion of Muhammad in the process. Apostasy does not apply to progression and acceptance of a next and anticipated Revelation. The Muslim converts from Judaism and Christianity were not considered apostates from their parent religion. Similarly, the followers of Bahá'u'lláh, often converts from Judaism, Christianity or Islam, cannot be considered apostates of any of these three religions, since the Faith of Bahá'u'lláh emphatically validates them all.

Blasphemy

In the Torah, blasphemy carries the death penalty:

> And he that blasphemeth the name of the Lord, he shall surely be put to death, and all the congregation shall certainly stone him: as well the stranger, as he that is born in the land, when he blasphemeth the name of the Lord, shall be put to death.[136]

Jesus was accused of blasphemy because He was not constrained by Jewish traditions and customs, this despite the transforming power of His influence.

> The Jews answered him, saying, For a good work we stone thee not; but for blasphemy; and because that thou, being a man, makest thyself God.[137]

In turn, Martin Luther charged the Jews with blasphemy, thus justifying the destruction of their synagogues, the restriction of their livelihoods, and banishment.[138]

Blasphemy in Islam is irreverent behaviour toward the Qur'án, holy personages, religious artifacts, customs, and beliefs that Muslims revere. The Qur'án regards misrepresentations by the Church and the literal interpretation of the Trinity as blasphemous. Notably, any assertion that a particular religion has sole custody and protector of truth to the exclusion of any future Revelation is also considered blasphemous:

> They say, 'Our hearts are the wrappings (which preserve God's word, we need no more).' Nay, God's curse is on them for their blasphemy; little is it they believe.[139]

> They have incurred divine displeasure): in that they broke their Covenant: that they rejected the Signs of God; that they slew the Messengers in defiance of right; that they said, 'Our hearts are the wrappings (which preserve God's Word; we need no more);' nay God hath set the seal on their hearts for their blasphemy, and little is it they believe.
> That they rejected faith . . .[140]

> The Jews say: 'God's hand is tied up.' Be their hands tied up and be they accursed for the (blasphemy) they utter. Nay, both His hands are widely outstretched: He giveth and spendeth (of His

bounty) as He pleaseth. But the revelation that cometh to thee from God increaseth in most of them their obstinate rebellion and blasphemy.[141]

The Qur'án and the *hadith* are silent concerning punishment for blasphemy. Jurists incorporated it into the Sharia. Under Sharia law the penalties for blasphemy can include fines, imprisonment, flogging, amputation, hanging, or beheading. Not infrequently, Muslim clerics call for the punishment of an alleged blasphemer by issuing a *fatwa*.

Bahá'ís have long endured a great deal of blasphemous attacks, but there is no concept in Bahá'í Writings of worldly punishment for those responsible for this injustice. Bahá'ís simply pray to be guarded 'from the aggressor, from him who hath become a shameless and blasphemous doer of wrong'.[142]

Modification of dietary laws

Judaism, Christianity, and Islam differ as to what foods are 'kosher', 'clean' or '*halál*'. Often, what had been forbidden previously became acceptable in a subsequent Dispensation.

The Torah is replete with dietary laws. These include the following:

> And the swine, because it divideth the hoof, yet cheweth not the cud, it is unclean unto you: ye shall not eat of their flesh, nor touch their dead carcass.[143]

> Nevertheless these ye shall not eat of them that chew the cud, or of them that divide the cloven hoof; as the camel, and the hare, and the coney: for they chew the cud, but divide not the hoof; therefore they are unclean unto you.[144]

> These shall ye eat of all that are in the waters: whatsoever hath fins and scales in the waters, in the seas, and in the rivers, them shall ye eat.
> And all that have not fins and scales in the seas, and in the rivers, of all that move in the waters, and of any living thing which is in the waters, they shall be an abomination unto you:
> Whatsoever hath no fins nor scales in the waters, that shall be an abomination unto you.[145]

The New Testament also contains dietary restrictions, but these are fewer and far less severe than those of the Mosaic Dispensation.

> For it seemed good to the Holy Ghost, and to us, to lay upon you no greater burden than these necessary things;
> That ye abstain from meats offered to idols, and from blood, and from things strangled, and from fornication: from which if ye keep yourselves, ye shall do well. Fare ye well.[146]

Certain foods are disallowed in the Qur'án. God's name is to be mentioned before the meat or food is eaten – but any food may be eaten in times of necessity.

> Say: 'I find not in the Message received by me by inspiration any (meat) forbidden to be eaten by one who wishes to eat it, unless it be dead meat, or blood poured forth, or the flesh of swine, for it is an abomination, or, what is impious, (meat) on which a name has been invoked, other than God's.' But (even so), if a person is forced by necessity, without willful disobedience, nor transgressing due limits, thy Lord is Oft-forgiving, Most Merciful.[147]

> He has only forbidden you what dies of itself, and blood, and flesh of swine, and that over which any other (name) than (that of) God has been invoked; but whoever is driven to necessity, not desiring, nor exceeding the limit, no sin shall be upon him; surely God is Forgiving, Merciful.[148]

Muslims are allowed to share the food of Jews and Christians.

> This day are (all) things Good and pure made lawful unto you. The food of the People of the Book is lawful unto you . . .[149]

It must also be borne in mind that the Qur'án teaches that God is displeased with those who forbid what is not specifically forbidden.

> But say not – for any false thing that your tongues may put forth, – 'This is lawful, and this is forbidden,' so as to ascribe false things to God. For those who ascribe false things to God, will never prosper.[150]

The Baháʼí Faith abrogates all the laws related to the cleanliness or uncleanliness (*halál* or kosher designations) of food.

> God hath, likewise, as a bounty from His presence, abolished the concept of 'uncleanness', whereby divers things and peoples have been held to be impure. He, of a certainty, is the Ever-Forgiving, the Most Generous.[151]

> As the change and alteration of conditions are necessities of the essence of beings, so laws also are changed and altered in accordance with the changes and alterations of the times. For example, in the time of Moses, His Law was conformed and adapted to the conditions of the time; but in the days of Christ these conditions had changed and altered to such an extent that the Mosaic Law was no longer suited and adapted to the needs of mankind; and it was, therefore, abrogated . . . After Christ four disciples, among whom were Peter and Paul, permitted the use of animal food forbidden by the Bible, except the eating of those animals which had been strangled, or which were sacrificed to idols, and of blood. They also forbade fornication. They maintained these four commandments. Afterward, Paul permitted even the eating of strangled animals, those sacrificed to idols, and blood, and only maintained the prohibition of fornication.[152]

Punishments for theft

Laws such as the punishment for theft vary from one religion to another and depend on prevailing conditions. The Torah prescribes compensation.

> If a man shall steal an ox, or a sheep, and kill it, or sell it; he shall restore five oxen for an ox, and four sheep for a sheep.
>
> If a thief be found breaking up, and be smitten that he die, there shall no blood be shed for him.
>
> If the sun be risen upon him, there shall be bloodshed for him; for he should make full restitution; if he have nothing, then he shall be sold for his theft.
>
> If the theft be certainly found in his hand alive, whether it be ox, or ass, or sheep; he shall restore double.[153]

The New Testament teaches that thieves are deprived of eternal salvation. There are however, no instructions as to how they should be punished by society.

> Nor thieves, nor covetous, nor drunkards, nor revilers, nor extortioners, shall inherit the kingdom of God.[154]

Presumably the culprits ought to be forgiven:

> And unto him that smiteth thee on the one cheek offer also the other; and him that taketh away thy cloak forbid not to take thy coat also.[155]

In the Qur'án the punishment for theft is particularly harsh, and although still carried out in some countries, clearly requires divine revision.

> As to the thief, male or female, cut off his or her hands: a punishment by way of example, from God, for their crime: and God is Exalted in Power.
> But if the thief repents after his crime, and amends his conduct, God turneth to him in forgiveness; for God if Oft-Forgiving, Most Merciful.[156]

In the Bahá'í Faith the penalty for theft must be in accordance with the seriousness of the offence and will be determined by the Universal House of Justice in the future. The Bahá'í Writings provide the following explanation about the harshness of the Law of Moses concerning punishment for theft, which would also apply to conditions in which the Qur'án was revealed:

> Moses lived in the wilderness and desert of Sinai; therefore, his ordinances and commandments were in conformity with those conditions. The penalty for theft was to cut off a man's hand. An ordinance of this kind was in keeping with desert life but not compatible with conditions of the present day. Such ordinances, therefore, constitute the second or non-essential division of the divine religions and are not of importance, for they deal with human transactions which are ever changing according to the requirements of time and place.[157]

19

PARTICIPATING IN THE RESURRECTION AND REBIRTH OF THE FAITH OF ISLAM

> Happy is the man who will arise to serve My Cause, and glorify My beauteous Name. Take hold of My Book with the power of My might, and cleave tenaciously to whatsoever commandment thy Lord, the Ordainer, the All-Wise, hath prescribed therein.
>
> Bahá'u'lláh[1]

Through the saving grace of Bahá'u'lláh's long-awaited Revelation, Muslims, as well as Jews, Christians and members of other religions, are invited to fulfil their destiny and to take part in the revival of the eternal truths of their cherished Faiths. They are all presented with the unique opportunity to partake not only of His transforming new social teachings but in the renewal of the essentials of faith through Bahá'u'lláh's prescription for this day and age, and to thereby play their part in a world-energizing and a world-redeeming divinely-ordained enterprise.

Love, unity and harmony

Christ taught that 'every good tree bringeth forth good fruit',[2] and St Paul added that the 'fruit of the Spirit is love, joy, peace, longsuffering, gentleness, goodness, faith'.[3] Jesus therefore gave His followers a new commandment: 'That ye love one another; as I have loved you, that ye also love one another.'[4] His disciples were to be known because they demonstrated 'love one to another'.[5] According to the New Testament, declaration of faith without love is futile: 'He that saith he is in the light, and hateth his brother, is in darkness,'[6] and 'He that loveth not knoweth not God; for God is love,'[7] 'for love is of God; and every one that loveth is born of God, and knoweth God.'[8] St Paul beseeched his Christian brethren 'that ye all speak the same thing, and that there be no divisions among you; but [that] ye be perfectly joined together in the same mind and in the same judgment,'[9] and further, 'Let nothing be done through strife or vainglory; but in lowliness of mind let each esteem other better than themselves.'[10] St Peter made a similar appeal: 'Finally, be ye all of one mind, having compassion one of another, love as brethren, be pitiful, be courteous.'[11] Although the exhortations defined primarily the intra-Christian community relations, Christ also commanded His followers: 'Love your enemies, bless them that curse you, do good to them that hate you, and pray for them which despitefully use you, and persecute you.'[12]

The Qur'án declares that 'The believers are but a single brotherhood.'[13] Hence, Muslims are exhorted to 'be not divided among yourselves; and remember with gratitude God's favour on you; for ye were enemies and He joined your hearts in love, so that by His Grace, ye became brethren . . .'[14] Muslims are warned: 'do not be like those who split up and differed (Jews and Christians) after the clear signs came to them'.[15] The Qur'án, moreover, equates the breaking of Islam into factions with the loss of its power: 'obey God and His Apostle; and fall into no disputes, lest ye lose heart and your power depart . . .'[16] Muslims are required to pray: 'Our Lord! forgive us, and our brethren who came before us into the Faith, and leave not, in our hearts, rancour (or sense of injury) against those who have believed. Our Lord! Thou art indeed Full of Kindness, Most Merciful.'[17] If divisions occur they are to 'make peace and reconciliation between your two (contending) brothers; and fear God, that ye may receive Mercy'.[18] A Muslim faction that unjustly seeks a quarrel must be restrained:

> If two parties among the believers fall into a quarrel, make ye peace between them: but if one of them transgresses beyond bounds against the other, then fight ye (all) against the one that transgresses until it complies with the command of God; but if it complies, then make peace between them with justice, and be fair: for God loves those who are fair (and just).[19]

Bahá'u'lláh revives the principle of love and unity and applies it to all humanity:

Consort with all men, O people of Bahá, in a spirit of friendliness and fellowship. If ye be aware of a certain truth, if ye possess a jewel, of which others are deprived, share it with them in a language of utmost kindliness and good-will. If it be accepted, if it fulfil its purpose, your object is attained. If anyone should refuse it, leave him unto himself, and beseech God to guide him. Beware lest ye deal unkindly with him. A kindly tongue is the lodestone of the hearts of men. It is the bread of the spirit, it clotheth the words with meaning, it is the fountain of the light of wisdom and understanding.[20]

O well-beloved ones! The tabernacle of unity hath been raised; regard ye not one another as strangers. Ye are the fruits of one tree, and the leaves of one branch. Verily I say, whatsoever leadeth to the decline of ignorance and the increase of knowledge hath been, and will ever remain, approved in the sight of the Lord of creation. Say: O people! Walk ye neath the shadow of justice and truthfulness and seek ye shelter within the tabernacle of unity.[21]

Consort with all religions with amity and concord, that they may inhale from you the sweet fragrance of God . . . All things proceed from God and unto Him they return. He is the source of all things and in Him all things are ended.[22]

It is Our wish and desire that every one of you may become a source of all goodness unto men, and an example of uprightness to mankind. Beware lest ye prefer yourselves above your neighbours. Fix your gaze upon Him Who is the Temple of God amongst men. He, in truth, hath offered up His life as a ransom for the redemption of the world. He, verily, is the All-Bountiful, the Gracious, the Most High. If any differences arise amongst you, behold Me standing before your face, and overlook the faults of one another for My name's sake and as a token of your love for My manifest and resplendent Cause. We love to see you at all times consorting in amity and concord within the paradise of My good-pleasure, and to inhale from your acts the fragrance of friendliness and unity, of loving-kindness and fellowship. Thus counselleth you the All-Knowing, the Faithful. We shall always be with you; if We inhale the perfume of your fellowship, Our heart will assuredly rejoice, for naught else can satisfy Us. To this beareth witness every man of true understanding.[23]

The unity of mankind

The germ of the oneness of humanity is evident in the Torah in the allegorical teaching of the birth of humanity from one father and mother, Adam and Eve. There is greater elaboration of this concept of equality in the New Testament, but, as we have seen in Chapter 18, the principle applies mainly to those who have accepted the Faith of Christ and are part of the new covenant – 'the community of saints' referred to in the Apostolic Creed.

> For there is no difference between the Jew and the Greek: for the same Lord over all is rich unto all that call upon him.[24]

> With all lowliness and meekness, with longsuffering, forbearing one another in love;
> Endeavouring to keep the unity of the Spirit in the bond of peace.
> There is one body, and one Spirit, even as ye are called in one hope of your calling;
> One Lord, one faith, one baptism,
> One God and Father of all, who is above all, and through all, and in you all.[25]

The oneness of mankind is also implied by the expectation that all humanity will partake of the future Divine Revelation:

> And I say unto you, That many shall come from the east and west, and shall sit down with Abraham, and Isaac, and Jacob, in the kingdom of heaven.[26]

The Qur'án reminds us that humanity shares a single set of parents, and that an individual's dignity and honour is not based on the colour of his or her skin, ethnicity or tribal allegiance, or even by professing a set of principles, but by living a life of sincere righteousness.

> O mankind! We created you from a single (pair) of a male and a female, and made you into nations and tribes, that ye may know each other (not that ye may despise each other). Verily the most honoured of you in the sight of God is (he who is) the most righteous of you. And God has full knowledge and is well acquainted (with all things).[27]

It explains that the removal of barriers to unity has been the aim of all God's Prophets, and that disunity and divisions creep in due to human perversity.

> Mankind was one single nation, and God sent Messengers with glad tidings and warnings; and with them He sent the Book in truth, to judge between people in matters wherein they differed; but the people of the Book, after the clear Signs came to them, did not differ among themselves, except through selfish contumacy. God by His Grace guided the believers to the Truth, concerning that wherein they differed. For God guides whom He will to a path that is straight.[28]

The Qur'án therefore reminds Muslims that there is 'one nation' (*ommatan wáhidatan*, see *Má'ida*, the Table Spread, 5:48) and that 'your nation is one nation (*ommatukum ommatan wáhidatan*, *Anbiyá'*, the Prophets, 21:92). However, similar to Christianity, the prescribed unity and non-sectarianism is reserved primarily for the *ummah* of Islam and for the Muslim brethren.

> Verily, this brotherhood of yours is a single brotherhood, and I am your Lord and Cherisher: therefore serve Me (and no other).[29]

The oneness of mankind is also implied by the expectation that God will gather and unite all humanity in 'the Day of Gathering' (*Húd*, the Prophet Húd, 11:103).

The oneness of all mankind is the principal aim of Bahá'u'lláh's Revelation. It is primarily a universal human rights issue and hence independent of religious affiliation or any other consideration. Today, all mankind is invited to reconcile its differences and promote this unity:

> The most glorious fruit of the tree of knowledge is this exalted word: Of one tree are ye all the fruit, and of one bough the leaves. Let not man glory in this that he loveth his country, let him rather glory in this that he loveth his kind.[30]

> An essential principle of Bahá'u'lláh's teaching is that religion must be the cause of unity and love amongst men . . . Religion is not intended to arouse enmity and hatred nor to become the source of tyranny and injustice. Should it prove to be the cause of hostility, discord and the alienation of mankind, assuredly the absence of religion would be preferable.[31]

The oneness of mankind is 'the pivot round which all other teachings of Bahá'u'lláh revolve':[32]

> In every Dispensation the light of Divine Guidance has been focused upon one central theme . . . In this wondrous Revelation, this glorious century, the foundation of the Faith of God, and the distinguishing feature of His Law, is the consciousness of the oneness of mankind.[33]

> [It] is no mere outburst of ignorant emotionalism or an expression of vague and pious hope. Its appeal is not to be merely identified with a reawakening of the spirit of brotherhood and good-will among men, nor does it aim solely at the fostering of harmonious cooperation among individual peoples and nations. Its implications are deeper, its claims greater than any which the Prophets of old were allowed to advance. Its message is applicable not only to the individual, but concerns itself primarily with the nature of those essential relationships that must bind all the states and nations as members of one human family. It does not constitute merely the enunciation of an ideal, but stands inseparably associated with an institution adequate to embody its truth, demonstrate its validity, and perpetuate its influence. It implies an organic change in the structure of present-day society, a change such as the world has not yet experienced. It constitutes a challenge, at once bold and universal, to outworn shibboleths of national creeds – creeds that have had their day and which must, in the ordinary course of events as shaped

and controlled by Providence, give way to a new gospel, fundamentally different from, and infinitely superior to, what the world has already conceived. It calls for no less than the reconstruction and the demilitarization of the whole civilized world – a world organically unified in all the essential aspects of its life, its political machinery, its spiritual aspiration, its trade and finance, its script and language, and yet infinite in the diversity of the national characteristics of its federated units.

It represents the consummation of human evolution – an evolution that has had its earliest beginnings in the birth of family life, its subsequent development in the achievement of tribal solidarity, leading in turn to the constitution of the city-state, and expanding later into the institution of independent and sovereign nations.

The principle of the Oneness of Mankind, as proclaimed by Bahá'u'lláh, carries with it no more and no less than a solemn assertion that attainment to this final stage in this stupendous evolution is not only necessary but inevitable, that its realization is fast approaching, and that nothing short of a power that is born of God can succeed in establishing it.[34]

Bahá'u'lláh thus exhorts humanity:

> O ye children of men! The fundamental purpose animating the Faith of God and His Religion is to safeguard the interests and promote the unity of the human race, and to foster the spirit of love and fellowship amongst men. Suffer it not to become a source of dissension and discord, of hate and enmity. This is the straight Path, the fixed and immovable foundation. Whatsoever is raised on this foundation, the changes and chances of the world can never impair its strength, nor will the revolution of countless centuries undermine its structure ... How long is chaos and confusion to reign amongst men? How long will discord agitate the face of society?... The winds of despair are, alas, blowing from every direction, and the strife that divideth and afflicteth the human race is daily increasing. The signs of impending convulsions and chaos can now be discerned, inasmuch as the prevailing order appeareth to be lamentably defective.[35]

The establishment of unity must be a concern of all of us:

Gird up the loins of your endeavor, O people of Bahá, that haply the tumult of religious dissension and strife that agitateth the peoples of the earth may be stilled, that every trace of it may be completely obliterated. For the love of God, and them that serve Him, arise to aid this most sublime and momentous Revelation. Religious fanaticism and hatred are a world-devouring fire, whose violence none can quench. The Hand of Divine power can, alone, deliver mankind from this desolating affliction . . .

The utterance of God is a lamp, whose light is these words: Ye are the fruits of one tree, and the leaves of one branch. Deal ye one with another with the utmost love and harmony, with friendliness and fellowship. He Who is the Day Star of Truth beareth Me witness! So powerful is the light of unity that it can illuminate the whole earth.[36]

That one indeed is a man who, today, dedicateth himself to the service of the entire human race . . . Blessed and happy is he that ariseth to promote the best interests of the peoples and kindreds of the earth . . . It is not for him to pride himself who loveth his own country, but rather for him who loveth the whole world. The earth is but one country, and mankind its citizens.[37]

The organic unity of mankind has been, and is, an evolving principle.

The Faith of Islám, the succeeding link in the chain of Divine Revelation, introduced, as Bahá'u'lláh Himself testifies, the conception of the nation as a unit and a vital stage in the organization of human society, and embodied it in its teaching. This indeed is what is meant by this brief yet highly significant and illuminating pronouncement of Bahá'u'lláh: 'Of old [Islámic Dispensation] it hath been revealed: "Love of one's country is an element of the Faith of God."' This principle was established and stressed by the Apostle of God, inasmuch as the evolution of human society required it at that time. Nor could any stage above and beyond it have been envisaged, as world conditions preliminary to the establishment of a superior form of organization were as yet unobtainable. The conception of nationality, the attainment to the state of nationhood, may, therefore, be said to be the distinguishing characteristics of the Muhammadan

Dispensation, in the course of which the nations and races of the world, and particularly in Europe and America, were unified and achieved political independence.[38]

The Bahá'í Faith has thus expanded the Quranic definition of 'brotherhood' to include all humanity, unconditionally and without exception.

> In cycles gone by, though harmony was established, yet, owing to the absence of means, the unity of all mankind could not have been achieved. Continents remained widely divided, nay even among the peoples of one and the same continent association and interchange of thought were well-nigh impossible. Consequently intercourse, understanding and unity amongst all the peoples and kindreds of the earth were unattainable. In this day, however, means of communication have multiplied, and the five continents of the earth have virtually merged into one ... In like manner all the members of the human family, whether peoples or governments, cities or villages, have become increasingly interdependent. For none is self-sufficiency any longer possible, inasmuch as political ties unite all peoples and nations, and the bonds of trade and industry, of agriculture and education, are being strengthened every day. Hence the unity of all mankind can in this day be achieved.[39]

> Unification of the whole of mankind is the hall-mark of the stage which human society is now approaching. Unity of family, of tribe, of city-state, and nation have been successively attempted and fully established. World unity is the goal towards which a harassed humanity is striving. Nation-building has come to an end. The anarchy inherent in state sovereignty is moving towards a climax. A world, growing to maturity, must abandon this fetish, recognize the oneness and wholeness of human relationships, and establish once for all the machinery that can best incarnate this fundamental principle of its life.[40]

Unity in diversity

Far from aiming at the subversion of the existing foundations of society, it [the Law of Bahá'u'lláh] seeks to broaden its basis, to remold its institutions in a manner consonant with the needs of an ever-changing world. It can conflict with no legitimate allegiances, nor can it undermine essential loyalties. Its purpose is neither to stifle the flame of a sane and intelligent patriotism in men's hearts, nor to abolish the system of national autonomy so essential if the evils of excessive centralization are to be avoided. It does not ignore, nor does it attempt to suppress, the diversity of ethnical origins, of climate, of history, of language and tradition, of thought and habit, that differentiate the peoples and nations of the world. It calls for a wider loyalty, for a larger aspiration than any that has animated the human race. It insists upon the subordination of national impulses and interests to the imperative claims of a unified world. It repudiates excessive centralization on one hand, and disclaims all attempts at uniformity on the other. Its watchword is unity in diversity . . .[41]

Religious freedom and removal of barriers to social intercourse

The Faith of Bahá'u'lláh upholds the right of the individual to choose his or her religion. The individual must be free to practise his or her faith without hindrance or persecution. At the same time the Bahá'í Faith discourages blind imitation, and addresses the root causes of religious rivalries.

Freedom from racial, class, colour, national, tribal, linguistic, economic, and religious prejudice

> A new religious principle is that prejudice and fanaticism – whether sectarian, denominational, patriotic or political – are destructive to the foundation of human solidarity; therefore man should release himself from such bonds in order that the oneness of the world of humanity may become manifest.[42]

> . . . the principle of the oneness of mankind which is the cornerstone of the message of Bahá'u'lláh is wholly incompatible with all forms of racial prejudice. Loyalty to this foundation principle of the Faith is the paramount duty of every believer and should be therefore whole-hearted and unqualified. For a Bahá'í racial prejudice, in

all its forms, is simply a negation of faith, an attitude wholly incompatible with the very spirit and actual teachings of the Cause.[43]

There can be no doubt whatever that the peoples of the world, of whatever race or religion, derive their inspiration from one heavenly Source, and are the subjects of one God. The difference between the ordinances under which they abide should be attributed to the varying requirements and exigencies of the age in which they were revealed. All of them, except a few which are the outcome of human perversity, were ordained of God, and are a reflection of His Will and Purpose. Arise and, armed with the power of faith, shatter to pieces the gods of your vain imaginings, the sowers of dissension amongst you. Cleave unto that which draweth you together and uniteth you.[44]

Gender equality and freedom from gender prejudice

Among the fundamental teachings of the Bahá'í Faith is that both sexes must be given the same opportunities, respect, and treatment:

> the world of humanity has two wings – one is women and the other men. Not until both wings are equally developed can the bird fly. Should one wing remain weak, flight is impossible. Not until the world of women becomes equal to the world of men in the acquisition of virtues and perfections, can success and prosperity be attained as they ought to be.[45]

> . . . as all are created in the image and likeness of the one God, there is no distinction as to sex in the estimation of God. He who is purest in heart, whose knowledge exceeds and who excels in kindness to the servants of God, is nearest and dearest to the Lord, our Creator, irrespective of sex . . . woman has not been afforded the same educational facilities as man. For if she had received the same opportunities for training and development as man has enjoyed, undoubtedly she would have attained the same station and level. In the estimate of God no distinction exists; both are as one and possess equal degrees of capacity. Therefore, through opportunity and development woman will merit and attain the same prerogatives.[46]

Men and women are taught to live by spiritual principles, but God's Faith today does not discriminate against women, nor does it dictate their choices or how they should lead their lives. No male dominance or subjugation is to be tolerated. Rather than being deprived of education, girls must be given preferential training, and the feminine counsel on human affairs is to be taken fully into account – world peace and prosperity are dependent on achieving this goal.

> The emancipation of women, the achievement of full equality between the sexes, is one of the most important, though less acknowledged prerequisites of peace. The denial of such equality perpetuates an injustice against one half of the world's population and promotes in men harmful attitudes and habits that are carried from the family to the workplace, to political life, and ultimately to international relations. There are no grounds, moral, practical, or biological, upon which such denial can be justified. Only as women are welcomed into full partnership in all fields of human endeavour will the moral and psychological climate be created in which international peace can emerge.[47]

> . . . there must be an equality of rights between men and women. Women shall receive an equal privilege of education. This will enable them to qualify and progress in all degrees of occupation and accomplishment. For the world of humanity possesses two wings: man and woman. If one wing remains incapable and defective, it will restrict the power of the other, and full flight will be impossible. Therefore, the completeness and perfection of the human world are dependent upon the equal development of these two wings.[48]

Consultation

'Mutual consultation' is recommended in the Qur'án (*Shúráa*, Consultation, 42:38). However, Bahá'u'lláh has established consultation as one of the fundamental principles of His Faith to be practised at all levels of administration of its affairs.

> The heaven of divine wisdom is illumined with the two luminaries of consultation and compassion. Take ye counsel together in all

matters, inasmuch as consultation is the lamp of guidance which leadeth the way, and is the bestower of understanding.⁴⁹

Essentials of Bahá'í consultation

... consultation must have for its object the investigation of truth. He who expresses an opinion should not voice it as correct and right but set it forth as a contribution to the consensus of opinion, for the light of reality becomes apparent when two opinions coincide. A spark is produced when flint and steel come together. Man should weigh his opinions with the utmost serenity, calmness and composure. Before expressing his own views he should carefully consider the views already advanced by others. If he finds that a previously expressed opinion is more true and worthy, he should accept it immediately and not wilfully hold to an opinion of his own. By this excellent method he endeavours to arrive at unity and truth. Opposition and division are deplorable.⁵⁰

... at the very root of the Cause lies the principle of the undoubted right of the individual to self-expression, his freedom to declare his conscience and set forth his views...

Let us also bear in mind that the keynote of the Cause of God is not dictatorial authority but humble fellowship, not arbitrary power, but the spirit of frank and loving consultation. Nothing short of the spirit of a true Bahá'í can hope to reconcile the principles of mercy and justice, freedom and submission, of the sanctity of the right of the individual and of self-surrender, of vigilance, discretion and prudence on the one hand, and fellowship, candor, and courage on the other...⁵¹

The prime requisites for them that take counsel together are purity of motive, radiance of spirit, detachment from all else save God, attraction to His Divine Fragrances, humility and lowliness amongst His loved ones, patience and long-suffering in difficulties and servitude to His exalted Threshold.⁵²

Complementary nature of science and faith

Scientific freedom and the acceptance of scientific truth must be unimpeded by preconceived religious beliefs. The Faith proclaimed by Bahá'u'lláh praises unrestricted pursuit of scientific enquiry. It teaches that 'religion must be in conformity with science and reason, so that it may influence the hearts of men. The foundation must be solid and must not consist of imitations.'[53] Science and religion both search for truth and therefore must not be in conflict. Rather, they should complement one the other.

> 'Alí, the son-in-law of Muhammad, said: 'That which is in conformity with science is also in conformity with religion.' Whatever the intelligence of man cannot understand, religion ought not to accept. Religion and science walk hand in hand, and any religion contrary to science is not the truth.[54]

Without faith, science can result in crass materialism and without science religion can sink into imitation, fanaticism and ignorance. The reconciliation of science and religion has only become possible in this day and age because of the application of the scientific method, and through the teachings of Bahá'u'lláh which have freed God's ancient Faith from superstition.

> Religion must stand the analysis of reason. It must agree with scientific fact and proof so that science will sanction religion and religion fortify science. Both are indissolubly welded and joined in reality. If statements and teachings of religion are found to be unreasonable and contrary to science, they are outcomes of superstition and imagination.[55]

> Science must be accepted. No one truth can contradict another truth. Light is good in whatsoever lamp it is burning! A rose is beautiful in whatsoever garden it may bloom! A star has the same radiance if it shines from the East or from the West. Be free from prejudice, so will you love the Sun of Truth from whatsoever point in the horizon it may arise![56]

If religion were contrary to logical reason then it would cease to be a religion and be merely a tradition. Religion and science are the two wings upon which man's intelligence can soar into the heights, with which the human soul can progress. It is not possible to fly with one wing alone! Should a man try to fly with the wing of religion alone he would quickly fall into the quagmire of superstition, whilst on the other hand, with the wing of science alone he would also make no progress, but fall into the despairing slough of materialism.[57]

Universal education and the spiritual training of children

Bahá'u'lláh declares that all human beings should attain knowledge and acquire an education. This is a necessary principle of religious belief and observance, characteristically new in this Dispensation.

> Bahá'u'lláh has announced that inasmuch as ignorance and lack of education are barriers of separation among mankind, all must receive training and instruction. Through this provision the lack of mutual understanding will be remedied and the unity of mankind furthered and advanced. Universal education is a universal law. It is, therefore, incumbent upon every father to teach and instruct his children according to his possibilities. If he is unable to educate them, the body politic, the representative of the people, must provide the means for their education.[58]

> And among the teachings of Bahá'u'lláh is the promotion of education. Every child must be instructed in sciences as much as is necessary. If the parents are able to provide the expenses of this education, it is well, otherwise the community must provide the means for the teaching of that child.[59]

The education of children is therefore compulsory in the Bahá'í Faith. They are required to receive 'systematic training' from earliest childhood, with explanations of the sciences through play and verbal interactive sessions, and not merely through reading books.[60] Education in the arts and sciences must be complemented by spiritual training and appreciation of ethical issues. Clearly, fathers have an important role in the upbringing of their children and acting as role models, but the early spiritual training and establishment of faith and certitude in the young is considered primarily the duty of the mother. This is among the reasons why the education of women and girls is of paramount importance.

> ... most important of all is the education of girl children, for these girls will one day be mothers, and the mother is the first teacher of the child. In whatever way she reareth the child, so will the child become, and the results of that first training will remain with the individual throughout his entire life, and it would be most difficult to alter them. And how can a mother, herself ignorant and untrained, educate her child? It is therefore clear that the education of girls is of far greater consequence than that of boys. This fact is extremely important, and the matter must be seen to with the greatest energy and dedication.[61]

> The girl's education is of more importance today than the boy's, for she is the mother of the future race. It is the duty of all to look after the children. Those without children should, if possible, make themselves responsible for the education of a child.[62]

Educators are encouraged to be particularly sensitive to the inclination, desire, and talents of a particular youth when considering long-term choices about contributing to society and earning a living.[63]

One universal language and one common script

To further facilitate evolution towards a global society and to eliminate prejudice, a universal language and one script, selected either from one of the existing languages or one that has been created, is to be taught in schools side by side with the mother tongue.

> Bahá'u'lláh enjoins the adoption of a universal language and script. His Writings envisage two stages in this process. The first stage is to consist of the selection of an existing language or an invented one which would then be taught in all the schools of the world as an auxiliary to the mother tongues. The governments of the world through their parliaments are called upon to effect this momentous

enactment. The second stage, in the distant future, would be the eventual adoption of one single language and common script for all on earth.[64]

A world commonwealth fortified by the principle of collective security

The unity of the human race, as envisaged by Bahá'u'lláh, implies the establishment of a world commonwealth in which all nations, races, creeds and classes are closely and permanently united, and in which the autonomy of its state members and personal freedom and initiative of the individuals that compose them are definitely and completely safeguarded. This commonwealth must, as far as we can visualize it, consist of a world legislature, whose members will, as the trustees of the whole of mankind, ultimately control the entire resources of all the component nations, and will enact such laws as shall be required to regulate the life, satisfy the needs and adjust the relationships of all races and peoples. A world executive, backed by an international Force, will carry out the decisions arrived at, and apply the laws enacted by, this world legislature, and will safeguard the organic unity of the whole commonwealth. A world tribunal will adjudicate and deliver its compulsory and final verdict in all and any disputes that may arise between the various elements constituting this universal system. A mechanism of world inter-communication will be devised, embracing the whole planet, freed from national hinderances and restrictions, and functioning with marvellous swiftness and perfect regularity. A world metropolis will act as the nerve centre of a world civilization, the focus towards which the unifying forces of life will converge and from which its energizing influences will radiate. A world language will either be invented or chosen from among the existing languages and will be taught in the schools of all the federated nations as an auxiliary to their mother tongue. A world script, a world literature, a uniform and universal system of currency, of weights and measures, will simplify and facilitate intercourse and understanding among the nations and races of mankind. In such a world society, science and religion, the two most potent forces in human life, will be reconciled, will cooperate, and will harmoniously develop. The press will, under such a system, while giving full scope to the expression of the diversified views and convictions of mankind, cease to be mischievously manipulated by vested interests, whether private or public, and will be liberated from the influence of contending governments and peoples. The economic resources of the world will be organized, its sources of raw materials will be tapped and fully utilized, its markets will be coordinated and developed, and the distribution of its products will be equitably regulated.[65]

Work as worship

O people of Bahá! It is incumbent upon each one of you to engage in some occupation – such as a craft, a trade or the like. We have exalted your engagement in such work to the rank of worship of the one true God. Reflect, O people, on the grace and blessings of your Lord, and yield Him thanks at eventide and dawn. Waste not your hours in idleness and sloth, but occupy yourselves with what will profit you and others.[66]

It is enjoined upon every one of you to engage in some form of occupation, such as crafts, trades and the like. We have graciously exalted your engagement in such work to the rank of worship unto God, the True One. Ponder ye in your hearts the grace and the blessings of God and render thanks unto Him at eventide and at dawn. Waste not your time in idleness and sloth. Occupy yourselves with that which profiteth yourselves and others . . .[67]

Rededication to spiritual transformation

Bahá'u'lláh exhorts His followers to consort, with amity and concord and without discrimination, with the adherents of all religions; warns them to guard against fanaticism, sedition, pride, dispute and contention; inculcates upon them immaculate cleanliness, strict truthfulness, spotless chastity, trustworthiness, hospitality, fidelity, courtesy, forbearance, justice and fairness; counsels them to be 'even as the fingers of one hand and the limbs of one body'; calls upon them to arise and serve His Cause; and assures them of His undoubted aid.[68]

Baháʼís are reminded that:

> Not by the force of numbers, not by the mere exposition of a set of new and noble principles, not by an organized campaign of teaching – no matter how worldwide and elaborate in its character – not even by the staunchness of our faith or the exaltation of our enthusiasm, can we ultimately hope to vindicate in the eyes of a critical and sceptical age the supreme claim of the Abhá Revelation. One thing and only one thing will unfailingly and alone secure the undoubted triumph of this sacred Cause, namely, the extent to which our own inner life and private character mirror forth in their manifold aspects the splendor of those eternal principles proclaimed by Baháʼuʼlláh.[69]

Truth and truthfulness

The Bible enjoins truthfulness,[70] and at the same time reminds believers that the source of truth is God. It is He Who guides the steps of humanity with His Revelations.

> Teach me your way, O Lord, that I may walk in your truth; unite my heart to fear your name.[71]

> Sanctify them in the truth; your word is truth.[72]

The Qurʼán expects Muslims, and specially the learned, to 'shun the word that is false'[73] and underlines the importance of truthfulness:

> Then woe that Day to those that treat (truth) as falsehood.[74]

> Ye People of the Book! why do ye clothe truth with falsehood, and conceal the truth, while ye have knowledge?[75]

> God will say: 'This is a day on which the truthful will profit from their truth: theirs are Gardens, with rivers flowing beneath, – their eternal home: God well-pleased with them, and they with God: that is the great Salvation.[76]

Truthfulness is also enjoined by ʻAlí Ibn Abí Tálib:

> Remember that inequity and falsehood bring disgrace to a man in this world and in the Hereafter.[77]

The Qur'án, moreover, points out that falsehood retreats when confronted with Divine Truth.

> Nay, We hurl the Truth against falsehood, and it knocks out its brain, and behold, falsehood doth perish! Ah! woe be to you for the (false) things ye ascribe (to Us).[78]

> Say: Truly my Lord sendeth forth the Truth: –Knower of things unseen!
> Say: Truth is come, and falsehood shall vanish and return no more.[79]

> And say: 'Truth has (now) arrived, and falsehood perished: for falsehood is (by its nature) bound to perish.'[80]

The Qur'án also promises that in Bahá'u'lláh's Day 'there shall they hear no vain discourse nor any falsehood' (*Nabáa*, the (Great) News, 78:30). An important version of 'truth' is the content of Divine Revelation, and in this context, Bahá'u'lláh's Revelation is the promised manifestation of the All-Truth (John 16:13):

> Verily this is that Most Great Beauty, foretold in the Books of the Messengers, through Whom truth shall be distinguished from error and the wisdom of every command shall be tested. Verily He is the Tree of Life that bringeth forth the fruits of God, the Exalted, the Powerful, the Great.
> . . . Whosoever desireth, let him turn aside from this counsel and whosoever desireth let him choose the path to his Lord.
> O people, if ye deny these verses, by what proof have ye believed in God?[81]

The followers of Bahá'u'lláh are also commanded to be true to themselves and honest with their fellowmen. Truthfulness is regarded as the foundation of all human virtues.

Beautify your tongues, O people, with truthfulness, and adorn your souls with the ornament of honesty. Beware, O people, that ye deal not treacherously with anyone. Be ye the trustees of God amongst His creatures, and the emblems of His generosity amidst His people.[82]

The purpose of the one true God in manifesting Himself is to summon all mankind to truthfulness and sincerity, to piety and trustworthiness, to resignation and submissiveness to the Will of God, to forbearance and kindliness, to uprightness and wisdom. His object is to array every man with the mantle of a saintly character, and to adorn him with the ornament of holy and goodly deeds.[83]

We beseech Him [God] – exalted be He – to aid everyone to become the essence of truthfulness, and to draw nigh unto Him. He, verily, is the Lord of strength and power. No God is there but Him, the All-Hearing, the Lord of Utterance, the Almighty, the All-Praised.[84]

Truthfulness must not only adorn the behaviour of each and every follower of the Faith of Bahá'u'lláh but must stand as a testimony to the transforming power of His Revelation.

The Day Star of Truth that shineth in its meridian splendor beareth Us witness! They who are the people of God have no ambition except to revive the world, to ennoble its life, and regenerate its peoples. Truthfulness and good-will have, at all times, marked their relations with all men. Their outward conduct is but a reflection of their inward life, and their inward life a mirror of their outward conduct. No veil hideth or obscureth the verities on which their Faith is established. Before the eyes of all men these verities have been laid bare, and can be unmistakably recognized. Their very acts attest the truth of these words.[85]

Justice and fairness

The Bible regrets the paucity of these virtues:

If thou seest the oppression of the poor, and violent perverting of

> judgment and justice in a province, marvel not at the matter: for he that is higher than the highest regardeth; and there be higher than they.[86]

> Thus saith the Lord, Keep ye judgment, and do justice: for my salvation is near to come, and my righteousness to be revealed.[87]

> None calleth for justice, nor any pleadeth for truth: they trust in vanity, and speak lies; they conceive mischief, and bring forth iniquity.[88]

> To do justice and judgment is more acceptable to the Lord than sacrifice.[89]

The Bible promises the advent of the 'Prince of Peace' who will usher in justice:

> Of the increase of his government and peace there shall be no end, upon the throne of David, and upon his kingdom, to order it, and to establish it with judgment and with justice from henceforth even forever. The zeal of the Lord of hosts will perform this.[90]

The Qur'án also enjoins justice:

> God doth command you to render back your trusts to those to whom they are due; and when ye judge between man and man, that ye judge with justice: verily how excellent is the teaching which He giveth you! for God is He who heareth and seeth all things.[91]

> O ye who believe! Stand out firmly for justice, as witnesses to God, even as against yourselves, or your parents, or your kin, and whether it be (against) rich or poor: for God can best protect both. Follow not the lusts (of your hearts), lest ye swerve, and if ye distort (justice) or decline to do justice, verily God is well-acquainted with all that ye do.[92]

> O ye who believe! Stand out firmly for God, as witnesses to fair dealing, and let not the hatred of others to you make you swerve to

wrong and depart from justice. Be just: that is next to piety: and fear God, for God is well-acquainted with all that ye do.[93]

Say: 'My Lord hath commanded justice . . .'[94]

. . . for God loves those who are fair (and just).[95]

Muslims must therefore avoid mischief and injustice:[96]

. . . do thou good, as God has been good to thee, and seek not (occasions for) mischief in the land: for God loves not those who do mischief.[97]

We sent aforetime Our apostles with Clear Signs (Revelation) and sent down with them The Book and the Balance (of right and wrong), that men may stand forth in justice . . .[98]

We shall set up scales of justice for the Day of Judgment, so that not a soul will be dealt with unjustly in the least. And if there be (no more than) the weight of a mustard seed, We will bring it (to account): And enough are We to take account.[99]

The Qur'án further teaches that an important reason why God sends His Messengers is to establish justice – it promises that comprehensive justice will be established on the 'Day of Resurrection'. As the Revelation of Bahá'u'lláh is the 'Day of Resurrection', its provisions are designed to ensure universal justice.

> O Son of Spirit! The best beloved of all things in My sight is Justice; turn not away therefrom if thou desirest Me, and neglect it not that I may confide in thee. By its aid thou shalt see with thine own eyes and not through the eyes of others, and shalt know of thine own knowledge and not through the knowledge of thy neighbor. Ponder this in thy heart; how it behooveth thee to be. Verily justice is My gift to thee and the sign of My loving-kindness. Set it then before thine eyes.[100]

> We beseech God to aid thee to be just and fair-minded, and to acquaint thee with the things that were hidden from the eyes of

men. He, in truth, is the Mighty, the Unconstrained. We ask thee to reflect upon that which hath been revealed, and to be fair and just in thy speech, that perchance the splendors of the day-star of truthfulness and sincerity may shine forth, and may deliver thee from the darkness of ignorance, and illumine the world with the light of knowledge.[101]

Bahá'u'lláh explains that the injustice He had to suffer is the cause of the justice that His Revelation will usher in.

> Glorified be the All-Merciful, the Revealer of so inestimable a bounty. Say: Because He bore injustice, justice hath appeared on earth, and because He accepted abasement, the majesty of God hath shone forth amidst mankind.[102]

Fear of God

Taqwá, awareness of the 'Presence of God' or the 'fear of God' must educate and regulate the actions of individuals.

The Bible instructs: 'fear thou God'[103] and the Qur'án explains that the future Revelation is destined for the God-fearing or '*muttaqin*', or 'those endowed with *taqwá*'.

> . . . submit then your wills to Him (in Islam) and give thou the Good News to those who humble themselves –
>
> To those whose hearts, when God is mentioned, are filled with fear, who show patient perseverance over their afflictions, keep up regular prayer, and spend (in charity) out of what we have bestowed upon them.[104]

> That is the Book; in it is guidance sure, without doubt, to those who fear God.[105]

> So fear God; For it is God that teaches you. And God is well acquainted with all things.[106]

> O ye that believe! fear God, and believe in His messenger, and He will bestow on you a double portion of His Mercy: He will provide

for you a light by which ye shall walk (straight in your path), and He will forgive you (your past): For God is Oft-Forgiving, Most Merciful.[107]

The actions of Bahá'ís are required to be guided by this virtue.

> We have admonished Our loved ones to fear God, a fear which is the fountain-head of all goodly deeds and virtues. It is the commander of the hosts of justice in the city of Bahá. Happy the man that hath entered the shadow of its luminous standard, and laid fast hold thereon.[108]

> By God! This people [followers of Bahá'u'lláh] have never been, nor are they now, inclined to mischief. Their hearts are illumined with the light of the fear of God, and adorned with the adornment of His love. Their concern hath ever been and now is for the betterment of the world. Their purpose is to obliterate differences, and quench the flame of hatred and enmity, so that the whole earth may come to be viewed as one country.[109]

Forbearance, contentment, and acquiescence in the Divine Will, reliance on God

Muslims are required to rely on God's Will:

> Put thy trust in God. For God loves those who put their trust (in Him).[110]

> If Thou punish them, lo! they are Thy slaves, and if Thou forgive them (lo! they are Thy slaves). Lo! Thou, only Thou, art the Mighty, the Wise.[111]

The Bahá'í teachings reaffirm and amplify this:

> Place not thy reliance on thy treasures. Put thy whole confidence in the grace of God, thy Lord. Let Him be thy trust in whatever thou doest, and be of them that have submitted themselves to His Will. Let Him be thy helper and enrich thyself with His treasures,

for with Him are the treasuries of the heavens and of the earth. He bestoweth them upon whom He will, and from whom He will He withholdeth them. There is none other God but Him, the All-Possessing, the All-Praised. All are but paupers at the door of His mercy; all are helpless before the revelation of His sovereignty, and beseech His favours.[112]

The virtues and attributes pertaining uto God are all evident and manifest, and have been mentioned and described in all the heavenly Books. Among them are trustworthiness, truthfulness, purity of heart while communing with God, forbearance, resignation to whatever the Almighty hath decreed, contentment with the things His Will hath provided, patience, nay, thankfulness in the midst of tribulation, and complete reliance, in all circumstances, upon Him. These rank, according to the estimate of God, among the highest and most laudable of all acts. All other acts are, and will ever remain, secondary and subordinate unto them . . .[113]

Immaculate cleanliness, a pure heart and a tranquil conscience

The Tanakh teaches the importance of spiritual purity and cleanliness of heart:

> Create in me a clean heart, O God; and renew a right spirit within me.
> Cast me not away from thy presence; and take not thy holy spirit from me.
> Restore unto me the joy of thy salvation; and uphold me with thy free spirit.
> Then will I teach transgressors thy ways; and sinners shall be converted unto thee.[114]

Christ promised that the 'pure in heart' will recognize the Divine Revelation.

> Blessed are the pure in heart, for they shall see God.[115]

The Qur'án reminds Muslims: 'For God loves those who turn to Him constantly and He loves those who keep themselves pure and clean,'[116] and 'Draw not near unto prayer . . . when ye are polluted . . .'[117]

Similarly, the Bahá'í Writings enjoin both physical cleanliness and spiritual purity:

> Create in me a pure heart, O my God, and renew a tranquil conscience within me, O my Hope! Through the spirit of power confirm Thou me in Thy Cause, O my Best-Beloved, and by the light of Thy glory reveal unto me Thy path, O Thou the Goal of my desire! Through the power of Thy transcendent might lift me up unto the heaven of Thy holiness, O Source of my being, and by the breezes of Thine eternity gladden me, O Thou Who art my God! Let Thine everlasting melodies breathe tranquillity on me, O my Companion, and let the riches of Thine ancient countenance deliver me from all except Thee, O my Master, and let the tidings of the revelation of Thine incorruptible Essence bring me joy, O Thou Who art the most manifest of the manifest and the most hidden of the hidden![118]

> It is easy to read the Holy Scriptures, but it is only with a clean heart and a pure mind that one may understand their true meaning.[119]

> To be pure and holy in all things is an attribute of the consecrated soul and a necessary characteristic of the unenslaved mind. The best of perfections is immaculacy and the freeing of oneself from every defect. Once the individual is, in every respect, cleansed and purified, then will he become a focal centre reflecting the Manifest Light.
>
> First in a human being's way of life must be purity, then freshness, cleanliness, and independence of spirit. First must the stream bed be cleansed, then may the sweet river waters be led into it. Chaste eyes enjoy the beatific vision of the Lord and know what this encounter meaneth; a pure sense inhaleth the fragrances that blow from the rose gardens of His grace; a burnished heart will mirror forth the comely face of truth.
>
> This is why, in Holy Scriptures, the counsels of heaven are likened to water, even as the Qur'án saith: 'And pure water send We down from Heaven' [*Furqán*, the Criterion, 25:48], and the Gospel: 'Except a man be baptized of water and of the spirit, he cannot

enter into the Kingdom of God' [John 3:5]. Thus it is clear that the Teachings which come from God are heavenly outpourings of grace; they are rain-showers of divine mercy, and they cleanse the human heart.[120]

Generosity, hospitality, and trustworthiness

Be generous in prosperity, and thankful in adversity. Be worthy of the trust of thy neighbour, and look upon him with a bright and friendly face. Be a treasure to the poor, an admonisher to the rich, an answerer to the cry of the needy, a preserver of the sanctity of thy pledge. Be fair in thy judgment, and guarded in thy speech. Be unjust to no man, and show all meekness to all men. Be as a lamp unto them that walk in darkness, a joy to the sorrowful, a sea for the thirsty, a haven for the distressed, an upholder and defender of the victim of oppression. Let integrity and uprightness distinguish all thine acts. Be a home for the stranger, a balm to the suffering, a tower of strength for the fugitive. Be eyes to the blind, and a guiding light unto the feet of the erring. Be an ornament to the countenance of truth, a crown to the brow of fidelity, a pillar of the temple of righteousness, a breath of life to the body of mankind, an ensign of the hosts of justice, a luminary above the horizon of virtue, a dew to the soil of the human heart, an ark on the ocean of knowledge, a sun in the heaven of bounty, a gem on the diadem of wisdom, a shining light in the firmament of thy generation, a fruit upon the tree of humility.[121]

Fidelity

Adorn your heads with the garlands of trustworthiness and fidelity, your hearts with the attire of the fear of God, your tongues with absolute truthfulness, your bodies with the vesture of courtesy.[122]

Courtesy, politeness, and consideration for others

The Tanakh views lack of consideration for the welfare of one's neighbour as evil:

The mind of a wicked person desires evil and has no consideration for his neighbour.[123]

St Peter in the New Testament teaches the Christians to be courteous:

> Finally, be ye all of one mind, having compassion one of another, love as brethren, be pitiful, be courteous.[124]

The Qur'án teaches that a Muslim's character must be adorned with courtesy and politeness:

> When a (courteous) greeting is offered you, meet it with a greeting still more courteous, (at least) of equal courtesy. God takes careful account of all things.[125]

Courtesy is enjoined on followers of the Faith of Bahá'u'lláh and is considered 'the prince of virtues':

> O people of God! I admonish you to observe courtesy, for above all else it is the prince of virtues. Well is it with him who is illumined with the light of courtesy and is attired with the vesture of uprightness. Whoso is endued with courtesy hath indeed attained a sublime station.[126]

> We, verily, have chosen courtesy, and made it the true mark of such as are nigh unto Him. Courtesy, is, in truth, a raiment which fitteth all men, whether young or old. Well is it with him that adorneth his temple therewith . . .[127]

Sanctity of family life and command to honour one's parents

The Tanakh:

> Honour your father and your mother, that your days may be long in the land that the Lord your God is giving you.[128]

The New Testament:

> Children, obey your parents in the Lord, for this is right.
> Honour thy father and mother; which is the first commandment with promise;
> That it may be well with thee, and thou mayest live long on the earth.
> And ye, fathers, provoke not your children to wrath: but bring them up in the nurture and admonition of the Lord.[129]

The Qur'án:

> We have enjoined on man kindness to his parents: in pain did his mother bear him, and in pain did she give him birth. The carrying of the (child) to his weaning is (a period of) thirty months. At length, when he reaches the age of full strength and attains forty years, He says, 'O my Lord! Grant me that I may be grateful for Thy favour which Thou hast bestowed upon me, and upon both my parents, and that I may work righteousness such as Thou mayest approve; And be gracious to me in my issue. Truly have I turned to Thee and truly do I bow (to Thee) in Islam.'[130]

The Bahá'í Faith:

> The fruits that best befit the tree of human life are trustworthiness and godliness, truthfulness and sincerity; but greater than all, after recognition of the unity of God, praised and glorified be He, is regard for the rights that are due to one's parents. This teaching hath been mentioned in all the Books of God, and reaffirmed by the Most Exalted Pen.[131]

Bahá'ís pray for pardon and forgiveness for their parents and seek their approval concerning their choice of spouse.

Bahá'í conduct in relation to others

This includes the spiritualization of one's social interactions and not preferring oneself to others:

> It is Our wish and desire that every one of you may become a source of all goodness unto men, and an example of uprightness to mankind. Beware lest ye prefer yourselves above your neighbours. Fix your gaze upon Him Who is the Temple of God amongst men. He, in truth, hath offered up His life as a ransom for the redemption of the world. He, verily, is the All-Bountiful, the Gracious, the Most High. If any differences arise amongst you, behold Me standing before your face, and overlook the faults of one another for My name's sake and as a token of your love for My manifest and resplendent Cause. We love to see you at all times consorting in amity and concord within the paradise of My good-pleasure, and to inhale from your acts the fragrance of friendliness and unity, of loving-kindness and fellowship.[132]

> And among the teachings of Bahá'u'lláh is voluntary sharing of one's property with others among mankind. This voluntary sharing is greater than equality, and consists in this, that man should not prefer himself to others, but rather should sacrifice his life and property for others. But this should not be introduced by coercion so that it becomes a law and man is compelled to follow it. Nay, rather should man voluntarily and of his own choice sacrifice his property and life for others, and spend willingly for the poor . . .[133]

A follower of the Faith of Bahá'u'lláh must not wish for others what he does not wish for himself:

> You must manifest complete love and affection toward all mankind. Do not exalt yourselves above others, but consider all as your equals, recognizing them as the servants of one God. Know that God is compassionate toward all; therefore, love all from the depths of your hearts, prefer all religionists before yourselves, be filled with love for every race, and be kind toward the people of all nationalities. Never speak disparagingly of others, but praise without distinction. Pollute not your tongues by speaking evil of another. Recognize your enemies as friends, and consider those who wish you evil as the wishers of good. You must not see evil as evil and then compromise with your opinion, for to treat in a smooth, kindly way one whom you consider evil or an enemy is hypocrisy, and this is not worthy

or allowable. You must consider your enemies as your friends, look upon your evil-wishers as your well-wishers and treat them accordingly. Act in such a way that your heart may be free from hatred. Let not your heart be offended with anyone. If some one commits an error and wrong toward you, you must instantly forgive him. Do not complain of others. Refrain from reprimanding them, and if you wish to give admonition or advice, let it be offered in such a way that it will not burden the bearer. Turn all your thoughts toward bringing joy to hearts. Beware! Beware! lest ye offend any heart. Assist the world of humanity as much as possible. Be the source of consolation to every sad one, assist every weak one, be helpful to every indigent one, care for every sick one, be the cause of glorification to every lowly one, and shelter those who are overshadowed by fear.

In brief, let each one of you be as a lamp shining forth with the light of the virtues of the world of humanity. Be trustworthy, sincere, affectionate and replete with chastity. Be illumined, be spiritual, be divine, be glorious, be quickened of God, be a Bahá'í.[134]

Cursing and execration are forbidden:

Defile not your tongues with the cursing and reviling of any soul, and guard your eyes against that which is not seemly. Set forth that which ye possess. If it be favourably received, your end is attained; if not, to protest is vain. Leave that soul to himself and turn unto the Lord, the Protector, the Self-Subsisting. Be not the cause of grief, much less of discord and strife . . . Ye are all the leaves of one tree and the drops of one ocean.[135]

Each one of the divine religions considers itself as belonging to a goodly and blessed tree, the tree of the Merciful, and all other religious systems as belonging to a tree of evil, the tree of Satan. For this reason they heap execration and abuse upon each other . . .

When the light of Bahá'u'lláh dawned . . . anathema and execration were utterly abrogated. He said, 'It is not becoming in man to curse another; it is not befitting that man should attribute darkness to another; it is not meet that one human being should consider another human being as bad; nay, rather, all mankind are the servants of one God; God is the Father of all; there is not a single exception to that law. There are no people of Satan; all belong to the Merciful. There is no darkness; all is light. All are the servants of God, and man must love humanity from his heart. He must, verily, behold humanity as submerged in the divine mercy.'[136]

It is the duty of a Bahá'í to bear witness to his Faith:

'This is the day in which to speak. It is incumbent upon the people of Bahá to strive, with the utmost patience and forbearance, to guide the peoples of the world to the Most Great Horizon. Every body calleth aloud for a soul. Heavenly souls must needs quicken, with the breath of the Word of God, the dead bodies with a fresh spirit. Within every word a new spirit is hidden. Happy is the man that attaineth thereunto, and hath arisen to teach the Cause of Him Who is the King of Eternity.' 'Say: O servants! The triumph of this Cause hath depended, and will continue to depend, upon the appearance of holy souls, upon the showing forth of goodly deeds, and the revelation of words of consummate wisdom.'[137]

Bahá'ís are required, among other things, to refer to the Holy Writings when differences arise, to recite the holy verses at morn and at eventide melodiously, to repent to God for one's sins, to distinguish oneself through good deeds, not to contend with those in authority; and to avoid losing one's temper.[138]

It is our ardent wish that the brief outline in the last two chapters of the spiritual and social laws for this Day, essential for the reanimation of earlier faiths, will serve an incentive for the true seeker to immerse himself in the ocean of Bahá'u'lláh's Revelation and discover for himself the Divine Plan for humanity in this age. For,

Today nothing but the power of the Word of God which encompasses the realities of things can bring the thoughts, minds, hearts and spirits under the shade of one Tree. He is the potent in all things, the vivifier of souls, the preserver and the controller of the world of mankind. Praise be to God, in this day the light of the Word of God has shone forth upon all regions; and from all sects, communities, nations, tribes, peoples, religions and denominations, souls have gathered together under the shadow of the Word of Oneness, and have in the utmost fellowship united and harmonized![139]

Glorified is He Who hath revealed His verses to those who understand. Glorified is He Who sendeth down His verses to those who perceive. Glorified is He Who guideth whomsoever He pleaseth unto His path. Say: I, verily, am the Path of God unto all who are in the heavens and all who are on the earth; well is it with them that hasten thereunto![140]

BIBLIOGRAPHY

'Abdu'l-Bahá. *'Abdu'l-Bahá in London* (1912, 1921). London: Bahá'í Publishing Trust, 1982.
— *Foundations of World Unity*. Wilmette, IL: Bahá'í Publishing Trust, 1968.
— *Paris Talks: Addresses given by 'Abdu'l-Bahá in 1911* (1912). London: Bahá'í Publishing Trust, 12th ed. 1995.
— *The Promulgation of Universal Peace: Talks Delivered by 'Abdu'l-Baha During His Visit to the United States and Canada in 1912* (1922, 1925). Comp. H. MacNutt. Wilmette, IL: Bahá'í Publishing Trust, 2nd ed. 1982.
— *The Secret of Divine Civilization*. Trans. M. Gail. Wilmette, IL: Bahá'í Publishing Trust, 1957.
— *Selections from the Writings of 'Abdu'l-Bahá*. Comp. Research Department of the Universal House of Justice. Haifa: Bahá'í World Centre, 1978.
— *Some Answered Questions* (1908). Comp. L. Clifford Barney. Wilmette, IL: Bahá'í Publishing Trust, 3rd ed. 1981.
— *Tablets of Abdul-Baha Abbas*. 3 vols. Chicago: Bahá'í Publishing Society, 1909–1916.
— *A Traveler's Narrative Written to Illustrate the Episode of the Báb* (1891). Trans. E. G. Browne. Wilmette, IL: Bahá'í Publishing Trust, rev. ed. 1980.

Affolter, Friedrich W. 'The Specter of Ideological Genocide: The Bahá'ís of Iran', in *War Crimes, Genocide and Crimes Against Humanity*, vol.1, no. 1 (Jan. 2005), pp. 59–89.

Ajram, Kasem. *The Miracle of Islamic Science*. Cedar Rapids: Knowledge House, 1992.

Aftab, Macksood. 'How Islam Influenced Science', in *The Islamic Herald*, March 1995.

'Alí Ibn Abí Tálib, *Nahjul Balaghah: Sermons, Letters and Sayings*. Qum, Islamic Republic of Iran: Ansariyan Publications.

Amanat, Abbas. 'The Historical Roots of the Persecution of the Babis and Baha'is in Iran', in Dominic P. Brookshaw and Seena B. Fazel: *The Baha'is of Iran: Socio-historical studies*. New York: Routledge, 2008.

The Báb. *Selections from the Writings of the Báb.* Comp. Research Department of the Universal House of Justice. Haifa: Bahá'í World Centre, 1976.

Bahá'í Education: A Compilation. Extracts from the Writings of Bahá'u'lláh, 'Abdu'l-Bahá, and Shoghi Effendi. Comp. Research Department of the Universal House of Justice. Wilmette, IL: Bahá'í Publishing Trust, 1977.

Bahá'í Prayers: A Selection of Prayers Revealed by Bahá'u'lláh, the Báb, and Abdu'l-Bahá. Wilmette, IL: Bahá'í Publishing Trust, rev. ed. 2002.

Bahá'u'lláh. *Epistle to the Son of the Wolf.* Trans. Shoghi Effendi. Wilmette, IL: Bahá'í Publishing Trust, rev. ed. 1976.
— *Gems of Divine Mysteries: Javáhiru'l-Asrár.* Haifa: Bahá'í World Centre, 2002.
— *Gleanings from the Writings of Bahá'u'lláh.* Trans. Shoghi Effendi. Wilmette, IL: Bahá'í Publishing Trust, 2nd ed. 1976.
— *The Hidden Words of Bahá'u'lláh.* Trans. Shoghi Effendi. Wilmette, IL: Bahá'í Publishing Trust, 1970; New Delhi: Bahá'í Publishing Trust, 1987.
— *The Kitáb-i-Aqdas: The Most Holy Book.* Haifa: Bahá'í World Centre, 1992.
— *Kitáb-i-Íqán: The Book of Certitude.* Trans. Shoghi Effendi. Wilmette, IL: Bahá'í Publishing Trust, 2nd ed. 1950, 1981.
— *Prayers and Meditations by Bahá'u'lláh.* Trans. Shoghi Effendi. Wilmette, IL: Bahá'í Publishing Trust, 1938, 1987.
— *The Seven Valleys and the Four Valleys.* Trans. M. Gail with A-K. Khan. Wilmette, IL: Bahá'í Publishing Trust, rev. ed. 1975.
— *The Summons of the Lord of Hosts: Tablets of Bahá'u'lláh.* Haifa: Bahá'í World Centre, 2002.
— *The Tabernacle of Unity.* Haifa: Bahá'í World Centre, 2006.
— *Tablets of Bahá'u'lláh Revealed after the Kitáb-i-Aqdas.* Comp. Research Department of the Universal House of Justice. Haifa: Bahá'í World Centre, 1978.

Balyuzi, H. M. *Muḥammad and the Course of Islám.* Oxford: George Ronald, 1976.

al-Báqir, Muḥammad ibn 'Alí. *Bihár Anwár Allámah Muhammad Báqir al-Majlisi*, vol. 13 (old ed.); vols. 51, 52, 53 (new ed.) Trans. Sayyid Athar Husain S.H. Rizvi. Mumbai, India: Ja'fari Propagation Centre. Arabic text available at: http://al-shia.org.

Barclay, William. *The Plain Man Looks at the Apostles' Creed.* London, Collins, 1967.

Berry, Gerald. *Religions of the World.* New York: Barnes and Noble, 1956.

Bible. *Holy Bible.* King James version. London: Eyre and Spottiswoode, various dates. The following translations are also quoted occasionally:
— *Douay-Rheims* (1609/1882), rev. Bishop Richard Challoner. Available online.
— *God's Word.* Ed. Eugene W. Bunkowska. Iowa Falls, Iowa: World Bible Publications, 1995.
— *New International Version (NIV).* Available at: http://www.biblica.com/en-us/the-niv-bible/.

Bhagavad Gita, Trans. Shri Purohit Swami. Woodstock, VT: Skylight Paths, 2001.

al-Bukhari, Abu Abdu'llah Muhammad ibn Isma'il. *Saḥīḥ*. Ed. L.K. Krehl, 4 vols. Leiden: E. J. Brill, 1962.

Cobb, Stanwood. *Islamic Contributions to Civilization*. Washington DC: Avalon Press, 1963.

The Compilation of Compilations. Prepared by the Universal House of Justice 1963–1990. 2 vols. Sydney: Bahá'í Publications Australia, 1991.

Digha Nikaya: The Long Discourses of the Buddha: A Translation of the Digha Nikaya. Trans. Maurice Walshe. Somerville, Mass: Wisdom Publications, 2nd ed. 1995.

Dowling, Rev. John W. *The History of Romanism: From the Earliest Corruptions of Christianity to the Present Time*. New York: E. Walker, 1845. Available at: http://onlinebooks.library.upenn.edu/.

Ebádi, Shirin. 'A Warning for Women of the Arab Spring', in *The Wall Street Journal*, 14 March 2012.

Esslemont, J. E. *Bahá'u'lláh and the New Era*. Wilmette: Bahá'í Publishing Trust, 5th rev. ed. 1987.

Foxe, John. *Foxe's Book of Martyrs*; original title: *Actes and Monuments of these Latter and Perillous Days, Touching Matters of the Church* (1563). Available at: www.johnfoxe.org.

Ghanea, Nazila. *Human Rights, the UN and the Bahá'ís in Iran*. Oxford: George Ronald, 2003.

The Great Papal Encyclicals (Series). Kansas City: Angelus Press, 2006.

Ghulam Ahmad of Qadian. *Jesus in India, Jesus' Escape from Death on the Cross and Journey to India*. Islamabad: Islam International Publications, 2012.

Gibbon, Edward. *The Decline and Fall of the Roman Empire*. New York: Everyman's Library, 2010.

Guillaume, Alfred. *The Life of Muhammad: A translation of Ibn Ishaq's Sirat Rasul Allah*. Oxford: Oxford University Press, 2013.

Hall, S. G. (ed). *Melito of Sardis: On Pascha and Fragments*. Oxford: Clarendon Press, 1979.

Harries, Jill; Wood, Ian (eds). *The Theodosian Code: Studies in the Imperial Law of Late Antiquity*. London: Bristol Classical Press, 2010.

Hillerbrand, Hans J. *The Reformation: A Narrative History Related by Contemporary Observers and Participants*. New York: Harper and Row, 1964.

Ibn-Hisham. Abu Muhammad 'Abd al-Malik. *Sirat an-Nabawiyya* (al-Sira al-Nabawiyya), vol. 4. Beirut: Dar al-Kitab al-'Arabi, 1987.

Ibsen, Henrik. *The Emperor Julian*, in *The Works of Henrik Ibsen*, vol. 6. Memphis, TN: General Books LLC, 2012.

Imam Malik. *Al-Muwatta*. Trans. A. Tarjumana; ed. Idris Mears. Norwich, UK: Diwan Press, 1982.

JPS Hebrew-English Tanakh. Philadelphia: Jewish Publication Society, 1999.

al-Khattab, Huda (ed.) *Musnad Imam Ahmad Bin Hanbal*, vol. 1. Darussalam: AhleSunnah Library, n.d. Available at: nmusba.wordpress.com.

Lights of Guidance: A Bahá'í Reference File. Comp. H. Hornby. New Delhi: Bahá'í Publishing Trust, 5th ed. 1997.

Luther, Martin. *On the Jews and Their Lies* (1543). Carshalton, Surrey, UK: The Historical Review Press, 2011.

Marcus, Della. *Her Eternal Crown: Queen Marie of Romania and the Bahá'í Faith*. Oxford: George Ronald, 2000.

Mesbah Uddin. 'Prophet Muhammad was Revered as the Jewish Messiah in Medina', in *MMN International*, 3 March 2008.

Nabíl-i- A'zam (Muḥammad-i-Zarandí). *The Dawn-Breakers: Nabíl's Narrative of the Early Days of the Bahá'í Revelation*. Trans. Shoghi Effendi. Wilmette, IL: Bahá'í Publishing Trust, 1932.

Perry, Marvin; Schweitzer, Frederick. *Anti-Semitism: Myth and Hate from Antiquity to the Present*. London: Palgrave Macmillan, 2002.

Phelps, Rev. Amos Augustus. 'Christianity vs. Churchianity', in *ZWT Reprints* (September 1883).

Qur'án. *The Holy Qur'an*. Trans. Abdullah Yusuf Ali (1934). Rev. ed. 2009/10. Available at sacred-texts.com.

Renan, Joseph Ernst. *Les Apôtres*. Paris: Calmann-Levy, 1883. Trans. William G. Hutchison: *The Apostles*. London: Watts, 1905.

Shoghi Effendi. *The Advent of Divine Justice* (1939). Wilmette, IL: Bahá'í Publishing Trust, 1984.
— *Bahá'í Administration: Selected Messages 1922–1932*. Wilmette: Bahá'í Publishing Trust, 1980.
— *Directives from the Guardian*. New Delhi: Bahá'í Publishing Trust, 1973.
— *God Passes By* (1944). Wilmette, IL: Bahá'í Publishing Trust, rev. ed. 1974.
— *Letters from the Guardian to Australia and New Zealand, 1923–1957*. Sydney: Australian Bahá'í Publishing, 1971.

— *The Light of Divine Guidance: The Messages from the Guardian of the Bahá'í Faith to the Bahá'ís of Germany and Austria*. 2 vols. Hofheim-Langenhain: Bahá'í-Verlag, 1982, 1985.
— *Messages of Shoghi Effendi to the Indian Subcontinent 1923–1957*. Comp. Iran Furutan Muhajír. New Delhi: Bahá'í Publishing Trust, rev. ed. 1995.
— *The Promised Day Is Come* (1941). Wilmette, IL: Bahá'í Publishing Trust, rev. ed. 1980.
— Summary Statement to the Special UM Committee on Palestine (1947).
— *The World Order of Bahá'u'lláh: Selected Letters by Shoghi Effendi* (1938). Wilmette, IL: Bahá'í Publishing Trust, 2nd rev. ed. 1974.

Sockett, Robert. 'Challenging Washington's Oldest Jewish Congregation', in *239 Days in America: A Social Media Documentary*, online, 2012. Available at: 239days.com.

Star of the West: The Bahai Magazine. Periodical, 25 vols. 1910–1935. Vols. 1–14 RP Oxford: George Ronald, 1978. Complete CD-ROM version: Talisman Educational Software/Special Ideas, 2001.

Taherzadeh, Adib. *The Revelation of Bahá'u'lláh*. 4 vols. Oxford: George Ronald, 1974–1987.

At-Tirmidhí, Abu 'Isa Muhammad. *Sunan*. 4 vols. Cairo, Maṭbaʻat al-Madani, 1875. Available at: hussainidalan.com/en/index.php/downloads/.

The Universal House of Justice. *Century of Light*. Haifa: Bahá'í World Centre, 2001.
— *Messages from the Universal House of Justice 1963–1986: The Third Epoch of the Formative Age*. Comp. Geoffry W. Marks. Wilmette, IL: Bahá'í Publishing Trust, 1996.
— Message to the World's Religious Leaders. Haifa, Bahá'í World Centre, 2002.
— *The Promise of World Peace*. Haifa: Bahá'í World Centre, 1985.

Vasicek, E. *The Origin of the Bible*, Part V: Manuscript Differences and Wrap-up. Indiana: Highland Park Church, 2010.

NOTES AND REFERENCES

Preface

1. Bahá'u'lláh, *Gleanings from the Writings of Bahá'u'lláh*, XCIX, p. 200.
2. Shoghi Effendi, *The Advent of Divine Justice*, p. 78.
3. Bahá'u'lláh, *Gleanings from the Writings of Bahá'u'lláh*, XLIII, pp. 92–3.
4. Shoghi Effendi, *The World Order of Bahá'u'lláh*, p. 169.
5. Bahá'u'lláh, *Gleanings from the Writings of Bahá'u'lláh*, C, p. 203.
6. Shoghi Effendi, *The World Order of Bahá'u'lláh*, p. 43.
7. 'Abdu'l-Bahá, *The Promulgation of Universal Peace*, pp. 438–9.
8. 'Abdu'l-Bahá, ibid. pp. 97–8.
9. Bahá'u'lláh, *Gleanings from the Writings of Bahá'u'lláh*, IV, p. 7.
10. Shoghi Effendi, *The World Order of Bahá'u'lláh*, p. 100.
11. ibid.
12. See Nabíl, *The Dawn-Breakers*, pp. 500–27.
13. See Shoghi Effendi, *God Passes By*, p. 101.
14. *Ál-i-'Imrán*, the Family of 'Imrán, 3:7:

هُوَ الَّذِيَ أَنزَلَ عَلَيْكَ الْكِتَابَ مِنْهُ آيَاتٌ مُحْكَمَاتٌ هُنَّ أُمُّ الْكِتَابِ وَأُخَرُ مُتَشَابِهَاتٌ فَأَمَّا الَّذِينَ في قُلُوبِهِمْ زَيْغٌ فَيَتَّبِعُونَ مَا تَشَابَهَ مِنْهُ ابْتِغَاءَ الْفِتْنَةِ وَابْتِغَاءَ تَأْوِيلِهِ وَمَا يَعْلَمُ تَأْوِيلَهُ إِلاَّ اللّهُ وَالرَّاسِخُونَ فِي الْعِلْمِ يَقُولُونَ آمَنَّا بِهِ كُلٌّ مِّنْ عِندِ رَبِّنَا وَمَا يَذَّكَّرُ إِلاَّ أُوْلُواْ الألْبَابِ

اوست کسی که این کتاب [=قرآن] را بر تو فرو فرستاد پاره‌ای از آن آیات محکم [=صریح و روشن] است آنها اساس کتابند و [پاره‌ای] دیگر متشابهاتند [که تاویل‌پذیرند] اما کسانی که در دلهایشان انحراف است برای فتنه‌جویی و طلب تاویل آن [به دلخواه خود] از متشابه آن پیروی می‌کنند با آنکه تاویلش را جز خدا و ریشه‌داران در دانش کسی نمی‌داند [آنان که] می‌گویند ما بدان ایمان آوردیم همه [چه محکم و چه متشابه] از جانب پروردگار ماست و جز خردمندان کسی متذکر نمی‌شود

15. Bahá'u'lláh, *Gleanings from the Writings of Bahá'u'lláh*, XXXIII, p. 77.
16. 'Abdu'l-Bahá, *The Promulgation of Universal Peace*, p. 454.
17. Heb. 1:1–2.

Foreword

1. The great-grandson of Bahá'u'lláh and the Guardian of the Bahá'í Faith (1921–1957).
2. Shoghi Effendi, *The Advent of Divine Justice*, p. 41.
3. ibid.
4. Letter written on behalf of Shoghi Effendi to an individual believer, 27 April 1936, excerpted in *Lights of Guidance*, no. 1664.
5. An eminent Bahá'í (1908–1980), and author of several publications including *Muḥammad and the Course of Islám*.

6 An American educator, a prominent Bahá'í, and author of *Islamic Contributions to Civilization*.
7 Cited in Bahá'u'lláh, *Kitáb-i-Íqán*, para. 215, p. 195. *'Ankabút*, the Spider, 29:69:

وَالَّذِينَ جَاهَدُوا فِينَا لَنَهْدِيَنَّهُمْ سُبُلَنَا وَإِنَّ اللَّهَ لَمَعَ الْمُحْسِنِينَ

و کسانی که در راه ما کوشیده‌اند به یقین راه‌های خود را بر آنان می‌نماییم و در حقیقت‌خدا با نیکوکاران است

8 Bahá'u'lláh, quoted in Shoghi Effendi, *The Promised Day Is Come*, p. 81.
9 Bahá'u'lláh, *Gleanings from the Writings of Bahá'u'lláh*, LXX. p. 136.
10 *Ḥajj*, the Pilgrimage, 22:78:

وَجَاهِدُوا فِي اللَّهِ حَقَّ جِهَادِهِ هُوَ اجْتَبَاكُمْ وَمَا جَعَلَ عَلَيْكُمْ فِي الدِّينِ مِنْ حَرَجٍ مِلَّةَ أَبِيكُمْ إِبْرَاهِيمَ هُوَ سَمَّاكُمُ الْمُسْلِمِينَ مِنْ قَبْلُ وَفِي هَذَا لِيَكُونَ الرَّسُولُ شَهِيدًا عَلَيْكُمْ وَتَكُونُوا شُهَدَاءَ عَلَى النَّاسِ فَأَقِيمُوا الصَّلَاةَ وَآتُوا الزَّكَاةَ وَاعْتَصِمُوا بِاللَّهِ هُوَ مَوْلَاكُمْ فَنِعْمَ الْمَوْلَى وَنِعْمَ النَّصِيرُ

در راه خدا چنانکه حق جهاد [در راه] اوست جهاد کنید اوست که شما را [برای خود] برگزیده و در دین بر شما سختی قرار نداده است آیین پدرتان ابراهیم [نیز چنین بوده است] او بود که قبلا شما را مسلمان نامید و در این [قرآن نیز همین مطلب آمده است] تا این پیامبر بر شما گواه باشد و شما بر مردم گواه باشید پس نماز را برپا دارید و زکات بدهید و به پناه خدا روید او مولای شماست چه نیکو مولایی و چه نیکو یاوری

11 *Má'ida*, the Table Spread, 5:64:

وَقَالَتِ الْيَهُودُ يَدُ اللَّهِ مَغْلُولَةٌ غُلَّتْ أَيْدِيهِمْ وَلُعِنُوا بِمَا قَالُوا بَلْ يَدَاهُ مَبْسُوطَتَانِ يُنْفِقُ كَيْفَ يَشَاءُ وَلَيَزِيدَنَّ كَثِيرًا مِنْهُمْ مَا أُنْزِلَ إِلَيْكَ مِنْ رَبِّكَ طُغْيَانًا وَكُفْرًا وَأَلْقَيْنَا بَيْنَهُمُ الْعَدَاوَةَ وَالْبَغْضَاءَ إِلَى يَوْمِ الْقِيَامَةِ كُلَّمَا أَوْقَدُوا نَارًا لِلْحَرْبِ أَطْفَأَهَا اللَّهُ وَيَسْعَوْنَ فِي الْأَرْضِ فَسَادًا وَاللَّهُ لَا يُحِبُّ الْمُفْسِدِينَ

و یهود گفتند دست‌خدا بسته است دست‌های خودشان بسته باد و به [سزای] آنچه گفتند از رحمت‌خدا دور شوند بلکه هر دو دست او گشاده است هر گونه بخواهد می‌بخشد و قطعا آنچه از جانب پروردگارت به سوی تو فرود آمده بر طغیان و کفر بسیاری از ایشان خواهد افزود و تا روز قیامت میانشان دشمنی و کینه افکندیم هر بار که آتشی برای پیکار برافروختند خدا آن را خاموش ساخت و در زمین برای فساد می‌کوشند و خدا مفسدان را دوست نمی‌دارد

12 Bahá'u'lláh, *Kitáb-i-Íqán*, para. 148, p. 137.
13 *Qiyámat*, the Resurrection, 75:16–19:
   Move not thy tongue concerning the (Qur'án) to make haste therewith,
   It is for Us to collect it and to promulgate it:
   But when We have promulgated it, follow thou Its recital
   Nay more, it is for us to explain it (and make it clear) …

لَا تُحَرِّكْ بِهِ لِسَانَكَ لِتَعْجَلَ بِهِ
إِنَّ عَلَيْنَا جَمْعَهُ وَقُرْآنَهُ
فَإِذَا قَرَأْنَاهُ فَاتَّبِعْ قُرْآنَهُ
ثُمَّ إِنَّ عَلَيْنَا بَيَانَهُ

زبانت را بخاطر عجله برای خواندن آن [قرآن] حرکت مده
چرا که جمع‌کردن و خواندن آن بر عهده ماست
پس هر گاه آن را خواندیم از خواندن آن پیروی کن
سپس بیان و توضیح آن نیز بر عهده ماست

14 Cited in Bahá'u'lláh, *Gleanings from the Writings of Bahá'u'lláh*, p. 185. *Qáf*, 50:16:

It was We Who created man, and We know what dark suggestions his soul makes to him: for We are nearer to him than (his) jugular vein.

وَلَقَدْ خَلَقْنَا الْإِنْسَانَ وَنَعْلَمُ مَا تُوَسْوِسُ بِهِ نَفْسُهُ وَنَحْنُ أَقْرَبُ إِلَيْهِ مِنْ حَبْلِ الْوَرِيدِ

و ما انسان را آفریده‌ایم و می‌دانیم که نفس او چه وسوسه‌ای به او می‌کند و ما از شاهرگ [او] به او نزدیکتریم

15 Bahá'u'lláh, *Kitáb-i-Íqán*, para. 213, p. 192.

Introduction

1 'Glory' may be translated in Arabic as Bahá – hence, this Bahá or Glory of God was with Christ and would be re-manifested.
2 See http://bahai-library.com/.
3 Bahá'u'lláh, quoted in Shoghi Effendi, *The World Order of Bahá'u'lláh*, pp. 186-7.
4 Matt. 7:17; *Ibráhím*, Abraham, 14:24.
5 'Abdu'l-Bahá, *Paris Talks*, ch. 40, p. 132.
6 Words spoken to Edward G. Browne, from his pen portrait of Bahá'u'lláh, quoted in Esslemont, *Bahá'u'lláh and the New Era*, pp. 39-40; and in *The Compilation of Compilations*, vol. II, p. 157.
7 Bahá'u'lláh, *Epistle to the Son of the Wolf*, p. 13.
8 Shoghi Effendi, *The World Order of Bahá'u'lláh*, pp. 196-7.
9 Bahá'u'lláh, *Gleanings from the Writings of Bahá'u'lláh*, XLIII, p. 97.
10 Shoghi Effendi, *The World Order of Bahá'u'lláh*, p. 186.
11 Jer. 6:16 (New International Version).
12 Matt. 7:13-14.
13 *Ṭá-Há*, 20:108-11 (M. M. Pickthall translation):

يَوْمَئِذٍ يَتَّبِعُونَ الدَّاعِيَ لَا عِوَجَ لَهُ وَخَشَعَتِ الْأَصْوَاتُ لِلرَّحْمَٰنِ فَلَا تَسْمَعُ إِلَّا هَمْسًا
يَوْمَئِذٍ لَا تَنْفَعُ الشَّفَاعَةُ إِلَّا مَنْ أَذِنَ لَهُ الرَّحْمَٰنُ وَرَضِيَ لَهُ قَوْلًا
يَعْلَمُ مَا بَيْنَ أَيْدِيهِمْ وَمَا خَلْفَهُمْ وَلَا يُحِيطُونَ بِهِ عِلْمًا
وَعَنَتِ الْوُجُوهُ لِلْحَيِّ الْقَيُّومِ

در آن روز [همه مردم] داعی [حق] را که هیچ انحرافی در او نیست پیروی می‌کنند و صداها در مقابل [خدای] رحمان خاشع می‌گردد و جز صدایی آهسته نمی‌شنوی
در آن روز شفاعت [به کسی] سود نبخشد مگر کسی را که [خدای] رحمان اجازه دهد و سخنش او را پسند آید
آنچه را که آنان در پیش دارند و آنچه را که پشتِ‌سر گذاشته‌اند می‌داند و حال آنکه ایشان بدان دانشی ندارند
و چهره‌ها برای آن [خدای] زنده پاینده خضوع می‌کنند و آن کس که ظلمی بر دوش دارد نومید می‌ماند

14 Bahá'u'lláh, *The Kitáb-i-Aqdas*, para. 182, p. 85.
15 *Rúm*, the Roman Empire, 30:37. See also Luke 18:19.
16 Ibsen, *The Emperor Julian*, Act III. Quoted by Shoghi Effendi, *The World Order of Bahá'u'lláh*, p. 114.
17 Mal. 4:5.
18 Isa. 40:5.
19 Isa. 9:6.
20 Isa. 11:1.
21 Isa. 9:7.
22 Isa. 51:9.

23 Isa. 2:4.
24 Isa. 11:4.
25 Isa. 11:12.
26 Ps. 24:7-10.
27 Hagg. 2:7.
28 Zech. 6:12.
29 ibid.
30 Ezek. 30:3-5; Joel 1:15.
31 Quoted in Shoghi Effendi, *God Passes By*, pp. 94-5.
32 John 16:12-14.
33 Heb. 1:1.
34 Matt. 6:10.
35 William Barclay, *The Plain Man Looks at the Apostles' Creed*, p. 178.
36 *Ḥajj*, the Pilgrimage, 22:67.
37 *Nisáa*, the Women, 4:164.
38 *Yá-Sín*, 36:68.
39 *Baqara*, the Heifer, 2:106-7:

مَا نَنسَخْ مِنْ آيَةٍ أَوْ نُنسِهَا نَأْتِ بِخَيْرٍ مِّنْهَا أَوْ مِثْلِهَا أَلَمْ تَعْلَمْ أَنَّ اللَّهَ عَلَىٰ كُلِّ شَيْءٍ قَدِيرٌ
أَلَمْ تَعْلَمْ أَنَّ اللَّهَ لَهُ مُلْكُ السَّمَاوَاتِ وَالْأَرْضِ وَمَا لَكُم مِّن دُونِ اللَّهِ مِن وَلِيٍّ وَلَا نَصِيرٍ

هر حکمی را نسخ کنیم یا آن را به [دست] فراموشی بسپاریم بهتر از آن یا مانندش را می‌آوریم مگر
ندانستی که خدا بر هر کاری تواناست
مگر ندانستی که فرمانروایی آسمانها و زمین از آن خداست و شما جز خدا سرور و یاوری ندارید

40 Shoghi Effendi, *God Passes By*, p. 96.
41 *Shúráa*, Consultation, 42:38.
42 *Lail*, the Night, 92:20-21.
43 Bahá'u'lláh, *Kitáb-i-Íqán*, para. 3, p. 4.
44 ibid. para. 156, pp. 147-8.
45 The Universal House of Justice, *The Promise of World Peace*, p. 6, quoting Shoghi Effendi, *The World Order of Bahá'u'lláh*, p. 42.
46 Bahá'u'lláh, Súriy-i-Haykal, para. 110, in Bahá'u'lláh, *The Summons of the Lord of Hosts*, p. 58.

1 The Summons of the Báb and Bahá'u'lláh and the 'Ajal' of the 'Ummah' of Islam

1 *Qamar*, the Moon, 54:6-8:

فَتَوَلَّ عَنْهُمْ يَوْمَ يَدْعُ الدَّاعِ إِلَىٰ شَيْءٍ نُكُرٍ
خُشَّعًا أَبْصَارُهُمْ يَخْرُجُونَ مِنَ الْأَجْدَاثِ كَأَنَّهُمْ جَرَادٌ مُّنتَشِرٌ
مُّهْطِعِينَ إِلَى الدَّاعِ يَقُولُ الْكَافِرُونَ هَٰذَا يَوْمٌ عَسِرٌ

پس از آنان روی برتاب روزی که داعی [حق] به سوی امری دهشتناک دعوت می‌کند
در حالی که دیدگان خود را فروهشته‌اند چون ملخهای پراکنده از گورها[ی خود] برمی‌آیند
به سرعت سوی آن دعوتگر می‌شتابند کافران می‌گویند امروز [چه] روز دشواری است

This verse is quoted by Bahá'u'lláh:
'He (Muhammad) hath revealed: "The day when the Summoner shall summon to a stern business."' (*Kitáb-i-Íqán*, p. 239)

NOTES AND REFERENCES

2 Shoghi Effendi, *The World Order of Bahá'u'lláh*, p. 60.
3 *Baqara*, the Heifer, 2:143:

وَكَذَلِكَ جَعَلْنَاكُمْ أُمَّةً وَسَطًا لِتَكُونُوا شُهَدَاءَ عَلَى النَّاسِ وَيَكُونَ الرَّسُولُ عَلَيْكُمْ شَهِيدًا ...

و بدین گونه شما را امتی میانه قرار دادیم تا بر مردم گواه باشید و پیامبر بر شما گواه باشد...

4 The Báb, the forerunner of Bahá'u'lláh, declared His Mission in Shiraz, Iran and proclaimed it in Mecca.
5 J. M. Rodwell: 'stern business'; M. M. Pickthall: 'painful thing'.
6 *A'ráf*, the Heights, 7:34-5:

وَلِكُلِّ أُمَّةٍ أَجَلٌ فَإِذَا جَاءَ أَجَلُهُمْ لَا يَسْتَأْخِرُونَ سَاعَةً وَلَا يَسْتَقْدِمُونَ
يَا بَنِي آدَمَ إِمَّا يَأْتِيَنَّكُمْ رُسُلٌ مِّنكُمْ يَقُصُّونَ عَلَيْكُمْ آيَاتِي فَمَنِ اتَّقَىٰ وَأَصْلَحَ فَلَا خَوْفٌ عَلَيْهِمْ وَلَا هُمْ يَحْزَنُونَ

و برای هر امتی اجلی است پس چون اجلشان فرا رسد نه [می‌توانند] ساعتی آن را پس اندازند و نه پیش
ای فرزندان آدم چون پیامبرانی از خودتان برای شما بیایند و آیات مرا بر شما بخوانند پس هر کس به پرهیزگاری و صلاح گراید نه بیمی بر آنان خواهد بود و نه اندوهگین می شوند

7 *'Ankabút*, the Spider, 29:5:

مَن كَانَ يَرْجُو لِقَاءَ اللَّهِ فَإِنَّ أَجَلَ اللَّهِ لَآتٍ وَهُوَ السَّمِيعُ الْعَلِيمُ

هرکس که به لقای الهی امید داشته باشد [بداند که] اجل مقرر الهی فرارسنده است و او شنوای داناست

8 *Rúm*, the Roman Empire, 30:8:

أَوَلَمْ يَتَفَكَّرُوا فِي أَنفُسِهِم مَّا خَلَقَ اللَّهُ السَّمَاوَاتِ وَالْأَرْضَ وَمَا بَيْنَهُمَا إِلَّا بِالْحَقِّ وَأَجَلٍ مُّسَمًّى وَإِنَّ كَثِيرًا مِّنَ النَّاسِ بِلِقَاءِ رَبِّهِمْ لَكَافِرُونَ

آیا در خودشان به تفکر نپرداخته‌اند خداوند آسمانها و زمین و آنچه را که میان آن دو است جز به حق و تا هنگامی معین نیافریده است و [با این همه] بسیاری از مردم لقای پروردگارشان را سخت منکرند

9 *Mursalát*, Those Sent Forth, 77:24-6:

وَيْلٌ يَوْمَئِذٍ لِّلْمُكَذِّبِينَ
أَلَمْ نَجْعَلِ الْأَرْضَ كِفَاتًا
أَحْيَاءً وَأَمْوَاتًا

آن روز وای بر تکذیب‌کنندگان
مگر زمین را محل اجتماع نگردانیدیم
چه برای مردگان چه زندگان

10 I Pet. 4:5.
11 Bahá'u'lláh, *Gleanings from the Writings of Bahá'u'lláh*, XVIII, p. 43.
12 See the Báb, *Selections from the Writings of the Báb*, 'Excerpts from the Qayyúmu'l-Asmá'.
13 Isa. 9:6-7.
14 Ps. 24:7-10.
15 Rev. 21:1-7.
16 The Báb, Qayyúmu'l-Asmá', ch. LXII, in *Selections from the Writings of the Báb*, p. 61; Shoghi Effendi, *The Promised Day is Come*, p. 85.

17 The Báb, Persian Bayán, VI:15, in *Selections from the Writings of the Báb*, p. 84.
18 The Báb, Tablet addressed to 'Him Who Will Be Made Manifest', in *Selections from the Writings of the Báb*, p. 3.
19 The Báb, Kitáb-i-Asmá', XVI:13, in *Selections from the Writings of the Báb*, p. 136.
20 Bahá'u'lláh, *Kitáb-i-Íqán*, para. 3, p. 4.
21 Bahá'u'lláh, *Gleanings from the Writings of Bahá'u'lláh*, XLIII, pp. 96-7.
22 Bahá'u'lláh, Short Obligatory Prayer, in *Prayers and Meditations*, p. 313:
    I bear witness, O my God, that Thou hast created me to know Thee and to worship Thee . . .
23 Bahá'u'lláh, *Kitáb-i-Íqán*, para. 110, p. 104.
24 Shoghi Effendi, *The World Order of Bahá'u'lláh*, pp. 196-7. Shoghi Effendi was the great-grandson of Bahá'u'lláh and the appointed Guardian and interpreter of His Faith.
25 Shoghi Effendi, *The Promised Day is Come*, p. 108.
26 Shoghi Effendi, *The World Order of Bahá'u'lláh*, pp. 197-8.
27 'Abdu'l-Bahá, *Selections from the Writings of 'Abdu'l-Bahá*, p. 2.
28 Bahá'u'lláh, Súriy-i-Haykal, in *The Summons of the Lord of Hosts*, p. 60.
29 *Baqara*, the Heifer, 2:87:

... أَفَكُلَّمَا جَاءَكُمْ رَسُولٌ بِمَا لاَ تَهْوَى أَنفُسُكُمُ اسْتَكْبَرْتُمْ فَفَرِيقًا كَذَّبْتُمْ وَفَرِيقًا تَقْتُلُونَ

...آيا هر زمان پيامبري بر خلاف هواي نفس شما آمد در برابر او تكبر كرديد (و از ايمان آوردن به او خود داري نموديد و به اين قناعت نكرديد بلكه) عدماي را تكذيب نموده، جمعي را بقتل رسانديد؟!

30 This is often deduced from the fact that the world centre of the Bahá'í Faith is in Israel, but this was merely because Bahá'u'lláh was banished initially to Baghdad by Nasir al-Din Shah Qajjár (Nasir'i-Din Shah) and later to Adrianople and Istanbul and finally to Akka in Palestine by a decree of the Sultan of the Ottoman Empire.
31 Shoghi Effendi, *God Passes By*, p. 146. The term 'misguided and detestable sect' was used by the Iranian foreign minister, Mírzá Sa'íd Khán, in a letter to the Iranian ambassador to the Sultan of the Ottoman Empire to describe the followers of Bahá'u'lláh. The denunciation is frequently used to this date by the clergy and government-controlled press in Iran. The term is also derived from a sermon given by Imám 'Alí ('Alí Ibn Abí Tálib) and refers more aptly to the state of Islam and Muslims, then and now, and as implied by the title of the sermon not applicable to the followers of the anticipated Revelation:
    About those who sit for dispensation of justice among people but are not fit for it.
    Among all the people the most detested before Allah are two persons. One is he who is devoted to his self. So he is deviated from the true path and loves speaking about (foul) innovations and inviting towards wrong path. He is therefore a nuisance for those who are enamoured of him, is himself misled from the guidance of those preceding him, misleads those who follow him in his life or after his death, carries the weight of others' sins and is entangled in his own misdeeds.
    The other man is he who has picked up ignorance. He moves among

the ignorant, is senseless in the thick of mischief and is blind to the advantages of peace. Those resembling like men have named him scholar but he is not so. He goes out early morning to collect things whose deficiency is better than plenty, till when he has quenched his thirst from polluted water and acquired meaningless things.

He sits among the people as a judge responsible for solving whatever is confusing to the others. If an ambiguous problem is presented before him he manages shabby argument about it of his own accord and passes judgement on its basis. In this way he is entangled in the confusion of doubts as in the spider's web, not knowing whether he was right or wrong. If he is right he fears lest he erred, while if he is wrong he hopes he is right. He is ignorant, wandering astray in ignorance and riding on carriages aimlessly moving in darkness. He did not try to find reality of knowledge. He scatters the traditions as the wind scatters the dry leaves.

By Allah, he is not capable of solving the problems that come to him nor is fit for the position assigned to him. Whatever he does not know he does not regard it worth knowing. He does not realise that what is beyond his reach is within the reach of others. If anything is not clear to him he keeps quiet over it because he knows his own ignorance. Lost lives are crying against his unjust verdicts, and properties (that have been wrongly disposed of) are grumbling against him.

I complain to Allah about persons who live ignorant and die misguided. For them nothing is more worthless than Qur'an if it is recited as it should be recited, nor anything more valuable than the Qur'an if its verses are removed from their places, nor anything more vicious than virtue nor more virtuous than vice. (*Nahjul Balághah,* Sermon 17)

32 *Fasád* is the crime of corruption or social disorder. Bahá'ís are often accused by the Islamic Republic of Iran as causing *fasád* and are hence labelled '*mofsede-fel-ardth*' or 'those who cause mischief, sedition or corruption on earth', an accusation that carries the threat of death under the penal code of the country. From the *Tafsir of Ibn Kathir*, '*fasád fi al-ardth*' (mischief or corruption in the land/on earth) is the act of disobedience to Allah.

Examples of Quranic verses from which the term is derived are as follows:
Baqara, the Heifer, 2:251:

> ... And did not God check one set of people by means of another, the earth would indeed be full of mischief. . .
>
> وَلَوْلَا دَفْعُ اللهِ النَّاسَ بَعْضَهُمْ بِبَعْضٍ لَفَسَدَتِ الْأَرْضَ ...
>
> ...و اگر خداوند، بعضی از مردم را به وسیله بعضی دیگر دفع نمی‌کرد، زمین را فساد فرامی‌گرفت...

See also *Má'ida,* the Table Spread, 5:32; *Baqara,* the Heifer, 2:11 and 2:27.

33 *Má'ida,* the Table Spread, 5:33:
The punishment of those who wage war against God and His Messenger, and strive with might and main for mischief through the land is: execution, or crucifixion, or the cutting off of hands and feet from opposite sides, or exile from the land: that is their disgrace in this world, and a heavy

punishment is theirs in the Hereafter.

إِنَّمَا جَزَاءُ الَّذِينَ يُحَارِبُونَ اللَّهَ وَرَسُولَهُ وَيَسْعَوْنَ فِي الْأَرْضِ فَسَادًا أَن يُقَتَّلُوا أَوْ يُصَلَّبُوا أَوْ تُقَطَّعَ أَيْدِيهِمْ وَأَرْجُلُهُم مِّنْ خِلَافٍ أَوْ يُنفَوْا مِنَ الْأَرْضِ ذَٰلِكَ لَهُمْ خِزْيٌ فِي الدُّنْيَا وَلَهُمْ فِي الْآخِرَةِ عَذَابٌ عَظِيمٌ

سزای کسانی که با خدا و پیامبر او می‌جنگند و در زمین به فساد می‌کوشند جز این نیست که کشته شوند یا بر دار آویخته گردند یا دست و پایشان در خلاف جهت‌یکدیگر بریده شود یا از آن سرزمین تبعید گردند این رسوایی آنان در دنیاست و در آخرت عذابی بزرگ خواهند داشت

34 Affolter, 'The Specter of Ideological Genocide: The Bahá'ís of Iran', in *War Crimes, Genocide and Crimes Against Humanity*, vol.1, no. 1, pp. 59–89; 'State to Appeal Ruling that Favours Egypt's Bahá'ís', *Khaleej Times*, Reuters, 3 May 2006.
35 'Worldwide Adherents of All Religions by Six Continental Areas, Mid-2002", in *The Britannica Book of the Year* (1992–present), Encyclopædia Britannica online.
36 Ṣaff, Battle Array, 61:8:

يُرِيدُونَ لِيُطْفِئُوا نُورَ اللَّهِ بِأَفْوَاهِهِمْ وَاللَّهُ مُتِمُّ نُورِهِ وَلَوْ كَرِهَ الْكَافِرُونَ

می‌خواهند نور خدا را با دهان خود خاموش کنند و حال آنکه خدا گر چه کافران را ناخوش افتد نور خود را کامل خواهد گردانید

37 *Muhammad* (the Prophet), 47:32:

إِنَّ الَّذِينَ كَفَرُوا وَصَدُّوا عَن سَبِيلِ اللَّهِ وَشَاقُّوا الرَّسُولَ مِن بَعْدِ مَا تَبَيَّنَ لَهُمُ الْهُدَىٰ لَن يَضُرُّوا اللَّهَ شَيْئًا وَسَيُحْبِطُ أَعْمَالَهُمْ

کسانی که کافر شدند و [مردم را] از راه خدا باز داشتند و پس از آنکه راه هدایت بر آنان آشکار شد با پیامبر [خدا] در افتادند هرگز به خدا گزندی نمی‌رسانند و به زودی [خدا] کرده‌هایشان را تباه خواهد کرد

38 *Ṣád*, 38:67–8:

قُلْ هُوَ نَبَأٌ عَظِيمٌ
أَنتُمْ عَنْهُ مُعْرِضُونَ

بگو این خبری بزرگ است
[که] شما از آن روی برمی‌تابید

39 *Háqqa*, the Sure Reality, 69:48–52:

وَإِنَّهُ لَتَذْكِرَةٌ لِّلْمُتَّقِينَ
وَإِنَّا لَنَعْلَمُ أَنَّ مِنكُم مُّكَذِّبِينَ
وَإِنَّهُ لَحَسْرَةٌ عَلَى الْكَافِرِينَ
وَإِنَّهُ لَحَقُّ الْيَقِينِ
فَسَبِّحْ بِاسْمِ رَبِّكَ الْعَظِيمِ

و آن پندآموزی برای پرهیزگاران است
و ما به یقین می‌دانیم که از میان شما تکذیب‌کنندگانی هستند
و آن [پیام]، مایه حسرتی بر کافران است
و آن یقین خالص است
پس به نام پروردگار بزرگ خود تسبیح گوی

40   Sockett, 'Challenging Washington's Oldest Jewish Congregation', in *239 Days in America, A Social Media Documentary*.
41   Bahá'u'lláh, quoted in Shoghi Effendi, *The World Order of Bahá'u'lláh*, p. 164; 'Abdu'l-Bahá, *Selections from the Writings of 'Abdu'l-Bahá*, pp. 98–9.
42   Bahá'u'lláh, *Gleanings from the Writings of Bahá'u'lláh*, XXXV, pp. 83–4.
43   From a Tablet of Bahá'u'lláh, quoted in *Messages of Shoghi Effendi to the Indian Subcontinent*, p. 434.
44   Bahá'u'lláh, *Kitáb-i-Íqán*, para. 40, p. 40; *Epistle to the Son of the Wolf*, p. 92.
45   Bahá'u'lláh, *Prayers and Meditations*, XXV, p. 29.
46   Bahá'u'lláh, *Kitáb-i-Íqán*, para. 40, p. 40.
47   'Abdu'l-Bahá, *The Secret of Divine Civilization*, p. 69.
48   'Abdu'l-Bahá, *The Promulgation of Universal Peace*, p. 126.
49   Bahá'u'lláh, *Kitáb-i-Íqán*, para. 172, p. 162.
50   'Abdu'l-Bahá, *Selections from the Writings of 'Abdu'l-Bahá*, no. 222, p. 281.
51   'Abdu'l-Bahá, *The Secret of Divine Civilization*, p. 5.
52   Bahá'u'lláh, *Kitáb-i-Íqán*, para. 25, p. 26.
53   Bahá'u'lláh, *Gleanings from the Writings of Bahá'u'lláh*, XXVIII, p. 69.
54   'Abdu'l-Bahá, *A Traveller's Narrative*, p. 32.
55   'Abdu'l-Bahá, *The Secret of Divine Civilization*, p. 99.
56   ibid. p. 87.
57   'Abdu'l-Bahá, *A Traveller's Narrative*, p. 74.
58   'Abdu'l-Bahá, *The Secret of Divine Civilization*, p. 53.
59   Bahá'u'lláh, *Gleanings from the Writings of Bahá'u'lláh*, XXIII, p. 57.
60   'Abdu'l-Bahá, *The Secret of Divine Civilization*, p. 27.
61   ibid. p. 53.
62   Bahá'u'lláh, *The Seven Valleys and the Four Valleys*, p. 2.
63   Bahá'u'lláh, Lawḥ-i-Maqṣúd, in *Tablets of Bahá'u'lláh*, p. 162.
64   Bahá'u'lláh, *Kitáb-i-Íqán*, para. 156, p. 147.
65   Shoghi Effendi, *The Promised Day Is Come*, pp. 108–9.
66   Shoghi Effendi, *The Advent of Divine Justice*, p. 49.
67   Shoghi Effendi, *Directives from the Guardian*, p. 64.
68   Shoghi Effendi, *The Promised Day Is Come*, pp. 108–9. Marie of Romania (1875–1938) was born at Eastwell Park in Kent, the eldest daughter of Prince Alfred, Duke of Edinburgh and Grand Duchess Maria Alexandrovna of Russia. Her father was the second-eldest son of Queen Victoria and Prince Albert. Her mother was the only surviving daughter of Alexander II of Russia and Maria Alexandrovna of Hesse. She was baptized in the Private Chapel of Windsor Castle on 15 December 1875 as a member of the Church of England, although she is known to have embraced the Orthodox Christian beliefs of Romanian nationals. In her later years, she was approached by Martha Root, a travelling teacher, on the topic of the Bahá'í Faith. Bahá'ís recognize Queen Marie of Romania as the first member of royalty to have declared her belief in Bahá'u'lláh. For further detail see Della Marcus, *Her Eternal Crown: Queen Marie of Romania and the Bahá'í Faith*.
69   Quoted by Shoghi Effendi, *The Promised Day Is Come*, p. 108.
70   ibid.
71   Shoghi Effendi, *The World Order of Bahá'u'lláh*, p. 114.

72 *Fátiḥa*, the Opening Chapter, 1:6:
   Show us the right way (path).

   اِهدِنَا الصِّرَاطَ المُستَقِيمَ

   ما را به راه راست هدایت فرما

73 Shoghi Effendi, *The Promised Day Is Come*, p. 99.
74 ibid. p. 112.
75 *Ḥujarát*, the Inner Apartments, 49:6:

   يَا أَيُّهَا الَّذِينَ آمَنُوا إِن جَاءكُمْ فَاسِقٌ بِنَبَإٍ فَتَبَيَّنُوا أَن تُصِيبُوا قَوْمًا بِجَهَالَةٍ فَتُصْبِحُوا عَلَى مَا فَعَلْتُمْ نَادِمِينَ

   ای کسانی که ایمان آورده‌اید اگر فاسقی برایتان خبری آورد نیک وارسی کنید مبادا به نادانی گروهی را آسیب برسانید و [بعد] از آنچه کرده‌اید پشیمان شوید

76 *'Ankabút*, the Spider, 29:69:

   وَالَّذِينَ جَاهَدُوا فِينَا لَنَهْدِيَنَّهُمْ سُبُلَنَا وَإِنَّ اللَّهَ لَمَعَ الْمُحْسِنِينَ

   و کسانی که در راه ما کوشیده‌اند به یقین راه‌های خود را بر آنان می‌نماییم و در حقیقت‌خدا با نیکوکاران است

77 *Muhammad* (the Prophet), 47:17:

   وَالَّذِينَ اهْتَدَوْا زَادَهُمْ هُدًى وَآتَاهُمْ تَقْوَاهُمْ

   و آنان که به هدایت گراییدند [خدا] آنان را هر چه بیشتر هدایت بخشید و [توفیق] پرهیزگاری‌شان داد

78 *Baqara*, the Heifer, 2:106:

   مَا نَنسَخْ مِنْ آيَةٍ أَوْ نُنسِهَا نَأْتِ بِخَيْرٍ مِّنْهَا أَوْ مِثْلِهَا أَلَمْ تَعْلَمْ أَنَّ اللَّهَ عَلَىٰ كُلِّ شَيْءٍ قَدِيرٌ

   هر حکمی را نسخ کنیم یا آن را به [دست] فراموشی بسپاریم بهتر از آن یا مانندش را می‌آوریم مگر ندانستی که خدا بر هر کاری تواناست

2 Islam: The Promise of the Bible

1 The Báb, *Kitáb-i-Asmá'*, XVI:3, in *Selections from the Writings of the Báb*, p. 137.
2 Mark 3:25.
3 Bahá'u'lláh, *Gems of Divine Mysteries, Javáhiru'l-Asrár*, para. 55, p. 40-41.
4 Bahá'u'lláh, *Kitáb-i-Íqán*, para. 25, p. 26.
5 II Pet. 1:19-21.
6 Deut. 4:2.
7 ibid. 12:32.
8 Shoghi Effendi, 'The Dispensation of Bahá'u'lláh', in *The World Order of Bahá'u'lláh*, p. 145.
9 Luke 10:23-4.
10 John 9:39.
11 Matt. 13:14-16.
12 For further Jewish objections to Jesus as the expected Messiah, see for example the extensive writings of Rabbi Maimonides (Rambam).

NOTES AND REFERENCES

13 John 5:46: 'For had ye believed Moses, ye would have believed me: for he wrote of me.'
14 *Ál-i-'Imrán*, the Family of 'Imrán, 3:84.
15 Bahá'u'lláh, *Gems of Divine Mysteries, Javáhiru'l-Asrár* para. 44, p. 33.
16 *A'ráf*, the Heights, 7:157:
    Those who follow the Messenger, the unlettered Prophet, whom they find mentioned in their own (Scriptures); in the law (Torah) and the Gospel for he commands them what is just and forbids them what is evil ...

    الَّذِينَ يَتَّبِعُونَ الرَّسُولَ النَّبِيَّ الْأُمِّيَّ الَّذِي يَجِدُونَهُ مَكْتُوبًا عِندَهُمْ فِي التَّوْرَاةِ وَالْإِنجِيلِ يَأْمُرُهُم بِالْمَعْرُوفِ وَيَنْهَاهُمْ عَنِ الْمُنكَرِ ...

    همانان که از این فرستاده پیامبر درس نخوانده که [نام] او را نزد خود در تورات و انجیل نوشته می‌یابند پیروی می‌کنند [همان پیامبری که] آنان را به کار پسندیده فرمان می‌دهد و از کار ناپسند باز می‌دارد...

17 Letter written on behalf of Shoghi Effendi to an individual believer, 27 April 1936, in *Lights of Guidance*, p. 495.
18 Please note that, as stated in Acts 3:22, this prophecy applies equally to Jesus, for He too abode by the Divine Will: 'Jesus answered them, and said, My doctrine is not mine, but his that sent me' (John 7:16).
19 *Moachiok*, or 'from brothers of thee' more aptly applies to the Arabs who are believed to have descended from Ishmael, the first son of Abraham. The Jews trace their ancestry from Isaac, the younger son of Abraham, and are called the 'seed of Abraham' in the Bible (cf. Deut. 1:8; 30:19; 34:4; Hebr. 11:17).
20 Deut. 18:15.
21 *kamuk*: this clearly is not a literal likeness as there are no records of the physical appearance and characteristics of Moses or Muhammad. The 'likeness' describes the identity of the Divine Purpose, the record that they all spoke only as bidden by God, and the similar transforming influence of their teachings.
    N.B. 'like unto me' is a translation of the Hebrew word *kamoni* which is similar to the Arabic word *kama* (like unto) used in the Qur'án to describe the similarity between the reactions to the Revelations of Moses and Muhammad:
    Baqara, the Heifer, 2:108:
    Would ye question your Apostle as Moses was questioned of old? But whoever changeth from Faith to unbelief, hath strayed without doubt from the even way.

    أَمْ تُرِيدُونَ أَن تَسْأَلُوا رَسُولَكُمْ كَمَا سُئِلَ مُوسَىٰ مِن قَبْلُ وَمَن يَتَبَدَّلِ الْكُفْرَ بِالْإِيمَانِ فَقَدْ ضَلَّ سَوَاءَ السَّبِيلِ

    آیا می‌خواهید از پیامبر خود همان را بخواهید که قبلا از موسی خواسته شد و هر کس کفر را با ایمان عوض کند مسلما از راه درست گمراه شده است

22 Deut. 18:18.
23 John 1:19–22.
24 Tanakh: *Eloahm*, from *teman*, he-is-coming.
25 Hab. 3:3.
26 Gen. 17:20.
27 Deut. 33:1–2. An explanation of this verse as follows:
    This means, four appearances of God (Divine Visitations); the first refers to the time when God appeared to Moses in Mount Sinai; the second, to

503

Christ . . . ; the third, to Mohammed from Mount Paran; and the fourth in Baha'o'llah, when He, God, 'The Almighty,' came with ten thousand of His Saints ('Abdu'l-Karim Effendi, in *Star of the West*, vol. 3, no. 14 (23 November 1912), p. 11).

28   The fig is associated with Abraham, Moses and the children of Israel (Jer. 24:5); the olive with Christ (Matt. 24:3; Luke 21:37) and also with the followers of Moses (Rom. 11:170); Mount Sinai is where Moses witnessed the Burning Bush and received the Ten Commandments (Exod. 19:20); while 'the 'safe land' refers to Mecca. See *Tín* , the Fig, 95:1–4:

التِّينِ وَالزَّيْتُونِ
وَطُورِ سِينِينَ
وَهَذَا الْبَلَدِ الْأَمِينِ
لَقَدْ خَلَقْنَا الْإِنسَانَ فِي أَحْسَنِ تَقْوِيمٍ

قسم به انجیر و زیتون (یا: قسم به سرزمین شام و بیت المقدس)،
و سوگند به «طور سینین»،
و قسم به این شهر امن (مکه)،
که ما انسان را در بهترین صورت و نظام آفریدیم

29   Literally, the Mount of Figs, associated with Abraham, Moses and Judaism; and the Mount of Olives associated with Jesus.

30   Bahá'u'lláh, Súriy-i-Ra'ís, para. 6, in *The Summons of the Lord of Hosts*, p. 143. The statement has a two-fold implication: (a) Bahá'u'lláh's Revelation is a re-statement of past Dispensations; and (b) the minister's hostility towards Him is identical to the opposition to past Prophets.

31   Isa. 11:6–9. See also 'Abdu'l-Bahá's explanation in *Some Answered Questions*, ch. 12, pp. 62–6.

32   *An'ám*, the Cattle, 6:38:

وَمَا مِن دَابَّةٍ فِي الْأَرْضِ وَلَا طَائِرٍ يَطِيرُ بِجَنَاحَيْهِ إِلَّا أُمَمٌ أَمْثَالُكُم مَّا فَرَّطْنَا فِي الْكِتَابِ مِن شَيْءٍ ثُمَّ إِلَىٰ رَبِّهِمْ يُحْشَرُونَ

و هیچ جنبنده‌ای در زمین نیست و نه هیچ پرندهای که با دو بال خود پرواز می‌کند مگر آنکه آنها [نیز] گروه‌هایی مانند شما هستند ما هیچ چیزی را در کتاب [لوح محفوظ] فروگذار نکرده‌ایم سپس [همه] به سوی پروردگارشان محشور خواهند گردید

33   'Abdu'l-Bahá, *Paris Talks*, ch. 13, p. 39.

34   A letter written on behalf of Shoghi Effendi, 26 December 1941, explains that 'References in the Bible to "Mt. Paran" and "Paraclete" refer to Muhammad's Revelation. Deuteronomy 33.2; Genesis 21.21.; Numbers 12.16; Numbers 13.3.; Genesis 17.20 refers to the twelve Imams and in the Revelation of St. John, Chap. 11.; where it mentions two witnesses, it refers to Muhammad and 'Alí' (*Letters from the Guardian to Australia and New Zealand, 1923-1957*, p. 41).

The Paraclete (Greek *parakletos*) or 'advocate', 'intercessor', 'teacher', 'helper', 'comforter' predicted to come after Christ is believed by Christians to refer to the 'Holy Spirit' or the 'Holy Ghost', but it should be noted that the Holy Spirit was present before and during Jesus's Mission, and operates through individuals and God's Chosen Ones. 'Paraclete' is believed by some to be a corruption of the Greek word periclytos, 'widely famed', similar to the Arabic word 'Ahmad, the

Highly Praised One' – a derivative of the name of Muhammad.

In reality all three, Muhammad, the Báb and Bahá'u'lláh are 'the Spirit of Truth' and fit the definitions of Paraclete – they have not spoken of themselves and have comforted humanity in their 'times' of distress.

35   John 14:16-17.
36   John 16:7-8; 12-15.
37   John 14:25-6.
38   John 15:26.
39   Explanation provided by 'Abdu'l-Bahá, 'Commentary on the Twelfth Chapter of the Revelation of St. John', in *Some Answered Questions*, ch. 13, pp. 67-72. The verses quoted here are from Rev. 12: 1-6.
40   The bride referred to in Revelation 21:2: 'And I John saw the holy city, new Jerusalem, coming down from God out of heaven, prepared as a bride adorned for her husband'; 'This woman is that bride,' 'Abdu'l-Bahá explains, 'the Law of God that descended upon Muhammad' (*Some Answered Questions*, ch. 13, p. 68).
41   Represents 'the two nations which are under the shadow of that Law, the Persian and Ottoman kingdoms; for the emblem of Persia is the sun, and that of the Ottoman Empire is the crescent moon' (ibid).
42   'These twelve stars are the twelve Imáms, who were the promoters of the Law of Muhammad and the educators of the people, shining like stars in the heaven of guidance' (ibid).
43   'These signs are an allusion to the dynasty of the Umayyads who dominated the Muhammadan religion. Seven heads and seven crowns mean seven countries and dominions over which the Umayyads had power: they were the Roman dominion around Damascus; and the Persian, Arabian and Egyptian dominions, together with the dominion of Africa – that is to say, Tunis, Morocco and Algeria; the dominion of Andalusia, which is now Spain; and the dominion of the Turks of Transoxania . . . The ten horns mean the names of the Umayyad rulers – that is, without repetition, there were ten names of rulers, meaning ten names of commanders and chiefs – the first is Abú Sufyán and the last Marván – but several of them bear the same name. So there are two Mu'áviya, three Yazíd, two Valíd, and two Marván; but if the names were counted without repetition there would be ten' (ibid. pp. 69-70).
44   'The Umayyads, of whom the first was Abú Sufyán, Amír of Mecca and chief of the dynasty of the Umayyads, and the last was Marván, destroyed the third part of the holy and saintly people of the lineage of Muhammad . . . The Umayyads were always waiting to get possession of the Promised One, Who was to come from the line of Muhammad, to destroy and annihilate Him; for they much feared the appearance of the promised Manifestation, and they sought to kill any of Muhammad's descendants who might be highly esteemed '(ibid. p. 70).
45   'This great son is the promised Manifestation Who was born of the Law of God and reared in the bosom of the divine teachings. The iron rod is a symbol of power and might – it is not a sword – and means that with divine power and might He will shepherd all the nations of the earth. This son is the Báb' (ibid).
46   'The Arabian Peninsula became the abode and dwelling place, and the centre of the Law of God' (ibid. p. 71).
47   'In the terminology of the Holy Book [see Num. 14:34, 'each day for a year' and

also Ezek. 4:6] these twelve hundred and sixty days mean the twelve hundred and sixty years that the Law of God was set up in the wilderness of Arabia, the great desert: from it the Promised One has come . . . Consider how the prophecies correspond to one another. In the Apocalypse, the appearance of the Promised One is appointed after forty-two months [Rev. 13:5], and Daniel [12:7] expresses it as three times and a half, which is also forty-two months, which are twelve hundred and sixty days . . . The Báb appeared in the year 1260 of the Hejira of Muhammad, which is the beginning of the universal era reckoning of all Islám' (ibid).

48 Explanation provided by 'Abdu'l-Bahá, 'Commentary on the Eleventh Chapter of the Revelation of St. John', in *Some Answered Questions,* ch. 11, pp. 45-61. The verses quoted here are from Rev.11:1-12.

49 'This reed is a Perfect Man . . . when the interior of a reed is empty and free from all matter, it will produce beautiful melodies; and as the sound and melodies do not come from the reed, but from the flute player who blows upon it, so the sanctified heart of that blessed Being is free and emptied from all save God, pure and exempt from the attachments of all human conditions, and is the companion of the Divine Spirit. Whatever He utters is not from Himself, but from the real flute player, and it is a divine inspiration' ('Abdu'l-Bahá, *Some Answered Questions,* ch. 11, p. 45).

50 'compare and measure . . . that is to say, investigate . . . what conditions, perfections, behaviour and attributes they possess; and make yourself cognizant of the mysteries of those holy souls who dwell in the Holy of Holies in purity and sanctity' (ibid. p. 46).

51 'In the beginning of the seventh century after Christ, when Jerusalem was conquered, the Holy of Holies was outwardly preserved – that is to say, the house which Solomon built; but outside the Holy of Holies the outer court was taken and given to the Gentiles' (ibid).

52 'This prophesies the duration of the Dispensation of Islám when Jerusalem was trodden under foot, which means that it lost its glory – but the Holy of Holies was preserved, guarded and respected – until the year 1260 . . . a prophecy of the manifestation of the Báb, the 'Gate' of Bahá'u'lláh, which took place in the year 1260 of the Hejira of Muhammad, and as the period of twelve hundred and sixty years has expired, Jerusalem, the Holy City, is now beginning to become prosperous, populous and flourishing' (ibid).

53 'Muhammad the Messenger of God, and 'Alí, son of Abú Tálib. In the Qur'án [*Fat-ḥ*, the Victory, 48:8] it is said that God addressed Muhammad, the Messenger of God, saying: "We made You a Witness, a Herald of good news, and a Warner" . . . These two souls are likened to olive trees because at that time all lamps were lighted by olive oil. The meaning is two persons from whom that spirit of the wisdom of God, which is the cause of the illumination of the world, appears . . . the candlestick is the abode of light, and from it the light shines forth. In the same way, the light of guidance would shine and radiate from these illumined souls' (ibid. pp. 48-9).

54 'this beast means the Umayyads who attacked them from the pit of error, and who rose against the religion of Muhammad and against the reality of 'Alí – in other words, the love of God. It is said, "The beast made war against these two witnesses" – that is to say, a spiritual war, meaning that the beast would act in

entire opposition to the teachings, customs and institutions of these two witnesses, to such an extent that the virtues and perfections which were diffused by the power of those two witnesses among the peoples and tribes would be entirely dispelled, and the animal nature and carnal desires would conquer. Therefore, this beast making war against them would gain the victory – meaning that the darkness of error coming from this beast was to have ascendency over the horizons of the world, and kill those two witnesses – in other words, that it would destroy the spiritual life which they spread abroad in the midst of the nation, and entirely remove the divine laws and teachings, treading under foot the Religion of God. Nothing would thereafter remain but a lifeless body without spirit' (ibid. p. 51).

55 '"Their bodies" means the Religion of God, and "the street" means in public view. The meaning of "Sodom and Egypt," the place "where also our Lord was crucified," is this region of Syria, and especially Jerusalem, where the Umayyads then had their dominions; and it was here that the Religion of God and the divine teachings first disappeared, and a body without spirit remained. "Their bodies" represents the Religion of God, which remained like a dead body without spirit' (ibid. p. 52).

56 'As it was before explained, in the terminology of the Holy Books three days and a half signify three years and a half, and three years and a half are forty and two months, and forty and two months twelve hundred and sixty days; and as each day by the text of the Holy Book signifies one year, the meaning is that for twelve hundred and sixty years, which is the cycle of the Qur'án, the nations, tribes and peoples . . . would make a spectacle of the Religion of God: though they would not act in accordance with it, still, they would not suffer their bodies – meaning the Religion of God – to be put in the grave. That is to say, that in appearance they would cling to the Religion of God, and not allow it to completely disappear from their midst . . . while outwardly preserving its name and remembrance . . . but the fundamental principles for the Religion of God . . . have disappeared . . . and the darkness of tyranny, oppression, satanic passions and desires has become victorious. The body of the Law of God, like a corpse, has been exposed to public view for twelve hundred and sixty days, each day being counted as a year, and this period is the cycle of Muhammad.

'The people forfeited all that these two persons had established, which was the foundation of the Law of God, and destroyed the virtues of the world of humanity, which are the divine gifts and the spirit of this religion, to such a degree that truthfulness, justice, love, union, purity, sanctity, detachment and all the divine qualities departed from among them . . . only prayers and fasting persisted . . .' (ibid. pp. 52–3).

57 1260 AH/1844 AD: 'these divine teachings, heavenly virtues, perfections and spiritual bounties were again renewed . . .' (ibid. p. 54).

58 'meaning that from the invisible heaven they heard the voice of God, saying: You have performed all that was proper and fitting in delivering the teachings and glad tidings; you have given My message to the people and raised the call of God, and have accomplished your duty . . . many of their enemies, after witnessing their martyrdom realized the sublimity of their station and the exaltation of their virtue, and testified to their greatness and perfection' (ibid. p. 55).

59 ibid. p. 47.

60 ibid.
61 Bahá'u'lláh, *The Seven Valleys and the Four Valleys*, p. 2.
62 I Cor. 4:5.
63 Isa. 12:4.
64 'Realistically speaking, the only people who could have found resonance in Muhammad's call for one unseen God are the Jews, believing in prophethood. Evidently, Muhammad's invitation to Yathrib came from a group of eminent Jews, and not from a few idolaters. Interestingly, various Jewish anecdotes still tell us that Muhammad's arrival in 622 C.E. was announced exuberantly from the rooftop of a Jewish dweller of Yathrib, saying: "here comes the Prophet". For about five years most Jewish people of Yathrib took Muhammad as their long awaited Messiah . . . Within a short while, their acceptance of Muhammad as their long awaited Prophet got symbolised in the name of the city. The powerful Jewish tribes, controlling the affairs of Yathrib, renamed the city as Medina-tun Nabi (City of the Prophet). Eventually, the name got shortened as Medina' (Mesbah Uddin, 'Prophet Muhammad was Revered as the Jewish Messiah in Medina', in *MMN International*, 3 March 2008).
65 Ṣaff, Battle Array, 61:6:

وَإِذْ قَالَ عِيسَى ابْنُ مَرْيَمَ يَا بَنِي إِسْرَائِيلَ إِنِّي رَسُولُ اللَّهِ إِلَيْكُم مُّصَدِّقًا لِّمَا بَيْنَ يَدَيَّ مِنَ التَّوْرَاةِ وَمُبَشِّرًا بِرَسُولٍ يَأْتِي مِن بَعْدِي اسْمُهُ أَحْمَدُ فَلَمَّا جَاءَهُم بِالْبَيِّنَاتِ قَالُوا هَذَا سِحْرٌ مُّبِينٌ

و هنگامی را که عیسی پسر مریم گفت ای فرزندان اسرائیل من فرستاده خدا به سوی شما هستم تورات را که پیش از من بوده تصدیق می‌کنم و به فرستاده‌ای که پس از من می‌آید و نام او احمد است بشارتگرم پس وقتی برای آنان دلایل روشن آورد گفتند این سحری آشکار است

66 The Báb, Dalá'il-i-Sab'ih, in *Selections from the Writings of the Báb*, p. 117.

3 Islam: A Testimony of Direct Divine Intervention in Human Affairs

1 Bahá'u'lláh, *Gleanings from the Writings of Bahá'u'lláh*, XX, p. 49.
2 Bahá'u'lláh, Súriy-i-Haykal, in *The Summons of the Lord of Hosts*, p. 101.
3 Bahá'u'lláh, *Kitáb-i-Íqán*, para. 231, p. 210.
4 A'ráf, the Heights, 7:157–8:

الَّذِينَ يَتَّبِعُونَ الرَّسُولَ النَّبِيَّ الْأُمِّيَّ الَّذِي يَجِدُونَهُ مَكْتُوبًا عِندَهُمْ فِي التَّوْرَاةِ وَالْإِنجِيلِ يَأْمُرُهُم بِالْمَعْرُوفِ وَيَنْهَاهُمْ عَنِ الْمُنكَرِ وَيُحِلُّ لَهُمُ الطَّيِّبَاتِ وَيُحَرِّمُ عَلَيْهِمُ الْخَبَائِثَ وَيَضَعُ عَنْهُمْ إِصْرَهُمْ وَالْأَغْلَالَ الَّتِي كَانَتْ عَلَيْهِمْ فَالَّذِينَ آمَنُوا بِهِ وَعَزَّرُوهُ وَنَصَرُوهُ وَاتَّبَعُوا النُّورَ الَّذِي أُنزِلَ مَعَهُ أُولَٰئِكَ هُمُ الْمُفْلِحُونَ قُلْ يَا أَيُّهَا النَّاسُ إِنِّي رَسُولُ اللَّهِ إِلَيْكُمْ جَمِيعًا الَّذِي لَهُ مُلْكُ السَّمَاوَاتِ وَالْأَرْضِ لَا إِلَٰهَ إِلَّا هُوَ يُحْيِي وَيُمِيتُ فَآمِنُوا بِاللَّهِ وَرَسُولِهِ النَّبِيِّ الْأُمِّيِّ الَّذِي يُؤْمِنُ بِاللَّهِ وَكَلِمَاتِهِ وَاتَّبِعُوهُ لَعَلَّكُمْ تَهْتَدُونَ

همانان که از این فرستاده پیامبر درس نخوانده که [نام] او را نزد خود در تورات و انجیل نوشته می‌یابند پیروی می‌کنند [همان پیامبری که] آنان را به کار پسندیده فرمان می‌دهد و از کار ناپسند باز می‌دارد و برای آنان چیزهای پاکیزه را حلال و چیزهای ناپاک را بر ایشان حرام می‌گرداند و از [دوش] آنان قید و بندهایی را که بر ایشان بوده است برمی‌دارد پس کسانی که به او ایمان آوردند و بزرگش داشتند و یاریش کردند و نوری را که با او نازل شده است پیروی کردند آنان همان رستگارانند

بگو ای مردم من پیامبر خدا به سوی همه شما هستم همان [خدایی] که فرمانروایی آسمانها و زمین از آن اوست هیچ معبودی جز او نیست که زنده می‌کند و می‌میراند پس به خدا و فرستاده او که پیامبر درس‌نخوانده‌ای است که به خدا و کلمات او ایمان دارد بگروید و او را پیروی کنید امید که هدایت‌شوید

5 Shoghi Effendi, *The World Order of Bahá'u'lláh*, p. 25.

NOTES AND REFERENCES

6 Shoghi Effendi, *The Advent of Divine Justice*, pp. 14-15.
7 Bahá'u'lláh, *Gleanings from the Writings of Bahá'u'lláh*, XCIX, p. 200.
8 'Abdu'l-Bahá, *The Promulgation of Universal Peace*, p. 367-8.
9 'Abdu'l-Bahá, *Paris Talks*, ch. 13, p. 39.
10 Isa. 11:6-9.
11 'Abdu'l-Bahá, *The Secret of Divine Civilization*, pp. 86-90.
12 Letter written on behalf of Shoghi Effendi to an individual believer, 27 April 1936, in *Lights of Guidance*, no. 1664.
13 Shoghi Effendi, *The Promised Day is Come*, p. 120.
14 During early Islam, Jews and Christians as people of the Book (*dhimmis*) enjoyed great privileges and their communities prospered, though they did not enjoy equal status with Muslims. There was no legislation or social barrier preventing them from conducting commercial activities. Many Jews migrated to areas newly conquered by Muslims and established communities there. This included the Iberian Peninsula under Muslim rule. The Jews in Spain were able to make great advances in mathematics, astronomy, philosophy, chemistry and philology. In contrast, the expulsion of Muslims from Spain, almost immediately followed by the expulsion of the Jews from Spain in 1492 (the Alhambra Decree), took place largely at the instigation of the Spanish Inquisition. The edict was not formally revoked until 1968 following the Second Vatican Council.
15 There are many sources of information concerning the scientific discoveries during the golden age of Islam. The examples here are excerpted and adapted from Ajram, 'Setting the Record Straight: What is Taught in the West About Science and What Should be Taught', Appendix B in his book, *The Miracle of Islamic Science*, p. 200; H. M. Balyuzi, *Muḥammad and the Course of Islám*; and Aftab, 'How Islam Influenced Science'.
16 'Abdu'l-Bahá, *Some Answered Questions*, ch. 7, pp. 23-4.

4 The Challenge and Failure of Islamic Fundamentalism and the Impotence of Liberal Secular Islam

1 Bahá'u'lláh, *Gleanings from the Writings of Bahá'u'lláh*, CXXXII, p. 288.
2 Words spoken to Edward G. Browne, from his pen portrait of Bahá'u'lláh, quoted in Esslemont, *Bahá'u'lláh and the New Era*, pp. 39-40; and in *The Compilation of Compilations*, vol. II, p. 157.
3 '*Salaf*' means ancestors; *Salafi* Islam is the religion of ancestral Islam, based strictly on the Qur'án, oral traditions and early history (*hadith*), and the biographies of Muhammad (*sira*).
4 '*Shar'ia*' or Sharia law is considered by many Muslims to be Divine law. When after the passing of Prophet Muhammad Islam united the tribes of the Arabian peninsula, the Sharia evolved to replace pre-Islamic tribal laws by a new common code of laws governing personal behaviour. Sharia law is based primarily on the teachings of the Qur'án and descriptions of the practices of Muhammad (*sunnah*).

The Sharia in Sunni Islam also depends on the consensus (*ijmá*) of the companions of Muhammad such a as Abu-Bakr and Islamic scholars and jurists (*ulemá*). In situations where no concrete rule exists in the sources, law scholars use *qiyas* – various forms of reasoning, including analogy, to derive law from the essence of divine principles and preceding rulings.

In Shí'ih Islam the sources of law (*usul al-fiqh*) are the Qur'án, anecdotes of Muhammad's practices and those of the twelve Imams, and the intellect (*'aql*). The practices called Sharia today, however, also have roots in comparative law and local customs (*urf*).

5   Also referred to in the West as '*salafi* Muslims', 'Islamic extremists', '*Jihádists*' or holy warriors, and 'radical Muslims'.

6   In France, the *Loi interdisant la dissimulation du visage dans l'espace public* (Act prohibiting concealment of the face in public space) was passed by the Senate on 14 September 2010 and came into force in April 2011, resulting in the ban on the wearing of face-covering headgear, including masks, helmets, balaclava, the *niqab* or other veils covering the face in public places such as the street, shops, museums, public transportation and parks. The ban also applies to the *burqa*, a full-body covering, if it covers the face. Veils such as the chador, scarves and other headwear that do not cover the face are not affected by this law and can be worn. The law applies to all citizens, including men and non-Muslims except under specified circumstances. A poll carried out by Pew Research Center leading up to the vote indicated that 80% of French voters supported the ban.

The wearing of all conspicuous religious symbols in public schools was previously banned in France in 2004 by a different law, the law on secularity and conspicuous religious symbols in schools. This affected the wearing of Islamic veils and headscarves in schools, as well as turbans and other distinctive items of dress.

In 2010, the Belgian lower house of parliament approved a bill to ban facial coverings, but this was not voted into law as the Belgian Government fell before the Senate could vote on it. In 2010, when the French law was being debated, partial bans were being discussed in the Netherlands and Spain; bans had been announced locally in Italy but were later declared unconstitutional, leading to a national law being proposed; and public debate on the issue was starting in Austria, while Germany, the United Kingdom and Switzerland did not consider legislation, although in the United Kingdom directives had been issued leaving the issue to the discretion of school directors and magistrates. In that country the debate still rages as to whether it is permissible for the face to be covered in a court of law or in school; lawyers and teachers argue that it is necessary to see the face of the witness or the student.

Many Muslims have stated that the face-covering veil is actually not Islamic and is not encouraged by the Qur'án. Instead, they say, it is part of Muslim cultural heritage.

7   For example, a headline in the *EU Times* of 26 September 2010 screamed: 'Angela Merkel: Germany will become Islamic State!' Of course, the German Chancellor had said nothing of the kind, but the article did reveal the extent of the transformation in European societies through the increasing number of Muslim residents and citizens in these countries:

> Chancellor Angela Merkel said that Germans have failed to grasp how Muslim immigration has transformed their country and will have to come to terms with more mosques than churches throughout the countryside, according to the *Frankfurter Allgemeine Zeitung* daily.

'Our country continues to change, and integration is also the task for society to deal with immigrants,' Ms. Merkel told the daily newspaper. 'For years we've been deceiving ourselves about this. Mosques, for example, are going to be a more prominent part of our cities than they were before.'

Germany, with a population of 4-5 million Muslims, has been divided in recent weeks by a debate over remarks by the Bundesbank's Thilo Sarrazin, who argued Turkish and Arab immigrants were failing to integrate and were swamping Germany with a higher birth rate.

The Chancellor's remarks represent the first official acknowledgment that Germany, like other European countries, is destined to become a stronghold of Islam.

In France 30% of children age 20 years and below are Muslims. The ratio in Paris and Marseilles has soared to 45%. In southern France there are more mosques than churches.

The situation within the United Kingdom is not much different. In last 30 years, the Muslim population there has climbed from 82,000 to 2.5 millions. Presently, there are over 1,000 mosques

In Belgium, 50% of newborns are Muslims and reportedly its Islamic population hovers around 25%. A similar statistic holds true for The Netherlands.

It's the same story in Russia where one in five inhabitants are Muslim . . .

8 For instance, the pronouncements of Anjem Choudary, a radical British Muslim. In April 2010 Erick Stakelbeck, CBN News Correspondent, travelled to London to interview Choudary and reported him as saying ' "You can't say that Islam is a religion of peace . . . There is a place for violence in Islam. There is a place for jihad in Islam." While Islamic radicals in the United States usually prefer to speak in more moderate tones while in public, masking their true agenda, Choudary has no such inhibitions.'

More recently, Choudary was in the news again:

The day after two young British converts to Islam, Michael Adebolajo and Michael Adebowale, were convicted of the horrific murder of the off-duty soldier Lee Rigby in a Woolwich street, Radio 4's Today programme ran an extensive interview with the extremist preacher Anjem Choudary, a spokesman for the minority Islamist group Islam4UK. Mr Choudary has been around for a while, and never in a style conducive to happy community relations: previously, he was the spokesman for Al-Muhajiroun before that organisation was banned by the British government.

Choudary has a way of popping up in the wake of horrific events, and what followed came as little surprise. He has learnt to say unacceptable things in a reasonable tone of voice, which spins him out more airtime than his views merit. In this case, what emerged from the discussion was that Choudary does not believe in democracy since 'sovereignty belongs to God'. He was not willing to condemn the murderers. And he calls, yet again, for the adoption of Sharia across the United Kingdom.

There is a nasty combination of victimhood, threat and doublespeak in his argument. He said he was 'very proud' of Adebolajo as a Muslim, but insisted, 'I can't control what the youth do,' as though we were talking of wayward rascals who had broken a window instead of almost beheading a man in broad daylight. I don't suppose he can fully control it, but he energetically provides the fuel of justification (both killers were former regulars at al-Muhijaroun meetings).

If I were a moderate British Muslim, my heart would plummet every time Choudary came on the television or radio. He speaks for a minority of British Muslims, yet likes to bandy the word 'Muslim' around as though he owns it. He deliberately enrages non-Muslims, since he seeks the oxygen – not only of publicity – but of conflict. And after Choudary has been rattling on, someone else . . . will inevitably appear to say that British Muslims really need to do and say more to condemn this kind of extremism.

Well, I've no doubt some do need to speak out more forcefully, and actively to resist the encroachment of extremism in their places of worship. Yet numerous British Muslims already strongly condemn Islamist violence. The Muslim Council of Britain, for example, called the murder of Lee Rigby 'truly a barbaric act' (for this, they are dismissed by Choudary as 'paid-up lackeys of the government'). Dr Taj Hargey, the imam of the Oxford Islamic Congregation, has persistently spoken out against 'Muslim McCarthyism' in Britain, including any idea that the veil is a religious necessity for women. In October, a number of prominent anti-extremist British Muslims – the journalist and film-maker Mohammed Ansar, the researcher Usama Hasan and the imam and broadcaster Ajmal Masroor – and their families were offered police protection after they were named and criticised in a video made by al-Shabaab, the group that carried out the Nairobi mall massacre.

It's a reminder that extremism is frightening, just as it was in 1930s Germany: British Muslims who openly oppose it already face pressure of the kind that the rest of us would prefer not to imagine. Yet part of the trouble is that the wider society, which should be uniting to offer such people stalwart support, is all over the place.

The media has a dirty little secret, for a start: it is attracted to extremists. The hot-heads get airtime because they are eager to appear, and they carry with them the forbidden frisson of street violence that broadcasters find exciting . . . And yet the more sustained exposure the likes of Choudary receive, the more – in some insidious way – they are treated as what they started out pretending to be: official representatives of true 'Muslim' thinking.

Instead of publicly uniting around agreed basic liberal values, along with those British Muslims who are also deeply grateful for them, British institutions have proved squelchy in the face of extremist demands. After brief resistance, Birmingham Metropolitan College permitted women earlier this year to wear full veils on campus (covering one's face, for any reason, had previously been banned). Universities UK recently gave in to the principle that speakers could demand sex segregation at their lectures, before it finally reversed the decision under public pressure.

NOTES AND REFERENCES

In response to the demands of Islamists, Britain seems to swing wildly between caving in to extremism or discussing Muslims as if they all hold similar views. Neither response is of any use, and nor is the media's penchant for Choudary. Increasingly, Islamist extremism is probing wider British values, and hoping to find mush.

To adapt that popular wartime slogan, we should keep calm, but flatly refuse to let it carry on. (Jenny McCartney, *The Telegraph online*, 21 December 2013)

9   Isi Leiber, 'Candidly speaking: Where are the voices of moderate Islam?' in *Jerusalem Post*, 2 February 2011. See ileibler@netvision.net.il.
10 For example, on Monday 1 December 2014 *The Independent* carried the following news story: 'Pope Francis has called on Muslim leaders, whether political, religious or academic, to issue a global condemnation of terrorism to help break the stereotype that Islam and violence are innately linked.'
11 See for example the article 'A warning for women of the Arab Spring' by the well-known lawyer Shirin Ebádi, in *Wall Street Journal*, 14 March 2012:

I hope that in the countries where people have risen against dictatorships, they will reflect on and learn from what happened to us in Iran.

I do not agree with the phrase 'Arab Spring'. The overthrow of dictatorships is not sufficient in itself. Only when repressive governments are replaced by democracies can we consider the popular uprisings in the Middle East to be a meaningful 'spring'.

Since women make up half of the region's population, any democratic developments must improve the social and legal status of women in the Arab world. It appears the Tunisian society has strong civil institutions, and there is much hope that democracy can take hold there. But in Egypt, many political actors are talking about returning to Islamic law, which could result in a regression of rights for women and girls similar to what we experienced in Iran in 1979.

There are interpretations of Shar'ia law that allow one to be a Muslim and enjoy equal gender rights – rights that we can exercise while participating in a genuinely democratic political system. Shar'ia law and women's rights do not have to be mutually exclusive. Although the 1979 revolution in Iran is often called an Islamic revolution, it can actually be said to be a revolution of men against women. Before the revolution, women's rights were recognized to some extent. But the revolution led to the enactment of numerous discriminatory laws against women.

After the revolution – even before drafting a new constitution or establishing parliament – the revolutionary councils changed the laws. When I first read the Islamic Penal Code instituted after the revolution, I couldn't believe my eyes. The drafters of this document had effectively taken us back 1,400 years.

Before the revolution, I was a presiding judge. When the revolution broke out, I was initially on the side of the revolutionaries and I believed in their cause. I was shocked when the revolutionaries decided that women could no longer hold my position. I was demoted to secretary – while many of my male colleagues who were not as professionally qualified were appointed judges.

In the 'green movement' protests after June 2009's disputed presidential elections, the world witnessed how many Iranian women were on the streets, and how strong our feminist movement is. More than 65% of university students are women, many university professors are women, and women are present in all important and sensitive social positions.

However, the law that is being enforced in Iran today does not consider women to be full human beings. Instead, it ascribes to women a value half that of a man. The testimony of two women in court equals the testimony of one man, for example. A man can marry four wives and can divorce his wife at will, but initiating divorce can be very difficult for a woman. A married woman even needs her husband's written consent to travel.

These discriminatory and misogynistic laws are not Islamic and cannot be found in the Quran. Iranian women from all walks of life oppose these laws – which is one reason why women are in the front lines of every protest.

Many Iranian religious authorities are against these laws. Yet the fundamentalists in power, because they belong to a patriarchal culture, insist on enforcing them. Iranian women are doubly oppressed, both by discriminatory laws and by unjust traditions…

12 *Baqara*, the Heifer, 2:28:

كَيْفَ تَكْفُرُونَ بِاللَّهِ وَكُنتُمْ أَمْوَاتًا فَأَحْيَاكُمْ ثُمَّ يُمِيتُكُمْ ثُمَّ يُحْيِيكُمْ ثُمَّ إِلَيْهِ تُرْجَعُونَ

چگونه خدا را منکرید با آنکه مردگانی بودید و شما را زنده کرد باز شما را می میراند [و] باز زنده می‌کند [و] آنگاه به سوی او بازگردانده می‌شوید

5 Religious Fanaticism and Intolerance

1 'Abdu'l-Bahá, *Paris Talks*, no. 40, pp. 132–3.
2 Shoghi Effendi, 'The Unfoldment of World Civilization', in *The World Order of Bahá'u'lláh*, pp. 197–8.
3 'Abdu'l-Bahá, *The Promulgation of Universal Peace*, p. 266.
4 The Universal House of Justice, *The Promise of World Peace*, p. 5.
5 'Abdu'l-Bahá, *Paris Talks*, no. 13, p. 37.
6 *Fátiha*, the Opening Chapter, 1:1:

بِسْمِ اللَّهِ الرَّحْمَنِ الرَّحِيمِ

به نام خداوند بخشنده و مهربان

7 *Baní Isrá-íl*, the Children of Israel, 17:37:

وَلاَ تَمْشِ فِي الأَرْضِ مَرَحًا إِنَّكَ لَن تَخْرِقَ الأَرْضَ وَلَن تَبْلُغَ الْجِبَالَ طُولًا

و در [روی] زمین به نخوت گام برمدار چرا که هرگز زمین را نمی‌توانی شکافت و در بلندی به کوهها نمی‌توانی رسید

NOTES AND REFERENCES

8 *Luqmán* (the Wise), 31:17-19:

يَا بُنَىَّ أَقِمِ الصَّلَاةَ وَأْمُرْ بِالْمَعْرُوفِ وَانْهَ عَنِ الْمُنْكَرِ وَاصْبِرْ عَلَى مَا أَصَابَكَ إِنَّ ذَلِكَ مِنْ عَزْمِ الْأُمُورِ وَلَا تُصَعِّرْ خَدَّكَ لِلنَّاسِ وَلَا تَمْشِ فِي الْأَرْضِ مَرَحًا إِنَّ اللَّهَ لَا يُحِبُّ كُلَّ مُخْتَالٍ فَخُورٍ وَاقْصِدْ فِي مَشْيِكَ وَاغْضُضْ مِنْ صَوْتِكَ إِنَّ أَنْكَرَ الْأَصْوَاتِ لَصَوْتُ الْحَمِيرِ

پسرم نماز را بر پا دار، و امر به معروف و نهى از منكر كن، و در برابر مصائبى كه به تو مى‌رسد با استقامت و شكيبا باش كه اين از كارهاى مهم است!

و رويت را از مردم [به تكبر] برمگردان و در زمين خرامان راه مرو، چرا كه خداوند ، هيچ متكبر فخرفروشى را دوست ندارد

[پسرم!] در راه رفتن اعتدال را رعايت كن، از صداى خود بكاه (و هرگز فرياد مزن) كه زشتترين صداها صداى خران است.

9   Prov. 20:3.
10 Lev. 19:18.
11 Matt. 5:9.
12 I Pet. 3:11.
13 Rom. 12:18.
14 Heb. 12:14.
15 Gal. 5:22.
16 James 3:18.
17 Rom. 12:17.
18 Rom. 14:19.
19 Luke 2:14.
20 Rom. 15:33.
21 I Thess. 5:15.
22 I Pet. 3:9.
23 Hag. 2:9.
24 Isa. 2:4.
25 *Nisáa*, the Women, 4:40:

إِنَّ اللَّهَ لَا يَظْلِمُ مِثْقَالَ ذَرَّةٍ وَإِنْ تَكُ حَسَنَةً يُضَاعِفْهَا وَيُؤْتِ مِنْ لَدُنْهُ أَجْرًا عَظِيمًا

در حقيقت خدا همـوزن ذره‌اى ستم نمى‌كند و اگر [آن ذره كار] نيكى باشد دو چندانش مى‌كند و از نزد خويش پاداشى بزرگ مى‌بخشد

26 *Naḥl*, Bees, 16:90:

إِنَّ اللَّهَ يَأْمُرُ بِالْعَدْلِ وَالْإِحْسَانِ وَإِيتَاءِ ذِي الْقُرْبَى وَيَنْهَى عَنِ الْفَحْشَاءِ وَالْمُنْكَرِ وَالْبَغْيِ يَعِظُكُمْ لَعَلَّكُمْ تَذَكَّرُونَ

در حقيقت خدا به دادگرى و نيكوكارى و بخشش به خويشاوندان فرمان مى‌دهد و از كار زشت و ناپسند و ستم باز مى‌دارد به شما اندرز مى‌دهد باشد كه پند گيريد

27 *An'ám*, Cattle, 6:115:

وَتَمَّتْ كَلِمَتُ رَبِّكَ صِدْقًا وَعَدْلًا لَا مُبَدِّلَ لِكَلِمَاتِهِ وَهُوَ السَّمِيعُ الْعَلِيمُ

و كلام پروردگار تو، با صدق و عدل، به حد تمام رسيد؛ هيچ كس نمى‌تواند كلمات او را دگرگون سازد؛ و او شنونده داناست

515

28 *Ḥá-Mím*, or *Fuṣṣilat*, 41:46:

مَنْ عَمِلَ صَالِحًا فَلِنَفْسِهِ وَمَنْ أَسَاءَ فَعَلَيْهَا وَمَا رَبُّكَ بِظَلَّامٍ لِّلْعَبِيدِ

هر که کار شایسته کند به سود خود اوست و هر که بدی کند به زیان خود است و پروردگار تو به بندگان [خود] ستمکار نیست

29 *Má'ida*, the Table Spread, 5:8:

يَا أَيُّهَا الَّذِينَ آمَنُواْ كُونُواْ قَوَّامِينَ لِلّهِ شُهَدَاءَ بِالْقِسْطِ وَلاَ يَجْرِمَنَّكُمْ شَنَآنُ قَوْمٍ عَلَى أَلاَّ تَعْدِلُواْ اعْدِلُواْ هُوَ أَقْرَبُ لِلتَّقْوَى وَاتَّقُواْ اللّهَ إِنَّ اللّهَ خَبِيرٌ بِمَا تَعْمَلُونَ

ای کسانی که ایمان آورده‌اید برای خدا به داد برخیزید [و] به عدالت شهادت دهید و البته نباید دشمنی گروهی شما را بر آن دارد که عدالت نکنید عدالت کنید که آن به تقوا نزدیکتر است و از خدا پروا دارید که خدا به آنچه انجام می‌دهید آگاه است

30 *Baqara*, the Heifer, 2:163:

وَإِلَهُكُمْ إِلَهٌ وَاحِدٌ لاَّ إِلَهَ إِلاَّ هُوَ الرَّحْمَنُ الرَّحِيمُ

و معبود شما معبود یگانه‌ای است که جز او هیچ معبودی نیست [و اوست] بخشایشگر مهربان

31 *Núr*, Light, 24:35:

اللَّهُ نُورُ السَّمَاوَاتِ وَالْأَرْضِ مَثَلُ نُورِهِ كَمِشْكَاةٍ فِيهَا مِصْبَاحٌ الْمِصْبَاحُ فِي زُجَاجَةٍ الزُّجَاجَةُ كَأَنَّهَا كَوْكَبٌ دُرِّيٌّ يُوقَدُ مِن شَجَرَةٍ مُّبَارَكَةٍ زَيْتُونِةٍ لَّا شَرْقِيَّةٍ وَلَا غَرْبِيَّةٍ يَكَادُ زَيْتُهَا يُضِيءُ وَلَوْ لَمْ تَمْسَسْهُ نَارٌ نُّورٌ عَلَى نُورٍ يَهْدِي اللَّهُ لِنُورِهِ مَن يَشَاءُ وَيَضْرِبُ اللَّهُ الْأَمْثَالَ لِلنَّاسِ وَاللَّهُ بِكُلِّ شَيْءٍ عَلِيمٌ

خدا نور آسمانها و زمین است مثل نور او چون چراغدانی است که در آن چراغی و آن چراغ در شیشه‌ای است آن شیشه گویی اختری درخشان است که از درخت خجسته زیتونی که نه شرقی است و نه غربی افروخته می‌شود نزدیک است که روغنش هر چند بدان آتشی نرسیده باشد روشنی بخشد روشنی بر روی روشنی است خدا هر که را بخواهد با نور خویش هدایت می‌کند و این مثلها را خدا برای مردم می‌زند و خدا به هر چیزی داناست

32 *Baqara*, the Heifer, 2:257:

اللّهُ وَلِيُّ الَّذِينَ آمَنُواْ يُخْرِجُهُم مِّنَ الظُّلُمَاتِ إِلَى النُّورِ وَالَّذِينَ كَفَرُواْ أَوْلِيَآؤُهُمُ الطَّاغُوتُ يُخْرِجُونَهُم مِّنَ النُّورِ إِلَى الظُّلُمَاتِ أُوْلَئِكَ أَصْحَابُ النَّارِ هُمْ فِيهَا خَالِدُونَ

خداوند، ولی و سرپرست کسانی است که ایمان آورده‌اند؛ آنها را از ظلمتها به سوی نور بیرون می‌برد. (اما) کسانی که کافر شدند، اولیای آنها طاغوتها هستند؛ که آنها را از نور، به سوی ظلمتها بیرون می‌برند؛ آنها اهل آتشند و همیشه در آن خواهند ماند.

33 Gen. 1:3.
34 I John 1:5.
35 Deut. 6:4, 5.
36 I Tim. 2:5.
37 Bahá'u'lláh, *Kitáb-i-Íqán*, para. 162, pp. 153–4.

38 *Baqara*, the Heifer, 2:113:

وَقَالَتِ الْيَهُودُ لَيْسَتِ النَّصَارَى عَلَىٰ شَيْءٍ وَقَالَتِ النَّصَارَى لَيْسَتِ الْيَهُودُ عَلَىٰ شَيْءٍ وَهُمْ يَتْلُونَ الْكِتَابَ كَذَٰلِكَ قَالَ الَّذِينَ لاَ يَعْلَمُونَ مِثْلَ قَوْلِهِمْ فَاللَّهُ يَحْكُمُ بَيْنَهُمْ يَوْمَ الْقِيَامَةِ فِيمَا كَانُوا فِيهِ يَخْتَلِفُونَ

و یهودیان گفتند : مسیحیان بر چیزی نیستند (آیینشان بی پایه و اساس است) و مسیحیان گفتند : یهودیان بر چیزی نیستند . این در حالی است که هر دو گروه کتاب آسمانی خود را می خوانند ، و می دانند که به حکم کتابشان این داوری صحیح نیست . مشرکان هم که دانشی ندارند مانند سخن اهل کتاب را بر زبان می آورند و می گویند : یهودیان و مسیحیان بر چیزی نیستند . پس خداوند روز قیامت میان آنان درباره آنچه بر سرش اختلاف کرده اند داوری خواهد کرد .

39 *Ál-i-'Imrán*, the Family of 'Imrán, 3:83–4:

أَفَغَيْرَ دِينِ اللَّهِ يَبْغُونَ وَلَهُ أَسْلَمَ مَن فِي السَّمَاوَاتِ وَالْأَرْضِ طَوْعًا وَكَرْهًا وَإِلَيْهِ يُرْجَعُونَ
قُلْ آمَنَّا بِاللَّهِ وَمَا أُنزِلَ عَلَيْنَا وَمَا أُنزِلَ عَلَىٰ إِبْرَاهِيمَ وَإِسْمَاعِيلَ وَإِسْحَاقَ وَيَعْقُوبَ وَالْأَسْبَاطِ وَمَا أُوتِيَ مُوسَىٰ وَعِيسَىٰ وَالنَّبِيُّونَ مِن رَّبِّهِمْ لاَ نُفَرِّقُ بَيْنَ أَحَدٍ مِّنْهُمْ وَنَحْنُ لَهُ مُسْلِمُونَ

آیا جز دین خدا را میجویند با آنکه هر که در آسمانها و زمین استخواه و ناخواه سر به فرمان او نهاده است و به سوی او بازگردانیده میشوید
بگو به خدا و آنچه بر ما نازل شده و آنچه بر ابراهیم و اسماعیل و اسحاق و یعقوب و اسباط نازل گردیده و آنچه به موسی و عیسی و انبیای [دیگر] از جانب پروردگارشان داده شده گرویدیم و میان هیچ یک از آنان فرق نمیگذاریم و ما او را فرمانبرداریم .

40 John 13:35.

41 *Qaṣaṣ*, the Narration, 28:52–3:

الَّذِينَ آتَيْنَاهُمُ الْكِتَابَ مِن قَبْلِهِ هُم بِهِ يُؤْمِنُونَ
وَإِذَا يُتْلَىٰ عَلَيْهِمْ قَالُوا آمَنَّا بِهِ إِنَّهُ الْحَقُّ مِن رَّبِّنَا إِنَّا كُنَّا مِن قَبْلِهِ مُسْلِمِينَ

کسانی که قبلا کتاب آسمانی به آنها دادهایم به آن (قرآن) ایمان میآورند .
و هنگامی که بر آنها خوانده میشود میگویند: به آن ایمان آوردیم، اینها همه حق است، و از سوی پروردگار ماست، ما قبل از این هم مسلمان بودیم .

42 *Yúnus*, Jonah, 10:71–2:

وَاتْلُ عَلَيْهِمْ نَبَأَ نُوحٍ إِذْ قَالَ لِقَوْمِهِ يَا قَوْمِ إِن كَانَ كَبُرَ عَلَيْكُم مَّقَامِي وَتَذْكِيرِي بِآيَاتِ اللَّهِ فَعَلَى اللَّهِ تَوَكَّلْتُ فَأَجْمِعُوا أَمْرَكُمْ وَشُرَكَاءَكُمْ ثُمَّ لاَ يَكُنْ أَمْرُكُمْ عَلَيْكُمْ غُمَّةً ثُمَّ اقْضُوا إِلَيَّ وَلاَ تُنظِرُونِ
فَإِن تَوَلَّيْتُمْ فَمَا سَأَلْتُكُم مِّنْ أَجْرٍ إِنْ أَجْرِيَ إِلاَّ عَلَى اللَّهِ وَأُمِرْتُ أَنْ أَكُونَ مِنَ الْمُسْلِمِينَ

بخوان بر آنها سرگذشت نوح را ، آن هنگام که به قوم خود گفت ای قوم من اگر موقعیت و یادآوری من نسبت به آیات الهی بر شما سنگین (و غیر قابل تحمل) است (هر کار از دستتان ساخته است بکنید) من بر خدا توکل کردهام فکر خود و قدرت معبودهایتان را جمع کنید و هیچ چیز بر شما مستور نماند سپس به حیات من پایان دهید (و لحظهای) مهلتم ندهید .
و اگر روی گردانیدید من مزدی از شما نمیطلبم پاداش من جز بر عهده خدا نیست و مامورم که از مسلمین باشم .

43 *Ál-i-'Imrán*, the Family of 'Imrán, 3:67:

مَا كَانَ إِبْرَاهِيمُ يَهُودِيًّا وَلاَ نَصْرَانِيًّا وَلَٰكِن كَانَ حَنِيفًا مُّسْلِمًا وَمَا كَانَ مِنَ الْمُشْرِكِينَ

ابراهیم نه یهودی بود و نه نصرانی، بلکه موحدی خالص و مسلمان بود، و هرگز از مشرکان نبود .

44 *J. M. Rodwell*: 'And Moses said: 'O my people! if ye believe in God, then put your trust in Him – if ye be Muslims.' *Yúnus*, Jonah, 10:84:

وَقَالَ مُوسَىٰ يَا قَوْمِ إِن كُنتُمْ آمَنتُم بِاللَّهِ فَعَلَيْهِ تَوَكَّلُوا إِن كُنتُم مُّسْلِمِينَ

و موسی گفت ای قوم من اگر به خدا ایمان آورده‌اید و اگر اهل تسلیمید بر او توکل کنید

45 *Yúsuf*, Joseph, 12:101:

رَبِّ قَدْ آتَيْتَنِي مِنَ الْمُلْكِ وَعَلَّمْتَنِي مِن تَأْوِيلِ الْأَحَادِيثِ فَاطِرَ السَّمَاوَاتِ وَالْأَرْضِ أَنتَ وَلِيِّي فِي الدُّنْيَا وَالْآخِرَةِ تَوَفَّنِي مُسْلِمًا وَأَلْحِقْنِي بِالصَّالِحِينَ

پروردگارا تو به من دولت دادی و از تعبیر خوابها به من آموختی ای پدیدآورنده آسمانها و زمین تنها تو در دنیا و آخرت مولای منی مرا مسلمان بمیران و مرا به شایستگان ملحق فرما

46 *Naml*, the Ants, 27:44:

قِيلَ لَهَا ادْخُلِي الصَّرْحَ فَلَمَّا رَأَتْهُ حَسِبَتْهُ لُجَّةً وَكَشَفَتْ عَن سَاقَيْهَا قَالَ إِنَّهُ صَرْحٌ مُّمَرَّدٌ مِّن قَوَارِيرَ قَالَتْ رَبِّ إِنِّي ظَلَمْتُ نَفْسِي وَأَسْلَمْتُ مَعَ سُلَيْمَانَ لِلَّهِ رَبِّ الْعَالَمِينَ

به او گفته شد داخل حیاط قصر شو، اما هنگامی که نظر به آن افکند پنداشت نهر آبی است و ساق پاهای خود را برهنه کرد (تا از آب بگذرد اما سلیمان) گفت (این آب نیست) بلکه قصری است از بلور صاف، (ملکه سبا) گفت پروردگارا! من به خود ستم کردم، و با سلیمان برای خداوندی که پروردگار عالمیان است اسلام آوردم.

47 *A'ráf*, the Heights, 7:120-26:

وَأُلْقِيَ السَّحَرَةُ سَاجِدِينَ
قَالُوا آمَنَّا بِرَبِّ الْعَالَمِينَ
رَبِّ مُوسَىٰ وَهَارُونَ
قَالَ فِرْعَوْنُ آمَنتُم بِهِ قَبْلَ أَنْ آذَنَ لَكُمْ إِنَّ هَٰذَا لَمَكْرٌ مَّكَرْتُمُوهُ فِي الْمَدِينَةِ لِتُخْرِجُوا مِنْهَا أَهْلَهَا فَسَوْفَ تَعْلَمُونَ
لَأُقَطِّعَنَّ أَيْدِيَكُمْ وَأَرْجُلَكُم مِّنْ خِلَافٍ ثُمَّ لَأُصَلِّبَنَّكُمْ أَجْمَعِينَ
قَالُوا إِنَّا إِلَىٰ رَبِّنَا مُنقَلِبُونَ
وَمَا تَنقِمُ مِنَّا إِلَّا أَنْ آمَنَّا بِآيَاتِ رَبِّنَا لَمَّا جَاءَتْنَا رَبَّنَا أَفْرِغْ عَلَيْنَا صَبْرًا وَتَوَفَّنَا مُسْلِمِينَ

و ساحران به سجده درافتادند
[و] گفتند به پروردگار جهانیان ایمان آوردیم
پروردگار موسی و هارون
فرعون گفت آیا پیش از آنکه به شما رخصت دهم به او ایمان آوردید قطعا این نیرنگی است که در شهر به راه انداخته‌اید تا مردمش را از آن بیرون کنید پس به زودی خواهید دانست
دستها و پاهایتان را یکی از چپ و یکی از راست خواهم برید سپس همه شما را به دار خواهم آویخت
گفتند ما به سوی پروردگارمان بازخواهیم گشت
و تو جز برای این ما را به کیفر نمی‌رسانی که ما به معجزات پروردگارمان وقتی برای ما آمد ایمان آوردیم پروردگارا بر ما شکیبایی فرو ریز و ما را مسلمان بمیران

48 *Ál-i-'Imrán*, the Family of 'Imrán, 3:52:

فَلَمَّا أَحَسَّ عِيسَىٰ مِنْهُمُ الْكُفْرَ قَالَ مَنْ أَنصَارِي إِلَى اللَّهِ قَالَ الْحَوَارِيُّونَ نَحْنُ أَنصَارُ اللَّهِ آمَنَّا بِاللَّهِ وَاشْهَدْ بِأَنَّا مُسْلِمُونَ

هنگامی که عیسی از آنان احساس کفر (و مخالفت) کرد، گفت: کیست که بلور من به سوی خدا (برای تبلیغ آیین او) گردد؟ حواریون (شاگردان مخصوص او) گفتند: ما یاوران خداییم، به خدا ایمان آوردیم، و تو (نیز) گواه باش که ما اسلام آورده‌ایم.

NOTES AND REFERENCES

49 *Máʾida,* the Table Spread, 5:111:

وَإِذْ أَوْحَيْتُ إِلَى الْحَوَارِيِّينَ أَنْ آمِنُوا بِي وَبِرَسُولِي قَالُوا آمَنَّا وَاشْهَدْ بِأَنَّنَا مُسْلِمُونَ

و [یاد کن] هنگامی را که به حواریون وحی کردم که به من و فرستاده‌ام ایمان آورید گفتند ایمان آوردیم و گواه باش که ما مسلمانیم

50 *Baqara,* the Heifer, 2:114:

وَمَنْ أَظْلَمُ مِمَّن مَّنَعَ مَسَاجِدَ اللَّهِ أَن يُذْكَرَ فِيهَا اسْمُهُ وَسَعَى فِي خَرَابِهَا أُولَٰئِكَ مَا كَانَ لَهُمْ أَن يَدْخُلُوهَا إِلَّا خَائِفِينَ لَهُمْ فِي الدُّنْيَا خِزْيٌ وَلَهُمْ فِي الْآخِرَةِ عَذَابٌ عَظِيمٌ

چه کسی ستمکارتر از کسانی است که از بردن نام خدا در مساجد او جلوگیری می‌کنند و سعی در ویرانی آنها دارند، شایسته نیست آنان جز با ترس و وحشت وارد این کانون‌های عبادت شوند، بهره آنها در دنیا رسوایی و در سرای دیگر عذاب عظیم است.

51 *Baqara,* the Heifer, 2:256:

لَا إِكْرَاهَ فِي الدِّينِ قَد تَّبَيَّنَ الرُّشْدُ مِنَ الْغَيِّ فَمَن يَكْفُرْ بِالطَّاغُوتِ وَيُؤْمِن بِاللَّهِ فَقَدِ اسْتَمْسَكَ بِالْعُرْوَةِ الْوُثْقَىٰ لَا انفِصَامَ لَهَا وَاللَّهُ سَمِيعٌ عَلِيمٌ

در دین هیچ اجباری نیست و راه از بیراهه بخوبی آشکار شده است پس هر کس به طاغوت کفر ورزد و به خدا ایمان آورد به یقین به دستاویزی استوار که آن را گسستن نیست چنگ زده است و خداوند شنوای داناست

52 *Furqán,* the Criterion, 25:63:

وَعِبَادُ الرَّحْمَٰنِ الَّذِينَ يَمْشُونَ عَلَى الْأَرْضِ هَوْنًا وَإِذَا خَاطَبَهُمُ الْجَاهِلُونَ قَالُوا سَلَامًا

بندگان واقعی خدای رحمان کسانی اند که روی زمین با خشوع گام برمی دارند (در معاشرت با مردم فروتنی می کنند) و هنگامی که نادانان با سخنی جاهلانه آنان را خطاب می کنند ، در پاسخ ، سخنی مسالمت آمیز بر زبان می آورند

53 *Furqán,* the Criterion, 25:72:

وَالَّذِينَ لَا يَشْهَدُونَ الزُّورَ وَإِذَا مَرُّوا بِاللَّغْوِ مَرُّوا كِرَامًا

و کسانی‌اند که گواهی دروغ نمی‌دهند و چون بر لغو بگذرند با بزرگواری می‌گذرند

54 *Qaṣaṣ,* the Narration, 28:55:

وَإِذَا سَمِعُوا اللَّغْوَ أَعْرَضُوا عَنْهُ وَقَالُوا لَنَا أَعْمَالُنَا وَلَكُمْ أَعْمَالُكُمْ سَلَامٌ عَلَيْكُمْ لَا نَبْتَغِي الْجَاهِلِينَ

و چون لغوی بشنوند از آن روی برمی‌تابند و می‌گویند کردارهای ما از آن ما و کردارهای شما از آن شماست‌سلام بر شما جویای [مصاحبت] نادانان نیستیم

55 *Ál-i-ʿImrán,* the Family of ʿImrán, 3:64:

قُلْ يَا أَهْلَ الْكِتَابِ تَعَالَوْا إِلَىٰ كَلِمَةٍ سَوَاءٍ بَيْنَنَا وَبَيْنَكُمْ أَلَّا نَعْبُدَ إِلَّا اللَّهَ وَلَا نُشْرِكَ بِهِ شَيْئًا وَلَا يَتَّخِذَ بَعْضُنَا بَعْضًا أَرْبَابًا مِّن دُونِ اللَّهِ فَإِن تَوَلَّوْا فَقُولُوا اشْهَدُوا بِأَنَّا مُسْلِمُونَ

بگو ای اهل کتاب بیایید بر سر سخنی که میان ما و شما یکسان است بایستیم که جز خدا را نپرستیم و چیزی را شریک او نگردانیم و بعضی از ما بعضی دیگر را به جای خدا به خدایی نگیرد پس اگر [از این پیشنهاد] اعراض کردند بگویید شاهد باشید که ما مسلمانیم

56 *An'ám*, Cattle, 6:108:

وَلاَ تَسُبُّوا الَّذِينَ يَدْعُونَ مِن دُونِ اللّهِ فَيَسُبُّوا اللّهَ عَدْوًا بِغَيْرِ عِلْمٍ كَذَلِكَ زَيَّنَّا لِكُلِّ أُمَّةٍ عَمَلَهُمْ ثُمَّ إِلَى رَبِّهِم مَّرْجِعُهُمْ فَيُنَبِّئُهُم بِمَا كَانُواْ يَعْمَلُونَ

و آنهایی را که جز خدا می‌خوانند دشنام مدهید که آنان از روی دشمنی [و] به نادانی خدا را دشنام خواهند داد این گونه برای هر امتی کردارشان را آراستیم آنگاه بازگشت آنان به سوی پروردگارشان خواهد بود و ایشان را از آنچه انجام می‌دادند آگاه خواهد ساخت

57 *Luqmán*, 31:23:

وَمَن كَفَرَ فَلَا يَحْزُنكَ كُفْرُهُ إِلَيْنَا مَرْجِعُهُمْ فَنُنَبِّئُهُم بِمَا عَمِلُوا إِنَّ اللَّهَ عَلِيمٌ بِذَاتِ الصُّدُورِ

و هر کس کفر ورزد نباید کفر او تو را غمگین گرداند بازگشتشان به سوی ماست و به [حقیقت] آنچه کرده‌اند آگاهشان خواهیم کرد در حقیقت‌خدا به راز دلها داناست

58 *Játhiya*, Bowing the Knee, 45:14:

قُل لِّلَّذِينَ آمَنُوا يَغْفِرُوا لِلَّذِينَ لَا يَرْجُونَ أَيَّامَ اللَّهِ لِيَجْزِيَ قَوْمًا بِما كَانُوا يَكْسِبُونَ

به کسانی که ایمان آورده‌اند بگو تا از کسانی که به روزهای [پیروزی] خدا امید ندارند درگذرند تا [خدا هر] گروهی را به [سبب] آنچه مرتکب می‌شده‌اند به مجازات رساند

59 *Ṭá-Há*, 20:43-4:

اذْهَبَا إِلَى فِرْعَوْنَ إِنَّهُ طَغَى
فَقُولَا لَهُ قَوْلًا لَّيِّنًا لَّعَلَّهُ يَتَذَكَّرُ أَوْ يَخْشَى

سوی فرعون بروید که او به سرکشی برخاسته
و با او سخنی نرم گویید شاید که پند پذیرد یا بترسد

60 *Nahjul Balághah*, Letter no. 19:

أَمَّا بَعْدُ، فَإِنَّ دَهَاقِينَ أَهْلِ بَلَدِكَ شَكَوْا مِنْكَ غِلْظَةً وَقَسْوَةً، وَاحْتِقَارًا وَجَفْوَةً، وَنَظَرْتُ فَلَمْ أَرَهُمْ أَهْلًا لِأَنْ يُدْنَوْا لِشِرْكِهِمْ، وَلَا أَنْ يُقْصَوْا وَيُجْفَوْا لِعَهْدِهِمْ، فَالْبَسْ لَهُمْ جِلْبَابًا مِنَ اللِّينِ تَشُوبُهُ بِطَرَفٍ مِنَ الشِّدَّةِ، وَدَاوِلْ لَهُمْ بَيْنَ الْقَسْوَةِ وَالرَّأْفَةِ، وَامْزُجْ لَهُمْ بَيْنَ التَّقْرِيبِ وَالْإِدْنَاءِ، وَالْإِبْعَادِ وَالْإِقْصَاءِ، إِنْ شَاءَ اللَّهُ.

61 Matt. 5:45.
62 Luke 11:4.
63 Matt. 8:5-13.
64 Luke 7:2-5.
65 Matt. 8:5-13.
66 The Universal House of Justice, *Message to the World's Religious Leaders*.
67 Letter from the Universal House of Justice to an individual Bahá'í, 3 January 1982, in *Messages from the Universal House of Justice, 1963-1986*, no. 308, p. 514; see also Shoghi Effendi, *The Advent of Divine Justice*, p. 66; and Bahá'u'lláh, *Gleanings from the Writings of Bahá'u'lláh*, CXXVIII, p. 279.
68 ibid. p. 513; see also Shoghi Effendi, *The Advent of Divine Justice*, p. 66.

NOTES AND REFERENCES

6 Sectarian Hostility and Violence

1. Bahá'u'lláh, *Gleanings from the Writings of Bahá'u'lláh*, CX, p. 215.
2. Countries with largest Sunni populations: Afghanistan, Algeria, Bangladesh, China, Egypt, Ehtiopia, Ghana, India, Indonesia, Iraq, Malaysia, Morocco, Niger, Nigeria, Pakistan, Russian Federation, Saudi Arabia, Senegal, Somalia, Sudan, Syria, Tanzania, Tunisia, Turkey, Uzbekistan and Yemen.
3. Estimated at 10-15% of the world's Muslims with 200 million followers worldwide. The majority countries are Iraq, Iran, Azerbaijan and Bahrain. Shí'ih Muslims also constitute over 35% of the population in Lebanon, over 45% in Yemen, over 40% in Kuwait, over 20% in Turkey, 10-15% in Pakistan, and over 20% in Afghanistan. Saudi Arabia hosts a number of distinct Shí'ih communities, including the Baharna in the Eastern Province, the Nakhawila of Medina, and the Sulaymani and Zaidiyyah of Najran. Significant communities exist on the coastal regions of West Sumatra and Aceh in Indonesia. A minority is present in Nigeria. East Africa holds several populations of Ismaili Shí'ih, primarily descendants of immigrants from South Asia during the colonial period.
4. Entitled *Amir Al-Múminin*, or 'Prince of Believers', the son-in-law of Muhammad, the first Imam of the Shí'ihs and the fourth Caliph of the Sunnis – one of the four *Al-Khulafah ar-Rashidun* or Rightly-Guided Caliphs.
5. *An'ám*, Cattle, 6:159:

إِنَّ الَّذِينَ فَرَّقُوا دِينَهُمْ وَكَانُوا شِيَعًا لَسْتَ مِنْهُمْ فِي شَيْءٍ إِنَّمَا أَمْرُهُمْ إِلَى اللَّهِ ثُمَّ يُنَبِّئُهُمْ بِمَا كَانُوا يَفْعَلُونَ

کسانی که آیین خود را پراکنده ساختند، و به دسته‌های گوناگون (و مذاهب مختلف) تقسیم شدند، تو هیچ گونه رابطه‌ای با آنها نداری! سر و کار آنها تنها با خداست؛ سپس خدا آنها را از آنچه انجام می‌دادند، با خبر می‌کند.

6. *Baqara*, the Heifer, 2:11:

وَإِذَا قِيلَ لَهُمْ لاَ تُفْسِدُواْ فِي الأَرْضِ قَالُواْ إِنَّمَا نَحْنُ مُصْلِحُونَ

و چون به آنان گفته شود در زمین فساد مکنید می‌گویند ما خود اصلاحگریم

7. *Múminún*, the Believers, 23:52-4:

وَإِنَّ هَذِهِ أُمَّتُكُمْ أُمَّةً وَاحِدَةً وَأَنَا رَبُّكُمْ فَاتَّقُونِ
فَتَقَطَّعُوا أَمْرَهُم بَيْنَهُمْ زُبُرًا كُلُّ حِزْبٍ بِمَا لَدَيْهِمْ فَرِحُونَ
فَذَرْهُمْ فِي غَمْرَتِهِمْ حَتَّى حِينٍ

و در حقیقت این امت‌شماست که امتی یگانه است و من پروردگار شمایم پس از من پروا دارید
تا کار [دین]شان را میان خود قطعه قطعه کردند [و] دسته دسته شدند هر دسته‌ای به آنچه نزدشان بود دل خوش کردند
پس آنها را در ورطه گمراهی‌شان تا چندی واگذار

8. *Maryam*, Mary, 19:37:

فَاخْتَلَفَ الأَحْزَابُ مِن بَيْنِهِمْ فَوَيْلٌ لِّلَّذِينَ كَفَرُوا مِن مَّشْهَدِ يَوْمٍ عَظِيمٍ

اما دسته‌ها[ی] گوناگون] از میان آنها به اختلاف پرداختند پس وای بر کسانی که کافر شدند از مشاهده روزی دهشتناک

9. *Rúm*, the Roman Empire, 30:32:

مِنَ الَّذِينَ فَرَّقُوا دِينَهُمْ وَكَانُوا شِيَعًا كُلُّ حِزْبٍ بِمَا لَدَيْهِمْ فَرِحُونَ

از کسانی که دین خود را قطعه قطعه کردند و فرقه فرقه شدند هر حزبی بدانچه پیش آنهاست دلخوش شدند

10. *Baiyina*, the Clear Evidence, 98:4:

وَمَا تَفَرَّقَ الَّذِينَ أُوتُوا الْكِتَابَ إِلَّا مِن بَعْدِ مَا جَاءَتْهُمُ الْبَيِّنَةُ

اهل کتاب (نیز در دین خدا) اختلاف نکردند مگر بعد از آنکه دلیل روشن برای آنان آمد!

11. *Ál-i-'Imrán*, the Family of 'Imrán, 3:105:

وَلاَ تَكُونُواْ كَالَّذِينَ تَفَرَّقُواْ وَاخْتَلَفُواْ مِن بَعْدِ مَا جَاءهُمُ الْبَيِّنَاتُ وَأُوْلَئِكَ لَهُمْ عَذَابٌ عَظِيمٌ

و چون کسانی مباشید که پس از آنکه دلایل آشکار برایشان آمد پراکنده شدند و با هم اختلاف پیدا کردند و برای آنان عذابی سهمگین است

12. *Shúráa*, Consultation, 42:14:

وَمَا تَفَرَّقُوا إِلَّا مِن بَعْدِ مَا جَاءَهُمُ الْعِلْمُ بَغْيًا بَيْنَهُمْ وَلَوْلَا كَلِمَةٌ سَبَقَتْ مِن رَّبِّكَ إِلَى أَجَلٍ مُّسَمًّى لَّقُضِيَ بَيْنَهُمْ وَإِنَّ الَّذِينَ أُورِثُوا الْكِتَابَ مِن بَعْدِهِمْ لَفِي شَكٍّ مِّنْهُ مُرِيبٍ

آنان پراکنده نشدند مگر بعد از آنکه علم و آگاهی به سراغشان آمد؛ و این تفرقه جویی بخاطر انحراف از حق بود؛ و اگر فرمانی از سوی پروردگارت صادر نشده بود که تا سرآمد معینی باشند، در میان آنها داوری می‌شد؛ و کسانی که بعد از آنها وارثان کتاب شدند نسبت به آن در شک و تردیدند، شکی همراه با بدبینی!

13. *Játhiya*, Bowing the Knee, 45:17:

وَآتَيْنَاهُم بَيِّنَاتٍ مِّنَ الْأَمْرِ فَمَا اخْتَلَفُوا إِلَّا مِن بَعْدِ مَا جَاءَهُمُ الْعِلْمُ بَغْيًا بَيْنَهُمْ إِنَّ رَبَّكَ يَقْضِي بَيْنَهُمْ يَوْمَ الْقِيَامَةِ فِيمَا كَانُوا فِيهِ يَخْتَلِفُونَ

و دلایل روشنی در امر [دین] به آنان عطا کردیم و جز بعد از آنکه علم برایشان [حاصل] آمد [آن هم] از روی رشک و رقابت میان خودشان دستخوش اختلاف نشدند قطعا پروردگارت روز قیامت میانشان در باره آنچه در آن اختلاف می‌کردند داوری خواهد کرد

14. *A'ráf*, the Heights, 7:142:

...وَأَصْلِحْ وَلاَ تَتَّبِعْ سَبِيلَ الْمُفْسِدِينَ

...و اصلاح کن و راه فسادگران را پیروی مکن

15. *Tauba*, Repentance, or *Baráat*, Immunity, 9:107:

وَالَّذِينَ اتَّخَذُواْ مَسْجِدًا ضِرَارًا وَكُفْرًا وَتَفْرِيقًا بَيْنَ الْمُؤْمِنِينَ وَإِرْصَادًا لِّمَنْ حَارَبَ اللّهَ وَرَسُولَهُ مِن قَبْلُ وَلَيَحْلِفَنَّ إِنْ أَرَدْنَا إِلاَّ الْحُسْنَى وَاللّهُ يَشْهَدُ إِنَّهُمْ لَكَاذِبُونَ

و آنهایی که مسجدی اختیار کردند که مایه زیان و کفر و پراکندگی میان مؤمنان است و [نیز] کمینگاهی است برای کسی که قبلا با خدا و پیامبر او به جنگ برخاسته بود و سخت‌سوگند یاد می‌کنند که جز نیکی قصدی نداشتیم و[لی] خدا گواهی می‌دهد که آنان قطعا دروغگو هستند

16 *Raḥmán*, (God) Most Gracious, 55:1-3:

الرَّحْمَنُ
عَلَّمَ الْقُرْآنَ
خَلَقَ الْإِنْسَانَ

[خدای] رحمان
قرآن را یاد داد
انسان را آفرید

17 *Tín*, the Fig, 95:4-5:

لَقَدْ خَلَقْنَا الْإِنْسَانَ فِي أَحْسَنِ تَقْوِيمٍ
ثُمَّ رَدَدْنَاهُ أَسْفَلَ سَافِلِينَ

براستی انسان را در نیکوترین اعتدال آفریدیم
سپس او را به پست‌ترین [مراتب] پستی بازگردانیدیم

18 *Baqara*, the Heifer, 2:28:

كَيْفَ تَكْفُرُونَ بِاللَّهِ وَكُنتُمْ أَمْوَاتًا فَأَحْيَاكُمْ ثُمَّ يُمِيتُكُمْ ثُمَّ يُحْيِيكُمْ ثُمَّ إِلَيْهِ تُرْجَعُونَ

چگونه خدا را منکرید با آنکه مردگانی بودید و شما را زنده کرد باز شما را می میراند [و] باز زنده می‌کند [و] آنگاه به سوی او بازگردانده می‌شوید

19 Amir Al-Mu'minin, 'Ali Ibn Abí Tálib, *Nahjul Balághah*, Sermon 102.
20 ibid. Sermon 369:

٣٦٩ _ وقال عليه السلام : يَأْتِي عَلَى النَّاسِ زَمَانٌ لَا يَبْقَى فِيهِمْ مِنَ الْقُرْآنِ إِلَّا رَسْمُهُ ، وَمِنَ الْإِسْلَامِ إِلَّا اسْمُهُ ، وَمَسَاجِدُهُمْ يَوْمَئِذٍ عَامِرَةٌ مِنَ الْبِنَاءِ، خَرَابٌ مِنَ الْهُدَى، سُكَّانُهَا وَعُمَّارُهَا شَرُّ أَهْلِ الْأَرْضِ، مِنْهُمْ تَخْرُجُ الْفِتْنَةُ ، وَإِلَيْهِمْ تَأْوِي الْخَطِيئَةُ ، يَرُدُّونَ مَنْ شَذَّ عَنْهَا فِيهَا ، وَيَسُوقُونَ مَنْ تَأَخَّرَ عَنْهَا إِلَيْهَا . يَقُولُ اللَّهُ سُبْحَانَهُ : فَبِي حَلَفْتُ لَأَبْعَثَنَّ عَلَى أُولَئِكَ فِتْنَةً تَتْرُكُ الْحَلِيمَ فِيهَا حَيْرَانَ ، وَقَدْ فَعَلَ ،وَنَحْنُ نَسْتَقِيلُ اللَّهَ عَثْرَةَ الْغَفْلَةِ .

21 ibid. Sermon 147, p. 538.
22 ibid. Sermon 103:

أَيُّهَا النَّاسُ ، سَيَأْتِي عَلَيْكُمْ زَمَانٌ يُكْفَأُ فِيهِ الْإِسْلَامُ ، كَمَا يُكْفَأُ الْإِنَاءُ بِمَا فِيهِ . أَيُّهَا النَّاسُ ، إِنَّ اللَّهَ قَدْ أَعَاذَكُمْ مِنْ أَنْ يَجُورَ عَلَيْكُمْ ، وَلَمْ يُعِذْكُمْ مِنْ أَنْ يَبْتَلِيَكُمْ (١٣٧٨) ، وَقَدْ قَالَ مِنْ قَائِلٍ : «إِنَّ فِي ذَلِكَ لَآيَاتٍ وَإِنْ كُنَّا لَمُبْتَلِينَ» .

23 *wa danaaneeruhum deenhum* – the dinar, unit of currency, will constitute their 'deen' or religion.

24 *Bihár Anwár Allámah Muhammad Báqir al-Majlisi*, vol. 22, section 453-4. Translation by Dr Khazeh Fananapazir. The Arabic text is available at http://al-shia.org/html/ara/books/lib-hadis/behar22/a46.html.

جع : قال رسول الله صلى الله عليه وآله : يأتي على الناس زمان وجوههم وجوه الآدميين ، وقلوبهم قلوب الشياطين ، كأمثال الذئاب الضواري ، سفاكون للدماء لا يتناهون عن منكر فعلوه ، إن تابعتهم ارتابوك ، وإن حدثتهم كذبوك ، وإن تواريت عنهم اغتابوك ، السنة فيهم بدعة ، والبدعة فيهم سنة ، والحليم بينهم غادر والغادر بينهم حليم ، المؤمن فيما بينهم مستضعف ، والفاسق فيما بينهم مشرف ، صبيانهم عارم ، ونساؤهم شاطر ، وشيخهم لا يأمر بالمعروف ، ولا ينهى عن المنكر ، والالتجاء إليهم خزي ، والاعتداد

(2) بهم ذل ، وطلب ما في أيديهم فقر ، فعند ذلك يحرمهم الله قطر السماء في أوانه ، وينزله في غير أوانه ، ويسلط عليهم شرارهم ، فيسومونهم سوء العذاب ، يذبحون أبناءهم ويستحيون نساءهم فيدعو خيارهم فلا يستجاب لهم .
قال رسول الله صلى الله عليه وآله : يأتي على الناس زمان بطونهم آلهتهم ونساؤهم قبلتهم ، و دنانيرهم دينهم ، وشرفهم متاعهم ، لا يبقى من الايمان إلا اسمه ، ولا من الاسلام إلا رسمه ، ولا من القرآن إلا درسه ، مساجدهم معمورة من البناء ، وقلوبهم خراب عن الهدى ، علماؤهم شر خلق الله على وجه الارض ، حينئذ ابتلاهم الله في هذا الزمان بأربع خصال : جور من السلطان ، وقحط من الزمان ، وظلم من الولاة والحكام فتعجبت الصحابة فقالوا : يا رسول الله أيعبدون الاصنام ؟ قال : نعم ، كل درهم عندهم صنم .
وقال النبي صلى الله عليه وآله : يأتي في آخر الزمان ناس

(3) من امتي يأتون المساجد يقعدون فيها حلقا ، ذكرهم الدنيا وحبها
(4) الدنيا لا تجالسون فليس لله بهم حاجة .
وقال رسول الله صلى الله عليه وآله : سيأتي زمان على الناس
(5) يفرون من العلماء كما يفر الغنم من الذئب ، ابتلاهم
(1) الله بثلاثة أشياء : الاول يرفع البركة من أموالهم والثاني سلط الله عليهم سلطانا جائرا ، والثالث يخرجون من الدنيا بلا إيمان .
عن أنس عن النبي صلى الله عليه وآله أنه قال : يأتي على الناس زمان الصابر منهم على دينه كالقابض على الجمرة .
وقال صلى الله عليه وآله يأتي على
(2) امتي زمان امراؤهم يكونون على الجور ، وعلماؤهم على الطمع ، وعبادهم على الرياء ، وتجارهم على أكل الربا ، ونساؤهم على زينة الدنيا ، وغلمانهم في التزويج ، فعند ذلك كساد امتي ككساد الاسواق وليس فيها مستقيم ، الاموات
(3) آيسون في قبورهم من خيرهم ، ولا يعيشون الاخيار فيهم ، فعند ذلك
(4) الهرب خير من القيام .
قال النبي صلى الله عليه وآله : سيأتي زمان على امتي لا يعرفون العلماء إلا بثوب حسن ولا يعرفون القرآن إلا بصوت حسن ، ولا يعبدون الله إلا في شهر رمضان ، فإذا كان كذلك سلط الله عليهم سلطانا لا علم له ولا حلم له ولا رحم له
(5) : توضيح : العارم : الخبيث الشرير والسيئ الخلق .
والشاطر : من أعيا أهله خبثا .
أقول : سيأتي كثير من الاخبار في ذلك في باب أشراط الساعة ، وباب علامات ظهور القائم عليه السلام

25 ibid. vol. 13 (old edition)/vols. 51-52-53 (new edition), ch. 30, pp. 78-9. Translation by Sayyid Athar Husain S.H. Rizvi, Ja'fari Propagation Centre.
26 ibid. p. 80.
27 ibid. pp. 88-9.
28 ibid. p. 89.
29 ibid. p. 90.
30 ibid. p. 92.

31 ibid. p. 140.
32 ibid. pp. 150–54.
33 ibid. pp. 155–6.
34 ibid. p. 157.
35 ibid. pp. 170–71.
36 ibid. p. 444.
37 Matt. 12:25.
38 John 17:21.
39 I Pet. 3:8.
40 Rom. 15:6.
41 I Cor. 1:10.
42 John 13:35.
43 Matt. 5:43–5.
44 The number of Christian denominations, independent organizations often with doctrinal differences, has increased exponentially in recent years (more than two-thirds of the independent churches are in Africa) – mushrooming according to the Center for the Study of Global Christianity at Gordon-Conwell Theological Seminary from an estimated 1,600 in the year 1900 to 34,000 in 2000 and 43,000 in 2012.
45 To name a few: Rev. John W. Dowling, *The History of Romanism* (1845), p. 542; also J. A. Wylie, *The History of Protestantism*; John Foxe, *Book of Martyrs*.
46 'Abdu'l-Bahá, *The Promulgation of Universal Peace*, pp. 265–6.
47 Barclay, *The Plain Man Looks at the Apostles' Creed*, pp. 294–5.
48 Matt. 7:21–3.
49 Matt. 8:11–12.
50 I Thess. 5:1–2, 4–8.
51 Jer. 23:12.
52 Isa. 24:21–2.
53 'Howlings': lit. 'sermon by wolves'. In Matt. 7:15 Jesus also warns Christians to be vigilant against 'wolves in sheep's clothing' i.e. those who are indistinguishable from the flock but who prey on the sheep.
54 Amos 8:3.
55 Bahá'u'lláh, *Gleanings from the Writings of Bahá'u'lláh*, CXI, p. 217.
56 Shoghi Effendi, 'The Unfoldment of World Civilization', in *The World Order of Bahá'u'lláh*, p. 198.
57 'Abdu'l-Bahá, *Paris Talks*, ch. 40, pp. 132–3.
58 'Abdu'l-Bahá, quoted in the Introduction to *The Kitáb-i-Aqdas*, pp. 4–5.
59 Isa. 60:20.
60 Rev. 22:4–5.
61 Rev. 21:23–7.
62 Bahá'u'lláh, Súriy-i-Haykal, para. 63, in *The Summons of the Lord of Hosts*, pp. 33–4.
63 'Abdu'l-Bahá, in *Bahá'í Prayers*, pp. 100–01.

7 Excessive Reliance on Religious Leaders for Guidance

1 Bahá'u'lláh, *Gleanings from the Writings of Bahá'u'lláh*, LXXV, p. 143.

2   *Luqmán* (the Wise), 31:30:

ذَلِكَ بِأَنَّ اللَّهَ هُوَ الْحَقُّ وَأَنَّ مَا يَدْعُونَ مِن دُونِهِ الْبَاطِلُ وَأَنَّ اللَّهَ هُوَ الْعَلِيُّ الْكَبِيرُ

این[ها همه] دلیل آن است که خدا خود حق است و غیر از او و هر چه را که می‌خوانند باطل است و خدا همان بلندمرتبه بزرگ است

3   *Yúnus*, Jonah, 10:32 and 35:

فَذَلِكُمُ اللَّهُ رَبُّكُمُ الْحَقُّ فَمَاذَا بَعْدَ الْحَقِّ إِلَّا الضَّلَالُ فَأَنَّى تُصْرَفُونَ
قُلْ هَلْ مِن شُرَكَائِكُم مَّن يَهْدِي إِلَى الْحَقِّ قُلِ اللَّهُ يَهْدِي لِلْحَقِّ أَفَمَن يَهْدِي إِلَى الْحَقِّ أَحَقُّ أَن يُتَّبَعَ أَمَّن لَّا يَهِدِّي إِلَّا أَن يُهْدَى فَمَا لَكُمْ كَيْفَ تَحْكُمُونَ

این است خدا پروردگار حقیقی شما و بعد از حقیقت جز گمراهی چیست پس چگونه [از حق] بازگردانیده می‌شوید
بگو آیا از شریکان شما کسی هست که به سوی حق رهبری کند بگو خداست که به سوی حق رهبری می‌کند پس آیا کسی که به سوی حق رهبری می‌کند سزاوارتر است مورد پیروی قرار گیرد یا کسی که راه نمی‌نماید مگر آنکه [خود] هدایت‌شود شما را چه شده چگونه داوری می‌کنید

4   *Má'ida*, the Table Spread, 5:16:

يَهْدِي بِهِ اللَّهُ مَنِ اتَّبَعَ رِضْوَانَهُ سُبُلَ السَّلَامِ وَيُخْرِجُهُم مِّنَ الظُّلُمَاتِ إِلَى النُّورِ بِإِذْنِهِ وَيَهْدِيهِمْ إِلَى صِرَاطٍ مُّسْتَقِيمٍ

خداوند به وسیله آن ، کسانی را که خشنودی او را دنبال می کنند به راه های سلامت که تأمین کننده نیکبختی آنهاست رهنمون می شود ، و آنان را در پرتو علم خود از تاریکی ها بیرون می آورد و به سوی روشنایی می برد و به راهی راست هدایتشان می کند .

5   *Fáṭir*, the Originator of Creation; or *Malá'ika*, the Angels, 35:31:

وَالَّذِي أَوْحَيْنَا إِلَيْكَ مِنَ الْكِتَابِ هُوَ الْحَقُّ مُصَدِّقًا لِّمَا بَيْنَ يَدَيْهِ إِنَّ اللَّهَ بِعِبَادِهِ لَخَبِيرٌ بَصِيرٌ

و آنچه از کتاب به سوی تو وحی کرده‌ایم خود حق [و] تصدیق‌کننده [کتابهای] پیش از آن است قطعا خدا نسبت به بندگانش آگاه بیناست

6   *Sabá*, the City of Sabá, 34:26:

قُلْ يَجْمَعُ بَيْنَنَا رَبُّنَا ثُمَّ يَفْتَحُ بَيْنَنَا بِالْحَقِّ وَهُوَ الْفَتَّاحُ الْعَلِيمُ

بگو پروردگارمان ما و شما را جمع خواهد کرد سپس میان ما به حق داوری می کند و اوست داور دانا

7   *Núr*, Light, 24:25:

يَوْمَئِذٍ يُوَفِّيهِمُ اللَّهُ دِينَهُمُ الْحَقَّ وَيَعْلَمُونَ أَنَّ اللَّهَ هُوَ الْحَقُّ الْمُبِينُ

آن روز خدا جزای شایسته آنان را به طور کامل می‌دهد و خواهند دانست که خدا همان حقیقت آشکار است

8   The 'Spirit of Truth' may be taken to apply to Muhammad, the Báb or Bahá'u'lláh, as all three proclaim one common Purpose and one common Faith. They did not 'speak of themselves' but conveyed a Divine Revelation to an expectant humanity. Again, all three glorified Christ and predicted the future. However, the prophecy perhaps applies more to Bahá'u'lláh as He represents the 'second coming' of Christ and the return of Christ in the Glory of the Father: 'For the Son of man shall come in the glory of his Father with his angels; and then he shall reward every man according to his works' (Matt. 16:27).

It is also to be noted that the appellation 'He' and 'Himself' is used nine

times – indicating the coming of a Divine Manifestation in human frame – One that 'hears' and 'speaks', and not a disembodied 'Holy Ghost' or 'Holy Spirit'.
9 John 16:12-14.
10 *Tatfīf*, Dealing in Fraud, 83:15:

كَلَّا إِنَّهُمْ عَن رَّبِّهِمْ يَوْمَئِذٍ لَّمَحْجُوبُونَ

چنین نیست که می‌پندارند، بلکه آنها در آن روز از پروردگارشان محجوبند

11 *Qáf*, 50:22:

لَقَدْ كُنتَ فِي غَفْلَةٍ مِّنْ هَذَا فَكَشَفْنَا عَنكَ غِطَاءكَ فَبَصَرُكَ الْيَوْمَ حَدِيدٌ

تو از این صحنه غافل بودی و ما پرده را از چشم تو کنار زدیم، و امروز چشمت کاملا تیزبین است!

12 *Ibráhím*, Abraham, 14:30:

وَجَعَلُواْ لِلّهِ أَندَاداً لِّيُضِلُّواْ عَن سَبِيلِهِ قُلْ تَمَتَّعُواْ فَإِنَّ مَصِيرَكُمْ إِلَى النَّارِ

آنان برای خدا همتایانی قرار دادند تا مردم را از راه او گمراه سازند و بدین وسیله از آنان بهره برند . ای پیامبر ، به آنان بگو : از دنیا بهره برید ولی بدانید که بازگشت شما به سوی آتش است.

13 'Shirk' is traditionally understood as referring to the Christian doctrine of the Trinity, but in the Bahá'í Writings it is often an allusion to clerics (divines) that have usurped divine authority.
14 M. M. Pickthall: 'unwarranted oppression'.
15 *A'ráf*, the Heights, 7:33:

قُلْ إِنَّمَا حَرَّمَ رَبِّيَ الْفَوَاحِشَ مَا ظَهَرَ مِنْهَا وَمَا بَطَنَ وَالإِثْمَ وَالْبَغْيَ بِغَيْرِ الْحَقِّ وَأَن تُشْرِكُواْ بِاللّهِ مَا لَمْ يُنَزِّلْ بِهِ سُلْطَانًا وَأَن تَقُولُواْ عَلَى اللّهِ مَا لاَ تَعْلَمُونَ

بگو: «خداوند، تنها اعمال زشت را، چه آشکار باشد چه پنهان، حرام کرده است؛ و (همچنین) گناه و ستم بناحق را؛ و اینکه چیزی را که خداوند دلیلی برای آن نازل نکرده، شریک او قرار دهید؛ و به خدا مطلبی نسبت دهید که نمی‌دانید.

16 Ps. 96:13.
17 Matt.12:35-6.
18 The Báb, Kitáb-i-Asmá', XVII:4, in *Selections from the Writings of the Báb*, p. 143.
19 Bahá'u'lláh, Tablet of Aḥmad, in most Bahá'í prayer books.
20 Bahá'u'lláh, Súriy-i-Vafá, in *Tablets of Bahá'u'lláh Revealed after the Kitáb-i-Aqdas*, p. 186.
21 Bahá'u'lláh, *Epistle to the Son of the Wolf*, p. 67.
22 Bahá'u'lláh, *Kitáb-i-Íqán*, para. 233, p. 211.
23 Bahá'u'lláh, quoted in Shoghi Effendi, *The Promised Day Is Come*, p. 81.
24 ibid. pp. 81-2.
25 Bahá'u'lláh, Lawḥ-i-Burhán, in *Tablets of Bahá'u'lláh Revealed after the Kitáb-i-Aqdas*, p. 211.
26 Amatul Rahman Omar: 'insolent leaders and well-to-do persons'; Tahir-ul-Qadri Mohammad: 'their chiefs and the affluent people among them'; Bilál

Muhammad: 'the elite among them'; Maududi: 'the affluent ones'.

27 Zukhruf, Gold Adornments, 43:22-5:

بَلْ قَالُوا إِنَّا وَجَدْنَا آبَاءَنَا عَلَىٰ أُمَّةٍ وَإِنَّا عَلَىٰ آثَارِهِم مُّهْتَدُونَ
وَكَذَٰلِكَ مَا أَرْسَلْنَا مِن قَبْلِكَ فِي قَرْيَةٍ مِّن نَّذِيرٍ إِلَّا قَالَ مُتْرَفُوهَا إِنَّا وَجَدْنَا آبَاءَنَا عَلَىٰ أُمَّةٍ وَإِنَّا عَلَىٰ آثَارِهِم مُّقْتَدُونَ
قَالَ أَوَلَوْ جِئْتُكُم بِأَهْدَىٰ مِمَّا وَجَدتُّمْ عَلَيْهِ آبَاءَكُمْ قَالُوا إِنَّا بِمَا أُرْسِلْتُم بِهِ كَافِرُونَ
فَانتَقَمْنَا مِنْهُمْ فَانظُرْ كَيْفَ كَانَ عَاقِبَةُ الْمُكَذِّبِينَ

[نه] بلکه گفتند ما پدران خود را بر آیینی یافتیم و ما [هم با] پی گیری از آنان راه یافتگانیم
و بدین گونه در هیچ شهری پیش از تو هشداردهنده‌ای نفرستادیم مگر آنکه خوشگذرانان آن گفتند ما پدران خود را بر آیینی [و راهی] یافته‌ایم و ما از پی ایشان راهسپریم
گفت هر چند هدایت کننده‌تر از آنچه پدران خود را بر آن یافته‌اید برای شما بیاورم گفتند ما [نسبت] به آنچه بدان فرستاده شده‌اید کافریم
پس از آنان انتقام گرفتیم پس بنگر فرجام تکذیب‌کنندگان چگونه بوده است

28 I Thess. 5:21.
29 II Tim. 4:3-4.
30 John 5:44.
31 Rom. 12:2.
32 Bahá'u'lláh, Súriy-i-Haykal, para. 232, in *The Summons of the Lord of Hosts*, p. 118.
33 'Abdu'l-Bahá, *The Secret of Divine Civilization*, p. 34.
34 Bahá'u'lláh, Súriy-i-Haykal, para. 232, in *The Summons of the Lord of Hosts*, p. 118.
35 *Baqara*, the Heifer, 2:145-7:

وَلَئِنْ أَتَيْتَ الَّذِينَ أُوتُوا الْكِتَابَ بِكُلِّ آيَةٍ مَّا تَبِعُوا قِبْلَتَكَ وَمَا أَنتَ بِتَابِعٍ قِبْلَتَهُمْ وَمَا بَعْضُهُم بِتَابِعٍ قِبْلَةَ بَعْضٍ وَلَئِنِ اتَّبَعْتَ أَهْوَاءَهُم مِّن بَعْدِ مَا جَاءَكَ مِنَ الْعِلْمِ إِنَّكَ إِذًا لَّمِنَ الظَّالِمِينَ
الَّذِينَ آتَيْنَاهُمُ الْكِتَابَ يَعْرِفُونَهُ كَمَا يَعْرِفُونَ أَبْنَاءَهُمْ وَإِنَّ فَرِيقًا مِّنْهُمْ لَيَكْتُمُونَ الْحَقَّ وَهُمْ يَعْلَمُونَ
الْحَقُّ مِن رَّبِّكَ فَلَا تَكُونَنَّ مِنَ الْمُمْتَرِينَ

سوگند که اگر هر گونه آیه (و نشانه و دلیلی) برای (ابن گروه) از اهل کتاب بیاوری از قبله تو پیروی نخواهند کرد، و تو نیز هیچگاه از قبله ی آنان پیروی نخواهی نمود (آنها نباید تصور کنند که بار دیگر تغییر قبله امکانپذیر است) و هیچ یک از آنها نیز از قبله دیگری پیروی نمی‌کنند. و اگر تو پس از این آگاهی مخالفت هوسهای آنها کنی مسلما از ستمگران خواهی بود.
کسانی که کتب آسمانی به آنان داده‌ایم او (پیامبر) را همچون فرزندان خود می‌شناسند (اگر چه) جمعی از آنان حق را آگاهانه کتمان می‌کنند.
این حکم حقی از طرف پروردگار تو است، بنابراین هرگز از تردید کنندگان در آن مباش

36 *Ál-i-'Imrán*, the Family of 'Imrán, 3:70-71:

يَا أَهْلَ الْكِتَابِ لِمَ تَكْفُرُونَ بِآيَاتِ اللَّهِ وَأَنتُمْ تَشْهَدُونَ
يَا أَهْلَ الْكِتَابِ لِمَ تَلْبِسُونَ الْحَقَّ بِالْبَاطِلِ وَتَكْتُمُونَ الْحَقَّ وَأَنتُمْ تَعْلَمُونَ

ای اهل کتاب! چرا به آیات خدا کافر می‌شوید، در حالی که (به درستی آن) گواهی می‌دهید؟!
ای اهل کتاب! چرا حق را با باطل (می‌آمیزید و) مشتبه می‌کنید (تا دیگران نفهمند و گمراه شوند)، و حقیقت را پوشیده می‌دارید در حالی که می‌دانید؟!

528

NOTES AND REFERENCES

37 *Ál-i-'Imrán*, the Family of 'Imrán, 3:98-9:

قُلْ يَا أَهْلَ الْكِتَابِ لِمَ تَكْفُرُونَ بِآيَاتِ اللّهِ وَاللّهُ شَهِيدٌ عَلَى مَا تَعْمَلُونَ
قُلْ يَا أَهْلَ الْكِتَابِ لِمَ تَصُدُّونَ عَن سَبِيلِ اللّهِ مَنْ آمَنَ تَبْغُونَهَا عِوَجًا وَأَنتُمْ شُهَدَاء وَمَا اللّهُ بِغَافِلٍ عَمَّا تَعْمَلُونَ

بگو ای اهل کتاب چرا به آیات خدا کفر می‌ورزید با آنکه خدا بر آنچه می‌کنید گواه است
بگو ای اهل کتاب چرا کسی را که ایمان آورده است از راه خدا بازمی‌دارید و آن [راه] را کج می‌شمارید با آنکه خود [به راستی آن] گواهید و خدا از آنچه می‌کنید غافل نیست

38 *Tauba*, Repentence; or *Baráat*, Immunity, 9:34:

يَا أَيُّهَا الَّذِينَ آمَنُواْ إِنَّ كَثِيرًا مِّنَ الأَحْبَارِ وَالرُّهْبَانِ لَيَأْكُلُونَ أَمْوَالَ النَّاسِ بِالْبَاطِلِ وَيَصُدُّونَ عَن سَبِيلِ اللّهِ وَالَّذِينَ يَكْنِزُونَ الذَّهَبَ وَالْفِضَّةَ وَلاَ يُنفِقُونَهَا فِي سَبِيلِ اللّهِ فَبَشِّرْهُم بِعَذَابٍ أَلِيمٍ

ای کسانی که ایمان آورده‌اید بسیاری از دانشمندان یهود و راهبان اموال مردم را به ناروا می‌خورند و [آنان را] از راه خدا باز می‌دارند و کسانی که زر و سیم را گنجینه می‌کنند و آن را در راه خدا هزینه نمی‌کنند ایشان را از عذابی دردناک خبر ده

39 Bahá'u'lláh, *Kitáb-i-Íqán*, paras. 15, 16, pp. 16-17.
40 *Tauba*, Repentence; or *Baráat*, Immunity, 9:31:

اتَّخَذُواْ أَحْبَارَهُمْ وَرُهْبَانَهُمْ أَرْبَابًا مِّن دُونِ اللّهِ وَالْمَسِيحَ ابْنَ مَرْيَمَ وَمَا أُمِرُواْ إِلاَّ لِيَعْبُدُواْ إِلَهًا وَاحِدًا لاَّ إِلَهَ إِلاَّ هُوَ سُبْحَانَهُ عَمَّا يُشْرِكُونَ

اینان دانشمندان و راهبان خود و مسیح پسر مریم را به جای خدا به الوهیت گرفتند با آنکه مامور نبودند جز اینکه خدایی یگانه را بپرستند که هیچ معبودی جز او نیست منزه است او از آنچه [با وی] شریک می‌گردانند

41 *Kahf*, the Cave, 18:57:

وَمَنْ أَظْلَمُ مِمَّن ذُكِّرَ بِآيَاتِ رَبِّهِ فَأَعْرَضَ عَنْهَا وَنَسِيَ مَا قَدَّمَتْ يَدَاهُ إِنَّا جَعَلْنَا عَلَى قُلُوبِهِمْ أَكِنَّةً أَن يَفْقَهُوهُ وَفِي آذَانِهِمْ وَقْرًا وَإِن تَدْعُهُمْ إِلَى الْهُدَى فَلَن يَهْتَدُوا إِذًا أَبَدًا

و کیست ستمکارتر از آن کس که به آیات پروردگارش پند داده شده و از آن روی برتافته و دستاورد پیشینه خود را فراموش کرده است ما بر دلهای آنان پوشش‌هایی قرار دادیم تا آن را درنیابند و در گوشهایشان سنگینی [نهادیم] و اگر آنها را به سوی هدایت فراخوانی باز هرگز به راه نخواهند آمد

42 *Zukhruf*, Gold Adornments, 43:40:

أَفَأَنتَ تُسْمِعُ الصُّمَّ أَوْ تَهْدِي الْعُمْيَ وَمَن كَانَ فِي ضَلَالٍ مُّبِينٍ

پس آیا تو می‌توانی کران را شنوا کنی یا نابینایان و کسی را که همواره در گمراهی آشکاری است راه نمایی

43 *Furqán*, the Criterion, 25:73:

وَالَّذِينَ إِذَا ذُكِّرُوا بِآيَاتِ رَبِّهِمْ لَمْ يَخِرُّوا عَلَيْهَا صُمًّا وَعُمْيَانًا

آنها کسانی هستند که هر گاه آیات پروردگارشان به آنها گوشزد شود کر و کور روی آن نمی‌افتند!

44 *Fáṭir*, the Originator of Creation; or *Maláika*, the Angels, 35:19–22:

وَمَا يَسْتَوِي الْأَعْمَىٰ وَالْبَصِيرُ
وَلَا الظُّلُمَاتُ وَلَا النُّورُ
وَلَا الظِّلُّ وَلَا الْحَرُورُ
وَمَا يَسْتَوِي الْأَحْيَاءُ وَلَا الْأَمْوَاتُ إِنَّ اللَّهَ يُسْمِعُ مَن يَشَاءُ وَمَا أَنتَ بِمُسْمِعٍ مَّن فِي الْقُبُورِ

و نابینا و بینا یکسان نیستند
و نه تیرگیها و روشنایی
و نه سایه و گرمای آفتاب
و زندگان و مردگان یکسان نیستند خداست که هر که را بخواهد شنوا می‌گرداند و تو کسانی را که در گورهایند نمی‌توانی شنوا سازی

45 *An'ám*, Cattle, 6:157:

أَوْ تَقُولُوا لَوْ أَنَّا أُنزِلَ عَلَيْنَا الْكِتَابُ لَكُنَّا أَهْدَىٰ مِنْهُمْ فَقَدْ جَاءَكُم بَيِّنَةٌ مِّن رَّبِّكُمْ وَهُدًى وَرَحْمَةٌ فَمَنْ أَظْلَمُ مِمَّن كَذَّبَ بِآيَاتِ اللَّهِ وَصَدَفَ عَنْهَا سَنَجْزِي الَّذِينَ يَصْدِفُونَ عَنْ آيَاتِنَا سُوءَ الْعَذَابِ بِمَا كَانُوا يَصْدِفُونَ

یا نگویید اگر کتاب بر ما نازل می‌شد قطعا از آنان هدایت‌یافته‌تر بودیم اینک حجتی از جانب پروردگارتان برای شما آمده و رهنمود و رحمتی است پس کیست‌ستمکارتر از آن کس که آیات خدا را دروغ پندارد و از آنها روی گرداند به زودی کسانی را که از آیات ما روی می‌گردانند به سبب [همین] اعراضشان به عذابی سخت مجازات خواهیم کرد

46 *Baqara*, the Heifer, 2:170:

وَإِذَا قِيلَ لَهُمُ اتَّبِعُوا مَا أَنزَلَ اللَّهُ قَالُوا بَلْ نَتَّبِعُ مَا أَلْفَيْنَا عَلَيْهِ آبَاءَنَا أَوَلَوْ كَانَ آبَاؤُهُمْ لَا يَعْقِلُونَ شَيْئًا وَلَا يَهْتَدُونَ

و چون به آنان گفته شود از آنچه خدا نازل کرده است پیروی کنید می‌گویند نه بلکه از چیزی که پدران خود را بر آن یافته‌ایم پیروی می‌کنیم آیا هر چند پدرانشان چیزی را درک نمی‌کرده و به راه صواب نمی‌رفته‌اند

47 *Luqmán* (the Wise), 31:21:

وَإِذَا قِيلَ لَهُمُ اتَّبِعُوا مَا أَنزَلَ اللَّهُ قَالُوا بَلْ نَتَّبِعُ مَا وَجَدْنَا عَلَيْهِ آبَاءَنَا أَوَلَوْ كَانَ الشَّيْطَانُ يَدْعُوهُمْ إِلَىٰ عَذَابِ السَّعِيرِ

و چون به آنان گفته شود آنچه را که خدا نازل کرده پیروی کنید می‌گویند [نه] بلکه آنچه که پدرانمان را بر آن یافته‌ایم پیروی می‌کنیم آیا هر چند شیطان آنان را به سوی عذاب سوزان فرا خواند

48 *Aḥzáb*, the Confederates, 33:66–8:

يَوْمَ تُقَلَّبُ وُجُوهُهُمْ فِي النَّارِ يَقُولُونَ يَا لَيْتَنَا أَطَعْنَا اللَّهَ وَأَطَعْنَا الرَّسُولَا
وَقَالُوا رَبَّنَا إِنَّا أَطَعْنَا سَادَتَنَا وَكُبَرَاءَنَا فَأَضَلُّونَا السَّبِيلَا
رَبَّنَا آتِهِمْ ضِعْفَيْنِ مِنَ الْعَذَابِ وَالْعَنْهُمْ لَعْنًا كَبِيرًا

در آن روز که صورتهای آنان در آتش (دوزخ) دگرگون خواهد شد (از کار خویش پشیمان می‌شوند و) می‌گویند: «ای کاش خدا و پیامبر را اطاعت کرده بودیم!»
و می‌گویند: «پروردگارا! ما از سران و بزرگان خود اطاعت کردیم و ما را گمراه ساختند!
پروردگارا! آنان را از عذاب، دو چندان ده و آنها را لعن بزرگی فرما!

NOTES AND REFERENCES

49   *Sabá*, the City of Sabá, 34:29-34:

وَيَقُولُونَ مَتَىٰ هَٰذَا الْوَعْدُ إِن كُنتُمْ صَادِقِينَ
قُل لَّكُم مِّيعَادُ يَوْمٍ لَّا تَسْتَأْخِرُونَ عَنْهُ سَاعَةً وَلَا تَسْتَقْدِمُونَ
وَقَالَ الَّذِينَ كَفَرُوا لَن نُّؤْمِنَ بِهَٰذَا الْقُرْآنِ وَلَا بِالَّذِي بَيْنَ يَدَيْهِ وَلَوْ تَرَىٰ إِذِ الظَّالِمُونَ مَوْقُوفُونَ عِندَ رَبِّهِمْ يَرْجِعُ بَعْضُهُمْ إِلَىٰ بَعْضٍ الْقَوْلَ يَقُولُ الَّذِينَ اسْتُضْعِفُوا لِلَّذِينَ اسْتَكْبَرُوا لَوْلَا أَنتُمْ لَكُنَّا مُؤْمِنِينَ
قَالَ الَّذِينَ اسْتَكْبَرُوا لِلَّذِينَ اسْتُضْعِفُوا أَنَحْنُ صَدَدْنَاكُمْ عَنِ الْهُدَىٰ بَعْدَ إِذْ جَاءَكُم ۖ بَلْ كُنتُم مُّجْرِمِينَ
وَقَالَ الَّذِينَ اسْتُضْعِفُوا لِلَّذِينَ اسْتَكْبَرُوا بَلْ مَكْرُ اللَّيْلِ وَالنَّهَارِ إِذْ تَأْمُرُونَنَا أَن نَّكْفُرَ بِاللَّهِ وَنَجْعَلَ لَهُ أَندَادًا ۚ وَأَسَرُّوا النَّدَامَةَ لَمَّا رَأَوُا الْعَذَابَ وَجَعَلْنَا الْأَغْلَالَ فِي أَعْنَاقِ الَّذِينَ كَفَرُوا ۚ هَلْ يُجْزَوْنَ إِلَّا مَا كَانُوا يَعْمَلُونَ
وَمَا أَرْسَلْنَا فِي قَرْيَةٍ مِّن نَّذِيرٍ إِلَّا قَالَ مُتْرَفُوهَا إِنَّا بِمَا أُرْسِلْتُم بِهِ كَافِرُونَ

و گویند اگر می‌گویید راست ابن وعده کی فرا می‌رسد
بگو برای شما موعد روزی مقرر است که نه از آن ساعتی پس افتید و نه پیش افتید
و کافران گویند هرگز به این قرآن، و به آنچه پیش از آن بود، ایمان نمی‌آوریم، و اگر ستمکاران را بنگری که نزد پروردگارشان بازداشته شوند، بعضی با بعضی دیگر گفتگو می‌کنند مستضعفان به مستکبران گویند اگر شما نبودید بی‌شک، ما مؤمن بودیم
مستکبران به مستضعفان گویند آیا ما شما را از هدایتی که به سراغ شما آمد بازداشتیم؟ چنین نیست، بلکه خودتان گناهکار بودید
و مستضعفان به مستکبران گویند چنین نیست، بلکه مکر [شما در] شب و روز بود، آنگاه که به ما فرمان می‌دادید که به خداوند کفر بورزیم و برای او شریک قائل شویم، و چون عذاب را ببینند پشیمانی خود را پنهان دارند، و غل‌ها را در گردن‌های کافران بگذاریم، آیا جز در برابر آنچه می‌کردند، جزا می‌یابند؟
و هیچ هشدار دهنده‌ای به هیچ شهری نفرستادیم مگر آنکه نازپروردگان آن گفتند ما رسالت شما را منکریم

50   *Furqán*, the Criterion, 25:17-19:

وَيَوْمَ يَحْشُرُهُمْ وَمَا يَعْبُدُونَ مِن دُونِ اللَّهِ فَيَقُولُ أَأَنتُمْ أَضْلَلْتُمْ عِبَادِي هَٰؤُلَاءِ أَمْ هُمْ ضَلُّوا السَّبِيلَ
قَالُوا سُبْحَانَكَ مَا كَانَ يَنبَغِي لَنَا أَن نَّتَّخِذَ مِن دُونِكَ مِنْ أَوْلِيَاءَ وَلَٰكِن مَّتَّعْتَهُمْ وَآبَاءَهُمْ حَتَّىٰ نَسُوا الذِّكْرَ وَكَانُوا قَوْمًا بُورًا
فَقَدْ كَذَّبُوكُم بِمَا تَقُولُونَ فَمَا تَسْتَطِيعُونَ صَرْفًا وَلَا نَصْرًا ۚ وَمَن يَظْلِم مِّنكُمْ نُذِقْهُ عَذَابًا كَبِيرًا

به خاطر بیاور روزی که همه آنها و معبودانی را که غیر از خدا پرستش می‌کردند جمع می‌کند، و به آنها می‌گوید: آیا شما این بندگان مرا گمراه کردید؟ یا خود گمراه شدند؟
آنها (در پاسخ) می‌گویند منزهی تو، برای ما شایسته نبود که غیر از تو اولیائی برگزینیم، ولی آنان و پدرانشان را از نعمت‌ها برخوردار نمودی تا اینکه آنها (به جای شکر نعمت) یاد تو را فراموش کردند، و هلاک شدند
(خداوند به آنها می‌گوید ببینید) این معبودان، شما در آنچه می‌گویید تکذیب کردند اکنون قدرت ندارید عذاب الهی را بر طرف سازید یا از کسی یاری بطلبید، و هر کس از شما ظلم و ستم کند عذاب شدیدی به او می‌چشانیم!

51   'Alí Ibn Abí Tálib, *Nahjul Balághah*, vol. 1, Sermon 18, p. 118.

ومن كلام له(عليه السلام) في ذمّ اختلاف العلماء في الفتيا [وفيه يذم أهل الرأي ويكل أمر الحكم في أمور الدين للقرآن]
تَرِدُ عَلَى أَحَدِهِمُ الْقَضِيَّةُ فِي حُكْمٍ مِنَ الْأَحْكَامِ فَيَحْكُمُ فِيهَا بِرَأْيِهِ، ثُمَّ تَرِدُ تِلْكَ الْقَضِيَّةُ بِعَيْنِهَا عَلَى غَيْرِهِ فَيَحْكُمُ فِيهَا بِخِلَافِ قَوْلِهِ، ثُمَّ يَجْتَمِعُ الْقُضَاةُ بِذَلِكَ عِنْدَ إمَامِهِمُ الَّذِي اسْتَقْضَاهُمْ(1)، فَيُصَوِّبُ آرَاءَهُمْ جَمِيعاً، وَإِلَهُهُمْ وَاحِدٌ! وَنَبِيُّهُمْ وَاحِدٌ! وَكِتَابُهُمْ وَاحِدٌ! أَفَأَمَرَهُمُ اللهُ ـ سُبْحَانَهُ ـ بِالْاِخْتِلَافِ فَأَطَاعُوهُ! أَمْ نَهَاهُمْ عَنْهُ فَعَصَوْهُ! أَمْ أَنْزَلَ اللهُ سُبْحَانَهُ دِيناً نَاقِصاً فَاسْتَعَانَ بِهِمْ عَلَى إِتْمَامِهِ! أَمْ كَانُوا شُرَكَاءَ لَهُ فَلَهُمْ أَنْ يَقُولُوا وَعَلَيْهِ أَنْ يَرْضَى! أَمْ أَنْزَلَ اللهُ سُبْحَانَهُ دِيناً تَامّاً فَقَصَّرَ الرَّسُولُ(صلى الله عليه وآله) عَنْ تَبْلِيغِهِ وَأَدَائِهِ؟ وَاللهُ سُبْحَانَهُ يَقُولُ: (مَا فَرَّطْنَا فِي الْكِتَابِ مِنْ شَيْءٍ) وَفِيهِ تِبْيَانٌ لِكُلِّ شَيْءٍ، وَذَكَرَ أَنَّ الْكِتَابَ يُصَدِّقُ بَعْضُهُ بَعْضاً، وَأَنَّهُ لَا اخْتِلَافَ فِيهِ، فَقَالَ سُبْحَانَهُ: (وَلَوْ كَانَ مِنْ عِنْدِ غَيْرِ اللهِ لَوَجَدُوا فِيهِ اخْتِلَافاً كَثِيراً). وَإِنَّ الْقُرْآنَ ظَاهِرُهُ أَنِيقٌ(1)، وَبَاطِنُهُ عَمِيقٌ، لَا تَفْنَى عَجَائِبُهُ، وَلَاتَنْقَضِي غَرَائِبُهُ، وَلَا تُكْشَفُ الظُّلُمَاتُ إِلَّا بِهِ.

52 Ezek. 34:2.
53 Ezek. 34:10.
54 Matt. 3:7.
55 Matt. 15:14.
56 Matt. 23:13–35.
57 Acts 24:1 and 5.
58 Matt. 23:9–12.
59 Matt. 24:5.
60 Matt. 7:15.
61 Matt. 7:15–20.
62 Matt. 11:6.
63 The Universal House of Justice, *Century of Light*, p. 59.
64 Bahá'u'lláh, *Kitáb-i-Íqán*, para. 15, p. 15.
65 *Mú-min*, the Believer, 40:59:

إِنَّ السَّاعَةَ لَآتِيَةٌ لَا رَيْبَ فِيهَا وَلَٰكِنَّ أَكْثَرَ النَّاسِ لَا يُؤْمِنُونَ

روز قیامت به طور مسلم خواهد آمد، شکی در آن نیست، ولی اکثر مردم ایمان نمی‌آورند.

66 *An'ám*, Cattle, 6:116:

وَإِن تُطِعْ أَكْثَرَ مَن فِي الْأَرْضِ يُضِلُّوكَ عَن سَبِيلِ اللَّهِ ۚ إِن يَتَّبِعُونَ إِلَّا الظَّنَّ وَإِنْ هُمْ إِلَّا يَخْرُصُونَ

اگر از بیشتر کسانی که در روی زمین هستند اطاعت کنی، تو را از راه خدا گمراه می کنند؛ (زیرا) آنها تنها از گمان پیروی می‌نمایند، و تخمین و حدس (واهی) می‌زنند.

67 *Má'ida*, the Table Spread, 5:100:

قُل لَّا يَسْتَوِي الْخَبِيثُ وَالطَّيِّبُ وَلَوْ أَعْجَبَكَ كَثْرَةُ الْخَبِيثِ ۚ فَاتَّقُوا اللَّهَ يَا أُولِي الْأَلْبَابِ لَعَلَّكُمْ تُفْلِحُونَ

بگو: ناپاک و پاک مساوی نیستند؛ هر چند فزونی ناپاکها، تو را به شگفتی اندازد! از خدا بپرهیزید ای صاحبان خرد، شاید رستگار شوید!

68 *Baqara*, the Heifer, 2:120:

وَلَن تَرْضَىٰ عَنكَ الْيَهُودُ وَلَا النَّصَارَىٰ حَتَّىٰ تَتَّبِعَ مِلَّتَهُمْ ۗ قُلْ إِنَّ هُدَى اللَّهِ هُوَ الْهُدَىٰ ۗ وَلَئِنِ اتَّبَعْتَ أَهْوَاءَهُم بَعْدَ الَّذِي جَاءَكَ مِنَ الْعِلْمِ ۙ مَا لَكَ مِنَ اللَّهِ مِن وَلِيٍّ وَلَا نَصِيرٍ

هرگز یهود و نصاری از تو راضی نخواهند شد، (تا به طور کامل، تسلیم خواسته‌های آنها شوی، و) از آیین (تحریف یافته) آنان، پیروی کنی. بگو: «هدایت، تنها هدایت الهی است!» و اگر از هوی و هوسهای آنان پیروی کنی، بعد از آنکه آگاه شده‌ای، هیچ سرپرست و یاوری از سوی خدا برای تو نخواهد بود.

69 *Qibla*: 'Cynosure' – the focal point of attention, guidance and admiration – the object towards which prayers and meditation are directed in every Dispensation. Some Qiblas point to the East and others to the West, i.e. the outward form and social teachings of different religions may be diametrically opposed to one another but it is important to consider that God is the Author of all Revelations.

70 *Baqara*, the Heifer, 2:142:

سَيَقُولُ السُّفَهَاءُ مِنَ النَّاسِ مَا وَلَّاهُمْ عَن قِبْلَتِهِمُ الَّتِي كَانُوا عَلَيْهَا ۚ قُل لِّلَّهِ الْمَشْرِقُ وَالْمَغْرِبُ ۚ يَهْدِي مَن يَشَاءُ إِلَىٰ صِرَاطٍ مُّسْتَقِيمٍ

به زودی مردم کم خرد خواهند گفت چه چیز آنان را از قبله‌ای که بر آن بودند رویگردان کرد بگو مشرق و مغرب از آن خداست هر که را خواهد به راه راست هدایت می‌کند

71 *Yúnus*, Jonah, 10:15:

وَإِذَا تُتْلَىٰ عَلَيْهِمْ آيَاتُنَا بَيِّنَاتٍ قَالَ الَّذِينَ لَا يَرْجُونَ لِقَاءَنَا ائْتِ بِقُرْآنٍ غَيْرِ هَٰذَا أَوْ بَدِّلْهُ قُلْ مَا يَكُونُ لِي أَنْ أُبَدِّلَهُ مِن تِلْقَاءِ نَفْسِي إِنْ أَتَّبِعُ إِلَّا مَا يُوحَىٰ إِلَيَّ إِنِّي أَخَافُ إِنْ عَصَيْتُ رَبِّي عَذَابَ يَوْمٍ عَظِيمٍ

و هنگامی که آیات روشن ما بر آنها خوانده می‌شود، کسانی که ایمان به لقای ما ندارند می‌گویند: «قرآنی غیر از این بیاور، یا آن را تبدیل کن! (و آیات نکوهش بتها را بردار)» بگو: «من حق ندارم که از پیش خود آن را تغییر دهم؛ فقط از چیزی که بر من وحی می‌شود، پیروی می‌کنم! من اگر پروردگارم را نافرمانی کنم، از مجازات روز بزرگ می‌ترسم!

72 The term also refers to certain scriptural statements, such as 'the Seal of the Prophets' (*Ahzáb*, the Confederates, 33:40), and 'I am the Way the Truth, and the Life: no man cometh unto the Father, but by me' (John 14:6), that by their apparent exclusivist nature are apt to hinder one from accepting God's next Revelation.

73 *Núh*, Noah, 71:7:
And every time I have called to them, that Thou mightest forgive them, they have (only) thrust their fingers into their ears, covered themselves up with their garments, grown obstinate, and given themselves up to arrogance.

وَإِنِّي كُلَّمَا دَعَوْتُهُمْ لِتَغْفِرَ لَهُمْ جَعَلُوا أَصَابِعَهُمْ فِي آذَانِهِمْ وَاسْتَغْشَوْا ثِيَابَهُمْ وَأَصَرُّوا وَاسْتَكْبَرُوا اسْتِكْبَارًا

و من هر بار که آنان را دعوت کردم تا ایشان را بیامرزی انگشتانشان را در گوشهایشان کردند و ردای خویشتن بر سر کشیدند و اصرار ورزیدند و هر چه بیشتر بر کبر خود افزودند

74 *Ahqáf*, Winding Sand-tracts, 46:26:
And We had firmly established them in a (prosperity and) power which We have not given to you; and We had endowed them with (faculties of) hearing, seeing, heart and intellect; but of no profit to them were their hearing, sight, and heart and intellect; when they went on rejecting the Signs of God; and they were (completely) encircled by that which they used to mock at!

وَلَقَدْ مَكَّنَّاهُمْ فِيمَا إِن مَّكَّنَّاكُمْ فِيهِ وَجَعَلْنَا لَهُمْ سَمْعًا وَأَبْصَارًا وَأَفْئِدَةً فَمَا أَغْنَىٰ عَنْهُمْ سَمْعُهُمْ وَلَا أَبْصَارُهُمْ وَلَا أَفْئِدَتُهُم مِّن شَيْءٍ إِذْ كَانُوا يَجْحَدُونَ بِآيَاتِ اللَّهِ وَحَاقَ بِهِم مَّا كَانُوا بِهِ يَسْتَهْزِئُونَ

ما به آنها (قوم عاد) قدرتی دادیم که به شما ندادیم، و برای آنان گوش و چشم و دل قرار دادیم؛ (اما) نه گوشها و چشمها و نه عقلهایشان برای آنان هیچ سودی نداشت، چرا که آیات خدا را انکار می‌کردند؛ و سرانجام آنچه را استهزا می‌کردند بر آنها وارد شد

75 Bahá'u'lláh, quoted in Shoghi Effendi, *The Promised Day Is Come*, p. 79.
76 Bahá'u'lláh, *Epistle to the Son of the Wolf*, p. 128.
77 Bahá'u'lláh, quoted in Shoghi Effendi, *The Promised Day Is Come*, p. 83.
78 ibid. p. 88.
79 ibid. p. 87.
80 ibid. p. 83.
81 Bahá'u'lláh, Lawh-i-Maqsúd, in *Tablets of Bahá'u'lláh Revealed after the Kitáb-i-Aqdas*, pp. 168–9.

82 *A'ráf*, the Heights, 7:55:

ادْعُواْ رَبَّكُمْ تَضَرُّعًا وَخُفْيَةً إِنَّهُ لاَ يُحِبُّ الْمُعْتَدِينَ

پروردگار خود را از روی تضرع، و در پنهانی، بخوانید! (و از تجاوز، دست بردارید که) او متجاوزان را دوست نمی‌دارد!

83 Bahá'u'lláh, quoted in Shoghi Effendi, *The Promised Day Is Come*, pp. 83-4.
84 Bahá'u'lláh, *Tablets of Bahá'u'lláh Revealed after the Kitáb-i-Aqdas*, p. 245.
85 Bahá'u'lláh, *Epistle to the Son of the Wolf*, p. 127.
86 Bahá'u'lláh, quoted in Shoghi Effendi, *The Promised Day Is Come*, p. 83.
87 ibid. p. 81.
88 ibid.
89 Bahá'u'lláh, *Kitáb-i-Íqán*, para. 114, pp. 108-9.
90 Bahá'u'lláh, *Súriy-i-Haykal*, para. 198, in *The Summons of the Lord of Hosts*, pp. 101-2.
91 Bahá'u'lláh, *Gleanings from the Writings of Bahá'u'lláh*, XXXV, p. 84.
92 '*khayru albariyyati*', as in *Baiyina*, the Clear Evidence, 98:7:
   Those who have faith and do righteous deeds, they are the best of creatures.

إِنَّ الَّذِينَ آمَنُوا وَعَمِلُوا الصَّالِحَاتِ أُولَٰئِكَ هُمْ خَيْرُ الْبَرِيَّةِ

در حقیقت کسانی که گرویده و کارهای شایسته کرده‌اند آنانند که بهترین آفریدگانند

93 Shoghi Effendi, *The Promised Day Is Come*, p. 81.
94 Bahá'u'lláh, quoted ibid. p. 82.
95 ibid. p. 83.
96 ibid. 79-80.
97 Abú 'Abdulláh Ja'far as Sádiq.
98 Bahá'u'lláh, *Kitáb-i-Íqán*, para. 275, pp. 247-8.
99 Bahá'u'lláh, *Gems of Divine Mysteries, Javáhiru'l-Asrár*, para. 54, pp. 39-40.
100 *Naḥl*, Bees, Súrah 16.
101 Bahá'u'lláh, *Epistle to the Son of Wolf*, pp. 15-16.
102 Joseph Ernest (Ernst) Renan (1823-92), *Les Apôtres*: 'le babisme ont eu des martyrs aussi nombreux, aussi exaltés, aussi résignés que le christianisme... Des milliers de martyrs sont accourus pour lui avec allégresse au-devant de la mort. Un jour sans pareil peut-être dans l'histoire du monde fut celui de la grande boucherie qui se fit des bâbis à Téhéran.'
103 Shoghi Effendi, *The Promised Day Is Come*, p. 75.
104 See Matt. 24:29.
105 Bahá'u'lláh, *Kitáb-i-Íqán*, para. 34, p. 36.
106 The supreme governing body of the Bahá'í Faith, the Universal House of Justice, wrote on 13 May 2014:
   A notable recent example has been the courageous efforts of a senior Iranian cleric, Ayatollah Abdol-Hamid Masoumi-Tehrani, who in April 2014 gave to the Bahá'ís of the world a calligraphic rendering of Bahá'í sacred verses along with a plea for religious 'co-existence'. At the heart of the work are the following words: 'Consort with the followers of all religions with amity and concord', a verse from Bahá'u'lláh's Kitáb-i-Aqdas, the 'Most Holy Book'.

> The illuminated calligraphic work was accompanied by a three-page statement, which, among other things, said: 'I present this precious symbol – an expression of sympathy and care from me and on behalf of all my open-minded fellow citizens who respect others for their humanity and not for their religion or way of worship – to all the Bahá'ís of the world, particularly to the Bahá'ís of Iran who have suffered in manifold ways as a result of blind religious prejudice.'

And in a letter to the Bahá'ís of Iran written on the same day, the Universal House of Justice commented that Ayatollah Tehrani's action was

> so dramatic, its implications so profound, and its reach so extensive that it has won the appreciation and support of religious figures, including Muslim leaders in other lands . . . Such spiritual leaders, detached from earthly matters, are extolled in the Bahá'í Writings as 'the bearers of God's mercy' and 'the tokens of His favour'; all sincere and pure souls who arise in service to humankind and promote the cause of universal peace are described in the same Writings as those who 'shall erelong shine like unto a brilliant star from the horizon of humankind and illuminate the whole earth'.

The assistant Secretary General of the Muslim Council of Britain, Ibrahim Mogra, who serves as an imam in Leicester, was reported by the *Guardian* newspaper as commenting that Ayatollah Masoumi-Tehrani,

> a prominent imam and scholar, has taken a stand for coexistence with the country's Bahá'í minority. He has reminded us that Islam is a religion of peace that recognises diversity of every kind as part of God's design for his creation. And it all came in the form of a gift – one which I am proud to endorse. . . The ayatollah offered his gift as a 'symbolic action to serve as a reminder of the importance of valuing human beings, of peaceful coexistence, of cooperation and mutual support, and avoidance of hatred, enmity and blind religious prejudice' . . . He has a long history of supporting peaceful coexistence between Muslims, Christians and Jews, including with illuminated calligraphic versions of the Qur'an, the Torah, the Psalms, the New Testament, and the Book of Ezra. I am proud, as a Muslim and as an imam, to celebrate this enlightened gift, which has such immense spiritual significance. The faiths of the world should be united in promoting coexistence to advance human civilisation. Six thousand Bahá'ís live in the UK and I am proud to count many as my friends. The community is respected for promoting interfaith harmony. I am sure that Iranian Bahá'ís have the same hopes to serve their country and to live in peace.

107 Bahá'u'lláh, quoted in Shoghi Effendi, *The Promised Day Is Come*, p. 111.
108 Bahá'u'lláh, *Epistle to the Son of Wolf*, pp. 16–17.
109 Bahá'u'lláh, quoted in Shoghi Effendi, *The Promised Day Is Come*, p. 111.
110 ibid.

8 Frustration of the Sacred Duty of Believers to Investigate the Truth and to Recognize their Lord

1 Bahá'u'lláh, *Kitáb-i-Íqán*, para. 176, pp. 164–5.
2 The Universal House of Justice, *The Promise of World Peace*, para. 32, p. 8.

3   The Universal House of Justice, *Message to the World's Religious Leaders.*
4   'Abdu'l-Bahá, *The Promulgation of Universal Peace*, p. 141.
5   The Universal House of Justice, *Message to the World's Religious Leaders.*
6   Bahá'u'lláh, Lawh-i-Maqsúd, in *Tablets of Bahá'u'lláh Revealed after the Kitáb-i-Aqdas*, p. 171.
7   Bahá'u'lláh, Kalimát-i-Firdawsíyyih, in *Tablets of Bahá'u'lláh Revealed after the Kitáb-i-Aqdas*, p. 62.
8   Esslemont, *Bahá'u'lláh and the New Era*, p. 131.
9   The Báb, Persian Bayán II: 16, in *Selections from the Writings of the Báb*, p. 77.
10   *Ál-i-'Imrán*, the Family of 'Imrán, 3:110:

كُنتُمْ خَيْرَ أُمَّةٍ أُخْرِجَتْ لِلنَّاسِ تَأْمُرُونَ بِالْمَعْرُوفِ وَتَنْهَوْنَ عَنِ الْمُنكَرِ وَتُؤْمِنُونَ بِاللَّهِ وَلَوْ آمَنَ أَهْلُ الْكِتَابِ لَكَانَ خَيْرًا لَّهُم مِّنْهُمُ الْمُؤْمِنُونَ وَأَكْثَرُهُمُ الْفَاسِقُونَ

شما بهترین امتی هستید که برای مردم پدیدار شده‌اید به کار پسندیده فرمان می‌دهید و از کار ناپسند بازمی‌دارید و به خدا ایمان دارید و اگر اهل کتاب ایمان آورده بودند قطعا برایشان بهتر بود برخی از آنان مؤمنند و[لی] بیشترشان نافرمانند

11   *Ál-i-'Imrán*, the Family of 'Imrán, 3:114:

يُؤْمِنُونَ بِاللَّهِ وَالْيَوْمِ الْآخِرِ وَيَأْمُرُونَ بِالْمَعْرُوفِ وَيَنْهَوْنَ عَنِ الْمُنكَرِ وَيُسَارِعُونَ فِي الْخَيْرَاتِ وَأُولَٰئِكَ مِنَ الصَّالِحِينَ

به خدا و روز قیامت ایمان دارند و به کار پسندیده فرمان می‌دهند و از کار ناپسند باز می‌دارند و در کارهای نیک شتاب می‌کنند و آنان از شایستگانند

12   *Ál-i-'Imrán*, the Family of 'Imrán, 3:104:

وَلْتَكُن مِّنكُمْ أُمَّةٌ يَدْعُونَ إِلَى الْخَيْرِ وَيَأْمُرُونَ بِالْمَعْرُوفِ وَيَنْهَوْنَ عَنِ الْمُنكَرِ وَأُولَٰئِكَ هُمُ الْمُفْلِحُونَ

و باید از میان شما گروهی [مردم را] به نیکی دعوت کنند و به کار شایسته وادارند و از زشتی بازدارند و آنان همان رستگاراند

13   *Tauba*, Repentance; or *Baráat*, Immunity, 9:71:

وَالْمُؤْمِنُونَ وَالْمُؤْمِنَاتُ بَعْضُهُمْ أَوْلِيَاءُ بَعْضٍ يَأْمُرُونَ بِالْمَعْرُوفِ وَيَنْهَوْنَ عَنِ الْمُنكَرِ وَيُقِيمُونَ الصَّلَاةَ وَيُؤْتُونَ الزَّكَاةَ وَيُطِيعُونَ اللَّهَ وَرَسُولَهُ أُولَٰئِكَ سَيَرْحَمُهُمُ اللَّهُ إِنَّ اللَّهَ عَزِيزٌ حَكِيمٌ

و مردان و زنان با ایمان دوستان یکدیگرند که به کارهای پسندیده وا می‌دارند و از کارهای ناپسند باز می‌دارند و نماز را بر پا می‌کنند و زکات می‌دهند و از خدا و پیامبرش فرمان می‌برند آنانند که خدا به زودی مشمول رحمتشان قرار خواهد داد که خدا توانا و حکیم است.

14   *Tauba*, Repentance; or *Baráat*, Immunity, 9:67:

الْمُنَافِقُونَ وَالْمُنَافِقَاتُ بَعْضُهُم مِّن بَعْضٍ يَأْمُرُونَ بِالْمُنكَرِ وَيَنْهَوْنَ عَنِ الْمَعْرُوفِ وَيَقْبِضُونَ أَيْدِيَهُمْ نَسُوا اللَّهَ فَنَسِيَهُمْ إِنَّ الْمُنَافِقِينَ هُمُ الْفَاسِقُونَ

مردان و زنان دو چهره [همانند] یکدیگرند به کار ناپسند وامی‌دارند و از کار پسندیده باز می‌دارند و دستهای خود را [از انفاق] فرو می‌بندند خدا را فراموش کردند پس [خدا هم] فراموششان کرد در حقیقت این منافقانند که فاسقند

NOTES AND REFERENCES

15 *An'ám*, Cattle, 6;108:

وَلاَ تَسُبُّواْ الَّذِينَ يَدْعُونَ مِن دُونِ اللّهِ فَيَسُبُّواْ اللّهَ عَدْوًا بِغَيْرِ عِلْمٍ كَذَلِكَ زَيَّنَّا لِكُلِّ أُمَّةٍ عَمَلَهُمْ ثُمَّ إِلَى رَبِّهِم مَّرْجِعُهُمْ فَيُنَبِّئُهُم بِمَا كَانُواْ يَعْمَلُونَ

و کسانی را که مشرکان به جای خدا می خوانند دشنام ندهید که آنان نیز خدا را از روی دشمنی که برخاسته از نادانی است دشنام می دهند . بدین سان برای هر امتی کردارشان را آراسته ایم ؛ پس به آنچه زیبا می دانند ناسزا مگویید . آن گاه بازگشت آنان به سوی پروردگارشان خواهد بود و او آنان را از حقیقت آنچه انجام می دادند با خبر خواهد ساخت .

16 Hadith Qudsi, relayed on the authority of Abu Dhar al-Ghifari(ra).
17 *Tauba*, Repentance; or *Baráat*, Immunity, 9:9:

اشْتَرَوْاْ بِآيَاتِ اللّهِ ثَمَنًا قَلِيلًا فَصَدُّواْ عَن سَبِيلِهِ إِنَّهُمْ سَاء مَا كَانُواْ يَعْمَلُونَ

آیات خدا را به بهای ناچیزی فروختند و [مردم را] از راه او باز داشتند به راستی آنان چه بد اعمالی انجام می دادند

18 Muḥammad ibn 'Alí al-Báqir, *Bihár Anwár Allámah Muhammad Báqir al-Majlisi*, p. 152.
19 Acts 20:28-9.
20 I Pet. 5:1-4.
21 The Catholic Code of Canon Law provides the following definition of clerics and laity: 'By divine institution, there are among the Christian faithful in the Church sacred ministers who in law are also called clerics; the other members of the Christian faithful are called lay persons.'
22 The Apostolic Constitutions (or Constitutions of the Holy Apostles, Lat. *Constitutiones Apostolorum*), 375–80 AD.
23 Codex Theodosianus (388 AD), 16.4.2, in Wood and Harries, *The Theodosian Code: Studies in the Imperial Law of Late Antiquity*.
24 Hillerbrand, *The Reformation*, pp. 474, 475.
25 Matt. 24:14.
26 Bahá'u'lláh, Súriy-i-Haykal, in Bahá'u'lláh, *The Summons of the Lord of Hosts*, p. 54.
27 Pope Pius IX, 'Qui pluribus', encyclical on faith and religion, 9 November 1846, in *The Great Papal Encyclicals*.
28 Martin Luther, *On the Jews and Their Lies* (1543), Part XI, pp. 111–12.
29 ibid. Part XII, p. 126.
30 Matt. 5:17-20.
31 *Húd* (the Prophet Húd), 11:109:

فَلاَ تَكُ فِي مِرْيَةٍ مِّمَّا يَعْبُدُ هَؤُلاء مَا يَعْبُدُونَ إِلاَّ كَمَا يَعْبُدُ آبَاؤُهُم مِّن قَبْلُ وَإِنَّا لَمُوَفُّوهُمْ نَصِيبَهُمْ غَيْرَ مَنقُوصٍ

پس در باره آنچه آنان [=مشرکان] می‌پرستند در تردید مباش آنان جز همان گونه که قبلا پدرانشان می‌پرستیدند نمی‌پرستند و ما بهره ایشان را تمام و ناکاسته خواهیم داد

32 See for example http//Christianity.stackexchange.com/questions/255530/: 'Why do Mormon missionaries travel in pairs? At its most basic, evangelizing in pairs builds accountability in a mutual commitment to a shared goal, reinforced by the social pressure of knowing another human being is aware of whether or not you are adhering to your commitment.'

33 John 9:18-22.
34 *Mu-minún*, the Believers, 23:23-4:

وَلَقَدْ أَرْسَلْنَا نُوحًا إِلَىٰ قَوْمِهِ فَقَالَ يَا قَوْمِ اعْبُدُوا اللَّهَ مَا لَكُم مِّنْ إِلَٰهٍ غَيْرُهُ أَفَلَا تَتَّقُونَ
فَقَالَ الْمَلَأُ الَّذِينَ كَفَرُوا مِن قَوْمِهِ مَا هَٰذَا إِلَّا بَشَرٌ مِّثْلُكُمْ يُرِيدُ أَن يَتَفَضَّلَ عَلَيْكُمْ وَلَوْ شَاءَ اللَّهُ لَأَنزَلَ مَلَائِكَةً مَّا سَمِعْنَا بِهَٰذَا فِي آبَائِنَا الْأَوَّلِينَ

و به یقین نوح را به سوی قومش فرستادیم پس [به آنان] گفت ای قوم من خدا را بپرستید شما را جز او خدایی نیست مگر این پروا ندارید
اشراف قومش که کافر بودند گفتند این [مرد] جز بشری چون شما نیست می‌خواهد بر شما برتری جوید و اگر خدا می‌خواست قطعا فرشتگانی می‌فرستاد [ما]در میان پدران نخستین خود چنین [چیزی] نشنیده‌ایم

35 *Mú-mín*, the Believer, 40:26:

وَقَالَ فِرْعَوْنُ ذَرُونِي أَقْتُلْ مُوسَىٰ وَلْيَدْعُ رَبَّهُ إِنِّي أَخَافُ أَن يُبَدِّلَ دِينَكُمْ أَوْ أَن يُظْهِرَ فِي الْأَرْضِ الْفَسَادَ

و فرعون گفت مرا بگذارید موسی را بکشم تا پروردگارش را بخواند من می‌ترسم آیین شما را تغییر دهد یا در این سرزمین فساد کند.

36 *Húd* (the Prophet Húd), 11:62:

قَالُوا يَا صَالِحُ قَدْ كُنتَ فِينَا مَرْجُوًّا قَبْلَ هَٰذَا أَتَنْهَانَا أَن نَّعْبُدَ مَا يَعْبُدُ آبَاؤُنَا وَإِنَّنَا لَفِي شَكٍّ مِّمَّا تَدْعُونَا إِلَيْهِ مُرِيبٍ

گفتند ای صالح به راستی تو پیش از این میان ما مایه امید بودی آیا ما را از پرستش آنچه پدرانمان می‌پرستیدند باز می‌داری و بی‌گمان ما از آنچه تو ما را بدان می‌خوانی سخت دچار شکیم

37 'Abdu'l-Bahá, *The Promulgation of Universal Peace*, p. 180.
38 ibid. p. 293.
39 Shoghi Effendi, *The Promised Day Is Come*, pp. v-vi.
40 Bahá'u'lláh, *Gleanings from the Writings of Bahá'u'lláh*, LXXV, p. 143.
41 *Falaq*, the Dawn, 113:1-3:

قُلْ أَعُوذُ بِرَبِّ الْفَلَقِ
مِن شَرِّ مَا خَلَقَ
وَمِن شَرِّ غَاسِقٍ إِذَا وَقَبَ

بگو پناه می‌برم به پروردگار سپیده دم
از شر آنچه آفریده
و از شر تاریکی چون فراگیرد

42 *Fátiḥa*, the Opening Chapter, 1:6:

اهدِنَا الصِّرَاطَ الْمُسْتَقِيمَ

ما را به راه راست هدایت فرما

43 *'Ankabút*, the Spider, 29:69:

وَالَّذِينَ جَاهَدُوا فِينَا لَنَهْدِيَنَّهُمْ سُبُلَنَا وَإِنَّ اللَّهَ لَمَعَ الْمُحْسِنِينَ

و کسانی که در راه ما کوشیده‌اند به یقین راه‌های خود را بر آنان می‌نماییم و در حقیقت خدا با نیکوکاران است

44 Bahá'u'lláh, *Kitáb-i-Íqán*, para. 215, p. 195.
45 Bahá'u'lláh, *Hidden Words*, Persian no. 7.
46 ibid. Arabic no. 5.

NOTES AND REFERENCES

47 *Baqara*, the Heifer, 2:186:

وَإِذَا سَأَلَكَ عِبَادِي عَنِّي فَإِنِّي قَرِيبٌ أُجِيبُ دَعْوَةَ الدَّاعِ إِذَا دَعَانِ فَلْيَسْتَجِيبُواْ لِي وَلْيُؤْمِنُواْ بِي لَعَلَّهُمْ يَرْشُدُونَ

و هرگاه بندگان من از تو در باره من بپرسند [بگو] من نزدیکم و دعای دعاکننده را به هنگامی که مرا بخواند اجابت می‌کنم پس [آنان] باید فرمان مرا گردن نهند و به من ایمان آورند که راه یابند

48 *Baqara*, the Heifer, 2:152:

فَاذْكُرُونِي أَذْكُرْكُمْ وَاشْكُرُواْ لِي وَلاَ تَكْفُرُونِ

پس مرا یاد کنید [تا] شما را یاد کنم و شکرانه‌ام را به جای آرید و با من ناسپاسی نکنید

49 *Mú-min*, the Believer, 40:60:

وَقَالَ رَبُّكُمُ ادْعُونِي أَسْتَجِبْ لَكُمْ إِنَّ الَّذِينَ يَسْتَكْبِرُونَ عَنْ عِبَادَتِي سَيَدْخُلُونَ جَهَنَّمَ دَاخِرِينَ

و پروردگارتان فرمود مرا بخوانید تا شما را اجابت کنم در حقیقت کسانی که از پرستش من کبر می‌ورزند به زودی خوار در دوزخ درمی‌آیند

50 Ezek. 14:3. *God's Word* translation: 'Son of man, these people are devoted to their idols, and they are allowing themselves to fall into sin. Should they be allowed to ask me for help?'
51 Jer. 6:16.
52 Isa. 55:6-9.
53 Ps. 69:32. *Douay-Rheims Bible* translation: 'Let the poor see and rejoice: seek ye God, and your soul shall live.'
54 Matt. 5:6.
55 ibid. 13:16-17.
56 ibid. 7:7-11.
57 I Pet. 2:2.
58 Matt. 5:3. *God's Word* translation: 'Blessed are those who recognize they are spiritually helpless. The kingdom of heaven belongs to them.'
59 I Thess. 5:17-21.
60 Eph. 5:10.
61 For instance, Bibleline Ministries, Christian Courier, or Cult Awareness and Information library. Such, however, is no longer the position of the mainstream Catholic and Protestant Churches.
62 Bahá'u'lláh, *Gleanings from the Writings of Bahá'u'lláh*, LXXV, p. 143.
63 *Sajda*, Adoration, 32:9:

ثُمَّ سَوَّاهُ وَنَفَخَ فِيهِ مِن رُوحِهِ وَجَعَلَ لَكُمُ السَّمْعَ وَالأَبْصَارَ وَالأَفْئِدَةَ قَلِيلاً مَّا تَشْكُرُونَ

آنگاه او را درست‌اندام کرد و از روح خویش در او دمید و برای شما گوش و دیدگان و دلها قرار داد چه اندک سپاس می‌گزارید

64 *'Ankabút*, the Spider, 29:2-3:

أَحَسِبَ النَّاسُ أَن يُتْرَكُوا أَن يَقُولُوا آمَنَّا وَهُمْ لَا يُفْتَنُونَ
وَلَقَدْ فَتَنَّا الَّذِينَ مِن قَبْلِهِمْ فَلَيَعْلَمَنَّ اللَّهُ الَّذِينَ صَدَقُوا وَلَيَعْلَمَنَّ الْكَاذِبِينَ

آیا مردم پنداشتند که تا گفتند ایمان آوردیم رها می‌شوند و مورد آزمایش قرار نمی‌گیرند
و به یقین کسانی را که پیش از اینان بودند آزمودیم تا خدا آنان را که راست گفته‌اند معلوم دارد و دروغگویان را [نیز] معلوم دارد

539

65　*Baqara*, the Heifer, 2:214:

أَمْ حَسِبْتُمْ أَن تَدْخُلُوا الْجَنَّةَ وَلَمَّا يَأْتِكُم مَّثَلُ الَّذِينَ خَلَوْا مِن قَبْلِكُم مَّسَّتْهُمُ الْبَأْسَاءُ وَالضَّرَّاءُ وَزُلْزِلُوا حَتَّى يَقُولَ الرَّسُولُ وَالَّذِينَ آمَنُوا مَعَهُ مَتَى نَصْرُ اللَّهِ أَلَا إِنَّ نَصْرَ اللَّهِ قَرِيبٌ

آیا پنداشتید که داخل بهشت می‌شوید و حال آنکه هنوز مانند آنچه بر [سر] پیشینیان شما آمد بر [سر] شما نیامده است آنان دچار سختی و زیان شدند و به [هول و] تکان درآمدند تا جایی که پیامبر [خدا] و کسانی که با وی ایمان آورده بودند گفتند پیروزی خدا کی خواهد بود هش دار که پیروزی خدا نزدیک است

66　Matt. 7:13-14.
67　Ps. 17:5.
68　*Najm*, the Star, 53:38:

لَّا تَزِرُ وَازِرَةٌ وِزْرَ أُخْرَى

که هیچ بردارنده‌ای بار گناه دیگری را بر نمی‌دارد

69　*Baqara*, the Heifer, 2:286:

لَا يُكَلِّفُ اللَّهُ نَفْسًا إِلَّا وُسْعَهَا لَهَا مَا كَسَبَتْ وَعَلَيْهَا مَا اكْتَسَبَتْ رَبَّنَا لَا تُؤَاخِذْنَا إِن نَّسِينَا أَوْ أَخْطَأْنَا رَبَّنَا وَلَا تَحْمِلْ عَلَيْنَا إِصْرًا كَمَا حَمَلْتَهُ عَلَى الَّذِينَ مِن قَبْلِنَا رَبَّنَا وَلَا تُحَمِّلْنَا مَا لَا طَاقَةَ لَنَا بِهِ وَاعْفُ عَنَّا وَاغْفِرْ لَنَا وَارْحَمْنَا أَنتَ مَوْلَانَا فَانصُرْنَا عَلَى الْقَوْمِ الْكَافِرِينَ

خداوند هیچ کس را جز به قدر توانایی‌اش تکلیف نمی‌کند. آنچه (از خوبی) به دست آورده به سود او، و آنچه (از بدی) به دست آورده به زیان اوست. پروردگارا، اگر فراموش کردیم یا به خطا رفتیم بر ما مگیر، پروردگارا، هیچ بار گرانی بر (دوش) ما مگذار؛ همچنانکه بر (دوش) کسانی که پیش از ما بودند نهادی. پروردگارا، و آنچه تاب آن نداریم بر ما تحمیل مکن؛ و از ما درگذر؛ و ما را ببخشای و بر ما رحمت آور؛ سرور ما تویی؛ پس ما را بر گروه کافران پیروز کن.

70　*An'ám*, Cattle, 6:164:

قُلْ أَغَيْرَ اللَّهِ أَبْغِي رَبًّا وَهُوَ رَبُّ كُلِّ شَيْءٍ وَلَا تَكْسِبُ كُلُّ نَفْسٍ إِلَّا عَلَيْهَا وَلَا تَزِرُ وَازِرَةٌ وِزْرَ أُخْرَى ثُمَّ إِلَى رَبِّكُم مَّرْجِعُكُمْ فَيُنَبِّئُكُم بِمَا كُنتُمْ فِيهِ تَخْتَلِفُونَ

بگو: «آیا غیر خدا، پروردگاری را بطلبم، در حالی که او پروردگار همه چیز است؟! هیچ کس، عمل (بدی) جز به زیان خودش، انجام نمی‌دهد؛ و هیچ گنهکاری گناه دیگری را متحمل نمی‌شود؛ سپس بازگشت همه شما به سوی پروردگارتان است؛ و شما را از آنچه در آن اختلاف داشتید، خبر خواهد داد.

71　*Nahl*, Bees, 16:25:

لِيَحْمِلُوا أَوْزَارَهُمْ كَامِلَةً يَوْمَ الْقِيَامَةِ وَمِنْ أَوْزَارِ الَّذِينَ يُضِلُّونَهُم بِغَيْرِ عِلْمٍ أَلَا سَاءَ مَا يَزِرُونَ

آنها باید روز قیامت، (هم) بار گناهان خود را بطور کامل بر دوش کشند؛ و هم سهمی از گناهان کسانی که بخاطر جهل، گمراهشان می‌سازند! بدانید آنها بار سنگین بدی بر دوش می‌کشند!

72　*Baní Isrá-íl*, the Children of Israel, 17:15:

مَّنِ اهْتَدَى فَإِنَّمَا يَهْتَدِي لِنَفْسِهِ وَمَن ضَلَّ فَإِنَّمَا يَضِلُّ عَلَيْهَا وَلَا تَزِرُ وَازِرَةٌ وِزْرَ أُخْرَى وَمَا كُنَّا مُعَذِّبِينَ حَتَّى نَبْعَثَ رَسُولًا

هر کس هدایت شود، برای خود هدایت یافته؛ و آن کس که گمراه گردد، به زیان خود گمراه شده است؛ و هیچ کس بار گناه دیگری را به دوش نمی‌کشد؛ و ما هرگز (قومی را) مجازات نخواهیم کرد، مگر آنکه پیامبری مبعوث کرده باشیم

73 *Fáṭir*, the Originator of Creation; or *Maláika*, the Angels, 35:18:

وَلَا تَزِرُ وَازِرَةٌ وِزْرَ أُخْرَىٰ وَإِن تَدْعُ مُثْقَلَةٌ إِلَىٰ حِمْلِهَا لَا يُحْمَلْ مِنْهُ شَيْءٌ وَلَوْ كَانَ ذَا قُرْبَىٰ إِنَّمَا تُنذِرُ الَّذِينَ يَخْشَوْنَ رَبَّهُم بِالْغَيْبِ وَأَقَامُوا الصَّلَاةَ وَمَن تَزَكَّىٰ فَإِنَّمَا يَتَزَكَّىٰ لِنَفْسِهِ وَإِلَى اللَّهِ الْمَصِيرُ

هیچ گنهکاری بار گناه دیگری را بر دوش نمی‌کشد؛ و اگر شخص سنگین‌باری دیگری را برای حمل گناه خود بخواند، چیزی از آن را بر دوش نخواهد گرفت، هر چند از نزدیکان او باشد! تو فقط کسانی را بیم‌می‌دهی که از پروردگار خود در پنهانی می‌ترسند و نماز برپا می‌دارند؛ و هر کس پاکی (و تقوا) پیشه کند، نتیجه آن به خودش بازمی‌گردد؛ و بازگشت (همگان) به سوی خداست!

74 *Zumar*, the Crowds, 39:7:

إِن تَكْفُرُوا فَإِنَّ اللَّهَ غَنِيٌّ عَنكُمْ وَلَا يَرْضَىٰ لِعِبَادِهِ الْكُفْرَ وَإِن تَشْكُرُوا يَرْضَهُ لَكُمْ وَلَا تَزِرُ وَازِرَةٌ وِزْرَ أُخْرَىٰ ثُمَّ إِلَىٰ رَبِّكُم مَّرْجِعُكُمْ فَيُنَبِّئُكُم بِمَا كُنتُمْ تَعْمَلُونَ إِنَّهُ عَلِيمٌ بِذَاتِ الصُّدُورِ

اگر کفر ورزید خدا از شما سخت بی‌نیاز است و برای بندگانش کفران را خوش نمی‌دارد و اگر سپاس دارید آن را برای شما می‌پسندد و هیچ بردارنده‌ای بار [گناه] دیگری را برنمی‌دارد آنگاه بازگشت‌تان به سوی پروردگارتان است و شما را به آنچه می‌کردید خبر خواهد داد که او به راز دلها داناست

75 Bahá'u'lláh, *Gleanings from the Writings of Bahá'u'lláh*, LII, p. 105.
76 Bahá'u'lláh, *Kitáb-i-Íqán*, paras. 153-4, pp. 145-6.
77 Muḥammad ibn 'Alí al-Báqir, *Bihár Anwár Allámah Muhammad Báqir al-Majlisi*, p. 127.
78 Phil. 3:13-15.
79 I Cor. 5:6-8.
80 Luke 5:36-8.
81 II Cor. 3:4-6.
82 Rev. 21:5.

9 Misinterpretation of the Divine Word

1 Bahá'u'lláh, *Gleanings from the Writings of Bahá'u'lláh*, LXXXVI, p. 171.
2 'Abdu'l-Bahá, *Some Answered Questions*, ch. 37, p. 149.
3 Shoghi Effendi, *The Promised Day Is Come*, p. 112.
4 Bahá'u'lláh, *Gleanings from the Writings of Bahá'u'lláh*, LXXXIX, p. 176.
5 ibid. pp. 175-6.
6 Bahá'u'lláh, *Kitáb-i-Íqán*, para. 16, p. 17.
7 'Abdu'l-Bahá, *The Promulgation of Universal Peace*, p. 291.
8 ibid. pp. 200-01.
9 John 9:39-41.
10 *Baqara*, the Heifer, 2:26:

إِنَّ اللَّهَ لَا يَسْتَحْيِي أَن يَضْرِبَ مَثَلًا مَّا بَعُوضَةً فَمَا فَوْقَهَا فَأَمَّا الَّذِينَ آمَنُوا فَيَعْلَمُونَ أَنَّهُ الْحَقُّ مِن رَّبِّهِمْ وَأَمَّا الَّذِينَ كَفَرُوا فَيَقُولُونَ مَاذَا أَرَادَ اللَّهُ بِهَٰذَا مَثَلًا يُضِلُّ بِهِ كَثِيرًا وَيَهْدِي بِهِ كَثِيرًا وَمَا يُضِلُّ بِهِ إِلَّا الْفَاسِقِينَ

خدای را از اینکه به پشه‌ای یا فروتر [یا فراتر] از آن مثل زند شرم نیاید پس کسانی که ایمان آورده‌اند می‌دانند که آن [مثل] از جانب پروردگارشان بجاست ولی کسانی که به کفر گراییده‌اند می‌گویند خدا از این مثل چه قصد داشته است [خدا] بسیاری را با آن گمراه و بسیاری را با آن راهنمایی می‌کند و[لی] جز نافرمانان را با آن گمراه نمی‌کند.

11 Ps. 115:4-6.
12 Ezek. 12:1-2.

13 Isa. 42:20.
14 Jer. 5:21.
15 Matt. 13:10-16.
16 ibid. 13:17.
17 I Cor. 2:9.
18 *Maryam,* Mary, 19:42:

إِذْ قَالَ لِأَبِيهِ يَا أَبَتِ لِمَ تَعْبُدُ مَا لَا يَسْمَعُ وَلَا يُبْصِرُ وَلَا يُغْنِي عَنكَ شَيْئًا

چون به پدرش گفت پدر جان چرا چیزی را که نمی‌شنود و نمی‌بیند و از تو چیزی را دور نمی‌کند می‌پرستی

19 *Baqara,* the Heifer, 2:18:

صُمٌّ بُكْمٌ عُمْيٌ فَهُمْ لاَ يَرْجِعُونَ

کرند لالند کورند بنابراین به راه نمی‌آیند

20 *Anfál,* the Spoils of War, 8:22:

إِنَّ شَرَّ الدَّوَابِّ عِندَ اللّهِ الصُّمُّ الْبُكْمُ الَّذِينَ لاَ يَعْقِلُونَ

قطعا بدترین جنبندگان نزد خدا کران و لالانی‌اند که نمی‌اندیشند

21 See for example Shoghi Effendi, *The Promised Day Is Come,* pp. 81-93.
22 ibid. p. 107.
23 Bahá'u'lláh, quoted ibid. p. 82.
24 ibid. p. 80.
25 ibid. p. 82.
26 *Baqara,* the Heifer, 2:79:

فَوَيْلٌ لِّلَّذِينَ يَكْتُبُونَ الْكِتَابَ بِأَيْدِيهِمْ ثُمَّ يَقُولُونَ هَذَا مِنْ عِندِ اللّهِ لِيَشْتَرُواْ بِهِ ثَمَنًا قَلِيلًا فَوَيْلٌ لَّهُم مِّمَّا كَتَبَتْ أَيْدِيهِمْ وَوَيْلٌ لَّهُمْ مِّمَّا يَكْسِبُونَ

پس وای بر کسانی که کتاب با دستهای خود می‌نویسند سپس می‌گویند این از جانب خداست تا بدان بهای ناچیزی به دست آرند پس وای بر ایشان از آنچه دستهایشان نوشته و وای بر ایشان از آنچه [از این راه] به دست می‌آورند

27 *Baqara,* the Heifer, 2:174:

إِنَّ الَّذِينَ يَكْتُمُونَ مَا أَنزَلَ اللّهُ مِنَ الْكِتَابِ وَيَشْتَرُونَ بِهِ ثَمَنًا قَلِيلًا أُولَئِكَ مَا يَأْكُلُونَ فِي بُطُونِهِمْ إِلاَّ النَّارَ وَلاَ يُكَلِّمُهُمُ اللّهُ يَوْمَ الْقِيَامَةِ وَلاَ يُزَكِّيهِمْ وَلَهُمْ عَذَابٌ أَلِيمٌ

کسانی که آنچه را خداوند از کتاب نازل کرده پنهان می‌دارند و بدان بهای ناچیزی به دست می‌آورند آنان جز آتش در شکمهای خویش فرو نبرند و خدا روز قیامت با ایشان سخن نخواهد گفت و پاکشان نخواهد کرد و عذابی دردناک خواهند داشت

28 Deut. 16:19.
29 II Cor. 2:17. *God's Word* translation: 'At least we don't go around selling an impure word of God like many others . . .'
30 Matt. 6:19-21.
31 Luke 9:58.
32 Mark 6:7-9.
33 Gen. 40:8.

NOTES AND REFERENCES

34 II Pet. 1:20-21.
35 I Cor. 4:4-5.
36 Matt. 15:14.
37 Luke 6:39.
38 *Ál-i-'Imrán*, the Family of 'Imrán, 3:7:

هُوَ الَّذِي أَنزَلَ عَلَيْكَ الْكِتَابَ مِنْهُ آيَاتٌ مُحْكَمَاتٌ هُنَّ أُمُّ الْكِتَابِ وَأُخَرُ مُتَشَابِهَاتٌ فَأَمَّا الَّذِينَ في قُلُوبِهِمْ زَيْغٌ فَيَتَّبِعُونَ مَا تَشَابَهَ مِنْهُ ابْتِغَاءَ الْفِتْنَةِ وَابْتِغَاءَ تَأْوِيلِهِ وَمَا يَعْلَمُ تَأْوِيلَهُ إِلَّا اللَّهُ وَالرَّاسِخُونَ في الْعِلْمِ يَقُولُونَ آمَنَّا بِهِ كُلٌّ مِّنْ عِندِ رَبِّنَا وَمَا يَذَّكَّرُ إِلَّا أُولُوا الْأَلْبَابِ

او کسی است که این کتاب را بر تو نازل کرد، که قسمتی از آن، آیات «محکم» (صریح و روشن) است، که اساس این کتاب میباشد. و قسمتی از آن، «متشابه» است. اما آنها که در قلوبشان انحراف است، به دنبال متشابهات اند، تا فتنهانگیزی کنند (و مردم را گمراه سازند)، و تفسیر (نادرستی) برای آن میطلبند؛ در حالی که تفسیر آنها را، جز خدا و راسخان در علم، نمیدانند. آنها میگویند: «ما به همه آن ایمان آوردیم، همه از طرف پروردگار ماست.» و جز صاحبان عقل، متذکر نمیشوند (و این حقیقت را درک نمیکنند).

39 The requisite 'knowledge' and 'understanding' refers more aptly to perception born of God rather than to learning acquired in institutions of theological training. Hence, 'those who are firmly grounded in knowledge'; and 'men of understanding' apply to those divine individuals who have a God-given mandate and ability to interpret the Word of God.

However, the Arabic súrahs of the Qur'án were not punctuated by commas and the sentences did not end in periods (full stops). Thus, this passage itself has been susceptible to conflicting interpretations – the placement of a period after 'God' in the English Sunni translation allows 'men of understanding', such as the twelve Imams, to explain the abstruse parts of the Qur'án.

40 Title of the Revelation of the Báb.
41 *Qiyámat*, the Resurrection, 75:16-19:

لَا تُحَرِّكْ بِهِ لِسَانَكَ لِتَعْجَلَ بِهِ
إِنَّ عَلَيْنَا جَمْعَهُ وَقُرْآنَهُ
فَإِذَا قَرَأْنَاهُ فَاتَّبِعْ قُرْآنَهُ
ثُمَّ إِنَّ عَلَيْنَا بَيَانَهُ

زبانت را بخاطر عجله برای خواندن آن [= قرآن] حرکت مده
چرا که جمعکردن و خواندن آن بر عهده ماست
پس هر گاه آن را خواندیم از خواندن آن پیروی کن
سپس بیان و توضیح آن نیز بر عهده ماست

42 *Ál-i-'Imrán*, the Family of 'Imrán, 3:23:

أَلَمْ تَرَ إِلَى الَّذِينَ أُوتُوا نَصِيبًا مِّنَ الْكِتَابِ يُدْعَوْنَ إِلَى كِتَابِ اللَّهِ لِيَحْكُمَ بَيْنَهُمْ ثُمَّ يَتَوَلَّى فَرِيقٌ مِّنْهُمْ وَهُم مُّعْرِضُونَ

آیا داستان کسانی را که بهرهای از کتاب یافتهاند ندانستهای که چون به سوی کتاب خدا فرا خوانده میشوند تا میانشان حکم کند آنگه گروهی از آنان به حال اعراض روی برمیتابند

43 *Yúnus*, Jonah, 10:39:

بَلْ كَذَّبُوا بِمَا لَمْ يُحِيطُوا بِعِلْمِهِ وَلَمَّا يَأْتِهِمْ تَأْوِيلُهُ كَذَلِكَ كَذَّبَ الَّذِينَ مِن قَبْلِهِمْ فَانظُرْ كَيْفَ كَانَ عَاقِبَةُ الظَّالِمِينَ

بلکه چیزی را تکذیب کردند که آگاهی از آن نداشتند، و هنوز واقعیتش بر آنان روشن نشده است! پیشینیان آنها نیز همین گونه تکذیب کردند؛ پس بنگر عاقبت کار ظالمان چگونه بود

44 *Ál-i-'Imrán*, the Family of 'Imrán, 3:94:

فَمَنِ افْتَرَىٰ عَلَى اللَّهِ الْكَذِبَ مِن بَعْدِ ذَٰلِكَ فَأُولَٰئِكَ هُمُ الظَّالِمُونَ

پس کسانی که بعد از این بر خدا دروغ بندند آنان خود ستمکارانند

45 *A'ráf*, the Heights, 7:52-3:

وَلَقَدْ جِئْنَاهُم بِكِتَابٍ فَصَّلْنَاهُ عَلَىٰ عِلْمٍ هُدًى وَرَحْمَةً لِّقَوْمٍ يُؤْمِنُونَ
هَلْ يَنظُرُونَ إِلَّا تَأْوِيلَهُ يَوْمَ يَأْتِي تَأْوِيلُهُ يَقُولُ الَّذِينَ نَسُوهُ مِن قَبْلُ قَدْ جَاءَتْ رُسُلُ رَبِّنَا بِالْحَقِّ فَهَل لَّنَا مِن شُفَعَاءَ
فَيَشْفَعُوا لَنَا أَوْ نُرَدُّ فَنَعْمَلَ غَيْرَ الَّذِي كُنَّا نَعْمَلُ قَدْ خَسِرُوا أَنفُسَهُمْ وَضَلَّ عَنْهُم مَّا كَانُوا يَفْتَرُونَ

ما کتابی برای آنها آوردیم که (اسرار و رموز) آن را با آگاهی شرح دادیم؛ (کتابی) که مایه هدایت و رحمت برای جمعیتی است که ایمان می‌آورند.
آیا آنها جز انتظار تأویل آیات (و فرا رسیدن تهدیدهای الهی) دارند؟ آن روز که تأویل آنها فرا رسد، (کار از کار گذشته، و پشیمانی سودی ندارد؛ و) کسانی که قبلا آن را فراموش کرده بودند می‌گویند:
«فرستادگان پروردگار ما، حق را آوردند؛ آیا (امروز) شفیعانی برای ما وجود دارند که برای ما شفاعت کنند؟ یا (به ما اجازه داده شود به دنیا) بازگردیم، و اعمالی غیر از آنچه انجام می‌دادیم، انجام دهیم؟!»
(ولی) آنها سرمایه وجود خود را از دست داده‌اند؛ و معبودهایی را که به دروغ ساخته بودند، همگی از نظرشان گم می‌شوند. (نه راه بازگشتی دارند، و نه شفیعانی!)

46 Bahá'u'lláh, *Gems of Divine Mysteries, Javáhiru'l-Asrár*, p. 26.
47 Dan. 12:4, 8-10.
48 Mark 13:32.
49 I Thess. 5:2.
50 Matt. 25:13.
51 See for example 'The "Great Disappointment"', Wikipedia, November 2012.
52 *Tatfif*, Dealing in Fraud, 83:22-6:

إِنَّ الْأَبْرَارَ لَفِي نَعِيمٍ
عَلَى الْأَرَائِكِ يَنظُرُونَ
تَعْرِفُ فِي وُجُوهِهِمْ نَضْرَةَ النَّعِيمِ
يُسْقَوْنَ مِن رَّحِيقٍ مَّخْتُومٍ
خِتَامُهُ مِسْكٌ وَفِي ذَٰلِكَ فَلْيَتَنَافَسِ الْمُتَنَافِسُونَ

براستی نیکوکاران در نعیم [الهی] خواهند بود
بر تختها [نشسته] می‌نگرند
از چهره‌هایشان طراوت نعمت [بهشت] را درمی‌یابی
از باده‌ای مهر شده نوشانیده شوند
باده‌ای که) مهر آن مشک است و در این [نعمتها] مشتاقان باید بر یکدیگر پیشی گیرند

53 Note 2 in Bahá'u'lláh, *The Kitáb-i-Aqdas*, p. 166.
54 Bahá'u'lláh, *Gleanings from the Writings of Bahá'u'lláh*, XIV, p. 34.
55 Reference to the Second Coming and to the Dispensation of Bahá'u'lláh.
56 Reference to the Dispensation of Christ.
57 John 4:23-4.
58 John 6:63.
59 I Cor. 2:13-14.
60 II Cor. 4:18.
61 ibid. 3:5-6.
62 Ps. 40:6, 11.
63 Ps. 119:18.
64 Isa. 42:18.

65 John 6:40.
66 Eph. 1:17-8.
67 Luke 3:6.
68 Rev. 1:7.
69 John 6:35, 48-51.
70 John 3:13.
71 John 6:58.
72 John 6:41-2.
73 John 8:51-3.
74 I John 3:14.
75 I Tim. 5:6.
76 Luke 9:60.
77 John 3:5.
78 John 3:6.
79 'Abdu'l-Bahá, *The Promulgation of Universal Peace*, p. 304.
80 John 8:56-9.
81 Acts 2:16, 19-20.
82 *'Ankabút*, the Spider, 29:63:

وَلَئِن سَأَلْتَهُم مَّن نَّزَّلَ مِنَ السَّمَاءِ مَاءً فَأَحْيَا بِهِ الْأَرْضَ مِن بَعْدِ مَوْتِهَا لَيَقُولُنَّ اللَّهُ قُلِ الْحَمْدُ لِلَّهِ بَلْ أَكْثَرُهُمْ لَا يَعْقِلُونَ

و اگر از آنان بپرسی چه کسی از آسمان آبی فرو فرستاده و زمین را پس از مرگش به وسیله آن زنده گردانیده است حتما خواهند گفت الله بگو ستایش از آن خداست با این همه بیشترشان نمی اندیشند

83 *Ḥá-Mím*, or *Fuṣṣilat*, 41:39:

وَمِنْ آيَاتِهِ أَنَّكَ تَرَى الْأَرْضَ خَاشِعَةً فَإِذَا أَنزَلْنَا عَلَيْهَا الْمَاءَ اهْتَزَّتْ وَرَبَتْ إِنَّ الَّذِي أَحْيَاهَا لَمُحْيِي الْمَوْتَىٰ إِنَّهُ عَلَىٰ كُلِّ شَيْءٍ قَدِيرٌ

از آیات او این است که زمین را خشک و خاضع می بینی، اما هنگامی که آب بر آن میفرستیم به جنبش در می آید و نمو می کند، همان کس که آنرا زنده کرد مردگان را نیز زنده میکند، او بر هر چیز تواناست.

84 *Ál-i-'Imrán*, the Family of 'Imrán, 3:27:

تُولِجُ اللَّيْلَ فِي النَّهَارِ وَتُولِجُ النَّهَارَ فِي اللَّيْلِ وَتُخْرِجُ الْحَيَّ مِنَ الْمَيِّتِ وَتُخْرِجُ الْمَيِّتَ مِنَ الْحَيِّ وَتَرْزُقُ مَن تَشَاءُ بِغَيْرِ حِسَابٍ

شب را به روز در می آوری و روز را به شب در می آوری و زنده را از مرده بیرون می آوری و مرده را از زنده خارج میسازی و هر که را خواهی بی حساب روزی میدهی

85 'Abdu'l-Bahá, *The Promulgation of Universal Peace*, pp. 291-3.
86 Bahá'u'lláh, *Kitáb-i-Íqán*, para. 88, p. 80, quoting the súrah *Furqán*, The Criterion, 25:7:

And they say: 'What sort of a messenger is this, who eats food, and walks through the streets? Why has not an angel been sent down to him to give admonition with him?'

وَقَالُوا مَالِ هَٰذَا الرَّسُولِ يَأْكُلُ الطَّعَامَ وَيَمْشِي فِي الْأَسْوَاقِ لَوْلَا أُنزِلَ إِلَيْهِ مَلَكٌ فَيَكُونَ مَعَهُ نَذِيرًا

و گفتند این چه پیامبری است که غذا میخورد و در بازارها راه میرود چرا فرشته ای به سوی او نازل نشده تا همراه وی هشداردهنده باشد

87 Bahá'u'lláh, *Gems of Divine Mysteries, Javáhiru'l-Asrár*, pp. 11-12.

10 Corruption of the Divine Message

1   Bahá'u'lláh, *Epistle to the Son of the Wolf*, p. 13.
2   *Baqara*, the Heifer, 2:75:

أَفَتَطْمَعُونَ أَن يُؤْمِنُواْ لَكُمْ وَقَدْ كَانَ فَرِيقٌ مِّنْهُمْ يَسْمَعُونَ كَلاَمَ اللّهِ ثُمَّ يُحَرِّفُونَهُ مِن بَعْدِ مَا عَقَلُوهُ وَهُمْ يَعْلَمُونَ

آیا انتظار دارید به (آئین) شما ایمان بیاورند، با اینکه عدّه‌ای از آنان، سخنان خدا را می‌شنیدند و پس از فهمیدن، آن را تحریف می‌کردند، در حالی که علم و اطّلاع داشتند؟!

3   *Má'ida*, the Table Spread, 5:41:

يَا أَيُّهَا الرَّسُولُ لاَ يَحْزُنكَ الَّذِينَ يُسَارِعُونَ فِي الْكُفْرِ مِنَ الَّذِينَ قَالُواْ آمَنَّا بِأَفْوَاهِهِمْ وَلَمْ تُؤْمِن قُلُوبُهُمْ وَمِنَ الَّذِينَ هِادُواْ سَمَّاعُونَ لِلْكَذِبِ سَمَّاعُونَ لِقَوْمٍ آخَرِينَ لَمْ يَأْتُوكَ يُحَرِّفُونَ الْكَلِمَ مِن بَعْدِ مَوَاضِعِهِ يَقُولُونَ إِنْ أُوتِيتُمْ هَذَا فَخُذُوهُ وَإِن لَّمْ تُؤْتَوْهُ فَاحْذَرُواْ وَمَن يُرِدِ اللّهُ فِتْنَتَهُ فَلَن تَمْلِكَ لَهُ مِنَ اللّهِ شَيْئًا أُوْلَـئِكَ الَّذِينَ لَمْ يُرِدِ اللّهُ أَن يُطَهِّرَ قُلُوبَهُمْ لَهُمْ فِي الدُّنْيَا خِزْيٌ وَلَهُمْ فِي الآخِرَةِ عَذَابٌ عَظِيمٌ

ای پیامبر کسانی که در کفر می‌کوشند تو را اندوهگین نکنند اینان از کسانی هستند که به زبان می‌گویند ایمان آوردهایم ولی دلشان ایمان نیاورده است همچنین از یهودیان، که عده‌ای پذیرا و شنوای دروغ و جاسوسان قومی دیگرند که به نزد شما [از در اسلام و تسلیم] نیامده‌اند اینان کلمات [کتاب آسمانی] را از مواضعش تحریف می‌کنند و [به همدیگر] می‌گویند اگر چنین [حکمی از سوی پیامبر] به شما داده شد، آن را بپذیرید و اگر داده نشد، از او کناره کنید، و کسی که خداوند سرگشتگی‌اش را خواسته باشد، هرگز برای او در برابر خداوند کاری نمی‌توانی کرد، اینان کسانی هستند که خداوند نخواسته است دلهایشان را پاکیزه بدارد، در دنیا خواری و در آخرت عذابی بزرگ [در پیش] دارند

4   The Bible was originally written in Hebrew and Aramaic. There are, however, numerous early texts in Greek with only minor variations among the manuscripts, such as alternative spellings, alternative word order, the presence or absence of an optional definite article ('the'), and so on. The King James version, completed in 1611 AD, was translated by 47 scholars, all of whom were members of the Church of England. In common with most other translations of the period, the New Testament was translated from Greek. There is less than 1 per cent difference between the King James and more modern English translations, and the differences do not affect doctrine – Christianity became divided into sects not because of minor differences in text but because of interpretation. There is no evidence that the relatively minor differences in the original Greek translations and subsequent English translations were deliberate, with the intention of preventing Jews and Christians from recognizing Muhammad. It would have been impossible to alter all the available copies – there are about 4,800 surviving Greek manuscripts of the New Testament, 8,000 ancient Latin copies (translated from the Greek), and 1,000 ancient copies in other languages (see Vasicek, *The Origin of the Bible*, Part V: *Manuscript Differences and Wrap-up*).
5   Shoghi Effendi, *God Passes By*, p. 139.
6   ibid. p. 100.
7   Bahá'u'lláh, *Kitáb-i-Íqán*, para. 93, p. 86. Some Muslim commentators have made similar observations. For instance, al-Bukhari in his book *Saḥīḥ*, commenting on the 85th súrah (*Burúj*, the Zodiacal Signs, 21-2) writes that Abdu'lláh Ibn 'Abbás, Muhammad's paternal cousin and one of His companions, stated that all God's revealed Books remain uncorrupted, for no one is able to change

any of the Divine Words, but the meaning of the Scriptures can be changed through interpretation: 'Nay, this is a Glorious Qur'án, (Inscribed) in a Tablet Preserved!'

صحیح البخاري
جزء6 الصفحة 264
55 - باب قول الله تعالى (بل هو قرآن مجید * فی لوح محفوظ) . (55) (والطور * وكتاب مسطور) .
قال قتادة مكتوب ، يسطرون يخطون فی (أم الكتاب) جملة الكتاب وأصله (ما يلفظ) ما يتكلم من شيء إلا كتب عليه . وقال ابن عباس يكتب الخير والشر ، (يحرفون) يزيلون ، وليس أحد يزيل لفظ كتاب من كتب الله عز وجل ، ولكنهم يحرفونه يتأولونه على غير تأويله ، دراستهم تلاوتهم ، (واعية) حافظة (وتعيها) تحفظها . (وأوحي إلى هذا القرآن لأنذركم به) يعنی أهل مكة ومن بلغ هذا القرآن فهو له نذير 9/196

And:

> How could there be any alteration in the Book whose word's sharpness has reached a great level of circulation among men. Every wise man can see that the alteration of the Bible was impossible for it was well circulated among men of different faiths and backgrounds. (ibid. vol. 3, p. 327)

8 Bahá'u'lláh, *Gems of Divine Mysteries*, *Javáhiru'l-Asrár*, p. 11.
9 Bahá'u'lláh, *Kitáb-i-Íqán*, para. 93, pp. 86-7.
10 *Ál-i-'Imrán*, the Family of 'Imrán, 3:23:

أَلَمْ تَرَ إِلَى الَّذِينَ أُوتُوا نَصِيبًا مِّنَ الْكِتَابِ يُدْعَوْنَ إِلَى كِتَابِ اللهِ لِيَحْكُمَ بَيْنَهُمْ ثُمَّ يَتَوَلَّى فَرِيقٌ مِّنْهُمْ وَهُم مُّعْرِضُونَ

آیا داستان کسانی را که بهره‌ای از کتاب [تورات] یافته‌اند ندانسته‌ای که چون به سوی کتاب خدا فرا خوانده می‌شوند تا میانشان حکم کند آنگه گروهی از آنان به حال اعراض روی برمی‌تابند

11 *Ál-i-'Imrán*, the Family of 'Imrán, 3:78:

وَإِنَّ مِنْهُمْ لَفَرِيقًا يَلْوُونَ أَلْسِنَتَهُم بِالْكِتَابِ لِتَحْسَبُوهُ مِنَ الْكِتَابِ وَمَا هُوَ مِنَ الْكِتَابِ وَيَقُولُونَ هُوَ مِنْ عِندِ اللهِ وَمَا هُوَ مِنْ عِندِ اللهِ وَيَقُولُونَ عَلَى اللهِ الْكَذِبَ وَهُمْ يَعْلَمُونَ

در میان آنها کسانی هستند که به هنگام تلاوت کتاب (خدا)، زبان خود را چنان می‌گردانند که گمان کنید (آنچه را می‌خوانند،) از کتاب (خدا) است؛ در حالی که از کتاب (خدا) نیست! (و با صراحت) می‌گویند: «آن از طرف خداست!» با اینکه از طرف خدا نیست، و به خدا دروغ می‌بندند در حالی که می‌دانند!

12 *Má'ida*, the Table Spread, 5:13:

فَبِمَا نَقْضِهِم مِّيثَاقَهُمْ لَعَنَّاهُمْ وَجَعَلْنَا قُلُوبَهُمْ قَاسِيَةً يُحَرِّفُونَ الْكَلِمَ عَن مَّوَاضِعِهِ وَنَسُوا حَظًّا مِّمَّا ذُكِّرُوا بِهِ وَلاَ تَزَالُ تَطَّلِعُ عَلَىَ خَآئِنَةٍ مِّنْهُمْ إِلاَّ قَلِيلاً مِّنْهُمُ فَاعْفُ عَنْهُمْ وَاصْفَحْ إِنَّ اللهَ يُحِبُّ الْمُحْسِنِينَ

ولی بخاطر پیمان‌شکنی، آنها را از رحمت خویش دور ساختیم؛ و دلهای آنان را سخت و سنگین نمودیم؛ سخنان (خدا) را از موردش تحریف می‌کنند؛ و بخشی از آنچه را به آنها گوشزد شده بود، فراموش کردند؛ و هر زمان، از خیانتی (تازه) از آنها آگاه می‌شوی، مگر عده کمی از آنان؛ ولی از آنها درگذر و صرف‌نظر کن، که خداوند نیکوکاران را دوست می‌دارد!

13 *Baqara*, the Heifer, 2:77-8:

أَوَلاَ يَعْلَمُونَ أَنَّ اللهَ يَعْلَمُ مَا يُسِرُّونَ وَمَا يُعْلِنُونَ
وَمِنْهُمْ أُمِّيُّونَ لاَ يَعْلَمُونَ الْكِتَابَ إِلاَّ أَمَانِيَّ وَإِنْ هُمْ إِلاَّ يَظُنُّونَ

آیا اینها نمی‌دانند خداوند آنچه را پنهان می‌دارند یا آشکار می‌کنند می‌داند!؟
و پاره‌ای از آنان عوامانی هستند که کتاب خدا را جز یک مشت خیالات و آرزوها نمی‌دانند؛ و تنها به پندار هایشان دل بسته‌اند.

14 *Mā'ida*, the Table Spread, 5:77:

قُلْ يَا أَهْلَ الْكِتَابِ لاَ تَغْلُوا۟ فِي دِينِكُمْ غَيْرَ الْحَقِّ وَلاَ تَتَّبِعُوا۟ أَهْوَاءَ قَوْمٍ قَدْ ضَلُّوا۟ مِن قَبْلُ وَأَضَلُّوا۟ كَثِيرًا وَضَلُّوا۟ عَن سَوَاءِ السَّبِيلِ

بگو: «ای اهل کتاب! در دین خود، غلو (و زیاده روی) نکنید! و غیر از حق نگویید! و از هوسهای جمعیتی که پیشتر گمراه شدند و دیگران را گمراه کردند و از راه راست منحرف گشتند، پیروی ننمایید!

15 See *Baqara*, the Heifer, 2:105:

It is never the wish of those without faith among the People of the Book, nor of the pagans, that anything good should come down to you from your Lord. But God will choose for His special Mercy whom He will, for God is Lord of grace abounding.

مَّا يَوَدُّ الَّذِينَ كَفَرُوا۟ مِنْ أَهْلِ الْكِتَابِ وَلاَ الْمُشْرِكِينَ أَن يُنَزَّلَ عَلَيْكُم مِّنْ خَيْرٍ مِّن رَّبِّكُمْ وَاللَّهُ يَخْتَصُّ بِرَحْمَتِهِ مَن يَشَاءُ وَاللَّهُ ذُو الْفَضْلِ الْعَظِيمِ

کافران اهل کتاب، و (همچنین) مشرکان، دوست ندارند که از سوی خداوند، خیر و برکتی بر شما نازل گردد؛ در حالی که خداوند، رحمت خود را به هر کس بخواهد، اختصاص می‌دهد؛ و خداوند، صاحب فضل بزرگ است

16 *Nisā'a*, the Women, 4:46:

مِّنَ الَّذِينَ هَادُوا۟ يُحَرِّفُونَ الْكَلِمَ عَن مَّوَاضِعِهِ وَيَقُولُونَ سَمِعْنَا وَعَصَيْنَا وَاسْمَعْ غَيْرَ مُسْمَعٍ وَرَاعِنَا لَيًّا بِأَلْسِنَتِهِمْ وَطَعْنًا فِي الدِّينِ وَلَوْ أَنَّهُمْ قَالُوا۟ سَمِعْنَا وَأَطَعْنَا وَاسْمَعْ وَانظُرْنَا لَكَانَ خَيْرًا لَّهُمْ وَأَقْوَمَ وَلَـٰكِن لَّعَنَهُمُ اللَّهُ بِكُفْرِهِمْ فَلاَ يُؤْمِنُونَ إِلاَّ قَلِيلاً

برخی از آنان که یهودی‌اند کلمات را از جاهای خود برمی‌گردانند و با پیچاندن زبان خود و به قصد طعنه زدن در دین [اسلام با درآمیختن عبری به عربی] می‌گویند شنیدیم و نافرمانی کردیم و بشنو [که کاش] ناشنوا گردی و [نیز از روی استهزا می‌گویند] راعنا [که در عربی یعنی به ما التفات کن ولی در عبری یعنی خبیث ما] و اگر آنان می‌گفتند شنیدیم و فرمان بردیم و بشنو و به ما بنگر قطعا برای آنان بهتر و درست‌تر بود ولی خدا آنان را به علت کفرشان لعنت کرد در نتیجه جز [گروهی] اندک ایمان نمی‌آورند

17 *Âl-i-'Imrán*, the Family of 'Imrán, 3:99-100:

قُلْ يَا أَهْلَ الْكِتَابِ لِمَ تَصُدُّونَ عَن سَبِيلِ اللَّهِ مَنْ آمَنَ تَبْغُونَهَا عِوَجًا وَأَنتُمْ شُهَدَاءُ وَمَا اللَّهُ بِغَافِلٍ عَمَّا تَعْمَلُونَ
يَا أَيُّهَا الَّذِينَ آمَنُوا۟ إِن تُطِيعُوا۟ فَرِيقًا مِّنَ الَّذِينَ أُوتُوا۟ الْكِتَابَ يَرُدُّوكُم بَعْدَ إِيمَانِكُمْ كَافِرِينَ

بگو: «ای اهل کتاب! چرا افرادی را که ایمان آورده‌اند، از راه خدا بازمی‌دارید، و می‌خواهید این راه را کج سازید؟! در حالی که شما (به درستی این راه) گواه هستید؛ و خداوند از آنچه انجام می‌دهید، غافل نیست!»
ای کسانی که ایمان آورده‌اید! اگر از گروهی از اهل کتاب، (که کارشان نفاق‌افکنی و شعلهورساختن آتش کینه و عداوت است) اطاعت کنید، شما را پس از ایمان، به کفر بازمی‌گردانند.

18 M. M. Pickthall: 'those who disbelieve among the people of the Scripture'.
19 *Baqara*, the Heifer, 2:146:

الَّذِينَ آتَيْنَاهُمُ الْكِتَابَ يَعْرِفُونَهُ كَمَا يَعْرِفُونَ أَبْنَاءَهُمْ وَإِنَّ فَرِيقًا مِّنْهُمْ لَيَكْتُمُونَ الْحَقَّ وَهُمْ يَعْلَمُونَ

کسانی که کتاب آسمانی به آنان داده‌ایم، او را همچون فرزندان خود می‌شناسند؛ جمعی از آنان، حق را آگاهانه کتمان می‌کنند!

NOTES AND REFERENCES

20 *Baqara*, the Heifer, 2:109:

وَدَّ كَثِيرٌ مِّنْ أَهْلِ الْكِتَابِ لَوْ يَرُدُّونَكُم مِّن بَعْدِ إِيمَانِكُمْ كُفَّارًا حَسَدًا مِّنْ عِندِ أَنفُسِهِم مِّن بَعْدِ مَا تَبَيَّنَ لَهُمُ الْحَقُّ فَاعْفُواْ وَاصْفَحُواْ حَتَّىٰ يَأْتِيَ اللَّهُ بِأَمْرِهِ إِنَّ اللَّهَ عَلَىٰ كُلِّ شَيْءٍ قَدِيرٌ

بسیاری از اهل کتاب، از روی حسد -که در وجود آنها ریشه دوانده- آرزو می‌کردند شما را بعد از اسلام و ایمان، به حال کفر باز گردانند؛ با اینکه حق برای آنها کاملا روشن شده است. شما آنها را عفو کنید و گذشت نمایید؛ تا خداوند فرمان خودش (فرمان جهاد) را بفرستد؛ خداوند بر هر چیزی تواناست

21 *Ál-i-ʿImrán*, the Family of *ʿImrán*, 3:69–72:

وَدَّت طَّائِفَةٌ مِّنْ أَهْلِ الْكِتَابِ لَوْ يُضِلُّونَكُمْ وَمَا يُضِلُّونَ إِلَّا أَنفُسَهُمْ وَمَا يَشْعُرُونَ
يَا أَهْلَ الْكِتَابِ لِمَ تَكْفُرُونَ بِآيَاتِ اللَّهِ وَأَنتُمْ تَشْهَدُونَ
يَا أَهْلَ الْكِتَابِ لِمَ تَلْبِسُونَ الْحَقَّ بِالْبَاطِلِ وَتَكْتُمُونَ الْحَقَّ وَأَنتُمْ تَعْلَمُونَ
وَقَالَت طَّائِفَةٌ مِّنْ أَهْلِ الْكِتَابِ آمِنُوا بِالَّذِي أُنزِلَ عَلَى الَّذِينَ آمَنُوا وَجْهَ النَّهَارِ وَاكْفُرُوا آخِرَهُ لَعَلَّهُمْ يَرْجِعُونَ

جمعی از اهل کتاب (از یهود)، دوست داشتند (و آرزو می‌کردند) شما را گمراه کنند؛ (اما آنها باید بدانند که نمی‌توانند شما را گمراه سازند)، آنها گمراه نمی‌کنند مگر خودشان را، و نمی‌فهمند!
ای اهل کتاب! چرا به آیات خدا کافر می‌شوید، در حالی که (به درستی آن) گواهی می‌دهید؟!
ای اهل کتاب! چرا حق را با باطل (می‌آمیزید و) مشتبه می‌کنید (تا دیگران نفهمند و گمراه شوند)، و حقیقت را پوشیده می‌دارید در حالی که می‌دانید؟!
و جمعی از اهل کتاب (از یهود) گفتند: «(بروید در ظاهر) به آنچه بر مؤمنان نازل شده، در آغاز روز ایمان بیاورید؛ و در پایان روز، کافر شوید (و باز گردید)! شاید آنها (از آیین خود) بازگردند! (زیرا شما را، اهل کتاب و آگاه از بشارات آسمانی پیشین می‌دانند؛ و این توطئه کافی است که آنها را متزلزل سازد).

22 *Baqara*, the Heifer, 2:121:

الَّذِينَ آتَيْنَاهُمُ الْكِتَابَ يَتْلُونَهُ حَقَّ تِلَاوَتِهِ أُولَٰئِكَ يُؤْمِنُونَ بِهِ وَمَن يَكْفُرْ بِهِ فَأُولَٰئِكَ هُمُ الْخَاسِرُونَ

کسانی که کتاب آسمانی به آنها داده‌ایم (یهود و نصاری) آن را چنان که شایسته آن است می‌خوانند؛ آنها به پیامبر اسلام ایمان می‌آورند؛ و کسانی که به او کافر شوند، زیانکارند.

23 *Ál-i-ʿImrán*, the Family of *ʿImrán*, 3:20:

فَإِنْ حَاجُّوكَ فَقُلْ أَسْلَمْتُ وَجْهِيَ لِلَّهِ وَمَنِ اتَّبَعَنِ وَقُل لِّلَّذِينَ أُوتُوا الْكِتَابَ وَالْأُمِّيِّينَ أَأَسْلَمْتُمْ فَإِنْ أَسْلَمُوا فَقَدِ اهْتَدَوا وَّإِن تَوَلَّوْا فَإِنَّمَا عَلَيْكَ الْبَلَاغُ وَاللَّهُ بَصِيرٌ بِالْعِبَادِ

اگر با تو، به گفتگو و ستیز برخیزند، (با آنها مجادله نکن! و) بگو: «من و پیروانم، در برابر خداوند (و فرمان او)، تسلیم شده‌ایم.» و به آنها که اهل کتاب هستند و بی‌سوادان بگو: «آیا شما هم تسلیم شده‌اید؟» اگر (در برابر فرمان و منطق حق)، تسلیم شوند، هدایت می‌یابند؛ و اگر سرپیچی کنند، (نگران مباش! زیرا) بر تو، تنها ابلاغ (رسالت) است؛ و خدا نسبت به (اعمال و عقاید) بندگان، بیناست .

24 *Má'ida*, the Table Spread, 5:66-9:

وَلَوْ أَنَّهُمْ أَقَامُوا التَّوْرَاةَ وَالْإِنجِيلَ وَمَا أُنزِلَ إِلَيْهِم مِّن رَّبِّهِمْ لَأَكَلُوا مِن فَوْقِهِمْ وَمِن تَحْتِ أَرْجُلِهِم مِّنْهُمْ أُمَّةٌ مُّقْتَصِدَةٌ وَكَثِيرٌ مِّنْهُمْ سَاءَ مَا يَعْمَلُونَ

يَا أَيُّهَا الرَّسُولُ بَلِّغْ مَا أُنزِلَ إِلَيْكَ مِن رَّبِّكَ وَإِن لَّمْ تَفْعَلْ فَمَا بَلَّغْتَ رِسَالَتَهُ وَاللَّهُ يَعْصِمُكَ مِنَ النَّاسِ إِنَّ اللَّهَ لَا يَهْدِي الْقَوْمَ الْكَافِرِينَ

قُلْ يَا أَهْلَ الْكِتَابِ لَسْتُمْ عَلَىٰ شَيْءٍ حَتَّىٰ تُقِيمُوا التَّوْرَاةَ وَالْإِنجِيلَ وَمَا أُنزِلَ إِلَيْكُم مِّن رَّبِّكُمْ وَلَيَزِيدَنَّ كَثِيرًا مِّنْهُم مَّا أُنزِلَ إِلَيْكَ مِن رَّبِّكَ طُغْيَانًا وَكُفْرًا فَلَا تَأْسَ عَلَى الْقَوْمِ الْكَافِرِينَ

إِنَّ الَّذِينَ آمَنُوا وَالَّذِينَ هَادُوا وَالصَّابِئُونَ وَالنَّصَارَىٰ مَنْ آمَنَ بِاللَّهِ وَالْيَوْمِ الْآخِرِ وَعَمِلَ صَالِحًا فَلَا خَوْفٌ عَلَيْهِمْ وَلَا هُمْ يَحْزَنُونَ

و اگر آنان، تورات و انجیل و آنچه را از سوی پروردگارشان بر آنها نازل شده (قرآن) برپا دارند، از آسمان و زمین، روزی خواهند خورد؛ جمعی از آنها، معتدل و میانه‌رو هستند، ولی بیشترشان اعمال بدی انجام می‌دهند.

ای پیامبر! آنچه از طرف پروردگارت بر تو نازل شده است، کاملا (به مردم) برسان! و اگر نکنی، رسالت او را انجام نداده‌ای! خداوند تو را از (خطرات احتمالی) مردم، نگاه می‌دارد؛ و خداوند، جمعیت کافران (لجوج) را هدایت نمی‌کند.

ای اهل کتاب! شما هیچ آیین صحیحی ندارید، مگر اینکه تورات و انجیل و آنچه را از طرف پروردگارتان بر شما نازل شده است، برپا دارید. ولی آنچه بر تو از سوی پروردگارت نازل شده، (نه تنها مایه بیداری آنها نمی‌گردد، بلکه) بر طغیان و کفر بسیاری از آنها می‌افزاید. بنابر این، از این قوم کافر، (و مخالفت آنها،) غمگین مباش!

آنها که ایمان آورده‌اند، و یهود و صابئان و مسیحیان، هرگاه به خداوند یگانه و روز جزا، ایمان بیاورند، و عمل صالح انجام دهند، نه ترسی بر آنهاست، و نه غمگین خواهند شد.

25 *An'ám*, Cattle, 6:34:

وَلَقَدْ كُذِّبَتْ رُسُلٌ مِّن قَبْلِكَ فَصَبَرُوا عَلَىٰ مَا كُذِّبُوا وَأُوذُوا حَتَّىٰ أَتَاهُمْ نَصْرُنَا وَلَا مُبَدِّلَ لِكَلِمَاتِ اللَّهِ وَلَقَدْ جَاءَكَ مِن نَّبَإِ الْمُرْسَلِينَ

پیش از تو نیز پیامبرانی تکذیب شدند؛ و در برابر تکذیبها، صبر و استقامت کردند؛ و (در این راه،) آزار دیدند، تا هنگامی که یاری ما به آنها رسید. و هیچ چیز نمی‌تواند سنن خدا را تغییر دهد؛ و اخبار پیامبران به تو رسیده است.

26 *An'ám*, Cattle, 6:115-16:

وَتَمَّتْ كَلِمَتُ رَبِّكَ صِدْقًا وَعَدْلًا لَّا مُبَدِّلَ لِكَلِمَاتِهِ وَهُوَ السَّمِيعُ الْعَلِيمُ
وَإِن تُطِعْ أَكْثَرَ مَن فِي الْأَرْضِ يُضِلُّوكَ عَن سَبِيلِ اللَّهِ إِن يَتَّبِعُونَ إِلَّا الظَّنَّ وَإِنْ هُمْ إِلَّا يَخْرُصُونَ

و کلام پروردگار تو، با صدق و عدل، به حد تمام رسید؛ هیچ کس نمی‌تواند کلمات او را دگرگون سازد؛ و او شنونده داناست.

اگر از بیشتر کسانی که در روی زمین هستند اطاعت کنی، تو را از راه خدا گمراه می کنند؛ (زیرا) آنها تنها از گمان پیروی می‌نمایند، و تخمین و حدس (واهی) می‌زنند.

27 *Yúnus*, Jonah, 10:64:

لَهُمُ الْبُشْرَىٰ فِي الْحَيَاةِ الدُّنْيَا وَفِي الْآخِرَةِ لَا تَبْدِيلَ لِكَلِمَاتِ اللَّهِ ذَٰلِكَ هُوَ الْفَوْزُ الْعَظِيمُ

در زندگی دنیا و در آخرت، شاد (و مسرور)ند؛ وعده‌های الهی تخلف ناپذیر است! این است آن رستگاری بزرگ!

28   *Qáf*, 50:28-9:

قَالَ لَا تَخْتَصِمُوا لَدَيَّ وَقَدْ قَدَّمْتُ إِلَيْكُم بِالْوَعِيدِ
مَا يُبَدَّلُ الْقَوْلُ لَدَيَّ وَمَا أَنَا بِظَلَّامٍ لِّلْعَبِيدِ

(خداوند) می‌گوید: «نزد من جدال و مخاصمه نکنید؛ من پیشتر به شما هشدار داده‌ام (و اتمام حجت کرده‌ام)!
سخن من تغییر ناپذیر است، و من هرگز به بندگان ستم نخواهم کرد!

29   *Húd* (the Prophet Húd), 11:1:
A. L. R: A Book with verses basic or fundamental further explained in detail, from One Who is Wise and well-Acquainted (with all things).

الر كِتَابٌ أُحْكِمَتْ آيَاتُهُ ثُمَّ فُصِّلَتْ مِن لَّدُنْ حَكِيمٍ خَبِيرٍ

الر، این کتابی است که آیاتش استحکام یافته؛ سپس تشریح شده و از نزد خداوند حکیم و آگاه (نازل گردیده) است!

Ibráhím, Abraham, 14:1:
A. L. R: A Book Which We have revealed unto thee, in order that thou mightest lead mankind out of the depths of darkness into light – by the leave of their Lord – to the Way of (Him) the Exalted in Power, Worthy of all Praise.

الر كِتَابٌ أَنزَلْنَاهُ إِلَيْكَ لِتُخْرِجَ النَّاسَ مِنَ الظُّلُمَاتِ إِلَى النُّورِ بِإِذْنِ رَبِّهِمْ إِلَى صِرَاطِ الْعَزِيزِ الْحَمِيدِ

الر، (این) کتابی است که بر تو نازل کردیم، تا مردم را از تاریکیها به سوی روشنایی بفرمان پروردگارشان در آوری، بسوی راه خداوند عزیز و حمید

30   *An'ám*, Cattle, 6:92:
And this is a Book which We have sent down, bringing blessings, and confirming (the revelations) which came before it: that thou mayest warn the Mother of Cities and all around her. Those who believe in the hereafter believe in this (Book), and they are constant in guarding their prayers.

وَهَذَا كِتَابٌ أَنزَلْنَاهُ مُبَارَكٌ مُّصَدِّقُ الَّذِي بَيْنَ يَدَيْهِ وَلِتُنذِرَ أُمَّ الْقُرَى وَمَنْ حَوْلَهَا وَالَّذِينَ يُؤْمِنُونَ بِالْآخِرَةِ يُؤْمِنُونَ بِهِ وَهُمْ عَلَى صَلَاتِهِمْ يُحَافِظُونَ

و این کتابی است که ما آن را نازل کردیم؛ کتابی است پربرکت، که آنچه پیش از آن آمده، تصدیق می‌کند؛ و تا (اهل) ام‌القری (مکه) و کسانی را که گرد آن هستند، بترسانی! (یقین بدان) آنها که به آخرت ایمان دارند، و به آن ایمان می‌آورند؛ و بر نمازهای خویش، مراقبت می کنند!

31   *An'ám*, Cattle, 6:114:
. . . He it is Who hath sent unto you the Book, explained in detail. . .

...وَهُوَ الَّذِي أَنزَلَ إِلَيْكُمُ الْكِتَابَ ...

...اوست که این کتاب آسمانی را، که همه چیز در آن آمده، به سوی شما فرستاده است...

32   As in *Tagábun*, Mutual Loss and Gain, 64:6:
That was because there came to them apostles with clear Signs, but they said: 'shall (mere) human beings direct us?' So they rejected (the Message) and turned away. But God can do without (them): and God is free of all needs, worthy of all praise.

ذَٰلِكَ بِأَنَّهُ كَانَت تَّأْتِيهِمْ رُسُلُهُم بِالْبَيِّنَاتِ فَقَالُوا أَبَشَرٌ يَهْدُونَنَا فَكَفَرُوا وَتَوَلَّوا وَّاسْتَغْنَى اللَّهُ وَاللَّهُ غَنِيٌّ حَمِيدٌ

این بخاطر آن است که رسولان آنها (پیوسته) با دلایل روشن به سراغشان می‌آمدند، ولی آنها (از روی کبر و غرور) گفتند: «آیا بشرهایی (مثل ما) می‌خواهند ما را هدایت کنند؟!» از این رو کافر شدند و روی برگرداندند؛ و خداوند (از ایمان و طاعتشان) بی نیاز بود، و خدا غنی و شایسته ستایش است!

33 *A'ráf*, the Heights, 7:35 (*J. M. Rodwell*'s translation):

يَا بَنِي آدَمَ إِمَّا يَأْتِيَنَّكُمْ رُسُلٌ مِّنكُمْ يَقُصُّونَ عَلَيْكُمْ آيَاتِي فَمَنِ اتَّقَىٰ وَأَصْلَحَ فَلَا خَوْفٌ عَلَيْهِمْ وَلَا هُمْ يَحْزَنُونَ

ای فرزندان آدم چون پیامبرانی از خودتان برای شما بیایند و آیات مرا بر شما بخوانند پس هر کس به پرهیزگاری و صلاح گراید نه بیمی بر آنان خواهد بود و نه اندوهگین می شوند

34 *Muhammad Asad*: 'whenever there comes to you apostles'; *Abdullah Yusuf Ali; Aisha Bewley; Ali Ünal; Amatul Rahman Omar; Syed Vickar Ahamed; Farook Malik*: 'whenever there come to you messengers'; *Thomas Ballantyne Irving*: 'whenever any messengers…come'; *M. M. Pickthall*: 'when messengers…come unto you'; *Muhammad Sarwar – Abdel-Haleem; Progressive Muslims; Shabbir Ahmed; Hasan Al-Fátih Qaribullah; Rashad Khalifa*: 'when messengers come to you', 'when messengers . . . come to you', or 'when messengers . . . come . . . to you'; *Al-Muntakhab:*'when there come to you Messengers'; *Ahmed Ali*: 'when apostles come to you'; *Wahiduddin Khan; Muhammad Taqqi Usmani; TahirulQadri Mohammad; Maududi; Maulana Muhammad Ali; Sher Ali*: 'if messengers come to you', or 'if messengers . . . come to you'; *Abdul Majid Daryabadi; Ali Quli Qara'i*: 'if there come unto you apostles'; *Umm Muhammad (Sahih International); Hillali and Khan*: 'if there come to you messengers'; *M. H. Shakir and Dr Kamal Omar*: 'if it happens that there come to you messengers'; *Faridul Haque*: 'if Noble Messengers from among you come to you'; *Muhammad Mahmoud Ghali*: 'in case ever there should definitely come up to you Messengers'.

35 See http://www.drmosad.com/index68.htm; http://www.banimalk.net/vb/banimalk44605-14/.

36 *A. J. Arberry*: 'If there should come to you'; *Edward Palmer*: 'verily, there will come to you Apostles'; *George Sale*: 'verily apostles from among you shall come unto you'; *J. M. Rodwell*: 'there shall come to you apostles'.

37 *Muhammad Ahmed – Samira*: 'if/whenever messengers . . . come to you'; *Dr Munir Munshey*: 'messengers will surely come to you'; *Bilal Muhammad*: 'there comes to you messengers'; *Hamid S. Aziz*: 'verily, there will come to you Messengers'.

38 *Baqara*, the Heifer, 2:38:

قُلْنَا اهْبِطُوا مِنْهَا جَمِيعًا فَإِمَّا يَأْتِيَنَّكُم مِّنِّي هُدًى فَمَن تَبِعَ هُدَايَ فَلَا خَوْفٌ عَلَيْهِمْ وَلَا هُمْ يَحْزَنُونَ

فرمودیم جملگی از آن فرود آیید پس اگر از جانب من شما را هدایتی رسد آنان که هدایتم را پیروی کنند بر ایشان بیمی نیست و غمگین نخواهند شد

39 *Ṭá-Há*, 20:123:

قَالَ اهْبِطَا مِنْهَا جَمِيعًا بَعْضُكُمْ لِبَعْضٍ عَدُوٌّ فَإِمَّا يَأْتِيَنَّكُم مِّنِّي هُدًى فَمَنِ اتَّبَعَ هُدَايَ فَلَا يَضِلُّ وَلَا يَشْقَىٰ

[و] فرمود همگی از آن [بهشت] پایین روید -برخی دشمن برخی دیگر و چون از سوی من رهنمودی برایتان آمد، هرکس که رهنمود مرا پیروی کند، نه گمراه شود و نه به رنج افتد

40 Other translations of *fa-imma ya/tiyannakum*:
    Sahih International: 'And when guidance comes to you from Me'; *M. M. Pickthall*: 'but verily there cometh unto you from Me a guidance'; *M. H. Shakir*: 'so surely there will come to you a guidance from Me'; *Muhammad Sarwar*: 'when Our guidance came to them'; *Muhsin Khan*: 'whenever there comes to you Guidance from Me'; *Arthur J. Arberry*: 'yet there shall come to you guidance from Me'; *George Sale*: 'hereafter, shall there come unto you a direction from me'.

    An'ám, Cattle, 6:114:

    أَفَغَيْرَ اللَّهِ أَبْتَغِي حَكَمًا وَهُوَ الَّذِي أَنزَلَ إِلَيْكُمُ الْكِتَابَ مُفَصَّلًا وَالَّذِينَ آتَيْنَاهُمُ الْكِتَابَ يَعْلَمُونَ أَنَّهُ مُنَزَّلٌ مِّن رَّبِّكَ بِالْحَقِّ فَلَا تَكُونَنَّ مِنَ الْمُمْتَرِينَ

    (با این حال،) آیا غیر خدا را به داوری طلبم؟! در حالی که اوست که این کتاب آسمانی را ، که همه چیز در آن آمده، به سوی شما فرستاده است؛ و کسانی که به آنها کتاب آسمانی داده‌ایم می‌دانند این کتاب، بحق از طرف پروردگارت نازل شده؛ بنابر این از تردیدکنندگان مباش!

41 Hadith 469, translated by Nasiruddin Al-Khattab, in al-Khattab (ed.), *Musnad Imam Ahmad Bin Hanbal*, vol. 1, p. 265.
42 ibid. Hadith 584.
43 ibid. Hadith 629.
44 Guillaume, *The Life of Muhammad: A translation of Ibn Ishaq's Sirat Rasul Allah*, p. 651; Ibn-Hisham, *Sirat an-Nabawiyya*, vol. 4, pp. 602-4.
45 At-Tirmidhi, *Sunan*, no. 3786.
46 *Shúráa*, Consultation, 42:47:

    اسْتَجِيبُوا لِرَبِّكُم مِّن قَبْلِ أَن يَأْتِيَ يَوْمٌ لَّا مَرَدَّ لَهُ مِنَ اللَّهِ مَا لَكُم مِّن مَّلْجَإٍ يَوْمَئِذٍ وَمَا لَكُم مِّن نَّكِيرٍ

    پیش از آن که روزی فرا رسد که از جانب خدا بازگشتی برای آن نیست ، فرمان پروردگارتان را اجابت کنید . آن روز در برابر عذاب خدا هیچ پناهگاهی نخواهید داشت و شما را راهی برای انکار آنچه کرده اید نخواهد بود.

    Please note the multiple insertions that serve only to reinforce the translator's view of the anticipated Day of the Lord or *Rabb*.

47 *Baqara*, the Heifer, 2:143:

    وَكَذَٰلِكَ جَعَلْنَاكُمْ أُمَّةً وَسَطًا لِّتَكُونُوا شُهَدَاءَ عَلَى النَّاسِ وَيَكُونَ الرَّسُولُ عَلَيْكُمْ شَهِيدًا وَمَا جَعَلْنَا الْقِبْلَةَ الَّتِي كُنتَ عَلَيْهَا إِلَّا لِنَعْلَمَ مَن يَتَّبِعُ الرَّسُولَ مِمَّن يَنقَلِبُ عَلَىٰ عَقِبَيْهِ وَإِن كَانَتْ لَكَبِيرَةً إِلَّا عَلَى الَّذِينَ هَدَى اللَّهُ وَمَا كَانَ اللَّهُ لِيُضِيعَ إِيمَانَكُمْ إِنَّ اللَّهَ بِالنَّاسِ لَرَءُوفٌ رَّحِيمٌ

    و بدین گونه شما را امتی میانه قرار دادیم تا بر مردم گواه باشید و پیامبر بر شما گواه باشد و قبله‌ای را که [چندی] بر آن بودی مقرر نکردیم جز برای آنکه کسی را که از پیامبر پیروی می‌کند از آن کس که از عقیده خود برمی‌گردد بازشناسیم هر چند [این کار] جز بر کسانی که خدا هدایت[شان] کرده گران بود و خدا بر آن نبود که ایمان شما را ضایع گرداند زیرا خدا [نسبت] به مردم دلسوز و مهربان است

    Note the obfuscation of '*ommatun wasatun*' or '*a middle umma*' ('*wasat*' is 'the middle part of anything') – and elimination of the possibility that the verse indicates that Islam is an *umma* inserted between past and future Revelations.

48 See for example YouTube, Islamic Republic of Iran, Zahraproductions.net, where the first paragraph is omitted and recitations begin with the second paragraph.
49 'Ayatollah Ali Khamenei Issues Edict Against Baha'i Faith In Iran', in *The Huffington Post*, 1 August 2013. Available at: www.huffingtonpost.com/2013/08/01/iran-bahai-fatwa 1 August 2013.

50   The Muslim Network for Baha'i Rights (BahaiRights.org) recently reported: Sheikh Yusuf Al-Qaradawi, President of the World Federation of Muslim Scholars, issued a formal legal opinion (fatwa) that it is illegal for a Muslim man to marry a Baha'i woman. He requested all those who marry abroad to provide written documents as proof of marriage to a Christian or Jewish [Kitabi] woman because some women do not follow any religion at all despite the fact that their official religion is Christianity, for example. He assured that the Baha'i religion is not recognized in the Qur'an. He also assured the right of some Muftis (those who provide formal legal opinions) to forbid the marriage of a Muslim man to a Kitabi woman in countries where Muslims are a minority, where a Muslim girl can only marry a Muslim man, and whereby the marriage of a Muslim man to a Kitabi woman would take away the chance of a Muslim woman to get a husband in that country, and this is what Omar Ibn Al-Khattab did. This fatwa was issued on the TV program 'understanding life' presented by Akram Kassab on 'ANA' channel during an episode about Muslim minorities. Available with a video at: http://is.gd/3zKWx.
51   See Ghanea, *Human Rights, the UN and the Bahá'ís in Iran*, p. 132; also Amanat, 'The Historical Roots of the Persecution of the Babis and Baha'is in Iran'; Fazel, *The Baha'is of Iran: Socio-historical studies*.
52   Jer. 3:21.
53   Eph. 4:29.
54   Matt. 16:4.
55   The Qur'án also warns against 'cheating', 'deception' and 'defrauding' – fraudulent explanations that will induce some to deny the Day of Resurrection' (*Tatfíf*, Dealing in Fraud, 83:1–17).
56   Heb. 1:1–3.
57   John 14:6.
58   Isa. 48:17.
59   Exod. 3:14.
60   John 1:23.
61   John 10:16.
62   I Cor. 4:5.
63   Shoghi Effendi, *The World Order of Bahá'u'lláh*, p. 20.
64   Justification for prejudice against Jews for the death of Jesus has been attributed to Matt. 27:24–5:
   When Pilate saw that he could prevail nothing, but that rather a tumult was made, he took water, and washed his hands before the multitude, saying, I am innocent of the blood of this just person: see ye to it.
   Then answered all the people, and said, His blood be on us, and on our children.
65   Some trace the origin of the charge that Jews are Christ- or God-killers to a sermon attributed to Melito of Sardis entitled 'Per Pascha' (on the Passover), see Hall (ed.), *Melito of Sardis*, p. 55. This homily formulated the charge of deicide, stating: 'the God has been murdered, the king of Israel has been put to death by an Israelite right hand' (Perry and Schweitzer, *Anti-Semitism: Myth and Hate from Antiquity to the Present*, p. 18).

66 'Declaration on the Relation of the Church to Non-Christian Religions', *Nostra Aetate*, proclaimed by Pope Paul VI on 28 October 1965.
67 Acts 3:19-21.
68 'Abdu'l-Bahá and Shoghi Effendi.
69 Shoghi Effendi, *The World Order of Bahá'u'lláh*, p. 22.

11 Christian–Islamic Doctrinal Conflicts

1 Bahá'u'lláh, *The Proclamation of Bahá'u'lláh*, p. 77.
2 Papal infallibility was dogmatically defined at the First Vatican Council of 1869-1870 during the pontificate of Pope Pius IX, at a time when the papacy was threatened by Italian Nationalist forces. Pope Pius IX is also noted for his denouncements of many basic trends in modernity. Notably, he created the Syllabus of Errors in 1864 which listed numerous ideas that Catholics were forbidden to accept, including rationalism, freedom of speech, freedom of worship/religion, national churches without papal authority, recognition of religions other than Catholicism, democracy, marriage as a civil institution, and secular schools run by the state. Pope Pius IX was also the pontiff addressed by Bahá'u'lláh.
3 Phelps, 'Christianity vs. Churchianity', in *ZWT Reprints* (September 1883) p. 533.
4 Berry, *Religions of the World*.
5 See Shoghi Effendi, *The World Order of Bahá'u'lláh*, pp. 56-7.
6 Mark 3:24-5:
   And if a kingdom be divided against itself, that kingdom cannot stand.
   And if a house be divided against itself, that house cannot stand.
7 Barclay, *The Plain Man Looks at the Apostles' Creed*, pp. 10-11: 'it is first actually called the Apostles Creed about A.D. 390. In the end legend and tradition came to believe that it was literally composed by the apostles . . . each contributing a clause he judged fitting . . .'
8 Gen. 1:1-3.
9 *Taláq*, Divorce, 65:12:

اللَّهُ الَّذِي خَلَقَ سَبْعَ سَمَاوَاتٍ وَمِنَ الْأَرْضِ مِثْلَهُنَّ يَتَنَزَّلُ الْأَمْرُ بَيْنَهُنَّ لِتَعْلَمُوا أَنَّ اللَّهَ عَلَى كُلِّ شَيْءٍ قَدِيرٌ وَأَنَّ اللَّهَ قَدْ أَحَاطَ بِكُلِّ شَيْءٍ عِلْمًا

خدا همان کسی است که هفت آسمان و همانند آنها هفت زمین آفرید فرمان [خدا] در میان آنها فرود می‌آید تا بدانید که خدا بر هر چیزی تواناست و به راستی دانش وی هر چیزی را در بر گرفته است

10 Bahá'u'lláh, Súriy-i-Haykal, para. 102, in Bahá'u'lláh, *The Summons of the Lord of Hosts*, pp. 54-5.
11 Isa. 65:17 and Rev. 21:1; Shoghi Effendi, 'The Unfoldment of World Civilization', in *The World Order of Bahá'u'lláh*, pp. 205-6.
12 John 1:12-13.
13 Rev. 21:7.
14 I Cor. 4:17.
15 Matt. 28:19.
16 I John 5:7.
17 The Nicene Creed was written by the First Ecumenical Council at Nicaea in 325 CE, with additions (the 3rd paragraph and following) by the first Council

of Constantinople (381). There is an unresolved controversy over the words 'and the Son' in the last paragraph (in Latin *filioque*). The *filioque* was accepted by the Catholic Church in 1014 CE and the revision has been part of its doctrine ever since. The *filioque*, the significance of Roman primacy, and geopolitical conflict led to the the Great Schism of 1053. To this day, the Eastern Orthodox Churches do not accept the *filioque* and raise this as one of many reasons that prevent reunification with the Roman Catholic Church. The text of the Nicene Creed is, according to a well-known translation:

> We believe in one God,
> the Father, the Almighty,
> maker of heaven and earth,
> of all that is seen and unseen.
> We believe in one Lord, Jesus Christ,
> the only Son of God,
> eternally begotten of the Father,
> God from God, Light from Light,
> true God from true God,
> begotten, not made, one in Being with the Father.
> Through him all things were made.
> For us men and for our salvation
> he came down from heaven:
> by the power of the Holy Spirit
> he was born of the Virgin Mary, and became man.
> For our sake he was crucified under Pontius Pilate,
> he suffered, died, and was buried.
> On the third day he rose again
> in fulfilment of the Scriptures;
> he ascended into heaven
> and is seated at the right hand of the Father.
> He will come again in glory to judge the living and the dead,
> and his kingdom will have no end.
> We believe in the Holy Spirit, the Lord, the giver of life,
> who proceeds from the Father and the Son.
> With the Father and the Son he is worshipped and glorified.
> He has spoken through the Prophets.
> We believe in one holy catholic and apostolic Church.
> We acknowledge one baptism for the forgiveness of sins.
> We look for the resurrection of the dead
> and the life of the world to come. Amen.

The Athanasian Creed is ascribed to Saint Athanasius of Alexandria (296–373 CE), and elaborates further on the doctrine of the Trinity:

> ... we venerate one God in the Trinity, and the Trinity in oneness; neither confounding the persons, nor dividing the substance; for there is one person of the Father, another of the Son, and another of the Holy Spirit; but the divine nature of the Father and of the Son and of the Holy Spirit is one, their glory is equal, their majesty is coeternal.
>
> Of such a nature as the Father is, so is the Son, so also is the Holy

Spirit; the Father is uncreated, the Son is uncreated, and the Holy Spirit is uncreated; the Father is infinite, the Son is infinite, and the Holy Spirit is infinite; the Father is eternal, the Son is eternal, and the Holy Spirit is eternal; and nevertheless there are not three eternals but one eternal; just as there are not three uncreated beings, nor three infinite beings, but one uncreated, and one infinite; similarly the Father is almighty, the Son is almighty, and the Holy Spirit is almighty; and yet there are not three almightys but one almighty; thus the Father is God, the Son is God, and the Holy Spirit is God; and nevertheless there are not three gods, but there is one God; so the Father is Lord, the Son is Lord, and the Holy Spirit is Lord; and yet there are not three lords, but there is one Lord; because just as we are compelled by Christian truth to confess singly each one person as God, and also Lord, so we are forbidden by the Catholic religion to say there are three gods or three Lords.

The Father was not made, nor created, nor begotten by anyone. The Son is from the Father alone, not made nor created, but begotten. The Holy Spirit is from the Father and the Son, not made, nor created, nor begotten, but proceeding.

There is, therefore, one Father, not three Fathers; one Son, not three Sons; one Holy Spirit, not three Holy Spirits; and in this Trinity there is nothing first or later, nothing greater or less, but all three Persons are coeternal and coequal with one another, so that in every respect, as has already been said above, both unity in Trinity, and Trinity in unity must be venerated. Therefore, let him who wishes to be saved, think thus concerning the Trinity.

18 Mark 12:28-30.
19 Matt. 23:9.
20 I Tim. 2:5.
21 I Tim. 1:17.
22 I Tim. 6:14-16.
23 I Cor. 8:4,6.
24 John 14:28.
25 John 4:23.
26 Mark 14:36 (Matt. 26:39).
27 John 6:38.
28 Mark 10:40.
29 Mark 13:32 (Matt. 24:36).
30 John 12:49-50.
31 John 14:24.
32 John 8:50.
33 John 8:54.
34 Luke 18:18-19.
35 John 5:30.
36 John 5:19.
37 John 8:28.
38 John 5:31.
39 I Tim. 6:13.

40 John 6:65.
41 John 12:44–5.
42 Heb. 1:1–3.
43 John 1:18.
44 John 14:20.
45 Matt. 12:31–2.
46 John 12:44.
47 John 10:37–8.
48 Luke 4:24.
49 John 7:40.
50 John 6:14 (Acts 7:37).
51 John 6:48.
52 John 6:49–51.
53 John 14:7.
54 John 14:8–10.
55 John 10:30–31.
56 Deut. 6:4.
57 Isa. 45:5–6.
58 Isa. 44:6 (Isa. 45:18; 45:21–2; 46:9).
59 Isa. 40:28.
60 John 10:33–7.
61 Hos. 1:10.
62 Hos. 11:1.
63 Gen. 6:1–2.
64 John 1:12–13.
65 I John 5:1.
66 Ps. 2:7.
67 John 1:18.
68 *Ikhláṣ*, Purity (of Faith), 112:1–4:

قُلْ هُوَ اللَّهُ أَحَدٌ
اللَّهُ الصَّمَدُ
لَمْ يَلِدْ وَلَمْ يُولَدْ
وَلَمْ يَكُنْ لَهُ كُفُوًا أَحَدٌ

بگو اوست خدای یگانه
خدای صمد [ثابت متعالی]
[کسی را] نزاده و زاده نشده است
و هیچ کس او را همتا نیست

69 *Ál-i-'Imrán*, the Family of 'Imrán, 3:6:

... لاَ إِلَهَ إِلاَّ هُوَ الْعَزِيزُ الْحَكِيمُ

... معبودی جز خداوند توانا و حکیم، نیست.

70 *Anbiyáa*, the Prophets, 21:25:

وَمَا أَرْسَلْنَا مِن قَبْلِكَ مِن رَّسُولٍ إِلَّا نُوحِي إِلَيْهِ أَنَّهُ لَا إِلَهَ إِلَّا أَنَا فَاعْبُدُونِ

و پیش از تو هیچ پیامبری نفرستادیم مگر اینکه به او وحی کردیم که خدایی جز من نیست پس مرا بپرستید

NOTES AND REFERENCES

71 *Baqara*, the Heifer, 2:116:

وَقَالُواْ اتَّخَذَ اللّهُ وَلَدًا سُبْحَانَهُ بَل لَّهُ مَا فِي السَّمَاوَاتِ وَالأَرْضِ كُلٌّ لَّهُ قَانِتُونَ

و گفتند خداوند فرزندی برای خود اختیار کرده است او منزه است بلکه هر چه در آسمانها و زمین است از آن اوست [و] همه فرمانپذیر اویند

72 *Má'ida*, the Table Spread, 5:72-74:

لَقَدْ كَفَرَ الَّذِينَ قَالُواْ إِنَّ اللّهَ هُوَ الْمَسِيحُ ابْنُ مَرْيَمَ وَقَالَ الْمَسِيحُ يَا بَنِي إِسْرَائِيلَ اعْبُدُواْ اللّهَ رَبِّي وَرَبَّكُمْ إِنَّهُ مَن يُشْرِكْ بِاللّهِ فَقَدْ حَرَّمَ اللّهُ عَلَيهِ الْجَنَّةَ وَمَأْوَاهُ النَّارُ وَمَا لِلظَّالِمِينَ مِنْ أَنصَارٍ
لَّقَدْ كَفَرَ الَّذِينَ قَالُواْ إِنَّ اللّهَ ثَالِثُ ثَلاَثَةٍ وَمَا مِنْ إِلَـهٍ إِلاَّ إِلَـهٌ وَاحِدٌ وَإِن لَّمْ يَنتَهُواْ عَمَّا يَقُولُونَ لَيَمَسَّنَّ الَّذِينَ كَفَرُواْ مِنْهُمْ عَذَابٌ أَلِيمٌ
أَفَلاَ يَتُوبُونَ إِلَى اللّهِ وَيَسْتَغْفِرُونَهُ وَاللّهُ غَفُورٌ رَّحِيمٌ

کسانی که گفتند خدا همان مسیح پسر مریم است قطعا کافر شده‌اند و حال آنکه مسیح می‌گفت ای فرزندان اسرائیل پروردگار من و پروردگار خودتان را بپرستید که هر کس به خدا شرک آورد قطعا خدا بهشت را بر او حرام ساخته و جایگاهش آتش است و برای ستمکاران یاورانی نیست
کسانی که [به تثلیث قائل شده و] گفتند خدا سومین [شخص از] سه [شخص یا سه اقنوم] است قطعا کافر شده‌اند و حال آنکه هیچ معبودی جز خدای یکتا نیست و اگر از آنچه می‌گویند باز نایستند به کافران ایشان عذابی دردناک خواهد رسید
چرا به درگاه خدا توبه نمی‌کنند و از وی آمرزش نمی‌خواهند و خدا آمرزنده مهربان است

73 *Ál-i-'Imrán*, the Family of 'Imrán, 3:64:

قُلْ يَا أَهْلَ الْكِتَابِ تَعَالَوْاْ إِلَى كَلَمَةٍ سَوَاء بَيْنَنَا وَبَيْنَكُمْ أَلاَّ نَعْبُدَ إِلاَّ اللّهَ وَلاَ نُشْرِكَ بِهِ شَيْئًا وَلاَ يَتَّخِذَ بَعْضُنَا بَعْضاً أَرْبَابًا مِّن دُونِ اللّهِ فَإِن تَوَلَّوْاْ فَقُولُواْ اشْهَدُواْ بِأَنَّا مُسْلِمُونَ

بگو ای اهل کتاب بیایید بر سر سخنی که میان ما و شما یکسان است بایستیم که جز خدا را نپرستیم و چیزی را شریک او نگردانیم و بعضی از ما بعضی دیگر را به جای خدا به خدایی نگیرد پس اگر [از این پیشنهاد] اعراض کردند بگویید شاهد باشید که ما مسلمانیم

74 *Tauba*, Repentance; or *Baráat*, Immunity, 9:31:

اتَّخَذُواْ أَحْبَارَهُمْ وَرُهْبَانَهُمْ أَرْبَابًا مِّن دُونِ اللّهِ وَالْمَسِيحَ ابْنَ مَرْيَمَ وَمَا أُمِرُواْ إِلاَّ لِيَعْبُدُواْ إِلَـهًا وَاحِدًا لاَّ إِلَـهَ إِلاَّ هُوَ سُبْحَانَهُ عَمَّا يُشْرِكُونَ

اینان دانشمندان و راهبان خود و مسیح پسر مریم را به جای خدا به الوهیت گرفتند با آنکه مامور نبودند جز اینکه خدایی یگانه را بپرستند که هیچ معبودی جز او نیست منزه است او از آنچه [با وی] شریک می‌گردانند

75 *Maryam*, Mary, 19:37-8:

فَاخْتَلَفَ الأَحْزَابُ مِن بَيْنِهِمْ فَوَيْلٌ لِّلَّذِينَ كَفَرُوا مِن مَّشْهَدِ يَوْمٍ عَظِيمٍ
أَسْمِعْ بِهِمْ وَأَبْصِرْ يَوْمَ يَأْتُونَنَا لَكِنِ الظَّالِمُونَ الْيَوْمَ فِي ضَلاَلٍ مُّبِينٍ

ولی (بعد از او) گروه‌هایی از میان پیروانش اختلاف کردند؛ وای به حال کافران از مشاهده روز بزرگ (رستاخیز)!
در آن روز که نزد ما می‌آیند، چه گوشهای شنوا و چه چشمهای بینایی پیدا می‌کنند! ولی این ستمگران امروز در گمراهی آشکارند!

76 Shoghi Effendi, *The Promised Day Is Come*, p. 123.
77 Bahá'u'lláh, *Epistle to the Son of the Wolf*, p. 57.
78 Shoghi Effendi, *The Light of Divine Guidance*, vol. 1, p. 123.
79 See Bahá'u'lláh: *Kitáb-i-Íqán*, p. 25; quoted in Shoghi Effendi, *The Promised Day Is Come*, p. 52; *Kitáb-i-Íqán*, p. 24; *Epistle to the Son of Wolf*, pp. 48, 171, 89.

80 Shoghi Effendi, *The World Order of Bahá'u'lláh*, p. 185.
81 Shoghi Effendi, *The Promised Day Is Come*, pp. 109-10.
82 Letter written on behalf of Shoghi Effendi to an individual believer, 19 May 1945, in *Lights of Guidance*, no. 1652, p. 492.
83 'Abdu'l-Bahá, *The Promulgation of Universal Peace*, pp. 173-4.
84 Bahá'u'lláh, *Gleanings from the Writings of Bahá'u'lláh*, XX, p. 49.
85 Bahá'u'lláh, *Kitáb-i-Íqán*, para. 110, pp. 103-4.
86 ibid. para. 109, p. 103.
87 Shoghi Effendi, *The World Order of Bahá'u'lláh*, p. 112.
88 Bahá'u'lláh, *Kitáb-i-Íqán*, paras. 104, 105, pp. 98-9.
89 Bahá'u'lláh, *Gleanings from the Writings of Bahá'u'lláh*, LXXXIV, pp. 166-7.
90 ibid. XCIV, pp. 192-3.
91 Bahá'u'lláh, quoted by Shoghi Effendi, *The World Order of Bahá'u'lláh*, p. 113.
92 Bahá'u'lláh, *Gleanings from the Writings of Bahá'u'lláh*, LXXXIV, p. 167.
93 'Abdu'l-Bahá, *Some Answered Questions*, ch. 27, pp. 113-15.
94 Heb. 7:1-3.
95 *Ḥadíd*, Iron, 57:27:

... وَقَفَّيْنَا بِعِيسَى ابْنِ مَرْيَمَ وَآتَيْنَاهُ الْإِنجِيلَ وَجَعَلْنَا فِي قُلُوبِ الَّذِينَ اتَّبَعُوهُ رَأْفَةً وَرَحْمَةً ...

... و عیسی پسر مریم را در پی [آنان] آوردیم و به او انجیل عطا کردیم و در دلهای کسانی که از او پیروی کردند رافت و رحمت نهادیم ...

96 *Anbiyáa*, the Prophets, 21:91:

وَالَّتِي أَحْصَنَتْ فَرْجَهَا فَنَفَخْنَا فِيهَا مِن رُّوحِنَا وَجَعَلْنَاهَا وَابْنَهَا آيَةً لِّلْعَالَمِينَ

و آن [زن را یاد کن] که خود را پاکدامن نگاه داشت و از روح خویش در او دمیدیم و او و پسرش را برای جهانیان آیتی قرار دادیم

97 *Maryam*, Mary, 19:17, 19-22:

فَاتَّخَذَتْ مِن دُونِهِمْ حِجَابًا فَأَرْسَلْنَا إِلَيْهَا رُوحَنَا فَتَمَثَّلَ لَهَا بَشَرًا سَوِيًّا
قَالَ إِنَّمَا أَنَا رَسُولُ رَبِّكِ لِأَهَبَ لَكِ غُلَامًا زَكِيًّا
قَالَتْ أَنَّى يَكُونُ لِي غُلَامٌ وَلَمْ يَمْسَسْنِي بَشَرٌ وَلَمْ أَكُ بَغِيًّا
قَالَ كَذَٰلِكِ قَالَ رَبُّكِ هُوَ عَلَيَّ هَيِّنٌ وَلِنَجْعَلَهُ آيَةً لِّلنَّاسِ وَرَحْمَةً مِّنَّا وَكَانَ أَمْرًا مَّقْضِيًّا
فَحَمَلَتْهُ فَانتَبَذَتْ بِهِ مَكَانًا قَصِيًّا

و در برابر آنان پرده‌ای بر خود گرفت پس روح خود را به سوی او فرستادیم تا به [شکل] بشری خوش‌اندام بر او نمایان شد
گفت من فقط فرستاده پروردگار توام برای اینکه به تو پسری پاکیزه ببخشم
گفت چگونه مرا پسری باشد با آنکه دست بشری به من نرسیده و بدکار نبوده‌ام
گفت [فرمان] چنین است پروردگار تو گفته که آن بر من آسان است و تا او را نشانه‌ای برای مردم و رحمتی از جانب خویش قرار دهیم و [این] دستوری قطعی بود
پس [مریم] به او [=عیسی] آبستن شد و با او به مکان دورافتاده‌ای پناه جست

98 The imperative 'Be' in the original Arabic is the word *kun*, consisting of the two letters 'K' or '*káf*' and 'N' or '*nún*'. The letters correspond to the letters 'B' and 'E' as translated by Shoghi Effendi, referring to the creative Power of God through His Command. In this Day, as attested by Bahá'u'lláh in the Obligatory Prayer, God has released the same creative Power through His revelation:

NOTES AND REFERENCES

> I testify . . . that Thou art God, that there is no God but Thee, and that He Who hath been manifested is the Hidden Mystery, the Treasured Symbol, through Whom the letters B and E (Be) have been joined and knit together. I testify that it is He whose name hath been set down by the Pen of the Most High, and Who hath been mentioned in the Books of God, the Lord of the Throne on high and of earth below.

99 *Maryam*, Mary, 19:34-6:

ذَٰلِكَ عِيسَى ابْنُ مَرْيَمَ قَوْلَ الْحَقِّ الَّذِي فِيهِ يَمْتَرُونَ
مَا كَانَ لِلَّهِ أَن يَتَّخِذَ مِن وَلَدٍ سُبْحَانَهُ إِذَا قَضَىٰ أَمْرًا فَإِنَّمَا يَقُولُ لَهُ كُن فَيَكُونُ
وَإِنَّ اللَّهَ رَبِّي وَرَبُّكُمْ فَاعْبُدُوهُ هَٰذَا صِرَاطٌ مُّسْتَقِيمٌ

این است [ماجرای] عیسی پسر مریم [همان] گفتار درستی که در آن شک می‌کنند
هرگز برای خدا شایسته نبود فرزندی انتخاب کند، منزه است او، هر گاه چیزی را فرمان دهد می‌گوید:
موجود باش، آن هم موجود می‌شود.
و خداوند پروردگار من و شماست، او را بپرستید کنید اینست راه راست.

100 *Ál-i-'Imrán*, the Family of 'Imrán, 3:59:

إِنَّ مَثَلَ عِيسَىٰ عِندَ اللَّهِ كَمَثَلِ آدَمَ خَلَقَهُ مِن تُرَابٍ ثُمَّ قَالَ لَهُ كُن فَيَكُونُ

در واقع مثل عیسی نزد خدا همچون مثل [خلقت] آدم است [که] او را از خاک آفرید سپس بدو گفت باش پس
وجود یافت

101 The doctrine was not dogmatically defined until 1854, by Pope Pius IX in his papal bull *Ineffabilis Deus*. It is rejected by Protestants generally. It is accepted by some Anglo-Catholics but not accepted by most in the Anglican Communion.
102 Shoghi Effendi, *The Promised Day Is Come*, p. 109.
103 Letter from Shoghi Effendi to an individual believer, 1 October 1935, in *Canadian Bahá'í News*, February 1968, p. 11.
104 *Nisáa*, the Women, 4:157-8:

وَقَوْلِهِمْ إِنَّا قَتَلْنَا الْمَسِيحَ عِيسَى ابْنَ مَرْيَمَ رَسُولَ اللَّهِ وَمَا قَتَلُوهُ وَمَا صَلَبُوهُ وَلَـٰكِن شُبِّهَ لَهُمْ وَإِنَّ الَّذِينَ اخْتَلَفُوا
فِيهِ لَفِي شَكٍّ مِّنْهُ مَا لَهُم بِهِ مِنْ عِلْمٍ إِلَّا اتِّبَاعَ الظَّنِّ وَمَا قَتَلُوهُ يَقِينًا
بَل رَّفَعَهُ اللَّهُ إِلَيْهِ وَكَانَ اللَّهُ عَزِيزًا حَكِيمًا

و گفت ایشان که ما مسیح عیسی بن مریم پیامبر خدا را کشتیم و حال آنکه آنان او را نکشتند و مصلوبش
نکردند لیکن امر بر آنان مشتبه شد و کسانی که در باره او اختلاف کردند قطعاً در مورد آن دچار شک شده‌اند
و هیچ علمی بدان ندارند جز آنکه از گمان پیروی می‌کنند و قطعاً او را نکشتند
بلکه خدا او را به سوی خود بالا برد و خدا توانا و حکیم است

105 *Ál-i-'Imrán*, the Family of 'Imrán, 3:55:

إِذْ قَالَ اللَّهُ يَا عِيسَىٰ إِنِّي مُتَوَفِّيكَ وَرَافِعُكَ إِلَيَّ وَمُطَهِّرُكَ مِنَ الَّذِينَ كَفَرُوا وَجَاعِلُ الَّذِينَ اتَّبَعُوكَ فَوْقَ الَّذِينَ كَفَرُوا
إِلَىٰ يَوْمِ الْقِيَامَةِ ثُمَّ إِلَيَّ مَرْجِعُكُمْ فَأَحْكُمُ بَيْنَكُمْ فِيمَا كُنتُمْ فِيهِ تَخْتَلِفُونَ

[یاد کن] هنگامی را که خدا گفت ای عیسی من تو را برگرفته و به سوی خویش بالا می‌برم و تو را از
[آلایش] کسانی که کفر ورزیده‌اند پاک می‌گردانم و تا روز رستاخیز کسانی را که از تو پیروی کرده‌اند فوق
کسانی که کافر شده‌اند قرار خواهم داد آنگاه فرجام شما به سوی من است پس در آنچه بر سر آن اختلاف
می‌کردید میان شما داوری خواهم کرد

106 *Ál-i-'Imrán*, the Family of 'Imrán, 3:38-9:

«هُنَالِكَ دَعَا زَكَرِيَّا رَبَّهُ قَالَ رَبِّ هَبْ لِي مِن لَّدُنْكَ ذُرِّيَّةً طَيِّبَةً إِنَّكَ سَمِيعُ الدُّعَاءِ
فَنَادَتْهُ الْمَلَائِكَةُ وَهُوَ قَائِمٌ يُصَلِّي فِي الْمِحْرَابِ أَنَّ اللَّهَ يُبَشِّرُكَ بِيَحْيَى مُصَدِّقًا بِكَلِمَةٍ مِّنَ اللَّهِ وَسَيِّدًا وَحَصُورًا وَنَبِيًّا مِّنَ الصَّالِحِينَ

آنجا [بود كه] زكريا پروردگارش را خواند [و] گفت پروردگارا از جانب خود فرزندى پاک و پسنديده به من عطا کن که تو شنونده دعايى
پس در حالى كه وى ايستاده [و] در محراب [خود] دعا مى‌كرد فرشتگان او را ندا دردادند كه خداوند تو را به [ولادت] يحيى كه تصديق كننده [حقانيت] كلمة الله [=عيسى] است و بزرگوار و خويشتندار [=هرگز هيچ زنده اى از آنان] و پيامبرى از شايستگان است مژده مى‌دهد

107 *Ál-i-'Imrán*, the Family of 'Imrán, 3:45:

إِذْ قَالَتِ الْمَلَائِكَةُ يَا مَرْيَمُ إِنَّ اللَّهَ يُبَشِّرُكِ بِكَلِمَةٍ مِّنْهُ اسْمُهُ الْمَسِيحُ عِيسَى ابْنُ مَرْيَمَ وَجِيهًا فِي الدُّنْيَا وَالْآخِرَةِ وَمِنَ الْمُقَرَّبِينَ

[ياد كن] هنگامى [را] كه فرشتگان گفتند اى مريم خداوند تو را به كلمه‌اى از جانب خود كه نامش مسيح عيسى‌بن‌مريم است مژده مى‌دهد در حالى كه [او] در دنيا و آخرت آبرومند و از مقربان [درگاه خدا] است

108 John 1:14.
109 *Yúnus*, Jonah, 10:82:

وَيُحِقُّ اللَّهُ الْحَقَّ بِكَلِمَاتِهِ وَلَوْ كَرِهَ الْمُجْرِمُونَ

و خدا با كلمات خود حق را ثابت مى‌گرداند هر چند بزهكاران را خوش نيايد

110 *Ṣáffát*, Those Ranged in Ranks, 37:171:

وَلَقَدْ سَبَقَتْ كَلِمَتُنَا لِعِبَادِنَا الْمُرْسَلِينَ

و قطعا فرمان ما در باره بندگان فرستاده ما از پيش [چنين] رفته است

111 Bahá'u'lláh, *The Kitáb-i-Aqdas*, para. 134, p. 67; see also note 155 in that book, p. 231.
112 The Nicene Creed used by Catholics in the Mass does not contain this statement which however is present in both the Apostles' Creed and the Athanasian Creed.
113 I Pet. 3:19.
114 I Sam. 2:6-8, Hebrew-English Tanakh.
115 Isa. 26:19, ibid.
116 Ezek. 37:4-5, ibid.
117 Mirza Ghulam Ahmad of Qadian, *Jesus in India: Jesus' escape from death on the cross and journey to India*. According to the late 19th-century writings of the founder of the Ahmadiyya sect of Islam, Jesus was only 'in a swoon' when he was taken down from the cross. Deut. 21:31 was interpreted as indicating that God would never allow one of His prophets to be hanged and brutally killed in such a degrading manner as crucifixion. It is recounted that following his ordeal, Jesus was cured of his wounds with a special ointment known as the 'ointment of Jesus' (*marham-i 'Ísá*). He then fled Palestine and settled in Kashmir where he died a natural death of old age, and was laid to rest in Srinagar, Kashmir.
118 Gibbon, *The Decline and Fall of the Roman Empire*, vol. 1, ch. 15, III. For the miraculous powers ascribed to the primitive Church, see pp. 520-21.
119 Luke 23:43.
120 'Abdu'l-Bahá, *Some Answered Questions*, ch. 23, pp. 103-5.

121 'Abdu'l-Bahá, *Tablets of Abdul-Baha*, p. 192.
122 ibid. pp. 193-4.
123 Letter written on behalf of Shoghi Effendi to an individual believer, 19 March 1938, in *Lights of Guidance*, p. 497.
124 I Cor. 12:12-14, 27:
> For as the body is one, and hath many members, and all the members of that one body, being many, are one body: so also is Christ.
> For by one Spirit are we all baptized into one body, whether we be Jews or Gentiles, whether we be bond or free; and have been all made to drink into one Spirit.
> For the body is not one member, but many.
> Now ye are the body of Christ, and members in particular.
125 'Abdu'l-Bahá, *The Promulgation of Universal Peace*, p. 395.
126 Bahá'u'lláh, *Gleanings from the Writings of Bahá'u'lláh*, XXXVI, p. 85.
127 John 6:38.
128 John 6.35.
129 John 6:41-2.
130 John 3:13.
131 'Abdu'l-Bahá, *Some Answered Questions*, ch. 23, pp. 103-4.
132 The Lord's Prayer, Matt. 6: 9-11.
133 I Thess. 4:16.
134 John 5:28-9.
135 *Ṭá-Há*, 20:55:

مِنْهَا خَلَقْنَاكُمْ وَفِيهَا نُعِيدُكُمْ وَمِنْهَا نُخْرِجُكُمْ تَارَةً أُخْرَىٰ

از این [زمین] شما را آفریده‌ایم در آن شما را بازمی‌گردانیم و بار دیگر شما را از آن بیرون می‌آوریم

136 Shoghi Effendi, *Directives from the Guardian*, no. 174, p. 65.
137 Bahá'u'lláh, *Gleanings from the Writings of Bahá'u'lláh*, CXIII, pp. 231-2.
138 Luke 4:16-22.
139 Gen. 1:1-2.
140 II Pet. 1:21.
141 I John 5: 7.
142 *Al-Hijr*, the Rocky Tract, 15:29:

فَإِذَا سَوَّيْتُهُ وَنَفَخْتُ فِيهِ مِن رُّوحِي فَقَعُوا لَهُ سَاجِدِينَ

پس وقتی او را درست اندام ساختم و از روح خود در او دمیدم، به خاک بیفتید و او را سجده کنید

143 *Sajda*, Adoration, 32:9:

ثُمَّ سَوَّاهُ وَنَفَخَ فِيهِ مِن رُّوحِهِ ۖ وَجَعَلَ لَكُمُ السَّمْعَ وَالْأَبْصَارَ وَالْأَفْئِدَةَ ۚ قَلِيلًا مَّا تَشْكُرُونَ

آنگاه او را درست‌اندام کرد و از روح خویش در او دمید و برای شما گوش و دیدگان و دلها قرار داد چه اندک سپاس می‌گزارید

144 *Naḥl*, Bees, 16:102:

قُلْ نَزَّلَهُ رُوحُ الْقُدُسِ مِن رَّبِّكَ بِالْحَقِّ لِيُثَبِّتَ الَّذِينَ آمَنُوا وَهُدًى وَبُشْرَىٰ لِلْمُسْلِمِينَ

بگو آن را روح القدس از طرف پروردگارت به حق فرود آورده تا کسانی را که ایمان آورده‌اند استوار گرداند و برای مسلمانان هدایت و بشارتی است

145 *Baqara*, the Heifer, 2:87: (also 2:253):

...وَآتَيْنَا عِيسَى ابْنَ مَرْيَمَ الْبَيِّنَاتِ وَأَيَّدْنَاهُ بِرُوحِ الْقُدُسِ...

...و به عیسی پسر مریم آن معجزات آشکار را عطا کردیم و او را با « روح القدس » تأیید نمودیم...

146 *Má'ida*, the Table Spread, 5:110:

إِذْ قَالَ اللَّهُ يَا عِيسَى ابْنَ مَرْيَمَ اذْكُرْ نِعْمَتِي عَلَيْكَ وَعَلَى وَالِدَتِكَ إِذْ أَيَّدتُّكَ بِرُوحِ الْقُدُسِ تُكَلِّمُ النَّاسَ فِي الْمَهْدِ وَكَهْلًا وَإِذْ عَلَّمْتُكَ الْكِتَابَ وَالْحِكْمَةَ وَالتَّوْرَاةَ وَالْإِنجِيلَ وَإِذْ تَخْلُقُ مِنَ الطِّينِ كَهَيْئَةِ الطَّيْرِ بِإِذْنِي فَتَنفُخُ فِيهَا فَتَكُونُ طَيْرًا بِإِذْنِي وَتُبْرِئُ الْأَكْمَهَ وَالْأَبْرَصَ بِإِذْنِي وَإِذْ تُخْرِجُ الْمَوْتَى بِإِذْنِي وَإِذْ كَفَفْتُ بَنِي إِسْرَائِيلَ عَنكَ إِذْ جِئْتَهُم بِالْبَيِّنَاتِ فَقَالَ الَّذِينَ كَفَرُواْ مِنْهُمْ إِنْ هَٰذَا إِلَّا سِحْرٌ مُّبِينٌ

[یاد کن] هنگامی را که خدا فرمود ای عیسی پسر مریم نعمت مرا بر خود و بر مادرت به یاد آور آنگاه که تو را به روح‌القدس تأیید کردم که در گهواره [به اعجاز] و در میانسالی [به وحی] با مردم سخن گفتی و آنگاه که تو را کتاب و حکمت و تورات و انجیل آموختم و آنگاه که به اذن من از گل [چیزی] به شکل پرنده می‌ساختی پس در آن می‌دمیدی و به اذن من از پرندهای می‌شد و کور مادرزاد و پیس را به اذن من شفا می‌دادی و آنگاه که مردگان را به اذن من از [زنده از قبر] بیرون می‌آوردی و آنگاه که [آسیب] بنی‌اسرائیل را هنگامی که به برای آنان حجتهای آشکار آورده بودی از تو باز داشتم پس کسانی از آنان که کافر شده بودند گفتند این[ها چیزی] جز افسونی آشکار نیست

147 *Mú-min*, the Believer, 40:15:

رَفِيعُ الدَّرَجَاتِ ذُو الْعَرْشِ يُلْقِي الرُّوحَ مِنْ أَمْرِهِ عَلَىٰ مَن يَشَاءُ مِنْ عِبَادِهِ لِيُنذِرَ يَوْمَ التَّلَاقِ

اوست آن که مرتبه های فرمانروایی اش بسی بلند است و صاحب عرش عظیم است . روح نبوت را که از امر اوست بر هر کس از بندگانش که بخواهد القا می کند و او را به رسالت برمی انگیزد تا مردم را از روز دیدارشان با خدا بیم دهد

148 *Mujádila*, the Woman who Pleads, 58:22:

لَّا تَجِدُ قَوْمًا يُؤْمِنُونَ بِاللَّهِ وَالْيَوْمِ الْآخِرِ يُوَادُّونَ مَنْ حَادَّ اللَّهَ وَرَسُولَهُ وَلَوْ كَانُوا آبَاءَهُمْ أَوْ أَبْنَاءَهُمْ أَوْ إِخْوَانَهُمْ أَوْ عَشِيرَتَهُمْ أُولَٰئِكَ كَتَبَ فِي قُلُوبِهِمُ الْإِيمَانَ وَأَيَّدَهُم بِرُوحٍ مِّنْهُ وَيُدْخِلُهُمْ جَنَّاتٍ تَجْرِي مِن تَحْتِهَا الْأَنْهَارُ خَالِدِينَ فِيهَا رَضِيَ اللَّهُ عَنْهُمْ وَرَضُوا عَنْهُ أُولَٰئِكَ حِزْبُ اللَّهِ أَلَا إِنَّ حِزْبَ اللَّهِ هُمُ الْمُفْلِحُونَ

قومی را نیابی که به خدا و روز بازپسین ایمان داشته باشند [و] کسانی را که با خدا و رسولش مخالفت کرده‌اند هر چند پدرانشان یا پسرانشان یا برادرانشان یا عشیره آنان باشند دوست بدارند در دل اینهاست که [خدا] ایمان را نوشته و آنها را با روحی از جانب خود تایید کرده است و آنان را به بهشتهایی که از زیر [درختان] آن جویهایی روان است در می‌آورد همیشه در آنجا ماندگارند خدا از ایشان خشنود و آنها از او خشنودند اینانند حزب خدا آری حزب خداست که رستگارانند

149 'Abdu'l-Bahá, *The Promulgation of Universal Peace*, p. 182.
150 ibid. p. 142.
151 ibid. p. 288.
152 William Barclay (1907-1978), was a Church of Scotland minister and a distinguished scholar; he was formerly Professor of Divinity and Biblical Criticism at Glasgow University. He was a member of the Advisory Committee working on the New English Bible and also a Member of the Apocrypha Panel of Translators.
153 Barclay, *The Plain Man Looks at the Apostles' Creed*, pp. 282-3.
154 ibid. pp. 293-4.
155 ibid. pp. 294-5.
156 Shoghi Effendi, *The Promised Day Is Come*, p. 105.

157 *Anbiyáa*, the Prophets, 21:92:

إِنَّ هَذِهِ أُمَّتُكُمْ أُمَّةً وَاحِدَةً وَأَنَا رَبُّكُمْ فَاعْبُدُونِ

این است امتشما که امتی یگانه است و منم پروردگار شما پس مرا بپرستید

158 'Abdu'l-Bahá, *Selections from the Writings of 'Abdu'l-Bahá*, no. 35, pp. 70-71.
159 I Kings 8:36.
160 II Chron. 6:30.
161 Ps. 85:2.
162 Ps. 86:5.
163 Matt. 6:12 (the Lord's Prayer).
164 Matt. 6:15.
165 John 20:23. Catholics also consider Matt. 9:2-8, 1 Cor. 11:27, and Matt. 16:17-20 to be among the Scriptural bases for the sacrament.
166 Matt. 6:6, 7, 9, 12.
167 *Nisáa*, the Women, 4:43, 4:99 and 4:149; *Ṭá-Há*, 20:82; *Ḥajj*, the Pilgrimage, 22:60; *Núr*, Light, 24:22, 24:33 and 24:62; *Furqán*, the Criterion, 25:6, 25:6, 25:6, and 25:70; *Ṣád*, 38:66; *Zumar*, the Crowds, 39:5; *Mu-min*, the Believer, 40:42; *Mujádila*, the Woman who Pleads, 58:2; *Núḥ*, Noah, 71:10.
168 Bahá'u'lláh, Bishárát (Glad-Tidings), in *Tablets of Bahá'u'lláh Revealed after the Kitáb-i-Aqdas*, p. 24.
169 Bahá'u'lláh, *The Kitáb-i-Aqdas*, para. 34, p. 30.
170 Clarification by Shoghi Effendi, ibid. note 58, p. 194.
171 Bahá'u'lláh, *Prayers and Meditations by Bahá'u'lláh*, CLXXXIV, p. 339.
172 Bahá'u'lláh, in *Baháʾí Prayers*, p. 163.
173 I Cor. 15:22.
174 Ezek. 18:19-22.
175 Rom. 2:5-6.
176 Rev. 20:13.
177 *Baní Isrá-íl*, the Children of Israel, 17:15:

مَّنِ اهْتَدَى فَإِنَّمَا يَهْتَدي لِنَفْسِهِ وَمَن ضَلَّ فَإِنَّمَا يَضِلُّ عَلَيْهَا وَلاَ تَزِرُ وَازِرَةٌ وِزْرَ أُخْرَى وَمَا كُنَّا مُعَذِّبِينَ حَتَّى نَبْعَثَ رَسُولاً

هر که هدایت یافت به سود خود هدایت یافته و هر که گمراه شد تنها به زیان خود گمراه شده است ، و هیچ گنهکاری بار گناه دیگری را بر دوش نمی گیرد ، و ما هیچ امّتی را پیش از آن که پیامبری به سویشان بفرستیم به عذاب های دنیوی عذاب نکرده ایم .

Also, *Fáṭir*, the Originator of Creation; or *Malá'ika*, the Angels. 35:18.

178 *Naḥl*, Bees, 16:111:

يَوْمَ تَأْتِي كُلُّ نَفْسٍ تُجَادِلُ عَن نَّفْسِهَا وَتُوَفَّى كُلُّ نَفْسٍ مَّا عَمِلَتْ وَهُمْ لاَ يُظْلَمُونَ

[یاد کن] روزی را که هر کس می‌آید [و] از خود دفاع می‌کند و هر کس به آنچه کرده بی کم و کاست پاداش می‌یابد و بر آنان ستم نمی‌رود

179 *Luqmán* (the Wise), 31:33:

يَا أَيُّهَا النَّاسُ اتَّقُوا رَبَّكُمْ وَاخْشَوْا يَوْمًا لَّا يَجْزِي وَالِدٌ عَن وَلَدِهِ وَلَا مَوْلُودٌ هُوَ جَازٍ عَن وَالِدِهِ شَيْئًا إِنَّ وَعْدَ اللَّهِ حَقٌّ فَلَا تَغُرَّنَّكُمُ الْحَيَاةُ الدُّنْيَا وَلَا يَغُرَّنَّكُم بِاللَّهِ الْغَرُورُ

ای مردم از پروردگارتان پروا بدارید و بترسید از روزی که هیچ پدری به کار فرزندش نمی‌آید و هیچ فرزندی [نیز] به کار پدرش نخواهد آمد آری وعده خدا حق است زنهار تا این زندگی دنیا شما را نفریبد و زنهار تا شیطان شما را مغرور نسازد

180 'Abdu'l-Bahá, *Some Answered Questions*, ch. 29, pp. 118-19.
181 Matt. 10:28.
182 John 6:63.
183 I John 3:14.
184 *Baqara*, the Heifer, 2:154:

وَلاَ تَقُولُواْ لِمَنْ يُقْتَلُ فِي سَبِيلِ اللّهِ أَمْوَاتٌ بَلْ أَحْيَاء وَلَكِن لاَّ تَشْعُرُونَ

و کسانی را که در راه خدا کشته می‌شوند مرده نخوانید بلکه زنده‌اند ولی شما نمی‌دانید

185 *Ál-i-'Imrán*, the Family of 'Imrán, 3:169:

وَلاَ تَحْسَبَنَّ الَّذِينَ قُتِلُواْ فِي سَبِيلِ اللّهِ أَمْوَاتًا بَلْ أَحْيَاء عِندَ رَبِّهِمْ يُرْزَقُونَ

هرگز کسانی را که در راه خدا کشته شده‌اند مرده مپندار بلکه زنده‌اند که نزد پروردگارشان روزی داده می‌شوند

186 *Baqara*, the Heifer, 2:28:

كَيْفَ تَكْفُرُونَ بِاللَّهِ وَكُنتُمْ أَمْوَاتاً فَأَحْيَاكُمْ ثُمَّ يُمِيتُكُمْ ثُمَّ يُحْيِيكُمْ ثُمَّ إِلَيْهِ تُرْجَعُونَ

چگونه خدا را منکرید با آنکه مردگانی بودید و شما را زنده کرد باز شما را می میراند [و] باز زنده می‌کند [و] آنگاه به سوی او باز گردانده می‌شوید

187 John 17:3.
188 John 6:40.
189 *Ál-i-'Imrán*, the Family of 'Imrán, 3:15,17:

قُلْ أَؤُنَبِّئُكُم بِخَيْرٍ مِّن ذَلِكُمْ لِلَّذِينَ اتَّقَوْا عِندَ رَبِّهِمْ جَنَّاتٌ تَجْرِي مِن تَحْتِهَا الأَنْهَارُ خَالِدِينَ فِيهَا وَأَزْوَاجٌ مُّطَهَّرَةٌ وَرِضْوَانٌ مِّنَ اللّهِ وَاللّهُ بَصِيرٌ بِالْعِبَادِ
الصَّابِرِينَ وَالصَّادِقِينَ وَالْقَانِتِينَ وَالْمُنفِقِينَ وَالْمُسْتَغْفِرِينَ بِالأَسْحَارِ

بگو آیا شما را به بهتر از اینها خبر دهم برای کسانی که تقوا پیشه کرده‌اند نزد پروردگارشان باغهایی است که از زیر [درختان] آنها نهرها روان است در آن جاودانه بمانند و همسرانی پاکیزه و [نیز] خشنودی خدا [را] دارند و خداوند به [امور] بندگان [خود] بیناست
[اینانند] شکیبایان و راستگویان و فرمانبرداران و انفاق‌کنندگان و آمرزش‌خواهان در سحرگاهان

190 Bahá'u'lláh, *Kitáb-i-Íqán*, para. 120, p. 113-14.
191 'Abdu'l-Bahá, *Some Answered Questions*, ch. 21, p. 98.
192 Bahá'u'lláh, *Hidden Words*, Arabic no. 4.
193 ibid. Persian no. 37.
194 Bahá'u'lláh, *Kitáb-i-Íqán*, para. 31, p. 34.

12 The 'Seal of the Prophets' (khátam al-nabiyyín) and the Finality of Islam

1 Bahá'u'lláh, *Kitáb-i-Íqán*, para. 3, p. 4.
2 'Abdu'l-Bahá, *Paris Talks*, ch. 13, p. 37.
3 *Aḥzáb*, the Confederates, 33:40:

مَّا كَانَ مُحَمَّدٌ أَبَا أَحَدٍ مِّن رِّجَالِكُمْ وَلَكِن رَّسُولَ اللَّهِ وَخَاتَمَ النَّبِيِّينَ وَكَانَ اللَّهُ بِكُلِّ شَيْءٍ عَلِيمًا

آ محمد پدر هیچ یک از مردان شما نبوده و نیست؛ ولی رسول خدا و ختم‌کننده و آخرین پیامبران است؛ و خداوند به همه چیز آگاه است!

566

4   *Ál-i-'Imrán*, the Family of 'Imrán, 3:19:

إِنَّ الدِّينَ عِندَ اللَّهِ الإِسْلَامُ ...

در حقیقت دین نزد خدا همان اسلام است ...

    E. H. Palmer:
        Verily, (the true) religion in God's sight is Islam . . .
    M. M. Pickthall:
        Lo! religion with God (is) the Surrender (to His Will and Guidance).

5   *Má'ida*, the Table Spread, 5:3:

...الْيَوْمَ أَكْمَلْتُ لَكُمْ دِينَكُمْ وَأَتْمَمْتُ عَلَيْكُمْ نِعْمَتِي وَرَضِيتُ لَكُمُ الإِسْلَامَ دِينًا

... امروز دینتان را برای شما کامل ساختم و نعمتم را بر شما تمام کردم و اسلام را آیین شما پسندیدم ...

6   This is one of the last verses revealed in the Qur'án and is a statement that follows completion of a final series of social laws. Hence, the perfection of the religion likely refers to perfection of the Dispensation of Islam.
Ál-i-'Imrán, the Family of 'Imrán, 3:85:

وَمَن يَبْتَغِ غَيْرَ الإِسْلَامِ دِينًا فَلَن يُقْبَلَ مِنْهُ وَهُوَ فِي الآخِرَةِ مِنَ الْخَاسِرِينَ

و هر که جز اسلام دینی [دیگر] جوید هرگز از وی پذیرفته نشود و وی در آخرت از زیانکاران است

7   *Tauba*, Repentance; or *Baráat*, Immunity, 9:32–3:

يُرِيدُونَ أَن يُطْفِئُوا نُورَ اللَّهِ بِأَفْوَاهِهِمْ وَيَأْبَى اللَّهُ إِلَّا أَن يُتِمَّ نُورَهُ وَلَوْ كَرِهَ الْكَافِرُونَ
هُوَ الَّذِي أَرْسَلَ رَسُولَهُ بِالْهُدَى وَدِينِ الْحَقِّ لِيُظْهِرَهُ عَلَى الدِّينِ كُلِّهِ وَلَوْ كَرِهَ الْمُشْرِكُونَ

می‌خواهند نور خدا را با سخنان خویش خاموش کنند ولی خداوند نمی‌گذارد تا نور خود را کامل کند هر چند کافران را خوش نیاید
او کسی است که رسولش را با هدایت و آیین حق فرستاد، تا آن را بر همه آیین‌ها غالب گرداند، هر چند مشرکان کراهت داشته باشند!

8   Bahá'u'lláh, *Kitáb-i-Íqán*, para. 3, p. 4.
9   Exod. 31:12–15.
10 Deut. 4:1–2.
11 Deut. 12:32; 13:1–4.
12 Josh. 1:7.
13 'Messiah' in Aramaic and 'Christ' in Greek both signify 'the Anointed One', referring to the return of King David who was anointed King of Israel by the High Priest Samuel.
14 Matt. 5:17–20.
15 Matt. 21:23.
16 Mark 2:24; 2:27–8.
17 Matt. 9:16–7.
18 John 5:19.
19 John 5:30.
20 John 6:38.
21 John 14:6.
22 Matt. 24:35; Mark 13:31; and Luke 21:33.

23 Rev. 22:18-19.
24 Bahá'u'lláh, *Gems of Divine Mysteries, Javáhiru'l-Asrár*, pp. 17-19.
25 *Baqara*, the Heifer, 2:111-12:

وَقَالُوا لَن يَدْخُلَ الْجَنَّةَ إِلَّا مَن كَانَ هُودًا أَوْ نَصَارَىٰ تِلْكَ أَمَانِيُّهُمْ قُلْ هَاتُوا بُرْهَانَكُمْ إِن كُنتُمْ صَادِقِينَ
بَلَىٰ مَنْ أَسْلَمَ وَجْهَهُ لِلَّهِ وَهُوَ مُحْسِنٌ فَلَهُ أَجْرُهُ عِندَ رَبِّهِ وَلَا خَوْفٌ عَلَيْهِمْ وَلَا هُمْ يَحْزَنُونَ

آنها گفتند: «هيچ کس، جز يهود يا نصاری، هرگز داخل بهشت نخواهد شد.» اين آرزوی آنهاست! بگو:
«اگر راست می‌گوييد، دليل خود را (بر اين موضوع) بياوريد!»
آری، کسی که از روی خود را تسليم خدا کند و نيکوکار باشد، پاداش او نزد پروردگارش ثابت است؛ نه ترسی
بر آنهاست و نه غمگين می‌شوند. (بنابر اين، بهشت خدا در انحصار هيچ گروهی نيست.)

26 *Má'ida*, the Table Spread, 5:64:

وَقَالَتِ الْيَهُودُ يَدُ اللَّهِ مَغْلُولَةٌ غُلَّتْ أَيْدِيهِمْ وَلُعِنُوا بِمَا قَالُوا بَلْ يَدَاهُ مَبْسُوطَتَانِ يُنفِقُ كَيْفَ يَشَاءُ وَلَيَزِيدَنَّ كَثِيرًا
مِنْهُم مَّا أُنزِلَ إِلَيْكَ مِن رَّبِّكَ طُغْيَانًا وَكُفْرًا...

و يهوديان گفتند : دست خدا بسته است ـ دست های خودشان بسته و بی اقتدار باد ، و به سزای آنچه گفتند
لعنت بر آنان باد ـ بلکه هر دو دست خدا باز است و قدرتش بی کران . هرگونه بخواهد می بخشد . و قطعاً
کتابی که از جانب پروردگارت به سوی تو فرو فرستاده شده است بر سرکشی و کفر بسياری از آنان می
افزايد ...

27 Bahá'u'lláh, *Kitáb-i-Íqán*, para. 172, p. 162.
28 Bahá'u'lláh, *Gems of Divine Mysteries, Javáhiru'l-Asrár*, p. 44.
29 *Saḥíḥ al-Bukhari*, 3455. Available at: http://sunnah.com/bukhari. Narrated by Abu Sa'íd. Book 60, Hadith 123; USC-MSA web (English) reference: vol. 4, Book 55, Hadith 662.
    As narrated by Abu Sa'id Al-Khudri:
    The Prophet said, 'You will follow the ways of those nations who were before you, span by span and cubit by cubit (i.e. inch by inch) so much so that if they entered a hole of a mastigure, you would follow them.' We said, 'O God's Apostle! (Do you mean) the Jews and Christians?' He said, 'Whom else?' (ibid. vol. 92, Book 9, Hadith 422)
    And in *Sunan Ibn Majah*:
    'You will most certainly follow the ways of those who came before you, arm's length by arm's length, forearm's length by forearm's length, hand span by hand span, until even if they entered a hole of a mastigure (lizard) you will enter it too.' They said: 'O Messenger of Allah, (do you mean) the Jews and the Christians?' He said: 'Who else?' (vol. 1, Book 36, Arabic ref. Hadith 4129; English ref. Hadith 3994)
30 Shoghi Effendi, Summary Statement to the Special UN Committee on Palestine, 1947.
31 Bahá'u'lláh, *Kitáb-i-Íqán*, para. 161, p. 153.
32 Shoghi Effendi, *The World Order of Bahá'u'lláh*, p. 58.
33 Bahá'u'lláh, *Kitáb-i-Íqán*, para. 110, p. 104.
34 Bahá'u'lláh, *Gleanings from the Writings of Bahá'u'lláh*, XXII, p. 54.
35 ibid. XCII, p. 183.

36 A'ráf, the Heights, 7:157-8:

الَّذِينَ يَتَّبِعُونَ الرَّسُولَ النَّبِيَّ الأُمِّيَّ الَّذِي يَجِدُونَهُ مَكْتُوبًا عِندَهُمْ فِي التَّوْرَاةِ وَالإِنْجِيلِ يَأْمُرُهُم بِالْمَعْرُوفِ وَيَنْهَاهُمْ عَنِ الْمُنكَرِ وَيُحِلُّ لَهُمُ الطَّيِّبَاتِ وَيُحَرِّمُ عَلَيْهِمُ الْخَبَائِثَ وَيَضَعُ عَنْهُمْ إِصْرَهُمْ وَالأَغْلالَ الَّتِي كَانَتْ عَلَيْهِمْ فَالَّذِينَ آمَنُوا بِهِ وَعَزَّرُوهُ وَنَصَرُوهُ وَاتَّبَعُوا النُّورَ الَّذِي أُنزِلَ مَعَهُ أُوْلَئِكَ هُمُ الْمُفْلِحُونَ قُلْ يَا أَيُّهَا النَّاسُ إِنِّي رَسُولُ اللَّهِ إِلَيْكُمْ جَمِيعًا الَّذِي لَهُ مُلْكُ السَّمَاوَاتِ وَالأَرْضِ لا إِلَهَ إِلا هُوَ يُحْيِي وَيُمِيتُ فَآمِنُوا بِاللَّهِ وَرَسُولِهِ النَّبِيِّ الأُمِّيِّ الَّذِي يُؤْمِنُ بِاللَّهِ وَكَلِمَاتِهِ وَاتَّبِعُوهُ لَعَلَّكُمْ تَهْتَدُونَ

مؤمنان کسانی اند که از این فرستاده ، پیامبر درس ناخوانده که اهل کتاب او را نزد خود با همین نام و نشان در تورات و انجیل درس نوشته می یابند ، پیروی می کنند . می یابند که آنان را به کار پسندیده فرمان می دهد و از کار ناپسند بازشان می دارد و پاکیزه ها را برای آنان حلال و پلیدها را بر آنان حرام می کند ، و بار گرانشان را از دوششان برمی دارد و بندها و زنجیر هایی را که بر آنان تحمیل شده است از آنان فرو می گذارد . پس کسانی که به او ایمان آورده و او را بزرگ داشته و یاری اش کرده اند و از قرآن ، این کتاب روشنگری که از جانب خدا نازل شده و قرین او و گواه راستگویی اوست پیروی نموده اند آنان نیکبخت خواهند بود .

بگو : ای مردم ، من فرستاده خدا به سوی همه شما هستم ؛ خدایی که فرمانروایی آسمان ها و زمین از آن اوست . معبودی شایسته پرستش جز او نیست . زنده می کند و می میراند . پس به خدا و رسول او ـ آن پیامبر درس ناخوانده که خود به خدا و سخنان او ایمان دارد ـ ایمان بیاورید و از او پیروی کنید ، باشد که به نیکبختی سرای آخرت راه یابید .

37 'He Who shall arise', expected by the Shí'ihs and a reference to the Báb. See Bahá'u'lláh, *Epistle to the Son of Wolf*, p. 112:
> Imám Ṣádiq hath said: 'When our Qá'im will arise, the earth will shine with the light of her Lord' [*Zumar*, or the Crowds, 39:69].

38 Bahá'u'lláh, *Gems of Divine Mysteries, Javáhiru'l-Asrár*, pp. 19-20. Here are the citations in the Qur'án for this passage:
> And all this, when the Day of Resurrection (*Sajda*, Adoration, 32:55; *Sabá*, the City of Sabá, 34:26; *Mú-min*, the Believer, 40:1-6) hath been ushered in, and the Trumpet hath been sounded (*Fáṭir*, the Originator of Creation; or *Maláika*, the Angels, 35:60; *Zumar*, the Crowds, 39:67-9; *Nabaa*, the (Great) News, 78:18; *Názi'át*, Those Who Tear Out, 79:6-9), and all the denizens of earth and heaven have been gathered together (*Ál-i-'Imrán*, the Family of 'Imrán, 3:9; *Nisáa*, the Women, 4:87; *Yúnus*, Jonah, 10:46; *Al-Hijr*, the Rocky Tract, 15:15), and the Balance (*Ál-i-'Imrán*, or the Family of 'Imrán 3:9; *Nisáa*, the Women, 4:87; *Yúnus*, Jonah, 10:46; *Al-Hijr*, the Rocky Tract, 15:15) hath been appointed, and the Bridge (Bukhari, vol. 1) hath been laid, and the Verses have been sent down (*Baní Isrá-íl*, the Children of Israel, 17:14), and the Sun hath shone forth (*Zumar*, the Crowds, 39:69), and the stars have been blotted out (*Mursalát*, or Those Sent Forth, 77:9), and the souls have been raised to life (*Mujádila*, the Woman who Pleads, 58:6; *Núh*, Noah, 71:18), and the breath of the Spirit hath blown (*Zumar*, the Crowds, 39:67-69; *Qáf*, 50:20; *Nabaa*, the (Great) News, 78:18; *Názi'át*, Those Who Tear Out, 79:6-9), and the angels have been arrayed in ranks (*Fajr*, the Break of Day, 89:22), and the Paradise hath been brought nigh (*Shu'aráa*, the Poets, 26:90), and Hell made to blaze! (*Baní Isrá-íl*, the Children of Israel, 17:97).

39 *Aḥzáb*, the Confederates, 33:40.

40 Bahá'u'lláh, *Kitáb-i-Íqán*, para. 196, p. 179.
41 *Naḥl*, Bees, 16:67:

وَمِن ثَمَرَاتِ النَّخِيلِ وَالأَعْنَابِ تَتَّخِذُونَ مِنْهُ سَكَرًا وَرِزْقًا حَسَنًا إِنَّ فِي ذَلِكَ لآيَةً لِّقَوْمٍ يَعْقِلُونَ

و از میوهٔ درختان خرما و انگور بادهٔ مستی‌بخش و خوراکی نیکو برای خود می‌گیرید قطعا در این[ها] برای مردمی که تعقل می‌کنند نشانه‌ای است

42 *Baqara*, the Heifer, 2:219:

يَسْأَلُونَكَ عَنِ الْخَمْرِ وَالْمَيْسِرِ قُلْ فِيهِمَا إِثْمٌ كَبِيرٌ وَمَنَافِعُ لِلنَّاسِ وَإِثْمُهُمَا أَكْبَرُ مِن نَّفْعِهِمَا .

در بارهٔ شراب و قمار از تو سؤال می‌کنند، بگو: «در آنها گناه و زیان بزرگی است؛ و منافعی برای مردم در بر دارد؛ (ولی) گناه آنها از نفعشان بیشتر است.

43 *Nisáa*, the Women, 4:43:

يَا أَيُّهَا الَّذِينَ آمَنُواْ لاَ تَقْرَبُواْ الصَّلاَةَ وَأَنتُمْ سُكَارَى حَتَّىَ تَعْلَمُواْ مَا تَقُولُونَ وَلاَ جُنُبًا إِلاَّ عَابِرِي سَبِيلٍ حَتَّىَ تَغْتَسِلُواْ وَإِن كُنتُم مَّرْضَى أَوْ عَلَى سَفَرٍ أَوْ جَاء أَحَدٌ مِّنكُم مِّنَ الْغَائِطِ أَوْ لاَمَسْتُمُ النِّسَاء فَلَمْ تَجِدُواْ مَاء فَتَيَمَّمُواْ صَعِيدًا طَيِّبًا فَامْسَحُواْ بِوُجُوهِكُمْ وَأَيْدِيكُمْ إِنَّ اللّهَ كَانَ عَفُوًّا غَفُورًا

ای کسانی که ایمان آورده‌اید در حال مستی به نماز نزدیک نشوید تا زمانی که بدانید چه می‌گویید و [نیز] در حال جنابت [وارد نماز نشوید] مگر اینکه راهگذر باشید تا غسل کنید و اگر بیمارید یا در سفرید یا یکی از شما از قضای حاجت آمد یا با زنان آمیزش کرده‌اید و آب نیافته‌اید پس بر خاکی پاک تیمم کنید و صورت و دستهایتان را مسح نمایید که خدا بخشنده و آمرزنده است

44 *Má'ida*, the Table Spread, 5:90–92:

يَا أَيُّهَا الَّذِينَ آمَنُواْ إِنَّمَا الْخَمْرُ وَالْمَيْسِرُ وَالأَنصَابُ وَالأَزْلاَمُ رِجْسٌ مِّنْ عَمَلِ الشَّيْطَانِ فَاجْتَنِبُوهُ لَعَلَّكُمْ تُفْلِحُونَ
إِنَّمَا يُرِيدُ الشَّيْطَانُ أَن يُوقِعَ بَيْنَكُمُ الْعَدَاوَةَ وَالْبَغْضَاء فِي الْخَمْرِ وَالْمَيْسِرِ وَيَصُدَّكُمْ عَن ذِكْرِ اللّهِ وَعَنِ الصَّلاَةِ فَهَلْ أَنتُم مُّنتَهُونَ
وَأَطِيعُواْ اللّهَ وَأَطِيعُواْ الرَّسُولَ وَاحْذَرُواْ فَإِن تَوَلَّيْتُمْ فَاعْلَمُواْ أَنَّمَا عَلَى رَسُولِنَا الْبَلاَغُ الْمُبِينُ

ای کسانی که ایمان آورده‌اید شراب و قمار و بتها و تیرهای قرعه پلیدند [و] از عمل شیطانند پس از آنها دوری گزینید باشد که رستگار شوید
همانا شیطان می‌خواهد با شراب و قمار میان شما دشمنی و کینه ایجاد کند و شما را از یاد خدا و از نماز باز دارد پس آیا شما دست برمی‌دارید
و اطاعت خدا و اطاعت پیامبر کنید و [از گناهان] برحذر باشید پس اگر روی گرداندید بدانید که بر عهدهٔ پیامبر ما فقط رساندن [پیام] آشکار است

45 *Anfál*, the Spoils of War, 8:65:

يَا أَيُّهَا النَّبِيُّ حَرِّضِ الْمُؤْمِنِينَ عَلَى الْقِتَالِ إِن يَكُن مِّنكُمْ عِشْرُونَ صَابِرُونَ يَغْلِبُواْ مِئَتَيْنِ وَإِن يَكُن مِّنكُم مِّئَةٌ يَغْلِبُواْ أَلْفًا مِّنَ الَّذِينَ كَفَرُواْ بِأَنَّهُمْ قَوْمٌ لاَّ يَفْقَهُونَ

ای پیامبر مؤمنان را به جهاد برانگیز اگر از [میان] شما بیست تن شکیبا باشند بر دویست تن چیره می‌شوند و اگر از شما یکصد تن باشند بر هزار تن از کافران پیروز می‌گردند چرا که آنان قومی‌اند که نمی‌فهمند

46 *Baqara*, the Heifer, 2:190–91:

وَقَاتِلُواْ فِي سَبِيلِ اللّهِ الَّذِينَ يُقَاتِلُونَكُمْ وَلاَ تَعْتَدُواْ إِنَّ اللّهَ لاَ يُحِبُّ الْمُعْتَدِينَ
وَاقْتُلُوهُمْ حَيْثُ ثَقِفْتُمُوهُمْ وَأَخْرِجُوهُم مِّنْ حَيْثُ أَخْرَجُوكُمْ وَالْفِتْنَةُ أَشَدُّ مِنَ الْقَتْلِ وَلاَ تُقَاتِلُوهُمْ عِندَ الْمَسْجِدِ الْحَرَامِ
حَتَّى يُقَاتِلُوكُمْ فِيهِ فَإِن قَاتَلُوكُمْ فَاقْتُلُوهُمْ كَذَلِكَ جَزَاء الْكَافِرِينَ

و در راه خدا با کسانی که با شما می‌جنگند بجنگید ولی از اندازه درنگذرید زیرا خداوند تجاوزکاران را دوست نمی‌دارد
و هر کجا بر ایشان دست‌یافتید آنان را بکشید و همان گونه که شما را بیرون راندند آنان را بیرون برانید [چرا که] فتنه [=شرک] از قتل بدتر است [با این همه] در کنار مسجد الحرام با آنان جنگ مکنید مگر آنکه با شما در آن جا به جنگ درآیند پس اگر با شما جنگیدند آنان را بکشید که کیفر کافران چنین است

47 *Nahjul Balághah*, vol. 2, Letter no. 14.
48 *Má'ida*, the Table Spread, 5:1:

... إِنَّ اللّهَ يَحْكُمُ مَا يُرِيدُ

... خدا هر چه بخواهد فرمان می‌دهد

49 *Anbiyáa*, the Prophets, 21:23:

لاَ يُسْأَلُ عَمَّا يَفْعَلُ وَهُمْ يُسْأَلُونَ

در آنچه [خدا] انجام می‌دهد چون و چرا راه ندارد و[لی] آنان [=انسانها] سؤال خواهند شد

50 *Ḥajj*, the Pilgrimage, 22:18:

... إِنَّ اللَّهَ يَفْعَلُ مَا يَشَاءُ

... خداوند هر کار را بخواهد (و صلاح بداند) انجام می‌دهد!

51 *Luqmán* (the Wise), 31:29 (a reference to the death and resurrection of a former Dispensation and its subsequent demise):

أَلَمْ تَرَ أَنَّ اللَّهَ يُولِجُ اللَّيْلَ فِي النَّهَارِ وَيُولِجُ النَّهَارَ فِي اللَّيْلِ وَسَخَّرَ الشَّمْسَ وَالْقَمَرَ كُلٌّ يَجْرِي إِلَى أَجَلٍ مُسَمًّى وَأَنَّ اللَّهَ بِمَا تَعْمَلُونَ خَبِيرٌ

آیا ندیده‌ای که خدا شب را در روز درمی‌آورد و روز را [نیز] در شب درمی‌آورد و آفتاب و ماه را تسخیر کرده است [که] هر یک تا وقت معلومی روانند و [نیز] خدا به آنچه می‌کنید آگاه است

52 Bahá'u'lláh, *Kitáb-i-Aqdas*, paras. 161-2, p. 77.
53 *Ra'd*, Thunder, 13:39:

يَمْحُو اللّهُ مَا يَشَاءُ وَيُثْبِتُ وَعِندَهُ أُمُّ الْكِتَابِ

خدا آنچه را بخواهد محو می‌کند یا اثبات می‌کند و اصل کتاب نزد اوست

54 *Naḥl*, Bees, 16:101:

وَإِذَا بَدَّلْنَا آيَةً مَّكَانَ آيَةٍ وَاللّهُ أَعْلَمُ بِمَا يُنَزِّلُ قَالُواْ إِنَّمَا أَنتَ مُفْتَرٍ بَلْ أَكْثَرُهُمْ لاَ يَعْلَمُونَ

و هنگامی که آیه‌ای را به آیه دیگر مبدل کنیم (حکمی را نسخ نماییم) -و خدا بهتر می‌داند چه حکمی را نازل کند- آنها می‌گویند: «تو افترا می‌بندی!» اما بیشترشان (حقیقت را) نمی‌دانند!

55 Visitation (*Ziyárat*) Address, *Al-Qummi, Mafátih,* 363. Available at: http://www.mezan.net/mawsouat/ali/ziyarat/z_ghadir.html:

اَلسَّلامُ عَلى مُحَمَّدٍ رَسُولِ اللهِ خاتَمِ النَّبِيِّينَ وَسَيِّدِ الْمُرْسَلِينَ
أمينِ اللهِ عَلى وَحْيِهِ وَعَزائِمِ أَمْرِهِ
وَالْخاتِمِ لِما سَبَقَ وَالْفاتِحِ لِمَا اسْتُقْبِلَ

56 Al-Báqir, *Bihár Anwár Allamah Muhammad Báqir al-Majlisi,* p. 127.
57 Bahá'u'lláh, *Kitáb-i-Íqán,* para. 272, pp. 243-4.
58 *Játhiya,* Bowing the Knee, 45:28:

وَتَرَى كُلَّ أُمَّةٍ جَاثِيَةً كُلُّ أُمَّةٍ تُدْعَى إِلَى كِتَابِهَا الْيَوْمَ تُجْزَوْنَ مَا كُنتُمْ تَعْمَلُونَ

در آن روز هر امتی را می‌بینی (که از شدت ترس و وحشت) بر زانو نشسته؛ هر امتی بسوی کتابش خوانده می‌شود، و (به آنها می‌گویند:) امروز جزای آنچه را انجام می‌دادید به شما می‌دهند!

59 *Qaṣaṣ,* the Narration, 28:59:

وَمَا كَانَ رَبُّكَ مُهْلِكَ الْقُرَى حَتَّى يَبْعَثَ فِي أُمِّهَا رَسُولًا يَتْلُو عَلَيْهِمْ آيَاتِنَا وَمَا كُنَّا مُهْلِكِي الْقُرَى إِلَّا وَأَهْلُهَا ظَالِمُونَ

و پروردگار تو هرگز شهرها و آبادیها را هلاک نمی‌کرد تا اینکه در کانون آنها پیامبری مبعوث کند که آیات ما را بر آنان بخواند؛ و ما هرگز آبادیها و شهرها را هلاک نکردیم مگر آنکه اهلش ظالم بودند!

60 *Shu'aráa,* the Poets, 26:208:

وَمَا أَهْلَكْنَا مِن قَرْيَةٍ إِلَّا لَهَا مُنذِرُونَ

ما هیچ شهر و دیاری را هلاک نکردیم مگر اینکه انذارکنندگانی (از پیامبران الهی) داشتند.

61 *Baqara,* the Heifer, 2:143:

وَكَذَلِكَ جَعَلْنَاكُمْ أُمَّةً وَسَطًا لِّتَكُونُواْ شُهَدَاء عَلَى النَّاسِ وَيَكُونَ الرَّسُولُ عَلَيْكُمْ شَهِيدًا وَمَا جَعَلْنَا الْقِبْلَةَ الَّتِي كُنتَ عَلَيْهَا إِلاَّ لِنَعْلَمَ مَن يَتَّبِعُ الرَّسُولَ مِمَّن يَنقَلِبُ عَلَى عَقِبَيْهِ وَإِن كَانَتْ لَكَبِيرَةً إِلاَّ عَلَى الَّذِينَ هَدَى اللّهُ وَمَا كَانَ اللّهُ لِيُضِيعَ إِيمَانَكُمْ إِنَّ اللّهَ بِالنَّاسِ لَرَؤُوفٌ رَّحِيمٌ

و بدین گونه شما را امتی میانه قرار دادیم تا بر مردم گواه باشید و پیامبر بر شما گواه باشد و قبله‌ای را که [چندی] بر آن بودی مقرر نکردیم جز برای آنکه کسی را که از پیامبر پیروی می‌کند از آن کس که از عقیده خود برمی‌گردد بازشناسیم هر چند [این کار] جز بر کسانی که خدا هدایت[شان] کرده سخت گران بود و خدا بر آن نبود که ایمان شما را ضایع گرداند زیرا خدا [نسبت] به مردم دلسوز و مهربان است

62 (M.M. Pickthall translation. Also translated as 'middle religion' by others such as *Wahiduddin Khan, Ali Quli Qara'i, Hamid S. Aziz, Shabbir Ahmed* and *E. H. Palmer. George Sale* translates it as 'intermediate nation', and *Aisha Bewley* translates it 'We have made you a middlemost community'. Several other translators interpret the verse to infer that Islam is a 'moderate', 'a medium, a reasonable' community, a 'community of middle way', 'just', or 'justly balanced' religion.)

Raḥmán, (God) Most Gracious, 55:1-4:

الرَّحْمَٰنُ
عَلَّمَ الْقُرْآنَ
خَلَقَ الْإِنسَانَ
عَلَّمَهُ الْبَيَانَ

[خدای] رحمان
قرآن را یاد داد
انسان را آفرید
به او بیان آموخت

63 Bahá'u'lláh, *Gleanings from the Writings of Bahá'u'lláh*, XXXIII, p. 77.
64 Title of the Revelation and of the Book of the Báb.
65 Bahá'u'lláh, *Gleanings from the Writings of Bahá'u'lláh*, XVIII, p. 44.
66 *Zumar*, the Crowds, 39:69:

وَأَشْرَقَتِ الْأَرْضُ بِنُورِ رَبِّهَا وَوُضِعَ الْكِتَابُ وَجِيءَ بِالنَّبِيِّينَ وَالشُّهَدَاءِ وَقُضِيَ بَيْنَهُم بِالْحَقِّ وَهُمْ لَا يُظْلَمُونَ

و زمین به نور پروردگارش روشن گردد و کارنامه [اعمال در میان] نهاده شود و پیامبران و شاهدان را بیاورند و میانشان به حق داوری گردد و مورد ستم قرار نگیرند

13 Promotion of True Religious Enquiry and Adherence to Valid Criteria for Ascertaining Truth

1 Bahá'u'lláh, *The Kitáb-i-Aqdas*, para. 1, p. 19.
2 *Ḥujurát*, the Inner Apartments, 49:6:

يَا أَيُّهَا الَّذِينَ آمَنُوا إِن جَاءَكُمْ فَاسِقٌ بِنَبَإٍ فَتَبَيَّنُوا أَن تُصِيبُوا قَوْمًا بِجَهَالَةٍ فَتُصْبِحُوا عَلَىٰ مَا فَعَلْتُمْ نَادِمِينَ

ای کسانی که ایمان آورده‌اید اگر فاسقی برایتان خبری آورد نیک وارسی کنید مبادا به نادانی گروهی را آسیب برسانید و [بعد] از آنچه کرده‌اید پشیمان شوید

3 Matt.13:13-15.
4 *An'ám*, Cattle, 6:158:

هَلْ يَنظُرُونَ إِلَّا أَن تَأْتِيَهُمُ الْمَلَائِكَةُ أَوْ يَأْتِيَ رَبُّكَ أَوْ يَأْتِيَ بَعْضُ آيَاتِ رَبِّكَ يَوْمَ يَأْتِي بَعْضُ آيَاتِ رَبِّكَ لَا يَنفَعُ نَفْسًا إِيمَانُهَا لَمْ تَكُنْ آمَنَتْ مِن قَبْلُ أَوْ كَسَبَتْ فِي إِيمَانِهَا خَيْرًا قُلِ انتَظِرُوا إِنَّا مُنتَظِرُونَ

آیا جز این انتظار دارند که فرشتگان به سویشان بیایند یا پروردگارت بیاید یا پاره‌ای از نشانه‌های پروردگارت بیاید [اما] روزی که پاره‌ای از نشانه‌های پروردگارت [پدید] آید کسی که قبلا ایمان نیاورده یا خیری در ایمان آوردن خود به دست نیاورده ایمان آوردنش سود نمی‌بخشد بگو منتظر باشید که ما [هم] منتظریم

5 *'Ankabút*, the Spider, 29:49:

بَلْ هُوَ آيَاتٌ بَيِّنَاتٌ فِي صُدُورِ الَّذِينَ أُوتُوا الْعِلْمَ وَمَا يَجْحَدُ بِآيَاتِنَا إِلَّا الظَّالِمُونَ

بلکه [قرآن] آیاتی روشن در سینه‌های کسانی است که علم [الهی] یافته‌اند و جز ستمگران منکر آیات ما نمی‌شوند

6. *Tauba*, Repentance; or *Barát*, Immunity, 9:80:

اسْتَغْفِرْ لَهُمْ أَوْ لاَ تَسْتَغْفِرْ لَهُمْ إِن تَسْتَغْفِرْ لَهُمْ سَبْعِينَ مَرَّةً فَلَن يَغْفِرَ اللّهُ لَهُمْ ذَلِكَ بِأَنَّهُمْ كَفَرُواْ بِاللّهِ وَرَسُولِهِ وَاللّهُ لاَ يَهْدِي الْقَوْمَ الْفَاسِقِينَ

چه برای آنان آمرزش بخواهی یا برایشان آمرزش نخواهی [یکسان است حتی] اگر هفتاد بار برایشان آمرزش طلب کنی هرگز خدا آنان را نخواهد آمرزید چرا که آنان به خدا و فرستاده‌اش کفر ورزیدند و خدا گروه فاسقان را هدایت نمی‌کند

7. *Taṭfīf*, Dealing in Fraud, 83:15:

كَلَّا إِنَّهُمْ عَن رَّبِّهِمْ يَوْمَئِذٍ لَّمَحْجُوبُونَ

زهی پندار که آنان در آن روز از پروردگارشان سخت محجوبند

8. II Tim. 4:3.
   God's Word translation:
   A time will come when people will not listen to accurate teachings. Instead, they will follow their own desires and surround themselves with teachers who tell them what they want to hear.

9. Bahá'u'lláh, *Kitáb-i-Íqán*, para. 2, p. 3.
10. Bahá'u'lláh, *Hidden Words*, Persian no. 11.
11. Bahá'u'lláh, *The Kitáb-i-Aqdas*, para. 157, p. 76.
12. ibid. para. 161, p. 77.
13. ibid. para. 99, p. 56. See also Bahá'u'lláh, *Epistle to the Son of Wolf*, p. 128.
14. *Baqara*, the Heifer, 2: 256:

لاَ إِكْرَاهَ فِي الدِّينِ قَد تَّبَيَّنَ الرُّشْدُ مِنَ الْغَيِّ فَمَنْ يَكْفُرْ بِالطَّاغُوتِ وَيُؤْمِن بِاللّهِ فَقَدِ اسْتَمْسَكَ بِالْعُرْوَةِ الْوُثْقَىَ لاَ انفِصَامَ لَهَا وَاللّهُ سَمِيعٌ عَلِيمٌ

در دین هیچ اجباری نیست و راه از بیراهه بخوبی آشکار شده است پس هر کس به طاغوت کفر ورزد و به خدا ایمان آورد به یقین به دستاویزی استوار که آن را گسستن نیست چنگ زده است و خداوند شنوای داناست

15. 'Abdu'l-Bahá, *The Promulgation of Universal Peace*, p. 293.
16. Bahá'u'lláh, Tablet of Aḥmad, in *Bahá'í Prayers*, p. 212.
17. *'Ankabút*, the Spider, 29:69:

وَالَّذِينَ جَاهَدُوا فِينَا لَنَهْدِيَنَّهُمْ سُبُلَنَا وَإِنَّ اللَّهَ لَمَعَ الْمُحْسِنِينَ

و آنها که در راه ما (با خلوص نیت) جهاد کنند قطعا هدایتشان خواهیم کرد و خدا با نیکوکاران است

18. *Baqara*, the Heifer, 2: 256:

لاَ إِكْرَاهَ فِي الدِّينِ ...

در دین هیچ اجباری نیست...

19. *Fáṭir*, the Originator of Creation; or *Malá'ika*, the Angels, 35:8:

أَفَمَن زُيِّنَ لَهُ سُوءُ عَمَلِهِ فَرَآهُ حَسَنًا فَإِنَّ اللَّهَ يُضِلُّ مَن يَشَاءُ وَيَهْدِي مَن يَشَاءُ فَلَا تَذْهَبْ نَفْسُكَ عَلَيْهِمْ حَسَرَاتٍ إِنَّ اللَّهَ عَلِيمٌ بِمَا يَصْنَعُونَ

آیا آن کس که زشتی کردارش برای او آراسته شده و آن را زیبا می‌بیند [مانند مؤمن نیکوکار است] خداست که هر که را بخواهد بیراه می‌گذارد و هر که را بخواهد هدایت می‌کند پس مبادا به سبب حسرت‌ها[ی] گوناگون] بر آنان جانت [از کف] برود قطعا خدا به آنچه می‌کنند داناست

20. The Báb, *Selections from the Writings of the Báb*, p. 120.

21 Exod. 6:30 and 7:1:
    And Moses said before the Lord, Behold, I am of uncircumcised lips (tendency to stammer), and how shall Pharaoh hearken unto me?
    And the Lord said unto Moses, See, I have made thee a god to Pharaoh: and Aaron thy brother shall be thy prophet.
22 John 1:38:
    And Jesus turned and saw them following, and said to them, 'What do you seek?' They said to Him, 'Rabbi (which translated means Teacher), where are You staying?'
23 Bahá'u'lláh, *Epistle to the Son of the Wolf*, p. 129.
24 Deut. 18:18-19.
25 John 5:30.
26 John 16:13.
27 *Najm*, the Star, 53:2-5:

مَا ضَلَّ صَاحِبُكُمْ وَمَا غَوَى
وَمَا يَنْطِقُ عَنِ الْهَوَى
إِنْ هُوَ إِلَّا وَحْيٌ يُوحَى
عَلَّمَهُ شَدِيدُ الْقُوَى

یار شما نه گمراه شده و نه در نادانی مانده
و از سر هوس سخن نمی‌گوید
این سخن بجز وحیی که وحی می‌شود نیست
آن را شدیدالقوی به او فرا آموخت

28 Bahá'u'lláh, *Epistle to the Son of the Wolf*, pp. 11-12, referring to the Súriy-i-Haykal, para. 192, in Bahá'u'lláh, *The Summons of the Lord of Hosts*, p. 98. Below is the powerful Arabic text:

يا سُلْطانُ إنِّي كُنْتُ كَأَحَدٍ مِنَ الْعِبادِ وَراقِداً عَلَى الْمِهادِ مَرَّتْ عَلَيَّ نَسائِمُ السُّبْحانِ وَعَلَّمَنِي عِلْمَ ما كانَ لَيْسَ هذا مِنْ عِنْدِي بَلْ مِنْ لَدُنْ عَزيزٍ عَليمٍ، وَأَمَرَنِي بِالنِّداءِ بَيْنَ الأَرْضِ وَالسَّماءِ وَبِذلِكَ وَرَدَ عَلَيَّ ما تَذَرَّفَتْ بِهِ عُيُونُ الْعارِفِينَ، ما قَرَأْتُ ما عِنْدَ النّاسِ مِنَ الْعُلُومِ وَما دَخَلْتُ الْمَدارِسَ فَسَلِ الْمَدِينَةَ الَّتِي كُنْتُ فيها لِتُوقِنَ بِأَنِّي لَسْتُ مِنَ الْكاذِبينَ، هذا وَرَقَةٌ حَرَّكَتْها أرْياحُ مَشِيَّةِ رَبِّكَ الْعَزيزِ الْحَمِيدِ هَلْ لَها اسْتِقْرارٌ عِنْدَ هُبُوبِ أرْياحٍ عاصِفاتٍ؟ لا وَمالِكِ الأَسْماءِ وَالصِّفاتِ بَلْ تُحَرِّكُها كَيْفَ تُرِيدُ، لَيْسَ لِلْعَدَمِ وُجُودٌ بِلْقاءِ الْقِدَمِ قَدْ جاءَ أَمْرُهُ الْمُبْرَمُ وَأَنْطَقَنِي بِذِكْرِهِ بَيْنَ الْعالَمينَ، إنِّي لَمْ أَكُنْ إلاّ كائِنَةً بِلْقاءِ أَمْرِهِ فَلْتُنْبِي بُدَّ إذاً يَرَ رَبُّكَ وُجُودٌ بِلْقاءِ الرَّحْمنِ الرَّجِيمِ، هَلْ يَقْدِرُ أَحَدٌ أَنْ يَتَكَلَّمَ مِنْ بِلْقاءِ نَفْسِهِ بِما يَعْتَرِضُ بِهِ عَلَيْهِ الْعِبادُ مِنْ كُلِّ وَضِيعٍ وَشَرِيفٍ؟ لا فَوالَّذِي عَلَّمَ الْقَلَمَ أَسْرارَ الْقِدَمِ إلاَّ مَنْ كانَ مُؤَيَّداً مِنْ لَدُنْ مُقْتَدِرٍ قَدِيرٍ، يُخاطِبُنِي الْقَلَمُ الأَعْلَى وَيَقُولُ لا تَخَفْ أَنْ اقْصُصْ لِحَضْرَةِ السُّلْطانِ ما وَرَدَ عَلَيْكَ إنَّهُ تَبَيَّنَ اسْتَعْصى رَبُّكَ الرَّحْمنُ لَعَلَّ تَشْتَرِقُ مِنْ أفْقِ قَلْبِهِ شَمْسُ الْعَدْلِ وَالإحْسانِ كَذلِكَ كانَ الْحُكْمُ مِنْ لَدى الْحَكِيمِ مَنْزُولاً.

29 Bahá'u'lláh, *Epistle to the Son of the Wolf*, p. 9.
30 Deut. 18:21-2.
31 John 1:11-3.
32 Matt. 12:33.
33 II Cor. 5:17.
34 Matt. 7:16-20.
35 John 1:1-4.
36 Mark 13:26.
37 Matt. 6:13.

38 *Ibráhím*, Abraham, 14:24-5, 27:

أَلَمْ تَرَ كَيْفَ ضَرَبَ اللّهُ مَثَلاً كَلِمَةً طَيِّبَةً كَشَجَرَةٍ طَيِّبَةٍ أَصْلُهَا ثَابِتٌ وَفَرْعُهَا فِي السَّمَاء
تُؤْتِي أُكُلَهَا كُلَّ حِينٍ بِإِذْنِ رَبِّهَا وَيَضْرِبُ اللّهُ الأَمْثَالَ لِلنَّاسِ لَعَلَّهُمْ يَتَذَكَّرُونَ
يُثَبِّتُ اللّهُ الَّذِينَ آمَنُواْ بِالْقَوْلِ الثَّابِتِ فِي الْحَيَاةِ الدُّنْيَا وَفِي الآخِرَةِ وَيُضِلُّ اللّهُ الظَّالِمِينَ وَيَفْعَلُ اللّهُ مَا يَشَاء

آیا ندیدی چگونه خداوند کلمه طیبه (و گفتار پاکیزه) را به درخت پاکیزه‌ای تشبیه کرده که ریشه آن (در زمین) ثابت و شاخه آن در آسمان است؟

میوه‌های خود را در هر زمان به اذن پروردگارش می‌دهد، و خداوند برای مردم مثلها می‌زند شاید متذکر شوند.

خداوند کسانی را که ایمان آوردند بخاطر گفتار و اعتقاد پایدارشان ثابت قدم می‌دارد، هم در این جهان و هم در سرای دیگر، و ستمگران را گمراه می‌سازد (و لطف خود را از آنها بر می‌گیرد) و خداوند هر چه کار را بخواهد (و صلاح بداند) انجام می‌دهد.

39 Bahá'u'lláh, *Gleanings from the Writings of Bahá'u'lláh*, XLIII, p. 97.
40 Bahá'u'lláh, Tablet of Aḥmad, in *Bahá'í Prayers*, p. 210.
41 Bahá'u'lláh, *Kitáb-i-Íqán*, para. 22, p. 22, quoting *Dahr*, Time, or *Insán*, Man, 76:9; *Má'ida*, the Table Spread, 5:117; *Ibráhím*, Abraham, 14:24. See also *Taṭfíf*, Dealing in Fraud, 83:22-25.
42 Shoghi Effendi, *The Advent of Divine Justice*, p. 15.
43 Dan. 12:9.
44 *Taṭfíf*, Dealing in Fraud, 83:25:
    Their thirst will be slaked with pure (choice) wine sealed:

يُسْقَوْنَ مِن رَّحِيقٍ مَّخْتُومٍ

آنها از شراب (طهور) زلال دست‌نخورده و سربسته‌ای سیراب می‌شوند

45 Bahá'u'lláh, *The Kitáb-i-Aqdas*, para. 5, p. 21.
46 Jer. 5:20-21.
47 Isa. 6:9-10.
48 John 12:37-40.
49 *Yúnus*, Jonah, 10, 41-3:

وَإِن كَذَّبُوكَ فَقُل لِّي عَمَلِي وَلَكُمْ عَمَلُكُمْ أَنتُمْ بَرِيئُونَ مِمَّا أَعْمَلُ وَأَنَاْ بَرِيءٌ مِّمَّا تَعْمَلُونَ
وَمِنْهُم مَّن يَسْتَمِعُونَ إِلَيْكَ أَفَأَنتَ تُسْمِعُ الصُّمَّ وَلَوْ كَانُواْ لاَ يَعْقِلُونَ
وَمِنْهُم مَّن يَنظُرُ إِلَيْكَ أَفَأَنتَ تَهْدِي الْعُمْيَ وَلَوْ كَانُواْ لاَ يُبْصِرُونَ

و اگر تو را تکذیب کردند بگو عمل من به من اختصاص دارد و عمل شما به شما اختصاص دارد شما از آنچه من انجام می‌دهم غیر مسؤولید و من از آنچه شما انجام نمی‌دهید غیر مسؤولم

و برخی از آنان کسانی‌اند که به تو گوش فرا می‌دهند آیا تو کران را هر چند در نیابند شنوا خواهی کرد

و از آنان کسی است که به سوی تو می‌نگرد آیا تو نابینایان را هر چند نبینند هدایت توانی کرد

50 *Muhammad* (the Prophet), 47:23:

أُوْلَئِكَ الَّذِينَ لَعَنَهُمُ اللَّهُ فَأَصَمَّهُمْ وَأَعْمَى أَبْصَارَهُمْ

اینان همان کسانند که خدا آنان را لعنت نموده و [گوش دل] ایشان را ناشنوا و چشمهایشان را نابینا کرده است

NOTES AND REFERENCES

51 *Ḥá-mím* (Abbreviated Letters), or *Ḥá-Mím Sajda*, or *Fuṣṣilat*, 41:44:

وَلَوْ جَعَلْنَاهُ قُرْآنًا أَعْجَمِيًّا لَّقَالُوا لَوْلَا فُصِّلَتْ آيَاتُهُ أَأَعْجَمِيٌّ وَعَرَبِيٌّ قُلْ هُوَ لِلَّذِينَ آمَنُوا هُدًى وَشِفَاءٌ وَالَّذِينَ لَا يُؤْمِنُونَ فِي آذَانِهِمْ وَقْرٌ وَهُوَ عَلَيْهِمْ عَمًى أُوْلَٰئِكَ يُنَادَوْنَ مِن مَّكَانٍ بَعِيدٍ

و اگر [این کتاب را] قرآنی غیر عربی گردانیده بودیم قطعا می‌گفتند چرا آیه‌های آن روشن نشده کتابی غیر عربی و [مخاطب آن] عرب زبان بگو این [کتاب] برای کسانی که ایمان آورده‌اند رهنمود و درمانی است و کسانی که ایمان نمی‌آورند در گوشهایشان سنگینی است و قرآن برایشان نامفهوم است و [گویی] آنان را از جایی دور ندا می‌دهند

52 *Baqara*, the Heifer, 2:18:

صُمٌّ بُكْمٌ عُمْيٌ فَهُمْ لَا يَرْجِعُونَ

کر و لال و کورند بنابراین به راه نمی‌آیند

53 John 1:5.
54 Translation by Aisha Bewley.
55 Translation by Muhammad Asad.
56 *Ibráhím*, Abraham, 14:26:

وَمَثَلُ كَلِمَةٍ خَبِيثَةٍ كَشَجَرَةٍ خَبِيثَةٍ اجْتُثَّتْ مِن فَوْقِ الْأَرْضِ مَا لَهَا مِن قَرَارٍ

(همچنین) «کلمه خبیثه» را به درخت ناپاکی تشبیه کرده که از روی زمین برکنده شده، و قرار و ثباتی ندارد.

57 *Mú-min*, the Believer, 40:51:

إِنَّا لَنَنصُرُ رُسُلَنَا وَالَّذِينَ آمَنُوا فِي الْحَيَاةِ الدُّنْيَا وَيَوْمَ يَقُومُ الْأَشْهَادُ

ما به یقین پیامبران خود و کسانی را که ایمان آورده‌اند، در زندگی دنیا و (در آخرت) روزی که گواهان به پا می‌خیزند یاری می‌دهیم!

58 *Mujádala*, the Woman who Pleads, 58:21:

كَتَبَ اللَّهُ لَأَغْلِبَنَّ أَنَا وَرُسُلِي إِنَّ اللَّهَ قَوِيٌّ عَزِيزٌ

خداوند چنین مقرر داشته که من و رسولانم پیروز می‌شویم؛ چرا که خداوند قوی و شکست‌ناپذیر است!

59 *Baní Isrá-íl*, the Children of Israel, 17:81:

وَقُلْ جَاءَ الْحَقُّ وَزَهَقَ الْبَاطِلُ إِنَّ الْبَاطِلَ كَانَ زَهُوقًا

و بگو حق آمد و باطل نابود شد آری باطل همواره نابودشدنی است

60 John 3:2.
61 *An'ám*, Cattle, 6:34:

وَلَقَدْ كُذِّبَتْ رُسُلٌ مِّن قَبْلِكَ فَصَبَرُواْ عَلَى مَا كُذِّبُواْ وَأُوذُواْ حَتَّى أَتَاهُمْ نَصْرُنَا وَلَا مُبَدِّلَ لِكَلِمَاتِ اللَّهِ وَلَقَدْ جَاءكَ مِن نَّبَإِ الْمُرْسَلِينَ

و پیش از تو نیز پیامبرانی تکذیب شدند ولی بر آنچه تکذیب شدند و آزار دیدند شکیبایی کردند تا یاری ما به آنان رسید و برای کلمات خدا هیچ تغییردهنده‌ای نیست و مسلما اخبار پیامبران به تو رسیده است

62 Bahá'u'lláh, *Kitáb-i-Íqán*, para. 257, p. 230.
63 ibid. pp. 230-31.

64 Bahá'u'lláh, Lawḥ-i-Dunyá, in *Tablets of Bahá'u'lláh Revelaed after the Kitáb-i-Aqdas*, p. 96.
65 Bahá'u'lláh, Súriy-i-Haykal, in *The Summons of the Lord of Hosts*, p. 98.
66 *Jumu'a*, the Assembly Prayer, 62:6-7:

قُلْ يَا أَيُّهَا الَّذِينَ هَادُوا إِن زَعَمْتُمْ أَنَّكُمْ أَوْلِيَاءُ لِلَّهِ مِن دُونِ النَّاسِ فَتَمَنَّوُا الْمَوْتَ إِن كُنتُمْ صَادِقِينَ
وَلَا يَتَمَنَّوْنَهُ أَبَدًا بِمَا قَدَّمَتْ أَيْدِيهِمْ وَاللَّهُ عَلِيمٌ بِالظَّالِمِينَ

بگو: «ای یهودیان! اگر گمان می‌کنید که (فقط) شما دوستان خدائید نه سایر مردم، پس آرزوی مرگ کنید اگر راست می‌گویید (تا به لقای محبوبتان برسید)!
ولی آنان هرگز تمنای مرگ نمی‌کنند بخاطر اعمالی که از پیش فرستاده‌اند؛ و خداوند ظالمان را بخوبی می‌شناسد!

67 Acts 7:54-60.
68 Bahá'u'lláh, *Epistle to the Son of the Wolf*, p. 92.
69 Bahá'u'lláh, *Bahá'í Prayers*, pp. 191-2.
70 Bahá'u'lláh, *Gleanings from the Writings of Bahá'u'lláh*, XCI, pp. 182-3.
71 Bahá'u'lláh, quoted in 'Abdu'l-Bahá, *A Traveller's Narrative*, pp. 66-7.
72 Shoghi Effendi, *God Passes By*, pp. 201-2.
73 Second son of 'Alí ibn Abi Tálib, and the grandson of Muhammad, whose return is awaited by Shí'ih Islam.
74 Taherzadeh, *Revelation of Bahá'u'lláh*, vol. 4, p. 349.
75 *Nisáa*, the Women, 4:82:

أَفَلَا يَتَدَبَّرُونَ الْقُرْآنَ وَلَوْ كَانَ مِنْ عِندِ غَيْرِ اللَّهِ لَوَجَدُوا فِيهِ اخْتِلَافًا كَثِيرًا

آیا در [معانی] قرآن نمی‌اندیشند اگر از جانب غیر خدا بود قطعا در آن اختلاف بسیاری می‌یافتند

76 Matt. 12:38-40.
77 Matt. 12:22-4.
78 *Ra'd*, Thunder, 13:27:

وَيَقُولُ الَّذِينَ كَفَرُوا لَوْلَا أُنزِلَ عَلَيْهِ آيَةٌ مِّن رَّبِّهِ قُلْ إِنَّ اللَّهَ يُضِلُّ مَن يَشَاءُ وَيَهْدِي إِلَيْهِ مَنْ أَنَابَ

و کسانی که کافر شده‌اند می‌گویند چرا از جانب پروردگارش معجزه‌ای بر او نازل نشده است بگو در حقیقت خداست که هر کس را بخواهد بی‌راه می‌گذارد و هر کس را که [به سوی او] بازگردد به سوی خود راه می‌نماید

79 *'Ankabút*, the Spider, 29:50-51:

وَقَالُوا لَوْلَا أُنزِلَ عَلَيْهِ آيَاتٌ مِّن رَّبِّهِ قُلْ إِنَّمَا الْآيَاتُ عِندَ اللَّهِ وَإِنَّمَا أَنَا نَذِيرٌ مُّبِينٌ
أَوَلَمْ يَكْفِهِمْ أَنَّا أَنزَلْنَا عَلَيْكَ الْكِتَابَ يُتْلَىٰ عَلَيْهِمْ إِنَّ فِي ذَٰلِكَ لَرَحْمَةً وَذِكْرَىٰ لِقَوْمٍ يُؤْمِنُونَ

و گفتند چرا بر او از جانب پروردگارش نشانه‌هایی [معجزه‌آسا] نازل نشده است بگو آن نشانه‌ها پیش خداست و من تنها هشداردهنده‌ای آشکارم
آیا برای ایشان بس نیست که این کتاب را که بر آنان خوانده می‌شود بر تو فرو فرستادیم در حقیقت در این [کار] برای مردمی که ایمان دارند رحمت و یادآوری است

80 'Abdu'l-Bahá, *Some Answered Question*, ch. 22, p. 100.
81 ibid. ch. 10, p. 36.
82 Isa. 40:5.
83 Isa. 52:15.

84 John 4:23-4.
85 I Cor. 2:12-14.
86 II Cor. 3:4-6.
87 II Cor. 4:18.
88 John 6:58, 60-63.
89 Matt. 8:21-2.
90 Matt. 13:15.
91 John 12:46.
92 *'Ankabút*, the Spider, 29:43:

وَتِلْكَ الْأَمْثَالُ نَضْرِبُهَا لِلنَّاسِ وَمَا يَعْقِلُهَا إِلَّا الْعَالِمُونَ

ما این مثل ها را برای همه مردم بیان می کنیم ، ولی حقیقت آنها را جز عالمانی که در حقایق امور می اندیشند ، درنمی یابند .

93 *An'ám*, Cattle, 6:36:

إِنَّمَا يَسْتَجِيبُ الَّذِينَ يَسْمَعُونَ وَالْمَوْتَى يَبْعَثُهُمُ اللَّهُ ثُمَّ إِلَيْهِ يُرْجَعُونَ

فقط کسانی که شنونده حق اند دعوت تو را اجابت می کنند ، نه آنان که چون مردگان ناشنوایند ؛ و خدا همه مردگان را در روز قیامت برمی انگیزد و حقیقت را به آنان می فهماند ، آن گاه به سوی او بازگردانده می شوند .

94 Shoghi Effendi, *The World Order of Bahá'u'lláh*, p. 54.

14 Responding to the Call of the Summoner

1 Bahá'u'lláh, *Gleanings from the Writings of Bahá'u'lláh*, III, p. 5.
2 Mark 2:21-2.
3 Bahá'u'lláh, *Gleanings from the Writings of Bahá'u'lláh*, XCIX, p. 200.
4 Shoghi Effendi, *The World Order of Bahá'u'lláh*, p. 61.
5 *Ál-i-'Imrán*, the Family of 'Imrán, 3:45:

إِذْ قَالَتِ الْمَلَائِكَةُ يَا مَرْيَمُ إِنَّ اللَّهَ يُبَشِّرُكِ بِكَلِمَةٍ مِنْهُ اسْمُهُ الْمَسِيحُ عِيسَى ابْنُ مَرْيَمَ وَجِيهًا فِي الدُّنْيَا وَالْآخِرَةِ وَمِنَ الْمُقَرَّبِينَ

[یاد کن] هنگامی [را] که فرشتگان گفتند ای مریم خداوند تو را به کلمه‌ای از جانب خود که نامش مسیح عیسی‌بن‌مریم است مژده می‌دهد در حالی که [او] در دنیا و آخرت آبرومند و از مقربان [درگاه خدا] است

6 John 1:1-5.
7 Bahá'u'lláh, *Gleanings from the Writings of Bahá'u'lláh*, XCIX, p. 200.
8 Bahá'u'lláh, *Súriy-i-Ra'ís*, in *The Summons of the Lord of Hosts*, p. 141.
9 Bahá'u'lláh, *Gleanings from the Writings of Bahá'u'lláh*, LXXIV, pp. 141-2.
10 Bahá'u'lláh, quoted in Shoghi Effendi, *The Advent of Divine Justice*, pp. 82-3.
11 Bahá'u'lláh, *Gleanings from the Writings of Bahá'u'lláh*, XXII, p. 51.
12 *Qáf*, 50:41:

وَاسْتَمِعْ يَوْمَ يُنَادِ الْمُنَادِ مِن مَّكَانٍ قَرِيبٍ

و روزی که منادی از جایی نزدیک ندا درمی‌دهد به گوش باش

Bahá'u'lláh declared His Mission in the Garden of Riḍván in Baghdad on 22 April 1863, close to where the verse was revealed.

13 A'ráf, the Heights, 7:44:

وَنَادَىٰ أَصْحَابُ الْجَنَّةِ أَصْحَابَ النَّارِ أَن قَدْ وَجَدْنَا مَا وَعَدَنَا رَبُّنَا حَقًّا فَهَلْ وَجَدتُم مَّا وَعَدَ رَبُّكُمْ حَقًّا قَالُوا نَعَمْ فَأَذَّنَ مُؤَذِّنٌ بَيْنَهُمْ أَن لَّعْنَةُ اللَّهِ عَلَى الظَّالِمِينَ

و بهشتیان به دوزخیان صدا میزنند که ما آنچه را پروردگارمان به ما وعده داده بود همه را حق یافتیم، آیا شما هم آنچه را پروردگارتان به شما وعده داده بود حق یافتید؟! در این هنگام ندا دهنده‌ای در میان آنها ندا می‌دهد که لعنت خدا بر ستمگران بادا

14 Qamar, the Moon, 54:6:

فَتَوَلَّ عَنْهُمْ يَوْمَ يَدْعُ الدَّاعِ إِلَىٰ شَيْءٍ نُكُرٍ

پس از آنان روی برتاب روزی که داعی [حق] به سوی امری دهشتناک دعوت می‌کند

15 Baní Isrá-íl, the Children of Israel, 17:52:

يَوْمَ يَدْعُوكُمْ فَتَسْتَجِيبُونَ بِحَمْدِهِ وَتَظُنُّونَ إِن لَّبِثْتُمْ إِلَّا قَلِيلًا

روزی که شما را فرا می‌خواند پس در حالی که او را ستایش می‌کنید اجابتش می‌نمایید و می‌پندارید که جز اندکی [در دنیا] نمانده‌اید

16 Aḥqáf, Winding Sand-tracts, 46:31:

يَا قَوْمَنَا أَجِيبُوا دَاعِيَ اللَّهِ وَآمِنُوا بِهِ يَغْفِرْ لَكُم مِّن ذُنُوبِكُمْ وَيُجِرْكُم مِّنْ عَذَابٍ أَلِيمٍ

ای قوم ما دعوت‌کننده خدا را پاسخ [مثبت] دهید و به او ایمان آورید تا [خدا] برخی از گناهانتان را بر شما ببخشاید و از عذابی پر درد پناهتان دهد

17 Aḥzáb, the Confederates, 33:45-7:

يَا أَيُّهَا النَّبِيُّ إِنَّا أَرْسَلْنَاكَ شَاهِدًا وَمُبَشِّرًا وَنَذِيرًا
وَدَاعِيًا إِلَى اللَّهِ بِإِذْنِهِ وَسِرَاجًا مُّنِيرًا
وَبَشِّرِ الْمُؤْمِنِينَ بِأَنَّ لَهُم مِّنَ اللَّهِ فَضْلًا كَبِيرًا

ای پیامبر، ما تو را به عنوان گواه فرستادیم و بشارت دهنده و انذار کننده
و تو را دعوت کننده به سوی الله به فرمان او و چراغ روشنی بخش
و مؤمنان را بشارت ده که برای آنها از سوی خدا فضل و پاداش بزرگی است.

18 Yúsuf, Joseph, 12:108:

قُلْ هَٰذِهِ سَبِيلِي أَدْعُو إِلَى اللَّهِ عَلَىٰ بَصِيرَةٍ أَنَا وَمَنِ اتَّبَعَنِي وَسُبْحَانَ اللَّهِ وَمَا أَنَا مِنَ الْمُشْرِكِينَ

بگو این است راه من که من و هر کس پیروی‌ام کرد با بینایی به سوی خدا دعوت می‌کنیم و منزه است‌خدا و من از مشرکان نیستم

19 Ál-i-'Imrán, the Family of 'Imrán, 3:193:

رَّبَّنَا إِنَّنَا سَمِعْنَا مُنَادِيًا يُنَادِي لِلْإِيمَانِ أَنْ آمِنُوا بِرَبِّكُمْ فَآمَنَّا رَبَّنَا فَاغْفِرْ لَنَا ذُنُوبَنَا وَكَفِّرْ عَنَّا سَيِّئَاتِنَا وَتَوَفَّنَا مَعَ الْأَبْرَارِ

پروردگارا ما شنیدیم که دعوتگری به ایمان فرا می‌خواند که به پروردگار خود ایمان آورید پس ایمان آوردیم پروردگارا گناهان ما را بیامرز و بدیهای ما را بزدای و ما را در زمره نیکان بمیران

NOTES AND REFERENCES

20 *Anbiyáa*, the Prophets, 21:104:

يَوْمَ نَطْوِي السَّمَاءَ كَطَيِّ السِّجِلِّ لِلْكُتُبِ كَمَا بَدَأْنَا أَوَّلَ خَلْقٍ نُعِيدُهُ وَعْدًا عَلَيْنَا إِنَّا كُنَّا فَاعِلِينَ

روزی که آسمان را همچون در پیچیدن صفحه نامه‌ها در می‌پیچیم همان گونه که بار نخست آفرینش را آغاز کردیم دوباره آن را بازمی‌گردانیم وعده‌ای است بر عهده ما که ما انجام‌دهنده آنیم

21 *Núr*, Light, 24:37:

رِجَالٌ لَّا تُلْهِيهِمْ تِجَارَةٌ وَلَا بَيْعٌ عَن ذِكْرِ اللَّهِ وَإِقَامِ الصَّلَاةِ وَإِيتَاءِ الزَّكَاةِ يَخَافُونَ يَوْمًا تَتَقَلَّبُ فِيهِ الْقُلُوبُ وَالْأَبْصَارُ

مردانی که نه تجارت و نه داد و ستدی آنان را از یاد خدا و برپا داشتن نماز و دادن زکات به خود مشغول نمی‌دارد و از روزی که دل‌ها و دیده‌ها در آن زیر و رو می‌شود می‌هراسند

22 *Baní Isrá-íl*, the Children of Israel, 17:13:

وَكُلَّ إِنسَانٍ أَلْزَمْنَاهُ طَائِرَهُ فِي عُنُقِهِ وَنُخْرِجُ لَهُ يَوْمَ الْقِيَامَةِ كِتَابًا يَلْقَاهُ مَنشُورًا

و هر انسانی، اعمالش را بر گردنش آویخته‌ایم؛ و روز قیامت، کتابی برای او بیرون می‌آوریم که آن را در برابر خود، گشوده می‌بیند!

The 'Book' referred to in this verse is often interpreted as a manuscript that tabulates the sins of individuals. However, everywhere else in the Qur'án the 'Book' signifies a distinct Revelation from God, and the 'People of the Book' the Jews and Christians who received their own specific divine Revelations. In addition, the new Revelation is also described by other designations such as a 'Call' and 'Great Announcement' in other parts of the Qur'án.

23 *Ḥajj*, the Pilgrimage, 22:16:

وَكَذَلِكَ أَنزَلْنَاهُ آيَاتٍ بَيِّنَاتٍ وَأَنَّ اللَّهَ يَهْدِي مَن يُرِيدُ

و بدین گونه [قرآن] را [به صورت] آیاتی روشنگر نازل کردیم و خداست که هر که را بخواهد راه می‌نماید

24 *Naḥl*, Bees, 16:101:

وَإِذَا بَدَّلْنَا آيَةً مَّكَانَ آيَةٍ وَاللَّهُ أَعْلَمُ بِمَا يُنَزِّلُ قَالُوا إِنَّمَا أَنتَ مُفْتَرٍ بَلْ أَكْثَرُهُمْ لَا يَعْلَمُونَ

و چون حکمی را به جای حکم دیگر بیاوریم و خدا به آنچه به تدریج نازل می‌کند داناتر است می‌گویند جز این نیست که تو دروغ‌بافی [نه] بلکه بیشتر آنان نمی‌دانند

25 Ezek. 36:25:
    Then will I sprinkle clean water upon you, and ye shall be clean: from all your filthiness, and from all your idols, will I cleanse you.
26 Isa. 65:17.
27 Isa. 43:19.
28 Joel 3:18.
29 Isa. 62:2.
30 Ezek. 36:26.
31 II Cor. 5:17.
32 Rev. 21:1.
33 Rev. 21:2.
34 Rev. 20:12.
35 Rev. 5:9 and 14:3.
36 Acts 3:20–21.
37 Rev. 21:5.

38 Rev. 21:6.
39 II Pet. 3:13.
40 Rev. 2:71.
41 Rev. 3:12.
42 Rev. 14:3.
43 Rev. 5:9.
44 Isa. 42:10.
45 John 16:7.
46 Isa. 42:16.
47 Isa. 66:22.
48 Isa. 65:71.
49 Rev. 20:12.
50 The Báb, Persian Bayán, IV:12, in *Selections From the Writings of the Báb*, pp. 105–6.
51 The Báb, Kitáb-i-Asmá', XVI:18, ibid. p. 139.
52 Bahá'u'lláh, *Gleanings from the Writings of Bahá'u'lláh*, IX, p. 12.
53 Bahá'u'lláh, Súriy-i-Haykal, para. 156, in *The Summons of the Lord of Hosts*, p. 82.
54 Bahá'u'lláh, *Epistle to the Son of the Wolf*, p. 137.
55 Bahá'u'lláh, *Gleanings from the Writings of Bahá'u'lláh*, VII, p. 11.
56 Bahá'u'lláh, quoted in Shoghi Effendi, *The World Order of Bahá'u'lláh*, p. 106.
57 Bahá'u'lláh, *Gleanings from the Writings of Bahá'u'lláh*, VII, pp. 10–11.
58 Bahá'u'lláh, Súriy-i-Mulúk, Tablet to the Kings, para. 58, in *The Summons of the Lord of Hosts*, p. 209.
59 Bahá'u'lláh, *The Kitáb-i-Aqdas*, para. 82, p. 49.
60 Bahá'u'lláh, Súriy-i-Haykal, paras. 102–3, in *The Summons of the Lord of Hosts*, pp. 54–5.
61 Bahá'u'lláh, quoted in Shoghi Effendi, *The Promised Day Is Come*, p. 108.
62 Matt. 8:11–12.
63 The reference applies not only to those who rejected Muhammad but also to those who deny the anticipated 'Day'.
64 Aḥqáf, Winding Sand-tracts, 46:31–5:

يَا قَوْمَنَا أَجِيبُوا دَاعِيَ اللَّهِ وَآمِنُوا بِهِ يَغْفِرْ لَكُم مِّن ذُنُوبِكُمْ وَيُجِرْكُم مِّنْ عَذَابٍ أَلِيمٍ
وَمَن لَّا يُجِبْ دَاعِيَ اللَّهِ فَلَيْسَ بِمُعْجِزٍ فِي الْأَرْضِ وَلَيْسَ لَهُ مِن دُونِهِ أَولِيَاءُ أُوْلَٰئِكَ فِي ضَلَالٍ مُّبِينٍ
أَوَلَمْ يَرَوْا أَنَّ اللَّهَ الَّذِي خَلَقَ السَّمَاوَاتِ وَالْأَرْضَ وَلَمْ يَعْيَ بِخَلْقِهِنَّ بِقَادِرٍ عَلَىٰ أَن يُحْيِيَ الْمَوْتَىٰ بَلَىٰ إِنَّهُ عَلَىٰ كُلِّ شَيْءٍ قَدِيرٌ
وَيَوْمَ يُعْرَضُ الَّذِينَ كَفَرُوا عَلَى النَّارِ أَلَيْسَ هَٰذَا بِالْحَقِّ قَالُوا بَلَىٰ وَرَبِّنَا قَالَ فَذُوقُوا الْعَذَابَ بِمَا كُنتُمْ تَكْفُرُونَ

ای قوم ما دعوت‌کنندۀ خدا را پاسخ [مثبت] دهید و به او ایمان آورید تا [خدا] برخی از گناهانتان را بر شما ببخشاید و از عذابی پر درد پناهتان دهد

و کسی که دعوت‌کنندۀ خدا را اجابت نکند در زمین درمانده‌کنندۀ [خدا] نیست و در برابر او دوستانی ندارد آنان در گمراهی آشکاری‌اند

مگر ندانسته‌اند که آن خدایی که آسمانها و زمین را آفریده و در آفریدن آنها درمانده نگردید می‌تواند مردگان را [نیز] زنده کند آری اوست که بر همه چیز تواناست

و روزی که کافران بر آتش عرضه می‌شوند [از آنان می‌پرسند] آیا این راست نیست می‌گویند سوگند به پروردگارمان که آری می‌فرماید پس به [سزای] آنکه انکار می‌کردید عذاب را بچشید

65   *Qamar*, the Moon, 54:7-8:

خُشَّعًا أَبْصَارُهُمْ يَخْرُجُونَ مِنَ الْأَجْدَاثِ كَأَنَّهُمْ جَرَادٌ مُنتَشِرٌ
مُهْطِعِينَ إِلَى الدَّاعِ يَقُولُ الْكَافِرُونَ هَذَا يَوْمٌ عَسِرٌ

در حالی که دیدگان خود را فروهشته‌اند چون ملخهای پراکنده از گور ها[ی خود] برمی‌آیند
به سرعت سوی آن دعوتگر می‌شتابند کافران می‌گویند امروز [چه] روز دشواری است

66   *Muhammad*, (the Prophet), 47:38:

... وَإِن تَتَوَلَّوْا يَسْتَبْدِلْ قَوْمًا غَيْرَكُمْ ثُمَّ لَا يَكُونُوا أَمْثَالَكُمْ

...و اگر روی برتابید [خدا] جای شما را به مردمی غیر از شما خواهد داد که مانند شما نخواهند بود

67   *Ma'árij*, the Ways of Ascent, 70:40-44:

فَلَا أُقْسِمُ بِرَبِّ الْمَشَارِقِ وَالْمَغَارِبِ إِنَّا لَقَادِرُونَ
عَلَى أَن نُّبَدِّلَ خَيْرًا مِّنْهُمْ وَمَا نَحْنُ بِمَسْبُوقِينَ
فَذَرْهُمْ يَخُوضُوا وَيَلْعَبُوا حَتَّى يُلَاقُوا يَوْمَهُمُ الَّذِي يُوعَدُونَ
يَوْمَ يَخْرُجُونَ مِنَ الْأَجْدَاثِ سِرَاعًا كَأَنَّهُمْ إِلَى نُصُبٍ يُوفِضُونَ
خَاشِعَةً أَبْصَارُهُمْ تَرْهَقُهُمْ ذِلَّةٌ ذَلِكَ الْيَوْمُ الَّذِي كَانُوا يُوعَدُونَ

[هرگز] به پروردگار خاوران و باختران سوگند یاد می‌کنم که ما توانائیم
که به جای آنان بهتر از ایشان را بیاوریم و بر ما پیشی نتوانند جست
پس بگذارشان یاوه گویند و بازی کنند تا روزی را که وعده داده شده‌اند ملاقات نمایند
روزی که از گور ها[ی خود] شتابان برآیند گویی که آنان به سوی پرچمهای افراشته می دوند
دیدگانشان فرو افتاده [غبار] مذلت آنان را فرو گرفته است این روزی است که به ایشان وعده داده
می‌شد

68   *Insán*, Man, 76:27-8:

إِنَّ هَؤُلَاءِ يُحِبُّونَ الْعَاجِلَةَ وَيَذَرُونَ وَرَاءَهُمْ يَوْمًا ثَقِيلًا
نَحْنُ خَلَقْنَاهُمْ وَشَدَدْنَا أَسْرَهُمْ وَإِذَا شِئْنَا بَدَّلْنَا أَمْثَالَهُم تَبْدِيلًا
إِنَّ هَذِهِ تَذْكِرَةٌ فَمَن شَاءَ اتَّخَذَ إِلَى رَبِّهِ سَبِيلًا

اینان دنیای زودگذر را دوست دارند و روزی گرانبار را [به غفلت] پشت سر می‌افکنند
ماییم که آنان را آفریده و پیوند مفاصل آنها را استوار کرده‌ایم و چون بخواهیم [آنان را] به نظایرشان تبدیل
می‌کنیم
این [آیات] پندنامه‌ای است تا هر که خواهد راهی به سوی پروردگار خود پیش گیرد

69   *Fátir*, the Originator of Creation; or *Maláika*, the Angels, 35:16:

إِن يَشَأْ يُذْهِبْكُمْ وَيَأْتِ بِخَلْقٍ جَدِيدٍ

اگر بخواهد شما را می‌برد و خلق جدیدی می‌آورد

70   *An'ám*, Cattle, 6:133-4:

وَرَبُّكَ الْغَنِيُّ ذُو الرَّحْمَةِ إِن يَشَأْ يُذْهِبْكُمْ وَيَسْتَخْلِفْ مِن بَعْدِكُم مَّا يَشَاءُ كَمَا أَنشَأَكُم مِّن ذُرِّيَّةِ قَوْمٍ آخَرِينَ
إِنَّ مَا تُوعَدُونَ لَآتٍ وَمَا أَنتُم بِمُعْجِزِينَ

پروردگارت بی‌نیاز و مهربان است: اگر بخواهد، همه شما را می‌برد؛ سپس هر کس را بخواهد جانشین شما
می‌سازد؛ همان‌طور که شما را از نسل اقوام دیگری به وجود آورد.
آنچه به شما وعده داده می‌شود، یقیناً می‌آید؛ و شما نمی‌توانید (خدا را) ناتوان سازید (و از عدالت و کیفر او
فرار کنید)!

71 *Ibráhím*, Abraham, 14:19-20:

أَلَمْ تَرَ أَنَّ اللَّهَ خَلَقَ السَّمَاوَاتِ وَالْأَرْضَ بِالْحَقِّ إِن يَشَأْ يُذْهِبْكُمْ وَيَأْتِ بِخَلْقٍ جَدِيدٍ وَمَا ذَلِكَ عَلَى اللَّهِ بِعَزِيزٍ

آیا در نیافته‌اى که خدا آسمانها و زمین را به حق آفریده اگر بخواهد شما را می‌برد و خلق تازه‌اى می‌آورد و این [کار] بر خدا دشوار نیست

72 *Ṭá-Há*, 20:108:

يَوْمَئِذٍ يَتَّبِعُونَ الدَّاعِيَ لَا عِوَجَ لَهُ وَخَشَعَتِ الْأَصْوَاتُ لِلرَّحْمَنِ فَلَا تَسْمَعُ إِلَّا هَمْسًا

در آن روز [همه مردم] داعى [حق] را که هیچ انحرافى در او نیست پیروى می‌کنند و صداها در مقابل [خداى] رحمان خاشع می‌گردد و جز صدایى آهسته نمی‌شنوى

73 *Húd*, (the Prophet Húd), 11:105:

يَوْمَ يَأْتِ لَا تَكَلَّمُ نَفْسٌ إِلَّا بِإِذْنِهِ فَمِنْهُمْ شَقِيٌّ وَسَعِيدٌ

روزى [است] که چون فرا رسد هیچ کس جز به اذن وى سخن نگوید آنگاه بعضى از آنان تیره‌بختند و [برخى] نیکبخت

74 Bahá'u'lláh, *Kitáb-i-Íqán*, para. 84, p. 77.
75 Bahá'u'lláh, *Gleanings from the Writings of Bahá'u'lláh*, XVII, p. 40.
76 ibid. XVIII, pp. 43-4.
77 ibid. VII, p. 11.
78 Bahá'u'lláh, *Epistle to the Son of the Wolf*, p. 101.
79 ibid. p. 92.
80 *Sabá*, the City of Sabá, 34:31:

وَقَالَ الَّذِينَ كَفَرُوا لَن نُّؤْمِنَ بِهَذَا الْقُرْآنِ وَلَا بِالَّذِي بَيْنَ يَدَيْهِ وَلَوْ تَرَى إِذِ الظَّالِمُونَ مَوْقُوفُونَ عِندَ رَبِّهِمْ يَرْجِعُ بَعْضُهُمْ إِلَى بَعْضٍ الْقَوْلَ يَقُولُ الَّذِينَ اسْتُضْعِفُوا لِلَّذِينَ اسْتَكْبَرُوا لَوْلَا أَنتُمْ لَكُنَّا مُؤْمِنِينَ

و کافران گویند هرگز به این قرآن، و به آنچه پیش از آن بود، ایمان نمی‌آوریم، و اگر ستمکاران [مشرک] را بنگرى که نزد پروردگارشان بازداشته شوند، بعضى با بعضى دیگر بگو مگو کنند مستضعفان به مستکبران گویند اگر شما نبودید بی‌شک، ما مؤمن بودیم

81 *Baqara*, the Heifer, 2:89:

وَلَمَّا جَاءَهُمْ كِتَابٌ مِّنْ عِندِ اللَّهِ مُصَدِّقٌ لِّمَا مَعَهُمْ وَكَانُوا مِن قَبْلُ يَسْتَفْتِحُونَ عَلَى الَّذِينَ كَفَرُوا فَلَمَّا جَاءَهُم مَّا عَرَفُوا كَفَرُوا بِهِ فَلَعْنَةُ اللَّهِ عَلَى الْكَافِرِينَ

و هنگامى که از جانب خداوند کتابى که مؤید آنچه نزد آنان است برایشان آمد و از دیرباز [در انتظارش] بر کسانى که کافر شده بودند پیروزى می‌جستند ولى همین که آنچه [که اوصافش] را می‌شناختند برایشان آمد انکارش کردند پس لعنت‌خدا بر کافران باد

82 *Mu-minún*, the Believers, 23:44:

ثُمَّ أَرْسَلْنَا رُسُلَنَا تَتْرَا كُلَّ مَا جَاءَ أُمَّةً رَّسُولُهَا كَذَّبُوهُ ...

باز فرستادگان خود را پیاپى روانه کردیم هر بار براى [هدایت] امتى پیامبرش آمد او را تکذیب کردند...

83 *Yá-Sín*, 36:30:

يَا حَسْرَةً عَلَى الْعِبَادِ مَا يَأْتِيهِم مِّن رَّسُولٍ إِلَّا كَانُوا بِهِ يَسْتَهْزِئُونَ

افسوس بر این بندگان که هیچ پیامبرى براى هدایت آنان نیامد مگر اینکه او را استهزا می‌کردند!

84 *An'ám*, the Cattle, 6:4:

وَمَا تَأْتِيهِم مِّنْ آيَةٍ مِّنْ آيَاتِ رَبِّهِمْ إِلاَّ كَانُواْ عَنْهَا مُعْرِضِينَ

هیچ نشانه و آیه‌ای از آیات پروردگارشان به آنها نمی‌رسد مگر اینکه از آن روی می‌گردانند!

85 *Mú-min*, the Believer, 40:5:

كَذَّبَتْ قَبْلَهُمْ قَوْمُ نُوحٍ وَالْأَحْزَابُ مِن بَعْدِهِمْ وَهَمَّتْ كُلُّ أُمَّةٍ بِرَسُولِهِمْ لِيَأْخُذُوهُ وَجَادَلُوا بِالْبَاطِلِ لِيُدْحِضُوا بِهِ الْحَقَّ فَأَخَذْتُهُمْ فَكَيْفَ كَانَ عِقَابِ

پیش از اینان قوم نوح و بعد از آنان دسته‌های مخالف [دیگر] به تکذیب پرداختند و هر امتی آهنگ فرستاده خود را کردند تا او را بگیرند و به [وسیله] باطل جدال نمودند تا حقیقت را با آن پایمال کنند پس آنان را فرو گرفتم آیا چگونه بود کیفر من

86 *Al-Hijr*, the Rocky Tract, 15:10–11:

وَلَقَدْ أَرْسَلْنَا مِن قَبْلِكَ فِي شِيَعِ الْأَوَّلِينَ
وَمَا يَأْتِيهِم مِّن رَّسُولٍ إِلاَّ كَانُواْ بِهِ يَسْتَهْزِؤُونَ

و به یقین پیش از تو [نیز] در گروه‌های پیشینیان [پیامبرانی] فرستادیم
و هیچ پیامبری برایشان نیامد جز آنکه او را به مسخره می‌گرفتند

87 *Mú-min*, the Believer, 40:34:

وَلَقَدْ جَاءكُمْ يُوسُفُ مِن قَبْلُ بِالْبَيِّنَاتِ فَمَا زِلْتُمْ فِي شَكٍّ مِّمَّا جَاءكُم بِهِ حَتَّى إِذَا هَلَكَ قُلْتُمْ لَن يَبْعَثَ اللَّهُ مِن بَعْدِهِ رَسُولًا كَذَلِكَ يُضِلُّ اللَّهُ مَنْ هُوَ مُسْرِفٌ مُّرْتَابٌ

و به یقین پیش از این دلایل آشکار برای شما آورد و از آنچه برای شما همواره در تردید بودید تا وقتی که از دنیا رفت گفتید خدا بعد از او هرگز فرستاده‌ای را برنخواهد انگیخت این گونه خدا هر که را افراطگر شکاک است بی راه می‌گذارد

88 *Anbiyáa*, the Prophets, 21:2:

مَا يَأْتِيهِم مِّن ذِكْرٍ مِّن رَّبِّهِم مُّحْدَثٍ إِلَّا اسْتَمَعُوهُ وَهُمْ يَلْعَبُونَ

هیچ پند تازه‌ای از پروردگارشان نیامد مگر اینکه بازیکنان آن را شنیدند

89 *Shu'aráa*, the Poets, 26:5:

وَمَا يَأْتِيهِم مِّن ذِكْرٍ مِّنَ الرَّحْمَنِ مُحْدَثٍ إِلَّا كَانُوا عَنْهُ مُعْرِضِينَ

و هیچ تذکر جدیدی از سوی [خدای] رحمان برایشان نیامد جز اینکه همواره از آن روی برمی‌تافتند

90 *An'ám*, Cattle, 6:112:

وَكَذَلِكَ جَعَلْنَا لِكُلِّ نِبِيٍّ عَدُوًّا شَيَاطِينَ الإِنسِ وَالْجِنِّ يُوحِي بَعْضُهُمْ إِلَى بَعْضٍ زُخْرُفَ الْقَوْلِ غُرُورًا وَلَوْ شَاء رَبُّكَ مَا فَعَلُوهُ فَذَرْهُمْ وَمَا يَفْتَرُونَ

و بدین گونه برای هر پیامبری دشمنی از شیطانهای انس و جن برگماشتیم بعضی از آنها به بعضی برای فریب [یکدیگر] سخنان آراسته القا می‌کنند و اگر پروردگار تو می‌خواست چنین نمی‌کردند پس آنان را با آنچه به دروغ می‌سازند واگذار

91 *Furqán*, the Criterion, 25:31:

وَكَذَلِكَ جَعَلْنَا لِكُلِّ نَبِيٍّ عَدُوًّا مِّنَ الْمُجْرِمِينَ وَكَفَى بِرَبِّكَ هَادِيًا وَنَصِيرًا

و این گونه برای هر پیامبری دشمنی از گناهکاران قرار دادیم و همین بس که پروردگارت راهبر و یاور توست

585

92 *Baqara*, the Heifer, 2:118:

...كَذَٰلِكَ قَالَ الَّذِينَ مِن قَبْلِهِم مِّثْلَ قَوْلِهِمْ تَشَابَهَتْ قُلُوبُهُمْ قَدْ بَيَّنَّا الْآيَاتِ لِقَوْمٍ يُوقِنُونَ

...کسانی که پیش از اینان بودند [نیز] مثل همین گفته ایشان را می‌گفتند دلها [و افکار]شان به هم می‌ماند ما نشانه‌ها[ی خود] را برای گروهی که یقین دارند نیک روشن گردانیده‌ایم

93 *Aḥqáf*, Winding Sand-tracts, 46:32.
94 *Anfál*, the Spoils of War, 8:36:

إِنَّ الَّذِينَ كَفَرُوا يُنفِقُونَ أَمْوَالَهُمْ لِيَصُدُّوا عَن سَبِيلِ اللَّهِ فَسَيُنفِقُونَهَا ثُمَّ تَكُونُ عَلَيْهِمْ حَسْرَةً ثُمَّ يُغْلَبُونَ وَالَّذِينَ كَفَرُوا إِلَىٰ جَهَنَّمَ يُحْشَرُونَ

بی‌گمان کسانی که کفر ورزیدند اموال خود را خرج می‌کنند تا [مردم را] از راه خدا بازدارند پس به زودی [همه] آن را خرج می‌کنند و آنگاه حسرتی بر آنان خواهد گشت‌سپس مغلوب می‌شوند و کسانی که کفر ورزیدند به سوی دوزخ گردآورده خواهند شد

95 Baháʼuʼlláh, *Kitáb-i-Íqán*, para. 6, p. 6.
96 *Ḥajj*, the Pilgrimage, 22:42-4:

وَإِن يُكَذِّبُوكَ فَقَدْ كَذَّبَتْ قَبْلَهُمْ قَوْمُ نُوحٍ وَعَادٌ وَثَمُودُ
وَقَوْمُ إِبْرَاهِيمَ وَقَوْمُ لُوطٍ
وَأَصْحَابُ مَدْيَنَ وَكُذِّبَ مُوسَىٰ فَأَمْلَيْتُ لِلْكَافِرِينَ ثُمَّ أَخَذْتُهُمْ فَكَيْفَ كَانَ نَكِيرِ

و اگر تو را تکذیب کنند، (امر تازه‌ای نیست؛) پیش از آنها قوم نوح و عاد و ثمود (پیامبرانشان را) تکذیب کردند.
و همچنین قوم ابراهیم و قوم لوط
و اصحاب مدین (قوم شعیب)؛ و نیز موسی (از سوی فرعونیان) تکذیب شد؛ اما من به کافران مهلت دادم، سپس آنها را مجازات کردم. دیدی چگونه (عمل آنها را) انکار نمودم (و چگونه به آنان پاسخ گفتم)؟!

97 *Zumar*, the Crowds, 39:59:

بَلَىٰ قَدْ جَاءَتْكَ آيَاتِي فَكَذَّبْتَ بِهَا وَاسْتَكْبَرْتَ وَكُنتَ مِنَ الْكَافِرِينَ

[به او گویند] آری نشانه‌های من بر تو آمد و آنها را تکذیب کردی و تکبر ورزیدی و از [جمله] کافران شدی

98 *Furqán*, the Criterion, 25:4 (see also 6:26, 23:83, 68:15 and 83:13):

وَقَالَ الَّذِينَ كَفَرُوا إِنْ هَٰذَا إِلَّا إِفْكٌ افْتَرَاهُ وَأَعَانَهُ عَلَيْهِ قَوْمٌ آخَرُونَ فَقَدْ جَاءُوا ظُلْمًا وَزُورًا

و کسانی که کفر ورزیدند گفتند این [کتاب] جز دروغی که آن را بربافته [چیزی] نیست و گروهی دیگر او را بر آن یاری کرده‌اند و قطعا [با چنین نسبتی] ظلم و بهتانی به پیش آوردند

99 *Naḥl*, Bees, 16:103:

وَلَقَدْ نَعْلَمُ أَنَّهُمْ يَقُولُونَ إِنَّمَا يُعَلِّمُهُ بَشَرٌ لِّسَانُ الَّذِي يُلْحِدُونَ إِلَيْهِ أَعْجَمِيٌّ وَهَٰذَا لِسَانٌ عَرَبِيٌّ مُّبِينٌ

و نیک می‌دانیم که آنان می‌گویند جز این نیست که بشری به او می‌آموزد [نه چنین نیست زیرا] زبان کسی که [این] نسبت را به او می‌دهند غیر عربی است و این [قرآن] به زبان عربی روشن است

100 *Furqán*, the Criterion, 25:32:

وَقَالَ الَّذِينَ كَفَرُوا لَوْلَا نُزِّلَ عَلَيْهِ الْقُرْآنُ جُمْلَةً وَاحِدَةً كَذَٰلِكَ لِنُثَبِّتَ بِهِ فُؤَادَكَ وَرَتَّلْنَاهُ تَرْتِيلًا

و کسانی که کافر شدند گفتند چرا قرآن یکجا بر او نازل نشده است این گونه [ما آن را به تدریج نازل کردیم] تا قلبت را به وسیله آن استوار گردانیم و آن را به آرامی [بر تو] خواندیم

101 *Naḥl*, Bees, 16:24:

وَإِذَا قِيلَ لَهُم مَّاذَا أَنزَلَ رَبُّكُمْ قَالُواْ أَسَاطِيرُ الْأَوَّلِينَ

و چون به آنان گفته شود پروردگارتان چه چیز نازل کرده است می‌گویند افسانه‌های پیشینیان است

102 *Anfál*, the Spoils of War, 8:31:

وَإِذَا تُتْلَىٰ عَلَيْهِمْ آيَاتُنَا قَالُوا قَدْ سَمِعْنَا لَوْ نَشَاءُ لَقُلْنَا مِثْلَ هَٰذَا إِنْ هَٰذَا إِلَّا أَسَاطِيرُ الْأَوَّلِينَ

و چون آیات ما بر آنان خوانده شود می‌گویند به خوبی شنیدیم اگر می‌خواستیم قطعا ما نیز همانند این را می‌گفتیم این جز افسانه‌های پیشینیان نیست

103 *Furqán*, the Criterion, 25:30:

وَقَالَ الرَّسُولُ يَا رَبِّ إِنَّ قَوْمِي اتَّخَذُوا هَٰذَا الْقُرْآنَ مَهْجُورًا

و پیامبر [خدا] گفت پروردگارا قوم من این قرآن را رها کردند

104 *Sabá*, the City of Sabá, 34:43:

وَإِذَا تُتْلَىٰ عَلَيْهِمْ آيَاتُنَا بَيِّنَاتٍ قَالُوا مَا هَٰذَا إِلَّا رَجُلٌ يُرِيدُ أَن يَصُدَّكُمْ عَمَّا كَانَ يَعْبُدُ آبَاؤُكُمْ وَقَالُوا مَا هَٰذَا إِلَّا إِفْكٌ مُفْتَرًى وَقَالَ الَّذِينَ كَفَرُوا لِلْحَقِّ لَمَّا جَاءَهُمْ إِنْ هَٰذَا إِلَّا سِحْرٌ مُبِينٌ

و چون آیات تابناک ما بر آنان خوانده می‌شود می‌گویند این جز مردی نیست که می‌خواهد شما را از آنچه پدرانتان می‌پرستیدند باز دارد و [نیز] می‌گویند این جز دروغی بربافته نیست و کسانی که به حق چون به سویشان آمد کافر شدند می‌گویند این جز افسونی آشکار نیست

105 *Furqán*, the Criterion, 25:4–5:

وَقَالَ الَّذِينَ كَفَرُوا إِنْ هَٰذَا إِلَّا إِفْكٌ افْتَرَاهُ وَأَعَانَهُ عَلَيْهِ قَوْمٌ آخَرُونَ فَقَدْ جَاءُوا ظُلْمًا وَزُورًا وَقَالُوا أَسَاطِيرُ الْأَوَّلِينَ اكْتَتَبَهَا فَهِيَ تُمْلَىٰ عَلَيْهِ بُكْرَةً وَأَصِيلًا

و کسانی که کفر ورزیدند گفتند این [کتاب] جز دروغی که آن را بربافته [چیزی] نیست و گروهی دیگر او را بر آن یاری کرده‌اند و قطعا [با چنین نسبتی] ظلم و بهتانی به پیش آوردند
و گفتند افسانه‌های پیشینیان است که آنها را برای خود نوشته و صبح و شام بر او املا می‌شود

106 *Má'ida*, the Table Spread, 5:70:

لَقَدْ أَخَذْنَا مِيثَاقَ بَنِي إِسْرَائِيلَ وَأَرْسَلْنَا إِلَيْهِمْ رُسُلًا كُلَّمَا جَاءَهُمْ رَسُولٌ بِمَا لَا تَهْوَىٰ أَنفُسُهُمْ فَرِيقًا كَذَّبُوا وَفَرِيقًا يَقْتُلُونَ

ما از بنی اسرائیل پیمان گرفتیم؛ و رسولانی به سوی آنها فرستادیم؛ (ولی) هر زمان پیامبری حکمی بر خلاف هوسها و دلخواه آنها می‌آورد، عده‌ای را تکذیب می‌کردند؛ و عده‌ای را می‌کشتند.

107 *Mu-minún*, the Believers, 23:26 (also, 23:39):

قَالَ رَبِّ انصُرْنِي بِمَا كَذَّبُونِ

گفت پروردگارا از آن روی که مرا دروغزن خواندند یاریم کن

108 *Ṣád*, 38:4:

وَعَجِبُوا أَن جَاءَهُم مُّنذِرٌ مِّنْهُمْ وَقَالَ الْكَافِرُونَ هَٰذَا سَاحِرٌ كَذَّابٌ

و از اینکه هشداردهنده‌ای از خودشان برایشان آمده درشگفتند و کافران می گویند این ساحری شیاد است

109 *Zukhruf*, Gold Adornments, 43:31-2:

وَقَالُوا لَوْلَا نُزِّلَ هَٰذَا الْقُرْآنُ عَلَىٰ رَجُلٍ مِّنَ الْقَرْيَتَيْنِ عَظِيمٍ

و گفتند چرا این قرآن بر مردی بزرگ از [آن] دو شهر فرود نیامده است

110 John 7:47-9.

111 *Baní Isrá-íl*, the Children of Israel, 17:47:

نَحْنُ أَعْلَمُ بِمَا يَسْتَمِعُونَ بِهِ إِذْ يَسْتَمِعُونَ إِلَيْكَ وَإِذْ هُمْ نَجْوَى إِذْ يَقُولُ الظَّالِمُونَ إِن تَتَّبِعُونَ إِلَّا رَجُلًا مَّسْحُورًا

هنگامی که به سوی تو گوش فرا می‌دارند ما بهتر می‌دانیم به چه [منظور] گوش می‌دهند و [نیز] آنگاه که به نجوا می‌پردازند وقتی که ستمگران گویند جز مردی افسون‌شده را پیروی نمی‌کنید

112 *Mu-minún*,, the Believers, 23:70:

أَمْ يَقُولُونَ بِهِ جِنَّةٌ بَلْ جَاءهُم بِالْحَقِّ وَأَكْثَرُهُمْ لِلْحَقِّ كَارِهُونَ

یا می‌گویند او جنونی دارد [نه] بلکه [او] حق را برای ایشان آورده و[لی] بیشترشان حقیقت را خوش ندارند

113 *Ṣáffát*, Those Ranged in Ranks, 37:35-6:

إِنَّهُمْ كَانُوا إِذَا قِيلَ لَهُمْ لَا إِلَهَ إِلَّا اللَّهُ يَسْتَكْبِرُونَ
وَيَقُولُونَ أَئِنَّا لَتَارِكُوا آلِهَتِنَا لِشَاعِرٍ مَّجْنُونٍ

چرا که آنان بودند که وقتی به ایشان گفته می‌شد خدایی جز خدای یگانه نیست تکبر می‌ورزیدند و می‌گفتند آیا ما برای شاعری دیوانه دست از خدایانمان برداریم

114 *Sabá*, the City of Sabá, 34:46:

قُلْ إِنَّمَا أَعِظُكُم بِوَاحِدَةٍ أَن تَقُومُوا لِلَّهِ ...
ثُمَّ تَتَفَكَّرُوا مَا بِصَاحِبِكُم مِّن جِنَّةٍ إِنْ هُوَ إِلَّا نَذِيرٌ لَّكُم بَيْنَ يَدَيْ عَذَابٍ شَدِيدٍ

بگو من فقط به شما یک اندرز می‌دهم ...
برای خدا به پا خیزید سپس بیندیشید که رفیق شما هیچ گونه دیوانگی ندارد او شما را از عذاب سختی که در پیش است جز هشداردهنده‌ای [بیش] نیست

115 Matt. 11:18.

116 Mark 3:22-5.

117 *Furqán*, the Criterion, 25:20:

وَمَا أَرْسَلْنَا قَبْلَكَ مِنَ الْمُرْسَلِينَ إِلَّا إِنَّهُمْ لَيَأْكُلُونَ الطَّعَامَ وَيَمْشُونَ فِي الْأَسْوَاقِ وَجَعَلْنَا بَعْضَكُمْ لِبَعْضٍ فِتْنَةً أَتَصْبِرُونَ وَكَانَ رَبُّكَ بَصِيرًا

و پیش از تو پیامبران [خود] را نفرستادیم جز اینکه آنان [نیز] غذا می‌خوردند و در بازارها راه می‌رفتند و برخی از شما را برای برخی دیگر [وسیله] آزمایش قرار دادیم آیا شکیبایی می‌کنید و پروردگار تو همواره بیناست

118 *Furqán*, the Criterion, 25:7:

وَقَالُوا مَالِ هَذَا الرَّسُولِ يَأْكُلُ الطَّعَامَ وَيَمْشِي فِي الْأَسْوَاقِ لَوْلَا أُنزِلَ إِلَيْهِ مَلَكٌ فَيَكُونَ مَعَهُ نَذِيرًا

و گفتند این چه پیامبری است که غذا می‌خورد و در بازارها راه می‌رود چرا فرشته‌ای به سوی او نازل نشده تا همراه وی هشداردهنده باشد

119 *Mu-minún*, the Believers, 23:33:

وَقَالَ الْمَلأُ مِن قَوْمِهِ الَّذِينَ كَفَرُوا وَكَذَّبُوا بِلِقَاء الآخِرَةِ وَأَتْرَفْنَاهُمْ فِي الْحَيَاةِ الدُّنْيَا مَا هَذَا إِلَّا بَشَرٌ مِّثْلُكُمْ يَأْكُلُ مِمَّا تَأْكُلُونَ مِنْهُ وَيَشْرَبُ مِمَّا تَشْرَبُونَ

ولی اشرافیان (خودخواه) از قوم او که کافر بودند، و دیدار آخرت را تکذیب می‌کردند، و در زندگی دنیا به آنان ناز و نعمت داده بودیم، گفتند: «این بشری است مثل شما؛ از آنچه می‌خورید می‌خورد؛ و از آنچه می‌نوشید می‌نوشد! (پس چگونه می‌تواند پیامبر باشد؟!)

120 *Baní Isrá-íl*, the Children of Israel, 17:94:

وَمَا مَنَعَ النَّاسَ أَن يُؤْمِنُواْ إِذْ جَاءهُمُ الْهُدَى إِلاَّ أَن قَالُواْ أَبَعَثَ اللّهُ بَشَرًا رَّسُولًا

تنها چیزی که بعد از آمدن هدایت مانع شد مردم ایمان بیاورند، این بود (که از روی نادانی و بی‌خبری) گفتند: «آیا خداوند بشری را بعنوان رسول فرستاده است»؟!

121 *Tagábun*, Mutual Loss and Gain, 64:6:

ذَلِكَ بِأَنَّهُ كَانَت تَّأْتِيهِمْ رُسُلُهُم بِالْبَيِّنَاتِ فَقَالُوا أَبَشَرٌ يَهْدُونَنَا فَكَفَرُوا وَتَوَلَّوا وَّاسْتَغْنَى اللَّهُ وَاللَّهُ غَنِيٌّ حَمِيدٌ

این [بدفرجامی] از آن روی بود که پیامبرانشان دلایل آشکار برایشان می‌آوردند و[لی] آنان [می‌]گفتند آیا بشری ما را هدایت می‌کند پس کافر شدند و روی گرداندند و خدا بی‌نیازی نمود و خدا بی‌نیاز ستوده‌است

122 Luke 7:34.
123 Matt. 9:14.
124 Bahá'u'lláh, *Kitáb-i-Íqán*, para. 80, pp. 72–3.
125 *Baqara*, the Heifer, 2:118:

وَقَالَ الَّذِينَ لاَ يَعْلَمُونَ لَوْلاَ يُكَلِّمُنَا اللّهُ أَوْ تَأْتِينَا آيَةٌ ...

افراد نادان گفتند چرا خدا با ما سخن نمی‌گوید یا برای ما معجزه‌ای نمی‌آید ...

126 *Shu'aráa*, the Poets, 26:154:

مَا أَنتَ إِلاَّ بَشَرٌ مِّثْلُنَا فَأْتِ بِآيَةٍ إِن كُنتَ مِنَ الصَّادِقِينَ

تو جز بشری مانند ما [بیش] نیستی اگر راست می‌گویی معجزه‌ای بیاور

127 *Ra'd*, the Thunder, 13:27:

وَيَقُولُ الَّذِينَ كَفَرُواْ لَوْلاَ أُنزِلَ عَلَيْهِ آيَةٌ مِّن رَّبِّهِ قُلْ إِنَّ اللّهَ يُضِلُّ مَن يَشَاءُ وَيَهْدِي إِلَيْهِ مَنْ أَنَابَ

و کسانی که کافر شده‌اند می‌گویند چرا از جانب پروردگارش معجزه‌ای بر او نازل نشده است بگو در حقیقت خداست که هر کس را بخواهد بی‌راه می‌گذارد و هر کس را که [به سوی او] بازگردد به سوی خود راه می‌نماید

128 *Furqán*, the Criterion, 25:21:

وَقَالَ الَّذِينَ لَا يَرْجُونَ لِقَاءنَا لَوْلَا أُنزِلَ عَلَيْنَا الْمَلَائِكَةُ أَوْ نَرَى رَبَّنَا لَقَدِ اسْتَكْبَرُوا فِي أَنفُسِهِمْ وَعَتَوْ عُتُوًّا كَبِيرًا

و کسانی که به لقای ما امید ندارند گفتند چرا فرشتگان بر ما نازل نشدند یا پروردگارمان را نمی‌بینیم قطعا در مورد خود تکبر ورزیدند و سخت‌سرکشی کردند

129 *Baní Isrá-íl*, the Children of Israel, 17:90–3:

وَقَالُوا لَن نُّؤْمِنَ لَكَ حَتَّىٰ تَفْجُرَ لَنَا مِنَ الْأَرْضِ يَنْبُوعًا
أَوْ تَكُونَ لَكَ جَنَّةٌ مِّن نَّخِيلٍ وَعِنَبٍ فَتُفَجِّرَ الْأَنْهَارَ خِلَالَهَا تَفْجِيرًا
أَوْ تُسْقِطَ السَّمَاءَ كَمَا زَعَمْتَ عَلَيْنَا كِسَفًا أَوْ تَأْتِيَ بِاللَّهِ وَالْمَلَائِكَةِ قَبِيلًا
أَوْ يَكُونَ لَكَ بَيْتٌ مِّن زُخْرُفٍ أَوْ تَرْقَىٰ فِي السَّمَاءِ وَلَن نُّؤْمِنَ لِرُقِيِّكَ حَتَّىٰ تُنَزِّلَ عَلَيْنَا كِتَابًا نَّقْرَؤُهُ قُلْ سُبْحَانَ رَبِّي هَلْ كُنتُ إِلَّا بَشَرًا رَّسُولًا

و گفتند: «ما هرگز به تو ایمان نمی‌آوریم تا اینکه چشمه‌جوشانی از این سرزمین (خشک و سوزان) برای ما خارج سازی...
یا باغی از نخل و انگور از آن تو باشد؛ و نهرها در لابه‌لای آن جاری کنی...
یا قطعاتی (سنگهای) آسمان را -آنچنان که می‌پنداری- بر سر ما فرود آری؛ یا خداوند و فرشتگان را در برابر ما بیاوری...
یا برای تو خانه‌ای پر نقش و نگار از طلا باشد؛ یا به آسمان بالا روی؛ حتی اگر به آسمان روی، ایمان نمی‌آوریم مگر آنکه نامه‌ای بر ما فرود آوری که آن را بخوانیم! «بگو:» منزه است پروردگارم (از این سخنان بی‌معنی)! مگر من جز انسانی فرستاده خدا هستم؟!»

130 *Anfál*, the Spoils of War, 8:32:

وَإِذْ قَالُوا اللَّهُمَّ إِن كَانَ هَٰذَا هُوَ الْحَقَّ مِنْ عِندِكَ فَأَمْطِرْ عَلَيْنَا حِجَارَةً مِّنَ السَّمَاءِ أَوِ ائْتِنَا بِعَذَابٍ أَلِيمٍ

و [یاد کن] هنگامی را که گفتند خدایا اگر این [کتاب] همان حق از جانب توست پس بر ما از آسمان سنگهایی ببباران یا عذابی دردناک بر سر ما بیاور

131 *Ál-i-'Imrán*, the Family of 'Imrán, 3:183:

الَّذِينَ قَالُوا إِنَّ اللَّهَ عَهِدَ إِلَيْنَا أَلَّا نُؤْمِنَ لِرَسُولٍ حَتَّىٰ يَأْتِيَنَا بِقُرْبَانٍ تَأْكُلُهُ النَّارُ قُلْ قَدْ جَاءَكُمْ رُسُلٌ
مِّن قَبْلِي بِالْبَيِّنَاتِ وَبِالَّذِي قُلْتُمْ فَلِمَ قَتَلْتُمُوهُمْ إِن كُنتُمْ صَادِقِينَ

(اینها) همان کسانی (هستند) که گفتند: «خداوند از ما پیمان گرفته که به هیچ پیامبری ایمان نیاوریم تا (این معجزه را انجام دهد، که) قربانی بیاورد، که آنس (صاعقه آسمانی) آن را بخورد!» بگو: «پیامبرانی پیش از من، برای شما آمدند؛ و دلایل روشن، و آنچه را گفتید؛ پس چرا آنها را به قتل رساندید اگر راست می‌گویید؟!»

132 Mark 8:11–12.
133 John 6:30–31.
134 *Aḥqáf*, Winding Sand-tracts, 46:6:

وَإِذَا حُشِرَ النَّاسُ كَانُوا لَهُمْ أَعْدَاءً وَكَانُوا بِعِبَادَتِهِمْ كَافِرِينَ

و هنگامی که مردم محشور می‌شوند، معبودهای آنها دشمنانشان خواهند بود؛ حتی عبادت آنها را انکار می‌کنند!

135 Bahá'u'lláh, *Súriy-i-Haykal*, paras. 55–6, in *The Summons of the Lord of Hosts*, pp. 28–9.
136 Bahá'u'lláh, *Kitáb-i-Íqán*, para. 257, pp. 230–31.
137 Bahá'u'lláh, *Epistle to the Son of the Wolf*, pp. 63–4.
138 Bahá'u'lláh, *Tablets of Bahá'u'lláh Revealed after the Kitáb-i-Aqdas*, p. 254.

139 *Má'ida,* the Table Spread, 5:33:

إِنَّمَا جَزَاءُ الَّذِينَ يُحَارِبُونَ اللَّهَ وَرَسُولَهُ وَيَسْعَوْنَ فِي الأَرْضِ فَسَادًا أَن يُقَتَّلُوا أَوْ يُصَلَّبُوا أَوْ تُقَطَّعَ أَيْدِيهِمْ وَأَرْجُلُهُم مِّنْ خِلَافٍ أَوْ يُنفَوْا مِنَ الأَرْضِ ذَلِكَ لَهُمْ خِزْيٌ فِي الدُّنْيَا وَلَهُمْ فِي الآخِرَةِ عَذَابٌ عَظِيمٌ

سزای کسانی که با [دوستداران] خدا و پیامبر او می‌جنگند و در زمین به فساد می‌کوشند جز این نیست که کشته شوند یا بر دار آویخته گردند یا دست و پایشان در خلاف جهت یکدیگر بریده شود یا از آن سرزمین تبعید گردند این رسوایی آنان در دنیاست و در آخرت عذابی بزرگ خواهند داشت

140 Bahá'u'lláh, quoted in Shoghi Effendi, *The Promised Day Is Come,* p. 87.
141 Bahá'u'lláh, *Gems of Divine Mysteries, Javáhiru'l-Asrár,* para. 68, pp. 48–9.
142 ibid. para. 61, p. 45.
143 Bahá'u'lláh, Tablet of Aḥmad, in *Bahá'í Prayers,* pp. 209–13.
144 Shoghi Effendi, *The Promised Day is Come,* p. 87.
145 Bahá'u'lláh, *Epistle to the Son of Wolf,* pp. 102–3.
146 Bahá'u'lláh, *Gleanings from the Writings of Bahá'u'lláh,* CVI, p. 213.
147 Shoghi Effendi, *The Promised Day Is Come,* p. 115.
148 Bahá'u'lláh, quoted ibid. p. 87.
149 ibid. p. 97.
150 Bahá'u'lláh, quoted in Shoghi Effendi, *Bahá'í Administration,* p. 174.
151 Bahá'u'lláh quoted by Shoghi Effendi, ibid. p. 173.
152 Bahá'u'lláh, *Gleanings from the Writings of Bahá'u'lláh,* XVIII, pp. 45–6.

15 Embracing 'the Great Announcement' of the Qur'án

1 Bahá'u'lláh, *Tablets of Bahá'u'lláh revealed after the Kitáb-i-Aqdas,* p. 254.
2 *Nabaa,* the (Great) News, 78:1–2:

عَمَّ يَتَسَاءَلُونَ
عَنِ النَّبَإِ الْعَظِيمِ

درباره چه چیز از یکدیگر می‌پرسند
از آن خبر بزرگ

3 *Wáqi'a,* the Inevitable Event, 56:1–2:

إِذَا وَقَعَتِ الْوَاقِعَةُ
لَيْسَ لِوَقْعَتِهَا كَاذِبَةٌ

آن واقعه چون وقوع یابد
[که] در وقوع آن دروغی نیست

4 *Ḥáqqa,* the Sure Reality, 69:15:

فَيَوْمَئِذٍ وَقَعَتِ الْوَاقِعَةُ

پس آن روز است که واقعه [آنچنانی] وقوع یابد

5 *Názi'át*, Those Who Tear Out, 79:34-41:

فَإِذَا جَاءَتِ الطَّامَّةُ الْكُبْرَى
يَوْمَ يَتَذَكَّرُ الْإِنْسَانُ مَا سَعَى
وَبُرِّزَتِ الْجَحِيمُ لِمَن يَرَى
فَأَمَّا مَن طَغَى
وَآثَرَ الْحَيَاةَ الدُّنْيَا
فَإِنَّ الْجَحِيمَ هِيَ الْمَأْوَى
وَأَمَّا مَنْ خَافَ مَقَامَ رَبِّهِ وَنَهَى النَّفْسَ عَنِ الْهَوَى
فَإِنَّ الْجَنَّةَ هِيَ الْمَأْوَى

پس آنگاه که آن هنگامه بزرگ دررسد
[آن] روز است که انسان آنچه را که در پی آن کوشیده است به یاد آورد
و جهنم برای هر که بیند آشکار گردد
اما هر که طغیان کرد
و زندگی پست دنیا را برگزید
پس جایگاه او همان آتش است
و اما کسی که از ایستادن در برابر پروردگارش هراسید و نفس خود را از هوس باز داشت
پس جایگاه او همان بهشت است

6 Bahá'u'lláh, *Gleanings from the Writings of Bahá'u'lláh*, CXXIX, p. 281.
7 Bahá'u'lláh, *Epistle to the Son of the Wolf*, pp. 143-4.
8 ibid. p. 132.
9 Isa. 52:5-7, 10.
10 Mark 1:1-3 (referring Isa. 40:3 and Mal. 3:1):
   The beginning of the gospel of Jesus Christ, the Son of God;
   As it is written in the prophets, Behold, I send my messenger before thy face, which shall prepare thy way before thee.
   The voice of one crying in the wilderness, Prepare ye the way of the Lord, make his paths straight.
11 Luke 11:2.
12 Mark 16:15.
13 Bahá'u'lláh, quoted by Shoghi Effendi, *The World Order of Bahá'u'lláh*, pp. 104-5.
14 *Tatfif*, Dealing in Fraud, 83:6:

يَوْمَ يَقُومُ النَّاسُ لِرَبِّ الْعَالَمِينَ

روزی که مردم در پیشگاه پروردگار جهانیان می‌ایستند.

15 Isa. 35:1-2, quoted by Bahá'u'lláh, *Epistle to the Son of the Wolf*, p. 146.
16 Isa. 2:10-11.
17 Bahá'u'lláh, *Gleanings from the Writings of Bahá'u'lláh*, X, p. 13.
18 Luke 12:37.
19 *Ál-i-'Imrán*, the Family of 'Imrán, 3:194:

رَبَّنَا وَآتِنَا مَا وَعَدتَّنَا عَلَى رُسُلِكَ وَلَا تُخْزِنَا يَوْمَ الْقِيَامَةِ إِنَّكَ لَا تُخْلِفُ الْمِيعَادَ

پروردگارا! آنچه را که به وسیله پیامبرانت به ما وعده فرمودی، به ما عطا کن! و ما را در روز رستاخیز، رسوا مگردان! زیرا تو هیچگاه از وعده خود، تخلف نمی‌کنی.

20 *Ál-i-'Imrán*, the Family of 'Imrán, 3:8:

رَبَّنَا لَا تُزِغْ قُلُوبَنَا بَعْدَ إِذْ هَدَيْتَنَا وَهَبْ لَنَا مِن لَّدُنكَ رَحْمَةً إِنَّكَ أَنتَ الْوَهَّابُ

[می‌گویند] پروردگارا پس از آنکه ما را هدایت کردی دلهایمان را دستخوش انحراف مگردان و از جانب خود رحمتی بر ما ارزانی دار که تو خود بخشایشگری

21 Also, a title of the Báb in the Bahá'í Writings.

22 *Lail*, the Night, 92:18-21:

الَّذِي يُؤْتِي مَالَهُ يَتَزَكَّىٰ
وَمَا لِأَحَدٍ عِندَهُ مِن نِّعْمَةٍ تُجْزَىٰ
إِلَّا ابْتِغَاءَ وَجْهِ رَبِّهِ الْأَعْلَىٰ
وَلَسَوْفَ يَرْضَىٰ

همان که مال خود را می‌دهد [برای آنکه] پاک شود
و هیچ کس را به قصد پاداش‌یافتن نعمت نمی‌بخشد
جز خواستن رضای پروردگارش که بسی برتر است [منظوری ندارد]
و قطعاً بزودی خشنود خواهد شد

23 *A'lá*, the Most High, 87:1:

سَبِّحِ اسْمَ رَبِّكَ الْأَعْلَى

به نام پروردگارت که بلندمرتبه است، تسبیح گوی

24 '*Amr*' or '*Hukm*' or 'Command' is a reference in the Qur'án to Revelation, as in *Ṭaláq*, Divorce, 65:12:
J. M. Rodwell:

> The Divine command cometh down through them all, that ye may know that God hath power over all things, and that God in his knowledge embraceth all things!

'*Amr*' has a similar connotation in the Bahá'í Writings, for example Bahá'u'lláh, *Kitáb-i-Íqán*, p. 153:

> These Countenances are the recipients of the Divine Command, and the Day Springs of His Revelation.

25 *Dahr*, Time; or *Insán*, Man, 76:24-6:

فَاصْبِرْ لِحُكْمِ رَبِّكَ وَلَا تُطِعْ مِنْهُمْ آثِمًا أَوْ كَفُورًا
وَاذْكُرِ اسْمَ رَبِّكَ بُكْرَةً وَأَصِيلًا
وَمِنَ اللَّيْلِ فَاسْجُدْ لَهُ وَسَبِّحْهُ لَيْلًا طَوِيلًا

پس در برابر فرمان پروردگارت شکیبایی کن و از آنان گناهکار یا ناسپاسگزار را فرمان مبر
و نام پروردگارت را بامدادان و شامگاهان یاد کن
و بخشی از شب را در برابر او سجده کن و شب[های] دراز او را به پاکی بستای

26 *Baqara*, the Heifer, 2:45-6:

وَاسْتَعِينُوا بِالصَّبْرِ وَالصَّلَاةِ وَإِنَّهَا لَكَبِيرَةٌ إِلَّا عَلَى الْخَاشِعِينَ
الَّذِينَ يَظُنُّونَ أَنَّهُم مُّلَاقُو رَبِّهِمْ وَأَنَّهُمْ إِلَيْهِ رَاجِعُونَ

از صبر و نماز یاری جوئید و این کار، جز برای خاشعان، گران است.
آنها کسانی هستند که می‌دانند دیدارکننده پروردگار خویشند، و به سوی او بازمی‌گردند.

27 A'ráf, the Heights, 7:50-51:

وَنَادَىٰ أَصْحَابُ النَّارِ أَصْحَابَ الْجَنَّةِ أَنْ أَفِيضُوا عَلَيْنَا مِنَ الْمَاءِ أَوْ مِمَّا رَزَقَكُمُ اللَّهُ قَالُوا إِنَّ اللَّهَ حَرَّمَهُمَا عَلَى الْكَافِرِينَ
الَّذِينَ اتَّخَذُوا دِينَهُمْ لَهْوًا وَلَعِبًا وَغَرَّتْهُمُ الْحَيَاةُ الدُّنْيَا فَالْيَوْمَ نَنسَاهُمْ كَمَا نَسُوا لِقَاءَ يَوْمِهِمْ هَٰذَا وَمَا كَانُوا بِآيَاتِنَا يَجْحَدُونَ

و دوزخیان بهشتیان را آواز می‌دهند که از آن آب یا از آنچه خدا روزی شما کرده بر ما فرو ریزید می‌گویند خدا آنها را بر کافران حرام کرده است
همانان که دین خود را سرگرمی و بازی پنداشتند و زندگی دنیا مغرورشان کرد پس همان گونه که آنان دیدار امروز خود را از یاد بردند و آیات ما را انکار می‌کردند ما [هم] امروز آنان را از یاد می‌بریم

28 Shúráa, Consultation, 42:17:

اللَّهُ الَّذِي أَنزَلَ الْكِتَابَ بِالْحَقِّ وَالْمِيزَانَ وَمَا يُدْرِيكَ لَعَلَّ السَّاعَةَ قَرِيبٌ

خداوند کسی است که کتاب را به حق نازل کرد و میزان (سنجش حق و باطل) را، اما تو چه می‌دانی شاید ساعت (قیام قیامت) نزدیک باشد

29 Raḥmán, (God) Most Gracious, 55:7-8:

وَالسَّمَاءَ رَفَعَهَا وَوَضَعَ الْمِيزَانَ
أَلَّا تَطْغَوْا فِي الْمِيزَانِ

و آسمان را بر افراشت و ترازو را گذاشت
تا مبادا از اندازه درگذرید

30 Ḥadid, Iron, 57:25:

لَقَدْ أَرْسَلْنَا رُسُلَنَا بِالْبَيِّنَاتِ وَأَنزَلْنَا مَعَهُمُ الْكِتَابَ وَالْمِيزَانَ لِيَقُومَ النَّاسُ بِالْقِسْطِ ...

ما رسولان خود را با دلایل روشن فرستادیم، و با آنها کتاب (آسمانی) و میزان (شناسایی حق از باطل و قوانین عادلانه) نازل کردیم تا مردم قیام به عدالت کنند...

31 A'ráf, the Heights, 7:8:

وَالْوَزْنُ يَوْمَئِذٍ الْحَقُّ فَمَن ثَقُلَتْ مَوَازِينُهُ فَأُولَٰئِكَ هُمُ الْمُفْلِحُونَ

وزن کردن در آن روز، حق است! کسانی که میزانهای (عمل) آنها سنگین است، همان رستگارانند!

32 Furqán, the Criterion, 25:26:

الْمُلْكُ يَوْمَئِذٍ الْحَقُّ لِلرَّحْمَٰنِ وَكَانَ يَوْمًا عَلَى الْكَافِرِينَ عَسِيرًا

حکومت در آن روز از آن خداوند رحمان است؛ و آن روز، روز سختی برای کافران خواهد بود!

33 Dan. 5:27.
34 John 8:32.
35 Bahá'u'lláh, *Gleanings from the Writings of Bahá'u'lláh*, XVII, p. 40.
36 Mark 13:32.
37 Bahá'u'lláh, *Kitáb-i-Íqán*, p. 192.
38 Baqara, the Heifer, 2:210:

هَلْ يَنظُرُونَ إِلَّا أَن يَأْتِيَهُمُ اللَّهُ فِي ظُلَلٍ مِّنَ الْغَمَامِ وَالْمَلَائِكَةُ وَقُضِيَ الْأَمْرُ وَإِلَى اللَّهِ تُرْجَعُ الْأُمُورُ

آیا انتظار دارند که خداوند و فرشتگان، در سایه‌هائی از ابرها به سوی آنان بیایند (و دلایل تازه‌ای در اختیارشان بگذارند)؟! با اینکه چنین چیزی محال است!) و همه چیز انجام شده، و همه کارها به سوی خدا بازمی‌گردد.

NOTES AND REFERENCES

    J. M. Rodwell:
        What can such expect but that God should come down to them overshadowed with clouds, and the angels also, and their doom be sealed? And to God shall all things return

39 Joel 2:1-2.
40 Zeph. 1:15.
41 Matt. 24:29.
42 Matt. 24:30.
43 Matt. 24:64.
44 Rev. 1:7.
45 *Takwír*, the Folding Up, 81:1:

إِذَا الشَّمْسُ كُوِّرَتْ

در آن هنگام که خورشید در هم پیچیده شود

46 *Qamar*, the Moon, 54:1:

اقْتَرَبَتِ السَّاعَةُ وَانشَقَّ الْقَمَرُ

قیامت نزدیک شد و ماه از هم شکافت!

47 *Qiyámat*, the Resurrection, 75:8-9:

وَخَسَفَ الْقَمَرُ
وَجُمِعَ الشَّمْسُ وَالْقَمَرُ

و ماه بی‌نور گردد،
و خورشید و ماه یک جا جمع شوند

48 *Ibráhím*, Abraham, 14:1:

الر كِتَابٌ أَنزَلْنَاهُ إِلَيْكَ لِتُخْرِجَ النَّاسَ مِنَ الظُّلُمَاتِ إِلَى النُّورِ بِإِذْنِ رَبِّهِمْ إِلَى صِرَاطِ الْعَزِيزِ الْحَمِيدِ

الر، (این) کتابی است که بر تو نازل کردیم، تا مردم را از تاریکیها به سوی روشنایی (ایمان و عدل و آگاهی،) بفرمان پروردگارشان در آوری، بسوی راه خداوند عزیز و حمید.

49 *Baqara*, the Heifer, 2:257:

اللَّهُ وَلِيُّ الَّذِينَ آمَنُواْ يُخْرِجُهُم مِّنَ الظُّلُمَاتِ إِلَى النُّورِ وَالَّذِينَ كَفَرُواْ أَوْلِيَآؤُهُمُ الطَّاغُوتُ يُخْرِجُونَهُم مِّنَ النُّورِ إِلَى الظُّلُمَاتِ أُوْلَـٰئِكَ أَصْحَابُ النَّارِ هُمْ فِيهَا خَالِدُونَ

خداوند، ولی و سرپرست کسانی است که ایمان آورده‌اند؛ آنها را از ظلمتها،به سوی نور بیرون می‌برد. (اما) کسانی که کافر شدند، اولیای آنها طاغوتها هستند؛ که آنها را از نور، به سوی ظلمتها بیرون می‌برند؛ آنها اهل آتشند و همیشه در آن خواهند ماند

50 *Ibráhím*, Abraham, 14:5:

وَلَقَدْ أَرْسَلْنَا مُوسَى بِآيَاتِنَا أَنْ أَخْرِجْ قَوْمَكَ مِنَ الظُّلُمَاتِ إِلَى النُّورِ وَذَكِّرْهُم بِأَيَّامِ اللَّهِ إِنَّ فِي ذَلِكَ لَآيَاتٍ لِّكُلِّ صَبَّارٍ شَكُورٍ

و در حقیقت موسی را با آیات خود فرستادیم [و به او فرمودیم] که قوم خود را از تاریکیها به سوی روشنایی بیرون آور و روزهای خدا را به آنان یادآوری کن که قطعا در این [یادآوری] برای هر شکیبای سپاسگزاری عبرتهاست

51   *Ḥadíd*, Iron, 57:9:

هُوَ الَّذِي يُنَزِّلُ عَلَى عَبْدِهِ آيَاتٍ بَيِّنَاتٍ لِيُخْرِجَكُم مِّنَ الظُّلُمَاتِ إِلَى النُّورِ وَإِنَّ اللَّهَ بِكُمْ لَرَؤُوفٌ رَّحِيمٌ

او همان کسی است که بر بنده خود آیات روشنی فرو می‌فرستد تا شما را از تاریکیها به سوی نور بیرون کشاند و در حقیقت‌خدا [نسبت] به شما سخت رئوف و مهربان است

52   *Yúnus*, Jonah, 10:27:

وَالَّذِينَ كَسَبُواْ السَّيِّئَاتِ جَزَاء سَيِّئَةٍ بِمِثْلِهَا وَتَرْهَقُهُمْ ذِلَّةٌ مَّا لَهُم مِّنَ اللَّهِ مِنْ عَاصِمٍ كَأَنَّمَا أُغْشِيَتْ وُجُوهُهُمْ قِطَعًا مِّنَ اللَّيْلِ مُظْلِمًا أُوْلَـئِكَ أَصْحَابُ النَّارِ هُمْ فِيهَا خَالِدُونَ

اما کسانی که مرتکب گناهان شدند، جزای بدی بمقدار آن دارند؛ و ذلت و خواری، چهره آنان را می‌پوشاند؛ و هیچ چیز نمی‌تواند آنها را از (مجازات) خدا نگه دارد! (چهره‌هایشان آنچنان تاریک است که) گویی با پاره‌هایی از شب تاریک، صورت آنها پوشیده شده! آنها اهل دوزخند؛ و جاودانه در آن خواهند ماند!

53   *Ḥadíd*, Iron, 57:6:

يُولِجُ اللَّيْلَ فِي النَّهَارِ وَيُولِجُ النَّهَارَ فِي اللَّيْلِ وَهُوَ عَلِيمٌ بِذَاتِ الصُّدُورِ

شب را در روز درمی‌آورد و روز را [نیز] در شب درمی‌آورد و او به راز دلها داناست

54   Isa. 13:10.
55   Isa. 24:23.
56   Isa. 60:1-2.
57   Joel 2:31.
58   Acts 2:15-20.
59   Mark 13:24.
60   John 12:46.
61   John 1:4-5.
62   Eph. 5:8-9.
63   I Tim. 4:1-3.
64   Luke 17:26-30.
65   I Thess. 2:3.
66   Isa. 42:20.
67   Ezek. 12:2 (Job 33:16, 36:15).
68   Amos 8:11-12.
69   Isa. 42:15.
70   Bahá'u'lláh, *Kitáb-i-Íqán*, para. 31, pp. 33-4.
71   ibid. para. 33, pp. 35-6, referring to the 'Lamentation' written by 'Alí Ibn Abí Tálib.
72   ibid. para. 38, p. 38.
73   Matt. 24:29.
74   Mark 13:25.
75   Luke 21:25.
76   *Infiṭár*, the Cleaving Asunder, 82:2:

وَإِذَا الْكَوَاكِبُ انتَثَرَتْ

و آنگاه که اختران پراکنده شوند

77 *Mursalát*, Those Sent Forth, 77:7–8:

إِنَّمَا تُوعَدُونَ لَوَاقِعٌ
فَإِذَا النُّجُومُ طُمِسَتْ

به اینها سوگند که آنچه به شما وعده داده می شود قطعاً تحقّق خواهد یافت .
پس آن گاه که ستارگان تاریک شوند و محو گردند

78 *Takwír*, the Folding Up, 81:2:

وَإِذَا النُّجُومُ انكَدَرَتْ

و آنگه که ستارگان همی‌تیره شوند

79 *Infiṭár*, the Cleaving Asunder, 82:3:

وَإِذَا الْكَوَاكِبُ انتَثَرَتْ

و آنگاه که اختران پراکنده شوند

80 Bahá'u'lláh, *Kitáb-i-Íqán*, paras. 34–5, pp. 36–7.
81 ibid. para. 41, p. 41.
82 Bahá'u'lláh, Lawḥ-i-Burhán, in *Tablets of Bahá'u'lláh Revealed after the Kitáb-i-Aqdas*, p. 211.
83 Bahá'u'lláh, Lawḥ-i-Aqdas, ibid. p. 14.
84 Shoghi Effendi, *The Promised Day is Come*, p. 103.
85 Bahá'u'lláh, Lawḥ-i-Dunyá, in *Tablets of Bahá'u'lláh Revealed after the Kitáb-i-Aqdas*, pp. 96–7.
86 Bahá'u'lláh, *Gleanings from the Writings of Bahá'u'lláh*, XCVI, p. 196.
87 Shoghi Effendi, *God Passes By*, p. 216.
88 *An'ám*, Cattle, 6:97:

وَهُوَ الَّذِي جَعَلَ لَكُمُ النُّجُومَ لِتَهْتَدُواْ بِهَا فِي ظُلُمَاتِ الْبَرِّ وَالْبَحْرِ قَدْ فَصَّلْنَا الآيَاتِ لِقَوْمٍ يَعْلَمُونَ

و اوست کسی که ستارگان را برای شما قرار داده تا به وسیله آنها در تاریکیهای خشکی و دریا راه یابید به یقین ما دلایل [خود] را برای گروهی که می‌دانند به روشنی بیان کرده‌ایم

89 *Ṣáffát*, Those Ranged in Ranks, 37:4–7:

إِنَّ إِلَهَكُمْ لَوَاحِدٌ
رَبُّ السَّمَاوَاتِ وَالْأَرْضِ وَمَا بَيْنَهُمَا وَرَبُّ الْمَشَارِقِ
إِنَّا زَيَّنَّا السَّمَاء الدُّنْيَا بِزِينَةٍ الْكَوَاكِبِ
وَحِفْظًا مِّن كُلِّ شَيْطَانٍ مَّارِدٍ

که قطعا معبود شما یگانه است
پروردگار آسمانها و زمین و آنچه میان آن دو است و پروردگار خاورها
ما آسمان این دنیا را به زیور اختران آراستیم
و [آن را] از هر شیطان سرکشی نگاه داشتیم

90 Taherzadeh, *The Revelation of Bahá'u'lláh*, vol. 2, p. 270. Bahá'u'lláh refers to this event in *Epistle to the Son of Wolf*, p. 132.
91 Dan. 12:3.
92 Num. 24:17.
93 Joel 2:10–11.

94 Joel 3:15.
95 Isa. 13:9–10.
96 *Ḥá-mím*, 41:42:

لَا يَأْتِيهِ الْبَاطِلُ مِن بَيْنِ يَدَيْهِ وَلَا مِنْ خَلْفِهِ تَنزِيلٌ مِّنْ حَكِيمٍ حَمِيدٍ

که هیچ گونه باطلی، نه از پیش رو و نه از پشت سر، به سراغ آن نمی‌آید؛ چرا که از سوی خداوند حکیم و شایسته ستایش نازل شده است!

97 I Pet. 5:4.
98 Rev. 21:23.
99 Rev. 21:25.
100 Rev. 22:4–5.
101 Isa. 60:19–22.
102 Isa. 30:26.
103 Mal. 4:2.
104 *Naml*, the Ants, 27:88:

وَتَرَى الْجِبَالَ تَحْسَبُهَا جَامِدَةً وَهِيَ تَمُرُّ مَرَّ السَّحَابِ صُنْعَ اللَّهِ الَّذِي أَتْقَنَ كُلَّ شَيْءٍ إِنَّهُ خَبِيرٌ بِمَا تَفْعَلُونَ

و کوه‌ها را می‌بینی [و] می‌پنداری که آنها بی‌حرکتند و حال آنکه آنها ابرآسا در حرکتند [این] صنع خدایی است که هر چیزی را در کمال استواری پدید آورده است در حقیقت او به آنچه انجام می‌دهید آگاه است

105 *Al-Qári'a*, the Day of Noise and Clamour, 101:5:

وَتَكُونُ الْجِبَالُ كَالْعِهْنِ الْمَنفُوشِ

و کوه‌ها مانند پشم رنگین حلاجی‌شده می‌گردد!

106 *Muzzammil*, Folded in Garments, 73:14:

يَوْمَ تَرْجُفُ الْأَرْضُ وَالْجِبَالُ وَكَانَتِ الْجِبَالُ كَثِيبًا مَّهِيلًا

در آن روز که زمین و کوه‌ها سخت به لرزه درمی‌آید، و کوه‌ها (چنان در هم کوبیده می‌شود که) به شکل توده‌هایی از شن نرم درمی‌آید!

107 *Ṭá-Há*, 20:105:

وَيَسْأَلُونَكَ عَنِ الْجِبَالِ فَقُلْ يَنسِفُهَا رَبِّي نَسْفًا

و از تو درباره کوه‌ها سؤال می‌کنند؛ بگو: «پروردگارم آنها را (متلاشی کرده) برباد می‌دهد!

108 *Wáqi'a*, the Inevitable Event, 56:5:

وَبُسَّتِ الْجِبَالُ بَسًّا

و کوه‌ها در هم کوبیده می‌شود

109 *Ḥáqqa*, the Sure Reality, 69:14:

وَحُمِلَتِ الْأَرْضُ وَالْجِبَالُ فَدُكَّتَا دَكَّةً وَاحِدَةً

و زمین و کوه‌ها از جای خود برداشته شوند و هر دوی آنها با یک تکان ریز ریز گردند

110 *Ma'árij*, the Ways of Ascent, 70:9:

وَتَكُونُ الْجِبَالُ كَالْعِهْنِ

و کوه‌ها چون پشم زده گردد

111 *Mursalát*, Those Sent Forth, 77:10:

وَإِذَا الْجِبَالُ نُسِفَتْ

و آنگاه که کوه‌ها از جا کنده شوند

112 *Nabaa*, the (Great) News, 78:20:

وَسُيِّرَتِ الْجِبَالُ فَكَانَتْ سَرَابًا

و کوه‌ها به حرکت درمی‌آید و بصورت سرابی می‌شود!

113 *Takwír*, the Folding Up, 81:3:

وَإِذَا الْجِبَالُ سُيِّرَتْ

و در آن هنگام که کوه‌ها به حرکت درآیند

114 Bahá'u'lláh, *Gleanings from the Writings of Bahá'u'lláh*, XVI, p. 39.
115 Bahá'u'lláh, Súriy-i-Haykal, para. 272, in Bahá'u'lláh, *The Summons of the Lord of Hosts*, p. 135.
116 Mic. 6:1–2.
117 Mic. 1:4.
118 *Kahf*, the Cave, 18:47:

وَيَوْمَ نُسَيِّرُ الْجِبَالَ وَتَرَى الْأَرْضَ بَارِزَةً وَحَشَرْنَاهُمْ فَلَمْ نُغَادِرْ مِنْهُمْ أَحَدًا

بخاطر بیاور روزی که کوه‌ها را به حرکت در می‌آوریم، و زمین را آشکار (و مسطح) می‌بینی، و همه آنها (انسان‌ها) را محشور می‌کنیم و احدی را فروگذار نخواهیم کرد.

119 *Ṭá-Há*, 20:105–8:

وَيَسْأَلُونَكَ عَنِ الْجِبَالِ فَقُلْ يَنسِفُهَا رَبِّي نَسْفًا
فَيَذَرُهَا قَاعًا صَفْصَفًا
لَّا تَرَى فِيهَا عِوَجًا وَلَا أَمْتًا
يَوْمَئِذٍ يَتَّبِعُونَ الدَّاعِيَ لَا عِوَجَ لَهُ وَخَشَعَتِ الْأَصْوَاتُ لِلرَّحْمَٰنِ فَلَا تَسْمَعُ إِلَّا هَمْسًا

و از تو درباره کوه‌ها سؤال می‌کنند؛ بگو: «پروردگارم آنها را (متلاشی کرده) برباد می‌دهد! سپس زمین را صاف و هموار و بی‌آب و گیاه رها می‌سازد... به گونه‌ای که در آن، هیچ پستی و بلندی نمی‌بینی!» در آن روز، همه از دعوت کننده الهی پیروی نموده، و قدرت بر مخالفت او نخواهند داشت (و همگی از قبرها برمی‌خیزند)؛ و همه صداها در برابر (عظمت) خداوند رحمان، خاضع می‌شود؛ و جز صدای آهسته چیزی نمی‌شنوی!

120 *Ḥáqqa*, the Sure Reality, 69:18:

يَوْمَئِذٍ تُعْرَضُونَ لَا تَخْفَىٰ مِنكُمْ خَافِيَةٌ

در آن روز شما [به پیشگاه خدا] عرضه می‌شوید [و] پوشیده‌ای از شما پوشیده نمی‌ماند

121 *Infiṭár*, the title of the 82nd Súrah of the Qur'án.
122 *Mursalát*, Those Sent Forth, 77:9:

وَإِذَا السَّمَاءُ فُرِجَتْ

و آنگاه که آسمان بشکافد

123 *Inshiqáq*, the Rendering Asunder, 84:1:

إِذَا السَّمَاءُ انْشَقَّتْ

آنگاه که آسمان ز هم بشکافد

124 *Infitár*, the Cleaving Asunder, 82:1:

إِذَا السَّمَاءُ انْفَطَرَتْ

آنگاه که آسمان ز هم بشکافد

125 *Muzzammil*, Folded in Garments, 73:18:

السَّمَاءُ مُنْفَطِرٌ بِهِ كَانَ وَعْدُهُ مَفْعُولًا

و آسمان از هم شکافته می‌شود، و وعده او شدنی و حتمی است.

126 *Rahmán*, (God) Most Gracious, 55:37:

فَإِذَا انْشَقَّتِ السَّمَاءُ فَكَانَتْ وَرْدَةً كَالدِّهَانِ

پس آنگاه که آسمان از هم شکافد و چون چرم گلگون گردد

127 Acts 2:19-20.
128 *Dukhán*, Smoke (or Mist), 44:10-14:

فَارْتَقِبْ يَوْمَ تَأْتِي السَّمَاءُ بِدُخَانٍ مُبِينٍ
يَغْشَى النَّاسَ هَذَا عَذَابٌ أَلِيمٌ
رَبَّنَا اكْشِفْ عَنَّا الْعَذَابَ إِنَّا مُؤْمِنُونَ
أَنَّى لَهُمُ الذِّكْرَى وَقَدْ جَاءَهُمْ رَسُولٌ مُبِينٌ
ثُمَّ تَوَلَّوْا عَنْهُ وَقَالُوا مُعَلَّمٌ مَجْنُونٌ

پس منتظر روزی باش که آسمان دود آشکاری پدید آورد...
که همه مردم را فرا‌می‌گیرد؛ این عذاب دردناکی است!
(می‌گویند:) پروردگارا! عذاب را از ما برطرف کن که ایمان می‌آوریم.
چگونه: و از کجا متذکر می‌شوند با اینکه رسول روشنگر (با معجزات و منطق روشن) به سراغشان آمد!
پس از او روی برتافتند و گفتند تعلیم‌یافته‌ای دیوانه است

129 Isa. 37:16.
130 Isa. 66:22.
131 Isa. 67:17.
132 II Pet. 3:13.
133 Rev. 21:1.
134 Matt. 24:7.
135 Isa. 29:6.
136 *Hajj*, the Pilgrimage, 22:1:

يَا أَيُّهَا النَّاسُ اتَّقُوا رَبَّكُمْ إِنَّ زَلْزَلَةَ السَّاعَةِ شَيْءٌ عَظِيمٌ

ای مردم! از (عذاب) پروردگارتان بترسید، که زلزله رستاخیز امر عظیمی است!

NOTES AND REFERENCES

137 *Zilzál*, the Convulsion, 99:1-5:

إِذَا زُلْزِلَتِ الْأَرْضُ زِلْزَالَهَا
وَأَخْرَجَتِ الْأَرْضُ أَثْقَالَهَا
وَقَالَ الْإِنْسَانُ مَا لَهَا
يَوْمَئِذٍ تُحَدِّثُ أَخْبَارَهَا
بِأَنَّ رَبَّكَ أَوْحَىٰ لَهَا

هنگامی که زمین شدیدا به لرزه درآید،
و زمین بارهای سنگینش را خارج سازد!
و انسان می‌گوید: زمین را چه می‌شود (که این گونه می‌لرزد)؟!
در آن روز زمین تمام خبرهایش را بازگو می‌کند؛
چرا که پروردگارت به او وحی کرده است!

138 *Zumar*, the Crowds, 39:67:

وَمَا قَدَرُوا اللَّهَ حَقَّ قَدْرِهِ وَالْأَرْضُ جَمِيعًا قَبْضَتُهُ يَوْمَ الْقِيَامَةِ وَالسَّمَاوَاتُ مَطْوِيَّاتٌ بِيَمِينِهِ سُبْحَانَهُ وَتَعَالَىٰ عَمَّا يُشْرِكُونَ

و خدا را آنچنان که باید به بزرگی نشناخته‌اند و حال آنکه روز قیامت زمین یکسره در قبضه [قدرت] اوست و آسمانها در پیچیده به دست اوست و منزه و برتر است از آنچه [با وی] شریک می‌گردانند

139 *Rúm*, the Roman Empire, 30:8:

أَوَلَمْ يَتَفَكَّرُوا فِي أَنفُسِهِم مَّا خَلَقَ اللَّهُ السَّمَاوَاتِ وَالْأَرْضَ وَمَا بَيْنَهُمَا إِلَّا بِالْحَقِّ وَأَجَلٍ مُّسَمًّى وَإِنَّ كَثِيرًا مِّنَ النَّاسِ بِلِقَاءِ رَبِّهِمْ لَكَافِرُونَ

آیا آنان با خود نیندیشیدند که خداوند، آسمانها و زمین و آنچه آن میان آن دو است جز بحق و برای زمان معینی نیافریده است؟! ولی بسیاری از مردم (رستاخیز و) لقای پروردگارشان را منکرند!

140 *Ibráhím*, Abraham, 14:48:

يَوْمَ تُبَدَّلُ الْأَرْضُ غَيْرَ الْأَرْضِ وَالسَّمَاوَاتُ وَبَرَزُوا لِلَّهِ الْوَاحِدِ الْقَهَّارِ

زمین به غیر این زمین و آسمان‌ها نیز به غیر این آسمان‌ها مبدل شوند ...

141 *Rúm*, the Roman Empire, 30:19:

يُخْرِجُ الْحَيَّ مِنَ الْمَيِّتِ وَيُخْرِجُ الْمَيِّتَ مِنَ الْحَيِّ وَيُحْيِي الْأَرْضَ بَعْدَ مَوْتِهَا وَكَذَٰلِكَ تُخْرَجُونَ

او زنده را از مرده بیرون می‌آورد، و مرده را از زنده، و زمین را پس از مردنش حیات می‌بخشد، و به همین گونه روز قیامت (از گورها) بیرون آورده می‌شوید!

142 *Yá-Sín*, 36:33:

وَآيَةٌ لَّهُمُ الْأَرْضُ الْمَيْتَةُ أَحْيَيْنَاهَا وَأَخْرَجْنَا مِنْهَا حَبًّا فَمِنْهُ يَأْكُلُونَ

زمین مرده برای آنها آیتی است، ما آن را زنده کردیم و دانه‌های (غذایی) از آن خارج ساختیم که از آن می‌خورند

143 *Zumar*, the Crowds, 39:69:

وَأَشْرَقَتِ الْأَرْضُ بِنُورِ رَبِّهَا وَوُضِعَ الْكِتَابُ وَجِيءَ بِالنَّبِيِّينَ وَالشُّهَدَاءِ وَقُضِيَ بَيْنَهُم بِالْحَقِّ وَهُمْ لَا يُظْلَمُونَ

و زمین (در آن روز) به نور پروردگارش روشن می‌شود، و نامه‌های اعمال را پیش می‌نهند و پیامبران و گواهان را حاضر می‌سازند، و میان آنها بحق داوری می‌شود و به آنان ستم نخواهد شد!

144 Isa. 2:11-12.
145 Isa. 40:3-5.
146 John the Baptist represented the first return of Elijah; the Báb represented His second coming. The Báb also represented the return of John the Baptist.
147 Luke 3:4-6.
148 Matt. 20:16.
149 *Wáqi'a*, the Inevitable Event, 56:4:

إِذَا رُجَّتِ الْأَرْضُ رَجًّا

چون زمین با تکان [سختی] لرزانده شود

150 The Báb, Persian Bayán, VII:9, in *Selections from the Writings of the Báb*, p. 92.
151 Bahá'u'lláh, *Gleanings from the Writings of Bahá'u'lláh*, XXXV, pp. 83-4.
152 Note no. 171, in Bahá'u'lláh, *The Kitáb-i-Aqdas*, pp. 239-40.
153 Bahá'u'lláh, *The Kitáb-i-Aqdas*, para. 157, pp. 75-6.
154 Shoghi Effendi, *God Passes By*, p. 230.
155 Isa. 40:3-6.
156 Isa. 2:1-3.

> A similar passage in Mic. 4:1-3 reads:
>
> But in the last days it shall come to pass, that the mountain of the house of Lord shall be established in the top of the mountains, and it shall be exalted above the hills; and many people shall flow unto it.
>
> And many nations shall come, and say, Come, and let us go up to the mountain of the Lord, and he will teach us his ways, and we will walk in his paths: for the law shall go forth of Zion, and the word of the Lord from Jerusalem.
>
> And he shall judge among many people, and rebuke strong nations afar off; and they shall beat their swords into plowshares, and their spears into pruninghooks: nation shall not lift up sword against nation, neither shall they learn war any more.

157 Isa. 52:15.
158 Zech. 14:9.
159 Rev. 1:7.
160 Isa. 60:3.
161 Isa. 11:10.
162 Joel 2:28.
163 Hag. 2:7.

16 Recognition of the Promised 'Day' and 'Hour'

1 Bahá'u'lláh, quoted in Shoghi Effendi, *God Passes By*, p. 99.
2 Bahá'u'lláh, quoted in Shoghi Effendi, *The Advent of Divine Justice*, p. 66.
3 ibid.
4 Bahá'u'lláh, *Gleanings from the Writings of Bahá'u'lláh*, XXV, p. 60.
5 Bahá'u'lláh, quoted in Shoghi Effendi, *The Advent of Divine Justice*, p. 65.
6 *Burúj*, the Zodiacal Signs, 85:2:

وَالْيَوْمِ الْمَوْعُودِ

و سوگند به آن روز موعود

NOTES AND REFERENCES

7   *Anbiyáa*, the Prophets, 21:103:

لَا يَحْزُنُهُمُ الْفَزَعُ الْأَكْبَرُ وَتَتَلَقَّاهُمُ الْمَلَائِكَةُ هَذَا يَوْمُكُمُ الَّذِي كُنْتُمْ تُوعَدُونَ

وحشت بزرگ، آنها را اندوهگین نمی‌کند؛ و فرشتگان به استقبالشان می‌آیند، (و می‌گویند:) این همان روزی است که به شما وعده داده می‌شد!

8   *Záriyát*, the Winds that Scatter, 51:60:

فَوَيْلٌ لِلَّذِينَ كَفَرُوا مِنْ يَوْمِهِمُ الَّذِي يُوعَدُونَ

پس وای بر کسانی که کافر شدند از روزی که به آنها وعده داده می‌شود!

9   *Ma'árij*, the Ways of Ascent, 70:42:

فَذَرْهُمْ يَخُوضُوا وَيَلْعَبُوا حَتَّى يُلَاقُوا يَوْمَهُمُ الَّذِي يُوعَدُونَ

آنان را به حال خود واگذار تا در باطل خود فروروند و بازی کنند تا زمانی که روز موعود خود را ملاقات نمایند!

10 *Wáqi'a*, the Inevitable Event, 56:50:

لَمَجْمُوعُونَ إِلَى مِيقَاتِ يَوْمٍ مَعْلُومٍ

قطعا همه در موعد روزی معلوم گرد آورده شوند

11 *Al-Hijr*, the Rocky Tract, 15:37-8:

قَالَ فَإِنَّكَ مِنَ الْمُنْظَرِينَ
إِلَى يَوْمِ الْوَقْتِ الْمَعْلُومِ

فرمود تو (ابلیس)
از مهلت‌یافتگانی
تا روز [و] وقت معلوم

12 *Insán*, Man, 76:11:

فَوَقَاهُمُ اللَّهُ شَرَّ ذَلِكَ الْيَوْمِ وَلَقَّاهُمْ نَضْرَةً وَسُرُورًا

خداوند آنان را از شر آن روز نگه می‌دارد و آنها را می‌پذیرد در حالی که غرق شادی و سرورند

13 *Zilzál*, the Convulsion, 99:3-4:

وَقَالَ الْإِنْسَانُ مَا لَهَا
يَوْمَئِذٍ تُحَدِّثُ أَخْبَارَهَا

و انسان گوید [زمین] را چه شده است
آن روز است که [زمین] خبرهای خود را باز گوید

14 *'Abasa*, He Frowned, 80:34-6:

يَوْمَ يَفِرُّ الْمَرْءُ مِنْ أَخِيهِ
وَأُمِّهِ وَأَبِيهِ
وَصَاحِبَتِهِ وَبَنِيهِ

روزی که آدمی از برادرش
و از مادرش و پدرش
و از همسرش و پسرانش می‌گریزد

15 *Zukhruf*, Gold Adornments, 43:67-8:

الأخِلَّاء يَوْمَئِذٍ بَعْضُهُمْ لِبَعْضٍ عَدُوٌّ إِلَّا الْمُتَّقِينَ
يَا عِبَادِ لَا خَوْفٌ عَلَيْكُمُ الْيَوْمَ وَلَا أَنتُمْ تَحْزَنُونَ

در آن روز یاران جز پرهیزگاران بعضی‌شان دشمن بعضی دیگرند
ای بندگان من امروز بر شما بیمی نیست و غمگین نخواهید شد

16 *Rúm*, the Roman Empire, 30:57:

فَيَوْمَئِذٍ لَّا يَنفَعُ الَّذِينَ ظَلَمُوا مَعْذِرَتُهُمْ وَلَا هُمْ يُسْتَعْتَبُونَ

آن روز عذرخواهی ظالمان سودی به حالشان ندارد، و توبه آنان پذیرفته نمی‌شود.

17 *Rúm*, the Roman Empire, 30:4:

...وَيَوْمَئِذٍ يَفْرَحُ الْمُؤْمِنُونَ

...و در آن روز است که مؤمنان از یاری خدا شاد می‌گردند

18 *Nisáa*, the Women, 4:42:

يَوْمَئِذٍ يَوَدُّ الَّذِينَ كَفَرُوا وَعَصَوُا الرَّسُولَ لَوْ تُسَوَّىٰ بِهِمُ الْأَرْضُ وَلَا يَكْتُمُونَ اللَّهَ حَدِيثًا

در آن روز، آنها که کافر شدند و با پیامبر بمخالفت برخاستند، آرزو می‌کنند که ای کاش (خاک بودند، و) خاک آنها با زمین‌های اطراف یکسان می‌شد (و بکلی محو و فراموش می‌شدند). در آن روز، سخنی را نمی‌توانند از خدا پنهان کنند.

19 *Húd* (the Prophet Húd), 11:105:

يَوْمَ يَأْتِ لَا تَكَلَّمُ نَفْسٌ إِلَّا بِإِذْنِهِ فَمِنْهُمْ شَقِيٌّ وَسَعِيدٌ

آن روز که فرا رسد، هیچ کس جز به اجازه او سخن نمی‌گوید؛ گروهی بدبختند و گروهی خوشبخت

20 *Nabaa*, the (Great) News, 78:34-9:

وَكَأْسًا دِهَاقًا
لَّا يَسْمَعُونَ فِيهَا لَغْوًا وَلَا كِذَّابًا
جَزَاءً مِّن رَّبِّكَ عَطَاءً حِسَابًا
رَّبِّ السَّمَاوَاتِ وَالْأَرْضِ وَمَا بَيْنَهُمَا الرَّحْمَٰنِ لَا يَمْلِكُونَ مِنْهُ خِطَابًا
يَوْمَ يَقُومُ الرُّوحُ وَالْمَلَائِكَةُ صَفًّا لَّا يَتَكَلَّمُونَ إِلَّا مَنْ أَذِنَ لَهُ الرَّحْمَٰنُ وَقَالَ صَوَابًا
ذَٰلِكَ الْيَوْمُ الْحَقُّ فَمَن شَاءَ اتَّخَذَ إِلَىٰ رَبِّهِ مَآبًا

در آنجا نه سخن لغو و بیهوده‌ای می‌شنوند و نه دروغی!
این کیفری است از سوی پروردگارت و عطیه‌ای است کافی!
همان پروردگار آسمانها و زمین و آنچه در میان آن دو است، پروردگار رحمان! و (در آن روز) هیچ کس حق ندارد بی اجازه او سخنی بگوید (یا شفاعتی کند)!
«روزی که «روح» و «ملائکه» در یک صف می‌ایستند و هیچ یک، جز به اذن خداوند رحمان، سخن نمی‌گویند، و (آنگاه که می‌گویند) درست می‌گویند.
آن روز حق است؛ هر کس بخواهد راهی به سوی پروردگارش برمی‌گزیند!

21 *Lail*, the Night, 92:2:

وَالنَّهَارِ إِذَا تَجَلَّىٰ

و قسم به روز هنگامی که تجلی کند،

NOTES AND REFERENCES

22 *Taṭfīf*, Dealing in Fraud, 83:5:

أَلَا يَظُنُّ أُولَٰئِكَ أَنَّهُم مَّبْعُوثُونَ لِيَوْمٍ عَظِيمٍ

مگر آنان گمان نمی‌دارند که برانگیخته خواهند شد [در] روزی بزرگ

23 *An'ām*, Cattle, 6:15:

قُلْ إِنِّي أَخَافُ إِنْ عَصَيْتُ رَبِّي عَذَابَ يَوْمٍ عَظِيمٍ

بگو: اگر نافرمانی پروردگارم کنم، از عذاب روزی بزرگ می‌ترسم

24 *Hūd* (the Prophet Hūd), 11:3:

وَأَنِ اسْتَغْفِرُوا رَبَّكُمْ ثُمَّ تُوبُوا إِلَيْهِ يُمَتِّعْكُم مَّتَاعًا حَسَنًا إِلَىٰ أَجَلٍ مُّسَمًّى وَيُؤْتِ كُلَّ ذِي فَضْلٍ فَضْلَهُ وَإِن تَوَلَّوْا فَإِنِّي أَخَافُ عَلَيْكُمْ عَذَابَ يَوْمٍ كَبِيرٍ

و اینکه از پروردگارتان آمرزش بخواهید سپس به درگاه او توبه کنید [تا اینکه] شما را با بهره‌مندی نیکویی تا زمانی معین بهره‌مند سازد، و به هر شایسته نعمتی از کرم خود عطا کند و اگر روی‌گردان شوید من از عذاب روزی بزرگ بر شما بیمناکم

25 *Mumtaḥana*, the Woman to be Examined, 60:6:

لَقَدْ كَانَ لَكُمْ فِيهِمْ أُسْوَةٌ حَسَنَةٌ لِّمَن كَانَ يَرْجُو اللَّهَ وَالْيَوْمَ الْآخِرَ وَمَن يَتَوَلَّ فَإِنَّ اللَّهَ هُوَ الْغَنِيُّ الْحَمِيدُ

برای شما در زندگی آنها اسوه حسنه (و سرمشق نیکویی) بود، برای کسانی که امید به خدا و روز قیامت دارند؛ و هر کس سرپیچی کند به خویشتن ضرر زده است، زیرا خداوند بی‌نیاز و شایسته ستایش است!

26 *'Ankabūt*, the Spider, 29:36:

وَإِلَىٰ مَدْيَنَ أَخَاهُمْ شُعَيْبًا فَقَالَ يَا قَوْمِ اعْبُدُوا اللَّهَ وَارْجُوا الْيَوْمَ الْآخِرَ وَلَا تَعْثَوْا فِي الْأَرْضِ مُفْسِدِينَ

و به سوی [مردم] مدین برادرشان شعیب را [فرستادیم] گفت ای قوم من خدا را بپرستید و به روز بازپسین امید داشته باشید و در زمین سر به فساد برمدارید

27 *Baqara*, the Heifer, 2:8-9:

وَمِنَ النَّاسِ مَن يَقُولُ آمَنَّا بِاللَّهِ وَبِالْيَوْمِ الْآخِرِ وَمَا هُم بِمُؤْمِنِينَ يُخَادِعُونَ اللَّهَ وَالَّذِينَ آمَنُوا وَمَا يَخْدَعُونَ إِلَّا أَنفُسَهُم وَمَا يَشْعُرُونَ

گروهی از مردم کسانی هستند که می‌گویند: «به خدا و روز رستاخیز ایمان آورده‌ایم.» در حالی که ایمان ندارند.

می‌خواهند خدا و مؤمنان را فریب دهند؛ در حالی که جز خودشان را فریب نمی‌دهند؛ (اما) نمی‌فهمند.

28 *Āl-i-'Imrān*, the Family of 'Imrān, 3:114:

يُؤْمِنُونَ بِاللَّهِ وَالْيَوْمِ الْآخِرِ وَيَأْمُرُونَ بِالْمَعْرُوفِ وَيَنْهَوْنَ عَنِ الْمُنكَرِ وَيُسَارِعُونَ فِي الْخَيْرَاتِ وَأُولَٰئِكَ مِنَ الصَّالِحِينَ

به خدا و روز قیامت ایمان دارند و به کار شایسته فرمان می‌دهند و از کار ناشایست باز می‌دارند و در کارهای نیک شتاب می‌کنند و آنان از شایستگانند

29 *Aḥzáb*, the Confederates, 33:21:

لَقَدْ كَانَ لَكُمْ فِي رَسُولِ اللَّهِ أُسْوَةٌ حَسَنَةٌ لِّمَن كَانَ يَرْجُو اللَّهَ وَالْيَوْمَ الْآخِرَ وَذَكَرَ اللَّهَ كَثِيرًا

مسلما برای شما در زندگی رسول خدا سرمشق نیکویی بود، برای آنها که امید به رحمت خدا و روز رستاخیز دارند و خدا را بسیار یاد می‌کنند.

30 Title of the 75th Súrah of the Qur'án.
31 *Rúm*, the Roman Empire, 30:56:

وَقَالَ الَّذِينَ أُوتُوا الْعِلْمَ وَالْإِيمَانَ لَقَدْ لَبِثْتُمْ فِي كِتَابِ اللَّهِ إِلَىٰ يَوْمِ الْبَعْثِ فَهَٰذَا يَوْمُ الْبَعْثِ وَلَٰكِنَّكُمْ كُنتُمْ لَا تَعْلَمُونَ

ولی کسانی که علم و ایمان به آنان داده شده می‌گویند: «شما بفرمان خدا تا روز قیامت درنگ کردید، و اکنون روز رستاخیز است، اما شما نمی‌دانستید

32 *Qiyámat*, the Resurrection, 75:5–7:

بَلْ يُرِيدُ الْإِنسَانُ لِيَفْجُرَ أَمَامَهُ
يَسْأَلُ أَيَّانَ يَوْمُ الْقِيَامَةِ
فَإِذَا بَرِقَ الْبَصَرُ

(انسان شک در معاد ندارد) بلکه او می‌خواهد (آزاد باشد و بدون ترس از دادگاه قیامت) در تمام عمر گناه کند
(از این رو) می‌پرسد: «قیامت کی خواهد بود»
آنگاه که دیدگان خیره شود

33 *Zumar*, the Crowds, 39:67:

وَمَا قَدَرُوا اللَّهَ حَقَّ قَدْرِهِ وَالْأَرْضُ جَمِيعًا قَبْضَتُهُ يَوْمَ الْقِيَامَةِ وَالسَّمَاوَاتُ مَطْوِيَّاتٌ بِيَمِينِهِ سُبْحَانَهُ وَتَعَالَىٰ عَمَّا يُشْرِكُونَ

و خدا را آنچنان که باید به بزرگی نشناخته‌اند و حال آنکه روز قیامت زمین یکسره در قبضه [قدرت] اوست و آسمانها در پیچیده به دست اوست و منزه است و برتر است از آنچه [با وی] شریک می‌گردانند

Bahá'u'lláh, *Kitáb-i-Íqán*, para. 51, p. 48:
   ... by the term 'earth' is meant the earth of understanding and knowledge, and by 'heavens' the heavens of divine Revelation. Reflect thou, how, in one hand, He hath, by His mighty grasp, turned the earth of knowledge and understanding, previously unfolded, into a mere handful, and, on the other, spread out a new and highly exalted earth in the hearts of men, thus causing the freshest and loveliest blossoms, and the mightiest and loftiest trees to spring forth from the illumined bosom of man.

34 *Wáqi'a*, the Inevitable Event, 56:56:

هَٰذَا نُزُلُهُمْ يَوْمَ الدِّينِ

این است پذیرایی آنان در روز جزا

35 *Fátiḥa*, the Opening Chapter, 1:4–6:

مَالِكِ يَوْمِ الدِّينِ
إِيَّاكَ نَعْبُدُ وَإِيَّاكَ نَسْتَعِينُ
اهْدِنَا الصِّرَاطَ الْمُسْتَقِيمَ

[و] خداوند روز جزاست
[بار الها] تنها تو را می‌پرستیم و تنها از تو یاری می‌جوییم
ما را به راه راست هدایت فرما

36 *Muddaththir*, One Wrapped Up, 74:41-7:

عَنِ الْمُجْرِمِينَ
مَا سَلَكَكُمْ فِي سَقَرَ
قَالُوا لَمْ نَكُ مِنَ الْمُصَلِّينَ
وَلَمْ نَكُ نُطْعِمُ الْمِسْكِينَ
وَكُنَّا نَخُوضُ مَعَ الْخَائِضِينَ
وَكُنَّا نُكَذِّبُ بِيَوْمِ الدِّينِ
حَتَّى أَتَانَا الْيَقِينُ

درباره مجرمان
چه چیز شما را در آتش [سقر] درآورد
گویند از نمازگزاران نبودیم
و بینوایان را غذا نمی‌دادیم
با هرزه‌درایان هرزه‌درایی می‌کردیم
و روز جزا را دروغ می‌شمردیم
تا مرگ ما در رسید

37 *Zumar*, the Crowds, 39:60:

وَيَوْمَ الْقِيَامَةِ تَرَى الَّذِينَ كَذَبُواْ عَلَى اللَّهِ وُجُوهُهُم مُّسْوَدَّةٌ أَلَيْسَ فِي جَهَنَّمَ مَثْوًى لِّلْمُتَكَبِّرِينَ

و روز قیامت کسانی را که بر خدا دروغ بستند می‌بینی که
صورت‌هایشان سیاه است؛ آیا در جهنم جایگاهی برای متکبران نیست؟!

38 *Záriyát*, the Winds that Scatter, 51:11-13:

الَّذِينَ هُمْ فِي غَمْرَةٍ سَاهُونَ
يَسْأَلُونَ أَيَّانَ يَوْمُ الدِّينِ
يَوْمَ هُمْ عَلَى النَّارِ يُفْتَنُونَ

کسانی که در نادانی فرو رفته و از حقیقت آنچه به آنان خبر می دهند ناآگاهند
همواره می پرسند : روز جزا کی خواهد بود ؟
روز جزا روزی است که آنان بر آتش سوخته می شوند

39 *Játhiya*, Bowing the Knee, 45:26:

قُلِ اللَّهُ يُحْيِيكُمْ ثُمَّ يُمِيتُكُمْ ثُمَّ يَجْمَعُكُمْ إِلَى يَوْمِ الْقِيَامَةِ لَا رَيْبَ فِيهِ وَلَكِنَّ أَكْثَرَ النَّاسِ لَا يَعْلَمُونَ

بگو: خداوند شما را زنده می‌کند، سپس می‌میراند، بار دیگر در روز قیامت که در آن تردیدی نیست
گردآوری می‌کند؛ ولی بیشتر مردم نمی‌دانند.

40 *Baqara*, the Heifer, 2:28:

كَيْفَ تَكْفُرُونَ بِاللَّهِ وَكُنتُمْ أَمْوَاتًا فَأَحْيَاكُمْ ثُمَّ يُمِيتُكُمْ ثُمَّ يُحْيِيكُمْ ثُمَّ إِلَيْهِ تُرْجَعُونَ

چگونه خدا را انکار می کنید ؟ در حالی که شما مردگانی بودید که خدا به شما حیات بخشیده است ،
سپس شما را می میراند و بار دیگر زنده می کند ، آن گاه به سوی او باز گردانده می شوید .

41 *Rúm*, the Roman Empire, 30:11:

اللَّهُ يَبْدَأُ الْخَلْقَ ثُمَّ يُعِيدُهُ ثُمَّ إِلَيْهِ تُرْجَعُونَ

خداوند آفرینش را آغاز می‌کند سپس آن را تجدید می‌نماید، سپس به سوی او باز می‌گردید.

42   The Báb, *Kitáb-i-Asmá'*, XVII: 2, in *Selections from the Writings of the Báb*, p. 140.

43   *Nabaa*, the (Great) News, 78:38–40:

يَوْمَ يَقُومُ الرُّوحُ وَالْمَلَائِكَةُ صَفًّا لَا يَتَكَلَّمُونَ إِلَّا مَنْ أَذِنَ لَهُ الرَّحْمَنُ وَقَالَ صَوَابًا
ذَلِكَ الْيَوْمُ الْحَقُّ فَمَنْ شَاءَ اتَّخَذَ إِلَى رَبِّهِ مَآبًا
إِنَّا أَنْذَرْنَاكُمْ عَذَابًا قَرِيبًا يَوْمَ يَنْظُرُ الْمَرْءُ مَا قَدَّمَتْ يَدَاهُ وَيَقُولُ الْكَافِرُ يَا لَيْتَنِي كُنْتُ تُرَابًا

روزی که روح و فرشتگان به صف می‌ایستند و [مردم] سخن نگویند مگر کسی که [خدای] رحمان به او رخصت دهد و سخن راست گوید
آن [روز] روز حق است پس هر که خواهد راه بازگشتی به سوی پروردگار خود بجوید
ما شما را از عذابی نزدیک هشدار دادیم روزی که آدمی آنچه را با دست‌خویش پیش فرستاده است بنگرد و کافر گوید کاش من خاک بودم

44   *Fajr*, the Break of Day, 89:22:

وَجَاءَ رَبُّكَ وَالْمَلَكُ صَفًّا صَفًّا

پروردگارت و فرشته[ها] صف‌درصف آیند

45   Bahá'u'lláh, *Kitáb-i-Íqán*, para. 86, pp. 78–9.

46   *Yúnus*, Jonah, 10:93:

وَلَقَدْ بَوَّأْنَا بَنِي إِسْرَائِيلَ مُبَوَّأَ صِدْقٍ وَرَزَقْنَاهُمْ مِنَ الطَّيِّبَاتِ فَمَا اخْتَلَفُوا حَتَّى جَاءَهُمُ الْعِلْمُ إِنَّ رَبَّكَ يَقْضِي بَيْنَهُمْ يَوْمَ الْقِيَامَةِ فِيمَا كَانُوا فِيهِ يَخْتَلِفُونَ

(سپس) بنی اسرائیل را در جایگاه صدق (و راستی) منزل دادیم؛ و از روزیهای پاکیزه به آنها عطا کردیم؛ و اختلاف نکردند، مگر بعد از آنکه علم و آگاهی به سراغشان آمد! پروردگار تو روز قیامت، در آنچه اختلاف می‌کردند، میان آنها داوری می‌کند!

47   *Ṣád*, 38:49–50, 53:

هَذَا ذِكْرٌ وَإِنَّ لِلْمُتَّقِينَ لَحُسْنَ مَآبٍ
جَنَّاتِ عَدْنٍ مُفَتَّحَةً لَهُمُ الْأَبْوَابُ ...
هَذَا مَا تُوعَدُونَ لِيَوْمِ الْحِسَابِ

این یادکردی است و قطعا برای پرهیزگاران فرجامی نیک است
باغهای همیشگی در حالی که در های [آنها] برایشان گشوده‌است
این است آنچه برای روز حساب به شما وعده داده می‌شد

48   *Ṣád*, 38:26:

يَا دَاوُودُ إِنَّا جَعَلْنَاكَ خَلِيفَةً فِي الْأَرْضِ فَاحْكُمْ بَيْنَ النَّاسِ بِالْحَقِّ وَلَا تَتَّبِعِ الْهَوَى فَيُضِلَّكَ عَنْ سَبِيلِ اللَّهِ إِنَّ الَّذِينَ يَضِلُّونَ عَنْ سَبِيلِ اللَّهِ لَهُمْ عَذَابٌ شَدِيدٌ بِمَا نَسُوا يَوْمَ الْحِسَابِ

ای داوود ما تو را در زمین خلیفه [و جانشین] گردانیدیم پس میان مردم به حق داوری کن و زنهار از هوس پیروی مکن که تو را از راه خدا به در کند در حقیقت کسانی که از راه خدا به در می‌روند به [سزای] آنکه روز حساب را فراموش کرده‌اند عذابی سخت‌خواهند داشت

49   *Ibráhím*, Abraham, 14:41:

رَبَّنَا اغْفِرْ لِي وَلِوَالِدَيَّ وَلِلْمُؤْمِنِينَ يَوْمَ يَقُومُ الْحِسَابُ

پروردگارا روزی که حساب برپا می‌شود بر من (ابراهیم) و پدر و مادرم و بر مؤمنان ببخشای

NOTES AND REFERENCES

50   *Nabaa*, the (Great) News, 78:17:

إِنَّ يَوْمَ الْفَصْلِ كَانَ مِيقَاتًا

روز جدایی (حق از باطل) وعدهگاه همه آنهاست!

51   *Dukhán*, Smoke (or Mist), 44:40:

إِنَّ يَوْمَ الْفَصْلِ مِيقَاتُهُمْ أَجْمَعِينَ

در حقیقت روز جدا سازی موعد همه آنهاست

52   Joel 3:14.
53   Zech. 14:7–8.
54   *Nisáa*, the Women, 4:59:

يَا أَيُّهَا الَّذِينَ آمَنُوا أَطِيعُوا اللَّهَ وَأَطِيعُوا الرَّسُولَ وَأُولِي الْأَمْرِ مِنكُمْ فَإِن تَنَازَعْتُمْ فِي شَيْءٍ فَرُدُّوهُ إِلَى اللَّهِ وَالرَّسُولِ إِن كُنتُمْ تُؤْمِنُونَ بِاللَّهِ وَالْيَوْمِ الْآخِرِ ذَٰلِكَ خَيْرٌ وَأَحْسَنُ تَأْوِيلًا

ای کسانی که ایمان آوردهاید خدا را اطاعت کنید و پیامبر و اولیای امر خود را [نیز] اطاعت کنید پس هر گاه در امری اختلاف نظر یافتید اگر به خدا و روز بازپسین ایمان دارید آن را به خدا و پیامبر [او] عرضه بدارید این بهتر و نیکفرجامتر است

55   *Húd* (the Prophet Húd), 11:103–4:

إِنَّ فِي ذَٰلِكَ لَآيَةً لِّمَنْ خَافَ عَذَابَ الْآخِرَةِ ذَٰلِكَ يَوْمٌ مَّجْمُوعٌ لَّهُ النَّاسُ وَذَٰلِكَ يَوْمٌ مَّشْهُودٌ وَمَا نُؤَخِّرُهُ إِلَّا لِأَجَلٍ مَّعْدُودٍ

قطعا در این [یادآوریها] برای کسی که از عذاب آخرت میترسد عبرتی است آن [روز] روزی است که مردم را برای آن گرد میآورند و آن [روز] روزی است که [جملگی در آن] حاضر میشوند و ما آن را جز تا زمان معینی به تاخیر نمیافکنیم

56   *Sajda*, the Adoration, 32:29:

قُلْ يَوْمَ الْفَتْحِ لَا يَنفَعُ الَّذِينَ كَفَرُوا إِيمَانُهُمْ وَلَا هُمْ يُنظَرُونَ

بگو روز پیروزی ایمان کسانی که کافر شدهاند سود نمیبخشد و آنان مهلت نمییابند

57   M. M. Pickthall translation; *Yusuf Ali* translates it as 'Day of decision'.
     Názi'át, Those Who Tear Out, 79:8:

قُلُوبٌ يَوْمَئِذٍ وَاجِفَةٌ

دلهایی در آن روز سخت مضطرب است

58   *Insán*, Man, 76:10:

إِنَّا نَخَافُ مِن رَّبِّنَا يَوْمًا عَبُوسًا قَمْطَرِيرًا

ما از پروردگارمان از روز عبوسی سخت هراسناکیم

59   *Muddaththir,* One Wrapped Up, 74:9:

فَذَٰلِكَ يَوْمَئِذٍ يَوْمٌ عَسِيرٌ

آن روز [چه] روز ناگواری است

609

60 *Maryam*, Mary, 19:39:

وَأَنذِرْهُمْ يَوْمَ الْحَسْرَةِ إِذْ قُضِيَ الْأَمْرُ وَهُمْ فِي غَفْلَةٍ وَهُمْ لَا يُؤْمِنُونَ

و آنان را از روز حسرت بیم ده آنگاه که داوری انجام گیرد و حال آنکه آنها [اکنون] در غفلتند و سر ایمان آوردن ندارند

61 *Húd* (the Prophet Húd), 11:26:

وَلَقَدْ أَرْسَلْنَا نُوحًا إِلَى قَوْمِهِ إِنِّي لَكُمْ نَذِيرٌ مُّبِينٌ
أَن لَّا تَعْبُدُوا إِلَّا اللَّهَ إِنِّي أَخَافُ عَلَيْكُمْ عَذَابَ يَوْمٍ أَلِيمٍ

و به راستی نوح را به سوی قومش فرستادیم [گفت] من برای شما هشداردهنده‌ای آشکارم که جز خدا را نپرستید زیرا من از عذاب روزی سهمگین بر شما بیمناکم

62 *Qiyámat*, the Resurrection, 75:24:

وَوُجُوهٌ يَوْمَئِذٍ بَاسِرَةٌ
تَظُنُّ أَن يُفْعَلَ بِهَا فَاقِرَةٌ

و در آن روز صورت‌هایی عبوس و در هم کشیده است
زیرا می‌داند عذابی در پیش دارد که پشت را در هم می‌شکند

63 *Ibráhím*, Abraham, 14:42:

وَلَا تَحْسَبَنَّ اللَّهَ غَافِلًا عَمَّا يَعْمَلُ الظَّالِمُونَ إِنَّمَا يُؤَخِّرُهُمْ لِيَوْمٍ تَشْخَصُ فِيهِ الْأَبْصَارُ

و خدا را از آنچه ستمکاران می‌کنند غافل مپندار جز این نیست که [کیفر] آنان را برای روزی به تاخیر می‌اندازد که چشم‌ها در آن خیره می‌شود

64 Isa. 2:10.
65 Zeph. 1:14-17.
66 Mal. 4:5.
67 *Insán*, Man, 76:11:

فَوَقَاهُمُ اللَّهُ شَرَّ ذَٰلِكَ الْيَوْمِ وَلَقَّاهُمْ نَضْرَةً وَسُرُورًا

خداوند آنان را از شر آن روز نگه می‌دارد و آنها را می‌پذیرد در حالی که غرق شادی و سرورند

68 *Qáf*, 50:20:

وَنُفِخَ فِي الصُّورِ ذَٰلِكَ يَوْمُ الْوَعِيدِ

و در «صور» دمیده می‌شود؛ آن روز، روز تحقق وعده وحشتناک است!

69 *Yá-Sín*, 36:51:

وَنُفِخَ فِي الصُّورِ فَإِذَا هُم مِّنَ الْأَجْدَاثِ إِلَىٰ رَبِّهِمْ يَنسِلُونَ

(بار دیگر) در «صور» دمیده می‌شود، ناگهان آنها از قبرها، شتابان به سوی (دادگاه) پروردگارشان می‌روند!

70 *Nabaa*, the (Great) News, 78:18:

يَوْمَ يُنفَخُ فِي الصُّورِ فَتَأْتُونَ أَفْوَاجًا

روزی که در «صور» دمیده می‌شود و شما فوج فوج می‌آیید!

NOTES AND REFERENCES

71 *Naml*, the Ants, 27:87:

وَيَوْمَ يُنفَخُ فِي الصُّورِ فَفَزِعَ مَن فِي السَّمَاوَاتِ وَمَن فِي الْأَرْضِ إِلَّا مَن شَاءَ اللَّهُ وَكُلٌّ أَتَوْهُ دَاخِرِينَ

روزی را که در «صور» دمیده می‌شود، و تمام کسانی که در آسمانها و زمین هستند در وحشت فرو می‌روند، جز کسانی که خدا خواسته؛ و همگی با خضوع در پیشگاه او حاضر می‌شوند!

72 Isa. 27:13.
73 Joel 2:1.
74 Matt. 24:31.
75 I Cor. 15:52.
76 I Thess. 4:16
77 *Zilzál*, the Convulsion, 99:1-2:

إِذَا زُلْزِلَتِ الْأَرْضُ زِلْزَالَهَا
وَأَخْرَجَتِ الْأَرْضُ أَثْقَالَهَا

آنگاه که زمین به لرزش [شدید] خود لرزانیده شود
و زمین بارهای سنگین خود را برون افکند

78 *Fajr*, the Break of Day, 89:22:

كَلَّا إِذَا دُكَّتِ الْأَرْضُ دَكًّا دَكًّا

چنان نیست که آنها خیال می‌کنند، در آن هنگام که زمین سخت در هم کوبیده شود.

79 *Názi'át*, Those Who Tear Out, 79:6-7, 9:

يَوْمَ تَرْجُفُ الرَّاجِفَةُ
تَتْبَعُهَا الرَّادِفَةُ ...
أَبْصَارُهَا خَاشِعَةٌ

در آن روز که زلزله‌های وحشتناک همه چیز را به لرزه در می‌آورند.
و از پی آن لرزه‌ای [دگر] افتد ...
و چشمهای آنان از شدت ترس فرو افتاده!

80 *Ibráhím*, Abraham, 14:48:

يَوْمَ تُبَدَّلُ الْأَرْضُ غَيْرَ الْأَرْضِ وَالسَّمَاوَاتُ وَبَرَزُوا لِلَّهِ الْوَاحِدِ الْقَهَّارِ

روزی که زمین به غیر این زمین و آسمانها [به غیر این آسمانها] مبدل گردد و [مردم] در برابر خدای یگانه قهار ظاهر شوند

81 *Nisáa*, the Women, 4:87:

اللَّهُ لَا إِلَهَ إِلَّا هُوَ لَيَجْمَعَنَّكُمْ إِلَى يَوْمِ الْقِيَامَةِ لَا رَيْبَ فِيهِ وَمَنْ أَصْدَقُ مِنَ اللَّهِ حَدِيثًا

خداوند، معبودی جز او نیست! و به یقین، همه شما را در روز رستاخیز -که شکی در آن نیست- جمع می‌کند! و کیست که از خداوند، راستگوتر باشد؟

82 *Tagábun*, Mutual Loss and Gain, 64:9:

يَوْمَ يَجْمَعُكُمْ لِيَوْمِ الْجَمْعِ ذَلِكَ يَوْمُ التَّغَابُنِ وَمَن يُؤْمِن بِاللَّهِ وَيَعْمَلْ صَالِحًا يُكَفِّرْ عَنْهُ سَيِّئَاتِهِ وَيُدْخِلْهُ جَنَّاتٍ تَجْرِي مِن تَحْتِهَا الْأَنْهَارُ خَالِدِينَ فِيهَا أَبَدًا ذَلِكَ الْفَوْزُ الْعَظِيمُ

روزی که شما را برای روز گردآوری گرد می‌آورد آن [روز] روز حسرت [خوردن] است و هر کس به خدا ایمان آورده و کار شایسته‌ای کرده باشد بدیهایش را از او بسترد و او را در بهشتهایی که از زیر [درختان] آن جویبارها روان است درآورد در آنجا بمانند این است همان کامیابی بزرگ

83 *Shúráa*, Consultation, 42:7:

...وَتُنذِرَ يَوْمَ الْجَمْعِ لَا رَيْبَ فِيهِ فَرِيقٌ فِي الْجَنَّةِ وَفَرِيقٌ فِي السَّعِيرِ.

...و آنها را از روزي که همه خلائق دور آن روز جمع مي‌شوند (روز محشر) و شک و ترديد در آن نيست بترساني همان روز که گروهي در بهشتند و گروهي در آتش!

84 *Bani Isrá-íl*, the Children of Israel, 17:71:

يَوْمَ نَدْعُو كُلَّ أُنَاسٍ بِإِمَامِهِمْ فَمَنْ أُوتِيَ كِتَابَهُ بِيَمِينِهِ فَأُولَٰئِكَ يَقْرَءُونَ كِتَابَهُمْ وَلَا يُظْلَمُونَ فَتِيلًا.

[ياد کن] روزي را که هر گروهي را با پيشوايشان فرا مي‌خوانيم پس هر کس کارنامه‌اش را به دست راستش دهند آنان کارنامه خود را مي‌خوانند و به قدر نخك هسته خرمايي به آنها ستم نمي‌شود

85 *Bani Isrá-íl*, the Children of Israel, 17:97:

وَمَن يَهْدِ اللَّهُ فَهُوَ الْمُهْتَدِ وَمَن يُضْلِلْ فَلَن تَجِدَ لَهُمْ أَوْلِيَاءَ مِن دُونِهِ وَنَحْشُرُهُمْ يَوْمَ الْقِيَامَةِ عَلَىٰ وُجُوهِهِمْ عُمْيًا وَبُكْمًا وَصُمًّا مَّأْوَاهُمْ جَهَنَّمُ كُلَّمَا خَبَتْ زِدْنَاهُمْ سَعِيرًا.

هر کس را خدا هدايت کند، هدايت يافته واقعي اوست؛ و هر کس را گمراه سازد، هاديان و سرپرستاني غير خدا براي او نخواهي يافت؛ و روز قيامت، آنها را بر صورتهايشان محشور مي‌کنيم، در حالي که نابينا و گنگ و کرند؛ جايگاهشان دوزخ است؛ هر زمان آتش آن فرونشيند، شعله تازه‌اي بر آنان مي‌افزاييم!

86 *Yúnus*, Jonah, 10:28:

وَيَوْمَ نَحْشُرُهُمْ جَمِيعًا ثُمَّ نَقُولُ لِلَّذِينَ أَشْرَكُوا مَكَانَكُمْ أَنتُمْ وَشُرَكَاؤُكُمْ فَزَيَّلْنَا بَيْنَهُمْ وَقَالَ شُرَكَاؤُهُم مَّا كُنتُمْ إِيَّانَا تَعْبُدُونَ.

و [ياد کن] روزي را که همه آنان را گرد مي‌آوريم آنگاه به کساني که شرک ورزيده‌اند مي‌گوييم شما و شريکانتان بر جاي خود باشيد پس ميان آنها جدايي مي‌افکنيم و شريکان آنان مي‌گويند در حقيقت شما ما را نمي‌پرستيديد

87 *Nás*, Mankind, 114:1-3:

قُلْ أَعُوذُ بِرَبِّ النَّاسِ
مَلِكِ النَّاسِ
إِلَٰهِ النَّاسِ

بگو پناه مي‌برم به پروردگار مردم
پادشاه مردم
معبود مردم

88 *Ál-i-'Imrán*, the Family of 'Imrán, 3:8-9:

رَبَّنَا لَا تُزِغْ قُلُوبَنَا بَعْدَ إِذْ هَدَيْتَنَا وَهَبْ لَنَا مِن لَّدُنكَ رَحْمَةً إِنَّكَ أَنتَ الْوَهَّابُ
رَبَّنَا إِنَّكَ جَامِعُ النَّاسِ لِيَوْمٍ لَّا رَيْبَ فِيهِ إِنَّ اللَّهَ لَا يُخْلِفُ الْمِيعَادَ.

[مي‌گويند] پروردگارا پس از آنکه ما را هدايت کردي دلهايمان را دستخوش انحراف مگردان و از جانب خود رحمتي بر ما ارزاني دار که تو خود بخشايشگري پروردگارا به يقين تو در روزي که هيچ ترديدي در آن نيست گردآورنده [جمله] مردماني قطعا خداوند در وعده [خود] خلاف نمي‌کند

89 *Taṭfíf*, Dealing in Fraud, 83:4–6:

أَلَا يَظُنُّ أُولَٰئِكَ أَنَّهُم مَّبْعُوثُونَ
لِيَوْمٍ عَظِيمٍ
يَوْمَ يَقُومُ النَّاسُ لِرَبِّ الْعَالَمِينَ

مگر آنان گمان نمی‌دارند که برانگیخته خواهند شد
[در] روزی بزرگ
روزی که مردم در برابر پروردگار جهانیان به پای ایستند

90 *Al-Ḥijr*, the Rocky Tract, 15:25:

وَإِنَّ رَبَّكَ هُوَ يَحْشُرُهُمْ إِنَّهُ حَكِيمٌ عَلِيمٌ

پروردگار تو، قطعا آنها را جمع و محشور می‌کند؛ چرا که او حکیم و داناست!

91 *Yúnus*, or Jonah, 10:45:

وَيَوْمَ يَحْشُرُهُمْ كَأَن لَّمْ يَلْبَثُوا إِلَّا سَاعَةً مِّنَ النَّهَارِ يَتَعَارَفُونَ بَيْنَهُمْ قَدْ خَسِرَ الَّذِينَ كَذَّبُوا بِلِقَاءِ اللَّهِ وَمَا كَانُوا مُهْتَدِينَ

و روزی که آنان را گرد می‌آورد گویی جز به اندازه ساعتی از روز درنگ نکرده‌اند با هم اظهار آشنایی می‌کنند قطعا کسانی که دیدار خدا را دروغ شمردند زیان کردند و [به حقیقت] راه نیافتند

'Meeting with God' is understood in the Baháʼí Writings as believing in or attaining unto the presence of the Divine Manifestation, as in the Tablet of Visitation of Baháʼuʼlláh, in *Prayers and Meditations*, CLXXX, p. 311:

> I bear witness that he who hath known Thee hath known God, and he who hath attained unto Thy presence hath attained unto the presence of God. Great, therefore, is the blessedness of him who hath believed in Thee, and in Thy signs, and hath humbled himself before Thy sovereignty, and hath been honoured with meeting Thee, and hath attained the good pleasure of Thy will, and circled around Thee, and stood before Thy throne.

92 *Sabá*, Sheba, or the City of Sabá, 34:26:

قُلْ يَجْمَعُ بَيْنَنَا رَبُّنَا ثُمَّ يَفْتَحُ بَيْنَنَا بِالْحَقِّ وَهُوَ الْفَتَّاحُ الْعَلِيمُ

بگو پروردگارمان ما و شما را جمع خواهد کرد سپس میان ما به حق داوری می کند و اوست داور دانا

93 *Sabá*, Sheba, or the City of Sabá, 34:40:

وَيَوْمَ يَحْشُرُهُمْ جَمِيعًا ...

یاد کن روزی را که خداوند همه آنان را گرد می آورد ...

94 *Húd* (the Prophet Húd), 11:103:

إِنَّ فِي ذَٰلِكَ لَآيَةً لِّمَنْ خَافَ عَذَابَ الْآخِرَةِ ذَٰلِكَ يَوْمٌ مَّجْمُوعٌ لَّهُ النَّاسُ وَذَٰلِكَ يَوْمٌ مَّشْهُودٌ

قطعا در این [یادآوری‌ها] برای کسی که از عذاب آخرت می‌ترسد عبرتی است آن [روز] روزی است که مردم را برای آن گرد می‌آورند و آن [روز] روزی است که [جملگی در آن] حاضر می‌شوند

95 *Qáf*, 50:44:

يَوْمَ تَشَقَّقُ الْأَرْضُ عَنْهُمْ سِرَاعًا ذَٰلِكَ حَشْرٌ عَلَيْنَا يَسِيرٌ

روزی که زمین به سرعت از روی آنها شکافته می‌شود و (از قبرها) خارج می‌گردند؛ و این جمع کردن برای ما آسان است!

96 *Má'ida*, the Table Spread, 5:109:

يَوْمَ يَجْمَعُ اللَّهُ الرُّسُلَ فَيَقُولُ مَاذَا أُجِبْتُمْ قَالُواْ لاَ عِلْمَ لَنَا إِنَّكَ أَنتَ عَلاَّمُ الْغُيُوبِ

روزی که خداوند، پیامبران را جمع می‌کند، و به آنها می‌گوید: «(در برابر دعوت شما) چه پاسخی به شما داده شد؟»، می‌گویند: «ما چیزی نمی‌دانیم؛ تو خود، از همه اسرار نهان آگاهی.»

97 *Baqara*, the Heifer, 2:148:

وَلِكُلٍّ وِجْهَةٌ هُوَ مُوَلِّيهَا فَاسْتَبِقُواْ الْخَيْرَاتِ أَيْنَ مَا تَكُونُواْ يَأْتِ بِكُمُ اللّهُ جَمِيعًا إِنَّ اللّهَ عَلَى كُلِّ شَيْءٍ قَدِيرٌ

هر طایفه‌ای قبله‌ای دارد که خداوند آن را تعیین کرده است؛ در نیکی‌ها و اعمال خیر، بر یکدیگر سبقت جویید! هر جا باشید، خداوند همه شما را حاضر می‌کند؛ زیرا او، بر هر کاری تواناست.

98 Ezek. 37:24 (see also 34:24).
99 Rev. 21:24.
100 Matt. 22:32.
101 John 10:16.
102 The Báb, *Selections from the Writings of the Báb*, p. 176.
103 *Takwír*, the Folding Up, 81:5:

وَإِذَا الْوُحُوشُ حُشِرَتْ

و در آن هنگام که وحوش جمع شوند

Yusuf Ali adds 'in human habitations', indicating that the verse refers to creation of zoological gardens.

104 Isa. 11:6–9.
105 *Rúm*, the Roman Empire, 30:14:

وَيَوْمَ تَقُومُ السَّاعَةُ يَوْمَئِذٍ يَتَفَرَّقُونَ

و روزی که رستاخیز برپا گردد آن روز [مردم] پراکنده می‌شوند

106 *Al-Qári'a*, the Day of Noise and Clamour, 101:1–3:

الْقَارِعَةُ
مَا الْقَارِعَةُ
وَمَا أَدْرَاكَ مَا الْقَارِعَةُ

آن در هم کوبنده !
چیست آن در هم کوبنده
و چه چیز تو را آگاه کرده است که آن در هم کوبنده چیست ؟

107 *Ra'd*, Thunder, 13:2:

... كُلٌّ يَجْرِي لِأَجَلٍ مُسَمًّى يُدَبِّرُ الأَمْرَ يُفَصِّلُ الآيَاتِ لَعَلَّكُم بِلِقَاء رَبِّكُمْ تُوقِنُونَ

...کارها را او تدبیر می‌کند؛ آیات را (برای شما) تشریح می‌نماید؛ شاید به لقای پروردگارتان یقین پیدا کنید!

108 *An'ám*, Cattle, 6:31:

قَدْ خَسِرَ الَّذِينَ كَذَّبُواْ بِلِقَاء اللّهِ حَتَّى إِذَا جَاءتْهُمُ السَّاعَةُ بَغْتَةً قَالُواْ يَا حَسْرَتَنَا عَلَى مَا فَرَّطْنَا فِيهَا وَهُمْ يَحْمِلُونَ أَوْزَارَهُمْ عَلَى ظُهُورِهِمْ أَلاَ سَاء مَا يَزِرُونَ

کسانی که لقای الهی را دروغ انگاشتند قطعا زیان دیدند تا آنگاه که قیامت بناگاه بر آنان دررسد می‌گویند ای دریغ بر ما بر آنچه در باره آن کوتاهی کردیم و آنان بار سنگین گناهانشان را به دوش می‌کشند چه بد است باری که می‌کشند

109 *'Ankabút*, the Spider, 29:5:

مَن كَانَ يَرْجُو لِقَاءَ اللَّهِ فَإِنَّ أَجَلَ اللَّهِ لَآتٍ وَهُوَ السَّمِيعُ الْعَلِيمُ

کسی که به دیدار خدا امید دارد [بداند که] اجل خدا آمدنی است و اوست شنوای دانا

110 *Sajda*, Adoration, 32:10:

وَقَالُوا أَئِذَا ضَلَلْنَا فِي الْأَرْضِ أَئِنَّا لَفِي خَلْقٍ جَدِيدٍ بَلْ هُم بِلِقَاءِ رَبِّهِمْ كَافِرُونَ

و گفتند آیا وقتی در زمین گم شدیم آیا [باز] ما در خلقت جدیدی خواهیم بود [نه] بلکه آنها به لقای پروردگارشان [و حضور او] کافرند

111 *'Ankabút*, the Spider, 29:23:

وَالَّذِينَ كَفَرُوا بِآيَاتِ اللَّهِ وَلِقَائِهِ أُولَٰئِكَ يَئِسُوا مِن رَّحْمَتِي وَأُولَٰئِكَ لَهُمْ عَذَابٌ أَلِيمٌ

و کسانی که آیات خدا و لقای او را منکر شدند آنانند که از رحمت من نومیدند و ایشان را عذابی پر درد خواهد بود

112 *Kahf*, the Cave, 18:105:

أُولَٰئِكَ الَّذِينَ كَفَرُوا بِآيَاتِ رَبِّهِمْ وَلِقَائِهِ فَحَبِطَتْ أَعْمَالُهُمْ فَلَا نُقِيمُ لَهُمْ يَوْمَ الْقِيَامَةِ وَزْنًا

[آری] آنان کسانی‌اند که آیات پروردگارشان و لقای او را انکار کردند در نتیجه اعمالشان تباه گردید و روز قیامت برای آنها [قدر و] ارزشی نخواهیم نهاد

113 *Yúnus*, Jonah, 10:11:

وَلَوْ يُعَجِّلُ اللَّهُ لِلنَّاسِ الشَّرَّ اسْتِعْجَالَهُم بِالْخَيْرِ لَقُضِيَ إِلَيْهِمْ أَجَلُهُمْ فَنَذَرُ الَّذِينَ لَا يَرْجُونَ لِقَاءَنَا فِي طُغْيَانِهِمْ يَعْمَهُونَ

و اگر خدا برای مردم به همان شتاب که آنان در کار خیر می‌طلبند در رساندن بلا به آنها شتاب می‌نمود قطعا اجلشان فرا می‌رسید پس کسانی را که به دیدار ما امید ندارند در طغیانشان رها می‌کنیم تا سرگردان بمانند

114 *Yúnus*, Jonah, 10:7-8:

إِنَّ الَّذِينَ لَا يَرْجُونَ لِقَاءَنَا وَرَضُوا بِالْحَيَاةِ الدُّنْيَا وَاطْمَأَنُّوا بِهَا وَالَّذِينَ هُمْ عَنْ آيَاتِنَا غَافِلُونَ أُولَٰئِكَ مَأْوَاهُمُ النَّارُ بِمَا كَانُوا يَكْسِبُونَ

کسانی که امید به دیدار ما ندارند و به زندگی دنیا دل خوش کرده و بدان اطمینان یافته‌اند و کسانی که از آیات ما غافلند
آنان به [کیفر] آنچه به دست می‌آوردند جایگاهشان آتش است.

115 Isa. 10:3.
116 Mic. 7:4.
117 I Pet. 2:12.
118 Jer. 30:7.
119 Zeph. 1:14.
120 Joel 1:15.
121 Mal. 3:1-2.
122 Isa. 9:6-7.
123 Luke 12:37.
124 Rev. 21:3.

125 *Al-Hijr*, the Rocky Tract, 15:85:

...وَإِنَّ السَّاعَةَ لَآتِيَةٌ...

...و ساعت موعود قطعاً فرا خواهد رسید!...

126 *Sabá*, Sheba, or the City of Sabá, 34:3:

وَقَالَ الَّذِينَ كَفَرُوا لَا تَأْتِينَا السَّاعَةُ قُلْ بَلَىٰ وَرَبِّي لَتَأْتِيَنَّكُمْ عَالِمِ الْغَيْبِ لَا يَعْزُبُ عَنْهُ مِثْقَالُ ذَرَّةٍ فِي السَّمَاوَاتِ وَلَا فِي الْأَرْضِ وَلَا أَصْغَرُ مِن ذَٰلِكَ وَلَا أَكْبَرُ إِلَّا فِي كِتَابٍ مُّبِينٍ

و کسانی که کافر شدند گفتند رستاخیز برای ما نخواهد آمد بگو سوگند به پروردگارم که حتماً برای شما خواهد آمد [همان] [همان] دانای نهان[ها] که هموزن ذرّه‌ای نه در آسمانها و نه در زمین از وی پوشیده نیست و نه کوچکتر از آن و نه بزرگتر از آن است مگر اینکه در کتابی روشن [درج شده] است

127 *Rúm*, the Roman Empire, 30:14:

وَيَوْمَ تَقُومُ السَّاعَةُ يَوْمَئِذٍ يَتَفَرَّقُونَ

و روزی که رستاخیز برپا گردد آن روز [مردم] پراکنده می‌شوند

See also: *A'ráf*, the Heights, 7:186-7; *Hajj*, the Pilgrimage, 22:54-6; *Ahzáb*, the Confederates, 33:63; *Sabá*, Sheba, or the City of Sabá, 34:27-9; *Fátir*, the Originator of Creation; or *Maláika*, the Angels, 35:42; *Mú-min*, the Believer, 40:61; *Muhammad* (the Prophet), 47:20; *Qiyámat*, the Resurrection, 75:34; *Na'ziát*, Those Who Tear Out, 79:42-6.

128 *Tá-Há*, 20:15:

إِنَّ السَّاعَةَ آتِيَةٌ أَكَادُ أُخْفِيهَا لِتُجْزَىٰ كُلُّ نَفْسٍ بِمَا تَسْعَىٰ

در حقیقت قیامت فرارسنده است می‌خواهم آن را پوشیده دارم تا هر کسی به [موجب] آنچه می‌کوشد جزا یابد

129 *A'ráf*, the Heights, 7:187:

يَسْأَلُونَكَ عَنِ السَّاعَةِ أَيَّانَ مُرْسَاهَا قُلْ إِنَّمَا عِلْمُهَا عِندَ رَبِّي لَا يُجَلِّيهَا لِوَقْتِهَا إِلَّا هُوَ ثَقُلَتْ فِي السَّمَاوَاتِ وَالْأَرْضِ لَا تَأْتِيكُمْ إِلَّا بَغْتَةً يَسْأَلُونَكَ كَأَنَّكَ حَفِيٌّ عَنْهَا قُلْ إِنَّمَا عِلْمُهَا عِندَ اللَّهِ وَلَٰكِنَّ أَكْثَرَ النَّاسِ لَا يَعْلَمُونَ

از تو در باره قیامت می‌پرسند [که] وقوع آن چه وقت است بگو علم آن تنها نزد پروردگار من است جز او [هیچ کس] آن را به موقع خود آشکار نمی‌گرداند [این حادثه] بر آسمانها و زمین گران است جز ناگهان به شما نمی‌رسد [باز] از تو می‌پرسند گویا تو از [زمان وقوع] آن آگاهی بگو علم آن تنها نزد خداست ولی بیشتر مردم نمی‌دانند

130 *Kahf*, the Cave, 18:21:

...أَنَّ وَعْدَ اللَّهِ حَقٌّ وَأَنَّ السَّاعَةَ لَا رَيْبَ فِيهَا...

...بدانند که وعده خداوند حق است؛ و در پایان جهان و قیام قیامت شکی نیست!...

131 *Há-Mím*, 41:47:

...إِلَيْهِ يُرَدُّ عِلْمُ السَّاعَةِ...

آگاهی از زمان برپایی قیامت فقط به خدا باز می گردد و جز او کسی از آن آگاه نیست ...

132 *Zukhruf*, Gold Adornments, 43:85:

وَتَبَارَكَ الَّذِي لَهُ مُلْكُ السَّمَاوَاتِ وَالْأَرْضِ وَمَا بَيْنَهُمَا وَعِندَهُ عِلْمُ السَّاعَةِ وَإِلَيْهِ تُرْجَعُونَ

و خجسته است کسی که فرمانروایی آسمانها و زمین و آنچه میان آن دو است از آن اوست و علم قیامت پیش اوست و به سوی او برگردانیده می‌شوید

NOTES AND REFERENCES

133 *Shúráa*, Consultation, 42:17-18:

...وَمَا يُدْرِيكَ لَعَلَّ السَّاعَةَ قَرِيبٌ يَسْتَعْجِلُ بِهَا الَّذِينَ لَا يُؤْمِنُونَ بِهَا وَالَّذِينَ آمَنُوا مُشْفِقُونَ مِنْهَا وَيَعْلَمُونَ أَنَّهَا الْحَقُّ أَلَا إِنَّ الَّذِينَ يُمَارُونَ فِي السَّاعَةِ لَفِي ضَلَالٍ بَعِيدٍ

... تو چه می‌دانی شاید ساعت (قیام قیامت) نزدیک باشد!
کسانی که به قیامت ایمان ندارند درباره آن شتاب می‌کنند؛ ولی آنها که ایمان آورده‌اند پیوسته از آن هراسانند، و می‌دانند آن حق است؛ آگاه باشید کسانی که در قیامت تردید می‌کنند، در گمراهی عمیقی هستند.

134 *Játhiya*, Bowing the Knee, 45:27:

وَلِلَّهِ مُلْكُ السَّمَاوَاتِ وَالْأَرْضِ وَيَوْمَ تَقُومُ السَّاعَةُ يَوْمَئِذٍ يَخْسَرُ الْمُبْطِلُونَ

مالکیت و حاکمیت آسمانها و زمین برای خداست؛ و آن روز که قیامت برپا شود اهل باطل زیان می‌بینند!

135 *Ḥajj*, the Pilgrimage, 22:1:

يَا أَيُّهَا النَّاسُ اتَّقُوا رَبَّكُمْ إِنَّ زَلْزَلَةَ السَّاعَةِ شَيْءٌ عَظِيمٌ

ای مردم از پروردگار خود پروا کنید چرا که زلزله رستاخیز امری هولناک است

136 *Ḥajj*, the Pilgrimage, 22:7:

وَأَنَّ السَّاعَةَ آتِيَةٌ لَا رَيْبَ فِيهَا وَأَنَّ اللَّهَ يَبْعَثُ مَن فِي الْقُبُورِ

و اینکه رستاخیز آمدنی است، و شکی در آن نیست؛ و خداوند تمام کسانی را که در قبرها هستند زنده می‌کند.

137 *Ḥajj*, the Pilgrimage, 22:55:

وَلَا يَزَالُ الَّذِينَ كَفَرُوا فِي مِرْيَةٍ مِّنْهُ حَتَّىٰ تَأْتِيَهُمُ السَّاعَةُ بَغْتَةً أَوْ يَأْتِيَهُمْ عَذَابُ يَوْمٍ عَقِيمٍ

و[لی] کسانی که کفر ورزیده‌اند همواره از آن در تردیدند تا بناگاه قیامت برای آنان فرا رسد یا عذاب روزی بدفرجام به سراغشان بیاید

138 *Furqán*, the Criterion, 25:11:

بَلْ كَذَّبُوا بِالسَّاعَةِ وَأَعْتَدْنَا لِمَن كَذَّبَ بِالسَّاعَةِ سَعِيرًا

بلکه رستاخیز را دروغ خواندند و برای هر کس که رستاخیز را دروغ خواند آتش سوزان آماده کرده‌ایم

139 *Rúm*, the Roman Empire, 30:12:

وَيَوْمَ تَقُومُ السَّاعَةُ يُبْلِسُ الْمُجْرِمُونَ

روزی که قیامت برپا شود مجرمان نومید می‌گردند

140 *Qamar*, the Moon, 54:46:

بَلِ السَّاعَةُ مَوْعِدُهُمْ وَالسَّاعَةُ أَدْهَىٰ وَأَمَرُّ

بلکه موعدشان قیامت است و قیامت [بسی] سخت‌تر و تلخ‌تر است

141 John 4:21.
142 John 4:23.
143 John 5:25.
144 John 5:28.

145 *Zumar*, the Crowds, 39:68:

وَنُفِخَ فِي الصُّورِ فَصَعِقَ مَن فِي السَّمَاوَاتِ وَمَن فِي الْأَرْضِ إِلَّا مَن شَاء اللَّهُ ثُمَّ نُفِخَ فِيهِ أُخْرَى فَإِذَا هُم قِيَامٌ يَنظُرُونَ

و در صور دمیده می‌شود پس هر که در آسمانی ها و هر که در زمین است بیهوش درمی‌افتد مگر کسی که خدا بخواهد سپس بار دیگر در آن دمیده می‌شود و بناگاه آنان بر پای ایستاده می‌نگرند

146 Bahá'u'lláh, *Tablets of Bahá'u'lláh Revealed after the Kitáb-i-Aqdas*, p. 244.
147 Bahá'u'lláh, *Gleanings from the Writings of Baha'u'llah*, XIV, p. 31.
148 Bahá'u'lláh, Kalimát-i-Firdaysíyyih (Words of Paradise), in *Tablets of Bahá'u'lláh Revealed after the Kitáb-i-Aqdas*, p. 61.
149 *Húd* (the Prophet Húd), 11:108:

وَأَمَّا الَّذِينَ سُعِدُواْ فَفِي الْجَنَّةِ خَالِدِينَ فِيهَا مَا دَامَتِ السَّمَاوَاتُ وَالأَرْضُ إِلاَّ مَا شَاء رَبُّكَ عَطَاء غَيْرَ مَجْذُوذٍ

و اما کسانی که نیکبخت‌شده‌اند تا آسمانی ها و زمین برجاست در بهشت جاودانند مگر آنچه پروردگار بخواهد [که این] بخششی است که بریدنی نیست

150 *Húd* (the Prophet Húd), 11:23:

إِنَّ الَّذِينَ آمَنُواْ وَعَمِلُواْ الصَّالِحَاتِ وَأَخْبَتُواْ إِلَى رَبِّهِمْ أُوْلَـئِكَ أَصْحَابُ الْجَنَّةِ هُمْ فِيهَا خَالِدُونَ

کسانی که ایمان آوردند و کارهای شایسته انجام دادند و در برابر پروردگارشان خضوع و خشوع کردند، آنها اهل بهشتند؛ و جاودانه در آن خواهند ماند!

151 *Raḥmán*, (God) Most Gracious, 55:46:

وَلِمَنْ خَافَ مَقَامَ رَبِّهِ جَنَّتَانِ

و برای کسی که از مقام پروردگارش بترسد، دو باغ بهشتی است

152 *Raḥmán*, (God) Most Gracious, 55:53-4:

فَبِأَيِّ آلَاء رَبِّكُمَا تُكَذِّبَانِ
مُتَّكِئِينَ عَلَى فُرُشٍ بَطَائِنُهَا مِنْ إِسْتَبْرَقٍ وَجَنَى الْجَنَّتَيْنِ دَانٍ

پس کدام یک از نعمتهای پروردگارتان را منکرید
بر بسترهایی که آستر آنها از ابریشم درشت‌بافت است تکیه زنند و چیدن میوه [از] آن دو باغ [به آسانی] در دسترس است

153 *Raḥmán*, (God) Most Gracious, 55:62:

وَمِن دُونِهِمَا جَنَّتَانِ

و پائین تر از آنها دو بهشت دیگر است.

154 The Báb, Persian Bayán, II:16, in *Selections from the Writings of the Báb*, p. 77.
155 ibid. VIII:14, p. 83.
156 Bahá'u'lláh, Tablet of Aḥmad, in *Bahá'í Prayers*, p. 210.
157 Bahá'u'lláh, Hidden Words, Persian no. 18.
158 *Raḥmán*, (God) Most Gracious, 55:50:

فِيهِمَا عَيْنَانِ تَجْرِيَانِ

در آن دو [باغ] دو چشمه روان است

159 *Raḥmán*, (God) Most Gracious, 55:19:

مَرَجَ الْبَحْرَيْنِ يَلْتَقِيَانِ

دو دریا را روان کرد [که] با هم برخورد کنند

    J. M. Rodwell: 'He hath let loose the two seas which meet each other.'
160 Bahá'u'lláh, *Prayers and Meditations*, LXV, p. 104.
161 Bahá'u'lláh, *Gleanings from the Writings of Bahá'u'lláh*, CLIII, p. 326.
162 Bahá'u'lláh, *Tablets of Bahá'u'lláh Revealed after the Kitáb-i-Aqdas*, p. 261.
163 Bahá'u'lláh, *Prayers and Meditations*, XL, p. 56.
164 '*Thumma*' ('then' or 'moreover') infers a further event separated in time.
165 *Nabaa*, the (Great) News, 78:1-5:

عَمَّ يَتَسَاءَلُونَ
عَنِ النَّبَإِ الْعَظِيمِ
الَّذِي هُمْ فِيهِ مُخْتَلِفُونَ
كَلَّا سَيَعْلَمُونَ
ثُمَّ كَلَّا سَيَعْلَمُونَ

آنها از چه چیز از یکدیگر سؤال می‌کنند؟!
از خبر بزرگ و پراهمیت (رستاخیز)!
همان خبری که پیوسته در آن اختلاف دارند!
چنین نیست که آنها فکر می‌کنند، و بزودی می‌فهمند!
باز هم چنین نیست که آنها می‌پندارند، و بزودی می‌فهمند (که قیامت حق است)!

166 *Ma'árij*, the Ways of Ascent, 70:40-41:
    M. M. Pickthall:
        'rising-places and the setting-places'
    Al-Hillali:
        'I swear by the Lord of all the points of sunrise and sunset in the East and the West'
    E. H. Palmer:
        'Lord of the Easts and the Wests'
167 *Raḥmán*, or (God) Most Gracious, 55:17:

رَبُّ الْمَشْرِقَيْنِ وَرَبُّ الْمَغْرِبَيْنِ

پروردگار دو خاور و پروردگار دو باختر

In the original Arabic, the words 'east' and 'west' are used in the dual, indicating that God is the Lord of two Easts (الْمَشْرِقَيْنِ) and two Wests (الْمَغْرِبَيْنِ).
Using the analogy of the sun, the Qur'án also describes God as the light of the heavens and the earth, and that He is the supreme Lord of the source or dawning place (East) and final illumination (West) of all Revelations (*Baqara*, the Heifer, 2:115 and 142; *Muzzammil*, Folded in Garments, 73:9). The Qur'án further explains that God is the Lord of many dawning places of Revelations (*Ṣáffát*, Those Ranged in Ranks, 37:5).
168 *Núr*, Light, 24:35.
169 Bahá'u'lláh, *Gleanings from the Writings of Bahá'u'lláh*, XXXVIII, pp. 87-8.
170 Rev. 11:3-11.
171 Bahá'u'lláh, *Gleanings from the Writings of Bahá'u'lláh*, XVII, pp. 40-42.
172 Bahá'u'lláh, *Epistle to the Son of the Wolf*, pp. 131-4.

17 Reaffirmation of the Unifying Principle of 'One Common Faith'

1. Rev. 3:21:
   ... and I will write upon him the name of my God, and the name of the city of my God, which is new Jerusalem, which cometh down out of heaven from my God ...
2. Bahá'u'lláh, *Gems of Divine Mysteries*, *Javáhiru'l-Asrár*, para. 44, pp. 33-4.
3. Chapter 11.
4. Exod. 3:14.
5. Isa. 40:28.
6. Job 36:26.
7. Rom. 11:33.
8. Isa. 45:15.
9. Isa. 40:18.
10. (1) *Ar-Rahmán*, The All-Compassionate; (2) *Ar-Rahim*, The All-Merciful; (3) *Al-Malik*, The Absolute Ruler or the Owner; (4) *Al-Quddus*, The Pure One; (5) *As-Salam*, The Source of Peace; (6) *Al-Mu'min*, The Inspirer of Faith; (7) *Al-Muhaymin*; The Guardian; (8) *Al-'Aziz*, The Victorious; (9) *Al-Jabbar*, The Compeller; (10) *Al-Mutakabbir*, The Greatest; (11) *Al-Khaliq*, The Creator; (12) *Al-Bari'*, The Maker of Order; (13) *Al-Musawwir*, The Shaper of Beauty; (14) *Al-Ghaffar*, The Forgiving; (15) *Al-Qahhar*, The Subduer; (16) *Al-Wahhab*, The Giver of All; (17) *Ar-Razzaq*, The Sustainer; (18) *Al-Fattah*, The Opener; (19) *Al-'Alim*, The Knower of All; (20) *Al-Qabid*, The Constrictor; (21) *Al-Basit*, The Reliever; (22) *Al-Khafid*, The Abaser; (23) *Ar-Rafi'*, The Exalter; (24) *Al-Mu'izz*, The Bestower of Honors; (25) *Al-Mudhill*, The Humiliator; (26) *As-Sami*, The Hearer of All; (27) *Al-Basir*, The Seer of All; (28) *Al-Hakam*, The Judge; (29) *Al-'Adl*, The Just; (30) *Al-Latif*, The Subtle One; (31) *Al-Khabir*, The All Aware; (32) *Al-Halim*, The Forebearing; (33) *Al-'Azim*, The Magnificent; (34) *Al-Ghafur*, The Forgiving and The Hider of Faults; (35) *Ash-Shakur*, The One Who Rewards Thankfulness; (36) *Al-'Ali*, The Highest; (37) *Al-Kabir*, The Greatest; (38) *Al-Hafiz*, The Preserver; (39) *Al-Muqit*, The Nourisher; (40) *Al-Hasib*, The Accounter; (41) *Al-Jalil*, The Mighty; (42) *Al-Karim*, The Generous; (43) *Ar-Raqib*, The Watchful One; (44) *Al-Mujib*, the Responder to Supplications; (45) *Al-Wasi'*, The All-Comprehending; (46) *Al-Hakim*, The Perfectly Wise; (47) *Al-Wadud*, The Loving One; (48) *Al-Majid*, The Majestic One; (49) *Al-Ba'ith*, The Resurrector; (50) *Ash-Sháhid*, The Witness; (51) *Al-Haqq*, The Truth; (52) *Al-Wakil*, The Trustee; (53) *Al-Qawi*, The Possessor of All-Strength; (54) *Al-Matin*, The Forceful One; (55) *Al-Wáli*, The Governor; (56) *Al-Hamid*, The Praised One; (57) *Al-Muhsi*, The Appraiser; (58) *Al-Mubdi*, The Originator; (59) *Al-Mu'id*, The Restorer; (60) *Al-Muhyi*, The Giver of Life; (61) *Al-Mumit*, The Taker of Life; (62) *Al-Hayy*; The Ever-Living One; (63) *Al-Qayyum*; The Self-Existing One; (64) *Al-Wajid*; The Finder; (65) *Al-Májid*, The Glorious; (66) *Al-Wahid*, The Only One; (67) *Al-Ahad*, The One, (68) *As-Samad*, The Satisfier of All Needs; (69) *Al-Qadir*, The All-Powerful; (70) *Al-Muqtadir*, The Creator of All Power; (71) *Al-Muqaddim*, The Expediter; (72) *Al-Mu'akhkhir*, The Delayer; (73) *Al-Awwal*, The First; (74) *Al-Akhir*, The Last; (75) *Az-Zahir*, The Manifest One; (76) *Al-Bátin*, The Hidden One; (77) *Al-Wali*, The Protecting Friend; (78) *Al-Muta'ali*, The Supreme One; (79) *Al-Barr*, The Doer of Good;

NOTES AND REFERENCES

(80) *At-Tawwib*, The Guide to Repentance; (81) *Al-Muntaqim*, The Avenger; (82) *Al-Afu*, The Forgiver; (83) *Ar-Ra'uf*, The Clement; (84) *Malik al-Mulk*, The Owner of All; (85) *Dhul-Jalali, Wal-Ikrám*, The Lord of Majesty and Bounty; (86) *Al-Muqsi*, The Equitable One; (87) *Al-Jami*, The Gatherer; (88) *Al-Ghani*, The Rich One; (89) *Al-Mughni*, The Enricher; (90) *Al-Mani*, The Preventer of Harm; (91) *Ad-Darr*, The Creator of the Harmful; (92) *An-Nafi*, The Creator of Good; (93) *An-Nur*, The Light; (94) *Al-Hadi*, The Guide; (95) *Al-Badi*, The Originator; (96) *Al-Baqi*, The Everlasting One; (97) *Al-Warith*, The Inheritor of All; (98) *Ar-Rashid*, The Righteous Teacher; and (99) *As-Sabur*, The Patient One.

11 Dan. 12:4.
12 Dan. 12:8–10.
13 John 10:10.
14 Rev. 20:12.
15 John 1:9.
16 'Abdu'l-Bahá, *Paris Talks*, ch. 41, p. 140.
17 John 14:2.
18 Mark 9:38–40.
19 Heb. 1:1–3.
20 Deut. 33:2.
21 John 16:12–14.
22 Rom. 2:109–20.
23 I Cor. 3:1–3.
24 I Tim. 6:13–16.
25 Isa. 9:10. Compared to bricks and sycamore wood the cut-stones and cedar wood provide relatively more robust and enduring structures. Bahá'u'lláh declares that this prophecy is fulfilled today:
> Zion trembleth and exulteth with joy at the Revelation of God, for it hath heard the Voice of God on every side. This Day Jerusalem hath attained unto a new Evangel, for in the stead of the sycamore standeth the cedar (*Epistle to the Son of the Wolf*, P. 145).
26 John 8:56–9.
27 John 5:45–7.
28 *Luqmán* (the Wise), 31:27:

وَلَوْ أَنَّمَا فِي الْأَرْضِ مِن شَجَرَةٍ أَقْلَامٌ وَالْبَحْرُ يَمُدُّهُ مِن بَعْدِهِ سَبْعَةُ أَبْحُرٍ مَّا نَفِدَتْ كَلِمَاتُ اللَّهِ إِنَّ اللَّهَ عَزِيزٌ حَكِيمٌ

و اگر همه درختان روی زمین قلم شود، و دریا برای آن مرکب گردد، و هفت دریاچه به آن افزوده شود، اینها همه تمام می‌شود ولی کلمات خدا پایان نمی‌گیرد؛ خداوند عزیز و حکیم است.

29 *Kahf*, the Cave, 18:109:

قُل لَّوْ كَانَ الْبَحْرُ مِدَادًا لِّكَلِمَاتِ رَبِّي لَنَفِدَ الْبَحْرُ قَبْلَ أَن تَنفَدَ كَلِمَاتُ رَبِّي وَلَوْ جِئْنَا بِمِثْلِهِ مَدَدًا

بگو اگر دریا برای کلمات پروردگارم مرکب شود پیش از آنکه کلمات پروردگارم پایان پذیرد قطعا دریا پایان می‌یابد هر چند نظیرش را به مدد [آن] بیاوریم

30 In the light of the scriptural teachings the contention that Christians should not use 'Alláh' in Arabic texts, because it is one of the many names of God used in the Qur'án, is ludicrous. The issue continues to be reported in the media:

The Christians who call God 'Allah'
Churches have been burnt down in Malaysia in a row over Christians using the word *Allah* for God.

The government had ruled that the word must not be used except to refer to God as worshipped by Muslims. But the high court declared that a Catholic newspaper, the *Herald*, could continue to use *Allah* in its Malay edition, since the people in Borneo that buy the paper have from time immemorial referred to God by that name. . . (Christopher Howse, *The Telegraph*, 30 January 2010)

There have been more attacks on churches in Malaysia, in a growing dispute over the use of the word Allah by non-Muslims . . .

Religious tensions in Malaysia have increased since a court ruled last month that a Roman Catholic newspaper could use the word Allah in its Malay-language edition to describe the Christian god . . .

Correspondents say some of Malaysia's majority Muslim community suspect Christians of wanting to use the word Allah to encourage Muslims to convert to Christianity.

The government has appealed against the ruling, in contrast to countries like Indonesia, Egypt and Syria where Christian minorities freely use the Arabic word to refer to God . . . (BBC News, 10 January 2010)

Christian Group: Malaysian Court's Decision to Ban Catholic Newspaper's Use of 'Allah' 'Seriously Flawed',
The interdenominational Christian Federation of Malaysia has warned that believers in the country face 'serious negative consequences' after the Supreme Court again confirmed that a Catholic newspaper is not allowed to use the word 'Allah' to refer to God.

'We continue to support that the decision of the Court of Appeal, upheld by the Federal Court, is seriously flawed in many respects. According to Justice, many erroneous and inaccurate observations had to be corrected. Now there will be serious negative consequences for the religious freedom of Christians in Malaysia,' . . .

The long-standing case concerns the Catholic weekly newspaper 'Herald', which was initially told in 2007 by Malaysian authorities to stop using the word 'Allah'. While in 2009 a lower court defended the newspaper's right to use the term, in October 2013 chief judge Mohamed Apandi Ali ruled that 'the usage of the word "Allah" is not an integral part of the faith in Christianity', and that it would 'cause confusion in the community'.

The federal court confirmed that verdict on Monday in a four to three decision, but clarified that Christians would still be allowed to use the word 'Allah' in church . . . (Stoyan Zaimov, *Christian Post*, 24 June 2014)

31 *Baqara*, the Heifer, 2:139:

قُلْ أَتُحَاجُّونَنَا فِي اللَّهِ وَهُوَ رَبُّنَا وَرَبُّكُمْ وَلَنَا أَعْمَالُنَا وَلَكُمْ أَعْمَالُكُمْ وَنَحْنُ لَهُ مُخْلِصُونَ

بگو: «آیا در باره خداوند با ما محاجه می‌کنید؟! در حالی که او، پروردگار ما و شماست؛ و اعمال ما از آن ما، و اعمال شما از آن شماست؛ و ما او را با اخلاص پرستش می‌کنیم

32 *Ibráhím*, Abraham, 14:5:

وَلَقَدْ أَرْسَلْنَا مُوسَىٰ بِآيَاتِنَا أَنْ أَخْرِجْ قَوْمَكَ مِنَ الظُّلُمَاتِ إِلَى النُّورِ وَذَكِّرْهُم بِأَيَّامِ اللَّهِ إِنَّ فِي ذَٰلِكَ لَآيَاتٍ لِّكُلِّ صَبَّارٍ شَكُورٍ

و در حقیقت موسی را با آیات خود فرستادیم [و به او فرمودیم] که قوم خود را از تاریکیها به سوی روشنایی بیرون آور و روزهای خدا را به آنان یادآوری کن که قطعا در این [یادآوری] برای هر شکیبای سپاسگزاری عبرتهاست

33 *Anbiyáa*, the Prophets, 21:48:

وَلَقَدْ آتَيْنَا مُوسَىٰ وَهَارُونَ الْفُرْقَانَ وَضِيَاءً وَذِكْرًا لِّلْمُتَّقِينَ

ما به موسی و هارون، «فرقان» (وسیله جدا کردن حق از باطل) و نور، و آنچه مایه یادآوری برای پرهیزگاران است، دادیم.

34 Notably, 'the Criterion' or '*Furqán*' and 'Message' or '*Dhikr*', which are applied to the Qur'án (*Ál-i-'Imrán*, the Family of 'Imrán, 3:4 and *Al-Hijr*, the Rocky Tract, 15:9) also describe the Dispensation of Moses. Hence the Qur'án is not the only criterion of truth.
Baqara, the Heifer, 2:87:

وَلَقَدْ آتَيْنَا مُوسَى الْكِتَابَ وَقَفَّيْنَا مِن بَعْدِهِ بِالرُّسُلِ وَآتَيْنَا عِيسَى ابْنَ مَرْيَمَ الْبَيِّنَاتِ وَأَيَّدْنَاهُ بِرُوحِ الْقُدُسِ ...

ما به موسی کتاب (تورات) دادیم، و بعد از او، پیامبرانی پشت سر هم فرستادیم؛ و به عیسی بن مریم دلایل روشن دادیم؛ و او را به وسیله روح القدس تایید کردیم...

35 *An'ám*, Cattle, 6:154-6:

ثُمَّ آتَيْنَا مُوسَى الْكِتَابَ تَمَامًا عَلَى الَّذِي أَحْسَنَ وَتَفْصِيلًا لِّكُلِّ شَيْءٍ وَهُدًى وَرَحْمَةً لَّعَلَّهُم بِلِقَاءِ رَبِّهِمْ يُؤْمِنُونَ
وَهَٰذَا كِتَابٌ أَنزَلْنَاهُ مُبَارَكٌ فَاتَّبِعُوهُ وَاتَّقُوا لَعَلَّكُمْ تُرْحَمُونَ
أَن تَقُولُوا إِنَّمَا أُنزِلَ الْكِتَابُ عَلَىٰ طَائِفَتَيْنِ مِن قَبْلِنَا وَإِن كُنَّا عَن دِرَاسَتِهِمْ لَغَافِلِينَ

سپس به موسی کتاب (آسمانی) دادیم؛ (و نعمت خود را) بر آنها که نیکوکار بودند، کامل کردیم؛ و همه چیز را (که مورد نیاز آنها بود، در آن) روشن ساختیم؛ کتابی که مایه هدایت و رحمت بود؛ شاید به لقای پروردگارشان ایمان بیاورند!
و این کتابی است پر برکت، که ما (بر تو) نازل کردیم؛ از آن پیروی کنید، و پرهیزگاری پیشه نمایید، باشد که مورد رحمت (خدا) قرار گیرید!
تا نگویید کتاب [آسمانی] تنها بر دو طایفه پیش از ما نازل شده و ما از آموختن آنان بی‌خبر بودیم

36 *Nisáa*, the Women, 4:163-5:

إِنَّا أَوْحَيْنَا إِلَيْكَ كَمَا أَوْحَيْنَا إِلَىٰ نُوحٍ وَالنَّبِيِّينَ مِن بَعْدِهِ وَأَوْحَيْنَا إِلَىٰ إِبْرَاهِيمَ وَإِسْمَاعِيلَ وَإِسْحَاقَ وَيَعْقُوبَ
وَالْأَسْبَاطِ وَعِيسَىٰ وَأَيُّوبَ وَيُونُسَ وَهَارُونَ وَسُلَيْمَانَ وَآتَيْنَا دَاوُودَ زَبُورًا
وَرُسُلًا قَدْ قَصَصْنَاهُمْ عَلَيْكَ مِن قَبْلُ وَرُسُلًا لَّمْ نَقْصُصْهُمْ عَلَيْكَ وَكَلَّمَ اللَّهُ مُوسَىٰ تَكْلِيمًا
رُّسُلًا مُّبَشِّرِينَ وَمُنذِرِينَ لِئَلَّا يَكُونَ لِلنَّاسِ عَلَى اللَّهِ حُجَّةٌ بَعْدَ الرُّسُلِ وَكَانَ اللَّهُ عَزِيزًا حَكِيمًا

ما همچنانکه به نوح و پیامبران بعد از او وحی کردیم به تو [نیز] وحی کردیم و به ابراهیم و اسماعیل و اسحاق و یعقوب و اسباط و عیسی و ایوب و یونس و هارون و سلیمان [نیز] وحی نمودیم و به داوود زبور بخشیدیم
و پیامبرانی [را] فرستادیم که در حقیقت [ماجرای] آنان را قبلا بر تو حکایت نمودیم و پیامبرانی [را نیز] برانگیخته‌ایم] که [سرگذشت] ایشان را بر تو بازگو نکرده‌ایم و خدا با موسی آشکارا سخن گفت
پیامبرانی که بشارتگر و هشداردهنده بودند تا برای مردم پس از [فرستادن] پیامبران در مقابل خدا [بهانه و] حجتی نباشد و خدا توانا و حکیم است

37 *Húd* (the Prophet Húd), 11:17:

أَفَمَن كَانَ عَلَىٰ بَيِّنَةٍ مِّن رَّبِّهِ وَيَتْلُوهُ شَاهِدٌ مِّنْهُ وَمِن قَبْلِهِ كِتَابُ مُوسَىٰ إِمَامًا وَرَحْمَةً أُوْلَـٰئِكَ يُؤْمِنُونَ بِهِ ...

آیا آن کس که دلیل آشکاری از پروردگار خویش دارد، و بدنبال آن، شاهدی از سوی او می‌باشد، و پیش از آن، کتاب موسی که پیشوا و رحمت بود (گواهی بر آن می‌دهد، همچون کسی است که چنین نباشد)؟! آنها (حق‌طلبان و حقیقت‌جویان) به او (که دارای این ویژگیهاست،) ایمان می‌آورند!...

38 *Baqara*, the Heifer, 2:89:

وَلَمَّا جَاءَهُمْ كِتَابٌ مِّنْ عِندِ اللّهِ مُصَدِّقٌ لِّمَا مَعَهُمْ وَكَانُواْ مِن قَبْلُ يَسْتَفْتِحُونَ عَلَى الَّذِينَ كَفَرُواْ فَلَمَّا جَاءَهُم مَّا عَرَفُواْ كَفَرُواْ بِهِ فَلَعْنَةُ اللَّهِ عَلَى الْكَافِرِينَ

و هنگامی که از جانب خداوند کتابی که مؤید آنچه نزد آنان است برایشان آمد و از دیرباز [در انتظارش] بر کسانی که کافر شده بودند پیروزی می‌جستند ولی همین که آنچه [که اوصافش] را می‌شناختند برایشان آمد انکارش کردند پس لعنت‌خدا بر کافران باد

39 *Yúnus*, Jonah, 10:37:

... هَذَا الْقُرْآنُ... تَصْدِيقَ الَّذِي بَيْنَ يَدَيْهِ وَتَفْصِيلَ الْكِتَابِ...

... این قرآن... تصدیق [کننده] آنچه پیش از آن است می‌باشد و توضیحی از آن کتاب است...

40 *Baqara*, the Heifer, 2:213:

كَانَ النَّاسُ أُمَّةً وَاحِدَةً فَبَعَثَ اللّهُ النَّبِيِّينَ مُبَشِّرِينَ وَمُنذِرِينَ وَأَنزَلَ مَعَهُمُ الْكِتَابَ بِالْحَقِّ لِيَحْكُمَ بَيْنَ النَّاسِ فِيمَا اخْتَلَفُواْ فِيهِ وَمَا اخْتَلَفَ فِيهِ إِلاَّ الَّذِينَ أُوتُوهُ مِن بَعْدِ مَا جَاءَتْهُمُ الْبَيِّنَاتُ بَغْيًا بَيْنَهُمْ فَهَدَى اللّهُ الَّذِينَ آمَنُواْ لِمَا اخْتَلَفُواْ فِيهِ مِنَ الْحَقِّ بِإِذْنِهِ وَاللّهُ يَهْدِي مَن يَشَاءُ إِلَى صِرَاطٍ مُّسْتَقِيمٍ

مردم (در آغاز) یک دسته بودند؛ خداوند، پیامبران را برانگیخت؛ تا مردم را بشارت و بیم دهند و کتاب آسمانی، که به سوی حق دعوت می‌کرد، با آنها نازل نمود؛ تا در میان مردم، در آنچه اختلاف داشتند، داوری کند. تنها کسانی که کتاب را دریافت داشته بودند، و نشانه‌های روشن به آنها رسیده بود، به خاطر انحراف از حق و ستمگری، در آن اختلاف کردند. خداوند، آنهایی را که ایمان آورده بودند، به حقیقت آنچه مورد اختلاف بود، به فرمان خودش، رهبری نمود. و خدا، هر کس را بخواهد، به راه راست هدایت می‌کند

41 *Baqara*, the Heifer, 2:136:

قُولُواْ آمَنَّا بِاللّهِ وَمَا أُنزِلَ إِلَيْنَا وَمَا أُنزِلَ إِلَى إِبْرَاهِيمَ وَإِسْمَاعِيلَ وَإِسْحَاقَ وَيَعْقُوبَ وَالأَسْبَاطِ وَمَا أُوتِيَ مُوسَى وَعِيسَى وَمَا أُوتِيَ النَّبِيُّونَ مِن رَّبِّهِمْ لاَ نُفَرِّقُ بَيْنَ أَحَدٍ مِّنْهُمْ وَنَحْنُ لَهُ مُسْلِمُونَ

بگویید ما به خدا و به آنچه بر ما نازل شده و به آنچه بر ابراهیم و اسماعیل و اسحاق و یعقوب و اسباط نازل آمده و به آنچه به موسی و عیسی داده شده و به آنچه به همه پیامبران از سوی پروردگارشان داده شده ایمان آورده‌ایم میان هیچ یک از ایشان فرق نمی‌گذاریم و در برابر او تسلیم هستیم

42 *Baqara*, the Heifer, 2:285:

آمَنَ الرَّسُولُ بِمَا أُنزِلَ إِلَيْهِ مِن رَّبِّهِ وَالْمُؤْمِنُونَ كُلٌّ آمَنَ بِاللّهِ وَمَلآئِكَتِهِ وَكُتُبِهِ وَرُسُلِهِ لاَ نُفَرِّقُ بَيْنَ أَحَدٍ مِّن رُّسُلِهِ وَقَالُواْ سَمِعْنَا وَأَطَعْنَا غُفْرَانَكَ رَبَّنَا وَإِلَيْكَ الْمَصِيرُ

پیامبر، به آنچه از سوی پروردگارش بر او نازل شده، ایمان آورده است و همه مؤمنان (نیز)، به خدا و فرشتگان او و کتابهای او و فرستادگانش، ایمان آورده‌اند؛ (و می‌گویند:) ما در میان هیچ یک از پیامبران او، فرق نمی‌گذاریم (و به همه ایمان داریم). و (مؤمنان) گفتند: «ما شنیدیم و اطاعت کردیم. پروردگارا! (انتظار) آمرزش تو را (داریم)؛ و بازگشت (ما) به سوی توست.»

43 *Sulaym ibn Qays*:
وسمعت رسول الله صلى الله عليه وآله يقول: لتركبن أمتي سنة بني إسرائيل حذو النعل بالنعل وحذو القذة بالقذة، شبرا بشبر وذراعا بذراع وباعا بباع، حتى لو دخلوا جحرا لدخلوا فيه معهم. إن التوراة والقرآن كتبه ملك واحد في رق واحد بقلم واحد، وجرت الأمثال والسنن سواء

44 *Shúráa*, Consultation, 42:13:
شَرَعَ لَكُم مِّنَ الدِّينِ مَا وَصَّىٰ بِهِ نُوحًا وَالَّذِي أَوْحَيْنَا إِلَيْكَ وَمَا وَصَّيْنَا بِهِ إِبْرَاهِيمَ وَمُوسَىٰ وَعِيسَىٰ أَنْ أَقِيمُوا الدِّينَ وَلَا تَتَفَرَّقُوا فِيهِ كَبُرَ عَلَى الْمُشْرِكِينَ مَا تَدْعُوهُمْ إِلَيْهِ اللَّهُ يَجْتَبِي إِلَيْهِ مَن يَشَاءُ وَيَهْدِي إِلَيْهِ مَن يُنِيبُ

آیینی را برای شما تشریع کرد که به نوح توصیه کرده بود؛ و آنچه را بر تو وحی فرستادیم و به ابراهیم و موسی و عیسی سفارش کردیم این بود که: دین را برپا دارید و در آن تفرقه ایجاد نکنید! و بر مشرکان گران است آنچه شما آنان را به سویش دعوت می‌کنید! خداوند هر کس را بخواهد برمی‌گزیند، و کسی را که به سوی او بازگردد هدایت می‌کند.

45 *Baqara*, the Heifer, 2:177:
لَّيْسَ الْبِرَّ أَن تُوَلُّوا وُجُوهَكُمْ قِبَلَ الْمَشْرِقِ وَالْمَغْرِبِ وَلَٰكِنَّ الْبِرَّ مَنْ آمَنَ بِاللَّهِ وَالْيَوْمِ الْآخِرِ وَالْمَلَائِكَةِ وَالْكِتَابِ وَالنَّبِيِّينَ وَآتَى الْمَالَ عَلَىٰ حُبِّهِ ذَوِي الْقُرْبَىٰ وَالْيَتَامَىٰ وَالْمَسَاكِينَ وَابْنَ السَّبِيلِ وَالسَّائِلِينَ وَفِي الرِّقَابِ وَأَقَامَ الصَّلَاةَ وَآتَى الزَّكَاةَ ...

نیکی، این نیست که (به هنگام نماز،) روی خود را به سوی مشرق و (یا) مغرب کنید؛ (و تمام گفتگوی شما، در باره قبله و تغییر آن باشد؛ و همه وقت خود را مصروف آن سازید؛) بلکه نیکی (و نیکوکار) کسی است که به خدا، و روز رستاخیز، و فرشتگان، و کتاب (آسمانی)، و پیامبران، ایمان آورده؛ و مال (خود) را، با همه علاقه‌ای که به آن دارد، به خویشاوندان و یتیمان و مسکینان و واماندگان در راه و سائلان و بردگان، انفاق می‌کند؛ نماز را برپا می‌دارد و زکات را می‌پردازد...

46 *Ḥajj*, the Pilgrimage, 22:67:
لِكُلِّ أُمَّةٍ جَعَلْنَا مَنسَكًا هُمْ نَاسِكُوهُ ...

برای هر امتی عبادتی قرار دادیم، تا آن عبادت را (در پیشگاه خدا) انجام دهند...

47 *Ra'd*, Thunder, 13:7:
وَيَقُولُ الَّذِينَ كَفَرُوا لَوْلَا أُنزِلَ عَلَيْهِ آيَةٌ مِّن رَّبِّهِ إِنَّمَا أَنتَ مُنذِرٌ وَلِكُلِّ قَوْمٍ هَادٍ

کسانی که کافر شدند می‌گویند: «چرا آیه (و معجزه‌ای) از پروردگارش بر او نازل نشده؟!» تو فقط بیم دهنده‌ای! و برای هر گروهی هدایت کننده‌ای است (؛و اینها همه بهانه است، نه برای جستجوی حقیقت)!

48 *Fáṭir*, the Originator of Creation; or *Maláika*, the Angels, 35:24:
إِنَّا أَرْسَلْنَاكَ بِالْحَقِّ بَشِيرًا وَنَذِيرًا وَإِن مِّنْ أُمَّةٍ إِلَّا خَلَا فِيهَا نَذِيرٌ

ما تو را بحق برای بشارت و انذار فرستادیم؛ و هر امتی در گذشته انذارکننده‌ای داشته است

49 *Naḥl*, Bees, 16:36:
وَلَقَدْ بَعَثْنَا فِي كُلِّ أُمَّةٍ رَّسُولًا أَنِ اعْبُدُوا اللَّهَ وَاجْتَنِبُوا الطَّاغُوتَ فَمِنْهُم مَّنْ هَدَى اللَّهُ وَمِنْهُم مَّنْ حَقَّتْ عَلَيْهِ الضَّلَالَةُ فَسِيرُوا فِي الْأَرْضِ فَانظُرُوا كَيْفَ كَانَ عَاقِبَةُ الْمُكَذِّبِينَ

ما در هر امتی رسولی برانگیختیم که: «خدای یکتا را بپرستید؛ و از طاغوت اجتناب کنید!» خداوند گروهی را هدایت کرد، و گروهی ضلالت و گمراهی دامانشان را گرفت؛ پس در روی زمین بگردید و ببینید عاقبت تکذیب‌کنندگان چگونه بود

50   *Nisáa*, the Women, 4:164:

وَرُسُلًا قَدْ قَصَصْنَاهُمْ عَلَيْكَ مِن قَبْلُ وَرُسُلًا لَّمْ نَقْصُصْهُمْ عَلَيْكَ ...

و پیامبرانی [را فرستادیم] که در حقیقت [ماجرای] آنان را قبلا بر تو حکایت نمودیم و پیامبرانی [را نیز برانگیخته‌ایم] که [سرگذشت] ایشان را بر تو بازگو نکرده‌ایم ...

51   *Mú-min*, the Believer, 40:78:

وَلَقَدْ أَرْسَلْنَا رُسُلًا مِّن قَبْلِكَ مِنْهُم مَّن قَصَصْنَا عَلَيْكَ وَمِنْهُم مَّن لَّمْ نَقْصُصْ عَلَيْكَ وَمَا كَانَ لِرَسُولٍ أَن يَأْتِيَ بِآيَةٍ إِلَّا بِإِذْنِ اللَّهِ فَإِذَا جَاءَ أَمْرُ اللَّهِ قُضِيَ بِالْحَقِّ وَخَسِرَ هُنَالِكَ الْمُبْطِلُونَ

ما پیش از تو رسولانی فرستادیم؛ سرگذشت گروهی از آنان را برای تو بازگفته، و گروهی را برای تو بازگو نکرده‌ایم؛ و هیچ پیامبری حق نداشت معجزه‌ای جز بفرمان خدا بیاورد و هنگامی که فرمان خداوند (برای مجازات آنها) صادر شود، بحق داوری خواهد شد؛ و آنجا اهل باطل زیان خواهند کرد

52   *Baqara*, the Heifer, 2:28:

كَيْفَ تَكْفُرُونَ بِاللَّهِ وَكُنتُمْ أَمْوَاتًا فَأَحْيَاكُمْ ثُمَّ يُمِيتُكُمْ ثُمَّ يُحْيِيكُمْ ثُمَّ إِلَيْهِ تُرْجَعُونَ

چگونه خدا را منکرید با آنکه مردگانی بودید و شما را زنده کرد باز شما را می میراند [و] باز زنده می‌کند [و] آنگاه به سوی او بازگردانده می‌شوید

53   *Ra'd*, Thunder, 13:38:

وَلَقَدْ أَرْسَلْنَا رُسُلًا مِّن قَبْلِكَ وَجَعَلْنَا لَهُمْ أَزْوَاجًا وَذُرِّيَّةً وَمَا كَانَ لِرَسُولٍ أَن يَأْتِيَ بِآيَةٍ إِلَّا بِإِذْنِ اللَّهِ لِكُلِّ أَجَلٍ كِتَابٌ

و قطعا پیش از تو [نیز] رسولانی فرستادیم و برای آنان زنان و فرزندانی قرار دادیم و هیچ پیامبری را نرسد که جز به اذن خدا معجزه‌ای بیاورد برای هر زمانی کتابی است

54   *Mu-minún*, the Believers, 23:44:

ثُمَّ أَرْسَلْنَا رُسُلَنَا تَتْرَا كُلَّ مَا جَاءَ أُمَّةً رَّسُولُهَا كَذَّبُوهُ فَأَتْبَعْنَا بَعْضَهُم بَعْضًا وَجَعَلْنَاهُمْ أَحَادِيثَ فَبُعْدًا لِّقَوْمٍ لَّا يُؤْمِنُونَ

باز فرستادگان خود را پیاپی روانه کردیم هر بار برای [هدایت] امتی پیامبرش آمد او را تکذیب کردند پس [ما امتهای سرکش را] یکی پس از دیگری آوردیم و آنها را مایه عبرت [و زبانزد مردم] گردانیدیم دور باد [از رحمت خدا] مردمی که ایمان نمی‌آورند

55   *Ál-i-'Imrán*, the Family of 'Imrán, 3:3-4:

نَزَّلَ عَلَيْكَ الْكِتَابَ بِالْحَقِّ مُصَدِّقًا لِّمَا بَيْنَ يَدَيْهِ وَأَنزَلَ التَّوْرَاةَ وَالْإِنجِيلَ مِن قَبْلُ هُدًى لِّلنَّاسِ وَأَنزَلَ الْفُرْقَانَ ...

این کتاب را در حالی که مؤید آنچه [از کتابهای آسمانی] پیش از خود می‌باشد به حق [و به تدریج] بر تو نازل کرد و تورات و انجیل را
پیش از آن برای رهنمود مردم فرو فرستاد و فرقان [=جداکننده حق از باطل] را نازل کرد ...

56   *Má'ida*, the Table Spread, 5:16:

يَهْدِي بِهِ اللَّهُ مَنِ اتَّبَعَ رِضْوَانَهُ سُبُلَ السَّلَامِ وَيُخْرِجُهُم مِّنَ الظُّلُمَاتِ إِلَى النُّورِ بِإِذْنِهِ وَيَهْدِيهِمْ إِلَى صِرَاطٍ مُّسْتَقِيمٍ

خدا هر که را از خشنودی او پیروی کند به وسیله آن [کتاب] به راههای سلامت رهنمون می‌شود و به توفیق خویش آنان را از تاریکیها به سوی روشنایی بیرون می‌برد و به راهی راست هدایتشان می‌کند

NOTES AND REFERENCES

57 *'Ankabút,* the Spider, 29:69:

وَالَّذِينَ جَاهَدُوا فِينَا لَنَهْدِيَنَّهُمْ سُبُلَنَا وَإِنَّ اللَّهَ لَمَعَ الْمُحْسِنِينَ

و کسانی که در راه ما کوشیده‌اند به یقین راه‌های خود را بر آنان می‌نماییم و در حقیقت خدا با نیکوکاران است

58 Matt. 7:13–14.

59 *An'ám,* Cattle, 6:153:

وَأَنَّ هَذَا صِرَاطِي مُسْتَقِيمًا فَاتَّبِعُوهُ وَلَا تَتَّبِعُوا السُّبُلَ فَتَفَرَّقَ بِكُمْ عَن سَبِيلِهِ ذَلِكُمْ وَصَّاكُم بِهِ لَعَلَّكُمْ تَتَّقُونَ

و [بدانید] این است راه راست من پس از آن پیروی کنید و از راه[ها]ی دیگر] که شما را از راه وی پراکنده می‌سازد پیروی مکنید اینهاست که [خدا] شما را به آن سفارش کرده است باشد که به تقوا گرایید

60 *Maryam,* Mary, 19:41–3.

وَاذْكُرْ فِي الْكِتَابِ إِبْرَاهِيمَ إِنَّهُ كَانَ صِدِّيقًا نَّبِيًّا
إِذْ قَالَ لِأَبِيهِ يَا أَبَتِ لِمَ تَعْبُدُ مَا لَا يَسْمَعُ وَلَا يُبْصِرُ وَلَا يُغْنِي عَنكَ شَيْئًا
يَا أَبَتِ إِنِّي قَدْ جَاءَنِي مِنَ الْعِلْمِ مَا لَمْ يَأْتِكَ فَاتَّبِعْنِي أَهْدِكَ صِرَاطًا سَوِيًّا

در این کتاب، ابراهیم را یاد کن، که او بسیار راستگو، و پیامبر (خدا) بود!
هنگامی که به پدرش گفت: «ای پدر! چرا چیزی را می‌پرستی که نه می‌شنود، و نه می‌بیند، و نه هیچ مشکلی را از تو حل می‌کند؟!
ای پدر! دانشی برای من آمده که برای تو نیامده است؛ بنابر این از من پیروی کن، تا تو را به راه راست هدایت کنم

61 *Húd* (the Prophet Húd), 11:56:

إِنِّي تَوَكَّلْتُ عَلَى اللَّهِ رَبِّي وَرَبِّكُم مَّا مِن دَابَّةٍ إِلَّا هُوَ آخِذٌ بِنَاصِيَتِهَا إِنَّ رَبِّي عَلَى صِرَاطٍ مُّسْتَقِيمٍ

من بر خدا که پروردگار خودم و پروردگار شماست توکل کرده ام . هیچ جنبنده‌ای نیست مگر اینکه او مهار هستی‌اش را در دست دارد به راستی پروردگار من بر راه راست است

62 *An'ám,* Cattle, 6:161:

قُلْ إِنَّنِي هَدَانِي رَبِّي إِلَى صِرَاطٍ مُّسْتَقِيمٍ دِينًا قِيَمًا مِّلَّةَ إِبْرَاهِيمَ حَنِيفًا وَمَا كَانَ مِنَ الْمُشْرِكِينَ

بگو آری پروردگارم مرا به راه راست هدایت کرده است دینی پایدار آیین ابراهیم حق‌گرای و او از مشرکان نبود

63 *Má'ida,* the Table Spread, 5:12:

وَلَقَدْ أَخَذَ اللَّهُ مِيثَاقَ بَنِي إِسْرَائِيلَ وَبَعَثْنَا مِنْهُمُ اثْنَيْ عَشَرَ نَقِيبًا وَقَالَ اللَّهُ إِنِّي مَعَكُمْ لَئِنْ أَقَمْتُمُ الصَّلَاةَ وَآتَيْتُمُ الزَّكَاةَ وَآمَنتُم بِرُسُلِي وَعَزَّرْتُمُوهُمْ وَأَقْرَضْتُمُ اللَّهَ قَرْضًا حَسَنًا لَّأُكَفِّرَنَّ عَنكُمْ سَيِّئَاتِكُمْ وَلَأُدْخِلَنَّكُمْ جَنَّاتٍ تَجْرِي مِن تَحْتِهَا الْأَنْهَارُ فَمَن كَفَرَ بَعْدَ ذَلِكَ مِنكُمْ فَقَدْ ضَلَّ سَوَاءَ السَّبِيلِ

در حقیقت خدا از فرزندان اسرائیل پیمان گرفت و از آنان دوازده سرکرده برانگیختیم و خدا فرمود من با شما هستم اگر نماز برپا دارید و زکات بدهید و به فرستادگانم ایمان بیاورید و یاریشان کنید و وام نیکویی به خدا بدهید قطعا گناهانتان را از شما می‌زدایم و شما را به باغهایی که از زیر [درختان] آن نهرها روان است در می‌آورم پس هر کس از شما بعد از این کفر ورزد در حقیقت از راه راست گمراه شده است

64 *Mu-minún,* the Believers, 23:43:

مَا تَسْبِقُ مِنْ أُمَّةٍ أَجَلَهَا وَمَا يَسْتَأْخِرُونَ

هیچ امتی نه از اجل خود پیشی می‌گیرد و نه باز پس می‌ماند

65 A'ráf, the Heights, 7:34:

وَلِكُلِّ أُمَّةٍ أَجَلٌ فَإِذَا جَاءَ أَجَلُهُمْ لاَ يَسْتَأْخِرُونَ سَاعَةً وَلاَ يَسْتَقْدِمُونَ

و برای هر امتی اجلی است پس چون اجلشان فرا رسد نه [می‌توانند] ساعتی آن را پس اندازند و نه پیش

66 Húd (the Prophet Húd), 11:104:

وَمَا نُؤَخِّرُهُ إِلاَّ لِأَجَلٍ مَّعْدُودٍ

و ما آن را جز تا زمان معینی به تاخیر نمی‌افکنیم

67 Al-Hijr, the Rocky Tract, 15:5:

مَا تَسْبِقُ مِنْ أُمَّةٍ أَجَلَهَا وَمَا يَسْتَأْخِرُونَ

هیچ امتی از اجل خویش نه پیش می‌افتد و نه پس می‌ماند

68 Yá-Sín, 36:68:

وَمَنْ نُعَمِّرْهُ نُنَكِّسْهُ فِي الْخَلْقِ أَفَلاَ يَعْقِلُونَ

و هر که را عمر دراز دهیم او را [از نظر] خلقت فروکاسته [و شکسته] گردانیم آیا نمی‌اندیشند

69 Baqara, the Heifer, 2:106:

مَا نَنْسَخْ مِنْ آيَةٍ أَوْ نُنْسِهَا نَأْتِ بِخَيْرٍ مِّنْهَا أَوْ مِثْلِهَا أَلَمْ تَعْلَمْ أَنَّ اللَّهَ عَلَى كُلِّ شَيْءٍ قَدِيرٌ

هر حکمی را نسخ کنیم یا آن را به [دست] فراموشی بسپاریم بهتر از آن یا مانندش را می‌آوریم مگر ندانستی که خدا بر هر کاری تواناست

70 Baqara, the Heifer, 2:272:

لَيْسَ عَلَيْكَ هُدَاهُمْ وَلَكِنَّ اللَّهَ يَهْدِي مَنْ يَشَاءُ وَمَا تُنْفِقُوا مِنْ خَيْرٍ فَلِأَنْفُسِكُمْ وَمَا تُنْفِقُونَ إِلاَّ ابْتِغَاءَ وَجْهِ اللَّهِ وَمَا تُنْفِقُوا مِنْ خَيْرٍ يُوَفَّ إِلَيْكُمْ وَأَنْتُمْ لاَ تُظْلَمُونَ

هدایت آنان بر عهده تو نیست، بلکه خدا هر که را بخواهد هدایت می‌کند، و هر مالی که انفاق کنید، به سود خود شماست، و(لی) جز برای طلب خشنودی خدا انفاق مکنید، و هر مالی را که انفاق کنید (پاداش آن) به طور کامل به شما داده خواهد شد و ستمی بر شما نخواهد رفت.

71 Muzzammil, Folded in Garments, 73:19:

إِنَّ هَذِهِ تَذْكِرَةٌ فَمَنْ شَاءَ اتَّخَذَ إِلَى رَبِّهِ سَبِيلاً

قطعا این [آیات] اندرزی است تا هر که بخواهد به سوی پروردگار خود راهی در پیش گیرد

Bahá'u'lláh delivers a similar admonition:
> Thus doth the Nightingale utter His call unto you from this prison. He hath but to deliver this clear message. Whosoever desireth, let him turn aside from this counsel and whosoever desireth let him choose the path to his Lord. (Tablet of Aḥmad, *Bahá'í Prayers*, p. 309)

72 Jumu'a, the Assembly (Friday) Prayer, 62:2:

هُوَ الَّذِي بَعَثَ فِي الْأُمِّيِّينَ رَسُولاً مِنْهُمْ يَتْلُو عَلَيْهِمْ آيَاتِهِ وَيُزَكِّيهِمْ وَيُعَلِّمُهُمُ الْكِتَابَ وَالْحِكْمَةَ وَإِنْ كَانُوا مِنْ قَبْلُ لَفِي ضَلاَلٍ مُبِينٍ

اوست آن کس که در میان بی‌سوادان فرستاده‌ای از خودشان برانگیخت تا آیات او را بر آنان بخواند و پاکشان گرداند و کتاب و حکمت بدیشان بیاموزد و [آنان] قطعا پیش از آن در گمراهی آشکاری بودند

73 *Yúnus*, Jonah, 10:37:

وَمَا كَانَ هَذَا الْقُرْآنُ أَن يُفْتَرَى مِن دُونِ اللَّهِ وَلَكِن تَصْدِيقَ الَّذِي بَيْنَ يَدَيْهِ وَتَفْصِيلَ الْكِتَابِ لاَ رَيْبَ فِيهِ مِن رَّبِّ الْعَالَمِينَ

و چنان نیست که این قرآن از جانب غیر خدا [و] به دروغ ساخته شده باشد بلکه تصدیق [کننده] آنچه پیش از آن است می‌باشد و توضیحی از آن کتاب است که در آن تردیدی نیست [و] از پروردگار جهانیان است

74 *Baqara*, the Heifer, 2:2:

ذَلِكَ الْكِتَابُ لاَ رَيْبَ فِيهِ هُدًى لِّلْمُتَّقِينَ

آن کتاب با عظمتی است که شک در آن راه ندارد؛ و مایه هدایت پرهیزکاران است.

75 *Ra'd*, Thunder, 13:39:

يَمْحُو اللَّهُ مَا يَشَاءُ وَيُثْبِتُ وَعِندَهُ أُمُّ الْكِتَابِ

خدا آنچه را بخواهد محو یا اثبات می‌کند و اصل کتاب نزد اوست

The Bahá'í Writings explain that the 'Mother Book' refers to both the Author of Revelation in every age, and to His Book. In the Bábí Dispensation, the Bayán is the Mother Book, and the Kitáb-i-Aqdas is the Mother Book of the Dispensation of Bahá'u'lláh. The Báb states that the Voice that addressed Moses speaks through Him:
> Hearken unto the Voice of Thy Lord calling from Mount Sinai, 'Verily there is no God but Him, and I am the Exalted One Who hath been veiled in the Mother Book according to the dispensations of Providence. (Qayyúmu'l-Asmá', ch. XIX, in *Selections from the Writings of the Báb*, p. 70)

And Bahá'u'lláh refers to the Revelation of the Báb (*Bayán*) as the 'Mother Book':
> Say: O people be obedient to the ordinances of God, which have been enjoined in the Bayán by the Glorious, the Wise One. Verily He is the King of the Messengers and His Book is the Mother Book did ye but know. (Bahá'u'lláh, Tablet of Aḥmad, in *Bahá'í Prayers* p. 308)

Bahá'u'lláh also describes His own Revelation as the 'Mother Book':
> Say: This, verily, is the heaven in which the Mother Book is treasured, could ye but comprehend it. (*Epistle to the Son of the Wolf*, p. 129)
> He is the sovereign Truth, the Knower of things unseen. The Mother Book is revealed and the Lord of Bounty is established upon the most blessed seat of Glory. The Dawn hath broken, yet the people understand not. (Kalimát-i-Firdaysíyyih, in *Tablets of Bahá'u'lláh Revealed after the Kitáb-i-Aqdas*, p. 75)

76 '*Wasaṭ*' simply means 'middle'; hence, the following translations: *M. M. Pickthall*: 'a middle nation'; *A. J. Arberry*: 'a midmost nation'; *J. M. Rodwell*: 'central people'. Others have translated the word to indicate a non-extreme or just nation; *Muhammad Sarwar*: 'moderate nation'; *Mohsin Khán*: 'just nation'; *Shákir*: 'a medium nation'; *Sahih International*: 'a just community'.

77 *Baqara*, the Heifer, 2:143:

وَكَذَلِكَ جَعَلْنَاكُمْ أُمَّةً وَسَطًا لِتَكُونُوا شُهَدَاءَ عَلَى النَّاسِ وَيَكُونَ الرَّسُولُ عَلَيْكُمْ شَهِيدًا وَمَا جَعَلْنَا الْقِبْلَةَ الَّتِي كُنْتَ عَلَيْهَا إِلَّا لِنَعْلَمَ مَنْ يَتَّبِعُ الرَّسُولَ مِمَّنْ يَنْقَلِبُ عَلَى عَقِبَيْهِ وَإِنْ كَانَتْ لَكَبِيرَةً إِلَّا عَلَى الَّذِينَ هَدَى اللَّهُ وَمَا كَانَ اللَّهُ لِيُضِيعَ إِيمَانَكُمْ إِنَّ اللَّهَ بِالنَّاسِ لَرَءُوفٌ رَحِيمٌ

و بدین گونه شما را امتی میانه قرار دادیم تا بر مردم گواه باشید و پیامبر بر شما گواه باشد و قبله‌ای را که [چندی] بر آن بودی مقرر نکردیم جز برای آنکه کسی را که از پیامبر پیروی می‌کند از آن کس که از عقیده خود برمی‌گردد بازشناسیم هر چند [این کار] جز بر کسانی که خدا هدایت[شان] کرده بسیار سخت گران بود و خدا بر آن نبود که ایمان شما را ضایع گرداند زیرا خدا [نسبت] به مردم دلسوز و مهربان است

78 The Báb, *Qayyúmu'l-Asmá'*, ch. IV, in *Selections from the Writings of the Báb*, p. 46.
79 Bahá'u'lláh, quoted in Shoghi Effendi, *The World Order of Bahá'u'lláh*, pp. 114–15.
80 Bahá'u'lláh, Tablet of Aḥmad, in *Bahá'í Prayers*, p. 310.
81 *The Dawn-Breakers: Nabíl's Narrative of the Early Days of the Bahá'í Revelation*, p. 447.
82 Bahá'u'lláh, Tablet of Visitation, in *Bahá'í Prayers*, pp. 328–9.
83 Bahá'u'lláh, *Gleanings from the Writings of Bahá'u'lláh*, XXII, p. 54.
84 *Fat-ḥ*, Victory, 48:10:

إِنَّ الَّذِينَ يُبَايِعُونَكَ إِنَّمَا يُبَايِعُونَ اللَّهَ يَدُ اللَّهِ فَوْقَ أَيْدِيهِمْ فَمَنْ نَكَثَ فَإِنَّمَا يَنْكُثُ عَلَى نَفْسِهِ وَمَنْ أَوْفَى بِمَا عَاهَدَ عَلَيْهُ اللَّهَ فَسَيُؤْتِيهِ أَجْرًا عَظِيمًا

در حقیقت کسانی که با تو بیعت می‌کنند جز این نیست که با خدا بیعت می‌کنند دست‌خدا بالای دست‌های آنان است پس هر که پیمان‌شکنی کند تنها به زیان خود پیمان می‌شکند و هر که بر آنچه با خدا عهد بسته وفادار بماند به زودی خدا پاداشی بزرگ به او می‌بخشد

85 *Ál-i-'Imrán*, the Family of 'Imrán, 3:31:

قُلْ إِنْ كُنْتُمْ تُحِبُّونَ اللَّهَ فَاتَّبِعُونِي يُحْبِبْكُمُ اللَّهُ وَيَغْفِرْ لَكُمْ ذُنُوبَكُمْ وَاللَّهُ غَفُورٌ رَحِيمٌ

بگو اگر خدا را دوست دارید از من پیروی کنید تا خدا دوستتان بدارد و گناهان شما را بر شما ببخشاید و خداوند آمرزنده مهربان است

86 *Anfál*, the Spoils of War, 8:17:

فَلَمْ تَقْتُلُوهُمْ وَلَكِنَّ اللَّهَ قَتَلَهُمْ وَمَا رَمَيْتَ إِذْ رَمَيْتَ وَلَكِنَّ اللَّهَ رَمَى وَلِيُبْلِيَ الْمُؤْمِنِينَ مِنْهُ بَلَاءً حَسَنًا إِنَّ اللَّهَ سَمِيعٌ عَلِيمٌ

این شما نبودید که آنها را کشتید؛ بلکه خداوند آنها را کشت! و این تو نبودی (ای پیامبر که خاک و سنگ به صورت آنها) انداختی؛ بلکه خدا انداخت! و خدا می‌خواست مؤمنان را به این وسیله امتحان خوبی کند؛ خداوند شنوا و داناست.

The verse refers to the Battle of Badr, the first of three defensive battles fought by Muslims, when an inexperienced and ill-equipped army of about a hundred Muslims defeated a superior professional invading Meccan army of about a thousand men.

87 John 14:8–9.
88 John 8:19.

89 John 14:7.
90 Matt. 5:8.
91 Exod. 4:15-16.
92 Num. 12:6-8.
93 Exod. 7:1.
94 Bahá'u'lláh, *Gleanings from the Writings of Bahá'u'lláh*, CXIII, p. 228.
95 Bahá'u'lláh, *Prayers and Meditations*, LXXVIII, p. 128.
96 Bahá'u'lláh, *Gleanings from the Writings of Bahá'u'lláh*, XXVII, pp. 67-8.
97 ibid. LXXXI, pp. 156–7.
98 Bahá'u'lláh, Lawḥ-i-Burhán, in *Tablets of Baha'u'llah Revealed after the Kitáb-i-Aqdas*, p. 212.
99 Bahá'u'lláh, *Tablets of Baha'u'llah Revealed after the Kitáb-i-Aqdas*, p. 255.
100 Bahá'u'lláh, *The Kitab-i-Aqdas*, para. 14, p. 24.
101 Bahá'u'lláh, *Gleanings from the Writings of Bahá'u'lláh*, CX, p. 215.
102 Bahá'u'lláh, *Tablets of Baha'u'llah Revealed after the Kitáb-i-Aqdas*, p. 254.
103 Bahá'u'lláh, *Gleanings from the Writings of Bahá'u'lláh*, XCIV, pp. 192-3.
104 Shoghi Effendi, *God Passes By*, p. 100.
105 For instance, from the Hindu scriptures:
> It is the same ancient Path that I have now revealed to thee . . .
> I (Lord Shri Krishna) have been born again and again, from time to time . . .
> I have no beginning. Though I am imperishable, as well as Lord of all that exists, yet by My own will and power do I manifest Myself.
> Whenever spirituality decays and materialism is rampant, then, O Arjuna, I reincarnate Myself!
> To protect the righteous, to destroy the wicked and to establish the kingdom of God, I am reborn from age to age. (Bhagavad Gita 4: 7-8)

And from the Buddhist scriptures:
> Suppressing his tears, Ananda said to the Buddha, 'Who shall teach us when You are gone?' And the Buddha advised him to regard His Teaching as the Master.
> The Buddha continued again: "I am not the first Buddha to come upon earth; nor shall I be the last. In due time, another Buddha will arise in this world, a Holy One, a Supremely Enlightened One, endowed with wisdom, in conduct auspicious, knowing the universe, an incomparable leader of men, a master of devas and men. He will reveal to you the same Eternal Truths which I have taught you. He will proclaim a religious life, wholly perfect and pure; such as I now proclaim.'
> 'How shall we know him?' asked Ananda. The Buddha replied, 'He will be known as *Maitreya* which means kindness or friendliness.' (Digha Nikaya IV:26)

106 Ibsen, *The Emperor Julian*, Act III, in *The Works of Henrik Ibsen*, vol. 6, p. 424; as quoted by Shoghi Effendi, *The World Order of Bahá'u'lláh*, p. 114.
107 Shoghi Effendi, *The World Order of Bahá'u'lláh*, pp. 57-8.
108 Bahá'u'lláh, *Gems of Divine Mysteries, Javáhiru'l-Asrár*, pp. 42-3.
109 Bahá'u'lláh, *Gleanings from the Writings of Bahá'u'lláh*, XVIII, p. 44.

110 'Abdu'l-Bahá, *Paris Talks*, ch. 18, p. 57.
111 Inscription written by 'Abdu'l-Bahá in Persian in the Bible at the City Temple, London, *'Abdu'l-Bahá in London*, p. 18.
112 *Baqara*, the Heifer, 2:253:

تِلْكَ الرُّسُلُ فَضَّلْنَا بَعْضَهُمْ عَلَى بَعْضٍ مِّنْهُم مَّن كَلَّمَ اللَّهُ وَرَفَعَ بَعْضَهُمْ دَرَجَاتٍ ...

برخی از آن پیامبران را بر برخی دیگر برتری بخشیدیم از آنان کسی بود که خدا با او سخن گفت و درجات بعضی از آنان را بالا برد ...

113 Shoghi Effendi, quoting Bahá'u'lláh, in *The World Order of Bahá'u'lláh*, p. 58.
114 *'Ankabút*, the Spider, 29:46:

وَلَا تُجَادِلُوا أَهْلَ الْكِتَابِ إِلَّا بِالَّتِي هِيَ أَحْسَنُ إِلَّا الَّذِينَ ظَلَمُوا مِنْهُمْ وَقُولُوا آمَنَّا بِالَّذِي أُنزِلَ إِلَيْنَا وَأُنزِلَ إِلَيْكُمْ وَإِلَهُنَا وَإِلَهُكُمْ وَاحِدٌ وَنَحْنُ لَهُ مُسْلِمُونَ

و با اهل کتاب جز به نیکوترین روش ، بحث نکنید . به آنان ، بگویید : ما به کتابی که بر خودمان نازل شده و نیز به کتابی که برای شما فرستاده شده است ایمان آورده ایم؛ معبود ما و معبود شما یکی است و ما تسلیم اوییم . البته با آن دسته از اهل کتاب که در بحث و مجادله ستم می کنند و رفق و مدارای شما را نشانه ضعف شما می پندارند این گونه بحث نکنید که کارساز نخواهد بود .

18 Submission to the Divine Will: Abrogation of the Dispensation of Muhammad, and the Suspension and Modification of its Social Laws by Bahá'u'lláh

1 Shoghi Effendi, *God Passes By*, p. 100.
2 'Abdu'l-Bahá, *The Promulgation of Universal Peace*, p. 393.
3 Shoghi Effendi, *The World Order of Bahá'u'lláh*, pp. 57-8.
4 Corresponding to the wineskins containing the wine of revelation referred to by Christ:
> Nor do people pour new wine into old wineskins. If they do, the skins burst, the wine runs out, and the skins are ruined. Rather, people pour new wine into fresh skins, and both are saved (Matt. 9:17, *God's Word* translation).
5 *Ibráhím*, Abraham, 14:5:
> We sent Moses with Our Signs, 'Bring out thy people from the depths of darkness into light, and teach them to remember the Days of God.' Verily in this there are Signs for such as are firmly patient and constant -- grateful and appreciative.

وَلَقَدْ أَرْسَلْنَا مُوسَى بِآيَاتِنَا أَنْ أَخْرِجْ قَوْمَكَ مِنَ الظُّلُمَاتِ إِلَى النُّورِ وَذَكِّرْهُم بِأَيَّامِ اللَّهِ إِنَّ فِي ذَلِكَ لَآيَاتٍ لِّكُلِّ صَبَّارٍ شَكُورٍ

و در حقیقت موسی را با آیات خود فرستادیم [و به او فرمودیم] که قوم خود را از تاریکیها به سوی روشنایی بیرون آور و روزهای خدا را به آنان یادآوری کن که قطعا در این [یادآوری] برای هر شکیبای سپاسگزاری عبرتهاست

Ar'áf, the Heights, 7:34:
> To every people is a term appointed: when their term is reached, not an hour can they cause delay, or (an hour) can they advance (it in anticipation).

وَلِكُلِّ أُمَّةٍ أَجَلٌ فَإِذَا جَاء أَجَلُهُمْ لاَ يَسْتَأْخِرُونَ سَاعَةً وَلاَ يَسْتَقْدِمُونَ

و برای هر امتی اجلی است پس چون اجلشان فرا رسد نه [می‌توانند] ساعتی آن را پس اندازند و نه پیش

Aḥqáf, Winding Sand-tracts, 46:3:
> We created not the heavens (spiritual principles) and the earth (social laws) and all between them but for just ends, and for a term appointed: but those who reject Faith turn away from that whereof they are warned.

مَا خَلَقْنَا السَّمَاوَاتِ وَالأَرْضَ وَمَا بَيْنَهُمَا إِلَّا بِالْحَقِّ وَأَجَلٍ مُّسَمًّى وَالَّذِينَ كَفَرُوا عَمَّا أُنذِرُوا مُعْرِضُونَ

ما آسمانها و زمین و آنچه را در میان این دو است جز بحق و برای سرآمد معینی نیافریدیم؛ اما کافران از آنچه انذار می‌شوند روی گردانند

An'ám, Cattle, 6:2:
> He it is who created you from clay, and then decreed a stated term (for you). And there is in His presence another determined term; yet ye doubt within yourselves!

هُوَ الَّذِي خَلَقَكُم مِّن طِينٍ ثُمَّ قَضَى أَجَلًا وَأَجَلٌ مُّسمًّى عِندَهُ ثُمَّ أَنتُمْ تَمْتَرُونَ

کسی است که شما را از گل آفرید؛ سپس مدتی مقرر داشت و اجل حتمی نزد اوست (و فقط او از آن آگاه است). با این همه، شما تردید می‌کنید!

6 Eccles. 3:1:
> To every thing there is a season, and a time to every purpose under the heaven:

Dan. 2:20–22:
> Daniel answered and said, Blessed be the name of God for ever and ever: for wisdom and might are his:
> And he changeth the times and the seasons: he removeth kings, and setteth up kings: he giveth wisdom unto the wise, and knowledge to them that know understanding:
> He revealeth the deep and secret things: he knoweth what is in the darkness, and the light dwelleth with him.

I Cor. 4:5:
> Therefore judge nothing before the time, until the Lord come . . .

Mark 13:32:
> But of that day and that hour knoweth no man, no, not the angels which are in heaven, neither the Son, but the Father.
> God, who at sundry times and in divers manners spake in time past unto the fathers by the prophets,
> Hath in these last days spoken unto us by his Son . . .

7 Shoghi Effendi, *God Passes By*, p. 25.
8 Shoghi Effendi, *The World Order of Bahá'u'lláh*, p. 42.
9 ibid. p. 22.
10 Bahá'u'lláh, *The Kitáb-i-Aqdas*, paras. 161–2, p. 77.
11 *Bihar al-Anwar*, vol. 13, ch. 30 (old edition), p. 127.
12 Exod. 23:22–5.
13 Gal. 3:28.

14 Matt. 7:6.
15 Matt. 10:5-6.
16 Matt. 15:22-8.
17 Rom. 1:16.
18 Rom. 2:9-11.
19 Eph. 6:5.
20 Col. 3:22.
21 I Tim. 6:1-8.
22 Titus 2:9-10.
23 I Pet. 2:18.
24 *Mā'ida*, the Table Spread, 5:51:

يَا أَيُّهَا الَّذِينَ آمَنُواْ لاَ تَتَّخِذُواْ الْيَهُودَ وَالنَّصَارَى أَوْلِيَاء بَعْضُهُمْ أَوْلِيَاء بَعْضٍ وَمَن يَتَوَلَّهُم مِّنكُمْ فَإِنَّهُ مِنْهُمْ إِنَّ اللّهَ لاَ يَهْدِي الْقَوْمَ الظَّالِمِينَ

ای کسانی که ایمان آورده‌اید! یهود و نصاری را ولی (و دوست و تکیه‌گاه خود،) انتخاب نکنید! آنها اولیای یکدیگرند؛ و کسانی که از شما با آنان دوستی کنند، از آنها هستند؛ خداوند، جمعیت ستمکار را هدایت نمی‌کند

25 *Mā'ida*, the Table Spread, 5:57:

يَا أَيُّهَا الَّذِينَ آمَنُواْ لاَ تَتَّخِذُواْ الَّذِينَ اتَّخَذُواْ دِينَكُمْ هُزُوًا وَلَعِبًا مِّنَ الَّذِينَ أُوتُواْ الْكِتَابَ مِن قَبْلِكُمْ وَالْكُفَّارَ أَوْلِيَاء وَاتَّقُواْ اللّهَ إِن كُنتُم مُّؤْمِنِينَ

ای کسانی که ایمان آورده‌اید! افرادی که آیین شما را به باد استهزاء و بازی می‌گیرند -از اهل کتاب و مشرکان- ولی خود انتخاب نکنید! و از خدا بپرهیزید اگر ایمان دارید!

26 *Baqara*, the Heifer, 2:178:

يَا أَيُّهَا الَّذِينَ آمَنُواْ كُتِبَ عَلَيْكُمُ الْقِصَاصُ فِي الْقَتْلَى الْحُرُّ بِالْحُرِّ وَالْعَبْدُ بِالْعَبْدِ وَالأُنثَى بِالأُنثَى ...

ای افرادی که ایمان آورده‌اید! حکم قصاص در مورد کشتگان، بر شما نوشته شده است: آزاد در برابر آزاد، و برده در برابر برده، و زن در برابر زن ...

   J. M. Rodwell:
   O believers! Retaliation for bloodshedding is prescribed to you: the free man for the free, and the slave for the slave, and the woman for the woman...
   M. M. Pickthall:
   O ye who believe! Retaliation is prescribed for you in the matter of the murdered, the freeman for the freeman, and the slave for the slave, and the female for the female...

27 *Mā'ida*, the Table Spread, 5:48:

...لِكُلٍّ جَعَلْنَا مِنكُمْ شِرْعَةً وَمِنْهَاجًا وَلَوْ شَاء اللّهُ لَجَعَلَكُمْ أُمَّةً وَاحِدَةً وَلَكِن لِّيَبْلُوَكُمْ فِي مَآ آتَاكُم فَاسْتَبِقُوا الخَيْرَاتِ إِلَى الله مَرْجِعُكُمْ جَمِيعًا فَيُنَبِّئُكُم بِمَا كُنتُمْ فِيهِ تَخْتَلِفُونَ

...برای هر یک از شما [امتها] شریعت و راه روشنی قرار داده‌ایم و اگر خدا می‌خواست شما را یک امت قرار می‌داد ولی [خواست] تا شما را در آنچه به شما داده است بیازماید پس در کارهای نیک بر یکدیگر سبقت گیرید بازگشت [همه] شما به سوی خداست

NOTES AND REFERENCES

28   *Húd* (the Prophet Húd), 11:118:

وَلَوْ شَاءَ رَبُّكَ لَجَعَلَ النَّاسَ أُمَّةً وَاحِدَةً وَلاَ يَزَالُونَ مُخْتَلِفِينَ

و اگر پروردگار تو می‌خواست قطعا همه مردم را امت واحدی قرار می‌داد در حالی که پیوسته در اختلافند

29   *Naḥl*, Bees, 16:93:

وَلَوْ شَاءَ اللَّهُ لَجَعَلَكُمْ أُمَّةً وَاحِدَةً وَلَكِن يُضِلُّ مَن يَشَاءُ وَيَهْدِي مَن يَشَاءُ وَلَتُسْأَلُنَّ عَمَّا كُنتُمْ تَعْمَلُونَ

و اگر خدا می‌خواست قطعا شما را امتی واحد قرار می‌داد ولی هر که را بخواهد بیراه و هر که را بخواهد هدایت می‌کند و از آنچه انجام می‌دادید حتما سؤال خواهید شد

30   *Shúráa*, Consultation, 42:8:

وَلَوْ شَاءَ اللَّهُ لَجَعَلَهُمْ أُمَّةً وَاحِدَةً وَلَكِن يُدْخِلُ مَن يَشَاءُ فِي رَحْمَتِهِ وَالظَّالِمُونَ مَا لَهُم مِّن وَلِيٍّ وَلَا نَصِيرٍ

و اگر خدا می‌خواست قطعا آنان را امتی یگانه می‌گردانید لیکن هر که را بخواهد به رحمت خویش درمی‌آورد و ستمگران نه یاری دارند و نه یاوری

31   Bahá'u'lláh, *The Kitáb-i-Aqdas*, para. 72, p. 45.
32   Deut. 21:10-14.
33   Deut. 21:15-17.
34   I Tim. 3:2.
35   Eph. 5:22–5.
36   Col. 3:18–19.
37   I Cor. 14:34–5; (1 Cor. 7:4).
38   I Tim. 2:9–15.
39   I Pet. 3:1–6.
40   *Nisáa*, the Women, 4:1:

يَا أَيُّهَا النَّاسُ اتَّقُوا رَبَّكُمُ الَّذِي خَلَقَكُم مِّن نَّفْسٍ وَاحِدَةٍ وَخَلَقَ مِنْهَا زَوْجَهَا وَبَثَّ مِنْهُمَا رِجَالًا كَثِيرًا وَنِسَاءً وَاتَّقُوا اللَّهَ الَّذِي تَسَاءَلُونَ بِهِ وَالْأَرْحَامَ إِنَّ اللَّهَ كَانَ عَلَيْكُمْ رَقِيبًا

ای مردم از پروردگارتان که شما را از نفس واحدی آفرید و جفتش را [نیز] از او آفرید و از آن دو مردان و زنان بسیاری پراکنده کرد پروا دارید و از خدایی که به [نام] او و همدیگر درخواست می‌کنید پروا نمایید و زنهار از خویشاوندان مبرید که خدا همواره بر شما نگهبان است

41   *Nisáa*, the Women, 4:34:

الرِّجَالُ قَوَّامُونَ عَلَى النِّسَاءِ بِمَا فَضَّلَ اللَّهُ بَعْضَهُمْ عَلَى بَعْضٍ وَبِمَا أَنفَقُوا مِنْ أَمْوَالِهِمْ ...

مردان، سرپرست و نگهبان زنانند، بخاطر برتریهایی که خداوند برای بعضی نسبت به بعضی دیگر قرار داده است، و بخاطر انفاقهایی که از اموالشان (در مورد زنان) می‌کنند...

M. M. Pickthall:
   Men are in charge of women, because God hath made the one of them to excel the other, and because they spend of their property (for the support of women)...

M. T. Al-Hilláli:
   Men are protectors and maintainers of women, because God has made one of them to excel the other, and because they spend (to support them) from their means...

J. M. Rodwell:
> Men are superior to women on account of the qualities with which God hath gifted the one above the other, and on account of the outlay they make from their substance for them...

George Sale:
> Men shall have pre-eminence above women, because of those advantages wherein God hath caused the one of them to excel the other, and for that which they expend of their substance in maintaining their wives...

42 *Nisáa*, the Women, 4:176:

يَسْتَفْتُونَكَ قُلِ اللّهُ يُفْتِيكُمْ فِي الْكَلَالَةِ إِنِ امْرُؤٌ هَلَكَ لَيْسَ لَهُ وَلَدٌ وَلَهُ أُخْتٌ فَلَهَا نِصْفُ مَا تَرَكَ وَهُوَ يَرِثُهَا إِن لَّمْ يَكُن لَّهَا وَلَدٌ فَإِن كَانَتَا اثْنَتَيْنِ فَلَهُمَا الثُّلُثَانِ مِمَّا تَرَكَ وَإِن كَانُواْ إِخْوَةً رِّجَالاً وَنِسَاءً فَلِلذَّكَرِ مِثْلُ حَظِّ الأُنثَيَيْنِ يُبَيِّنُ اللّهُ لَكُمْ أَن تَضِلُّواْ وَاللّهُ بِكُلِّ شَيْءٍ عَلِيمٌ

از تو [در باره کلاله] فتوا می‌طلبند بگو خدا در باره کلاله فتوا می‌دهد اگر مردی بمیرد و فرزندی نداشته باشد و خواهری داشته باشد نصف میراث از آن اوست و آن [مرد نیز] از او ارث می‌برد اگر برای او [=خواهر] فرزندی نباشد پس اگر [ورثه فقط] دو خواهر باشند دو سوم میراث برای آن دو است و اگر [چند] خواهر و برادرند پس نصیب مرد مانند نصیب دو زن است خدا برای شما توضیح می‌دهد تا مبادا گمراه شوید و خداوند به هر چیزی داناست

43 *Má'ida*, the Table Spread, 5:5:

الْيَوْمَ أُحِلَّ لَكُمُ الطَّيِّبَاتُ وَطَعَامُ الَّذِينَ أُوتُواْ الْكِتَابَ حِلٌّ لَّكُمْ وَطَعَامُكُمْ حِلٌّ لَّهُمْ وَالْمُحْصَنَاتُ مِنَ الْمُؤْمِنَاتِ وَالْمُحْصَنَاتُ مِنَ الَّذِينَ أُوتُواْ الْكِتَابَ مِن قَبْلِكُمْ إِذَا آتَيْتُمُوهُنَّ أُجُورَهُنَّ مُحْصِنِينَ غَيْرَ مُسَافِحِينَ وَلاَ مُتَّخِذِي أَخْدَانٍ وَمَن يَكْفُرْ بِالإِيمَانِ فَقَدْ حَبِطَ عَمَلُهُ وَهُوَ فِي الآخِرَةِ مِنَ الْخَاسِرِينَ

امروز چیزهای پاکیزه برای شما حلال شده و طعام کسانی که اهل کتابند برای شما حلال و طعام شما برای آنان حلال است و [بر شما حلال است ازدواج با] زنان پاکدامن از مسلمان و زنان پاکدامن از کسانی که پیش از شما کتاب [آسمانی] به آنان داده شده به شرط آنکه مهر هایشان را به ایشان بدهید در حالی که خود پاکدامن باشید نه زناکار و نه آنکه زنان را در پنهانی دوست خود بگیرید و هر کس در ایمان خود شک کند قطعا عملش تباه شده و در آخرت از زیانکاران است

44 *Núr*, Light, 24:32:

وَأَنكِحُوا الأَيَامَى مِنكُمْ وَالصَّالِحِينَ مِنْ عِبَادِكُمْ وَإِمَائِكُمْ إِن يَكُونُوا فُقَرَاء يُغْنِهِمُ اللَّهُ مِن فَضْلِهِ وَاللَّهُ وَاسِعٌ عَلِيمٌ

بی‌همسران خود و غلامان و کنیزان درستکارتان را همسر دهید اگر تنگدستند خداوند آنان را از فضل خویش بی‌نیاز خواهد کرد و خدا گشایشگر داناست

45 *Baqara*, the Heifer, 2:221:

وَلاَ تَنكِحُواْ الْمُشْرِكَاتِ حَتَّى يُؤْمِنَّ وَلأَمَةٌ مُّؤْمِنَةٌ خَيْرٌ مِّن مُّشْرِكَةٍ وَلَوْ أَعْجَبَتْكُمْ وَلاَ تُنكِحُواْ الْمُشِرِكِينَ حَتَّى يُؤْمِنُواْ وَلَعَبْدٌ مُّؤْمِنٌ خَيْرٌ مِّن مُّشْرِكٍ وَلَوْ أَعْجَبَكُمْ أُوْلَـئِكَ يَدْعُونَ إِلَى النَّارِ وَاللّهُ يَدْعُوَ إِلَى الْجَنَّةِ وَالْمَغْفِرَةِ بِإِذْنِهِ وَيُبَيِّنُ آيَاتِهِ لِلنَّاسِ لَعَلَّهُمْ يَتَذَكَّرُونَ

و با زنان مشرک ازدواج مکنید تا ایمان بیاورند قطعا کنیز با ایمان بهتر از زن مشرک است هر چند [زیبایی] او شما را به شگفت آورد و به مردان مشرک زن مدهید تا ایمان بیاورند قطعا برده با ایمان بهتر از مرد آزاد مشرک است هر چند شما را به شگفت آورد آنان [شما را] به سوی آتش فرا می‌خوانند و خدا به فرمان خود [شما را] به سوی بهشت و آمرزش می‌خواند و آیات خود را برای مردم روشن می‌گرداند باشد که متذکر شوند

46 *Nisáa*, the Women, 4:3:
وَإِنْ خِفْتُمْ أَلاَّ تُقْسِطُوا فِي الْيَتَامَى فَانكِحُوا مَا طَابَ لَكُم مِّنَ النِّسَاء مَثْنَى وَثُلاَثَ وَرُبَاعَ فَإِنْ خِفْتُمْ أَلاَّ تَعْدِلُوا فَوَاحِدَةً أَوْ مَا مَلَكَتْ أَيْمَانُكُمْ ذَلِكَ أَدْنَى أَلاَّ تَعُولُوا

و اگر می‌ترسید که (بهنگام ازدواج با دختران یتیم،) عدالت را رعایت نکنید، (از ازدواج با آنان، چشم‌پوشی کنید و) با زنان پاک (دیگر) ازدواج نمائید، دو یا سه یا چهار همسر و اگر می‌ترسید عدالت را (درباره همسران متعدد) رعایت نکنید، تنها یک همسر بگیرید، و یا از زنانی که مالک آنهائید استفاده کنید، این کار، از ظلم و ستم بهتر جلوگیری می‌کند.

47 Deut. 24:1.
48 Matt. 5:31–2.
49 *Ahzáb*, the Confederates, 33:49:
يَا أَيُّهَا الَّذِينَ آمَنُوا إِذَا نَكَحْتُمُ الْمُؤْمِنَاتِ ثُمَّ طَلَّقْتُمُوهُنَّ مِن قَبْلِ أَن تَمَسُّوهُنَّ فَمَا لَكُمْ عَلَيْهِنَّ مِنْ عِدَّةٍ تَعْتَدُّونَهَا فَمَتِّعُوهُنَّ وَسَرِّحُوهُنَّ سَرَاحًا جَمِيلًا

ای کسانی که ایمان آورده‌اید! هنگامی که با زنان با ایمان ازدواج کردید و قبل از همبستر شدن طلاق دادید، عده‌ای برای آنها نیست که بخواهید حساب آن را نگاه دارید؛ آنها را با هدیه مناسبی بهره‌مند سازید و بطرز شایسته‌ای رهایشان کنید

50 *Baqara*, the Heifer, 2:229–30:
الطَّلَاقُ مَرَّتَانِ فَإِمْسَاكٌ بِمَعْرُوفٍ أَوْ تَسْرِيحٌ بِإِحْسَانٍ ...
فَإِن طَلَّقَهَا فَلاَ تَحِلُّ لَهُ مِن بَعْدُ حَتَّى تَنكِحَ زَوْجًا غَيْرَهُ فَإِن طَلَّقَهَا فَلاَ جُنَاحَ عَلَيْهِمَا أَن يَتَرَاجَعَا إِن ظَنَّا أَن يُقِيمَا حُدُودَ اللَّهِ وَتِلْكَ حُدُودُ اللَّهِ يُبَيِّنُهَا لِقَوْمٍ يَعْلَمُونَ

طلاق [رجعی] دو بار است پس از آن یا [باید زن را] بخوبی نگاه داشتن یا بشایستگی آزاد کردن...
و اگر [شوهر برای بار سوم] او را طلاق گفت پس از آن دیگر [آن زن] برای او حلال نیست تا اینکه با شوهری غیر از او ازدواج کند [و با او هم‌خوابگی نماید] پس اگر [شوهر دوم] وی را طلاق گفت اگر آن دو [همسر سابق] پندارند که حدود خدا را برپا می‌دارند گناهی بر آن دو نیست که به یکدیگر بازگردند و اینها حدود الهی احکام خدا است که آن را برای قومی که می‌دانند بیان می‌کند

51 Imam Malik, *Al-Muwatta*, Book 28, no. 28.7, p. 248.
52 *Baqara*, the Heifer, 2:231–2:
وَإِذَا طَلَّقْتُمُ النِّسَاء فَبَلَغْنَ أَجَلَهُنَّ فَأَمْسِكُوهُنَّ بِمَعْرُوفٍ أَوْ سَرِّحُوهُنَّ بِمَعْرُوفٍ وَلاَ تُمْسِكُوهُنَّ ضِرَارًا لَّتَعْتَدُوا وَمَن يَفْعَلْ ذَلِكَ فَقَدْ ظَلَمَ نَفْسَهُ وَلاَ تَتَّخِذُوا آيَاتِ اللَّهِ هُزُوًا وَاذْكُرُوا نِعْمَتَ اللَّهِ عَلَيْكُمْ وَمَا أَنزَلَ عَلَيْكُم مَّنَ الْكِتَابِ وَالْحِكْمَةِ يَعِظُكُم بِهِ وَاتَّقُوا اللَّهَ وَاعْلَمُوا أَنَّ اللَّهَ بِكُلِّ شَيْءٍ عَلِيمٌ
وَإِذَا طَلَّقْتُمُ النِّسَاء فَبَلَغْنَ أَجَلَهُنَّ فَلاَ تَعْضُلُوهُنَّ أَن يَنكِحْنَ أَزْوَاجَهُنَّ إِذَا تَرَاضَوْا بَيْنَهُم بِالْمَعْرُوفِ ذَلِكَ يُوعَظُ بِهِ مَن كَانَ مِنكُمْ يُؤْمِنُ بِاللَّهِ وَالْيَوْمِ الْآخِرِ ذَلِكُمْ أَزْكَى لَكُمْ وَأَطْهَرُ وَاللَّهُ يَعْلَمُ وَأَنتُمْ لاَ تَعْلَمُونَ

و چون آنان را طلاق گفتید و به پایان عده خویش رسیدند پس بخوبی نگاهشان دارید یا بخوبی آزادشان کنید و [به] برای [آزار و] زیان رساندن [به ایشان] نگاه مدارید تا [به حقوقشان] تعدی کنید و هر کس چنین کند قطعا بر خود ستم نموده است و آیات خدا را به ریشخند مگیرید و نعمت خدا را بر خود و آنچه را که از کتاب و حکمت بر شما نازل کرده و به [وسیله] آن به شما اندرز می‌دهد به یاد آورید و از خدا پروا داشته باشید و بدانید که خدا به هر چیزی داناست
و چون زنان را طلاق گفتید و عده خود را به پایان رساندند آنان را از ازدواج با همسران [سابق] خود چنانچه بخوبی با یکدیگر تراضی نمایند جلوگیری مکنید هر کس از شما به خدا و روز بازپسین ایمان دارد به این [دستورها] پند داده می‌شود [مراعات] این امر برای شما پربرکت‌تر و پاکیزه‌تر است و خدا می‌داند و شما نمی‌دانید

53 *Baqara*, the Heifer, 2:228:

وَالْمُطَلَّقَاتُ يَتَرَبَّصْنَ بِأَنفُسِهِنَّ ثَلَاثَةَ قُرُوءٍ وَلَا يَحِلُّ لَهُنَّ أَن يَكْتُمْنَ مَا خَلَقَ اللَّهُ فِي أَرْحَامِهِنَّ إِن كُنَّ يُؤْمِنَّ بِاللَّهِ وَالْيَوْمِ الْآخِرِ وَبُعُولَتُهُنَّ أَحَقُّ بِرَدِّهِنَّ فِي ذَٰلِكَ إِنْ أَرَادُوا إِصْلَاحًا وَلَهُنَّ مِثْلُ الَّذِي عَلَيْهِنَّ بِالْمَعْرُوفِ وَلِلرِّجَالِ عَلَيْهِنَّ دَرَجَةٌ وَاللَّهُ عَزِيزٌ حَكِيمٌ

و زنان طلاق داده شده باید مدت سه پاکی انتظار کشند و اگر به خدا و روز بازپسین ایمان دارند برای آنان روا نیست که آنچه را خداوند در رحم آنان آفریده پوشیده دارند و شوهرانشان اگر سر آشتی دارند به بازآوردن آنان در این [مدت] سزاوارترند و مانند همان [وظایفی] که بر عهده زنان است به طور شایسته به نفع آنان [بر عهده مردان] است و مردان بر آنان درجه برتری دارند و خداوند توانا و حکیم است

54 See also *Taláq*, Divorce, 65:4.
    Note 100 in Bahá'u'lláh, *The Kitáb-i-Aqdas*, p. 211.
55 I Tim. 4:1-3.
56 I Cor. 7:1-4.
57 I Cor. 7:8-11.
58 I Cor. 7:32-4.
59 *Ḥadíd*, Iron, 57:27:

ثُمَّ قَفَّيْنَا عَلَىٰ آثَارِهِم بِرُسُلِنَا وَقَفَّيْنَا بِعِيسَى ابْنِ مَرْيَمَ وَآتَيْنَاهُ الْإِنجِيلَ وَجَعَلْنَا فِي قُلُوبِ الَّذِينَ اتَّبَعُوهُ رَأْفَةً وَرَحْمَةً وَرَهْبَانِيَّةً ابْتَدَعُوهَا مَا كَتَبْنَاهَا عَلَيْهِمْ إِلَّا ابْتِغَاءَ رِضْوَانِ اللَّهِ فَمَا رَعَوْهَا حَقَّ رِعَايَتِهَا فَآتَيْنَا الَّذِينَ آمَنُوا مِنْهُمْ أَجْرَهُمْ وَكَثِيرٌ مِّنْهُمْ فَاسِقُونَ

سپس پیامبران دیگر خود را نیز بر طریقه آنان پی در پی فرستادیم ، و عیسی پسر مریم را از پی آنان آوردیم و به او انجیل را عطا کردیم ، و در دل های کسانی که از او پیروی کردند مهربانی و رحمت قرار دادیم . آنان رهبانیّت (عزلت برای عبادت) را از پیش خود درآوردند ، ما آن را در آیینشان مقرر نکردیم ولی به آن روی آوردند تا خشنودی خدا را بجویند ، اما حدّ و مرز آن را چنان که باید رعایت نکردند؛ پس به کسانی از آنان که ایمان آوردند اجرشان را عطا کردیم و بسیاری از آنان از مرز دین خارج شدند .

60 Bahá'u'lláh, Bishárát (Glad-Tidings), in *Tablets of Bahá'u'lláh Revealed after the Kitáb-i-Aqdas*, p. 24.
61 Bahá'u'lláh, Súriy-i-Haykal, para. 136, in Bahá'u'lláh, *The Summons of the Lord of Hosts*, p. 69.
62 Deut. 22:10-21.
63 Lev. 19:20.
64 Deut. 21:22-4.
65 I Tim. 2:9-15.
66 Titus 2:3-5.
67 I Pet. 3:1-7.

68 *Nūr*, Light, 24:31:

وَقُل لِّلْمُؤْمِنَاتِ يَغْضُضْنَ مِنْ أَبْصَارِهِنَّ وَيَحْفَظْنَ فُرُوجَهُنَّ وَلَا يُبْدِينَ زِينَتَهُنَّ إِلَّا مَا ظَهَرَ مِنْهَا وَلْيَضْرِبْنَ بِخُمُرِهِنَّ عَلَىٰ جُيُوبِهِنَّ وَلَا يُبْدِينَ زِينَتَهُنَّ إِلَّا لِبُعُولَتِهِنَّ أَوْ آبَائِهِنَّ أَوْ آبَاءِ بُعُولَتِهِنَّ أَوْ أَبْنَائِهِنَّ أَوْ أَبْنَاءِ بُعُولَتِهِنَّ أَوْ إِخْوَانِهِنَّ أَوْ بَنِي إِخْوَانِهِنَّ أَوْ بَنِي أَخَوَاتِهِنَّ أَوْ نِسَائِهِنَّ أَوْ مَا مَلَكَتْ أَيْمَانُهُنَّ أَوِ التَّابِعِينَ غَيْرِ أُولِي الْإِرْبَةِ مِنَ الرِّجَالِ أَوِ الطِّفْلِ الَّذِينَ لَمْ يَظْهَرُوا عَلَىٰ عَوْرَاتِ النِّسَاءِ وَلَا يَضْرِبْنَ بِأَرْجُلِهِنَّ لِيُعْلَمَ مَا يُخْفِينَ مِن زِينَتِهِنَّ وَتُوبُوا إِلَى اللَّهِ جَمِيعًا أَيُّهَ الْمُؤْمِنُونَ لَعَلَّكُمْ تُفْلِحُونَ

و به زنان با ایمان بگو دیدگان خود را [از هر نامحرمی] فرو بندند و پاکدامنی ورزند و زیورهای خود را آشکار نگردانند مگر آن چه که طبعا از آن پیداست و باید روسری خود را بر سینه خویش [فرو] اندازند و زیور هایشان را جز برای شوهرانشان یا پدرانشان یا پدران شوهرانشان یا پسرانشان یا پسران شوهرانشان یا برادرانشان یا پسران برادرانشان یا پسران خواهرانشان یا زنان [همکیش] خود یا کنیزانشان یا خدمتکاران مرد که [از زن] بی‌نیازند یا کودکانی که بر عورتهای زنان وقوف حاصل نکرده‌اند آشکار نکنند و پاهای خود را [به گونه‌ای به زمین] نکوبند تا آن چه از زینتشان نهفته می‌دارند معلوم گردد ای مؤمنان همگی [از مرد و زن] به درگاه خدا توبه کنید امید که رستگار شوید

69 *Aḥzāb*, the Confederates, 33:59:

يَا أَيُّهَا النَّبِيُّ قُل لِّأَزْوَاجِكَ وَبَنَاتِكَ وَنِسَاءِ الْمُؤْمِنِينَ يُدْنِينَ عَلَيْهِنَّ مِن جَلَابِيبِهِنَّ ذَٰلِكَ أَدْنَىٰ أَن يُعْرَفْنَ فَلَا يُؤْذَيْنَ وَكَانَ اللَّهُ غَفُورًا رَّحِيمًا

ای پیامبر! به همسران و دخترانت و زنان مؤمنان بگو: «جلبابها خود را بر خویش فروافکنند، این کار برای اینکه شناخته شوند و مورد آزار قرار نگیرند بهتر است؛ خداوند همواره آمرزنده رحیم است.

Al-Hillāli:
> O Prophet! Tell your wives and your daughters and the women of the believers to draw their cloaks (veils) all over their bodies (i.e. screen themselves completely except the eyes or one eye to see the way). That will be better, that they should be known (as free respectable women) so as not to be annoyed. And Allāh is Ever Oft-Forgiving, Most Merciful.

Amatul Rahmán Omar:
> Prophet! tell your wives, your daughters and women of the believers that (while going out of their houses) they should draw lower upon them the portions of their (loose) outer coverings from over their heads on to their bosoms (so as to veil therewith the arms, the neck, the hair and ornaments worn over them). This practice is more likely to help them to be distinguished (from other women who make a display of their beauty and ornamentation) and so saves them from trouble. God is Great Protector, Ever Merciful.

Dr Munir Munshey:
> O Prophet! Ask your wives and daughters and the women of the believers to wrap a loose outer garment completely around their bodies (leaving the face and the figure unobservable). That way they are more likely to be recognised and won´t be harassed. God is the most Forgiving and the most Merciful.

M. M. Pickthall:
> O Prophet! Tell thy wives and thy daughters and the women of the believers to draw their cloaks close round them (when they go abroad). That will be better, so that they may be recognised and not annoyed. God is ever Forgiving, Merciful."

Shakir:
> O Prophet! say to your wives and your daughters and the women of the believers that they let down upon them their over-garments; this will be more proper, that they may be known, and thus they will not be given trouble; and God is Forgiving, Merciful.

70 *Núr*, Light, 24:60:

وَالْقَوَاعِدُ مِنَ النِّسَاءِ اللَّاتِي لَا يَرْجُونَ نِكَاحًا فَلَيْسَ عَلَيْهِنَّ جُنَاحٌ أَن يَضَعْنَ ثِيَابَهُنَّ غَيْرَ مُتَبَرِّجَاتٍ بِزِينَةٍ وَأَن يَسْتَعْفِفْنَ خَيْرٌ لَّهُنَّ وَاللَّهُ سَمِيعٌ عَلِيمٌ

و بر زنان از کار افتاده‌ای که [دیگر] امید زناشویی ندارند گناهی نیست که پوشش خود را کنار نهند [به شرطی که] زینتی را آشکار نکنند و عفت ورزیدن برای آنها بهتر است و خدا شنوای داناست

71 *Núr*, Light, 24:23:

إِنَّ الَّذِينَ يَرْمُونَ الْمُحْصَنَاتِ الْغَافِلَاتِ الْمُؤْمِنَاتِ لُعِنُوا فِي الدُّنْيَا وَالْآخِرَةِ وَلَهُمْ عَذَابٌ عَظِيمٌ

بی‌گمان کسانی که به زنان پاکدامن بی‌خبر و با ایمان نسبت زنا می‌دهند در دنیا و آخرت لعنت‌شده‌اند و برای آنها عذابی سخت خواهد بود

72 *Núr*, Light, 24:4:

وَالَّذِينَ يَرْمُونَ الْمُحْصَنَاتِ ثُمَّ لَمْ يَأْتُوا بِأَرْبَعَةِ شُهَدَاءَ فَاجْلِدُوهُمْ ثَمَانِينَ جَلْدَةً وَلَا تَقْبَلُوا لَهُمْ شَهَادَةً أَبَدًا وَأُولَٰئِكَ هُمُ الْفَاسِقُونَ

و کسانی که نسبت زنا به زنان شوهردار می‌دهند سپس چهار گواه نمی‌آورند هشتاد تازیانه به آنان بزنید و هیچ‌گاه شهادتی از آنها نپذیرید و اینانند که خود فاسقند

73 *Núr*, Light, 24:6-9:

وَالَّذِينَ يَرْمُونَ أَزْوَاجَهُمْ وَلَمْ يَكُن لَّهُمْ شُهَدَاءُ إِلَّا أَنفُسُهُمْ فَشَهَادَةُ أَحَدِهِمْ أَرْبَعُ شَهَادَاتٍ بِاللَّهِ إِنَّهُ لَمِنَ الصَّادِقِينَ
وَالْخَامِسَةُ أَنَّ لَعْنَتَ اللَّهِ عَلَيْهِ إِن كَانَ مِنَ الْكَاذِبِينَ وَيَدْرَأُ
عَنْهَا الْعَذَابَ أَن تَشْهَدَ أَرْبَعَ شَهَادَاتٍ بِاللَّهِ إِنَّهُ لَمِنَ الْكَاذِبِينَ
وَالْخَامِسَةَ أَنَّ غَضَبَ اللَّهِ عَلَيْهَا إِن كَانَ مِنَ الصَّادِقِينَ

و کسانی که همسران خود را (به عمل منافی عفت) متهم می‌کنند، و گواهانی جز خودشان ندارند، هر یک از آنها باید چهار مرتبه به نام خدا شهادت دهد که از راستگویان است؛
و در پنجمین بار بگوید که لعنت خدا بر او باد اگر از دروغگویان باشد.
آن زن نیز می‌تواند کیفر (زنا) را از خود دور کند، به این طریق که چهار بار خدا را به شهادت طلبد که آن مرد (در این نسبتی که به او می‌دهد) از دروغگویان است.
و بار پنجم بگوید که غضب خدا بر او باد اگر آن مرد از راستگویان باشد.

74 *Nisáa*, the Women, 4:15-16:

وَاللَّاتِي يَأْتِينَ الْفَاحِشَةَ مِن نِّسَائِكُمْ فَاسْتَشْهِدُوا عَلَيْهِنَّ أَرْبَعَةً مِّنكُمْ فَإِن شَهِدُوا فَأَمْسِكُوهُنَّ فِي الْبُيُوتِ حَتَّىٰ يَتَوَفَّاهُنَّ الْمَوْتُ أَوْ يَجْعَلَ اللَّهُ لَهُنَّ سَبِيلًا
وَاللَّذَانِ يَأْتِيَانِهَا مِنكُمْ فَآذُوهُمَا فَإِن تَابَا وَأَصْلَحَا فَأَعْرِضُوا عَنْهُمَا إِنَّ اللَّهَ كَانَ تَوَّابًا رَّحِيمًا

و از زنان شما کسانی که مرتکب زنا می‌شوند چهار تن از میان خود بر آنان گواه گیرید پس اگر شهادت دادند آنان [=زنان] را در خانه‌ها نگاه دارید تا مرگشان فرا رسد یا خدا راهی برای آنان قرار دهد
و از میان شما دو تن را که مرتکب زشتکاری می‌شوند آزارشان دهید پس اگر توبه کردند و درستکار شدند از آنان صرف‌نظر کنید زیرا خداوند توبه‌پذیر مهربان است

Some translators such as *Al-Hillálí* translate this as 'two' i.e. the man and the woman. As details of the punishments are not provided some also assume that this opens the way for less severe legislative pronouncements.

75 *Núr*, Light, 24:2:

الزَّانِيَةُ وَالزَّانِي فَاجْلِدُوا كُلَّ وَاحِدٍ مِّنْهُمَا مِئَةَ جَلْدَةٍ وَلَا تَأْخُذْكُم بِهِمَا رَأْفَةٌ فِي دِينِ اللَّهِ إِن كُنتُمْ تُؤْمِنُونَ بِاللَّهِ وَالْيَوْمِ الْآخِرِ وَلْيَشْهَدْ عَذَابَهُمَا طَائِفَةٌ مِّنَ الْمُؤْمِنِينَ

هر یک از زن و مرد زناکار را صد تازیانه بزنید؛ و نباید رأفت (و محبت کاذب) نسبت به آن دو شما را از اجرای حکم الهی مانع شود، اگر به خدا و روز جزا ایمان دارید! و باید گروهی از مؤمنان مجازاتشان را مشاهده کنند!

76 J. M. Rodwell.

77 *Núr*, Light, 24:3:

الزَّانِي لَا يَنكِحُ إِلَّا زَانِيَةً أَوْ مُشْرِكَةً وَالزَّانِيَةُ لَا يَنكِحُهَا إِلَّا زَانٍ أَوْ مُشْرِكٌ وَحُرِّمَ ذَٰلِكَ عَلَى الْمُؤْمِنِينَ

مرد زناکار جز با زن زناکار یا مشرک ازدواج نمی‌کند؛ و زن زناکار را، جز مرد زناکار یا مشرک، به ازدواج خود درنمی‌آورد؛ و این کار بر مؤمنان حرام شده است!

78 *Núr*, Light, 24:26:

الْخَبِيثَاتُ لِلْخَبِيثِينَ وَالْخَبِيثُونَ لِلْخَبِيثَاتِ وَالطَّيِّبَاتُ لِلطَّيِّبِينَ وَالطَّيِّبُونَ لِلطَّيِّبَاتِ أُولَٰئِكَ مُبَرَّءُونَ مِمَّا يَقُولُونَ لَهُم مَّغْفِرَةٌ وَرِزْقٌ كَرِيمٌ

زنان ناپاک از آن مردان ناپاکند، و مردان ناپاک نیز به زنان ناپاک تعلق دارند؛ و زنان پاک از آن مردان پاک، و مردان پاک از آن زنان پاکند! اینان از نسبتهای ناروایی که (ناپاکان) به آنان می‌دهند مبرا هستند؛ و برای آنان آمرزش (الهی) و روزی پرارزشی است!

79 *Nisáa*, the Women, 4:34:

... فَالصَّالِحَاتُ قَانِتَاتٌ حَافِظَاتٌ لِّلْغَيْبِ بِمَا حَفِظَ اللَّهُ وَاللَّاتِي تَخَافُونَ نُشُوزَهُنَّ فَعِظُوهُنَّ وَاهْجُرُوهُنَّ فِي الْمَضَاجِعِ وَاضْرِبُوهُنَّ فَإِنْ أَطَعْنَكُمْ فَلَا تَبْغُوا عَلَيْهِنَّ سَبِيلًا إِنَّ اللَّهَ كَانَ عَلِيًّا كَبِيرًا

... زنان شایسته آنانند که مطیع و به حفظ الهی در نهان خویشتندار هستند، و زنانی که از نافرمانیشان نگرانید، باید نصیحتشان کنید و [سپس] در خوابگاهها از آنان دوری کنید [و سپس اگر لازم افتاد] آنان را ترک کنید آنگاه اگر از شما اطاعت کردند، دیگر بهانه جویی [و زیاده‌روی] نکنید، خداوند بلندمرتبه بزرگوار است

80 Malik Ghulam Farid (ed.), *The Holy Qur'án*, p. 201.
81 Bahá'u'lláh, *Gleanings from the Writings of Bahá'u'lláh*, LX, p. 118.
82 Shoghi Effendi, *The Advent of Divine Justice*, p. 25.
83 ibid. p. 28.
84 Lev. 10:9.
85 Prov. 20:1.
86 Isa. 5:11.
87 Isa. 5:22.
88 Luke 1:15.
89 I Cor. 5:11.
90 I Cor. 6:9–10.
91 Gal. 5:21.
92 Eph. 5:18.

93　Bahá'u'lláh, *The Kitáb-i-Aqdas*, para. 119, p. 62.
94　Note 144 in Bahá'u'lláh, *The Kitáb-i-Aqdas*, pp. 226-7.
95　ibid.
96　Exod. 21:23-36.
97　Lev. 24:17-21.
98　Deut. 19:21.
99　Matt. 5:21-2.
100　Matt. 4:44-5.
101　Matt. 22:17-21.
102　Shoghi Effendi, *The Promised Day Is Come*, pp. 119-20.
103　*Baqara*, the Heifer, 2:179:

وَلَكُمْ فِي الْقِصَاصِ حَيَاةٌ يَا أُولِيْ الْأَلْبَابِ لَعَلَّكُمْ تَتَّقُونَ

و برای شما در قصاص، حیات و زندگی است، ای صاحبان خرد! شاید شما تقوا پیشه کنید.

104　*Baqara*, the Heifer, 2:178:

يَا أَيُّهَا الَّذِينَ آمَنُواْ كُتِبَ عَلَيْكُمُ الْقِصَاصُ فِي الْقَتْلَى الْحُرُّ بِالْحُرِّ وَالْعَبْدُ بِالْعَبْدِ وَالْأُنثَى بِالْأُنثَى فَمَنْ عُفِيَ لَهُ مِنْ أَخِيهِ شَيْءٌ فَاتِّبَاعٌ بِالْمَعْرُوفِ وَأَدَاءٌ إِلَيْهِ بِإِحْسَانٍ ذَلِكَ تَخْفِيفٌ مِّن رَّبِّكُمْ وَرَحْمَةٌ فَمَنِ اعْتَدَى بَعْدَ ذَلِكَ فَلَهُ عَذَابٌ أَلِيمٌ

ای کسانی که ایمان آورده‌اید در باره کشتگان بر شما [حق] قصاص مقرر شده آزاد عوض آزاد و بنده عوض بنده و زن عوض زن و هر کس که از جانب برادر [دینی]اش [یعنی ولی مقتول] چیزی [از حق قصاص] به او گذشت‌شود [باید از گذشت ولی مقتول] به طور پسندیده پیروی کند و با [رعایت] احسان [خونبها را] به او بپردازد این [حکم] تخفیف و رحمتی از پروردگار شماست پس هر کس بعد از آن از اندازه درگذرد وی را عذابی دردناك است

> M. M. Pickthall:
> O ye who believe! Retaliation is prescribed for you in the matter of the murdered...
>
> M. Muhammad Ali:
> O ye who believe, retaliation is prescribed for you in the matter of the slain...
>
> Al-Hilláli:
> O ye who believe! Al-Qisás (the Law of Equality in punishment) is prescribed for you in case of murder...

105　*Baqara*, the Heifer, 2:194:

الشَّهْرُ الْحَرَامُ بِالشَّهْرِ الْحَرَامِ وَالْحُرُمَاتُ قِصَاصٌ فَمَنِ اعْتَدَى عَلَيْكُمْ فَاعْتَدُواْ عَلَيْهِ بِمِثْلِ مَا اعْتَدَى عَلَيْكُمْ وَاتَّقُواْ اللَّهَ وَاعْلَمُواْ أَنَّ اللَّهَ مَعَ الْمُتَّقِينَ

این ماه حرام در برابر آن ماه حرام است و [هتك] حرمتها قصاص دارد پس هر کس بر شما تعدی کرد همان گونه که بر شما تعدی کرده بر او تعدی کنید و از خدا پروا بدارید و بدانید که خدا با تقواپیشگان است

> Al-Hilláli:
> The Sacred month is for the sacred month, and for the prohibited things, there is the Law of equality (*Qisás*). Then whoever transgresses the prohibition against you, you transgress likewise against him, and know that God is with the pious.

106 *Naḥl*, Bees, 16:126-7:

وَإِنْ عَاقَبْتُمْ فَعَاقِبُوا بِمِثْلِ مَا عُوقِبْتُم بِهِ وَلَئِن صَبَرْتُمْ لَهُوَ خَيْرٌ لِّلصَّابِرِينَ
وَاصْبِرْ وَمَا صَبْرُكَ إِلَّا بِاللَّهِ وَلَا تَحْزَنْ عَلَيْهِمْ وَلَا تَكُ فِي ضَيْقٍ مِّمَّا يَمْكُرُونَ

و هر گاه خواستید مجازات کنید، تنها بمقداری که به شما تعدی شده کیفر دهید! و اگر شکیبایی کنید، این کار برای شکیبایان بهتر است.

صبر کن، و صبر تو فقط برای خدا و به توفیق خدا باشد! و بخاطر (کارهای) آنها، اندوهگین و دلسرد مشو! و از توطئه‌های آنها، در تنگنا قرار مگیر!

> M. M. Pickthall:
> If ye punish, then punish with the like of that wherewith ye were afflicted. But if ye endure patiently, verily it is better for the patient.
> Endure that patiently. Thine endurance is only by God. Grieve not for them, and be not in distress because of that which they devise.
>
> J. M. Rodwell:
> If ye make reprisals, then make them to the same extent that ye were injured: but if ye can endure patiently, best will it be for the patiently enduring.
> Endure then with patience. But thy patient endurance must be sought in none by God. And be not grieved about the infidels, and be not troubled at their devises; for God is with those who fear him and do good deeds.

107 Bahá'u'lláh, Súriy-i-Haykal, para. 213, in Bahá'u'lláh, *The Summons of the Lord of Hosts*, p. 110.
108 'Abdu'l-Bahá, *Selections from the Writings of 'Abdu'l-Baha*, no. 35, p. 73.
109 Matt. 10:34-6.
110 'Abdu'l-Bahá, *Some Answered Questions*, ch. 7, pp. 18-21.
111 *An'ám*, Cattle, 6:151:

وَلَا تَقْتُلُوا أَوْلَادَكُم مِّنْ إِمْلَاقٍ ۖ نَّحْنُ نَرْزُقُكُمْ وَإِيَّاهُمْ ...
وَلَا تَقْتُلُوا النَّفْسَ الَّتِي حَرَّمَ اللَّهُ إِلَّا بِالْحَقِّ ۚ ذَٰلِكُمْ وَصَّاكُم بِهِ لَعَلَّكُمْ تَعْقِلُونَ

... و فرزندانتان را در اثر تنگدستی مکشید ، زیرا ماییم که به شما و آنان روزی می دهیم ، ...و انسانی را که خدا کشتن او را حرام کرده است جز به حق مکشید . اینهاست که خدا شما را به آن سفارش کرده است ، باشد که دریابید

112 *Baqara*, the Heifer, 2:256:

لَا إِكْرَاهَ فِي الدِّينِ ۖ قَد تَّبَيَّنَ الرُّشْدُ مِنَ الْغَيِّ ۚ فَمَن يَكْفُرْ بِالطَّاغُوتِ وَيُؤْمِن بِاللَّهِ فَقَدِ اسْتَمْسَكَ بِالْعُرْوَةِ الْوُثْقَىٰ لَا انفِصَامَ لَهَا ۗ وَاللَّهُ سَمِيعٌ عَلِيمٌ

در دین هیچ اجباری نیست و راه از بیراهه بخوبی آشکار شده است پس هر کس به طاغوت کفر ورزد و به خدا ایمان آورد به یقین به دستاویزی استوار که آن را گسستن نیست چنگ زده است و خداوند شنوای داناست

113 *Anfál*, the Spoils of War, 8:61:

وَإِن جَنَحُوا لِلسَّلْمِ فَاجْنَحْ لَهَا وَتَوَكَّلْ عَلَى اللَّهِ ۚ إِنَّهُ هُوَ السَّمِيعُ الْعَلِيمُ

و اگر تمایل به صلح نشان دهند، تو نیز از در صلح درآی؛ و بر خدا توکل کن، که او شنوا و داناست!

114 *Yūnus*, Jonah, 10:99-100:

وَلَوْ شَاءَ رَبُّكَ لَآمَنَ مَن فِي الْأَرْضِ كُلُّهُمْ جَمِيعًا أَفَأَنتَ تُكْرِهُ النَّاسَ حَتَّىٰ يَكُونُوا مُؤْمِنِينَ
وَمَا كَانَ لِنَفْسٍ أَن تُؤْمِنَ إِلَّا بِإِذْنِ اللَّهِ وَيَجْعَلُ الرِّجْسَ عَلَى الَّذِينَ لَا يَعْقِلُونَ

و اگر پروردگار تو می‌خواست، تمام کسانی که روی زمین هستند، همگی به(اجبار) ایمان می‌آوردند؛ آیا تو می‌خواهی مردم را مجبور سازی که ایمان بیاورند؟! (ایمان اجباری چه سودی دارد؟!)
(اما) هیچ کس نمی‌تواند ایمان بیاورد، جز به فرمان خدا (و توفیق و یاری و هدایت او)! و پلیدی (کفر و گناه) را بر کسانی قرار می‌دهد که نمی‌اندیشند.

115 *Ḥajj*, the Pilgrimage, 22:67-9:

لِكُلِّ أُمَّةٍ جَعَلْنَا مَنسَكًا هُمْ نَاسِكُوهُ فَلَا يُنَازِعُنَّكَ فِي الْأَمْرِ وَادْعُ إِلَىٰ رَبِّكَ إِنَّكَ لَعَلَىٰ هُدًى مُّسْتَقِيمٍ
وَإِن جَادَلُوكَ فَقُلِ اللَّهُ أَعْلَمُ بِمَا تَعْمَلُونَ
اللَّهُ يَحْكُمُ بَيْنَكُمْ يَوْمَ الْقِيَامَةِ فِيمَا كُنتُمْ فِيهِ تَخْتَلِفُونَ

برای هر امتی عبادتی قرار دادیم، تا آن عبادت را (در پیشگاه خدا) انجام دهند؛ پس نباید در این امر با تو به نزاع برخیزند! بسوی پروردگارت دعوت کن، که بر هدایت مستقیم قرار داری (و راه راست همین است که تو می‌پویی).
و اگر آنان با تو به جدال برخیزند، بگو: «خدا از کارهایی که شما انجام می‌دهید آگاه‌تر است!
خدا روز قیامت در مورد آنچه با یکدیگر در آن اختلاف می‌کردید داوری خواهد کرد

116 *Nisáa*, the Women, 4:94:

يَا أَيُّهَا الَّذِينَ آمَنُوا إِذَا ضَرَبْتُمْ فِي سَبِيلِ اللَّهِ فَتَبَيَّنُوا وَلَا تَقُولُوا لِمَنْ أَلْقَىٰ إِلَيْكُمُ السَّلَامَ لَسْتَ مُؤْمِنًا تَبْتَغُونَ عَرَضَ الْحَيَاةِ الدُّنْيَا فَعِندَ اللَّهِ مَغَانِمُ كَثِيرَةٌ كَذَٰلِكَ كُنتُم مِّن قَبْلُ فَمَنَّ اللَّهُ عَلَيْكُمْ فَتَبَيَّنُوا إِنَّ اللَّهَ كَانَ بِمَا تَعْمَلُونَ خَبِيرًا

ای کسانی که ایمان آورده‌اید! هنگامی که در راه خدا گام می‌زنید (و به سفری برای جهاد می‌روید)، تحقیق کنید! و بخاطر اینکه سرمایه ناپایدار دنیا (و غنایمی) به دست آورید، به کسی که اظهار صلح و اسلام می‌کند نگویید: «مسلمان نیستی» زیرا غنیمتهای فراوانی (برای شما) نزد خداست. شما قبلا چنین بودید؛ و خداوند بر شما منت نهاد (و هدایت شدید). پس، (بشکرانه این نعمت بزرگ،) تحقیق کنید! خداوند به آنچه انجام می‌دهید آگاه است

117 *Má'ida*, the Table Spread, 5:32:

مِنْ أَجْلِ ذَٰلِكَ كَتَبْنَا عَلَىٰ بَنِي إِسْرَائِيلَ أَنَّهُ مَن قَتَلَ نَفْسًا بِغَيْرِ نَفْسٍ أَوْ فَسَادٍ فِي الْأَرْضِ فَكَأَنَّمَا قَتَلَ النَّاسَ جَمِيعًا وَمَنْ أَحْيَاهَا فَكَأَنَّمَا أَحْيَا النَّاسَ جَمِيعًا وَلَقَدْ جَاءَتْهُمْ رُسُلُنَا بِالْبَيِّنَاتِ ثُمَّ إِنَّ كَثِيرًا مِّنْهُم بَعْدَ ذَٰلِكَ فِي الْأَرْضِ لَمُسْرِفُونَ

به همین جهت، بر بنی اسرائیل مقرر داشتیم که هر کس، انسانی را بدون ارتکاب قتل یا فساد در روی زمین بکشد، چنان است که گویی همه انسانها را کشته؛ و هر کس، انسانی را از مرگ رهایی بخشد، چنان است که گویی همه مردم را زنده کرده است. و رسولان ما، دلایل روشن برای بنی اسرائیل آوردند، اما بسیاری از آنها، پس از آن در روی زمین، تعدی و اسراف کردند.

118 *Baqara*, the Heifer, 2:244:

وَقَاتِلُوا فِي سَبِيلِ اللَّهِ وَاعْلَمُوا أَنَّ اللَّهَ سَمِيعٌ عَلِيمٌ

و در راه خدا کارزار کنید و بدانید که خداوند شنوای داناست

119 *Nisáa*, the Women, 4:95:

NOTES AND REFERENCES

لاَ يَسْتَوِي الْقَاعِدُونَ مِنَ الْمُؤْمِنِينَ غَيْرُ أُولِي الضَّرَرِ وَالْمُجَاهِدُونَ فِي سَبِيلِ اللّهِ بِأَمْوَالِهِمْ وَأَنفُسِهِمْ فَضَّلَ اللّهُ الْمُجَاهِدِينَ بِأَمْوَالِهِمْ وَأَنفُسِهِمْ عَلَى الْقَاعِدِينَ دَرَجَةً وَكُلاًّ وَعَدَ اللّهُ الْحُسْنَى وَفَضَّلَ اللّهُ الْمُجَاهِدِينَ عَلَى الْقَاعِدِينَ أَجْرًا عَظِيمًا

(هرگز) افراد باایمانی که بدون بیماری و ناراحتی، از جهاد بازنشستند، با مجاهدانی که در راه خدا با مال و جان خود جهاد کردند، یکسان نیستند! خداوند، مجاهدانی را که با مال و جان خود جهاد نمودند، بر قاعدان (ترک‌کنندگان جهاد) برتری مهمی بخشیده...

120 *Anfál*, the Spoils of War, 8:65:

يَا أَيُّهَا النَّبِيُّ حَرِّضْ الْمُؤْمِنِينَ عَلَى الْقِتَالِ إِن يَكُن مِّنكُمْ عِشْرُونَ صَابِرُونَ يَغْلِبُواْ مِئَتَيْنِ وَإِن يَكُن مِّنكُم مِّئَةٌ يَغْلِبُواْ أَلْفًا مِّنَ الَّذِينَ كَفَرُواْ بِأَنَّهُمْ قَوْمٌ لاَّ يَفْقَهُونَ

ای پیامبر مؤمنان را به جهاد برانگیز اگر از [میان] شما بیست تن شکیبا باشند بر دویست تن چیره می‌شوند و اگر از شما یکصد تن باشند بر هزار تن از کافران پیروز می‌گردند چرا که آنان قومی‌اند که نمی‌فهمند

121 *Anfál,* the Spoils of War, 8:39:

وَقَاتِلُوهُمْ حَتَّى لاَ تَكُونَ فِتْنَةٌ وَيَكُونَ الدِّينُ كُلُّهُ لِلّهِ فَإِنِ انتَهَوْاْ ...

و با آنان بجنگید تا فتنه‌ای بر جای نماند و دین یکسره از آن خدا گردد ...

122 *Baqara*, the Heifer, 2:216-17:

كُتِبَ عَلَيْكُمُ الْقِتَالُ وَهُوَ كُرْهٌ لَّكُمْ وَعَسَى أَن تَكْرَهُواْ شَيْئًا وَهُوَ خَيْرٌ لَّكُمْ وَعَسَى أَن تُحِبُّواْ شَيْئًا وَهُوَ شَرٌّ لَّكُمْ وَاللّهُ يَعْلَمُ وَأَنتُمْ لاَ تَعْلَمُونَ
يَسْأَلُونَكَ عَنِ الشَّهْرِ الْحَرَامِ قِتَالٍ فِيهِ قُلْ قِتَالٌ فِيهِ كَبِيرٌ وَصَدٌّ عَن سَبِيلِ اللّهِ وَكُفْرٌ بِهِ وَالْمَسْجِدِ الْحَرَامِ وَإِخْرَاجُ أَهْلِهِ مِنْهُ أَكْبَرُ عِندَ اللّهِ وَالْفِتْنَةُ أَكْبَرُ مِنَ الْقَتْلِ وَلاَ يَزَالُونَ يُقَاتِلُونَكُمْ حَتَّىَ يَرُدُّوكُمْ عَن دِينِكُمْ إِنِ اسْتَطَاعُواْ وَمَن يَرْتَدِدْ مِنكُمْ عَن دِينِهِ فَيَمُتْ وَهُوَ كَافِرٌ فَأُوْلَئِكَ حَبِطَتْ أَعْمَالُهُمْ فِي الدُّنْيَا وَالآخِرَةِ وَأُوْلَئِكَ أَصْحَابُ النَّارِ هُمْ فِيهَا خَالِدُونَ

جهاد در راه خدا، بر شما مقرر شده، در حالی که برایتان ناخوشایند است. چه بسا چیزی را خوش نداشته باشید، حال آنکه خیر شما در آن است. و یا چیزی را دوست داشته باشید، حال آنکه شر شما در آن است. و خدا می‌داند، و شما نمی‌دانید.
از تو، درباره جنگ کردن در ماه حرام، سؤال می‌کنند، بگو: جنگ در آن، (گناهی) بزرگ است، ولی جلوگیری از راه خدا (و گرایش مردم به آیین حق) و کفر ورزیدن نسبت به او و هتک احترام مسجد الحرام، و اخراج ساکنان آن، نزد خداوند مهمتر از آن است، و ایجاد فتنه، (و محیط نامساعد، که مردم را به کفر، تشویق و از ایمان باز می‌دارد) حتی از قتل بالاتر است. و مشرکان، پیوسته با شما می‌جنگند، تا اگر بتوانند شما را از آیینتان برگردانند، ولی کسی که از آیینش برگردد، و در حال کفر بمیرد، تمام اعمال نیک (گذشته) او، در دنیا و آخرت، بر باد می‌رود، و آنان اهل دوزخند، و همیشه در آن خواهند بود.

123 *Tauba*, Repentance; or *Baráat*, Immunity, 9:5:

... فَاقْتُلُواْ الْمُشْرِكِينَ حَيْثُ وَجَدتُّمُوهُمْ وَخُذُوهُمْ وَاحْصُرُوهُمْ وَاقْعُدُواْ لَهُمْ كُلَّ مَرْصَدٍ فَإِن تَابُواْ وَأَقَامُواْ الصَّلاَةَ وَآتَوُاْ الزَّكَاةَ فَخَلُّواْ سَبِيلَهُمْ إِنَّ اللّهَ غَفُورٌ رَّحِيمٌ

... مشرکان را هر کجا یافتید بکشید و آنان را دستگیر کنید و به محاصره درآورید و در هر کمینگاهی به کمین آنان بنشینید پس اگر توبه کردند و نماز برپا داشتند و زکات دادند راه برایشان گشاده گردانید زیرا خدا آمرزنده مهربان است

124 *Muhammad* (the Prophet), 47:4:

فَإِذَا لَقِيتُمُ الَّذِينَ كَفَرُوا فَضَرْبَ الرِّقَابِ حَتَّى إِذَا أَثْخَنتُمُوهُمْ فَشُدُّوا الْوَثَاقَ فَإِمَّا مَنًّا بَعْدُ وَإِمَّا فِدَاء حَتَّى تَضَعَ الْحَرْبُ أَوْزَارَهَا ذَلِكَ وَلَوْ يَشَاءُ اللَّهُ لَانتَصَرَ مِنْهُمْ وَلَكِن لِّيَبْلُوَ بَعْضَكُم بِبَعْضٍ وَالَّذِينَ قُتِلُوا فِي سَبِيلِ اللَّهِ فَلَن يُضِلَّ أَعْمَالَهُمْ

پس چون با کسانی که کفر ورزیده‌اند برخورد کنید گردنها[یشان] را بزنید تا چون آنان را [در کشتار] از پای درآوردید پس [اسیران را] استوار در بند کشید سپس یا [بر آنان] منت نهید [و آزادشان کنید] و یا فدیه [و عوض از ایشان بگیرید] تا در جنگ اسلحه بر زمین گذاشته شود این است [دستور خدا] و اگر خدا می‌خواست از ایشان انتقام می‌کشید ولی [فرمان پیکار داد] تا برخی از شما را به وسیله برخی [دیگر] بیازماید و کسانی که در راه خدا کشته شده‌اند هرگز کار هایشان را ضایع نمی‌کند

125 *Tauba*, Repentance; or *Baráat*, Immunity, 9:73:

يَا أَيُّهَا النَّبِيُّ جَاهِدِ الْكُفَّارَ وَالْمُنَافِقِينَ وَاغْلُظْ عَلَيْهِمْ وَمَأْوَاهُمْ جَهَنَّمُ وَبِئْسَ الْمَصِيرُ

ای پیامبر با کافران و منافقان جهاد کن و بر آنان سخت بگیر و جایگاهشان دوزخ است و چه بد سرانجامی است

(See also 9:123.)

126 *Anfál*, the Spoils of War, 8:57-8:

فَإِمَّا تَثْقَفَنَّهُمْ فِي الْحَرْبِ فَشَرِّدْ بِهِم مَّنْ خَلْفَهُمْ لَعَلَّهُمْ يَذَّكَّرُونَ وَإِمَّا تَخَافَنَّ مِن قَوْمٍ خِيَانَةً فَانبِذْ إِلَيْهِمْ عَلَى سَوَاء إِنَّ اللَّهَ لاَ يُحِبُّ الْخَائِنِينَ

پس اگر در جنگ بر آنان دست‌یافتی با [عقوبت] آنان کسانی را که در پی ایشانند تاروماز کن با شد که عبرت گیرند

و اگر از گروهی بیم خیانت داری [پیمانشان را] به سویشان بینداز [تا طرفین] به طور یکسان [بدانند که پیمان گسسته است] زیرا خدا خائنان را دوست نمی‌دارد

127 Poll tax imposed on Jews and Christians that replaced tithing (*zakát*), and participation in *jihád*.

128 *Tauba*, Repentance; or *Baráat*, Immunity, 9:29:

قَاتِلُوا الَّذِينَ لاَ يُؤْمِنُونَ بِاللّهِ وَلاَ بِالْيَوْمِ الآخِرِ وَلاَ يُحَرِّمُونَ مَا حَرَّمَ اللّهُ وَرَسُولُهُ وَلاَ يَدِينُونَ دِينَ الْحَقِّ مِنَ الَّذِينَ أُوتُواْ الْكِتَابَ حَتَّى يُعْطُواْ الْجِزْيَةَ عَن يَدٍ وَهُمْ صَاغِرُونَ

با کسانی از اهل کتاب که به خدا و روز بازپسین ایمان نمی‌آورند و آنچه را خدا و فرستاده‌اش حرام گردانیده‌اند حرام نمی‌دارند و متدین به دین حق نمی‌گردند کارزار کنید تا با [کمال] خواری به دست خود جزیه دهند

129 *Tauba*, Repentance; or *Baráat*, Immunity, 9:36:

... وَقَاتِلُواْ الْمُشْرِكِينَ كَآفَّةً كَمَا يُقَاتِلُونَكُمْ كَآفَّةً وَاعْلَمُواْ أَنَّ اللّهَ مَعَ الْمُتَّقِينَ

... و همگی با مشرکان بجنگید چنانکه آنان همگی با شما می‌جنگند و بدانید که خدا با پرهیزگاران است

130 Baha'u'lláh, *Bishárát* (Glad-Tidings), in *Tablets of Bahá'u'lláh Revealed after the Kitáb-i-Aqdas*, p. 21.
131 Bahá'u'lláh, *Epistle to the Son of the Wolf*, p. 25.
132 Bahá'u'lláh, *Gleanings from the Writings of Bahá'u'lláh*, CXXXIX, pp. 303-4.
133 Note 87 (quoting Shoghi Effendi) in Bahá'u'lláh, *The Kitab-i-Aqdas*, p. 204.

NOTES AND REFERENCES

134 A recent example that made the headlines illustrates this issue (the individual in question was eventually freed following international pressure): Ibrahim was sentenced to 100 lashes for adultery and to death for apostasy this month. She told a court in Khartoum that she had been brought up as a Christian, and refused to renounce her faith. She and Wani married in 2011, but the court ruled that the union was invalid and that Ibrahim was guilty of adultery. Ibrahim, a graduate of Sudan University's school of medicine, has been told that her death sentence will be deferred for two years to allow her to nurse her baby (Harriet Sherwood, *The Guardian*, 30 May 2014).

135 *Muhammad* (the Prophet), 47:25:

إِنَّ الَّذِينَ ارْتَدُّوا عَلَى أَدْبَارِهِم مِّن بَعْدِ مَا تَبَيَّنَ لَهُمُ الْهُدَى الشَّيْطَانُ سَوَّلَ لَهُمْ وَأَمْلَى لَهُمْ

بی‌گمان کسانی که پس از آنکه [راه] هدایت بر آنان روشن شد [به حقیقت] پشت کردند شیطان آنان را فریفت و به آرزوهای دور و درازشان انداخت

136 Lev. 24:16.
137 John 10:32–3.
138 Martin Luther, *On the Jews and Their Lies*, Part X.
139 *Baqara*, the Heifer, 2:88:

وَقَالُوا قُلُوبُنَا غُلْفٌ بَل لَّعَنَهُمُ اللَّه بِكُفْرِهِمْ فَقَلِيلًا مَّا يُؤْمِنُونَ

گفتند: دلهای ما در غلاف است! خداوند آنها را به خاطر کفرشان، از رحمت خود دور ساخته، (به همین دلیل، چیزی درک نمی‌کنند؛) و کمتر ایمان می‌آورند.

140 *Nisáa*, the Women, 4:155–6:

فَبِمَا نَقْضِهِم مِّيثَاقَهُمْ وَكُفْرِهِم بآيَاتِ اللَّهِ وَقَتْلِهِمُ الأَنبِيَاءَ بِغَيْرِ حَقٍّ وَقَوْلِهِمْ قُلُوبُنَا غُلْفٌ بَلْ طَبَعَ اللَّهُ عَلَيْهَا بِكُفْرِهِمْ فَلاَ يُؤْمِنُونَ إِلاَّ قَلِيلاً
وَبِكُفْرِهِم ...

پس به [سزای] پیمان‌شکنی‌شان و انکارشان نسبت به آیات خدا و کشتار ناحق آنان [از] انبیا و گفتارشان که دلهای ما در غلاف است بلکه خدا به خاطر کفرشان بر دلهایشان مهر زده و در نتیجه جز شماری اندک [از ایشان] ایمان نمی‌آورند
و [نیز] به سزای کفرشان ...

141 *Ma'ida*, the Table Spread, 5:64:

وَقَالَتِ الْيَهُودُ يَدُ اللّهِ مَغْلُولَةٌ غُلَّتْ أَيْدِيهِمْ وَلُعِنُواْ بِمَا قَالُواْ بَلْ يَدَاهُ مَبْسُوطَتَانِ يُنفِقُ كَيْفَ يَشَاءُ وَلَيَزِيدَنَّ كَثِيرًا مِّنْهُم مَّا أُنزِلَ إِلَيْكَ مِن رَّبِّكَ طُغْيَانًا وَكُفْرًا وَأَلْقَيْنَا بَيْنَهُمُ الْعَدَاوَةَ وَالْبَغْضَاء إِلَى يَوْمِ الْقِيَامَةِ كُلَّمَا أَوْقَدُواْ نَارًا لِّلْحَرْبِ أَطْفَأَهَا اللّهُ وَيَسْعَوْنَ فِي الأَرْضِ فَسَادًا وَاللّهُ لاَ يُحِبُّ الْمُفْسِدِينَ

و یهود گفتند دست خدا بسته است دست‌های خودشان بسته باد و به [سزای] آنچه گفتند از رحمت خدا دور شوند بلکه هر دو دست او گشاده است هر گونه بخواهد می‌بخشد و قطعا آنچه از جانب پروردگارت به سوی تو فرود آمده بر طغیان و کفر بسیاری از ایشان خواهد افزود و تا روز قیامت میانشان دشمنی و کینه افکندیم هر بار که آتشی برای پیکار برافروختند خدا آن را خاموش ساخت و در زمین برای فساد می‌کوشند و خدا مفسدان را دوست نمی‌دارد

142 'Abdu'l-Bahá, *Selections from the Writings of 'Abdu'l-Bahá*, no. 190, p. 224.
143 Deut. 14:8.

144 Deut. 18:7.
145 Lev. 11:9-12.
146 Acts 15:28-9.
147 *An'ám*, Cattle, 6:145 (also, *Má'ida*, the Table Spread, 5:3; *Naḥl*, Bees, 16:115):

قُل لاَّ أَجِدُ فِي مَا أُوْحِيَ إِلَيَّ مُحَرَّمًا عَلَى طَاعِمٍ يَطْعَمُهُ إِلاَّ أَن يَكُونَ مَيْتَةً أَوْ دَمًا مَّسْفُوحًا أَوْ لَحْمَ خِنزِيرٍ فَإِنَّهُ رِجْسٌ أَوْ فِسْقًا أُهِلَّ لِغَيْرِ اللّهِ بِهِ فَمَنِ اضْطُرَّ غَيْرَ بَاغٍ وَلاَ عَادٍ فَإِنَّ رَبَّكَ غَفُورٌ رَّحِيمٌ

بگو: «در آنچه بر من وحی شده، هیچ غذای حرامی نمی‌یابم، بجز اینکه مردار باشد، یا خونی که (از بدن حیوان) بیرون ریخته، یا گوشت خوک ـ که اینها همه پلیدند ـ یا حیوانی که به گناه، هنگام سر بریدن، نام غیر خدا (نام بتها) بر آن برده شده است.» اما کسی که مضطر (به خوردن این محرمات) شود، بی آنکه خواهان لذت باشد و یا زیاده روی کند (گناهی بر او نیست)؛ زیرا پروردگارت، آمرزنده مهربان است.

148 *Má'ida*, the Table Spread, 5:3:

حُرِّمَتْ عَلَيْكُمُ الْمَيْتَةُ وَالْدَّمُ وَلَحْمُ الْخِنْزِيرِ وَمَا أُهِلَّ لِغَيْرِ اللّهِ بِهِ وَالْمُنْخَنِقَةُ وَالْمَوْقُوذَةُ وَالْمُتَرَدِّيَةُ وَالنَّطِيحَةُ وَمَا أَكَلَ السَّبُعُ إِلاَّ مَا ذَكَّيْتُمْ وَمَا ذُبِحَ عَلَى النُّصُبِ وَأَن تَسْتَقْسِمُواْ بِالأَزْلاَمِ ذَلِكُمْ فِسْقٌ الْيَوْمَ يَئِسَ الَّذِينَ كَفَرُواْ مِن دِينِكُمْ فَلاَ تَخْشَوْهُمْ وَاخْشَوْنِ الْيَوْمَ أَكْمَلْتُ لَكُمْ دِينَكُمْ وَأَتْمَمْتُ عَلَيْكُمْ نِعْمَتِي وَرَضِيتُ لَكُمُ الإِسْلاَمَ دِينًا فَمَنِ اضْطُرَّ فِي مَخْمَصَةٍ غَيْرَ مُتَجَانِفٍ لِّإِثْمٍ فَإِنَّ اللّهَ غَفُورٌ رَّحِيمٌ

بر شما حرام شده است مردار و خون و گوشت‌خوک و آنچه به نام غیر خدا کشته شده باشد و [حیوان حلال گوشت] خفه شده و به چوب مرده و از بلندی افتاده و به ضرب شاخ مرده و آنچه درنده از آن خورده باشد مگر آنچه را [که زنده دریافته و خود] سر ببرید و [همچنین] آنچه برای بتان سر بریده شده و [نیز] قسمت کردن شما [چیزی را] به وسیله تیرهای قرعه این [کارها همه] نافرمانی [خدا]ست امروز کسانی که کافر شده‌اند از [کارشکنی در] دین شما نومید گردیده‌اند پس از ایشان مترسید و از من بترسید امروز دین شما را برایتان کامل و نعمتخود را بر شما تمام گردانیدیم و اسلام را برای شما [به عنوان] آیینی برگزیدم و هر کس دچار گرسنگی شود بی‌آنکه به گناه متمایل باشد [اگر از آنچه منع شده است بخورد] بی تردید خدا آمرزنده مهربان است

149 *Má'ida*, the Table Spread, 5:5:

الْيَوْمَ أُحِلَّ لَكُمُ الطَّيِّبَاتُ وَطَعَامُ الَّذِينَ أُوتُواْ الْكِتَابَ حِلٌّ لَّكُمْ وَطَعَامُكُمْ حِلُّ لَّهُمْ ...

امروز چیزهای پاکیزه برای شما حلال شده و طعام کسانی که اهل کتابند برای شما حلال و طعام شما برای آنان حلال است ...

150 *Naḥl*, Bees, 16:116:

وَلاَ تَقُولُواْ لِمَا تَصِفُ أَلْسِنَتُكُمُ الْكَذِبَ هَذَا حَلاَلٌ وَهَذَا حَرَامٌ لِّتَفْتَرُواْ عَلَى اللّهِ الْكَذِبَ إِنَّ الَّذِينَ يَفْتَرُونَ عَلَى اللّهِ الْكَذِبَ لاَ يُفْلِحُونَ

و برای آنچه زبان شما به دروغ می‌پردازد مگویید این حلال است و آن حرام تا بر خدا دروغ بندید زیرا کسانی که بر خدا دروغ می‌بندند رستگار نمی‌شوند

151 Baháʼuʼlláh, *The Kitáb-i-Aqdas*, para. 75, p. 47.
152 ʻAbduʼl-Bahá, *Some Answered Questions*, ch. 20, p. 93.
153 Exod. 22:1-4.
154 I Cor. 6:10.
155 Luke 6:29.

156 *Ma'ida*, the Table Spread, 5:38-9:

وَالسَّارِقُ وَالسَّارِقَةُ فَاقْطَعُواْ أَيْدِيَهُمَا جَزَاءً بِمَا كَسَبَا نَكَالاً مِّنَ اللّهِ وَاللّهُ عَزِيزٌ حَكِيمٌ
فَمَن تَابَ مِن بَعْدِ ظُلْمِهِ وَأَصْلَحَ فَإِنَّ اللّهَ يَتُوبُ عَلَيْهِ إِنَّ اللّهَ غَفُورٌ رَّحِيمٌ

و مرد و زن دزد را به سزای آنچه کرده‌اند دستمان را به عنوان کیفری از جانب خدا ببرید و خداوند توانا و حکیم است

پس هر که بعد از ستمکردنش توبه کند و به صلاح آید خدا توبه او را می‌پذیرد که خدا آمرزنده مهربان است

157 'Abdu'l-Bahá, *The Promulgation of Universal Peace*, p. 393.

19 Participating in the Resurrection of Faith

1 Bahá'u'lláh, *Gleanings from the Writings of Bahá'u'lláh*, XXVIII, p. 69.
2 Matt. 7:17.
3 Gal. 5:22.
4 John 13:34; also, John 15:12.
5 John 13:35.
6 I John 2:9-11.
7 I John 4:8.
8 I John 4:7.
9 I Cor. 1:10.
10 Phil. 2:3.
11 I Peter 3:8.
12 Matt. 5:44-5.
13 *Ḥujurát*, the Inner Apartments, 49:10:

إِنَّمَا الْمُؤْمِنُونَ إِخْوَةٌ فَأَصْلِحُوا بَيْنَ أَخَوَيْكُمْ وَاتَّقُوا اللَّهَ لَعَلَّكُمْ تُرْحَمُونَ

در حقیقت مؤمنان با هم برادرند پس میان برادرانتان را سازش دهید و از خدا پروا بدارید امید که مورد رحمت قرار گیرید

14 *Ál-i-'Imrán*, the Family of 'Imrán, 3:103:

... وَلاَ تَفَرَّقُواْ وَاذْكُرُواْ نِعْمَتَ اللّهِ عَلَيْكُمْ إِذْ كُنتُمْ أَعْدَاءً فَأَلَّفَ بَيْنَ قُلُوبِكُمْ فَأَصْبَحْتُم بِنِعْمَتِهِ إِخْوَانًا ...

... و از اختلاف و پراکندگی بپرهیزید ، و نعمت خدا را بر خود یاد کنید، آن گاه که دشمن یکدیگر بودید و او میان دل های شما الفت انداخت و در پرتو نعمت و با یکدیگر برادر شدید

15 *Ál-i-'Imrán*, the Family of 'Imrán, 3:105:

وَلاَ تَكُونُواْ كَالَّذِينَ تَفَرَّقُواْ وَاخْتَلَفُواْ مِن بَعْدِ مَا جَاءهُمُ الْبَيِّنَاتُ وَأُوْلَـئِكَ لَهُمْ عَذَابٌ عَظِيمٌ

و چون کسانی مباشید که پس از آنکه دلایل آشکار برایشان آمد پراکنده شدند و با هم اختلاف پیدا کردند و برای آنان عذابی سهمگین است

16 *Anfál*, the Spoils of War, 8:46:

... وَلاَ تَنَازَعُواْ فَتَفْشَلُواْ وَتَذْهَبَ رِيحُكُمْ وَاصْبِرُواْ إِنَّ اللّهَ مَعَ الصَّابِرِينَ

... و با هم نزاع مکنید که سست‌شوید و مهابت‌شما از بین برود و صبر کنید که خدا با شکیبایان است

17 *Ḥashr*, the Gathering, 59:10:

... رَبَّنَا اغْفِرْ لَنَا وَلِإِخْوَانِنَا الَّذِينَ سَبَقُونَا بِالْإِيمَانِ وَلَا تَجْعَلْ فِي قُلُوبِنَا غِلًّا لِّلَّذِينَ آمَنُوا رَبَّنَا إِنَّكَ رَءُوفٌ رَّحِيمٌ

... پروردگارا بر ما و بر آن برادرانمان که در ایمان آوردن بر ما پیشی گرفتند ببخشای و در دلهایمان نسبت به کسانی که ایمان آورده‌اند [هیچ گونه] کینه‌ای مگذار پروردگارا راستی که تو رئوف و مهربانی

18 *Ḥujurát*, the Inner Apartments, 49:10:

إِنَّمَا الْمُؤْمِنُونَ إِخْوَةٌ فَأَصْلِحُوا بَيْنَ أَخَوَيْكُمْ وَاتَّقُوا اللَّهَ لَعَلَّكُمْ تُرْحَمُونَ

در حقیقت مؤمنان با هم برادرند پس میان برادرانتان را سازش دهید و از خدا پروا بدارید امید که مورد رحمت قرار گیرید

19 *Ḥujurát*, the Inner Apartments, 49:9:

الْأُخْرَى فَقَاتِلُوا الَّتِي تَبْغِي حَتَّى تَفِيءَ إِلَى أَمْرِ اللَّهِ فَإِن فَاءَتْ فَأَصْلِحُوا بَيْنَهُمَا بِالْعَدْلِ وَأَقْسِطُوا إِنَّ اللَّهَ يُحِبُّ الْمُقْسِطِينَ

و اگر دو طایفه از مؤمنان با هم بجنگند میان آن دو را اصلاح دهید و اگر [باز] یکی از آن دو بر دیگری تعدی کرد با آن [طایفه‌ای] که تعدی می‌کند بجنگید تا به فرمان خدا بازگردد پس اگر باز گشت میان آنها را دادگرانه سازش دهید و عدالت کنید که خدا دادگران را دوست می‌دارد

20 Bahá'u'lláh, *Epistle to the Son of the Wolf*, p. 15.
21 Bahá'u'lláh, *The Tabernacle of Unity*, p. 9.
22 Bahá'u'lláh, *The Kitáb-i-Aqdas*, para. 144, p. 72.
23 Bahá'u'lláh, *Gleanings from the Writings of Bahá'u'lláh*, CXLVI, p. 315-16.
24 Rom. 10:12.
25 Eph. 4:1-6.
26 Matt. 8:11.
27 *Ḥujurát*, the Inner Apartments, 49:13:

يَا أَيُّهَا النَّاسُ إِنَّا خَلَقْنَاكُم مِّن ذَكَرٍ وَأُنثَى وَجَعَلْنَاكُمْ شُعُوبًا وَقَبَائِلَ لِتَعَارَفُوا إِنَّ أَكْرَمَكُمْ عِندَ اللَّهِ أَتْقَاكُمْ إِنَّ اللَّهَ عَلِيمٌ خَبِيرٌ

ای مردم! ما شما را از یک مرد و زن آفریدیم و شما را تیره‌ها و قبیله‌ها قرار دادیم تا یکدیگر را بشناسید؛ (اینها ملاک امتیاز نیست،) گرامی‌ترین شما نزد خداوند با تقواترین شماست؛ خداوند دانا و آگاه است.

28 *Baqara*, the Heifer, 2:213:

كَانَ النَّاسُ أُمَّةً وَاحِدَةً فَبَعَثَ اللَّهُ النَّبِيِّينَ مُبَشِّرِينَ وَمُنذِرِينَ وَأَنزَلَ مَعَهُمُ الْكِتَابَ بِالْحَقِّ لِيَحْكُمَ بَيْنَ النَّاسِ فِيمَا اخْتَلَفُوا فِيهِ وَمَا اخْتَلَفَ فِيهِ إِلَّا الَّذِينَ أُوتُوهُ مِن بَعْدِ مَا جَاءَتْهُمُ الْبَيِّنَاتُ بَغْيًا بَيْنَهُمْ فَهَدَى اللَّهُ الَّذِينَ آمَنُوا لِمَا اخْتَلَفُوا فِيهِ مِنَ الْحَقِّ بِإِذْنِهِ وَاللَّهُ يَهْدِي مَن يَشَاءُ إِلَى صِرَاطٍ مُّسْتَقِيمٍ

مردم امتی یگانه بودند پس خداوند پیامبران را نویدآور و بیم‌دهنده برانگیخت و با آنان کتاب [خود] را بحق فرو فرستاد تا میان مردم در آنچه با هم اختلاف داشتند داوری کند و جز کسانی که [کتاب] به آنان داده شد پس از آنکه دلایل روشن برای آنان آمد به خاطر ستم [و حسدی] که میانشان بود [هیچ کس] در آن اختلاف نکرد پس خداوند آنان را که ایمان آورده بودند به توفیق خویش به حقیقت آنچه که در آن اختلاف داشتند هدایت کرد و خدا هر که را بخواهد به راه راست هدایت می‌کند

29 *Anbiyáa*, the Prophets, 21:92:

إِنَّ هَذِهِ أُمَّتُكُمْ أُمَّةً وَاحِدَةً وَأَنَا رَبُّكُمْ فَاعْبُدُونِ

این است امت شما که امتی یگانه است و منم پروردگار شما پس مرا بپرستید

30 Bahá'u'lláh, Ishráqát, in *Tablets of Bahá'u'lláh Revealed after the Kitáb-i-Aqdas*, pp. 127–8.
31 'Abdu'l-Bahá, *The Promulgation of Universal Peace*, p. 394.
32 Shoghi Effendi, *The World Order of Bahá'u'lláh*, p. 42.
33 Bahá'u'lláh, quoted in Shoghi Effendi, *The Promised Day is Come*, p. 119.
34 Shoghi Effendi, *The World Order of Bahá'u'lláh*, pp. 43–4.
35 Bahá'u'lláh, *Gleanings from the Writings of Bahá'u'lláh*, CX, pp. 215–16.
36 ibid. CXXXII, p. 288.
37 ibid. CXVII, p. 250.
38 Shoghi Effendi, *The Promised Day is Come*, p. 120.
39 'Abdu'l-Bahá, quoted ibid.
40 Shoghi Effendi, *The World Order of Bahá'u'lláh*, p. 202.
41 ibid. p. 41–2.
42 'Abdu'l-Bahá, *The Promulgation of Universal Peace*, p. 455.
43 Letter written on behalf of Shoghi Effendi to an individual, 22 November 1936, in *Lights of Guidance*, no. 1812, p. 533.
44 Bahá'u'lláh, *Gleanings from the Writings of Bahá'u'lláh*, CXI, p. 217.
45 'Abdu'l-Bahá, *Selections from the Writings of 'Abdu'l-Bahá*, no. 227, p. 302.
46 'Abdu'l-Bahá, *The Promulgation of Universal Peace*, p. 394.
47 The Universal House of Justice, *The Promise of World Peace*, letter to the Peoples of the World, October 1985.
48 'Abdu'l-Bahá, *The Promulgation of Universal Peace*, p. 318.
49 Bahá'u'lláh, Lawḥ-i-Maqṣúd, in *Tablets of Bahá'u'lláh Revealed after the Kitáb-i-Aqdas*, p. 168. See also Note 52, in Bahá'u'lláh, *The Kitáb-i-Aqdas*, p. 190.
50 'Abdu'l-Bahá, *The Promulgation of Universal Peace*, p. 72.
51 Shoghi Effendi, *Bahá'í Administration*, pp. 63–4.
52 'Abdu'l-Bahá, *Selections from the Writings of 'Abdu'l-Bahá*, no. 43, p. 87.
53 ibid. no. 227, p. 299.
54 'Abdu'l-Bahá, *Paris Talks*, ch. 40, p. 133.
55 'Abdu'l-Bahá, *The Promulgation of Universal Peace*, p. 175.
56 'Abdu'l-Bahá, *Paris Talks*, ch. 41, p. 140.
57 ibid. ch. 44, p. 147.
58 'Abdu'l-Bahá, *The Promulgation of Universal Peace*, p. 300.
59 'Abdu'l-Bahá, *Selections from the Writings of 'Abdu'l-Bahá*, no. 227, p. 304.
60 'Abdu'l-Bahá, in *Bahá'í Education*, p. 73.
61 'Abdu'l-Bahá, ibid. p. 46; also in *The Compilation of Compilations*, vol. I, no. 635, p. 285.
62 'Abdu'l-Bahá, *'Abdu'l-Bahá in London*, p. 91.
63 'Abdu'l-Bahá, in *Bahá'í Education*, p. 42.
64 Note 193, in Bahá'u'lláh, *The Kitáb-i-Aqdas*, p. 250.
65 Shoghi Effendi, *The World Order of Bahá'u'lláh*, pp. 203–4.
66 Bahá'u'lláh, *The Kitáb-i-Aqdas*, para. 33, p. 30.

67 Bahá'u'lláh, Bi<u>sh</u>árát (Glad-Tidings), *in Tablets of Bahá'u'lláh Revealed after the Kitáb-i-Aqdas*, p. 26.
68 Shoghi Effendi, *God Passes By*, pp. 214-15.
69 Shoghi Effendi, *Bahá'í Administration*, p. 66.
70 Zech. 8:16:
> These are the things that you shall do: Speak the truth to one another; render in your gates judgments that are true and make for peace
>
> Eph. 4:25:
> Therefore, having put away falsehood, let each one of you speak the truth with his neighbor, for we are members one of another.
71 Ps. 86:11.
72 John 17:17.
73 *Ḥajj*, the Pilgrimage, 22:30, i.e. 'refrain from deceptive speech' (T. B. Irving translation):

... وَاجْتَنِبُوا قَوْلَ الزُّورِ

... و از گفتار باطل اجتناب ورزید

74 *Ṭúr*, the Mount, 52:11:

فَوَيْلٌ يَوْمَئِذٍ لِلْمُكَذِّبِينَ

پس وای بر تکذیب‌کنندگان در آن روز

75 *Ál-i-'Imrán*, the Family of 'Imrán, 3:71:

يَا أَهْلَ الْكِتَابِ لِمَ تَلْبِسُونَ الْحَقَّ بِالْبَاطِلِ وَتَكْتُمُونَ الْحَقَّ وَأَنتُمْ تَعْلَمُونَ

ای اهل کتاب! چرا حق را با باطل (بی آمیزید و) مشتبه می کنید (تا دیگر آن نفهمند و گمراه شوند)، و حقیقت را پوشیده می دارید در حالی که می دانید؟

76 *Má'ida*, the Table Spread, 5:119-20:

قَالَ اللَّهُ هَذَا يَوْمُ يَنفَعُ الصَّادِقِينَ صِدْقُهُمْ لَهُمْ جَنَّاتٌ تَجْرِي مِن تَحْتِهَا الْأَنْهَارُ خَالِدِينَ فِيهَا أَبَدًا رَّضِيَ اللَّهُ عَنْهُمْ وَرَضُوا عَنْهُ ذَلِكَ الْفَوْزُ الْعَظِيمُ

خدا فرمود این روزی است که راستگویان را راستی‌شان سود بخشد برای آنان باغهایی است که از زیر [درختان] آن نهرها روان است همیشه در آن جاودانند خدا از آنان خشنود است و آنان [نیز] از او خشنودند این است رستگاری بزرگ

77 'Alí Ibn Abí Ṭálib, *Nahjul Balá<u>gh</u>ah*, Letter no. 48.
78 *Anbiyá*, the Prophets, 21:18:

بَلْ نَقْذِفُ بِالْحَقِّ عَلَى الْبَاطِلِ فَيَدْمَغُهُ فَإِذَا هُوَ زَاهِقٌ وَلَكُمُ الْوَيْلُ مِمَّا تَصِفُونَ

بلکه ما حق را بر سر باطل می‌کوبیم تا آن را هلاک سازد؛ و این گونه، باطل محو و نابود می‌شود! اما وای بر شما از توصیفی که می‌کنید!

79 *Sabá,* Sheba, or the City of Sabá, 34:48-9:

قُلْ إِنَّ رَبِّي يَقْذِفُ بِالْحَقِّ عَلَّامُ الْغُيُوبِ
قُلْ جَاءَ الْحَقُّ وَمَا يُبْدِئُ الْبَاطِلُ وَمَا يُعِيدُ

بگو بی‌گمان پروردگارم حقیقت را القا می‌کند [اوست] دانای نهانها
بگو حق آمد و [دیگر] باطل از سر نمی‌گیرد و برنمی‌گردد

80 *Baní Isrá-il,* the Children of Israel, 17:81:

وَقُلْ جَاءَ الْحَقُّ وَزَهَقَ الْبَاطِلُ إِنَّ الْبَاطِلَ كَانَ زَهُوقًا

و بگو حق آمد و باطل نابود شد آری باطل همواره نابودشدنی است

81 Bahá'u'lláh, Tablet of Aḥmad, in *Bahá'í Prayers*, pp. 210-11.
82 Bahá'u'lláh, *Gleanings from the Writings of Bahá'u'lláh*, CXXXVI, p. 297.
83 ibid. CXXXVII, p. 299.
84 Bahá'u'lláh, *Epistle to the Son of the Wolf,* p. 119.
85 Bahá'u'lláh, *Gleanings from the Writings of Bahá'u'lláh,* CXXVI, pp. 270-71.
86 Eccl. 5:8.
87 Isa. 56:1.
88 Isa. 59:4.
89 Prov. 21:3.
90 Isa. 9:7.
91 *Nisáa,* the Women, 4:58:

إِنَّ اللَّهَ يَأْمُرُكُمْ أَن تُؤَدُّواْ الأَمَانَاتِ إِلَى أَهْلِهَا وَإِذَا حَكَمْتُم بَيْنَ النَّاسِ أَن تَحْكُمُواْ بِالْعَدْلِ إِنَّ اللَّهَ نِعِمَّا يَعِظُكُم بِهِ إِنَّ اللَّهَ كَانَ سَمِيعًا بَصِيرًا

خداوند به شما فرمان می‌دهد که امانتها را به صاحبان آن برسانید و هنگامی که میان مردم داوری می‌کنید از روی عدالت داوری کنید، خداوند پند و اندرزهای خوبی به شما می‌دهد، خداوند شنوا و بیناست.

92 *Nisáa,* the Women, 4:135:

يَا أَيُّهَا الَّذِينَ آمَنُواْ كُونُواْ قَوَّامِينَ بِالْقِسْطِ شُهَدَاءَ لِلّهِ وَلَوْ عَلَى أَنفُسِكُمْ أَوِ الْوَالِدَيْنِ وَالأَقْرَبِينَ إِن يَكُنْ غَنِيًّا أَوْ فَقَيرًا فَاللّهُ أَوْلَى بِهِمَا فَلاَ تَتَّبِعُواْ الْهَوَى أَن تَعْدِلُواْ وَإِن تَلْوُواْ أَوْ تُعْرِضُواْ فَإِنَّ اللّهَ كَانَ بِمَا تَعْمَلُونَ خَبِيرًا

ای کسانی که ایمان آورده‌اید پیوسته به عدالت قیام کنید و برای خدا گواهی دهید هر چند به زیان خودتان یا [به زیان] پدر و مادر و خویشاوندان [شما] باشد اگر [یکی از دو طرف دعوا] توانگر یا نیازمند باشد باز خدا به آن دو [از شما] سزاوارتر است پس از پی هوس نروید که [درنتیجه از حق] عدول کنید و اگر به انحراف گرایید یا اعراض نمایید قطعا خدا به آنچه انجام می‌دهید آگاه است

93 *Má'ida,* the Table Spread, 5:8:

يَا أَيُّهَا الَّذِينَ آمَنُواْ كُونُواْ قَوَّامِينَ لِلّهِ شُهَدَاءَ بِالْقِسْطِ وَلاَ يَجْرِمَنَّكُمْ شَنَآنُ قَوْمٍ عَلَى أَلاَّ تَعْدِلُواْ اعْدِلُواْ هُوَ أَقْرَبُ لِلتَّقْوَى وَاتَّقُواْ اللّهَ إِنَّ اللّهَ خَبِيرٌ بِمَا تَعْمَلُونَ

ای کسانی که ایمان آورده‌اید برای خدا به داد برخیزید [و] به عدالت شهادت دهید و البته نباید دشمنی گروهی شما را بر آن دارد که عدالت نکنید عدالت کنید که آن به تقوا نزدیکتر است و از خدا پروا دارید که خدا به آنچه انجام می‌دهید آگاه است

94   *A'ráf,* the Heights, 7:29:

قُلْ أَمَرَ رَبِّي بِالْقِسْطِ ...

بگو: «پروردگارم امر به عدالت کرده است...

95   *Ḥujurát,* the Inner Apartments, 49:9:

وَإِن طَائِفَتَانِ مِنَ الْمُؤْمِنِينَ اقْتَتَلُوا فَأَصْلِحُوا بَيْنَهُمَا فَإِن بَغَتْ إِحْدَاهُمَا عَلَى الْأُخْرَى فَقَاتِلُوا الَّتِي تَبْغِي حَتَّى تَفِيءَ إِلَى أَمْرِ اللَّهِ فَإِن فَاءَتْ فَأَصْلِحُوا بَيْنَهُمَا بِالْعَدْلِ وَأَقْسِطُوا إِنَّ اللَّهَ يُحِبُّ الْمُقْسِطِينَ

و هرگاه دو گروه از مؤمنان با هم به نزاع و جنگ بپردازند، آنها را آشتی دهید؛ و اگر یکی از آن دو بر دیگری تجاوز کند، با گروه متجاوز پیکار کنید تا به فرمان خدا بازگردد؛ و هرگاه بازگشت (، در میان آن دو به عدالت صلح برقرار سازید؛ و عدالت پیشه کنید که خداوند عدالت پیشگان را دوست می‌دارد.

96   *Zulm:* cruel or unjust acts of exploitation, oppression and wrongdoing, whereby a person either deprives others of their rights or does not fulfil his obligations towards them; people who commit *zulm* are labeled *zálim-een.*

97   *Qaṣaṣ,* the Narration, 28:77:

وَابْتَغِ فِيمَا آتَاكَ اللَّهُ الدَّارَ الْآخِرَةَ وَلَا تَنسَ نَصِيبَكَ مِنَ الدُّنْيَا وَأَحْسِن كَمَا أَحْسَنَ اللَّهُ إِلَيْكَ وَلَا تَبْغِ الْفَسَادَ فِي الْأَرْضِ إِنَّ اللَّهَ لَا يُحِبُّ الْمُفْسِدِينَ

و با آنچه خدایت داده سرای آخرت را بجوی و سهم خود را از دنیا فراموش مکن و همچنانکه خدا به تو نیکی کرده نیکی کن و در زمین فساد مجوی که خدا فسادگران را دوست نمی‌دارد

98   *Ḥadíd,* Iron, 57:25:

لَقَدْ أَرْسَلْنَا رُسُلَنَا بِالْبَيِّنَاتِ وَأَنزَلْنَا مَعَهُمُ الْكِتَابَ وَالْمِيزَانَ لِيَقُومَ النَّاسُ بِالْقِسْطِ وَأَنزَلْنَا الْحَدِيدَ فِيهِ بَأْسٌ شَدِيدٌ وَمَنَافِعُ لِلنَّاسِ وَلِيَعْلَمَ اللَّهُ مَن يَنصُرُهُ وَرُسُلَهُ بِالْغَيْبِ إِنَّ اللَّهَ قَوِيٌّ عَزِيزٌ

ما رسولان خود را با دلایل روشن فرستادیم، و با آنها کتاب (آسمانی) و میزان (شناسایی حق از باطل و قوانین عادلانه) نازل کردیم تا مردم قیام به عدالت کنند؛ و آهن را نازل کردیم که در آن نیروی شدید و منافعی برای مردم است، تا خداوند بداند چه کسی او و رسولانش را یاری می‌کند بی‌آنکه او را ببینند؛ خداوند قوی و شکست‌ناپذیر است!

99   *Anbiyáa,* the Prophets, 21:47:

وَنَضَعُ الْمَوَازِينَ الْقِسْطَ لِيَوْمِ الْقِيَامَةِ فَلَا تُظْلَمُ نَفْسٌ شَيْئًا وَإِن كَانَ مِثْقَالَ حَبَّةٍ مِّنْ خَرْدَلٍ أَتَيْنَا بِهَا وَكَفَى بِنَا حَاسِبِينَ

ما ترازوهای عدل را در روز قیامت برپا می‌کنیم؛ پس به هیچ کس کمترین ستمی نمی‌شود؛ و اگر بمقدار سنگینی یک دانه خردل (کار نیک و بدی) باشد، ما آن را حاضر می‌کنیم؛ و کافی است که ما حساب‌کننده باشیم

100 Bahá'u'lláh, *Hidden Words,* Arabic no. 2.
101 Bahá'u'lláh, *Epistle to the Son of Wolf,* p. 10.
102 Bahá'u'lláh, *The Kitáb-i-Aqdas,* para. 158, p. 76.
103 Eccl. 5:7.

NOTES AND REFERENCES

104 *Ḥajj*, the Pilgrimage, 22:34-5:

وَلِكُلِّ أُمَّةٍ جَعَلْنَا مَنسَكًا لِيَذْكُرُوا اسْمَ اللَّهِ عَلَىٰ مَا رَزَقَهُم مِّن بَهِيمَةِ الْأَنْعَامِ فَإِلَٰهُكُمْ إِلَٰهٌ وَاحِدٌ فَلَهُ أَسْلِمُوا وَبَشِّرِ الْمُخْبِتِينَ

الَّذِينَ إِذَا ذُكِرَ اللَّهُ وَجِلَتْ قُلُوبُهُمْ وَالصَّابِرِينَ عَلَىٰ مَا أَصَابَهُمْ وَالْمُقِيمِي الصَّلَاةِ وَمِمَّا رَزَقْنَاهُمْ يُنفِقُونَ

و برای هر امتی مناسکی قرار دادیم تا نام خدا را بر دامهای زبان‌بسته‌ای که روزی آنها یاد گردانیده یاد کنند پس [بدانید که] خدای شما خدایی یگانه است پس به [فرمان] او گردن نهید و فروتنان را بشارت ده همانان که چون [نام] خدا یاد شود دلهایشان خشیت‌یابد و [آنان که] بر هر چه برسرشان آید صبر پیشه‌گانند و برپا دارندگان نمازند و از آنچه روزیشان داده‌ایم انفاق می‌کنند

105 *Baqara*, the Heifer, 2:2:

ذَٰلِكَ الْكِتَابُ لَا رَيْبَ فِيهِ هُدًى لِّلْمُتَّقِينَ

آن کتاب با عظمتی است که شک در آن راه ندارد؛ و مایه هدایت پرهیزکاران است.

106 *Baqara*, the Heifer, 2:282:

... وَاتَّقُوا اللَّهَ وَيُعَلِّمُكُمُ اللَّهُ وَاللَّهُ بِكُلِّ شَيْءٍ عَلِيمٌ

... و از خدا پروا کنید، و خدا (بدین گونه) به شما آموزش می‌دهد، و خدا به هر چیزی داناست.

J. M. Rodwell:
But fear God and God will give you knowledge, for God hath knowledge of all things.

107 *Ḥadíd*, Iron, 57:28:

يَا أَيُّهَا الَّذِينَ آمَنُوا اتَّقُوا اللَّهَ وَآمِنُوا بِرَسُولِهِ يُؤْتِكُمْ كِفْلَيْنِ مِن رَّحْمَتِهِ وَيَجْعَل لَّكُمْ نُورًا تَمْشُونَ بِهِ وَيَغْفِرْ لَكُمْ وَاللَّهُ غَفُورٌ رَّحِيمٌ

ای کسانی که ایمان آورده‌اید! تقوای الهی پیشه کنید و به رسولش ایمان بیاورید تا دو سهم از رحمتش به شما ببخشد و برای شما نوری قرار دهد که با آن (در میان مردم و در مسیر زندگی خود) راه بروید و گناهان شما را ببخشد؛ و خداوند غفور و رحیم است.

108 Bahá'u'lláh, *Epistle to the Son of the Wolf*, p. 135.
109 ibid. pp. 122-3.
110 *Ál-i-'Imrán*, the Family of 'Imrán, 3:159:

... فَتَوَكَّلْ عَلَى اللَّهِ إِنَّ اللَّهَ يُحِبُّ الْمُتَوَكِّلِينَ ...

... بر خدا توکل کن زیرا خداوند توکل‌کنندگان را دوست می‌دارد ...

111 *Má'ida*, the Table Spread, 5:118:

إِن تُعَذِّبْهُمْ فَإِنَّهُمْ عِبَادُكَ وَإِن تَغْفِرْ لَهُمْ فَإِنَّكَ أَنتَ الْعَزِيزُ الْحَكِيمُ

اگر آنها را مجازات کنی، بندگان توانند و اگر آنان را ببخشی، توانا و حکیمی!

112 Bahá'u'lláh, *Gleanings from the Writings of Bahá'u'lláh*, CXIV, p. 234.
113 ibid. CXXXIII, p. 290.
114 Ps. 51, 10-13.
115 Matt. 5:8.

116 *Baqara*, the Heifer, 2:222:

... إِنَّ اللَّهَ يُحِبُّ ... الْمُتَطَهِّرِينَ

...خداوند،... پاکان را دوست دارد.

117 *Nisáa*, the Women, 4:43:

يَا أَيُّهَا الَّذِينَ آمَنُواْ لاَ تَقْرَبُواْ الصَّلاَةَ وَأَنتُمْ سُكَارَى حَتَّىَ تَعْلَمُواْ مَا تَقُولُونَ وَلاَ جُنُبًا إِلاَّ عَابِرِي سَبِيلٍ حَتَّىَ تَغْتَسِلُواْ وَإِن كُنتُم مَّرْضَى أَوْ عَلَى سَفَرٍ أَوْ جَاء أَحَدٌ مَّنكُم مِّنَ الْغَآئِطِ أَوْ لاَمَسْتُمُ النِّسَاء فَلَمْ تَجِدُواْ مَاء فَتَيَمَّمُواْ صَعِيدًا طَيِّبًا فَامْسَحُواْ بِوُجُوهِكُمْ وَأَيْدِيكُمْ إِنَّ اللَّهَ كَانَ عَفُوًّا غَفُورًا

ای کسانی که ایمان آورده‌اید! در حال مستی به نماز نزدیک نشوید، تا بدانید چه می‌گویید! و همچنین هنگامی که جنب هستید -مگر اینکه مسافر باشید- تا غسل کنید. و اگر بیماريد، یا مسافر، و یا «قضای حاجت» کرده‌اید، و یا با زنان آمیزش جنسی داشته‌اید، و در این حال، آب (برای وضو یا غسل) نیافتید، با خاک پاکی تیمم کنید! (به این طریق که) صورتها و دستهایتان را با آن مسح نمایید. خداوند، بخشنده و آمرزنده است.

118 Bahá'u'lláh, *Prayers and Meditations*, CLV, p. 248.
119 'Abdu'l-Bahá, *Paris Talks*, ch. 16, p. 49.
120 'Abdu'l-Bahá, *Selections from the Writings of 'Abdu'l-Bahá*, no. 129, p. 146.
121 Bahá'u'lláh, *Epistle to the Son of the Wolf*, p. 95.
122 Bahá'u'lláh, *The Kitáb-i-Aqdas*, para. 120, p. 62.
123 Prov. 21:10. (*God's Word* translation).
124 I Pet. 3:8.
125 *Nisáa*, the Women, 4:86:

وَإِذَا حُيِّيْتُم بِتَحِيَّةٍ فَحَيُّواْ بِأَحْسَنَ مِنْهَا أَوْ رُدُّوهَا إِنَّ اللّهَ كَانَ عَلَى كُلِّ شَيْءٍ حَسِيبًا

هرگاه به شما تحیت گویند، پاسخ آن را بهتر از آن بدهید؛ یا (لااقل) به همان گونه پاسخ گویید! خداوند حساب همه چیز را دارد.

126 Bahá'u'lláh, Lawḥ-i-Dunyá (Tablet of the World), in *Tablets of Bahá'u'lláh Revealed after the Kitáb-i-Aqdas*, p. 88.
127 Bahá'u'lláh, Súriy-i-Haykal, para. 137, in *The Summons of the Lord of Hosts*, pp. 71-2.
128 Exod. 20:12.
129 Eph. 6:1-4.
130 *Aḥqáf*, Winding Sand-tracts, 46:15:

وَوَصَّيْنَا الْإِنسَانَ بِوَالِدَيْهِ إِحْسَانًا حَمَلَتْهُ أُمُّهُ كُرْهًا وَوَضَعَتْهُ كُرْهًا وَحَمْلُهُ وَفِصَالُهُ ثَلَاثُونَ شَهْرًا حَتَّى إِذَا بَلَغَ أَشُدَّهُ وَبَلَغَ أَرْبَعِينَ سَنَةً قَالَ رَبِّ أَوْزِعْنِي أَنْ أَشْكُرَ نِعْمَتَكَ الَّتِي أَنْعَمْتَ عَلَيَّ وَعَلَى وَالِدَيَّ وَأَنْ أَعْمَلَ صَالِحًا تَرْضَاهُ وَأَصْلِحْ لِي فِي ذُرِّيَّتِي إِنِّي تُبْتُ إِلَيْكَ وَإِنِّي مِنَ الْمُسْلِمِينَ

ما به انسان توصیه کردیم که به پدر و مادرش نیکی کند، مادرش او را با ناراحتی حمل می‌کند و با ناراحتی بر زمین می‌گذارد؛ و دوران حمل و از شیر بازگرفتنش سی ماه است؛ تا زمانی که به کمال قدرت و رشد برسد و به چهل سالگی بالغ گردد می‌گوید: «پروردگارا! مرا توفیق ده تا شکر نعمتی را که به من و پدر و مادرم دادی بجا آورم و کار شایسته‌ای انجام دهم که از آن خشنود باشی، و فرزندان مرا صالح گردان؛ من به سوی تو بازمی‌گردم و توبه می‌کنم، و من از مسلمانانم

131 Bahá'u'lláh, 'Questions and Answers', no. 106, in *The Kitáb-i-Aqdas*, p. 139.
132 Bahá'u'lláh, *Gleanings from the Writings of Bahá'u'lláh*, CXLVI, p. 315.

NOTES AND REFERENCES

133 'Abdu'l-Bahá, *Selections from the Writings of 'Abdu'l-Bahá*, no. 227, p. 302.
134 'Abdu'l-Bahá, *The Promulgation of Universal Peace*, p. 453.
135 Bahá'u'lláh, *Bishárát* (Glad-Tidings), in *Tablets of Bahá'u'lláh Revealed after the Kitáb-i-Aqdas*, p. 27.
136 'Abdu'l-Bahá, *The Promulgation of Universal Peace*, p. 266.
137 Bahá'u'lláh, quoted by Shoghi Effendi, *The Advent of Divine Justice*, pp. 69–70.
138 'Synopsis and Codification', in Bahá'u'lláh, *The Kitáb-i-Aqdas*, p. 160.
139 'Abdu'l-Bahá, Tablet to the Hague, in 'Abdu'l-Bahá, *Foundations of World Unity*, p. 33.
140 Bahá'u'lláh, Súriy-i-Haykal, in *The Summons of the Lord of Hosts*, p. 3.

ABOUT THE AUTHOR

Dr Lameh Fananapazir was born in Iran and spent his youth in Africa. He is a graduate of Edinburgh Medical School, where he trained in Cardiovascular Diseases and was elected as a Fellow of the Royal College of Physicians of Edinburgh. He further specialized in Electrophysiology at Duke Medical Center in the United States, following which he was recruited to study causes of sudden death in athletes and patients with familial hypertrophic cardiomyopathy at the National Institutes of Health where he became the chief of the Section of Inherited Heart Diseases. He has authored and presented several hundred articles. He spent two and a half years in Haifa, Israel where he was the director of the Health Services at the Bahá'í World Centre and Visiting Professor of Molecular Genetics at Technion, Israel Institute of Technology. Dr Fananapazir is currently in private practice as cardiologist and electrophysiologist in Cumberland, Maryland.

The Bahá'í principles of the oneness of God, of faith, and of mankind have been particularly relevant in his life: his father and mother were respectively from Muslim and Zoroastrian backgrounds. An indelible experience of his early childhood in Iran was the persecution of the Iranian Bahá'ís in 1955-6 when their properties were destroyed or confiscated, Bahá'í centres looted and Bahá'í cemeteries desecrated. Several Bahá'ís were killed, some hacked to pieces, Bahá'í women were abducted and forced to marry Muslims, and Bahá'ís were expelled and dismissed from schools and employment. The National Bahá'í Center in Tehran, a beautiful place with peacocks that he loved to visit as a child, was occupied by the military and its dome destroyed.

In Africa, he attended a Methodist school in Gambia and became familiar with the Bible through the efforts of Christian missionaries; the family moved for a while to Morocco where he witnessed an abrupt persecution of the Bahá'ís (1962-3), and finally to Kenya. In 1968 he travelled to Scotland, a country which was a bastion of Protestantism and had been responsible for a great deal of the missionary activity that he had witnessed in Africa. He became acutely aware of the tensions between Protestants and Catholics in Britain, particularly apparent because of the vicious sectarian violence in Northern Ireland at this time. In 1974 he married Karen Sutherland, whose grandfather had been a minister of the Free Church of Scotland, known for its ultra-Protestant commitments.

On 11 September 2001, while in the middle of a heart catheterization procedure, he became aware of the coordinated attack on the United States by a band of Muslims. While his research held the promise of saving a few lives, religious fanaticism had suddenly ended the lives of so many. Two years later while living in Israel he witnessed the almost daily acts of violence between the Jews and Palestinian Muslims, which stood in sharp contrast to the harmoniuos relationships among over 500 Bahá'ís from diverse national and religious backgrounds working together at the Bahá'í World Centre in Haifa. This book was born out of his curiosity concerning the root causes of religious fanaticism and increasing certitude that Bahá'u'lláh's teachings represent the only possible remedy.

www.ingramcontent.com/pod-product-compliance
Lightning Source LLC
Chambersburg PA
CBHW021712300426
44114CB00009B/107